Daily Giving Service

Daily Giving Service

A History of the Diocesan Girls' School, Hong Kong

Author: Moira M. W. Chan-Yeung

Contributors: Amy Ng
                Vanessa Leung
                Wun Tsz Sum
                Janice Tsang
                Grace Chiang
                Robyn Lamsam
                Andrea Lai
                Yvonne Chan
                Sheilah Chatjaval

Hong Kong University Press
The University of Hong Kong
Pok Fu Lam Road
Hong Kong
https://hkupress.hku.hk

© 2023 Hong Kong University Press

ISBN 978-988-8754-31-1 (*Paperback*)

All rights reserved. No portion of this publication may be reproduced or transmitted in any form or by any means, electronic or mechanical, including photocopying, recording, or any information storage or retrieval system, without prior permission in writing from the publisher.

British Library Cataloguing-in-Publication Data
A catalogue record for this book is available from the British Library.

Front cover image: DGS view from Jordan Road, c. 1913. Source: Bob Tatz, *Lost in the Battle for Hong Kong, December 1941: A Memoir of Survival, Identity and Success 1931–1959*, second edition. Reprinted with permission.

Back cover image: Line drawing of the DGS campus. Source: 黃棣才，《圖說香港歷史建築 1946–1997》。香港：中華書局 [Richard Tai Choi Wong, *Illustrating Hong Kong Historical Buildings 1946–1997*. Hong Kong: Chunghwa Book Co.]. Reprinted with permission.

Digitally printed

To Our Heavenly Father and the DGS Family Past and Present

Contents

Forewords

The Most Reverend Andrew Chan, Chairman of the Council of the Diocesan Girls' School — ix

Mrs Doris Ho, School Supervisor, Diocesan Girls' School and Diocesan Girls' Junior School — xi

Mrs Stella Lau, Headmistress of Diocesan Girls' School — xiii

Mrs Annie Lee, Headmistress of Diocesan Girls' Junior School — xv

Preface — xvi

Acknowledgements — xx

List of Abbreviations — xxii

Part I. Chronological Perspective — 1
Moira M. W. Chan-Yeung (1955)

Chapter 1. Historical Background: 1859 to 1898 — 3

Chapter 2. Laying the Foundation: 1899 to 1924 — 31

Chapter 3. Coping with Social Changes: 1925 to 1938 — 54

Chapter 4. The Imminent War and Japanese Occupation: 1939 to 1945 — 73

Chapter 5. Post-war Rehabilitation: 1946 to 1953 — 89

Chapter 6. The Great Expansion: 1953 to 1985 — 110

Chapter 7. Consolidation and New Challenges: 1985 to 1999 — 158

Chapter 8. The Turbulent Modern Era: 1999 to 2019 — 192

Chapter 9. "We Reap What They Have Sown" — 233

Part II. An Interlude: Metamorphosis in Bricks and Mortar — 253
Vanessa Leung (1986)

Part III. Various Aspects ... 265
   Editors: Amy Ng (1991) and Moira M. W. Chan-Yeung (1955)

Chapter 10. Spiritual Life at DGS ... 267
   Wun Tsz Sum (2007)

Chapter 11. Scholastic Activities ... 280
   Janice Tsang (1992)

Chapter 12. Musical Life ... 297
   Grace Chiang (1999)

Chapter 13. Sports ... 317
   Robyn Lamsam (1994)

Chapter 14. School Life ... 335
   Amy Ng (1991)

Chapter 15. Teaching and Non-teaching Staff ... 347
   Andrea Lai (1990) and Moira M. W. Chan-Yeung (1955)

Chapter 16. Diocesan Old Girls' Association ... 370
   Yvonne Chan (1980) and Andrea Lai (1990)

Chapter 17. Diocesan Girls' School Parent Teacher Association ... 384
   Sheilah Chatjaval (1978)

Appendixes

Appendix 1: Chronicle of Major Events ... 399

Appendix 2: Members of the School Council from 1860 to the Present ... 405

Appendix 3: The Teaching Staff, from 1860/1861 to the Present ... 409

Appendix 4: Head Girls, 1922 to 2019 ... 426

Bibliography ... 428

Index ... 433

Foreword

The Most Reverend Andrew Chan
Chairman of the Council of the Diocesan Girls' School

History is a great teacher, and *Daily Giving Service: A History of the Diocesan Girls' School, Hong Kong* is a significant publication that has given me much insight into how a great school based on sound Christian principles came to be. DGS is regarded as a leading school for girls within the Hong Kong SAR, and I must say that I derived great pleasure and satisfaction upon reading this remarkable book.

The book offers us a written tour of the School's immense history, from its spiritual life to the diverse scholastic activities, its music and sports, and the sense of community and collegiality that binds all girls and staff together. All these reflect the underlying Christian concept of education through the holistic development of girls, for the glory of our Heavenly Father.

All contemporary education institutions emphasise the claim that they provide a "holistic education", but what does this actually entail? Some may fall under the idea that holistic education merely requires a list of boxes to be checked: that as long as there are morning assemblies, there is moral education; that a high academic achievement is proof of intellectual education; physical education inevitably arises from the encouragement of sports activities; community education is achieved through inter-class collaborations; aesthetic education is accomplished via the visual arts classes; and religious education takes place through spiritual activities. The idea is that by presenting a long list of activities, we can claim that we have achieved the goal of holistic education. This idea, however, is very far from the truth.

So what exactly is holistic education? This review of the development of DGS over the past 160 years may give us some indication.

In terms of overall planning, this book reveals how DGS places great emphasis on the healthy development of students through the promotion of a school wellness plan. Healthy development does not merely refer to the absence of illness, as the plan encourages students to maintain a wholesome approach towards the body, the mind, and the school community. Career planning is greatly emphasised as through it, students reason why they should study hard, strive for excellence, and dare to dream and plan their future. The school also places strong emphasis on integrating the latest innovation and technology into the students' learning curriculum. Such ideals go beyond the achievement of better results in academic courses, extracurricular activities, or systemic procedures. In effect, the school has applied its ideals of holistic development in all its teaching and activities, and for this we give praise and thanks to our Heavenly Father for DGS. Through Him, we are able to appreciate the staff, teachers, and our predecessors for their tireless toil and intellectual acuity in achieving these lofty ideals.

As a church school, and especially an Anglican school, we always believe that the human body, mind, and spirit are each and all part of a complete unit. The education we provide allows the next generation to fully attain balanced growth physically, mentally, and spiritually.

Life has its own cycle of completeness, and it is a continuous entity. From the moment a person comes into being, he or she never ceases growing. For human life, like any other life forms, growing is the only way forward. This book documents the process of growth and maturation of the DGS family. Through the book, we can appreciate the hard work of our students, while recognising that this family has greatly benefited from the support and dedication of countless parents, teachers, and friends. Through such nurturing from parents, teachers, and fellow peers, growth is made possible. Hence, we can visualise the life of each DGS girl as a gift from countless people: their lives have become blessings, as they recognise the importance of paying forward the blessings they have received. This vitality also propels them to strive for excellence in whatever they do. The nature of successful growth is such that it leads to a successful life of accomplishments and fulfilment. Long may these lives pass on their blessings to new cohorts that come afterwards, for it is in giving that we receive.

DGS family members, let us pray that the Lord will continue to lead us in the days to come, so we may bring direction and meaning to our lives through holistic education. Give us the true knowledge that can only come from our Heavenly Father, that we may embody the spirit of our school song, that the flowers of our DGS life may bloom ever more splendidly.

> They reap not where they laboured;
> We reap what they have sown;
> Our harvest may be garnered
> By ages yet unknown.
> The days of old have dowered us
> With gifts beyond all praise;
> Our Father, make us faithful
> To serve the coming days.

Foreword

Mrs Doris Ho
School Supervisor, Diocesan Girls' School and Diocesan Girls' Junior School

DGS is a school like no other, one that evokes very strong feelings of pride, camaraderie, and sense of belonging among all who have passed through its gate. There are few educational institutions in the world that can claim to celebrate their one hundred sixtieth anniversary in 2020. I wholeheartedly commend the collaborative effort of the many past and current members of the DGS family from all walks of life spanning different continents who, tasked with the onerous responsibility of condensing these 160 years of history into one book, generously shared their memories to distil the essence of what school life at DGS was like over the years, from a twenty-first-century perspective.

A tremendous debt of gratitude goes to the numerous pioneer members of the DGS family, many of whom remain unnamed, who were either school leaders, members of staff, or past students of the school. Through their visionary zeal and dedication, our predecessors went against the convention of their day and proved that, given the right environment and opportunity, girls could excel academically and contribute meaningfully to society in a professional capacity.

From its humble origin as a small school for girls in 1860, DGS has evolved to become one of the top girls' schools in Hong Kong. All the while, the school went through the countless challenges and events that took place in Hong Kong over the passage of time. These included the First and Second World Wars, the territory being administered under British colonial rule for one-and-a-half centuries, the return to Chinese sovereignty to become a Special Administrative Region of the People's Republic of China, as well as other major events. Through it all, the school has always stood by its Christian principles and beliefs, producing hundreds of thousands of women of excellence in every field, from loving mothers to a wide range of professionals, caring and contributing to the society with a worldwide vision.

I cannot but feel an overwhelming sense of pride and satisfaction at how far we have come over the many years as a school and, indeed, as a family. The key to this continuous success is, in my opinion, the school's unwavering commitment to excellence as well as the utmost concern for our students' psychological and physical harmony, based upon the provision of an all-round Christian education.

At the same time, one cannot deny that many challenges will continue to confront the school in the future. At the time of writing, the world is coping with the second year of the COVID-19 pandemic, which inevitably has impacted school life, necessitating the adoption of online-based learning for much of the time. Thankfully, the redevelopment of the school campus from 2009 to 2011 has equipped it with the latest IT networking infrastructure, which has greatly facilitated the delivery of blended learning during the pandemic. And like other places in the world, Hong Kong has had its share of complexities to contend with, partly due to its historical backdrop and significance.

But if the lessons from the long and illustrious history of our school is any guide, it is that through God's providence, members of the DGS family have been gifted with the calmness of heart and mind, as well as the wisdom to plan ahead and thrive amidst the ever-changing landscape. As the pandemic subsides, there are plans afoot to offer places for up to sixty boarders at the newly established boarding facility within our campus, thus rekindling our roots as a boarding sanctuary for girls.

I hope that the essence captured in this history book will serve as a useful reminder of how we came to be where we are today as a school, and as a family. We will continue to uphold our fundamentals of education through keeping to our precious and dearest Christian values, which give us an incomparable source of strength and serenity. With this energy and direction, we will forge ahead with renewed vigour and confidence to fulfil our mission of delivering educational excellence to girls in Hong Kong, China, and the world.

Finally, I wish with all my heart that the school will continue to prosper, hold fast to the DGS legacy, and strive to reach new heights over the next 160 years.

Foreword

Mrs Stella Lau
Headmistress of Diocesan Girls' School

As we celebrate the one hundred sixtieth anniversary of Diocesan Girls' School, it seems appropriate that a book that provides an account of our school's long and illustrious history should be published to mark this milestone of our journey. Being one of the oldest girls' schools in Hong Kong, DGS has played an important role in the education of girls in the city. Over the years, the school has adapted to the changing needs of society whilst retaining its core ethos and traditions of providing a well-rounded Christian education to girls. Because of the tremendous support from school members and members of society, old girls, parents, and friends over the years, the school remains internationally recognised as a leading girls' school in the region. Yet, to date, there has not been a comprehensive record of our rich tradition and the people that have shaped the school. A history book such as this would be a tribute to the institutions we have been, and pays homage to all students, teachers, staff, friends whom we are blessed to have as members of the DGS family over the past decades and century. Such a book would help readers to understand how DGS has evolved over the years to become this happy and thriving school today.

The idea of this book began to take shape when we realised we had, in our midst, an accomplished old girl and an eminent medical professor, who happens also to be an excellent writer and historian, Professor Moira Chan-Yeung. However, no one could have imagined the effect of the COVID-19 pandemic. Air travel was severely disrupted and restrictive quarantine measures were imposed by nations throughout the world to contain the pandemic. As Moira is based in Canada, it was unlikely that she could be enlisted to take on such a project, since neither she, nor others we hoped to invite to help, would be able to visit archives in Hong Kong to research documents related to the history of the school. Nor would they be able to confer or visit the school during the production of the book because of the pandemic. In spite of the difficulties, we invited her to take on the project in early April 2020, and she readily accepted.

While Moira was to deal with the main narrative of the history, others were enlisted to deal in greater details with the different facets of student life. A team of contributors was assembled, comprising old girls from different walks of life, and a few members of staff. Among the contributors, many old girls were based overseas in different parts of the world. Because of this, most of the work and coordination for the production of the history book was done remotely using a cloud-based archive to share scanned information like documents, photographs, copies of past school magazines, etc. Despite the difficulty of not being able to be physically present together to discuss the project, work progressed smoothly. What you have before you is the fruit of their combined labour, which, I feel, offers the most complete history of our school to date.

As headmistress, I know that this book has enriched my understanding of our school's history, particularly the chapters on the work of my predecessors. I am in profound admiration of our past loyal and dedicated teaching staff who have served tirelessly for the betterment of our school throughout its long history. I hope that in some small way this book can serve as a fitting tribute to them, as well as to all past and current stakeholders, including current and old girls, parents, friends of the school, and members of society who have dedicated themselves to furthering the cause of DGS education in Hong Kong.

After reading this book, I begin to realise how far the school has come since its early days and how, over the years throughout its history, the legacy of DGS has always been synonymous with the pursuit of excellence, whether in academics, sports, music, or other domains. The quest for excellence continues to this day. As I write this, the world is captivated by the defiant display of athletes from all over the world during the 2020 Tokyo Olympics, which is now taking place in the summer of 2021, delayed for months because of the pandemic. I feel particularly proud that two of our old girls made history by capturing the Bronze Olympic medal in the women's Table Tennis Team Competition, a first for DGS, and a first for the Hong Kong SAR. Their journey to overcome the odds and realise their dreams by standing on the podium amongst the world's elite exemplifies that pursuit of excellence amongst DGS girls, and validates the extra support given by the school to our athletes over the years.

On behalf of the school, I would like to convey my deepest gratitude to all members of the DGS history book project for their insight, hard work, and contribution. Together, they have amply demonstrated through their action our school motto *Daily Giving Service* as they volunteered their valuable time and talent in writing this history of our school.

Finally, I would like to dedicate this history book to Our Father in Heaven. Through Him, all things are made possible.

Foreword

Mrs Annie Lee
Headmistress of Diocesan Girls' Junior School

History always lends us a multi-dimensional view on the details and turns of events as these are slowly carved along the spectrum of time. Since 1860, nineteen years into the history of Hong Kong growing from a fishing village into the metropolitan city we see today, Diocesan Girls' School has been a witness and participant of this miraculous and blessed journey.

Despite the destruction and sufferings of the Wars, and in the midst of the successive challenges that have continued till this very day, the School has stood securely and never failed to grow and bear fruit because Father God is with us all along, fully prepared to calm our storms and bless us abundantly.

As we turn the pages and savour the very first history book of the School, let us also give thanks for all the faithful school heads, teachers, parents, old girls, and friends who have helped weave this beautiful fabric of excellence in perseverance, joy for learning, service to the community, and love for one another. Let us recount these moments of significance and relive the vivid memories that touch us personally.

"We love because He first loved us." (1 John 4:19)
"For the Lord is good, and His love endures forever;
His faithfulness continues through all generations." (Psalm 100:5)

Preface

There have been two attempts to have a history of DGS: "Diocesan Girls' School, Kowloon. A Brief History 1860–1977" written by Dr C. J. Symons, which was published in a booklet in 1978, and a manuscript on "Diocesan Girls' School 1, Jordan Road, Kowloon, Hong Kong: A Brief History 1860–2006", which was prepared by a brilliant Form 6 student, Lo Yee Sum, but was not published. Towards the end of the summer of 2019, Mrs Stella Lau discussed with me her wish to have a school history book which was long overdue. I am a DGS alumna, but I was reluctant to take on such a huge project on my own. When she opened up the project to involve other DGS alumnae, I agreed to prepare the chronological part of the school history. A talented team of alumnae, including Amy Ng, Vanessa Leung, Wun Tsz Sum, Janice Tsang, Grace Chiang, Robyn Lamsam, Andrea Lai, Yvonne Chan, and Sheilah Chatjaval, was formed to write on the various aspects of the school and its development. Mrs Stella Lau acted as our most efficient coordinator and Professor Jane Lai our wise counsellor to the project.

The information in this book came from the following sources: (1) information on the Diocesan Native Female Training School from the annual reports and minutes of meetings of the Society of Promoting Female Education for Girls in the East, covering the period from 1834 to 1879 and from 1880 to 1939. This information was found in the Church Missionary Society Archives, in the Special Collections of the Hong Kong University Library; (2) minutes of the School Committee Meetings of the Diocesan Home and Orphanage, with references to the Diocesan Native Female Training School from the book written by the Reverend W. T. Featherstone entitled *The Diocesan Boys' School and Orphanage, Hong Kong. The History and Records 1869 to 1929*; (3) minutes of the School Council meetings and general correspondence, 1945 to 1999, from the Bishop's House Archives; (4) minutes of School Council meetings, 1999 to 2019, from the School Archives; (5) records of the school's correspondence with the government, 1911 to 1960, from the Hong Kong Public Records Office; (6) historical newspapers: *South China Morning Post, China Mail, Hong Kong Daily, Hong Kong Telegraph, Kung Sheng Daily*, and *Wah Kiu Yat Po* from the University of Hong Kong Library and the Electronic Resources of the Multimedia Information Service of

Hong Kong Public Libraries; and (7) the school magazine *Quest* from 1941 to 2016–2018 and the Speech Day Booklets available after the war from the School Archives.

Because all the pre-war records of the school had been destroyed during the Japanese Occupation when the school was used as the headquarters of the Japanese Gendarmerie, the story of DGS during this period was reconstructed from the above resources and supplemented by several books written about the school during the pre-war era, some of them by DGS alumnae: *The Private Life of Old Hong Kong: Western Women in the British Colony, 1841–1941* by Susanna Hoe; *Lady Victoria Jubilee Lo* 中西融和：羅何錦姿 by Leung Hung Kei; *Intercultural Reminiscences* by Irene Cheng; *Eastern Windows, Western Skies* by Jean Gittins; *My Memories* by Florence Yeo; *Looking at the Stars: Memoirs of Catherine Joyce Symons* by C. J. Symons; and two books by Frances Wong, *China Bound and Unbound: History in the Making* and *The Lost Schools*. In addition, the reports of the two headmistresses, Miss Elizabeth Skipton and Miss Dorothy Sawyer, to the *Outpost*, an interim newsletter of the Diocese of Victoria, Hong Kong and South China, and interviews of alumnae of the school in the 1930s by the members of the DOGA were used as source materials.

While most of the materials from the Hong Kong Public Records Office, Bishop's House Archives, HKU Library Special Collections, and Hong Kong Public Libraries were collected by myself when I was in Hong Kong, the rest of the materials were made available through the modern world of technology to overcome the inability to travel as a result of lockdown of cities by the COVID-19 pandemic. The minutes of the School Council Meetings after 1999, the school magazines *Quest* and the Speech Day Booklets, old photographs, and other materials from the School Archives were uploaded by Mrs Carmen Ho of the IT Department onto the school computer drive to be accessed by myself and contributors who are living in Hong Kong or in other parts of the world. Other materials were sent by various people through emails, and Professor Nicholas Chan has been most kind in this regard. Interviews of past and present headmistresses, current and past teachers, and alumnae were carried out by telephone or through the internet. In fact, the research had been carried out much more expeditiously than by one person alone.

In recent years, some of us have become aware of the modest origin of DGS, the Diocesan Native Female Training School (DNFTS), founded in 1860 by Mrs Lydia Smith, wife of the first Bishop of Victoria and South China of the Anglican Church. The story was first told by Professor Nicholas Chan, a DBS alumnus, in a lecture which was aired in October 2020 and more recently by Professors Nicholas Chan (陳煒舜) and Fong Wing Chung (方穎聰) in their book *A Brief History of the "Female Diocesan School", Hong Kong, 1860–1869 and Beyond* (女仔館興衰：香港拔萃書室的史前史, *1860–1869*) published by Hong Kong Open Page Publishing Company Limited (香港中和出版有限公司). Their latest research revealed that Mrs Lydia Smith also established the Day Girls' School in 1858/1859 in the same building as DNFTS at Albany Terrace, and it was likely the precursor of DNFTS. The Day Girls' School was referred to as the Bishop's Diocesan Girls' School by the Rev. Ernest John Eitel, the Inspector of Schools of Hong Kong at that time. Because of the success of the Day Girls' School, Mrs Smith turned it into a boarding school to enable the girls to have more opportunities of learning the English language and Anglican Church customs, before their marriages to St. Paul's College graduates who were becoming ministers to spread the faith. We believe that the one hundred sixtieth anniversary of the school should be celebrated earlier in 2019 rather than 2020. This school history book therefore pauses the chronicle at the end of the academic year 2018/2019, in July 2019.

In writing the chronological part of the school history, I was constantly reminded that mistakes might occur. Thus, the manuscript was reviewed for accuracy by a number of people: the current and former headmistresses including Mrs Stella Lau, Mrs Elim Lau, Mrs Rebecca Yip, Mrs Emily Dai, and Mrs Annie Lee, Professor Jane Lai, Mrs Paulina Hui, Ms Yvonne Chan, and several old boys of DBS including Professors Fung Yee Wang and Nicholas Chan. While the participation of alumni of DGS and DBS might give the impression that the preparation of the school history is a family enterprise, we are very fortunate to have a distinguished panel of advisors—two of them are not our alumni—to keep us on the right path: Professor Chan Lau Kit Ching, retired Professor of History at HKU, and Dr Li Yuet Ting, former Director of Education. Professor Elizabeth Sinn, a DGS alumna and a renowned historian of Hong Kong, was the third advisor. They offered invaluable advice.

The first part of the book is a chronicle of the development of DGS in the context of the cultural, social, political, and economic settings of the community of different eras and how the school responded over the years to the needs of society and to various challenges. During each one of these challenges, the School Council, the headmistresses, and the teaching staff fought hard to keep the tradition and ethos of the school alive and to adhere to the school's original aim—to provide a well-rounded education based on Christian principles.

The second part of the book addresses the development of various aspects of the school, including the campus, spiritual life, scholastic, musical and sports activities, school life, the Diocesan Old Girls' Association, and the DGS Parent Teacher Association. The details in these chapters are inevitably linked to the main narrative, and we tried hard to avoid repetition in the two parts.

As the school's function is to provide education to girls in the community, and it has received consistent financial and moral support from the community since its inception, we feel that it would be appropriate to describe how DGS graduates contributed to Hong Kong in return. In Chapter 9, we presented the career paths of some DGS alumnae. Because the school did not keep an archive of its graduates until recently, the result of our attempt to track the career of our graduates was only patchy. The list of alumnae who made their mark in various professions was compiled by a number of alumnae including the headmistresses,

Preface

current and past. We know that there are many who contributed to society both locally and overseas, many of whom we have lost touch with, or we have no knowledge of. Since no list is exhaustive to encompass them all, we have chosen to name a few to show the diverse domains that our alumnae have worked in, and apologise for the many omissions. We have also approached all surviving individuals on the original list for their permission to name them in the history book; not surprisingly, a few modest but very worthwhile alumnae declined.

We hope the book will offer the general public some insights of how the school interacts with the community. For teachers and staff, both past and present, parents, and friends, the book marks traces of their efforts, their generosity, and their love. For the alumnae, the book may bring back some happy memories of their school days and help them understand the education they received in their formative years. For the current students, we hope to bring them an understanding of the tradition and ethos of the school and to remind them of Mrs Symons' speech during the school's centenary celebration:

> We have inherited an old and revered school, we have been given magnificent buildings, but with them, we have been handed the future of this school. You have grown to admire and love these buildings, but you are the school. Remember our motto, "Daily Giving Service".

Moira M. W. Chan-Yeung
Vancouver
April 2022

Acknowledgements

This history book is hardly an effort of my own but a composite endeavour of many people. The number of contributors to the project as detailed in the table of contents reveals the love of the alumnae for the school and their wish for the story of the school to be documented. Mrs Stella Lau, Headmistress of DGS, organised the whole project and mobilised the staff of the school to assist with the preparation of the manuscript. Among the staff who kindly supported the project were: Paulina Hui who responded to my numerous requests and fulfilled them expeditiously from various sources; Sharon Chu who worked so efficiently and diligently to gather data from various sources and to prepare the tables on School Council members, staff, and head prefects over the years, and assisted in formatting the manuscripts for publication; Carmen Ho who organised and uploaded information on the school computer drive; Grace Chiang who meticulously researched the years of the founding of various extracurricular activities; Azeem Ebrahim who obtained information on the graduates essential to the preparation of parts of Chapter 9; Joe Oddie who searched for information from the School Archives on various aspects of the school history; Alice Cheung who prepared the graphs in Chapter 9 and checked all the graphs and tables; Shirley Ping who tirelessly acted as my guide to various personnel resources, and, together Pearl Kam and the A-V team, improved all the photographs in the book; and Yvonne Chan and Andrea Lai who reviewed and checked the manuscript, the captions, notes, sources of photographs, tables, and appendices. A number of DGS old girls also sent in various useful information about the school. I wish to express my sincere gratitude to everyone involved, especially to those who helped to proofread the manuscript. The efficiency with which they completed their tasks enabled the smooth and timely completion of the project.

The enthusiastic support of many DBS alumni has been most heartening. Professor Fung Yee Wang, who guided the development of the book, reviewed the manuscript during different stages and gave his valuable comments, especially on education and extracurricular activities. In addition to providing the references on the Diocesan Native Female Training School (DNFTS) and other useful information already mentioned, Professor Nicholas Chan very kindly also reviewed Chapters 1 to 5. Dr Kenneth Suen kindly reviewed the manuscript and Mr Hanson Huang graciously sent over important titbits of DGS history.

Acknowledgements

Mr Kevin Lau scanned the book by Mary Goodban, daughter of Gerald Goodban, former DBS Headmaster, for my reference. Mr Gordon Loch, an old boy and former teacher of DBS, edited the manuscript of the first part of the book. Gordon had edited the manuscript of DBS school history previously. Their valuable contributions are greatly appreciated.

I wish to thank the current and former headmistresses of DGS: Mrs Stella Lau, Mrs Elim Lau, Mrs Rebecca Yip, Mrs Emily Dai, and Mrs Annie Lee for their assistance in providing information, taking part in interviews, and reviewing the manuscript. A number of past and present teachers participated in interviews. Their detailed answers to my questions and their frankness in expressing their views were most helpful.

I am especially indebted to Professor Peter Cunich of the University of Hong Kong (HKU) for providing the data of the number of DGS graduates from the Arts Faculty of HKU before the Second World War and for offering a number of most useful suggestions to improve the manuscript. My deepest gratitude also goes to our three highly supportive advisors: Professor Chan-Lau Kit Ching, Dr Li Yuet Ting, and Professor Elizabeth Sinn, and the two anonymous reviewers for their invaluable and constructive comments.

Finally, I would like to gratefully acknowledge the chief advisor of the project, Professor Jane Lai, whose humour, support, and wisdom, in addition to reviewing the manuscript numerous times, helped us to navigate our way through the project smoothly and successfully.

Moira M. W. Chan-Yeung
Vancouver
April 2022

Abbreviations

AAT	Academic Aptitude Test
A-level	Advanced Level
AS-level	Advanced Supplementary Level
BCG	Bacillus Calmette-Guérin
BHA	Bishop's House Archives
CCP	Chinese Communist Party
CDC	Curriculum Development Committee
CM	Certificated Mistress/Certificated Master
CMS	Church Missionary Society
CUHK	Chinese University of Hong Kong, The
DBS	Diocesan Boys' School
DGS	Diocesan Girls' School
DGJS	Diocesan Girls' Junior School
DHO	Diocesan Home and Orphanage
DNFTS	Diocesan Native Female Training School
DOGA	Diocesan Old Girls' Association
DPS	Diocesan Preparatory School
DSO	Diocesan School and Orphanage
DSS	Direct Subsidy Scheme
EC	Education Commission
ECA	Extracurricular activities
ECR	Education Commission Report
ED	Education Department
EDB	Education Bureau
EMB	Education and Manpower Bureau
FES	Female Education Society (Society for Promoting Female Education in the East)
GCE	General Certificate of Examination
GDP	Gross Domestic Product

GSC	Grant Schools Council
HKALE	Hong Kong Advanced Level Examination
HKAR	Hong Kong Administrative Reports
HKCEE	Hong Kong Certificate of Education Examination
HKDSE	Hong Kong Diploma of Secondary Education
HKPRO	Hong Kong Public Records Office
HKSAR	Hong Kong Special Administrative Region
HKSKH	Hong Kong Sheng Kung Hui
HKSP	Hong Kong Sessional Papers
HKU	University of Hong Kong, The
HKUST	Hong Kong University of Science and Technology, The
ICAC	Independent Commission Against Corruption
ICT	Information and Communication Technology
IL	Inland Lot
IT	Information Technology
JSEA	Junior Secondary Education Assessment
KIL	Kowloon Inland Lot
LegCo	Legislative Council
LMS	London Missionary Society
MCL	Ministering Children's League
MMLC	Multimedia Learning Centre
MOI	Medium of Instruction
NSS	New Senior Secondary
OECD	Organization for Economic Cooperation and Development
OLE	Other Learning Experience
O-Level	Ordinary Level
PRC	People's Republic of China
PTA	Parent Teacher Association
PTH	Putonghua
RAF	Royal Air Force
SARS	Severe Acute Respiratory Syndrome
SCMP	South China Morning Post
SIP	School Improvement Plan
SMC	School Management Committee
SMI	School Management Initiative
SSEE	Secondary School Entrance Examination
STEM	Science, Technology, Engineering, Mathematics
SSPA	Secondary School Placement Allocation

TOC	Target Oriented Curriculum
TSA	Territory-Wide System Assessment
UK	United Kingdom
US	United States of America
YMCA	Young Men's Christian Association
YWCA	Young Women's Christian Association

Part I

Chronological Perspective

Moira M. W. Chan-Yeung (1955)

Chapter 1

Historical Background: 1859 to 1898

Go ye therefore, and make disciples of all the nations.

—Matthew 28: 19–20

Over the centuries, Christians have responded to the spiritual injunction to become missionaries. Overseas missions began as early as the late seventeenth century and blossomed during the last quarter of the nineteenth century, when a dynamic combination of three elements in the Western world—university education, personal Christian awakening, and the call to missionary service—conjoined in the English-speaking world.[1] In England itself, the evangelical revival coincided with the imperialistic expansion of the British Empire, leading to a proliferation of overseas missionary activities. Because of its vast population, China presented both a challenge and an opportunity for Christian missionaries; and because of its mystique, it was also a source of fascination for missionary societies.

The missionaries aimed to teach people about Jesus Christ and His great commandment to love God and to love others. In achieving this aim, they needed to overcome the prejudice and suspicion of local people from a completely different culture and to gain access behind closed doors by practising "love in action" through service to the community. It was thought that medical missions might be the best way for missionaries to show "love in action" by healing the sick while simultaneously spreading the gospel in hospitals and clinics. Yet they were not highly successful in winning converts to Christianity. Most of the time, medical missionaries found that they spent all their time healing with no time for evangelical duties during their brief contact with people. Moreover, in some countries,

---

1. Robin Boyd, *The Witness of the Student Christian Movement* (London: Society of Promoting Christian Knowledge, 2007), 1.

especially in China, local people did not consult them because of their distrust in Western medicine.

Education, on the other hand, provided opportunities for the missionaries to teach the love of Christ through prolonged contact. There was also a demand for the locals to learn English for trade. The missionaries established schools mostly for boys in the beginning. At that time, girls were not given an education in many parts of the world. In China, women had no legal rights and were confined in their homes. The task of educating girls was problematic and indeed impossible for male missionaries. Nevertheless, the missionaries believed that by giving girls education, they could eventually improve the position of women in society. This unenviable and difficult task fell on the shoulders of wives of missionaries and female missionaries, who contributed greatly to the development of girls' education not only in Hong Kong and China but also in other parts of the world.

Diocesan Girls' School (DGS) was founded in the mid-nineteenth century by the wife of the first Bishop of Victoria and South China who believed in "love in action" by serving others. Her work was subsequently continued by other female Christians, equally enthusiastic in giving service to others despite multiple trials and tribulations throughout DGS's long history. They all enacted the school motto, "Daily Giving Service".

The Sociocultural and Political Backdrop: When East Meets West

In the mid-eighteenth century, Britain's Industrial Revolution proved to be the catalyst for the nation's expansionist policy, resulting in the establishment of dominions, colonies, protectorates, mandates and territories across the globe; by the nineteenth century, Britain was the largest and most powerful empire in the world. In 1842, Hong Kong Island became a colonial administration under Britain after the Chinese Qing empire lost the First Opium War.

At that time, China was facing a number of problems even before the Opium War. The population surged from 200 million to 400 million between the sixteenth and eighteenth centuries, which was not accompanied by an increase in agricultural production. By the nineteenth century, the food shortage had become evident. The Opium War was not just a political upheaval; it also had economic and social repercussions. Together with the destructive Taiping Rebellion, which started in 1850 and lasted till 1864, the Opium War led to the disintegration of what remained of the Qing empire.

In its early days, Hong Kong had only about 7,000 people, mostly farmers and fishermen. As the British began to build the City of Victoria, more Chinese arrived from the hinterland looking for opportunities to make a living. The majority of this immigrant influx comprised labourers, coolies, stonecutters, builders, hawkers, and others attending to such a pioneering population (cooks, fortune tellers, and entertainers, for example),

Historical Background: 1859 to 1898

mainly from the lower strata of society, all hoping to make a future for themselves and for their families. The two races were encouraged, and at times forced, to segregate, with the Chinese crowded in the Tai Ping Shan, or the steeper, western area where running water and proper sewage were lacking, whilst initially the Europeans mostly tended to live on the east of Pottinger Street and gradually moved along the Mid-Levels to the west. As the population in Hong Kong increased, the European population moved to the Peak, where the Chinese were forbidden unless they were servants of the European residents.

From the outset, the mercantile community had a clear vision for the purpose of Hong Kong's establishment as a colonial outpost. It was to facilitate and control trade into China. At first, the colonial government instituted a small, but effective, administration to transform Hong Kong into the "Emporium of the Far East"; however, this enterprise failed to materialise in the early years partly because of rampant piracy in the nearby waters around Hong Kong as well as competition from several Treaty Ports, such as Shanghai, Guangzhou, Ningpo, Foochow, and Amoy in China that opened up at the same time. Another reason was that wealthy Chinese merchants found it advantageous to live in Guangzhou.

With Hong Kong established as a free port, the government received little revenue, while public works expenses towards developing infrastructure from scratch were huge. British merchants in Hong Kong believed that their government should bear all such development expenses and that they should be free from governmental interference. Although the British government did give a small grant, the financial aid was discontinued in the 1850s, and as a result, there was little to spend on any public service, let alone medical or education services for the native population.

Shortly after the establishment of Hong Kong as a colonial administrative region, missionaries from various societies arrived, intent on introducing Christianity to China, combining the Christian ideals with educational and Western medical services, which the Chinese communities sorely lacked. At that time, most missionaries regarded Hong Kong as a stepping stone to a wider conversion objective in China, but some stayed in Hong Kong and contributed greatly to the territory's system of education by founding missionary schools, introducing Western medical services, and building hospitals and clinics, and even establishing the Hong Kong College of Medicine for Chinese, which later became the Faculty of Medicine of the University of Hong Kong. The first missionary society to arrive was the Morrison Education Society, which transferred its school from Macau to Hong Kong in 1842. The Catholic Church, the London Missionary Society (LMS), and the Anglican Church followed.

Foreign missionaries were not the first to introduce the concept of schooling to the Chinese in Hong Kong; a few small private schools called *sishu* (私塾) were already in operation before their arrival. A *sishu*, along the lines of traditional Chinese village schools, typically consisted of one teacher tutoring about a dozen boys on a curriculum of basic literacy and Confucian classics, with some form of mathematics and general knowledge taught, but no physical education or music. At that time, girls did not attend school, and their learning was restricted to housework, embroidery, and crafts taught by elders at home. Unsurprisingly, the first two schools founded by missionaries were for boys only: the first was founded by the Rev. James Legge of the LMS, who moved the Anglo-Chinese College from Malacca to Hong Kong in 1843, later known as Ying Wah College; the second was St Paul's College, founded by the Rev. Vincent Stanton of the Anglican Church in 1851 to teach Chinese boys English, with the aim of training them to spread the gospel among the Chinese people. The establishment of St Paul's Convent School in 1854 by the Sisters of St Paul de Chartres followed but was limited to educating girls who grew up in their orphanage.

In Britain, before the 1850s, few children, apart from the upper classes and clergy, received a formal education. Most boys who went to school were educated to become teachers, lawyers, or clergymen. By contrast, most girls, if they went to school, received only a general education, which was deemed sufficient as they were expected to be married, serving men as wives, with no greater role to play in society. If a woman without independent means remained single, she would become a nanny or governess or teacher of young children. But, as industrialisation gave men increasing opportunities for work in many new areas, such as engineering, medicine, sciences, and trade, the role of teaching was, by default, left to women. As a result, girls required a higher level of education to support a system that enhanced men's superior academic and professional positioning in the patriarchal British society at the time. However, by 1868, universities opened their doors for women, and by 1880, education became compulsory for all children aged five to ten.

By contrast, in Hong Kong and China, women had virtually no legal rights and were relegated to an inferior role, confined in their households. Their social position was constricted by the Confucian concept of a woman's role in the family. They were expected to follow the doctrine of "Three Obediences": to obey their fathers in childhood, their husbands when married, and their sons when older. Female subjugation even extended to the blotting out of the personal given name by the use of the woman's familial role in much social discourse. She bore her husband's surname and was addressed as "the wife of [X]" or "the mother of [Y]".

Girls did chores in the family or worked to contribute to the family income. Even those from well-to-do or genteel families who did not have to work were, for the most part, not spared a role in supporting a male-dominated society. Under the Song dynasty (tenth century AD), the cruel practice of foot-binding began among court dancers and courtesans. The long, torturous procedure began early in a girl's life when her toes were bent, forced under her foot and bound, so that her feet were permanently disfigured and maimed to enhance her figure, movement, and gait for the purpose of satisfying what was considered

Historical Background: 1859 to 1898

an erotic appeal to the Chinese male.[2] The practice became widespread and developed into something of a status symbol of wealth and a genteel upbringing. Though attempts were made by the late Qing authorities to ban the practice, it persisted into the early twentieth century in some families in Hong Kong, much to the consternation of Western missionaries and educationalists who held that the point of a woman's existence was not just to serve the desires of men.

Diocesan Native Female Training School, 1860 to 1869

When Mrs Lydia Smith, wife of George Smith, Bishop of Victoria and South China (Bishop 1849–1866), arrived in Hong Kong with her husband in 1849, she found herself in a society dominated by Confucian thought and conventional Chinese norms. As a member of the Society of Promoting Female Education for Girls in the East (FES), Mrs Smith was keenly interested in education for girls. The FES was a Protestant Christian missionary society that was involved in sending missionary workers to China and other Asian countries during the late Qing dynasty (late nineteenth to early twentieth centuries). In 1858, Mrs Smith had the opportunity to establish the Girls' Day School in Hong Kong. Accordingly, she hired a school mistress and appealed to the FES for assistance and support. Luckily, the FES was highly supportive and granted £25 to help run the school. The school, which was opened on 18 April 1858 in Albany Terrace near the hillside of the present Zoological Gardens in a new house provided by the government, had nine Chinese girls,[3] and the number increased the following year. Despite her dedication and passion for the education of young women, Mrs Smith only considered the Girls' Day School as an experiment. The unwillingness of the Chinese lower classes to entrust foreigners with the education of their female children put the potential success of the project into jeopardy. Given the cultural background of Hong Kong dominated by Confucian teaching, the school was, indeed, a brave venture.

Attesting to the success of Mrs Smith's academic venture about a year after its establishment was the realisation that the school no longer required the grant of £25 to sustain operations. Since there was adequate local subscription for the school, Bishop Smith wrote to the FES cancelling the grant and mentioned that he hoped to expand opportunities for female education through the establishment of a boarding school for girls and an application to the Society for a teacher.[4] The popularity of the Girls' Day School encouraged

---

2. J. Preston Maxwell, "On the Evil of Chinese Foot-Binding", in *The China Medical Journal* 30 (1916): 393–396; Wang Ping, *Aching for Beauty: Foot-Binding in China* (Minneapolis/London: University of Minnesota Press, 2000), 32.

3. Entry 2950, Minutes of the Committee of the Society of Promoting Female Education for Girls in the Far East (FES), 11 March 1858.

4. Entry 3160, Minutes of the Committee of FES, 16 July 1859.

Mrs Smith to go ahead with her second project following the above exchange between her husband and the FES. In 1860, she founded the Diocesan Native Female Training School (DNFTS), an institution she hoped would educate girls from a higher social class, as stated in its first annual report:

> The object of the institution is not to provide for the friendless and the destitute: there are other and excellent establishments which have this in view. The present is rather an effort to introduce among a somewhat superior class of native females the blessings of Christianity and religious training . . . and they were to occupy positions of influence and usefulness.

There is some evidence to indicate that Mrs Smith changed the name of the Girls' Day School (which in 1892 was referred to by the Rev. E. J. Eitel, the then Inspector of Education, as "Bishop's Diocesan Girls' School"—the first time the name Diocesan Girls' School was used) to DNFTS, a boarding school, located in the same building.[5] The FES also considered that DNFTS evolved from the Girls' Day School.[6] A motivating factor to educate these girls at that time was to make them suitable wives for the young male converts (referring to the graduates of St Paul's College),[7] as evidenced by the Ladies Committee's report to the FES in December 1863:

> course of education has embraced instruction in Chinese and English reading, writing, plain needlework, geography, and Bible history, and more especially a training in the religious truths and moral habits of the Christian faith. The object aimed at has been to prepare the girls for taking hereafter a position of usefulness in native society as the future wives and mothers of the rising generation of Chinese inhabitants in the colony.[8]

When Mrs Smith applied to the FES for support for her new venture and to send out an agent to organise the school, she received an enthusiastic response.[9] One of the members, who had longed to be a missionary in China, was Miss Susan Harriet Baxter, second daughter of Mr Robert Baxter, a parliamentary solicitor located in Westminster, a man of

---

5. E. J. Eitel, "Materials for a History of Education", in *China Review or Notes and Queries on the Far East*, XIX (1892): 361–395, CO129/254. Eitel wrote "that the Board of Education at that time, when they approved Dr. Legge's draft of that circular (2nd April, 1861), resolved that the Bishop's Diocesan Girls' School, which had been placed under the Board as a grant-in-aid school 15 months previous (12 December 1859) could not remain under the Board's Superintendence 'being a Christian School and constituted differently from the Government schools'. The institution called by James Legge as 'the Bishop's Diocesan Girls' school' in December 1859 before the founding of DNFTS is most likely the Girls' Day School ran by Lady Smith. The Girls' Day School was most likely the preparatory phase of DNFTS."

6. Patricia P. K. Chiu, "A Position of Usefulness: Gendering History of Girls' Education in Colonial Hong Kong (1850s–1890s)", in *History of Education* 17, no. 6 (2008): 789–805.

7. *The Female Missionary Intelligencer* 1 (1858): 173.

8. *The Female Missionary Intelligencer* 7 (July 1864): 143.

9. Entry 3220, Minutes of the Committee of FES, 5 December 1895.

Historical Background: 1859 to 1898

strong religious convictions and, most importantly, independent financial means. Upon learning of Mrs Smith's proposal, Miss Baxter agreed to undertake the organisation and the superintendence of DNFTS using her own resources.[10] In the meantime, there was a great deal of support locally for Mrs Smith's proposal. DNFTS opened in March 1860 with the timely arrival of Miss Wilson, a schoolmistress from England, who became the temporary superintendent of DNFTS until Miss Baxter's arrival, upon which Miss Wilson planned to step down and pass along control of the institution.[11]

The Wilson Years (March 1860–December 1862)

The school, operating under the guidance of a women-only team called the Ladies Committee, was situated in Albany Terrace, the same building as the Girls' Day School.[12] It was inaugurated with a student body of nine Chinese girls, all with small feet, characteristic of foot-binding to indicate that they were from upper-class families.[13] The school was considered a great success even during its first year of operation, as some Chinese teachers from government schools brought their daughters forward for admission. The following year, it became more popular as the number of Chinese girls increased to fifteen. The school's underlying Christian values were illustrated by the "baptism of two older girls in the school and their Christian conduct and deportment",[14] to the satisfaction of the Committee of Ladies.

When Miss Baxter arrived in April 1860, she did not take over the superintendentship of DNFTS from Miss Wilson as expected. Rather, Baxter was disappointed with DNFTS. Having determined to devote her life to the poor and destitute in China, she found that DNFTS's aim of teaching a privileged and wealthy class of girls did not square with her principles to help the less fortunate. Using her own resources, she established four small schools: an English school on Mosque Street for children of British soldiers, a school for European orphans and children of mixed race, a Chinese girls' day school on Staunton Street, and a boarding school for orphaned children in her own house on Bonham Road. The Chinese girls in her schools were taught in a traditional Chinese curriculum by Pong Shi, a young Chinese widow, while Baxter herself taught prayers and simple scriptural

---

10. Susanna Hoe, *The Private Life of Old Hong Kong* (Hong Kong: Oxford University Press, 1991), 112.

11. Hoe, *The Private Life of Old Hong Kong*, 111.

12. Hoe, *The Private Life of Old Hong Kong*, 110.

13. Hoe, *The Private Life of Old Hong Kong*, 111.

14. W. T. Featherstone, The First Annual Report of DNFTS, in W. T. Featherstone, *The Diocesan Boys' School and Orphanage: The History and Records, 1969 to 1929*, 14.

passages.[15] Baxter quickly became a friend to all the needy, from soldiers' wives to poor Chinese families, and she often visited, with Mrs Smith, the lodging houses of European and American sailors in the back streets of Victoria. After a while, she learned to speak colloquial Cantonese fluently from conversing constantly with Chinese women.[16]

Although she did not become the superintendent of the school, Miss Baxter still remained closely associated with DNFTS, teaching their students in Sunday School at St John's Cathedral. She also helped her younger colleague, Miss Mary Anne Winifred Eaton, who became the superintendent of DNFTS after Miss Wilson's departure. In fact, Baxter provided strong behind-the-scenes spiritual and moral support in upholding the school.[17] DNFTS measured its success by its students' conversions to Christianity, and during the second year, two more girls publicly declared their faith, and seven out of sixteen students of DNFTS were baptised the following year. In the eyes of the church, Miss Wilson did a wonderful job with the school, and she thought highly of the children who reciprocated her trust and affection. In her report to the FES, she wrote, "Although I have not been well lately, things have gone very nicely. I think the children are the best in the world."[18]

At the end of the third year of DNFTS's operation, in December 1862, Miss Wilson left Hong Kong because of poor health. Indeed, Hong Kong was far from being a comfortable place to live then. The city was known for its unsanitary living conditions, especially in the Tai Ping Shan area where the poverty-stricken Chinese congregated. There was no running water, proper refuse disposal, or adequate sewage. Infectious diseases, including malaria, cholera, dysentery, and smallpox, were rampant and, at that time, without any known treatment. Average life expectancy was low, generally under forty years. The exhausting summer heat and humidity forced many Europeans to leave after a couple of years, unable to tolerate the hostile weather and poor sanitary conditions.

To express their gratitude to Miss Wilson for a job well done, the Ladies Committee raised funds for a first-class boat ticket for her return to England. The public responded generously, so much so that a relatively large sum still remained even after Miss Wilson's travels had been paid for. Unfortunately, the decision of the committee to retain the leftover money for future use of the school resulted in an extensive debate in the *China Mail*, some agreeing with the decision of the committee while others denounced it. The latter group argued that the funds were raised for Miss Wilson and the entire amount should be given

---

15. Patricia P. K. Chiu, "Female Education and the Early Development of St. Stephen's Church, Hong Kong [1865–1900s]", in *Christian Encounter with Chinese Culture: Essays on Anglican and Episcopal History in China*, ed. Philip Wickeri (Hong Kong: Hong Kong University Press, 2015), 53–54.

16. Hoe, *The Private Life of Old Hong Kong*, 112.

17. Hoe, *The Private Life of Old Hong Kong*, 113.

18. 28th Annual Report of the FES, January 1862.

Historical Background: 1859 to 1898

to her. This incident left the public to question the judgement of the Ladies Committee.[19] With few things to occupy them in those days, the British colonists often amused themselves by writing to the press, thus making mountains out of molehills and inflating the significance of trivial issues.

The Eaton Years (January 1863–December 1865)

Miss Mary A. W. Eaton arrived from England in January 1863 to succeed Miss Wilson as the superintendent of DNFTS, just in time to witness the move of the school from Albany Terrace to a hired house in Mosque Street and subsequently to the new schoolhouse on Bonham Road. With its initial success, DNFTS was granted a site from the government (IL831) at the corner of Bonham Road and Eastern Street. The cost of the building was about HK$8,000, covered by donations from the Chinese public and the government. On 14 July 1863,[20] the institution was opened by Bishop Smith, in the presence of His Excellency, acting Governor William Thomas Mercer, and their wives, together with Miss Baxter and members of the Ladies Committee.

By this time, the student body had reached thirty girls, educated in Chinese and English reading, writing, plain needle work, geography, Bible reading, and training "in the religious truths and moral habits of the Christian faith".[21] The number of students had increased to the point that Miss Eaton could not execute her responsibilities alone and was in desperate need of an assistant. Although attempts were made by the FES to secure the appointment of Miss Bailey, a friend of Miss Eaton, to come from England to help, this plan unfortunately did not materialise, and the service of another assistant was sought.

Lydia Leung, who took her Christian name, "Lydia", from Mrs Lydia Smith, and was the eldest student in the school, described her typical day at the school as follows:

> rise early in the morning, arrange bedroom, prepare Chinese lessons before breakfast, first hour after breakfast devoted to family prayer, Scripture lesson (Mimpriss), and repetition of hymns. Followed by English reading with questioning both on meaning of the words and on the subject of the lesson, writing, simple arithmetic or object lesson, concluded with singing, geography or the elements of grammar; an hour in middle of day lunch, each girl have ten cash, half a penny given her. Assu (interpreter) teaches Chinese and at the same time explain the lesson from Mimpress reading in the

---

19. *China Mail*, 18 January 1863 and 22 January 1863.
20. 30th Annual Report of FES, April 1864, 7.
21. Hoe, *The Private Life of Old Hong Kong*, 114, quoted from *The Female Missionary Intelligencer*, vols. 7–9 (2 May 1864): 90.

Figure 1.1: Miss M. A. W. Eaton and the girls of DNFTS. Source: *The Female Missionary Intelligencer* Volume VII, May 1864, Original Title: "Diocesan Native Female Training School, Hong Kong".

Figure 1.2: Lydia Leung, one of the first pupils, and three other girls of DNFTS. Source: *The Female Missionary Intelligencer* VII, January 1864, cover, original title: "Girls in the Diocesan Native Female Training School, Hong Kong".

Historical Background: 1859 to 1898

morning, and the children are examined and instructed upon it. Needlework occupies the remainder of the afternoon. Four thirty dinner; eight o'clock to bed.[22]

During the week, Lydia, being the eldest, would see to it that every girl swept and dusted in rotation and that two of the girls waited on the schoolmistress. Occasionally, a day or portion of a day would be devoted to cooking, washing, ironing, and finishing needlework. On Sunday mornings the girls attended Sunday School in St John's Cathedral and stayed for morning service. In the afternoon, they sang and read.

Miss Eaton's second year (1864) as superintendent was marked by an event that aroused a great deal of interest and hope. Lydia married a Chinese catechist. This event was chronicled in *The Female Missionary Intelligencer* on 1 August 1864:[23]

> Miss Eaton was unable to go to the house of the bride, so Miss Baxter went instead and accompanied the bride's chair the two miles to the Cathedral. There she supported the bride as the smallness of her feet rendered it painful for her to stand for a long time. Miss Eaton was near to her as well as some members of the School Committee . . . Lady Robinson stopped to speak to the bride at the Church door. After the ceremony, there was a Chinese entertainment, organized by the committee, in the Bishop's dining room at St. Paul's College, and then they all moved to the drawing room where Mrs. Stringer, wife of the Colonial Chaplain, played the piano and sang. Lydia and her new husband stayed for a couple of days until they left for his new job in Foochow.

Thus, the ultimate purpose envisaged for DNFTS, to provide suitable marriage partners for male converts of St Paul's College, was realised for the first time. In Foochow, Lydia successfully helped run a girls' boarding school and set up a girls' day school under the FES.[24]

During the same year, two other girls left the school for different parts of Guangdong province, presumably to teach or to launch their own schools, as Miss Eaton wrote, "They are young and inexperienced, but have, I trust, 'put on the Lord.'" The FES Committee in London regarded the event with gratitude and hope, marking this as the beginning of a "native female agency" in Hong Kong.[25] However, despite these good tidings, not all was well at DNFTS. Six months after her arrival, Miss Eaton expressed grave doubts to the Ladies Committee regarding the utility of teaching the girls English. She did not feel that their progress reflected the time spent on learning English, and the girls did not understand English sufficiently to receive lessons in grammar or geography as suggested by Mrs Smith. Miss Eaton suggested that the girls should be taught differently and start to learn English

---

22. Chiu, "A Position of Usefulness: Gendering History of Girls' Education in Colonial Hong Kong (1850s–1890s)", 794–795.

23. *The Female Missionary Intelligencer*, vol. 7–9 (1 August 1864): 159–160; Susanna Hoe, *The Private Life of Old Hong Kong*, 114.

24. 31st Annual Reports of FES, January 1865, 7.

25. 31st Annual Report of FES, January 1865, 8.

afresh.[26] Yet she was told by the Ladies Committee that limited academic achievement was expected of the girls.

Towards the end of 1864, an unexpected event occurred that precipitated a crisis in the school and led to its ultimate decline. On the evening of Sunday 4 December 1864, Miss Eaton was returning home from the chapel in her sedan chair (then the only mode of transport other than walking), and on Caine Road between where the garden behind the Hong Kong Museum of Medical Sciences is today and the school, a gang of ruffians sprang from the hillside on the sound of a whistle and viciously attacked the chair-bearers. Some tried hard to turn the chair over, and others, armed with knives, overpowered the chair-coolies, forcefully dragging the frightened Miss Eaton onto the road, trying to take her watch. Miss Eaton struggled violently and shrieked for help. For several minutes she fought the assailants with all her might, and as they pulled her uphill, she managed to free herself and escape to the school. She received no assistance from anyone else despite her repeated and desperate cries for help.[27] DNFTS was considered far out of town and the roads lonely and dangerous, without motors, rickshaws, or Sikh police. It was dangerous for a woman to travel without protection.

The purpose of the attack was not necessarily to rob Miss Eaton of her watch but to punish her for her association with the teaching of English to Chinese girls and, by extension, their degradation. The disdain for the education of Chinese children in English partly stemmed from the humiliating treaty at the conclusion of the Second Opium War, which ended with the Convention of Peking in 1860. The agreement resulted in the cession of Kowloon south of the Boundary Street to the British, together with the opening of Tianjin as a port, the legalisation of the opium trade, and indemnities to Britain and France of 8 million taels of silver. This demeaning political moment led to considerable hostility among the Chinese towards the British, and therefore, very few Chinese wanted to send their boys, let alone their girls, to learn English.

As a result of this racial tension, and despite a prosperous start, the school had not been able to continuously secure girls from a good social class and was forced to accept girls from families of inferior economic standing. In 1865, it was reported that after graduating from school, some of these lower-class young women were sold by their parents to become "household companions" of foreigners, a less provocative term denoting kept mistresses, formerly known as "protected women". Because they could communicate in English, these girls were very attractive to that demographic of the male European community, who purchased them as companions. When one of the girls from DNFTS was sold for a high price

---

26. Minute Book of the Local Committee dated 1 July 1863 from Featherstone, *The Diocesan Boys' School and Orphanage: The History and Records*, 92.

27. "Desperate Attack on a Lady", *Hong Kong Daily Press*, 6 December 1864.

of $500,[28] the school discontinued English education, as teaching English to the Chinese girls was considered to be fatal to their character and only fostered the local system of concubinage.[29] Without a doubt, few DNFTS students wished to be sold or to become mistresses of foreigners.

In the same era, the treaty ports opened up to foreign powers for trade and became the melting pots for intermarriage, legal or otherwise. Most of the large British corporations or "Hongs" had a "ten-year rule" for young men who ventured to outposts such as Hong Kong: they were forbidden to marry until they had been away from home for ten years. This rule, not surprisingly, resulted in many kept mistresses,[30] and, of course, many unwanted babies. Many Eurasian children born out of wedlock became orphans without familial support when their fathers left the Far East, creating problems for the mothers and for the local community—a social issue that the next bishop, Bishop Richard Charles Alford (Bishop of Victoria and South China 1867–1874), hoped to solve.

Apart from the removal of the English language from the curriculum, the school bore other consequences of the attack on Miss Eaton. After her assault, she reported the incident the following day to the Ladies Committee and to the police, requesting the committee to give her holidays at once instead of at Christmas. However, she did not receive an answer nor were there any measures taken for her protection over the following three days. On 8 December, the parents of the older girls insisted on removing their daughters from the school, fearing that the girls might be attacked. Younger students also asked permission to leave, and on receiving no reply or protection from anyone, Miss Eaton gave them permission to do so.

At about this time, Miss Eaton was informed by Mrs Stringer, Secretary of the Ladies Committee, that she was dismissed on account of want of judgement and disregard of the school.[31] Apparently, the Ladies Committee met on 8 December. While it agreed to give Miss Eaton her holidays at once rather than wait until Christmas, it also decided that the girls should not go away at that time. Miss Baxter had promised to send Mrs Ainsworth, a teacher from Miss Baxter's school, to supervise the girls at DNFTS during Miss Eaton's absence. The committee also made a request to the governor to protect the school and agreed to subscribe a sum of money to be given to the chair-bearers, who were overcome

---

28. Extracts from the Minute Book of the Local Committee of DNFTS, dated 19 July 1865, Featherstone, *The Diocesan Boys' School and Orphanage: The History and Records*, 95.

29. Eitel to the Colonial Secretary, 5 July 1889, CO 129/242, 80.

30. Yee Wang Fung and Moira Chan-Yeung, *To Serve and to Lead: A History of the Diocesan Boys' School* (Hong Kong: Hong Kong University Press, 2009), 18.

31. Entry 4250, Minutes of the Committee of the FES, 9 February 1865.

by the ruffians in their efforts to fight them off.[32] The committee, however, was angered by Miss Eaton giving permission to the students to leave school on her own initiative and dismissed her on that count. In the end, Miss Eaton apologised to the Ladies Committee and the committee reinstated her, although several members of the committee resigned as a result.

The attack on Miss Eaton and her dismissal caused a commotion in Hong Kong and a debate raged in the *Daily Press* newspaper. While most people were sympathetic to Miss Eaton, others sided with the committee's decision to fire her. The most significant outcome of this episode was that DNFTS lost public support. Subscriptions failed to flow in, partly because the school's reputation had been tarnished by girls being sold after leaving the school, and partly because of the administrative blunders of the Ladies Committee. The second consequence was the resignation of the entire Ladies Committee and its replacement by a committee composed only of men (the School Committee). Miss Eaton received strong support from the FES, who thought the Ladies Committee lacked sympathy and Christian forbearance. The final result of this saga was that fewer and fewer families requested admission for their daughters.

On 29 June 1865, Miss Baxter passed away.[33] This made matters worse for DNFTS. Miss Baxter was a pillar of the community who had provided spiritual guidance and support to the school and to Miss Eaton. Her death left her own schools in a most unsettled state. Since DNFTS was not fully occupied, it was decided that the girls in Baxter's boarding school could move into the empty wing of DNFTS under the supervision of Miss M. J. Oxlad, Baxter's assistant. Miss Eaton continued to serve in the school until the end of the year when she resigned, prior to her marriage to the Rev. E. J. Eitel, a German sinologist, who became the Inspector of Schools in Hong Kong. The resignation of Miss Eaton put Miss Oxlad in charge of DNFTS.

The Diocesan Female School under Miss Oxlad (1866–1869)

At the beginning of 1866, the name of the school was changed to the Diocesan Female School, and it began to admit European students and those from mixed marriages. Children were still segregated by race, with the Chinese in one wing and the Europeans and mixed races in the opposite wing, with the teachers' residence in between. For a while, there was talk of amalgamating Baxter's Chinese Girls' School and Diocesan Female School; however, this union did not take place because of the terms laid down by Miss

---

32. Minute Book of the Local Committee, 8 December 1864, Featherstone, *The Diocesan Boys' School and Orphanage: The History and Records*, 94.

33. *Hong Kong Daily Press*, 2 August 1865.

Historical Background: 1859 to 1898

Figure 1.3: Miss Oxlad, Louisa and Bessie Rickomartz, and Johanna of Diocesan Female School. Source: *The Female Missionary Intelligencer* XI, February 1868. Note: Louisa and Bessie Rickomartz were orphans of a Japanese Christian father and a British mother. They entered DNFTS when their parents died. When Miss Oxlad left, Louisa, with a Chinese Christian teacher, carried on the teaching at Baxter's vernacular day school, while Bessie assisted the missionaries in daily chores and care for the sick children and took part in the Sunday school. Later Bessie took up a job as a nursery governess for a European family and moved to France with them. Note the girls were wearing Western dresses.

Baxter before her death. Her father, Mr Robert Baxter, who had supported his late daughter's schools, followed her wish and asked Miss Oxlad to re-establish herself with Baxter's students in a small house and to call the institution the "Baxter Female Mission". However, the Diocesan Female School Committee did not permit Miss Oxlad to take up missionary work outside the school, and Miss Oxlad chose to stay as a permanent teacher in Diocesan Female School instead.[34]

The Diocesan Female School under Miss Oxlad also had some of Baxter's girls under its care. The Rev. Warren, a missionary from the Church Missionary Society (CMS) and a member of the School Committee, who had been responsible for teaching the children scripture and to prepare those willing for baptism, was able to arrange a few baptisms among the girls in the school in 1866 and 1867, which demonstrated the school's success in the eyes of the European community.[35] In 1867, the School Committee agreed to provide a

---

34. Minute Book of the Local Committee, 3 September 1866, Featherstone, *The Diocesan Boys' School and Orphanage: The History and Records*, 95.
35. Letter from the Reverend Warren to Mr Penn, 10 May 1867, CMS/C/CH/O90/36.

salary, room, and board for Miss Oxlad for another year, but her health was sadly deteriorating. On hearing this news, the FES Committee decided to send a teacher to the school to give time for further local arrangement. Miss Rendle, therefore, arrived on the scene to relieve Miss Oxlad of her duties. Miss Oxlad retired to the position of matron in the Diocesan Female School.[36]

In the meantime, the financial situation of Diocesan Female School worsened as the number of students continued to decline and subscriptions dwindled. With the retirement of Bishop Smith, Bishop Alford was appointed. He was also interested in female education but had yet to arrive from England. The local acting colonial chaplain was unable to grant to the school a general offertory from St John's Cathedral, which was a decision that only the Bishop could make on his arrival. The School Committee wrote to the Bishop about the school's financial difficulties and that its closure would be imminent without further funding. The Bishop replied that he could not be of immediate help, so by November, with no funding, the School Committee decided to dismiss the majority of its Chinese students, except the orphans and those who could pay $3 per month. Even though a bazaar was organised to raise funds, the amount generated was insufficient to pay Miss Rendle. Miss Oxlad was asked once again to take over teaching duties as well as to continue her role as matron. With no further responses from the Bishop, the School Committee decided to dissolve itself and informed the bishop of its actions on 9 December 1867.[37]

Bishop Alford finally arrived in Hong Kong and met with the School Committee, leading to the withdrawal of its letter of dissolution. The Bishop organised an extraordinary meeting of the friends of Diocesan Female School, which was held at St Paul's College on 8 January 1868. During the meeting, the Bishop proposed to take the entire management of the school into his own hands in conjunction with the colonial chaplain as a temporary measure until other arrangements could be made. The academic year of 1868/1869 proceeded with many difficulties under the superintendentship of Miss Oxlad at a diminishing budget of about $1,900, partly from donations and subscriptions given in response to the appeal from the Bishop. With very few students, the future of the school became uncertain. The FES Committee decided to ask Miss Oxlad to return to England for a visit, believing that she had enough anxiety and burden on her shoulders from the last five years in Hong Kong and that a rest in England would strengthen and refresh her physical and mental health.[38] Miss Oxlad was asked by Bishop Alford to remain in the institution until the arrival of the new superintendent and his wife to head the institution.[39] The departure

---

36. Entry 4697, Minutes of FES Committee, 21 March 1867.

37. Minute Books of Local Committee, 9 December 1867, Featherstone, *The Diocesan Boys' School and Orphanage: The History and Records*, 97.

38. Entry 5007, Minutes of the Committee of FES, 10 December 1868.

39. Entry 5082, Minutes of the Committee of FES, 20 May 1869.

of Miss Oxlad to England marked the end of Diocesan Female School, which would soon be replaced by another institution, the Diocesan Home and Orphanage (DHO), which the Bishop thought would be better supported by the public.

The Diocesan Home and Orphanage: A Co-educational Institution

The Taiping Rebellion (1850–1864), the bloodiest rebellion in world history that resulted in millions of deaths, altered the characteristics of the Chinese population in Hong Kong. During the rebellion there was an influx of immigrants from a completely different socio-economic stratum into the territory. These newcomers were better educated and sought political stability for their families as well as education for their children. In 1860, Kowloon was ceded to Britain, increasing the size of the administrative region. Britain appointed a governor who would oversee the overall affairs of Hong Kong, rather than one whose main duty was to supervise trade in China. Sir Hercules Robinson (Governor, 1859–1865), the first such governor, took up his appointment in 1859 and began to develop not just infra-structure but also education and other basic social services.

Before Robinson's arrival, there was an Education Committee chaired by Bishop Smith to deal with all education matters in Hong Kong. Robinson established the Board of Education to replace the Education Committee and appointed the Rev. James Legge as acting chairman because of the frequent absences of the Bishop. The Rev. Legge was a member of the LMS, which was made up of dissenting Protestant churches that often found themselves at odds with the established Church of England in general and the CMS in particular. His personal values showed a stark departure from the church's traditional view on education: he advocated education for its own sake rather than for the spread of the gospel. He also recognised the practical value of English in China and promoted the teaching of English. During his time on the board, two schools were established that even-tually became elite schools in Hong Kong: Central School (the present Queen's College, established in 1862) and the DHO (established in 1870). The Central School was the first school established by the government under Legge as a model school in Hong Kong. Its headmaster, Frederick Stewart, a young man of 24, was also appointed Inspector of Schools. The school had access to greater government resources for its development over the years than the missionary schools.[40]

By the late 1860s, the humiliation of the Convention of Peking as a result of the Second Opium War was a distant memory for most of the Chinese in Hong Kong. With British trade flourishing, Hong Kong became increasingly important as a point of entry into the Mainland. The city began to prosper, and it also became apparent that there was an

---

40. Fung and Chan-Yeung, *To Serve and to Lead*, 7–8.

increasing need for individuals who were fluent in both English and Chinese and with a sound knowledge of both cultures. In China, there was also a growing demand for young men who were competent in English to go abroad for further education in Western sciences and engineering. These two factors led to an expansion of education in Hong Kong, with an emphasis on the English language.

Government Education Initiatives

In the early colonial period, the missionary schools established in the territory did not receive support from the colonial government. When Bishop Alford became Bishop of Victoria and South China, he was concerned with the status of various missionary schools in Hong Kong and their poor financial health, as both St Paul's College and the Diocesan Female School were in debt. Both institutions were highly dependent on subscriptions. Bishop Alford met Governor Sir Richard MacDonnell about these missionary schools. The governor promised that he would help but only as an individual parishioner of the church.[41]

However, as trade pressed for the demand of an education in English, the government introduced a grant-in-aid scheme in 1873 to assist voluntary efforts in providing education for the city. The amount of grant money in relation to the total expenditure of the schools was meagre,[42] and the conditions of the scheme were restrictive: (1) the school must have an attendance of no fewer than twenty students, must be opened for inspection by government inspectors at all times, and must be represented by a manager who could communicate with the government inspector; (2) the school must give secular instruction for not less than four hours each day; and (3) grants were to be paid according to the results of an annual examination on secular subjects by the inspector. The scheme was modelled on the 1870 Education Act in Britain, which aimed at reducing the role of religious teaching. Of course, this aspect was unpopular among missionary schools, and only five such schools joined the scheme.

In 1878, two major initiatives took place in Hong Kong that were crucial to the development of education. The first was the organisation of an Education Conference, presided over by Sir John Pope Hennessy, who was known for his liberal views, and attended by Frederick Stewart, the Rev. E. J. Eitel, and several members of the Legislative Council. The conference declared the importance of learning English and resolved that all students in government schools should be given five hours of compulsory English lessons and

---

41. Charles Richard Alford, "China and Japan, A Charge", delivered in the Cathedral Church of St John, Victoria, Hong Kong (London: Noronha and Sons, 1869).

42. Patricia P. K. Chiu, *A History of Grant Schools Council, Hong Kong* (Hong Kong: Grant Schools Council, 2013), 4–5.

two-and-a-half hours of optional Chinese studies each day. The second step forward was the 1878 revision of the grant-in-aid scheme of 1873, when the restrictive elements of the curriculum were removed. Four hours of teaching secular subjects each day were no longer mandatory, and the limitation on the number of student attendances was also removed. Since the grant schools had been providing education for a large number of children in Hong Kong with little financial help from the government, the government wisely decided not to interfere with religious teaching. Altogether, seventeen missionary schools joined the scheme to become "grant-in-aid" schools in 1878, including DHO.[43]

The Birth of the Diocesan Home and Orphanage

Bishop Alford had not forgotten the Diocesan Female School during the difficult year of 1868. He gradually formulated an idea to develop an institution that would appeal to the sentiments of the time and the conscience of the British colonists in Hong Kong. In early February 1869, the Bishop issued a circular inviting support to establish an orphanage in Hong Kong for orphans and children of destitute Europeans and children of mixed parentage. As we have seen, the need for an orphanage in Hong Kong was great at that time, because it was common for irresponsible fathers of various foreign nationalities to leave their mistresses and their illegitimate children behind as they headed home. The orphanage would be directed under the auspices of the acting governor, Vice Admiral Keppel, Major General Brunker, and the chief justice—the most important people from the government, army, navy, and legal system to ensure the success of the institution. The circular stated:

> many children of European and half-caste parentage are to be found living under very deplorable circumstances in Hong Kong, China and Japan; and it is urged as a duty to consider what can be done on their behalf. One of the objectives of the Female Diocesan School (Diocesan Female School) in Hong Kong is to offer a permanent home for a limited number of Orphans and other Children in necessitous circumstances. The Education of Chinese Girls in Hong Kong on Anglo-Chinese principles having been found undesirable, it is proposed to extend the benefits of the Education given in the Female Diocesan School (Diocesan Female School) to a few such Children of both sexes as has been described—reserving one wing for the Boys and the other for the Girls, and to give them, with board and lodging, an education which may fit them for useful service. The Children must be without deformity, and generally healthy and strong in mind and body.[44]

---

43. Chiu, *A History of Grant Schools Council*, 5.
44. Alford, "China and Japan, A Charge".

Bishop Alford's proposal was received with much enthusiasm as he was addressing an important social problem that British imperialism had helped to perpetuate. The Diocesan Home and Orphanage was therefore established in January 1870 and a School Committee was organised, consisting of fourteen members that included the four dignitaries mentioned above, members of the church, and members of the business community.

The School Committee met on 11 April 1870 and decided that the institution be called the Diocesan Home and Orphanage and that the institution could admit children whose parents were able to pay towards the expense of their maintenance. The rules as approved on 18 January 1870 and revised on 11 April 1870 were clearly stated:

> That the Institution be called "The Diocesan Home and Orphanage." That the objects of the Institution be to receive orphan children of both sexes, sound both in body and mind of European, Chinese and half-caste parentage, and such as they become capable of education; and to board, clothe and instruct them with a view to industrial life and the Christian faith according to the teachings of the Church of England.[45]

The DHO was therefore constituted as a co-educational institution, with accommodation for both boys and girls; meanwhile, the girls of the school remained in the same school building. It occupied the land (IL831) that had been granted to DNFTS by the government in 1863. Mr William M. B. Arthur and his wife, Mrs Arthur, were appointed master and matron of the DHO respectively.

Figure 1.4: Mr and Mrs W. M. B. Arthur, Headmaster (right) and Matron (left) of DHO (1869–1878). Source: Marguerite Logie, the great-great-granddaughter of Mr and Mrs Arthur, courtesy of Dr Nicholas Chan.

---

45. The Diocesan Home and Orphanage, Rules as approved, 18 January 1870 and revised 11 April 1870, found in Bishop House Archive (BHA), Diocesan Girls' School, General File, 1956.

Historical Background: 1859 to 1898

In 1871, the DHO had eighteen boys and eleven girls, and through the years of Mr Arthur's administration it grew only slowly. At the time of Mr Arthur's departure in 1878, there were twenty-seven boys and ten girls.[46] The school's annual expenditure was about $5,000, deriving its financial support from payment of fees from parents and guardians of the children, collections from St John's Cathedral, and subscriptions and donations from residents, mostly expatriates, of the city. A sum of $1,500 was raised by voluntary contributions during the year and spent mainly on repairs. It joined the grant-in-aid scheme in 1873 and received a small subsidy from the government.

The school could only afford a three-person staff: Mr and Mrs Arthur and a Chinese teacher. The Arthurs received a salary of $120 per month,[47] which was hardly adequate, and Mr Arthur had to supplement his salary by working as an organist at the Cathedral. His salary was a long way from the salary of $3,120 per year ($260/month) of Frederick Stewart, headmaster of Central School.[48] With such a meagre budget and salary for the staff, how could the DHO be expected to grow?

The church provided little support in terms of funds or personnel. There was constant dispute in the School Committee between those members from the business community and those from the Anglican Church over the lack of church support.[49] Since the DHO was no longer an institution sponsored by the FES, the FES saw no reason to send an agent or a teacher to the institution. Moreover, the FES had a problem with Bishop Alford's handling of Miss Oxlad when the DHO was established.

As described above, Miss Oxlad, a very capable young agent from the FES, who was very much respected and loved by the members of the Society, served the Diocesan Female School during its most difficult years after the departure of Miss Eaton in 1865. When the school lost support from the community and went bankrupt, she kept the school alive. In December 1869, the FES asked Miss Oxlad to return to England for a rest before returning to Hong Kong whilst the school was being reconstituted to become the DHO. The FES was willing to send Miss Oxlad back to the DHO to be fully in control of the female student body. But Bishop Alford requested Miss Oxlad to be only a teacher under the supervision of Mr Arthur. Not only did Miss Oxlad disagree with this proposal but so did the members of the FES Committee. When Bishop Alford failed to change his position, Miss Oxlad declined to work in the DHO. She reopened the school on Staunton Street, which was closed after Miss Baxter's death, and founded two new schools, one in Sai Ying

---

46. Education, Hong Kong Blue Book, 1878, 142.
47. Education, Hong Kong Blue Book, 1878, 142.
48. Education, Hong Kong Blue Book, 1878, 140.
49. Fung and Chan-Yeung, *To Serve and to Lead*, 21.

Pun and the other in Tai Ping Shan, in 1873 with a total attendance of 133. She later left for Japan as an agent of the FES.[50]

Miss Oxlad's situation reflected that of many other female teachers at the time in the West. While teaching provided new employment opportunities for women, it also reaffirmed their secondary position: paid less than men, they were kept in the lower ranks and were always under the supervision of male administrators, rarely gaining seniority or administrative responsibility. They were mainly young women, who usually ended up leaving their teaching positions by their own volition or were released when they married.[51]

The Crisis of 1878

After serving for eight years as headmaster of the DHO, Mr Arthur, with no prospect of advancement either in position or in salary, decided in 1878 to leave for a position at Central School, which offered him a salary of $1,680 per year ($140/month). The reason he provided for his departure was that his wife was unable to carry on as the matron because of ill health. In 1889, Mr Arthur left Central School;[52] he then worked as the first clerk in the magistracy in Hong Kong from which he retired in 1900.[53]

The resignation of Mr and Mrs Arthur created a crisis, as conflict surfaced between the two factions in the DHO Committee. By then, Bishop Alford had retired, and Bishop John Shaw Burdon (Bishop of Victoria and South China 1874–1897) was the new chair of the School Committee. During the committee meeting on 26 March 1878, Bishop Burdon proposed to alter the constitution of the DHO and revert it to Mrs Lydia Smith's (wife of the first bishop) original vision of an all-girls' school. In this way, the DHO might be placed on a more permanent footing by reconnecting it with the FES, which, the Bishop thought, would be willing to supply at least one teacher of their own to the school under the superintendence of the bishop. The committee agreed to this on condition that the change would be gradual so that no injustice would be done to the boys then present in the school.[54] The Bishop promised to make other provisions for the boys who would remain when the proposed change became known. He believed that the expenses of the school, such as the

---

50. Entry 5315, Minutes of the Committee of FES, 14 July 1870; Entry 5473, Minutes of the Committee of FES, 19 May 1871; Entry 5614, Minutes of the Committee of FES, 28 February 1872, 9.

51. "Women and Education", *Canadian Encyclopedia*, accessed 13 March 2020, https://www.thecanadianencyclopedia.ca/en/article/women-and-education.

52. Education, Hong Kong Blue Book, 1888 and 1889.

53. Fung and Chan-Yeung, *To Serve and to Lead*, 21.

54. Minutes of DHO School Committee, 26 March 1878, Featherstone, *The Diocesan Boys' School and Orphanage: The History and Records*, 101–102.

Historical Background: 1859 to 1898

boarding of the girls, salaries of the Chinese teachers, and repairs of the building, would be financed by local contributions.

With the committee's agreement, Bishop Burdon wrote to the FES and requested two English women to be sent to Hong Kong to reorganise the school and rename it as Diocesan Female School. During the next committee meeting, on 9 May 1878, the Bishop announced that he had received a reply from Mrs Smith, who offered her own services and those of her daughter to take charge of the school for no more than two years during the period of transition and that, in the meantime, the school should reconnect with the FES.[55] Delighted at the prospect that her dream might be realised, Mrs Smith decided to travel with her daughter at their own expense to take responsibility for the school, while the FES made the necessary preparations for an agent to take over the school under the new conditions.

Bishop Burdon was about to propose the implementation of this plan when Mr William Keswick of Jardine Matheson Co Ltd, an influential member of the committee who had been absent from Hong Kong, returned. Keswick objected strongly to the change and urged further consideration. He denounced the change as an injustice to the subscribers who had for years given large sums towards the support of the institution and to the class of children whom it was now proposed to exclude. He also doubted whether the committee had the power to give the school building in Hong Kong to a society in England, and he had reasons to believe that if the change were carried out it would probably be disputed in the courts.[56]

The meeting was adjourned at that point until the following day when Mr Wilberforce Wilson, the only representative of the original DNFTS trustees left in Hong Kong, was present by request. No longer willing to challenge Keswick with his influence on the committee, Bishop Burdon withdrew his proposal. However, Bishop Burdon still advised that reorganisation of the home should take place because of the difficulty of running the institution for both boys and girls since a co-educational boarding school was then unheard of.[57] The committee then agreed to rescind the 26 March decision and to communicate immediately with the FES and Mrs Smith to explain the situation. Messrs William Keswick, Henry Lowcock, and Cecil Smith would be responsible for finding the replacements for Mr and Mrs Arthur.

Bishop Burdon wrote to Mrs Smith explaining the situation and that the committee would reimburse her for any loss that might have occurred as a result of the cancellation of

---

55. Minutes of DHO School Committee, 15 July 1878, Featherstone, *The Diocesan Boys' School and Orphanage: The History and Records*, 102.

56. Ibid.

57. Minutes of DHO School Committee, 16 July 1878, Featherstone, *The Diocesan Boys' School and Orphanage: The History and Records*, 103.

her trip. In the letter, he also expressed his earnest desire to establish a boarding school for Chinese girls in Hong Kong and asked the FES to consider taking up the proposal and to send out an agent to organise it. To the latter request, the FES declined with regret because of the heavy liabilities to the Society but offered to advertise the project in the hope that a suitable woman with independent means would devote herself to the work.[58]

In May 1879, the School Committee unanimously declared that no more girls be received into the DHO as boarders and that a limited number of Chinese boys be admitted as day scholars at a fee of about $2 per month. At the same time, Mr Wilberforce Wilson, the only trustee left from DNFTS, requested that the institution be vested in the Bishop of Victoria and the colonial chaplain either with or without himself as a third trustee.[59]

DHO Turned into a Boys' School

Mr George H. Piercy became the headmaster of the DHO in 1879, and during his administration the DHO gradually turned into a boys' school. The DHO first stopped admitting girls as boarders, but girls continued to attend as day students. At the same time, a limited number of Chinese boys attended as day students. Occasionally, when there were some urgent applications for the admission of girls, the DHO took them in as day students and asked Miss Margaret Johnstone of Baxter Mission, who lived nearby, to take them in as boarders.[60] At other times, some girls were lodged with the Rev. and Mrs J. B. Ost in the neighbourhood, the former being a member of the DHO Committee.[61]

In 1892, Mr Piercy transferred the remaining ten female day students from the DHO to Fairlea School, supervised by Miss Johnstone.[62] Miss Johnstone had opened a small boarding school in a rented house at the West End Terrace for Chinese girls in 1883, and in 1886 the school moved to the Fairlea House and became known as Fairlea School.[63] The history of Fairlea School would become interconnected with three other Anglican girls' schools in Hong Kong: Diocesan Girls' School, Victoria Home and Orphanage, and St

---

58. Entry 6972, Minutes of Committee of FES, 9 January 1879.

59. Minutes of DHO School Committee, 31 May 1879, Featherstone, *The Diocesan Boys' School and Orphanage: The History and Records*, 102–103.

60. Minutes of DHO School Committee, 13 April 1883, Featherstone, *The Diocesan Boys' School and Orphanage: The History and Records*, 104.

61. Minutes of DHO School Committee, 1888–1889 Annual Report, Featherstone, *The Diocesan Boys' School and Orphanage: The History and Records*, 27.

62. Featherstone, *The Diocesan Boys' School and Orphanage: The History and Records*, 2.

63. "Fairlea School Celebrations: Next Week's Jubilee Opened as Boarding", *South China Morning Post*, 15 October 1936.

Figure 1.5: Mr and Mrs G. Piercy, Headmaster and Matron of DHO (1879–1918). Source: Mrs Angela Ridge, the great-granddaughter of Mr Piercy, courtesy of Dr Nicholas Chan.

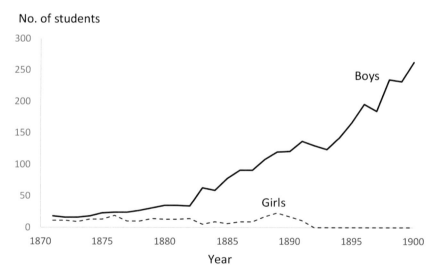

Figure 1.6: Number of boys and girls in DHO, 1871 to 1900. Source: Education, *Hong Kong Blue Book*, 1871 to 1900.

Stephen's Girls' College.[64] There were racial and class divides in these three schools: DGS was for Eurasians and Europeans, St Stephen's Girls' College for wealthy Chinese girls, and Victoria Home and Orphanage for Chinese girls rescued from a life of misery and destitution and girls from poor families. At the time, there was strong prejudice against Eurasians among the "pure" Europeans and Chinese. The Chinese also looked down on individuals in a lower social class. The parents of St Stephen's College students would send their daughters to a school made exclusive by high fees.[65] The Anglican Church helped perpetuate the attitude of discrimination over the years by establishing separate schools for different races and social classes. The situation changed during the post-war era when there were less racial and social class differences in schools, although Eurasians, by tradition, would enter DGS. Chinese girls would enter St Stephen's College and Heep Yunn School, which was established in 1936 from the amalgamation of Fairlea School and Victoria Home and Orphanage.

The DHO became an exclusively boys' school after 1892, with no more girls, changing its name to the Diocesan School and Orphanage (DSO).

Figure 1.7: Diocesan Boys' School in 1924, occupying the premises of DNFTS on IL 831, Bonham Road. Source: *To Serve and to Lead: A History of Diocesan Boys' School* (Hong Kong: Hong Kong University Press, 2009), 41. Reprinted with permission by Mr Ronnie Cheng, Headmaster of DBS.

---

64. Patricia P. K. Chiu, *Promoting All-Round Education for Girls: A History of Heep Yunn School in Hong Kong* (Hong Kong: Hong Kong University Press, 2020), 14.
65. Report of the Educational Visiting Committee, CMS Discussion on Education in 1911, Hong Kong Public Records Office (HKPRO), HKMS94-1-06.

Historical Background: 1859 to 1898   29

On 28 May 1892, an ordinance for the incorporation of the Chairman of the Committee of the Diocesan School and Orphanage was enacted, known as the Diocesan School and Orphanage Incorporation Ordinance 1892 (Chapter 1017). In it, The Chairman of the Committee of DSO would become a corporate body with perpetual succession and all the legal powers to deal with all the possessions, land, money, and securities of the DSO. The land (IL831) and its buildings in Hong Kong, which were vested in the names of Thomas Stringer, Wilberforce Wilson, and William Chesterman Hunter as Trustees of Diocesan Female School, were transferred to and vested in the Corporation of The Chairman of the Committee of the DSO.[66]

It is hard to believe that the church would allow the business community to use the property, which was granted for girls' education, exclusively for boys' education without raising any objection.

Diocesan Girls' School and Orphanage: Rebirth of English Education for Girls

Bishop Burdon and his successor, Bishop Joseph Charles Hoare (Bishop of Victoria and South China 1898–1906), the colonial chaplain, and other members of the Anglican Church had not given up the hope of reviving a school for girls in accordance with the dream of Mrs Smith to promote continuity and progress in female education in Hong Kong. The dream was realised in 1899, seven years after all the girls had left the DHO to be housed in Fairlea School, when Rose Villa West, situated opposite the DSO on Bonham Road, became vacant. The building was leased to become Diocesan Girls' School and Orphanage, which then received back all the European and Eurasian girls from Fairlea School. The following year (1900), the school changed its name to Diocesan Girls' School and registered with the government under this name.

In summary, many government publications indicated that DGS had been established in 1900. Most people were unaware of its long history before 1900, which can be traced back to 1860 when DNFTS, a boarding school for upper-class Chinese girls, was founded by Mrs Lydia Smith, wife of Bishop Smith. DNFTS changed its name to Diocesan Female School in 1866. Lack of students and funds led to its closure in 1869. On the same premises, Bishop Alford created the DHO for orphans, boys, and girls of European or mixed parentage. Because of the difficulties of having both boys and girls in one boarding school, in 1879 it was decided not to admit girls as boarders and to admit Chinese day students instead. In 1892, all the remaining day girls in the DHO were transferred to Fairlea School, a school constituted for Chinese girls only. In 1898, six years later, Bishop Hoare revived Diocesan Female School as Diocesan Girls' School and Orphanage for European and Eurasian girls.

---

66. Enclosure 2, Report by the Attorney General on Ordinance 3, 1892, CO 129/255, 285.

The institution dropped the word "orphanage" from its name in 1900. The name Diocesan Girls' School has been used ever since. In 1902, the DSO also changed its name to Diocesan Boys' School and Orphanage and also dropped the word "orphanage" sometime later and became known as Diocesan Boys' School (DBS).

DGS is closely linked to DBS in terms of its historical development, as both were derived from the DHO, a co-educational institution, which, in turn, stemmed from DNFTS. Because DNFTS was an institution for girls only, DBS claims its origins from the DHO and that DNFTS is the forerunner of DHO. Being a female institution, DGS, also derived from the DHO, could legitimately call itself a direct descendant of DNFTS, with a history dating back to 1860, or even earlier in 1859 as there is some evidence to suggest that DNFTS evolved from the Girls' Day School of Mrs Smith (referred to as Bishop's Diocesan Girls' School by Eitel), even though the school was only registered in 1900 with the government as Diocesan Girls' School.

Chapter 2

Laying the Foundation: 1899 to 1924

When Mrs Lydia Smith founded the Diocesan Native Female Training School (DNFTS) in 1860, it was meant "to introduce among a somewhat superior class of native females the blessings of Christianity and religious training . . . and they were to occupy positions of influence and usefulness". For some forty years, like all organisations, the school adapted to the needs of the social, cultural, and economic circumstances of the time. Towards the turn of the century, the school was able to proceed towards its initial goal. Its commitment to the care and education of its male charges were taken care of by the Diocesan School and Orphanage (1892), then Diocesan Boys' School and Orphanage (1902), and later, Diocesan Boys' School. While keeping to its Christian commitment and ethos, and providing support and education for girls, the Diocesan Female School was revived by Bishop Hoare as the Diocesan Girls' School and Orphanage (1899), and later, as Diocesan Girls' School (1900).

While the above transformation was taking place in the school, Hong Kong also found itself evolving against the backdrop of political and social changes in China and Sino-British relations.

Towards the end of the nineteenth century, despite its attempt to revive itself, the Qing dynasty continued to decline. Following the destruction of its entire navy by the Japanese during the First Sino-Japanese War in 1894–1895, the Qing government was forced to sign the Treaty of Shimonoseki on 17 April 1895. This ceded the Liaodong Peninsula and Taiwan to Japan "in perpetuity" and granted the Japanese people the right to trade and reside at the Treaty Ports and to engage in cotton manufacture in the international settlement in Shanghai. The weakness of Qing China lay itself open to Western imperialism with major European powers carving out areas of special influence in the country. In 1898, the British acquired a 99-year lease of 922 square kilometres of land (known as the New Territories) adjoining Kowloon Peninsula opposite the island of Victoria, thereby enlarging the British holding in the region almost tenfold. Britain further secured the opening of all of China's inland waterways to foreign steamers, thus greatly facilitating British trading opportunities in China and Asia.

In 1898, the young Emperor Guangxu began to implement a broad series of radical reforms proposed by Kang Youwei, a prominent political thinker, and his student Liang Qichao. These reforms involved extensive restructuring of education, the introduction of Western learning, the promotion and development of commerce and industry, and the establishment of a new army. So ambitious and so rapidly introduced were these reforms that they were rejected by the old conservative factions in the Qing government. They came to a screeching halt in one hundred days when Empress Dowager organised a coup that resulted in the imprisonment of the young emperor and the cancellation of the reforms. The abrupt termination of the much-needed advancements and the fiasco of the Boxer Rebellion against foreign powers in 1900 plunged many Chinese into despair. Many gave up the hope of progress under the Qing dynasty and embraced the idea of overthrowing the Manchu by revolution.

The Xinhai Revolution took place in 1911 and the Republic of China was founded in 1912, but these events did not improve the lives of ordinary people. The country rapidly deteriorated into the Warlord Period (1916–mid-1930s), dividing China into various military factions. Sun Yat-sen, the father of the revolution, died in 1925 before the country could be reunited. In 1927, his successor, Chiang Kai-shek, reinvigorated Sun Yat-sen's objective by leading an expeditionary force in a joint effort with the Chinese Communist Party (CCP), established in 1921, to reunite the country. Yet before the expedition ended, Chiang began to persecute the CCP members, marking the beginning of the Chinese civil war. The political instability in China resulted in the influx of more refugees to Hong Kong, greatly increasing the population and the demand for modern education.

Events Leading to the Founding of Diocesan Girls' School and Orphanage

In Hong Kong, in the late nineteenth century, as a result of the influx of immigrants, many private schools were opened in tenement houses for children living nearby. The number of grant-in-aid schools increased from six in 1873 to ninety-six in 1899. The majority of these schools provided a Chinese education, with varying standards of performance. To control and supervise different types of school in the territory, an Education Ordinance was enacted in 1913 to register all schools and to ensure that they met a certain standard in sanitation, discipline, and educational attainment. A less costly subsidy system was also introduced in the same year for private vernacular schools.[1] In 1921, the government decided to abandon the grant-in-aid scheme, with the exception of a few competent schools, which were mostly missionary schools, providing Western education in English. They remained in the grant system and were called grant schools. By 1938, only fourteen English schools and three upper-grade vernacular schools remained under the Grant Code.[2]

In the early twentieth century, however, the Education Department carried out overall reviews in an attempt to improve education in Hong Kong. The report of the first overall review of education was published in 1902.[3] As a result, a Revised Grant Code was adopted in 1903, which consisted of the following elements: (1) the grants awarded were to be based not on examination results but on the inspector's observations throughout the year; (2) schools employing a well-educated staff would be given special recognition, and to meet this requirement, the staff must be partly composed of European teachers or Chinese teachers trained outside Hong Kong; and (3) Chinese education should be taught using modern Western methods rather than rote memorisation, and only English and Chinese could be used as languages of instruction.[4]

Another review was carried out in 1910 focusing on the staffing of schools and the results were published in the same year with the following recommendations to improve instruction: (1) the high cost of recruiting European staff from England should be minimised in government and grant schools by employing Chinese teachers who had been trained for three years at a technical institute; (2) the maximum number of students who could be taught efficiently by one English or Chinese master was determined to be forty; (3) the proportion of English and Chinese masters in the school should be two to three; and (4) the schools should have a number of teachers with a set number of years of teaching experience.[5]

The grant given by the government to the missionary schools was vital for the development of Hong Kong's school system, and DGS was one of the beneficiaries. The grant schools' freedom to use either Chinese or English as the medium of instruction, their broad and diverse curricula, and regulations that would improve classroom instruction all facilitated the development of education in Hong Kong in the late nineteenth and early twentieth centuries.

In the meantime, a shift occurred in attitudes towards women in China, brought about by the influx of missionaries since the opening of the Treaty Ports after the First Opium War in 1842. While making little headway with their agenda of Christian conversion in

---

1. The Educational Report for 1914, Hong Kong Administrative Report (HKAR) online, 1914, 210.
2. Patricia P. K. Chiu, *A History of the Grant Schools Council* (Hong Kong: Grant Schools Council, 2013), 7.
3. Education Committee Report 1902, Hong Kong Sessional Paper (HKSP), no. 14/1902, 371–328.
4. Chiu, *A History of the Grant Schools Council*, 6.
5. Education Committee Report 1910, HKAR 1910, 25.

China, the foreign missionaries greatly influenced Chinese attitudes towards women. They established schools for girls and formed anti-foot-binding societies to eradicate a practice that had kept women subservient to men in various Treaty Ports as well as in Hong Kong. There was also a change in societal attitudes regarding the education of Chinese girls. In 1866, there were 1,870 students in Hong Kong, of whom 45 (2.4 per cent) were girls, the corresponding numbers in 1873 were 2,282 students with 304 girls (13.3 per cent), and in 1883, 5,597 students with 1,477 girls (26.4 per cent), demonstrating a gradual increase in the number of students and in the proportion of girls. However, in 1883, there were 12,980 children of school age, only 43 per cent of whom were in school. Eitel, the Inspector of Schools, concluded that more changes were necessary in order to further raise the number of children attending schools, especially among girls.[6] The low school attendance was due to rampant child labour in those days, especially among the working class. The Industrial Employment of Children Ordinance, which defined the age limit of child labour and determined the legal minimal age for each category of work (10 years old for factories, 12 years old for carrying loads, and 15 years old for dangerous industries), was only enacted in 1922.[7]

In the 1860s and 1870s, English education was offered only to boys in Hong Kong. As mentioned in Chapter 1, girls were not given an English education since it was believed that this would lead to the degradation of their character as they became mistresses of foreigners. The government was against teaching girls English on those grounds, claiming that this type of education would promote concubinage and polygamy.[8] The DNFTS founded by Mrs Smith was closed in 1869 partly because of this reason. In those days, girls drifting into concubinage had no opportunity to learn English, and so they crowded into the DNFTS when the school failed to attract girls from the higher social classes. By the late 1880s, there were a number of evening schools scattered throughout Hong Kong where girls who wished to become "protected women" could learn the English they required. On the other hand, a number of Chinese boys, who had received Western education abroad, failed to find suitable wives of compatible intellectual ability and education. Because of the above observations, Eitel believed that the chances of degradation of Chinese girls from learning English were very low. At his recommendation, the government started a government girls' school on 1 March 1890, offering to girls of all nationalities an elementary English education on the principles of the Government Central School. A headmistress was to be hired from England to organise the school.[9]

---

6. Educational Report of 1883, HKSP, 1884.

7. Industrial Employment of Children Ordinance of 1922, Historical Laws of Hong Kong Online, accessed 9 April 2020, https://oelawhk.lib.hku.hk/items/show/1355.

8. The Educational Report 1888, HKSP 1889, no. 3/89, 103.

9. "Girls' School", Education Department, HKSP 1888, no 18/89, 275–277.

Laying the Foundation: 1899 to 1924

In response to the change in the attitude of the government and the community in Hong Kong towards female education, and to fulfil Mrs Smith's and his own wish to promote female education, Bishop Hoare organised a public meeting on 9 February 1899 at St Paul's College. At the meeting, the following resolution was unanimously passed:

> That it is desirable to establish in Hongkong a boarding and day School for girls, more especially for Eurasian children, such school to aim at giving a liberal education according to the doctrines of the Church of England, and that this meeting pledges itself to do all it can in support of that scheme.[10]

The proposal was supported by the following people present at the meeting: Bishop Joseph Charles Hoare (Bishop of Victoria), the Rev. R. F. Cobbold (Chaplain of St John's Cathedral), Sir John W. Carrington (Chief Justice of Hong Kong), the Hon. Francis Henry May (Captain Superintendent of the Hong Kong Police Force, later Governor), Mr Thomas Jackson (Chief Manager of Hong Kong Shanghai Bank), Mr Robert Ho Tung, and Miss Margaret Johnstone. The need for the establishment of the proposed school was well known and was made more apparent when Miss Johnstone became unable to provide for European or Eurasian girls at Fairlea School. At the same time, Bishop Hoare and Mrs Hoare also wanted to revive the Diocesan Female School for the education of European and Eurasian girls.[11]

Fairlea was a large house on Bonham Road where the Baxter Mission, a centre for women's work, was based. The mission sent out Chinese Bible women—Chinese Christian women dedicated to evangelistic work—into the community to visit Chinese families and women in hospital and in prison in order to convert them. In 1892, when the Diocesan Home and Orphanage (DHO) no longer accepted girls and was turned into a boys' school, Miss Johnstone took responsibility for the girls, moving them to Fairlea. In 1895, there were thirty-five Chinese girls, thirteen Eurasians, and five Europeans at Fairlea School.[12] The Baxter Mission was intended for Chinese girls only and with the rise in admission applications there was no room left for others. Miss Johnstone, who had been providing education for European and Eurasian girls at a very low cost, had to give up that part of her work. By the end of 1899, twenty European and Eurasian girls, then cared for at Fairlea, would be without room and board and education.[13]

---

10. Diocesan Girls' School and Orphanage Under the Patronage of Her Excellency Lady Blake, Hong Kong, March 1899, Hong Kong Public Record Office (HKPRO), HKMS94-1-06.

11. Discussion on Education Leading to the Founding of Diocesan Girls' School and Orphanage. Under the Patronage of Her Excellency Lady Blake, Hong Kong March 1899, HKPRO, HKMS94-1-06.

12. Susanna Hoe, *The Private Life of Old Hong Kong: Western Women in the British Colony, 1841–1941* (Hong Kong: Oxford University Press, 1991), 211–212.

13. Diocesan Girls' School and Orphanage Under the Patronage of Her Excellency Lady Blake, Hong Kong, March 1899, HKPRO, HKMS94-1-06.

A public appeal for HK$3,000 was made to enable a school for European and Eurasian girls to be established. The first School Committee (School Council today) was constituted of eighteen individuals, all female, except for the Bishop and the Rev. Cobbold. They were:

Mrs J. M. Atkinson	Mrs J. J. Bell Irving
Lady Carrington	Mrs T. Jackson
Mrs C. W. Dickson	Miss M. Johnstone
Mrs Fletcher	Mrs A. P. MacEwen
Mrs Gascoigne	Mrs F. H. May
Mrs W. M. Goodman	Mrs W. Poate
Mrs W. C. H. Hastings	Mrs H. A Ritchie
Mrs V. A. C. Hawkins	Rev. R. F. Cobbold
Mrs Hoare	Bishop Joseph Charles Hoare

Bishop Hoare and the Rev. Cobbold were to become the school supervisors.[14]

Rose Villa West on Bonham Road, the property of Mr Granville Sharp, a successful banker, was leased for the school. The Diocesan Girls' School and Orphanage came into being in 1899, and Miss Elizabeth D. Skipton from England was appointed superintendent or headmistress.[15] It was a girls' school that aimed to provide a Christian upbringing and education for girls of European and mixed parentage. In 1900, one year after its founding, the word "orphanage" was dropped from the name and the school from then on was known as Diocesan Girls' School (DGS) and registered with the government as such in the same year.

DGS under Miss Elizabeth D. Skipton (November 1899–August 1921)

Miss Elizabeth D. Skipton and Miss Maud I. Hawker arrived in November 1899 from England to take up their positions as headmistress and teacher respectively. Miss Skipton was neither a Church Missionary Society (CMS) missionary nor an agent of the Society of Promoting Female Education for Girls in the East (FES); we have no information on

---

14. Diocesan Girls' School and Orphanage Under the Patronage of Her Excellency Lady Blake, Hong Kong, March 1899, HKPRO, HKMS94-1-06.

15. Diocesan Girls' School and Orphanage Under the Patronage of Her Excellency Lady Blake, Hong Kong, March 1899, HKPRO, HKMS94-1-06.

Figure 2.1: Rose Villa, c. 1900. Source: Royal Asiatic Society Hong Kong Branch.

Miss Hawker. They were the only two European teachers in DGS in the beginning, though they were joined by other European staff as the school expanded. In 1910, Miss Doble, a trained certified teacher, and Miss Lovegrove, a matron, joined the staff;[16] and in 1912, Miss Swinton, a trained nurse, replaced Miss Lovegrove as matron.[17] In later years, other European teachers were appointed, including Mrs Pope, Mrs Jenkinson, Miss Roberts, Miss Catherine Ferguson, and Miss Nora Bascombe.

We know very little about Miss Skipton because all the documents about the school before the Second World War have been destroyed. However, from a few books written about the school, an idea of Miss Skipton as a person emerges. Mrs Maria Fincher (née Kacker), then a young orphan girl from the school, describes her as a "lovely person, but a martinet . . . nice looking, with deep set piercing blue eyes".[18] Irene Cheng (née Ho Tung), daughter of Sir Robert and Lady Ho Tung, was a DGS student from 1914 to 1918. In her book *Intercultural Reminiscences*,[19] she wrote:

> Miss Skipton was not a cloistered missionary, but she lived like one and had never married. She had a B.A. from London University and was already fairly elderly when we girls were at DGS because she retired soon after we left school. She was a dedicated headmistress who looked every inch the part, being tall and thin with drawn-back grey

---

16. "Diocesan Girls' School", *South China Morning Post*, 10 November 1910.
17. "Diocesan Girls' School Prize Distribution", *South China Morning Post*, 20 December 1912.
18. Hoe, *The Private Life of Old Hong Kong*, 212.
19. Irene Cheng, *Intercultural Reminiscences* (Hong Kong: Hong Kong Baptist University, 1996), 81–82.

hair. Because there was little in the way of clerical assistance in those days, she would work hard in her office every night, catching up with all the paperwork. Even after she finished, her day was not complete, for she would then take a lantern on a round of all the dormitories, just to make sure that none of the girls had kicked off her blanket. If she found one uncovered, Miss Skipton would gently replace the blanket.

Jean Gittins, a younger daughter of the Ho Tungs and a DGS student in the late 1910s, remembers Miss Skipton as "a dedicated woman who tempered a stern discipline with the warmness of a kind and gentle heart" in her book *Eastern Windows, Western Skies*.[20] These students' accounts show Miss Skipton's dedication to her job and her pupils.

The difficulties of starting the school can be seen from Miss Skipton's report published in the *Outpost*, an interim newsletter of the Diocese of Victoria, Hong Kong, and South China for the period July to December 1922. In 1900, DGS had twenty-four boarders and two to three day-students. There was no timetable and few books, except for Royal Readers, and some books of arithmetic which had examples without answers. Miss Skipton and Miss Hawker had to start from scratch. Fortunately, there were two pupil-teachers aged 15 and 16 to help them. Clearly the two teachers did well, and by November 1901 there were forty boarders and twelve day-students. After that, the number increased steadily. The vacations were one month in February varying with Chinese New Year, six weeks in July and August, and a few days at Christmas and Easter.[21]

The school also provided clothing for most of the girls. Twice a year, in spring and autumn, there was a trying on of frocks to see who needed new clothes. There was no uniform because of lack of funds, and it was hard to obtain materials for clothing; so, the school had to make do with what was sent to them from England. It also proved difficult to find a matron locally. At last, one came from England, and this set a precedent for English matrons to look after the housekeeping and the health of the students, especially when a student developed an infectious disease. Luckily, the Government Civil Hospital was quite close to the school, and the doctors and sisters were very kind to the children and always willing to visit the sick children on request. The matron also taught the girls to do things for themselves.[22]

In 1903, Rose Villa East, the property next to DGS, became vacant. The School Committee decided to lease the property, adding more student accommodation to the

---

20. Jean Gittins, *Eastern Windows, Western Skies* (Hong Kong: *South China Morning Post*, 1969). Also in Hoe, *The Private Life of Old Hong Kong*, 212.

21. "Correspondence. Diocesan Girls' School", *South China Morning Post*, 15 December 1903.

22. Elizabeth Skipton, "The Diocesan Girls' School, Hong Kong 1900–1921", *The Outpost* (July–December 1922): 18–21.

campus and increasing the student body.[23] In 1904, DGS began to admit a few small boys, who left school when they turned nine.

In 1900, the school became a grant-in-aid school. Initially the grant payment was conditional on examination results, but by 1903 grants were made according to the observations of government inspectors.[24] In 1910, the school was recommended for the highest government grant. This was just as well, since the rent for the two buildings was high, and the school supported a number of non-paying orphans, since in keeping with the school's mission, students were never rejected on account of their inability to pay the fees.[25] The school fees for those families who could pay included a tuition fee of HK$3 per month. Together with board, laundry, and clothing, the total came to HK$20 per month. Despite the efficiency with which it was run, in 1911 the school had a deficit of HK$2,193, and the Bishop made a public appeal for funds to cover the deficit.[26]

From the beginning, DGS stood out from other schools in Hong Kong in offering an English education only to European and Eurasian girls. The school was therefore criticised for discrimination against the Chinese, but there were already a number of schools for Chinese girls in Hong Kong other than the Fairlea School and the St Stephen's Girls' College, whereas there were at the time no schools specifically for Eurasian children. DGS was also criticised for only giving prizes to Eurasian students and not to British girls. However, there was much praise for the school as well.[27]

The New School at 1 Jordan Road, Kowloon

Rose Villas were located opposite the Diocesan School and Orphanage on Bonham Road. Situated on the outskirts of the city of Victoria, Rose Villas were quiet, and the schoolchildren used the garden as a playground. The number of students in DGS increased with time. In 1910, there were fifty-four boarders and sixty-seven day-scholars. By 1912, however, the school had become overcrowded as the space was originally intended for only sixty-four girls. During the same year, Rose Villas were sold to Chinese investors, who proceeded to build a number of houses on the garden site. The crowded neighbourhood and the loss of the playground made it no longer suitable for a school.

---

23. Notes drafted by the Rev. H. T. Johnson, Rector of Little Casterton, formerly Chaplain of St John's Cathedral, Hong Kong, on Bishop Hoare (1898–1906), HKPRO, HKMS94-1-05.

24. Report of the Director of Education 1903, HKSP 1904, 113.

25. "The Bishop's Appeal, Diocesan Girls' School", *South China Morning Post*, 23 July 1909.

26. "The Diocesan Girls' School and Orphanage", *South China Morning Post*, 24 February 1911.

27. Elizabeth Skipton, "The Diocesan Girls' School, Hong Kong 1900–1921", *The Outpost*, July–December 1922, 18–21.

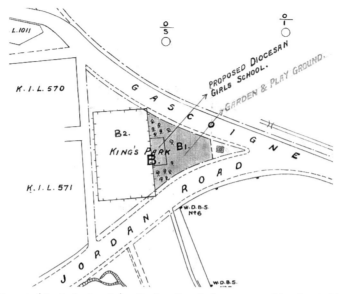

Figure 2.2: K.I.L. 1281 (shaded triangle), 1 Jordan Road, the proposed lot for DGS. Source: CO 129/388,160, the National Archives, UK.

To address the need to relocate DGS, the School Council approached Governor Sir Frederick Lugard for a new site. The grant of land must have been helped by Lady Flora Lugard, a journalist and a writer who promoted education and helped her husband establish the University of Hong Kong (HKU). Sir Frederick took up the project with great interest and vigour. He was able to secure a grant of land of 33,000 square feet from the Secretary of State for the Colonies[28] at the intersection of Jordan Road and Gascoigne Road (KIL 1281, 1 Jordan Road) for the establishment of the new school, which remains the site of DGS today (Figure 2.2). The new lot was granted to The Chairman of the Committee of the Diocesan School and Orphanage, an incorporated company,[29] which also held the properties of the Diocesan School and Orphanage, IL831 granted to DNFTS.

DGS was neither the first nor the last school to move to Kowloon in 1913. The lack of building space on Hong Kong Island in the early twentieth century prompted a more general shift of population from Hong Kong to Kowloon in search of more spacious and affordable accommodation. Many of the middle-class families, European and Eurasian, moved to Kowloon, and a number of the grant-in-aid schools followed, initially to Tsim Sha Tsui area, then to Ho Man Tin, and later still to Kowloon Tong, the Garden City.[30] In

---

28. From Lugard to Lewis Harcourt on KIL 1281, 25 January 1912, CO 129/388, 167.
29. Document found among copies of documents with Ordinance 3 of 1892 for the incorporation of The Chairman of the Committee of the Diocesan School and Orphanage, Bishop's House Archives, DGS General Files, 1948.
30. Chiu, *History of the Grant Schools Council*, 49.

Laying the Foundation: 1899 to 1924

1936, Heep Yunn School was founded on its current Kowloon site as a result of relocation of Fairlea School and its amalgamation with Victoria Home and Orphanage.[31]

The School Council of Diocesan Girls' School and Orphanage met with its counterpart, the Diocesan Boys' School and Orphanage, to discuss the building of the girls' school. Given that the boys' school had taken over the premises of the Diocesan Native Training School since 1878, and had been enjoying the rent-free premises while the girls' school had been struggling to pay a high rent since 1899, the Diocesan Boys' School agreed to contribute $10,000 towards the building of the girls' school. In addition, the government promised a building grant of up to $10,000 under the Grant Code. The school building—designed by Leigh and Orange, one of the most prominent architectural firms in the city, who had designed many of the magnificent new Edwardian baroque structures on the central reclamation and the Main Building of HKU—included the principal's house, dormitories, schoolrooms, and sickrooms and was estimated to cost around $30,000 to erect. A successful appeal for funds was made and the building was scheduled to be completed by September 1913.[32]

The construction was unexpectedly delayed by the military authorities, which made a claim on the land. In the end, the school paid the military compensation of 12.5 cents per square foot of land. In the few months left before September 1913, the builders Wong Tong Kee and Cheung Kam Po worked furiously to ensure the completion of the building before the new term. The building charges were $39,000, and together with payment to the military and the architectural fees, the total came to $45,075.[33]

According to a report in the South China Morning Post, the school was well designed and built with quality materials from different parts of the world. The building expenses exceeded the budget for the project by $17,000—a huge sum at that time. Maria Fincher remembered morning prayers after the move into the new school, when all boarders lowered their sleepy heads meekly in prayer: "Dear God, please help us to pay this awful dreadful debt."[34]

The new school building occupied the western end of the triangular plot of land and was designed to extend along the northern side of the site to form an L-shaped block. The two-storey building consisted of a large central hall, 74 feet by 30 feet, on the ground floor. The hall was divided into three large rooms by sliding partitions. It was well lit on both sides by French windows opening onto the verandas with large bay windows at either end. In the centre of the west side was a small private classroom. At the south end were the

---

31. Patricia P. K. Chiu, *Promoting All-Round Education for Girls: A History of Heep Yunn School in Hong Kong* (Hong Kong: Hong Kong University Press, 2020), 32.

32. "The Diocesan Girls' School", *South China Morning Post*, 3 September 1912.

33. "The Diocesan Girls' School. To Be Opened Today", *South China Morning Post*, 10 September 1913.

34. Hoe, *The Private Life of Old Hong Kong*, 212.

Figure 2.3: DGS view from Jordan Road, c. 1913. Source: Mr Bob Tatz, old boy of DGS in the late 1930s to onset of war.

headmistress's quarters, which had a separate entrance, a waiting room, sitting room, two bedrooms, and bathrooms. Behind were the kitchen, pantry, and two large drying rooms or storerooms. The main entrance included the principal staircase with two sitting rooms for the matron, and the staff room was situated on the north-east side of the school building.[35] On the first floor were three large airy dormitories to accommodate sixty to seventy boarders, three small bedrooms, a sick ward, and a teacher's bedroom. All the dormitories were accessible from the east and west verandas by French windows so that they could be supervised by the matron and the teachers. The lavatories, washrooms, and amah's room were on a separate block connected by covered walkways. In the garden, which was enclosed by a wall to secure privacy, was a full-sized tennis court and a playground. The schoolrooms (excluding the dining room) contained an area of about 1,800 square feet, providing sufficient seating accommodation for 150 students under the regulation of the Education Code.

The staff and girls were transferred from Rose Villas in time for the new term to begin in September 1913, and on 11 September the opening ceremony of the newly built DGS was attended by the Administrator of Government, Mr Claud Severn, Bishop Gerard Heath

---

35. "The Diocesan Girls' School. To Be Opened Today", *South China Morning Post*, 10 September 1913.

Laying the Foundation: 1899 to 1924

Figure 2.4: DGS in the early 1920s, with new extension in 1918, a three-storey building on the right side. Source: The-Monument-and-DGS, CO1069/473, the National Archives, UK.

Lander (Bishop of Victoria and South China 1907–1920), and Mrs Lander, together with many dignitaries of Hong Kong. After the dedication service conducted by the Bishop, a key of the front door of the school was presented to Mr Severn who performed the opening ceremony.

The school accommodated fifty to sixty boarders, one superintendent, one matron and four other teachers. Anticipating a rise in the student population in the years ahead, the school was constructed with the view for further expansion, and, in 1917, as predicted, the school was no longer able to accommodate all students requesting admission. A new wing was planned with a new school room, a new dormitory, a new sick room, and additional teachers' rooms.[36] Renovations were completed in 1918 at a cost of $23,500, and the school was once again in debt, owing $7,500 (Figure 2.4).[37]

---

36. "The Diocesan Girls' School and Orphanage", *South China Morning Post*, 3 March 1917.
37. "Diocesan Girls' School", *South China Morning Post*, 26 April 1918.

School Life in the Early Days

One can catch a glimpse of school life at DGS in the 1900s from the biography of Lady Victoria Jubilee Lo,[38] the eldest daughter of Sir Robert and Lady Ho Tung. Victoria entered DGS in January 1903. At that time all schools in Hong Kong began the new school year after Chinese New Year. Her home was close to the school, and she walked to school every day. After the family moved to the Peak, she was taken on a sedan chair every morning from her home to the Peak Tram Station where she took a tram to the Kennedy Road Station. From there she was carried once again on a chair to Rose Villas. DGS had only foreign teachers then and instruction was given in English; Chinese was not taught. As we have seen, the students were Europeans and Eurasians and were permitted to speak only in English. Victoria received private Chinese lessons at home from a Chinese scholar, a *xiucai* (秀才)—a scholar who passed the provincial level of the Imperial Examination of the Qing dynasty. She was only five-and-a-half years old when she started school at DGS and she graduated at the age of 15, much younger than other students in her class, whose average age was 19.[39]

In the 1910s, DGS gradually garnered a glowing reputation as a school where girls learned good English. Lady Ho Tung followed the trend and sent all her daughters to DGS. In 1914, Eva, aged 11, was placed in Class 4; Irene, one year younger, was assigned to Class 5; and Daisy, who had a learning disability, was enrolled in Class 6 even though she was already 14. The remaining three girls in the family, Jean, Grace, and Florence, were enrolled into DGS in the late 1910s and early 1920s. Apart from Daisy, all the girls thrived academically and often came first in the class or took prizes in various subjects. Eva and Irene were the first two of the three Chinese female students admitted to HKU.[40] After graduation from the university, both realised highly successful careers in life.

In her book *Intercultural Reminiscences* Irene Cheng describes her student days at DGS. At that time, there was no entrance examination, but all potential students had to take a placement test. As in the previous decade, the school structure was as follows: Class 1 was the highest class in the school. Classes 1 to 5 were called the Upper school, and Classes 6, 7, and 8 (which were divided into Upper 8, Middle 8, and Lower 8) were the Lower School. Altogether there were ten classes, which normally took students a decade to complete. Some classes were quite small; for instance, Class 1 had only four students in Irene's days. Classes 1 to 5 all had their desks arranged in separate rows in the "big school room", the

---

38. 梁雄姬，《中西融和：羅何錦姿》（香港：三聯書店有限公司，2013）。Leung Hung Kei, *Lady Victoria Jubilee Lo* (Hong Kong: Joint Publishing Hong Kong Co. Ltd., 2013).

39. 梁雄姬，《中西融和：羅何錦姿》，68–72。

40. Cheng, *Intercultural Reminiscences*, 105. Lai Po Chuen from another school was the third Chinese female student. She entered the Medical Faculty.

Laying the Foundation: 1899 to 1924   45

partitioned great hall. She went on to describe the assembly hall and how roll call was conducted in the morning:

> Class One was nearest the left-hand side as we sat down facing the teacher and Class Five, where I was a student, was at the far right-hand side of the hall. We all went to our desks for roll call, which would be conducted by either Miss Skipton, our headmistress; Miss Ferguson, second mistress; or Miss Bascombe, one of the teachers. They just called the Christian names or "given" names of the girls, not the surnames, as they checked attendance[41]
>
> Our large assembly hall was partitioned into three sections: the home room with five classes at one end; the dining room, which was also used for singing and other lessons of the Upper school, at the other end; and a middle classroom in the centre. These were all separated from each other by movable wooden partitions.[42]

Mrs E. Dunbar (later Mrs Matthews), an old girl, an old staff member, and a member of the School Council in 1947, also gives us a hint of the life at DGS at that time. Miss Skipton taught the students to appreciate their blessings and never failed to impress on them that all privileges beget responsibilities, and so the students learned to share in the running of the school and home. The older girls were school mothers to the younger ones—keeping an eye on them, mending, and doing for them generally as any mother's help. Each of the older girls was delegated some household duty—the sweeping, dusting, and tidying of the various rooms in the building, the setting of tables for meals, and the preparation for tea. Mrs Dunbar had three school mothers doting on her in her younger days.[43]

The school day started with the rising bell at 6:30 am and prayers at 7:30 am. Breakfast was at 8:00 am, accompanied by piano music. After breakfast, it was bed-making before school. After school, the boarders joined in games and a daily walk in the neighbourhood. Tea, the last meal of the day, was at 5:30 pm, and evening prayer at 6:30 pm followed by an hour of homework. Bedtime was 8:00 pm except for Class 1, for which it was 8:30 pm. At that time the school was attached to St Peter's Church, West Point, where DGS girls and DBS boys went on Sundays to worship. When the school moved to Kowloon, St Andrew's Church became their church for Sunday worship.[44] Both St Peter's Church and St Andrew's Church were staffed by CMS missionaries.

Florence Yeo (née Ho Tung) was the youngest daughter of the Ho Tungs to enter DGS kindergarten in 1919 at the age of four. At that time two of her elder sisters, Jean and Grace, were still at school. The trip from home at the Peak to school took over an hour, consisting

---

41. Cheng, *Intercultural Reminiscences*, 75.
42. Cheng, *Intercultural Reminiscences*, 76.
43. Mrs Dunbar, "A Glimpse of the DGS in Days Gone By", *The Quest* (1950): 45.
44. Mrs Dunbar, "A Glimpse of the DGS in Days Gone By", *The Quest* (1950): 45.

of different modes of transport—rickshaw rides or donkey, tram, and ferry.[45] Because of the distance and the long journey each way, Lady Ho Tung felt that it would be better for the 4-year-old Florence to be a boarder. In her book *My Memories*, [46] Florence described her traumatic experience as a boarder:

> I hadn't yet quite learned to feed myself properly and can still remember how difficult it was to put on my own shoes . . . I suppose all this was because my amah had always spoilt me . . . Each day at school, I would scream and cry and cling on to my sisters who were going home. This upsets them, so that they had to steal away without my knowing. "Cry baby, sissy" this would greet me most mornings from the girl on the next bed in the dormitory as I would wake up on the cold floor, having fallen out of bed at night. I woke up cold, lost and desolate.

She also remembered the misery of being given a bath in a cold concrete tub without any privacy and the feeling of hunger that gripped her in the evening and at night because the last meal of the day at tea time consisted only of bread, margarine, and jam.[47] From Florence's story, we learn about the spartan life of the boarders in those days.

According to Irene, her older sister, Florence, a sensitive and nervous child by nature, had several unfortunate incidents in her early life that added to her problems in later life, the most important being that after her birth, their mother was occupied by the poor health of her husband, Sir Robert, and other things happening around the same time and so had no time for Florence. To make up for this, her mother hired two amahs to look after her, but this failed to compensate for the lack of attention from her mother.[48] Even in those days, it was considered by many to be far too early to send a child of such a tender age to be a boarder.

In memory of Bishop Hoare and other founders of the school, Miss Skipton observed Founders' Day every year on 18 September each year. Bishop Hoare and his students from St Paul's College lost their lives off the coast of Castle Peak during one of the worst typhoons that struck Hong Kong when they were on a preaching tour on a sampan on 18 September 1906.[49]

Scholastic Activities: An Initial Curriculum for Domestic Life

As for the curriculum, Irene Cheng believed that the school's English teaching was based on the assumption that the girls would eventually marry and go to England. This was

---

45. Gittins, *Eastern Windows, Western Skies*, 86.
46. Florence Yeo, *My Memories* (Pittsburgh: Dorrance Publishing, 1994), 17.
47. Florence Yeo, *My Memories*, 17–18.
48. Irene Cheng, *Intercultural Reminiscences*, 87.
49. Mrs Dunbar, "A Glimpse of the DGS in Days Gone By", *The Quest* (1950): 46.

Laying the Foundation: 1899 to 1924

probably true for the British children but not for the Eurasians, as most of them remained in Hong Kong:

> Mama knew of DGS only as a good school for teaching English, and that is why she sent us there, in spite of its being partly or mainly the intention of the founders to provide a good Christian education and orphanage for children of mixed parentage. I suppose the founders thought that many of these children would eventually go to England and the curriculum was designed to meet their needs. When we enrolled in 1914, there were only two Chinese staff members who instructed the lower classes. One Miss Poon from Australia taught us needlework while the other, Miss Allen, gave us 30 minutes of dictation each week and spent most of her time teaching the little ones. The other staff were mostly English teachers recruited from the United Kingdom. In 1914 the school was probably not as generously funded as it and many other local establishments would be in later years. Consequently, the headmistress at DGS must have a very tight budget, which explains why she had little or no clerical assistance.[50]

> As ours was a Christian school the first lesson preceding all classes was a half hour of learning the Scriptures, with each class generally studying one or more books of the Bible thoroughly. For this lesson, all classes but two—which used the far sides of the big schoolroom and had separate blackboards—moved to other rooms in the building.[51]

As the school increased in size, it was necessary to augment its teaching staff. Even though Hong Kong had a technical institute that had provided a teacher training course since 1907, there were no teachers for DGS because of its English-only education. Besides scripture, which was taught by Anglican clergymen, the girls had lessons in English literature, composition, grammar, and dictation. Of mathematics, only arithmetic was taught in the school, and it was a struggle to prepare the students for the Oxford Local Examinations.

As girls were not allowed to enter HKU before 1921, the highest level of public examination open to the girls was the Senior Local Examination, which did not require examination on all branches of mathematics, such as algebra, geometry, and trigonometry. Irene Cheng described how Miss Bascombe encouraged the girls to learn mathematics even though it was not necessary for examination. Irene enjoyed the challenge of learning mathematics and appreciated Miss Bascombe's efforts.

The school also taught history, geography, nature studies, hygiene, domestic science, singing (with several classes combined in the dining room), and needlework. Irene Cheng remembered learning English history and geography, which both focused on the British Empire. She observed how impractical and unrealistic the syllabus was for children living in Hong Kong to study only the geography of the British Empire and to learn history through the British lens:

---

50. Cheng, *Intercultural Reminiscences*, 81.
51. Cheng, *Intercultural Reminiscences*, 76.

I remember in Class Five we studied English history from 1066, beginning with the Norman Conquest, and for geography, we studied British South Africa—which, at the time, struck me as being rather odd.

Most of the curriculum at DGS was based on what English children would learn "back home" . . . Fortunately, when we were in Class Two, Miss Ferguson taught us the geography of Asia, including China, a subject that I was keenly interested. I particularly remember learning that China had rich mineral resources that had not been developed and that the Middle Kingdom had only a tiny rail system despite the vast areas that desperately needed to be opened up.[52]

In 1916, when Lady Ho Tung refused to send her younger daughters to DGS because she wanted them to learn Chinese in addition to English, Miss Skipton agreed to find a suitable Chinese teacher. Unfortunately, the teacher she hired was just not good enough, and the girls did not learn much from him.[53]

After the school became a grant-in-aid school in 1900, government inspection was required. During the 1904 inspection, the inspector reported that the girls in DGS were admitted to a higher grade than they deserved based on their academic achievements (or lack thereof). While English was well taught, the girls did not sufficiently practise their reading and were often inaudible when asked to read. While the writing, composition, and grammar of the girls were good on the whole, they failed badly in arithmetic. The inspector did find something nice to say, remarking that the girls' notebooks were neatly kept and their map drawing satisfactory.[54]

Two years later the government inspector reported that, while the campus was adequate for sixty-four students, the school was over capacity at eighty-five students. More significantly, the students' academic performance remained unchanged and quite poor. While reading English had improved, spelling was notably weak; the achievement of the girls in arithmetic was far below average. Geography and history had been introduced, but the inspector noted that the teacher did not make use of the maps adequately in the lower grades, and facts were learned by rote memorisation, a teaching method that discourages critical thinking. The only subjects in which students appeared to excel were hygiene and needlework.[55]

Hong Kong first participated in the Cambridge Local Examinations which was administered by the Cambridge Local Examinations syndicate as public examinations in 1886, because HKU was founded only in 1911. In 1889, the Cambridge Local Examinations

---

52. Cheng, *Intercultural Reminiscences*, 77.

53. Cheng, *Intercultural Reminiscences*, 82–83.

54. Appendix D, Detailed Reports on Schools 1904: A. Government Schools; B. Grant Schools, HKSP 1905, 532–540.

55. Reports of the Inspector of Schools 1906, HKSP 1907, No. 28/1907, 533–534.

Laying the Foundation: 1899 to 1924

were replaced by the Oxford Local Examinations. After passing these examinations, a few boys left Hong Kong to study in Britain if their families could afford it, though it was out of the question for most boys or any girl to go abroad for studies. Indeed, the results of the students in these examinations served only as an indication of the academic standing of the school.

In 1909, three DGS students, Mollie Mooney, Leila Lace, and May Palmer, passed the preliminary Oxford Local Examinations out of six students who took part in the examination that year.[56] But none took part in the Senior Oxford Local Examination. Nevertheless, this was an indication that the standard of the school had improved.

One can conclude that at the beginning of the school's history the performance of DGS girls was, at best, only satisfactory. This was perhaps a natural and inevitable outcome of the school's mission, to function as a boarding school for European and Eurasian girls to learn English with a curriculum to prepare them for a domestic life at home. DGS was not an academic school, and there was no demand for it to be anything beyond its stated mission.

Gradually the scholastic standard of the school improved, and classes were extended to cover secondary school education level, although the number of students in each of the upper classes was small. Further improvement in the scholastic achievement of DGS began with the admission in the late 1910s and 1920s of the Ho Tung girls and girls of families of a higher social stratum, such as the daughters of Mr and Mrs Robert Kotewall and Mr and Mrs Lo Man Kam. Kotewall and Lo were to receive their knighthood in 1938 and 1948 respectively.

In the meantime, the examination system in Hong Kong also changed. During the First World War, the Oxford Local Examinations were discontinued because of the difficulties of sending the question papers from England to Hong Kong and to return the answers. In the academic year of 1913/1914, two years after it was founded, HKU introduced its own Matriculation and Junior Local Examinations to replace the Oxford Local Examinations. Students were to take the Junior Local Examinations after Class II and the Matriculation Examinations after Class I. For those who did not wish to enter university, a certificate would be given to them if they passed their own school examinations in Class I.

In 1916, five DGS girls participated in the Oxford Local Examination, when it was last held, and passed. In 1918, 11 girls entered the HKU examinations. Those who entered the Junior Local Examinations all passed, and five of them received six distinctions. Eva and Irene Ho Tung, who took the Matriculation Examinations, also passed but were not admitted to HKU until three years later.

In England, many of the universities founded in the Victorian era, including the red-brick universities of the early twentieth century, were from the start co-educational

---

56. "Diocesan Girls' School. The Bishop's Appeal", *South China Morning Post*, 23 July 1909.

by name but not in practice. The University of London was the first in Britain to award degrees to women in 1878, but there were no female students in HKU until 1921. A couple of years earlier, DGS had asked HKU if it would be willing to let a very bright female student of German and Chinese parentage to attend as an external student, but the request was denied. No one dared to ask about letting the Ho Tung girls enter HKU. In 1921, Mr Edward Alexander Irving, who had served as HKU's first registrar, became the director of education. His daughter, Rachel, who had previously obtained a Social Science Certificate at Bedford College, London University, wanted to complete her education at HKU. The university at first declined her application solely on account of her gender. The matter was referred to the attorney general, who examined the university statutes, which stated "any person who had passed the prescribed examination and is over 16 years of age may, on payment of the prescribed fee, be admitted to the university". Consequently, the Senate of HKU resolved to admit Miss Irving to the third-year arts course but exempted her from residence as there was no hostel accommodation for girls. Eva and Irene, who had each passed nine matriculation subjects when the requirement was only five, were permitted to enter HKU in the same year.[57] Henceforth, university education became a possibility for upper-class local girls in Hong Kong.

Limited Extracurricular Activities

In the nineteenth century, extracurricular activities were not considered important for either boys or girls in Hong Kong or China. It was considered most "unladylike" for girls to be active or to take part in any sport. At DGS, there were, however, a few extracurricular activities, such as girl guiding.

One of the most memorable events for the girls was Empire Day in 1909. On that day, the students of DGS and DBS were supposedly in for a treat, but they in fact were being trained to become worthy citizens of the British Empire. They assembled early that morning at their respective schools to sing the British National Anthem and were afterwards put on launches to explore the outlying islands in Hong Kong at the invitation of the Hon. Mr Edward Osborne and Hon. Mr Edbert Ansgar Hewett respectively for the two schools, followed by a swim in the ocean and a picnic lunch. In the evening, Mr A. O. Brawn, a teacher at DBS, gave a lecture on the significance of Empire Day and on the vastness of the British Empire compared with Hong Kong Island. The lecture was even illustrated by Mr Henry Sykes, a teacher at DBS, using a lantern borrowed from the government.[58]

---

57. Cheng, *Intercultural Reminiscences*, 105. Irene Ho Tung entered HKU in September 1921 and Eva Ho Tung in January 1922 as she was away from Hong Kong in September 1921.

58. "Scholars and Empire Day", *South China Morning Post*, 26 May 1909.

Laying the Foundation: 1899 to 1924

In the report that appeared in July–December 1922 in the *Outpost*, Miss Skipton reported on students' whereabouts and careers after graduation. Many had married and left for different parts of the world—Treaty Ports in China, Siam, Japan, India, the United States of America, France, Germany, Denmark, and Scandinavia and had their own homes and children. Others worked as secretaries in firms, offices, and shops; some of them rose in rank to become pivotal members of corporations. A few became nurses and teachers.

In 1921, after being headmistress for twenty-two years, Miss Skipton left the school for a well-earned retirement. She sailed away on the *Empress of Russia* on 18 August with the good will and affection of all the girls and their parents.[59] She continued to take an active interest in the school after retirement, and it was customary for her to interview new members of staff before they came out from England until 1946, four years before she passed away.[60]

DGS under Miss Catherine A. Ferguson (September 1921–July 1924)

Miss Catherine A. Ferguson, a well-known teacher at DGS, succeeded Miss Skipton as headmistress. Ferguson returned from vacation in September 1921 to take up the position. During her first year, there was also a change of staff, whereby Miss H. Dorothy Sawyer, who would become the next headmistress, arrived as the senior mistress. Miss Aspinall took charge of kindergarten, and Miss McGill replaced Mrs Jenkinson as matron. Mrs Jenkinson, a very capable housekeeper, looked after the children as her own and was much loved by the girls in return. She seemingly had the magic of making one thousand little problems that crept up every day in the boarding school disappear into thin air with great ease.[61]

Miss Ferguson grew up during the women's suffrage era when women demanded a political voice in Britain. The First World War also advanced the feminist cause because of women's sacrifices during the war, and so women began to seek legislative reform against female discrimination and gender inequality. Miss Ferguson took the education of young women seriously and encouraged her students to take part in matriculation examinations and to enter HKU for higher education when feasible. She had a gift for languages and a sense of musical appreciation. The school opened up to Chinese girls under Miss Ferguson. A "Remove" class was started where Chinese girls learned English for one year before joining the regular classes.[62]

Extracurricular activities expanded during Miss Ferguson's administration. She encouraged learning for the sake of learning rather than for converting students to Christianity,

---

59. "Diocesan Girls' School, Departure of Miss Skipton", *South China Morning Post*, 17 July 1921.
60. "Miss E. D. Skipton Former Headmistress of DGS Dead", *South China Morning Post*, 9 August 1950.
61. "DGS, Annual Speech Day", *South China Morning Post*, 3 December 1923.
62. Mrs Dunbar, "A Glimpse of the DGS in Days Gone By", *The Quest* (1950): 47.

and she also encouraged gardening.[63] The *South China Morning Post* reported on 18 February 1925 that DGS published a school magazine in 1924 with two issues, in April and October. Unfortunately, these have not been located to date.[64] *The Quest Magazine of the Diocesan Girls' School* (*The Quest*), was first published in 1941, just before the Second World War. It is unclear whether school magazines were published in between.

Miss Ferguson also broke accepted social norms by insisting on promoting sports in the school, an activity, as we have seen, that had until then been considered the prerogative of boys. Due to lack of space, she approached the Kowloon Football Club for the use of their grounds for hockey, and the school had quite a few matches there. Tennis became much more popular than before, and six classes competed for the Lady Ho Tung Challenge Cup. Sir Robert Ho Tung even donated a new tennis court to the school in 1924. In the summer, the school took students on swimming picnics. The Girl Guides Troop, which began at the time of Miss Skipton, expanded. In 1924, a competition took place among different troops: DGS, Central British School in Kowloon, Murray Company, and Wan Chai Company. The students were tested on first aid, tracking, knot tying, laws and promises of the Girl Guides, and they were inspected at the end of the day. DGS came second, tied with Murray Company. The Central British School in Kowloon gained the highest mark.[65]

Miss Ferguson did much to influence the future policies of the school by introducing social service activities and seeking the cooperation of parents. Although she served as headmistress for only a short time, she left a legacy at DGS by admitting Chinese girls and setting the motto of the school "Daily Giving Service"—a typical Christian pledge and also an acronym for Diocesan Girls' School. Many extracurricular activities organised outside class were related to social service, such as organising a boys' and girls' club for children whose families could not afford to send them to school. DGS students taught these children reading and writing and served them a light meal after the lessons. The Bishop of Victoria and South China, Charles Ridley Duppuy (Bishop 1920–1932), once remarked: "The purpose of attending school for children was not just studying their lessons but the main object was how to face life and if the girls could carry into life their school motto, they will have learned the biggest lesson."[66]

Sadly, in July 1924, Miss Ferguson became ill and returned to England for treatment. She had planned to resume her work after her recovery, but this was not to happen. She passed

---

63. "Diocesan Girls' School Annual Prize-Giving", *South China Morning Post*, 8 March 1924.

64. "Diocesan Girls' School, Prize Distribution. The Bishop's Remarks", *South China Morning Post*, 28 February 1925.

65. "Hong Kong Girl Guides, Competition at Government House", *South China Morning Post*, 24 April 1924.

66. "Diocesan Girls' School, Prize Distribution. The Bishop's Remarks", *South China Morning Post*, 28 February 1925.

away from her illness in 1925. Miss Sawyer, the senior mistress, who acted on her behalf in her absence, was appointed the next headmistress.

Miss Elizabeth Skipton inaugurated the revival of the Diocesan Female School as the Diocesan Girls' School and Orphanage almost single-handedly. Her dedication to the school overcame many challenges during the first twenty years. The school grew steadily, with an enrolment of 26 at its inauguration to 180, and a teaching staff of around eight to nine in 1921 at the time of her retirement. The school blossomed, growing from a school for orphans and abandoned Europeans and children of mixed marriages to learn good English to one where girls from the upper social class would attend. She gradually elevated the academic standing of the school, which was limited initially to primary education, to secondary level, preparing students for a university education. As a result of her efforts, two of her students were admitted into HKU. Due to the strength of her personality and dedication to the church, Miss Skipton imparted a strong moral tone to the school. Miss Catherine Ferguson, the next headmistress, had a short tenure of only four years due to her illness and subsequent demise. She consolidated all the achievements of the school in academic work, opened up the school to Chinese girls, and introduced extracurricular activities. She left her mark by giving the school its motto "Daily Giving Service". These two headmistresses laid the foundation for DGS to grow as an academic institution and to develop into one of the elite schools in Hong Kong today.

Chapter 3

Coping with Social Changes: 1925 to 1938

During the first part of the twentieth century, China's political turmoil continued relentlessly despite the founding of the Republic of China. The country rapidly fell into the chaos and degeneracy of the warlord period, during which more immigrants settled in Hong Kong, increasing its population and need for education. In the meantime, Hong Kong flourished as a trading post. Under British colonial administration, it used English for its governance and also for business communication. The Eurasians in the territory were of assistance to the relatively small number of British expatriate officials; and those with English and a little Chinese, as well as those Chinese with some knowledge of the English language, were in great demand. English therefore became an important school subject, and an English education much desired. DGS's original purpose of providing an English education thus supported demands from all social classes, not just those who could afford it, but also those of modest means.

From its founding as a colonial administrative region, Hong Kong was China's main gateway to the West, and it prospered during the First World War in particular. After the war, inflation and a rapid rise in the cost of living caused the poorly paid working class a great deal of hardship. The early 1920s were plagued by a series of labour strikes for better wages, which, happily, were resolved in favour of the workers. The 1922 Seamen's Strike led to a general strike, with 120,000 workers taking part. Although this almost paralysed Hong Kong, it was the 1925–1926 strike-boycott that almost destroyed the economy. Early in 1925, a Chinese labourer was killed by a Japanese foreman, and on 30 May, the British Shanghai Municipal Police opened fire on Chinese students who protested against the killing. This shooting sparked nationwide anti-foreigner demonstrations and riots. In Hong Kong, anti-British sentiments further escalated after another incident of police violence took place: on 23 June, in Shameen, Guangzhou, the British opened fire on demonstrators and killed scores of workers and students. The workers responded with a strike-boycott, which continued until May 1926 and bankrupted many individuals and companies. DBS and St Paul's Girls' School both went into serious debt as a result of subscribers' inability to come up with funds for the new school buildings that were being constructed. DGS and other schools were also affected by low enrolment as many families could not afford to send their children to school.

After testing their aggression against China in the 1920s, when the country was still fragmented and constantly at civil war, the Japanese finally invaded the country in 1931 and eventually took control of Manchuria. Soon afterwards, Japanese forces gradually penetrated into North China. In 1937, after the Marco Polo Bridge Incident, when the Nationalist Army fired at the Japanese troops as the latter moved close to the bridge which is not far from Beijing, China declared war on Japan, marking the beginning of the Second Sino-Japanese War. The Imperial Japanese Army marched southward and very quickly took over the coastal areas of China. By 1938, Guangzhou had fallen into the hands of the Japanese. As Britain was not at war with Japan, the Japanese Army halted at the border of Hong Kong in Shenzhen. However, although Hong Kong had not yet been invaded, many British felt that war was imminent and therefore left the city or sent home their families.

In this bleak scenario, one movement seemed to gain support from many different sides—the change in perspective on gender roles. The suffragette movement in the West had led to positive change in the perception of women's rights, and women's issues received attention as part of the new thinking in China. In Hong Kong, women's social status also improved. Physical education rose in popularity among the Westernised Chinese: the Young Men's Christian Association (YMCA) and the Young Women's Christian Association (YWCA), founded by missionaries, provided facilities for young people to engage in physical exercise and helped instil awareness of its importance. This change of perspective on women's rights was a significant turning point.

DGS under Miss H. Dorothy Sawyer

Miss H. Dorothy Sawyer, who acted as Headmistress when Miss Catherine Ferguson was ill, was appointed to the headship of the school when Miss Ferguson passed away in 1925.[1] Miss Sawyer, like Miss Elizabeth Skipton, was dedicated to the school but was extremely overworked because she was given no clerical assistance; she often worked in her office late into the night. Miss Sawyer believed in discipline. When presenting her school report in 1935, she urged parents to have absolute confidence in and to offer total support to the

---

1. "School Prizes: Diocesan Girls' School's Annual Function", *South China Morning Post*, 15 March 1926.

Figure 3.1: Miss H. Dorothy Sawyer (Headmistress 1925–1938). Source: School Archives.

Figure 3.2: DGS staff and students, 1926. Source: School Archives. Note: School uniform was not mandatory then. There were 222 students in 1926.

school staff. She likened the parental acceptance of school discipline to the private relationship between parents and their child: the child's views should not take precedence over school authority any more than her mother's views should prevail over the authority of her father.[2] Although this might sound like the last blast of Victorian authority, discipline was what the public expected during this era.

Miss Sawyer was tall, austere, and had "yellow" hair. While her appearance might have been formidable for many young children, at times she showed moments of softness. In 1930, Patricia (Patsy) Fenton (née Kotewall) was the youngest in her class in DGS. She recalled occasions when she sat on her teacher's lap while Miss Sawyer was reading or reciting. One form of punishment handed out by Miss Sawyer to offending students was

---

2. "Diocesan Girls' School. Headmistress's Outspoken and Interesting Report. Lady Southorn's Tribute", *South China Morning Post*, 12 July 1935.

to send them on short errands, such as to buy a small item from outside school. Patsy recollected that such a punishment, instead of being a hardship, was rather enjoyable for students, who felt far from being chastised.[3] Miss Sawyer was ahead of her time in believing that too much emphasis was placed on examinations and marks, and that promotions and prizes should not be based on test results but rather on the cumulative progress over a year. In 1935, she started to put this belief into practice in the way she distributed prizes.[4]

DGS remained a grant-in-aid school, receiving a grant every year from the government. The amount received was based on the school inspector's annual assessment of the school rather than solely on the results of examinations. During Miss Sawyer's administration, school enrolment steadily increased from 177 in 1922 to 339 in 1938 when she retired. Because of the economic recession that followed the strike-boycott, the number of students in the school dropped temporarily in 1926 and 1927, but by 1928, the school saw some gradual growth in student enrolment (Figure 3.3). Miss Sawyer planned for a number of years to extend the school building to relieve overcrowding and to create new facilities, but because of the shortage of funds, her plan did not materialise while she was in office.

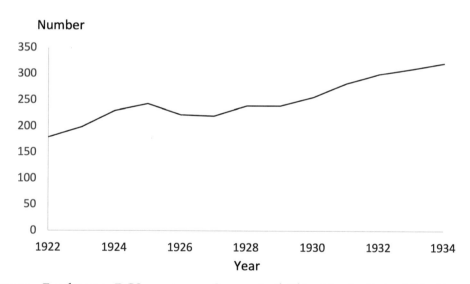

Figure 3.3: Enrolment in DGS, 1922 to 1934. Source: *South China Morning Post* published in respective years.

---

3. "One Family Unbroken—Across Three Generations—The Fentons", Interview by DOGA, accessed 26 July 2020, http://www.doga.org.hk/index.php/doga-news/conversations/old-girls-profiles/112-interviews/old-girls-profiles/136-the-fentons.
4. "Diocesan Girls' School Headmistress's Outspoken and Interesting Report", *South China Morning Post*, 12 July 1935.

As mentioned previously, Miss Sawyer's headship came about at the same time as the advancement in women's rights, when education for girls was being treated more sympathetically by government and community alike. The school was built on a triangular lot (KIL 1281) that was formed by the junction of Gascoigne Road and Jordan Road. In 1927, Miss Sawyer was able to obtain more land for a playground for students by extending the base of the triangle westward.[5] The Recreation Grounds Committee granted this land to the school as a playground on an annual basis, and also allowed the school to enclose it with a substantial wall, indicating the government's intention of allowing the school to occupy the area for an indefinite period, even though the permit only extended until 16 September 1931.[6] The ground was awarded to the school free of charge, on condition that no structure was built on it without permission from the Director of Public Works and that the area was only to be used for the purpose of a playground in connection with the school. The permit was renewed every five years, the date of the last renewal being 17 September 1936 for a period of five years, thus expiring just before the Second World War.[7] In 1928, Miss Sawyer applied to the Director of Education to build a covered pavilion on a section of the playground and requested a building grant of HK$2,350, which was half the cost of construction.[8] Little did she expect that by the turn of the twenty-first century, the whole playground would be occupied by several new school buildings.

The pavilion was opened by Mrs Southorn, wife of Mr Wilfred Thomas Southorn, the Acting Governor, on 13 December 1928, the same day as the school bazaar. The school was decorated with flags, and its entrance pillars were covered with blue and white ribbons. Mrs Southorn, who performed the opening ceremony for the pavilion, was met and welcomed by Bishop Duppuy, and Miss Sawyer at the entrance of the playground. Her route was lined by the school's Girl Guides Company. At the entrance to the pavilion, Mrs Southorn ceremoniously cut the ribbons and walked inside amid music and dances presented by the girls. The pavilion was equipped for gymnastics; drills, organised by the new physical education mistress, who joined the staff in 1929, could be conducted there even on rainy days.[9] With this new facility, the school was finally successful in persuading girls to take part in sports—an uncommon opportunity in those days.

The school had a small and poorly run library until 1934 when it was completely revamped. Old books were discarded and new ones added, and a proper system of organisation was introduced. It is unclear who was responsible for its management, but each pupil

---

5. This large playground did not have a plot number and was assigned KIL 6329 in 1949.

6. Public Works Department to Colonial Secretary, 13 December 1927, HKPRO, HKRS58-1-60 (70).

7. Lands Officer to Colonial Secretary, 9 November 1937, HKPRO, HKRS58-1-60 (70).

8. Dorothy Sawyer to A. E. Wood, Director of Education, 3 November 1928, HKPRO, HKRS58-1-60 (70).

9. "New Pavilion: Diocesan Girls' School Building Opened", *South China Morning Post*, 13 December 1928.

Figure 3.4a: The covered playground or "Greek Temple", 1929. Source: School Archives.

Figure 3.4b: Girls exercising in their winter uniform. Source: School Archives.

contributed 80 cents a term to the library towards its expenses, and this led to a feeling of ownership and responsibility among the students.

A notable event in DGS history was the establishment of an off-site kindergarten on 14 September 1933 under the auspices of the school. This was located at 3 Duke Street, Kowloon Tong, in the same building as an Anglican Church. St Peter's Church in Sai Ying Pun had closed, as most of its congregation had moved to Kowloon Tong, and the church on Duke Street was a stopgap measure to house the congregation from St Peter's until a new church, Christ Church, was eventually built on Waterloo Road to replace it. In later years, the primary school sponsored by Christ Church was a feeder school for DGS for a period. The new kindergarten in Kowloon Tong was limited to thirty girls, from ages four to eight, and the fees were $6 per month payable quarterly. It was established to reduce the large class sizes at the kindergarten on the Jordan Road main campus. This was considered to be an experiment, with the proviso that if the need was not there it would be closed.[10] But the new facility did well, because Mrs Langley, an experienced kindergarten teacher, was put in charge. During 1934, the number of students reached thirty, with many old girls' children among them.[11] Unfortunately, the kindergarten on Duke Street was not restored after the Second World War.

Scholastic Activities: An "English Only" Curriculum

Under Miss Sawyer there were twelve teachers at DGS. Few among them were university graduates or trained in teaching colleges—as was common in the 1920s and 1930s—although some of them were innately skilled in teaching.[12] It was therefore a most unusual occurrence when Dr Baldwin Lee, who had returned from the United States having obtained a doctoral degree from Columbia University, joined the teaching staff.[13]

In 1925, when Miss Sawyer took over, the school was run along the lines of an English school. It was divided into three divisions: kindergarten, middle, and senior schools. The kindergarten (Class 9) had about sixty children who were divided into three levels. It was run by a fully trained English mistress, usually with three helpers. Children were admitted

---

10. "Diocesan Girls' Kindergarten. Kowloon Tong to Have New School. An Experiment", *South China Morning Post*, 27 July 1933.

11. "Diocesan Girls' School. Miss Sawyer's Work Praised", *South China Morning Post*, 26 March 1934.

12. Susanna Hoe, *The Private Life of Old Hong Kong: Western Women in the British Colony, 1841–1941* (Hong Kong: Hong Kong Oxford Press, 1911), 213.

13. Frances Wong, *China Bound and Unbound: History in the Making* (Hong Kong: Hong Kong University Press, 2009), 16.

at the age of four and few could speak English. Yet all the teaching was carried out in English and, according to Miss Sawyer, standard up-to-date kindergarten methods were used.[14]

In 1928, the middle school, comprising classes from Class 8 to 6, was the largest division with a total of around 120 children; some were Chinese, but they were mostly Eurasians. A "Remove", Class 5, was established for Chinese girls who entered the school with no English but received previous education in Chinese: they were taught English for a year before they were placed in the regular classes. The senior school had fourteen in Class 3, twelve in Class 2, and seven in Class 1. DGS was a boarding school with room for forty-five to fifty boarders.[15]

As DGS was a grant-in-aid school, all students in Class 2 took the Hong Kong Junior Examination, while students in Class 1 participated in the Hong Kong Senior Examination at the end of the school year. In the lower classes, students were taught English, Bible studies, history, and geography. According to Mrs Joyce Symons (née Anderson, Headmistress from 1953 to 1985):

> Class Four academic work became diverse and interesting. I started to learn French and enjoyed speaking and reading that language. We also studied algebra, geometry and trigonometry, which I absorbed quite easily, but found dull.[16]

Students were forbidden to speak Chinese in school, and if Miss Sawyer found anyone who was not communicating in English, she would punish her by having her write a hundred lines. The practice of "English only" persisted after the war until Mrs Symons's time. DGS girls' standard of English was the highest among Hong Kong students but was achieved at the expense of learning Chinese.[17]

In order to increase student care, and on the instruction of the government, the school introduced a hygiene programme during the 1920s. When Hong Kong was first founded, the government paid scant attention to sanitation, and later attempts to improve it was met with little success. The city thus became infamous for its insanitary conditions, especially in the Tai Ping Shan area. After plague struck Hong Kong in 1894, recurring regularly for almost thirty years, the government realised the importance of public health in preventing the spread of disease and finally began to implement sanitation measures, such as increasing water supply, improving environmental sanitation, educating the public on hygiene, and complying with sanitary regulations. Schools were encouraged to teach hygiene, and interschool competitions on hygiene were organised by the government to stimulate interest in the topic and to stress its importance. Additionally, the government emphasised

---

14. H. D. Sawyer, "Diocesan Girls' School, Kowloon, Hongkong", *The Outpost* (January 1928): 6–7.
15. H. D. Sawyer, "Diocesan Girls' School, Kowloon, Hongkong", *The Outpost* (January 1928): 6–7.
16. C. J. Symons, *Looking at the Stars: Memoirs by Catherine Joyce Symons* (Hong Kong: Pegasus Books, 1996), 15.
17. Wong, *China Bound and Unbound*, 14.

the significance of physical exercise in strengthening students' general well-being and immune systems. Mr William T. Featherstone, Headmaster of DBS, actively promoted sports.[18]

In 1924, the government went a step further and organised a school health programme (then called the school hygiene programme) for the first time, following the policy of the "home country" where a similar programme was already well established. In England and Wales, the Education (Administrative Provisions) Act of 1907 permitted local authorities to undertake medical examination and treatment of school children.[19]

The school hygiene programme was carried out in government schools first and then in grant schools. It consisted of the medical examination of schoolchildren and inspection of the school environment. In the first part of the programme, all students were examined, and those with health problems were referred to school clinics for treatment. Almost 80 per cent of students were found to have dental caries,[20] and about 10 per cent suffered from visual defects, either myopia or astigmatism or both. Free glasses were given to those who needed them.[21]

The second part of the programme was inspection of the school environment. This took place at DGS in 1927 and was conducted by Dr de Martin, Medical Officer of Schools, who made valuable suggestions about improving the campus's conditions. In 1929, a detailed report on the school premises was submitted to the school by Dr E. M. Minette after his inspection. He found that the classrooms and dormitories were large and had excellent ventilation. The single-flush toilets were clean and in good working condition. Water closets were not found in most homes in those days, and the children needed to learn to flush the toilets after use. Dr Minette made an interesting remark about the amount of face cream and powder found in the dormitories, and was surprised to learn from Miss Sawyer that most girls carried out the ritual of thoroughly "creaming" their faces every night. After inspecting the kitchen and the pantry, and finding them tidy and clean, he partook in the school's midday lunch, which he thought was a well-balanced meal of meat, greens, and starchy vegetables. He heaped praise on the physical education programme, which included drills that took place on the covered playground even on rainy days, and applauded the emphasis that was placed on physical exercise and its relationship with student health.[22]

---

18. W. T. Featherstone, *The Diocesan Boys' School and Orphanage, Hong Kong, The History and Records, 1869 to 1929*, compiled by W. E. Featherstone, 57–58.

19. J. Boyd Barrett, "Medical Examination of School Children Studies", *An Irish Quarterly Review* 2 (1913): 73–80.

20. "Summary of a Report and the Main Findings of the Survey on the Oral and Dental Conditions of Chinese Children in Hong Kong", Medical Report 1939, HKAR 1939, M101, Appendix I(a).

21. Medical Report 1925, HKAR, 1925, M(1)30.

22. "Diocesan Girls' Medical Officer's Tribute to the School", *South China Morning Post*, 22 July 1929.

At the request of the Board of Education, domestic science was introduced in 1929. Part of the servants' quarters and kitchen were renovated so they could be used as a kitchen where girls' domestic science classes could take place. Personal hygiene and domestic science were the only scientific subjects offered in the school; "real" science was taught in boys' schools. In 1934, the school invited Mr Smith of the Kowloon-Canton Railway to lecture to the girls on some science subjects. To make the topics interesting and interactive, he took the children on field trips to a workshop and to a factory. He also conducted some simple experiments in the school to demonstrate several scientific principles.[23]

In 1932, the Board of Education recommended to the government that the Senior and Junior Local Examinations should be abolished, and a School-Leaving Certificate Examination should be introduced instead.[24] The School Certificate Examination was initiated in June 1935, to be conducted by the University of Hong Kong (HKU).[25] The University then abolished the Senior and Junior Local Examinations and, at the same time, issued the criteria for admission to the University's various courses. The examination subjects included English, Chinese (for Chinese candidates), physics, chemistry (or domestic science), mathematics, history, and geography (or biblical knowledge, drawing, or needlework). The subjects tested varied depending on the faculty the student wished to enter. To secure a matriculation pass, a higher standard was required than that for passing the School Certificate.[26]

In 1937, the Board of Education changed its policy again. The School Certificate Examination was to be taken after Class 2 by all English grant-in-aid schools, and it was to be controlled by a syndicate under the chairmanship of the Inspector of Schools. HKU would continue with the matriculation examination after Class 1, which became the matriculation class and was only open to those who had passed the School Certificate Examination.[27] With the School Certificate Examination taking place at the end of Class 2, those who did not wish to enter university had the option to graduate a year earlier. In order to adequately prepare students for the real world, Miss Sawyer introduced a business course in 1937 for those who did not plan to go to university but still wanted to learn more practical skills, such as shorthand, typing, and business correspondence.[28]

---

23. "Diocesan Girls' School. Miss H.D. Sawyer's Work Praised", *South China Morning Post*, 26 March 1934.

24. "Local Education. Senior and Junior Exams May be Abolished. Certificate Plan", *South China Morning Post*, 5 February 1932.

25. "The School Leaving Certificates. Plan Postponed Locally until 1935", *South China Morning Post*, 9 December 1932.

26. "The Hong Kong School Certificate. Conditions of Recognition by University", *South China Morning Post*, 1 August 1933.

27. "School Certificate Examinations. Class Two Test for Students Being Introduced", *South China Morning Post*, 16 July 1936.

28. "Diocesan Girls' School. Business Course to Be Started", *South China Morning Post*, 16 January 1937.

In January 1928, Miss Sawyer reported to the *Outpost* the outcomes for those who had graduated from the school.[29] These were very similar to those reported by Miss Skipton in 1922. However, Miss Sawyer was proud that at least two DGS graduates had completed their university education. Later, one of these girls became a medical doctor (Eva Ho Tung) and the other became the Chief School Inspector in Hong Kong (Irene Ho Tung).

With unceasing hard work on the part of Miss Sawyer and the teaching staff, more girls were admitted to HKU in the 1930s. In 1939, after Miss Sawyer retired, seven girls entered the HKU Arts Faculty and a few were accepted to study medicine.[30]

School Life: With International Flavour

In the 1920s, DGS was quite a multinational community, teachers and students included. Jean English, a student then, recalled: "DGS was quite multiracial with white Russians and Germans, French, Spanish and Portuguese, Filipinos and Greeks, Parsees, Japanese and Danes and, of course, heaps of Chinese girls and just a smattering of English." She claimed that the interaction between individuals of different cultures and backgrounds was the reason her father sent her and her sister to DGS instead of Central British School.[31]

Mrs Cecily Zimmern (née Kotewall, older sister of Patricia Kotewall), a DGS student in the 1930s, recalled that she lived on Hong Kong Island, where several other girls also lived. They crossed the harbour on the Star Ferry each morning, and a school bus waiting at the Ferry Terminal took them to school at 1 Jordan Road. These Hong Kong girls became a close and friendly community: they had good fun on this journey, and made use of the ferry ride to collaborate on their homework instead of doing it independently at home.[32]

During the school day, a bell rang after each session to signal a change of activities. The day began when the first bell rang for chapel, where students had morning prayers and sang hymns. The school hymn at this time was "Blest Are the Pure in Heart". Lessons followed. School lasted the whole day, and a Western-style lunch was provided in the dining hall at cost. The menu consisted of meat or fish served with potatoes at every meal. As there was no tuck shop, students had to bring their own snacks for breaktimes.[33]

---

29. The *Outpost* was an interim newsletter of the Dioceses of Victoria, Hong Kong, and South China that was published about three times each year from 1920 to 1975.

30. Personal communication from Professor Peter Cunich, HKU.

31. Jean English, *A Vanished World: My Memories* (private circulation, n.d.), 22–23.

32. Mrs Cicely Kotewall Zimmern, "A Collection of Memories of DGS in the 1930s". Interview by DGS Old Girls Association, accessed 26 July 2020, http://www.doga.org.hk/index.php/conversations/112-interviews/old-girls-profiles/144.

33. Interview of Mrs Cicely Kotewall Zimmern, DOGA.

The school hymn: "Blest Are the Pure in Heart"

> Blest are the pure in heart,
> for they shall see our God;
> the secret of the Lord is theirs,
> their soul is Christ's abode.
>
> The Lord, who left the heavens
> our life and peace to bring,
> to dwell in lowliness with men,
> their pattern and their King;
>
> Still to the lowly soul
> He doth Himself impart,
> and for His dwelling and His throne
> chooseth the pure in heart.
>
> Lord, we Thy presence seek;
> may ours this blessing be;
> give us a pure and lowly heart,
> a temple meet for Thee.

Young boys were also admitted to DGS, but they were a minority—as described by Mrs Symons in her memoirs.[34] She herself had entered DGS in 1926 as a pupil in the "baby class". As space was a major problem at this time, her classroom was shared by three classes. She described the layout of the school and the difficulties of having lessons when classrooms were separated only by sliding partitions:

> To the east of the hall was the staff room, flanked by wide verandahs, which afforded no privacy for the poor teachers. Next were two classrooms divided only by a thin partition, which provided no acoustic barriers at all. We quickly learned to switch off one set of sounds but could not fail to be distracted by hearing some child next door being scolded or punished.
>
> Access to the first floor was by a wide flight of granite stairs. The Headmistress's [Miss Sawyer] terrifying lair was above the dining room. At the back of the school were two sets of toilets—dark, unpleasant, and often foul smelling. We called them "Hell". Yet beyond them was "Heaven"—a full-sized hockey pitch, surrounded by exciting trees, and grassy lawn, and one building, a copy of the Parthenon in Athens, which became our play-shed.[35]
>
> . . . our Class 5 was in the middle third of the hall—known as the "Black Hole of Calcutta"—which was only good for dozing during a dull lesson. Our eyes must have suffered considerably, particularly on dull days, when the blackboard could not be seen at all. I remember asking the teacher, on the urging of other class members, why we did

---

34. Symons, *Looking at the Stars*, 9.

35. Symons, *Looking at the Stars*, 9.

not have any light over the blackboard so that we could see it properly. I was sent to see Miss Sawyer who lectured me on being cheeky.[36]

Mrs Symons, who was also a former head girl, recalled how one of her class teachers commanded the attention of her students, not by making the lessons interesting or inviting participation, but by physical methods:

> She was Scots of ample proportions, who had the lethal habit of throwing a tennis ball at pupils when she wanted their attention. She towered over us from her high, Victorian desk and would fly with that ball at anyone she caught day-dreaming or playing. It was quite frightening and anyone who dared to find it funny would be the next target. Just once, she caught me day-dreaming and I instantly became a target. Yet, although my mind might have been miles away, my reflexes were not, and almost automatically, I caught the ball before it thumped down on my desk. In dead silence, I walked up to her, still seated at her desk, and in a shaky voice declared that I was returning the tennis ball. I remember the rest of the class gasped and waited, but nothing happened.[37]

Mrs Symons as a student often crossed swords with Miss Sawyer, a frequent occurrence when two strong personalities collide. The last and most serious encounter was when Miss Sawyer refused to sign Joyce's scholarship application until confronted by her persuasive father. Joyce wrote in her memoir: "I left DGS with mixed feelings. I knew I would miss some of the teachers—those who had shown me great kindness, but I would certainly not miss being criticized by Miss Sawyer."[38]

On the other hand, Frances Wong, who entered DGS in 1928 when she was four and remained a student for twelve years, recalled a different experience. Frances later worked in the Intelligence Department of the Foreign Ministry of China in the early 1950s. In her book *China Bound and Unbound*, Frances attributed her successes in life to schooling at DGS and wrote how the school had influenced her life and her love of poetry:

> I spent twelve happy years in this school and looking back I can see that the school shaped me and made me what I am today. Every achievement I have made belongs to DGS, just as Plato once said, "The direction which education starts a man will determine his future life." The one subject that interested me most was poetry and this has remained with me throughout my life. I always looked forward to our poetry class. I like the melody and thoughts in poetry and I was able to connect them to myself.[39]

Frances Wong describes how domestic science as well as singing were important to her:

---

36. Symons, *Looking at the Stars*, 14.
37. Symons, *Looking at the Stars*, 10.
38. Symons, *Looking at the Stars*, 17–18.
39. Wong, *China Bound and Unbound*, 11.

Today, girls' schools do not pay much attention to sewing, but the sewing and knitting I learnt at DGS helped me to set up my hobby of making my own garments which I often boast about to my friends. Singing class was also a joy. Mr. Baldwin taught us famous folk songs and classical songs which now I often hum to myself even though I do not have a good voice or talent for music.[40]

She also recalled the international atmosphere of the school, remembering fondly the international choirs and group performances in a series of public concerts. Among the numerous representatives were English, Scots, Welsh, Irish, Swiss, French, German, Spanish, Portuguese, Norwegian, Danish, Swedish, and Russian choirs. She was thrilled to see so many different nationalities.[41]

The two students quoted in this section, Joyce and Frances, attended DGS at around the same time, yet their memories of the school were very different. Writing when she was a retired teacher and Headmistress, Mrs Symons recalled the poor methods of teaching and the inappropriate curriculum during her school days. These weaknesses made her determined to reform the school and to bring the best education to the children under her care. On the other hand, Frances Wong's years at DGS were happy, carefree, and idyllic in comparison with what awaited in her adult life. She and her husband went to China in 1949 to serve the country, where no doubt she experienced many hardships during those difficult years on the Mainland.

In the 1930s, there was a prefect in each class. From Class 7, the girls themselves voted for the prefects, who enjoyed much clout and a few perks; for example, the rooftop of the 1940 Wing was reserved for the prefects and their friends.[42] One of the prefects' duties was to mete out punishment, such as writing lines when a student was heard speaking Chinese in school.

There was an optional school uniform at this time, quite different from the current requirements. In the summer, a sleeveless white dress with a collar and blue trimming around the waist and at the bottom was worn; in the winter, the shirt was white but the tunic was dark blue, as was the blazer. No tie was used (Figure 3.5).[43]

Extracurricular Activities: Introduction of Sports, Music, School Bazaar, and Others

Given the comparatively more liberal social attitude of this period, extracurricular activities flourished during Miss Sawyer's administration. The school, which had gained a tennis

---

40. Wong, *China Bound and Unbound*, 14.
41. Wong, *China Bound and Unbound*, 14–16.
42. Interview of the Fentons, DOGA.
43. School uniform described in Interview of the Fentons, DOGA.

Figure 3.5a: Summer uniform in the 1930s, C. J. Anderson, second from the left back row. Source: courtesy of DOGA.

Figure 3.5b: Winter uniform in the 1930s, P. Kotewall, holding the ball. Source: courtesy of DOGA.

Coping with Social Changes: 1925 to 1938

court with its move to the Kowloon campus, held many sports matches. In time, tennis became a favourite game for a number of girls. DGS also held annual sports meetings on the school grounds in the 1930s, including track and field (50 yards, 100 yards, and 200 yards), a relay race, an obstacle course, long and high jump, a potato race, and a three-legged race for kindergarten girls.[44] There were hockey games within the school and interschool matches that competed for the Brawn Cup.[45]

DGS also staged an annual gymnastic display in the 1930s. In 1932, this commenced with routines performed by kindergarteners. Class 1 and Class 2 displayed faultless drill exercises, while the intermediate classes performed choreographed dumbbell exercises to music. More colourful performances with costumes and dances to music won the praise and applause of the spectators.[46]

During breaks and what remained of lunchtimes, the girls chatted and played games, such as rope games. They played netball, rounders, and hockey. The girls formed their own teams, because there was no house system as there is now. According to Mrs Cecily Zimmern, DGS girls were in general quite athletic and energetic, and were known to be good sportswomen, fair, open, and fun to be with.[47]

Girl Guide activities continued to be an important part of school life, and each year the school's Girl Guide Company competed for the Prince of Wales banner, which was presented to the winner during the Annual Prize Giving. In addition, the Society for the Prevention of Cruelty to Animals (SPCA) Cup was awarded to the girl who wrote the best essay on a subject assigned by the Girl Guides Society. In 1929, Phyllis Anderson, Joyce Anderson's elder sister and also a DGS girl, won this award. Over the years, many leaders of the Girl Guides at the school were old girls.[48]

For those who were not drawn to sports, the school encouraged drawing and music. Since the late 1920s, the school had sponsored candidates in the annual Royal Drawing Society Examination. In 1928, the school entered 187 candidates, and 113 secured honours and 68 passes, while only 6 failed. One candidate even won a prize in Division 2.[49] The school's musical tradition also began early. In 1930, the school entered the Trinity College, London Music Examinations for the first time. Of the ten candidates, seven passed.[50]

---

44. "School Sports: Diocesan Girls' School Annual Meeting List of Winners", *South China Morning Post*, 10 April 1936.

45. "Brawn Cup Matches", *South China Morning Post*, 10 February 1936.

46. "School Gymnastics. Diocesan Girls' Annual Exercises Yesterday, Excellent Display", *South China Morning Post*, 17 December 1932.

47. Interview with Mrs Cicely Kotewall Zimmern, DOGA.

48. "School Prizes. Distribution at Diocesan Girls' School. Year Reviewed", *South China Morning Post*, 2 March 1929.

49. "Diocesan Girls. Results of Royal Drawing Society Examinations, Excellent Results", *South China Morning Post*, 10 December 1928.

50. "Diocesan Girls. The Era of Woman", *South China Morning Post*, 17 February 1930.

DGS belonged to the school branch of the Ministering Children's League (MCL), which was an imperial international youth movement that had begun in Britain, reminiscent of the Girl Guides and the YWCA. The MCL was founded by the Countess of Meath in London in 1885 to teach the children of wealthy families to be charitable and kind to children of the disadvantaged. The society's mission spread to different parts of the British Empire, including Hong Kong. Lady May, wife of Governor Sir Francis Henry May (in post 1912–1919), championed charitable work in Hong Kong, and the wives of succeeding governors continued to practise this type of humanitarian activity. Other schools that belonged to MCL included St Stephen's Girls' College, Belilios Public School, Fairlea, and St Paul's Girls' Schools (later St Paul's Coeducational College).[51]

It is not surprising that many extracurricular activities of the school centred around social work. The students established a "Boys' Club" for newspaper boys in Kowloon and taught them about an hour of Chinese every evening, serving them a light meal afterwards. Frances Wong also reported that the school opened an orphanage, which took in the unwanted babies in town. After classes, the girls visited, to knit, sew, and look after the babies. On Saturdays and Sundays, they sold flowers for buttonholes to raise money for the institution.[52] Unfortunately, we have been unable to find out more about the orphanage and who was responsible for its operation.

The annual school bazaar was also organised to raise funds for the less fortunate, and in addition it provided a social occasion. In 1928, the bazaar made a total of HK$1,331 (equivalent to the purchasing power of HK$20,737 in 2021, taking inflation into consideration). Out of this amount, HK$600 was assigned to meet school needs and the rest was given to various charities, such as the leper colonies in Pakhoi, the Victoria Home and Orphanage in Kowloon, the SPCA in Hong Kong and Kowloon, Po Leung Kuk, an institution founded to provide shelter and education of abducted women and children, the Eyre Refuge in Kowloon, almshouses in Kowloon, the Home for the Blind, and others.[53] The school bazaar offered great opportunities for parents, their children, alumni, and teachers to work together towards a common goal, and encouraged an *esprit de corps*.

The Founding of the Diocesan Old Girls' Association

The Diocesan Old Girls' Association (DOGA) was formed in 1926, and the first annual meeting took place the following year. Initially, the association organised entertainment and sports activities, such as bathing picnics for members. Soon after, its activities expanded to

---

51. "Address by Lady Lugard, Ministering Children's League", *South China Morning Post*, 7 March 1911.

52. Wong, *China Bound and Unbound*, 9.

53. "Bazaar Results. Success of Diocesan Girls' School Effort. The Distribution", *South China Morning Post*, 18 December 1928.

Coping with Social Changes: 1925 to 1938

those which engaged with existing students, in order to foster a closer fellowship between the past and present members of the school. Miss Skipton served as Honorary President of DOGA in the second and third year. In 1929, Mrs Lo Man Kam became President, Miss Maria Kacker Vice-President, Miss Phyllis Anderson Hon. Secretary, and Miss W. Robinson Hon. Treasurer.[54] During 1932, DOGA raised funds for an endowment, and the interest from investments was used for a scholarship, awarded annually to students in Class 4.[55] It continued to provide enthusiastic support for the school over the years.

Retirement of Miss Sawyer

Miss Sawyer was nearing retirement age when the Japanese Army marched southward into China. In 1938, she requested the School Council to relieve her of the headship, a position she had held for sixteen years. She felt that she had given her best to the school, and would not be able to cope with the modern difficulties and problems of a large school in a way she felt was appropriate. The school was overcrowded and required an extension, but she had not been able to devote sufficient time or energy to realising the plan. After much thought, she had made the tough decision to step down. Indeed, it required a great deal of stamina not only to run the school, which was always short of staff and funds, and had little clerical help, but also to modify the curriculum according to the changing needs of the community. To expand the school would need much more effort and manpower, which she was unable to muster.

Miss Sawyer did not leave Hong Kong immediately but stayed on to help with school administration before the arrival of the new Headmistress, Miss Gibbins, during the Christmas of 1938. Miss Sawyer then took charge of the kindergarten in Kowloon Tong until the repatriation of British women and children began in 1940, when she retired to England. She was not eligible for a pension in England because her service was overseas, and she received no pension from the Hong Kong government as headmistress of a grant school: a provident fund for grant schools was not established until after the Second World War. In 1953, the school recognised Miss Sawyer's contribution and devotion to the school by sending her £16 each month (roughly about HK$350 per month, approximately half of a headmistress's salary in a grant school in the early 1950s), and this amount increased with inflation until she passed away in 1965. A memorial service was held in the school chapel

---

54. "Diocesan Old Girls' Association Holds Its Annual Meeting. A Successful Year", *South China Morning Post*, 16 April 1929.

55. "Diocesan Girls' School Prize-Giving, Progressive Work of Last Year Reviewed: Changes in Staff. Old Girls Association's Help", *South China Morning Post*, 17 October 1932.

by Bishop Ronald Owen Hall (Bishop of Victoria and South China 1932–1966) when the news reached Hong Kong.[56]

By the end of Miss Sawyer's administration, DGS had become a leading educational institution in Hong Kong and held a premier position among girls' schools for its teaching of English. The academic standing of the school had risen considerably, with an increasing number of girls entering HKU after graduation. By 1939, DGS girls dominated the female student population in the Arts Faculty at HKU. Miss Sawyer maintained the moral, spiritual, and physical development of its students. She should also be remembered for her dedication and for her foresight in obtaining the playing field for the school. Without this, the school would not have been able to expand within the same location, at 1 Jordan Road, after the war.

---

56. Minutes of School Council Meeting, 27 July 1965.

Chapter 4

The Imminent War and Japanese Occupation: 1939 to 1945

Despite the impending war in Europe, Miss Elizabeth Mary Gibbins accepted the position of Headmistress of DGS and arrived in Hong Kong around Christmas 1938, about two months after Guangzhou had fallen to the Imperial Japanese Army. As previously mentioned, the Army had stopped at the border of Shenzhen because Japan was not then at war with Britain. However, most people felt a Japanese invasion of Hong Kong was inevitable, and just a matter of time. Repatriation of British subjects and other foreign nationals began in 1940. By the summer of 1941, most expatriate families had left Hong Kong. Finally, on 7 December 1941, the long-dreaded day arrived. The Japanese launched an all-out offensive, with a battle-hardened army of 60,000 troops striking Hong Kong as they simultaneously attacked Pearl Harbour, marking the beginning of the Second World War. The vigorous resistance (the Battle of Hong Kong) put up by the small number of British, Canadian, and Indian forces as well as the Hong Kong Volunteer Defence Corps surprised the Japanese, and after seventeen days of ferocious fighting, Hong Kong surrendered to the Imperial Japanese Army. Many young men, mostly British and Eurasians who had joined the Volunteer Defence Corps, were killed during the battle, among them Donald Anderson, a brilliant lawyer and the beloved brother of Joyce Anderson.[1] Hong Kong then entered a long, dark period of three years and eight months of harsh Japanese Occupation.

In 1939, despite the imminence of war, most aspects of life in Hong Kong carried on in much the same way as before, including education. As DGS was a grant-in-aid school, it was given a capitation grant each year according to the number of students in the school. Earlier, in 1938, the government had proposed replacing this grant with a deficiency grant

---

1. C. J. Symons, *Looking at the Stars: Memoirs by Catherine Joyce Symons* (Hong Kong: Pegasus Books, 1996), 25.

to give the government more control over the considerable public spending on grant schools. Under this proposal, the government would base their grant calculation on the difference between income and approved expenditure, both controlled by the government, thereby leaving no margin for the school to expand. The qualification and the salary scales of teachers would be fixed, and the proportion of religious teachers to lay teachers would be limited to not more than 50 per cent—a serious blow to the finances of Catholic schools in Hong Kong.[2] This proposal was met with protests from grant schools, especially over the limitation of the number of religious teachers. A number of the principals of grant schools who served on the Board of Education, including Father George Byrne, SJ (Wah Yan College Hong Kong), the Rev. Christopher B. R. Sargent (Diocesan Boys' School), the Rev. Frank Short (Ying Wah College), and Miss Edna S. Atkins (St Stephen's Girls' College), decided to form an umbrella organisation, the Grant Schools Council (GSC), to represent all grant schools across all denominations to negotiate with the government. After protracted discussions of more than a year, the government withdrew the section on religious orders but not the basis of grant calculation. The GSC accepted this revised grant code, which was finally approved by the Secretary of State for the Colonies on 4 June 1940: it was known as the 1941 Grant Code.[3] However it was not implemented as the war broke out.

DGS under Miss Elizabeth Mary Gibbins (1939–1941, 1945)

A graduate of Westfield College, London, with First Class Honours in History and First Class Honours in the Cambridge Certificate in Education, Miss Gibbins had prior experience as a staff member at St Brandon's School, Bristol, before she joined DGS.[4] At the age of 26, she became the youngest Headmistress of DGS.[5] She certainly did not suspect what was to lie ahead for her and the school in the very near future.

In 1939, there were 340 students enrolled at DGS and 23 teachers, giving a student–teacher ratio of 14.8:1, which is sound by today's standards. In the academic year of 1939/1940, Miss Gibbins recruited Joyce Anderson (Mrs Symons), a recent graduate of the Faculty of Arts, Hong Kong University (HKU), as a teacher for Forms 1 and 2. Miss Gibbins and Miss Anderson became fast friends.

---

2. Patricia P. K. Chiu, *A History of the Grant Schools Council* (Hong Kong: Grant Schools Council, 2013), 82–83.
3. Chiu, *A History of the Grant Schools Council*, 86.
4. Miss E. M. Gibbins, "New Head of Diocesan Girls' School", *South China Morning Post*, 10 October 1938.
5. Bishop Hall DGS Speech Day Address.

Figure 4.1: Miss Elizabeth Mary Gibbins (1939–1941, 1945). Source: *Portrait of Miss Gibbins* (St Mary's School (Calne) Old Girls Association, 1993), 4.

Figure 4.2: DGS teachers in 1939. Source: Mrs Patricia Fenton (née Kotewall).
From left to right:
Sitting: 2nd Miss Cunningham, 5th Miss Wentworth, 6th Miss E. M. Gibbins, 7th Miss Allen, 9th Miss Lee (PE)
Standing: 4th Miss Helen Ho, 5th Miss Chiu (botany), 7th Miss Jessie Wong (sports), 10th Miss C. J. Anderson. (The missing ones are teachers who could not be identified.)

Building the New Extension: A Proper Classroom for Each Class

One of Miss Gibbins's first tasks was to complete the long-awaited expansion of the overcrowded school. The original school building had been constructed in 1913 to accommodate 150 students, and the small extension in 1918 had added only one classroom, one dormitory, and a teachers' room. By 1939, DGS had 340 students, so Bishop Hall, who was also the Chairman of the School Council of DGS, pushed the expansion project to its completion.[6] He addressed the parents at the Annual Prize Giving Day in 1939 and told them that with DGS's 80th birthday rapidly approaching, the school buildings should reflect the excellence of the student body. Plans to expand were already prepared, but DGS still lacked the budget to finance the HK$40,000 construction. The Bishop was willing to borrow money to have this extension built.[7]

Despite the tense political situation at the time, the government provided a building grant, together with generous donations from parents, old girls, and friends of the school, and construction of the new wing began in early 1940. It was completed by December 1940.[8] The new wing, designed by the architect Mr H. S. Tam, added seven classrooms,

Figure 4.3: The 1940 School extension, later renamed Gibbins Wing. Source: School Archives.

---

6. Moira Chan-Yeung, *The Practical Prophet: Bishop Ronald O. Hall and His Legacies* (Hong Kong: Hong Kong University Press, 2015).
7. "Scholars Receive Prizes DGS and St. Stephen's", *South China Morning Post*, 10 July 1939.
8. "Diocesan Girls' School, Prize-Giving and Foundation Stone Function Postponed", *South China Morning Post*, 8 July 1940.

The Imminent War and Japanese Occupation: 1939 to 1945

an art room, and a science laboratory. On the ground floor were the laboratory and two classrooms with splinter-proof glass windows, on the first floor two classrooms and an arts room, and on the top floor three more classrooms.[9] As a result, the assembly hall was no longer partitioned to accommodate three classes at the same time, and students could enjoy their lessons in proper classrooms.[10]

The new laboratory was memorable for students. Rose Woo, a Class 3 student, described its modern features and compared it with the old one, which was totally inadequate and unsuitable for conducting scientific experiments:

> When I first entered the new lab of our school, I felt a thrill of joy in me, the joy of light, air and efficient equipment which had been lacking so badly in our former lab. The thought of being at last free from the inadequate low, dark room with boisterous street surroundings, the room which was supposed to be our lab, was a great delight. To be relieved from the embarrassment of being the audience and object of street passers-by was also a great relief.
>
> In our new laboratory we have now three long benches, each of which allows twelve students to sit on individual round stools. In our former laboratory, however, there were so few places obtainable that our class of thirty students had to be split into two groups because we could not possibly squeeze ourselves into the tiny room. Water taps and gas taps are convenient because they are fixed on the benches and are within the reach of all seated students . . . There is a fume cupboard in one corner of the lab into which we put smelling stuffs.[11]

With the opening of the new wing, the school library had, for the first time, a room of its own that was bright and spacious. A bookcase was set aside for reference books, including a set of encyclopedia, dictionaries, and other books of general knowledge. A number of magazines and a daily newspaper were available. Although there were only a few books initially, more were added later through donations.[12]

Scholastic Activities: A More Academic Curriculum

Shortly after her arrival, Miss Gibbins was dismayed to discover that the academic standard of DGS was low compared with schools in England, and she was determined to make changes.[13] Despite her finding, the number of DGS girls entering HKU Arts Faculty

---

9. "Diocesan Girls' School, New Wing Expected to Be Completed by December", *South China Morning Post*, 3 September 1940.

10. Miss E. M. Gibbins, DGS Archive.

11. Rose Woo, "Our Lab", *The Quest Magazine of the Diocesan Girls' School* (shortened to *The Quest* hereafter) (1941): 13.

12. "The School Library", *The Quest* (1941): 11.

13. Symons, *Looking at the Stars*, 87.

continued to increase in the 1930s: five in 1938 and seven in 1939. Further increase occurred during the second year of Miss Gibbins' administration—seven in 1940 and nine in 1941—accounting for 32 per cent and 23 per cent of all females who were admitted to HKU during these respective years. In the year 1941/1942 (the year before the Japanese Occupation), DGS girls made up 25 per cent of the female population in the Faculty of Arts, higher than any other girls' school in Hong Kong.[14]

Miss Gibbins made significant changes to the school, the most important being to break the long-standing tradition of teaching English only. She introduced Chinese into the school curriculum at the request of the Director of Education, who stated that Chinese students must receive Chinese education. During Joyce Anderson's school days, the majority of children were Eurasians or Europeans with only a handful of Chinese, but in the 1930s, the school admitted more Chinese girls. Some parents, such as Lady Ho Tung, removed her daughter Florence from the school because of the lack of Chinese tuition. Clearly there was a pressing need to change the English-only teaching policy.[15]

In the beginning, Chinese language classes were restricted to Chinese girls. However, Miss Gibbins believed that all students, irrespective of ancestry, should learn Chinese, because children growing up in Hong Kong would invariably encounter two of the world's dominant cultures, Chinese and English. She felt that the school should reflect the best that Chinese and English civilisations could offer to prepare the students for the future, and to contribute in a special way towards international cooperation and peace for the cross-cultural communication they would undoubtedly face. Miss Gibbins appointed Mr Tsang Kwai Ming, formerly Headmaster of Kwangsi Middle School, to head the Chinese Department, assisted by Mr C. Y. Lin and Miss Leung, and hoped to introduce Chinese to all students in due course.[16]

In addition to Chinese, Miss Gibbins added botany, then biology, to the curriculum. A more in-depth mathematics syllabus and more professional approaches to the study of English literature, history, and geography were added to prepare the students for a university education. In doing this, she had the assistance of Joyce Anderson and a few other dedicated and well-qualified teachers, along with many intelligent students.[17] Mrs Symons recalled her time as a teacher at DGS in 1939:

> In those days before specialization, a form teacher taught most subjects especially in the lower forms. I taught Scripture, English, History, Geography, Mathematics, Physical Training, Art and Needlework to a class of 30 Chinese, Eurasian and expatriate 11-year-old children. I admitted to the girls in the class that I could hardly draw or sew and

---

14. Personal communication from Professor Peter Cunich.

15. Florence Yeo, *My Memories* (Pittsburgh: Dorrance Publishing, 1994), 27.

16. "Scholars Receive Prizes. DGS and St. Stephen's", *South China Morning Post*, 16 July 1939.

17. Symons, *Looking at the Stars*, 87.

would need help from the best in the class. After studying the rather vague syllabuses for each subject, I decided to plan projects to help link many of the subjects and submitted them to the Head for approval. We also pooled materials and resources from my home and those of the girls to create a thriving class library . . . The children were very lively and keen to work and fortunately my ideas found favour with both Miss Gibbins and parents. I was so enthusiastic about my new career.[18]

These two years were quite significant to Joyce Anderson as she found her love for teaching and her future career.

School Life and Extracurricular Activities

A significant moment for DGS was the decision to make the hymn "Our Father by Whose Servants" the school hymn in 1941:[19]

Our Father, by whose servants
Our house was built of old,
Whose hand hath crowned her children
With blessings manifold,
For Thine unfailing mercies
Far-strewn along our way,
With all who passed before us,
We praise Thy name to-day.

The changeful years unresting
Their silent course have sped,
New comrades ever bringing
In comrades' steps to tread;
And some are long forgotten,
Long spent their hopes and fears;
Safe rest they in Thy keeping,
Who changest not with years.

They reap not where they laboured,
We reap what they have sown;
Our harvest may be garnered
By ages yet unknown.
The days of old have dowered us
With gifts beyond all praise,
Our father, make us faithful
To serve the coming days.

---

18. Symons, *Looking at the Stars*, 22.
19. Miss E. M. Gibbins, DGS Archive.

> Before us and beside us,
> Still holden in Thine hand,
> A cloud unseen of witness,
> Our elder comrades stand:
> One family unbroken,
> We join, with one acclaim,
> One heart, one voice uplifting,
> To glorify Thy name.

The school hymn, which plays an important role in bonding students together and fostering a community, is sung at the beginning and end of term and on special and important occasions. The hymn, which expresses that the school is a large family with many children, interconnected and unbroken over the years, reflects the ethos of the school. Just as the school motto "Daily Giving Service" does, the hymn reminds students that they should serve others and be mindful of God's manifold blessings and be thankful. Old girls may not remember other hymns or songs they learned during their school days, but they always remember the school hymn and sing it during reunions or gatherings, often with emotion, displaying their togetherness, their loyalty, and their pride in belonging to the school.

The musical life of staff and students alike vastly improved with the arrival of Mr Gerald Archer Goodban, Headmaster of the DBS, who promoted music among all students in Hong Kong. In 1940, he took the lead in forming the Hong Kong Schools' Music Association.[20] All students and teachers were welcome to join, paying a fee of $3 or $5 per year respectively. In 1941, five major concerts—two orchestral, two vocal, and one instrumental—were organised for the enjoyment and delight of all music lovers, and in another concert, members participated in the music-making. These concerts brought students and teachers from different schools together for the first time.[21] A school choral society, string orchestra, and musical competitions were planned, but all these efforts came to an end because of the war.[22]

Another innovation was the formation of a religious discussion group by members of senior classes in which they discussed their religious beliefs among themselves. The group invited Mrs Mary Goodban, wife of Mr Goodban, and the Dean of St John's Cathedral as speakers on a few occasions.[23]

In 1940, DGS decided to do something more than just collecting donations for charity, and started a club for poor children aged between seven and fourteen. This was to be run

---

20. Yee Wang Fung and Moira Chan-Yeung, *To Serve and to Lead: A History of Diocesan Boys' School* (Hong Kong: Hong Kong University Press, 2009), 55.

21. "The Hong Kong Schools' Music Association", *The Quest* (1941): 14.

22. "The Hong Kong Schools' Music Association", *The Quest* (1947): 43.

23. *The Quest* (1941): 3.

The Imminent War and Japanese Occupation: 1939 to 1945

by the students and Miss Lai, a paid leader, who attended the club every night. Two girls assisted each evening. The club started at 5:00 pm and finished at 7:00 pm, with a meal served at 6:30 pm. Funds were supplied by the staff and students—40 cents and 10 cents a month respectively. The club was opened on 17 February 1940 with sixteen children. The children entered the Young Women's Christian Association singing competition and were highly commended.[24]

The Girl Guides continued their usual activities, but the numbers dwindled because of the evacuation of British women and children from Hong Kong. However, a few girls joined during the year, increasing the number somewhat.[25]

Despite the winds of war, life went on as usual at DGS before the war erupted. In terms of sports, the school had a strong hockey team in 1941 that played against a number of different teams and won six out of its seven matches. In netball, the senior team likewise did well against other school teams that year.[26]

The school magazine, *The Quest Magazine of the Diocesan Girls' School* (shortened to *The Quest* in the footnotes) was first published sometime in 1941. It had an English and a Chinese section, each with a student editor.[27] There was also an editorial committee of six, four teachers and two students. The magazine stopped publication with the closure of the school during the Japanese Occupation.

Japanese Invasion and the Occupation of Hong Kong

With the expected war, the British began to evacuate women and children from Hong Kong throughout 1940. In September 1940, the school term began with the indefinite closure of all British schools. DGS remained open, with all the Chinese children returning, but about twenty-five British girls left. The three British teachers who departed were replaced temporarily by substitute teachers. Total enrolment reached 340. Before the new wing's completion in December 1940, the junior and kindergarten classes occupied the hall of St Andrew's Church during the September term.[28]

The school has no record of wartime activities by DGS girls and old girls. Presumably most of the girls followed their families: some left for Free China, some such as Joyce Anderson escaped to Macau, while the rest remained in Hong Kong. Shortly after the declaration of war with the Japanese, a number of Chinese universities in the coastal area

---

24. "The DGS Girls' Club", *The Quest* (1941): 15.

25. "The Girl Guides", *The Quest* (1941): 17.

26. "Hockey, Netball", *The Quest* (1941): 18–20.

27. *The Quest* (1941).

28. "Summer Vacation Ends: Chinese Students Returning, All British Schools to Remain Closed Indefinitely", *South China Morning Post*, 3 September 1940.

of China moved to the south-west region, which remained unoccupied by the Japanese during the war. Arrangements were made by HKU for their students to continue their education in some of these universities.[29] Some old girls who were HKU undergraduates probably followed this route.

The bravery of some alumnae and teachers during the war deserves mention. Dr Eva Ho Tung, who was the first female graduate from the Faculty of Medicine, HKU in 1927, resigned from her position as the first assistant to Professor of Department of Obstetrics and Gynaecology at HKU in October 1938 to take part in the war efforts against the Japanese in China. She became a member of the China Defence League, which was started by Madame Soong Ching Ling, widow of Dr Sun Yat Sen, and worked tirelessly for the organization.[30] Later Eva joined the Medical Relief Corps of the Chinese Red Cross and worked under Dr Robert Lim, a physiology professor of Peking Union Medical College, in Kweiyang.[31] There she commanded a field unit to provide medical care and anti-epidemic work[32] and served her country until the war ended. Rebecca Ho Wai Chan (née Chung) received training as a nurse after graduating from DGS in 1938. During the war, she enlisted with the Flying Tigers in the United States Army. In 1943–1944, she flew over the Himalayas between Calcutta and Chongqing about fifty times on propeller aeroplanes, looking after the wounded at the risk of losing her own life (see Chapter 9). Phyllis Anderson, the elder sister of Joyce Anderson, received the King's Medal for her undercover work during the war.[33] Helen Ho worked tirelessly in arranging relief, both legal and secret, for the camps, especially Bowen Road Military Hospital, during the Japanese Occupation. She was imprisoned on three occasions for this but survived the war to be honoured with an OBE (Order of the British Empire).[34] Miss E. A. Allen, a Eurasian English teacher at DGS, opened a little school, the Play Centre, for the children of internees at the Stanley and Sham Shui Po camps. This school was supervised by Dr Percy Selwyn Selwyn-Clarke, who was the Director of Medical and Sanitary Services before the war. When Dr Selwyn-Clarke was arrested by the Japanese for suspected spying and for arranging a loan to obtain supplies for internees and prisoners of war, Miss Allen continued to teach the dependents

---

29. Gordon King, "An Episode in the History of the University", in *Dispersal and Renewal: Hong Kong University during the War Years*, ed. Clifford Matthews and Oswald Cheung (Hong Kong: Hong Kong University Press, 1998), 83–93.

30. Israel Epstein, *Woman in World History: Life and Times of Soong Ching Ling (Mme. Sun Yat-sen)* (Beijing: New World Press, distributed by China International Book Trading Co., 1995), 365.

31. Lindsay Ride, "The Test of War". In *Dispersal and Renewal: Hong Kong University During the War Years*, ed. Clifford Matthews and Oswald Cheung (Hong Kong: Hong Kong University Press, 1998), 12.

32. "Anti-epidemic War: Dr. Eva Ho Tung Among Chungking Workers, Kweiyang Read Cross", *South China Morning Post*, 30 May 1939.

33. Symons, *Looking at the Stars*, 29.

34. Helen Ho, accessed 15 October 2021, https://gwulo.com/node/20249.

The Imminent War and Japanese Occupation: 1939 to 1945

of prisoners of war, civil internees, and the British Red Cross at Rosary Hill, which was the Dominican House of Studies for the Far East, situated at the foot of Mount Nicholson. During the war, Rosary Hill opened its doors to these children, who were mainly Europeans and Eurasians, and was managed by the International Red Cross.[35] The above are just some examples, and there must be other old girls whose courageous deeds we have no knowledge of.

During the Japanese Occupation, Miss Gibbins was interned together with other expatriate British civilians in the Stanley Camp where many developed malnutrition, beriberi, scurvy, and signs of other vitamin deficiencies. Even then, the prisoners of war in Stanley Camp fared better than those in other camps such as Sham Shui Po, because they were far away from the city and did not experience the more serious epidemics of infectious diseases, particularly diphtheria, which killed many prisoners of war in other camps. In the Stanley Camp, Miss Gibbins patiently and calmly supported everyone around her with her strong Christian faith and, at the same time, gave interesting lectures on different aspects of history to fellow internees to keep up their spirits.[36] Another internee was Jean Gittins (née Ho Tung), a DGS old girl and a Eurasian. Jean's husband, a Eurasian engineer, was taken as a prisoner of war, because he fought in the Hong Kong Volunteer Defence Corps, and was interned in Sham Shui Po Camp. Jean went voluntarily into Stanley Camp, hoping there would be an exchange of prisoners of war and she would be able to join her children in Australia. Just as Miss Gibbins was, Jean was an exemplary internee, always helpful to others.[37] In 1983, she published a book, *Stanley: Behind Barbed Wire*, about her experience during internment.[38]

In the meantime, the school became the headquarters of the Japanese Gendarmerie, the much-dreaded and much-hated Japanese military police, who imprisoned, tortured, and killed many.

Reclaiming the School from the Japanese: An Act of Courage and Foresight

On 15 August 1945, Japan surrendered. When Miss Gibbins heard the news, she walked out of the camp and headed for the school, without interference from the Japanese.

---

35. "Report on Miss Allen's Retirement", *The Quest* (1956): 24. Dr Selwyn-Clarke, the Director of Medical and Sanitary Services before the war, worked in the same position for about one-and-a-half years during the Japanese Occupation because he felt that he would be far more useful to the community by working outside Stanley Camp. He worked hard to obtain food and medical supplies for the internees and prisoners of war until he was arrested by the Japanese and thrown into prison where he suffered grievously.

36. Symons, *Looking at the Stars*, 30.

37. Geoffrey Charles Emerson, *Hong Kong Internment, 1942 to 1945: Life in the Japanese Civilian Camp at Stanley* (Hong Kong: Hong Kong University Press, 2008), 2.

38. Jean Gittins, *Stanley: Behind Barbed Wire* (Hong Kong: Hong Kong University Press, 1983).

Accompanied by an old friend, Lancelot Forster, Professor of Education at HKU, they courageously gathered their strength, despite their poor physical condition, and walked ten miles from the Stanley peninsula to the north shore of the harbour and to the site of the old Star Ferry. No one stopped them when they were on the road. When they arrived, the ferries were not running, not surprisingly, but they were able to convince some military personnel to take them across the harbour. On the Kowloon side, they continued to trek the last mile to the school.[39]

The Japanese were obviously displeased when Miss Gibbins arrived with Professor Forster to reclaim possession of the school. The Japanese commandant, who had had no orders from his superiors on how to handle such a situation, bluntly refused to leave.[40] Miss Gibbins and Professor Forster stubbornly stayed in the school compound the whole night in an attempt to protect the grounds. The following day, Miss Gibbins hailed some Royal Air Force (RAF) personnel to send a signal to a senior officer, who later ordered a contingent to march into the school compound to officially accept the surrender of the Japanese. Miss Gibbins then wisely invited the RAF to "adopt" the school and to provide guards so that no looting would occur and to protect the school before she left for England to recuperate.

Reopening of the School

As families returned from the Mainland, schooling for children became a problem. Rear-Admiral Cecil H. J. Harcourt set up a military government and restored British administration very quickly and efficiently ensuring the restoration of essential services and law and order in the territory—but he was unable to take immediate steps to revive education. It was missionaries and conscientious private citizens who reopened schools as soon as possible, recognising the importance of not letting children and young people miss more schooling than they already had, and keeping them off the streets. By September 1945, schools such as DGS, Ying Wah Girls' School, Kowloon Wah Yan College, St Stephen's Girls' College, and St Paul's Co-educational College had placed an advertisement in Wah Kiu Yat Po (華僑日報) advertising the entrance examination date and that they would reopen on 1 October 1945.[41] During the same month, twelve grant-in-aid schools and twenty-seven private schools also re-established themselves one by one.[42] Schools including Munsang College,

---

39. Symons, *Looking at the Stars*, 30.

40. "Teachers Take Over. DGS Preserved", *South China Morning Post*, 7 September 1945. "Former Headmistress: Courage of Miss E. M. Gibbins at DGS Recalled", *South China Morning Post*, 7 January 1960.

41. Kit-ching Chan Lau and Peter Cunich, *The Impossible Dream: Hong Kong University from Foundation to Re-establishment 1910 to 1950* (Hong Kong: Oxford University Press, 2002), 246.

42. "Education Revived: Schools Being Re-opened All Over Colony", *South China Morning Post*, 6 October 1945.

The Imminent War and Japanese Occupation: 1939 to 1945

Pui Ching Middle School, Hong Kong Lingnan Secondary School, and Ling Ying College opened at the beginning of the second academic term in early 1946.[43] However, some of the government schools, such as Queen's College and Belilios Girls' School, had been looted or bombed, and they remained closed until reconstruction could take place. The story of DGS during this period provides an example of how these schools operated during the immediate post-war period with little help from the government.

Although in a dilapidated state, DGS was spared from serious looting after the war. As a result, it was one of the first schools to reopen. Very soon after the war ended, Joyce Anderson was surprised by a telegram from Miss Gibbins, urging her to return to DGS as soon as possible. Joyce immediately left Macao where she had sought refuge with her family during the war. The city that greeted her was war-torn and depopulated, with Nathan Road completely deserted at around 5 pm.[44] At the sight of Joyce, Miss Gibbins ran out excitedly to meet her, and the two old friends spent hours catching up on the events of the Japanese Occupation. When Miss Gibbins left for England to recuperate in September 1945, she handed over the control of the school to Joyce, who was glad to be protected by the RAF personnel during those unsettling weeks. In the days ahead, the Royal Navy, and the RAF all helped rebuild the school by contributing supplies that were necessary for it to reopen.

Miss Joyce Anderson's job was to reopen the school as soon as possible, but without a letter of appointment, contract, and salary, she could only offer the returned staff the opportunity to work until they could be paid by the GSC or the government. In the meantime, without any resources, she set about obtaining the most basic provisions, including food for herself and for anyone who returned to the school, using Miss Gibbins's ration card.[45]

Soon, some of the staff returned: Miss Phyllis Lang and Miss Phyllis Sinn who taught Chinese, Miss Sarah Abdullah who taught mathematics, and Mrs Lydia Moo Wong who taught English. Mona Swanston, an alumna, also returned to the school to work as the secretary. The housekeeping staff also gradually reappeared. Then Miss Anderson began interviewing prospective students, most of them having been students there before the war.[46] On 1 October 1945, DGS reopened.

Even though the school building did not suffer too badly, it was cluttered with concrete structures that made rehabilitation difficult and costly. One classroom had been used as a blacksmith's shop, and stables and pigsties were set up on the school grounds. While the wooden floor remained intact, all the furniture, fittings, and equipment had been

---

43. Chan Lau and Cunich, *The Impossible Dream*, 246.
44. Symons, *Looking at the Stars*, 29.
45. Symons, *Looking at the Stars*, 31.
46. Symons, *Looking at the Stars*, 31.

Figure 4.4: DGS gate in the 1950s. Source: School Archives.

removed.[47] One of the most pressing problems was the lack of desks and chairs, which had been removed for firewood. The school had to make do with tables, stools, and benches borrowed from the Royal Navy or RAF, or donated by various sources.

The Japanese had opened a gate on Gascoigne Road that became an easy night-time entry to the school for looters. It was therefore blocked. The main entrance on Jordan Road, which had been narrowed to a mere doorway by the Japanese, was restored to its original width.[48]

As the war had ended, Bishop Hall hastily left England on 14 September 1945, where he was on leave from Free China, to return to Hong Kong as soon as possible, so he could rebuild the Anglican Church and re-establish the Anglican schools. Assisting him during the challenging years that followed was the faithful and indefatigable Rev. George She, who became the supervisor of many schools and helped them to become re-established as soon as possible. The Rev. George She became the Headmaster of DBS from 1955 to 1961.

During the Occupation, DBS had been turned into a military hospital by the Japanese, and it remained in the hands of the military after the war until 1946. When DGS reopened on 1 October, Bishop Hall asked Miss Anderson to take over twenty senior boys from DBS

---

47. "Diocesan Girls' School Observes the First Post-war Speech Day: Trial at Co-education", *South China Morning Post*, 14 December 1946.
48. Headmistress's Report, 25 November 1946.

The Imminent War and Japanese Occupation: 1939 to 1945

together with some of their teachers, including Mr James Lawrence Young Saye, one of the most dedicated teachers at DBS.[49] These boys were preparing for the matriculation class of HKU. For the first time, Miss Anderson had the opportunity to teach senior students geography, English, scripture, and physical training, which was a satisfying experience for her even though she had no textbooks to prepare her lessons. As she recalled in her memoir, by the time it was published in 1996, those who matriculated in 1947 were highly placed in their respective professions in Hong Kong.[50]

Bishop Hall commented on this brief period of co-education in his address during DGS's first post-war speech day on 13 December 1945, believing it to have been a success that contributed to the strong family spirit in the school. There was a healthy rivalry between girls and boys in their work, and their relations were happy and natural. The prefects that year in DGS were both girls and boys. The boys had been trained under Mr Goodban, the Headmaster of DBS, who was interned during the war and had returned to England for recuperation when the school was still in the hands of the military.[51]

The first post-war DGS School Council meeting took place on 11 December 1945 in the Bishop's House, chaired by Bishop Hall, with Major Samuel M. Churn, Mrs A. E. Matthews, Mr A. Stewart, Dr Yeo Kok Cheang (husband of Florence Ho Tung, an old girl, later Director of the Medical and Health Department), and Miss Joyce Anderson (Acting Headmistress) in attendance. During the meeting, the Bishop announced that Miss Gibbins was unable to return because her mother was ill. At the request of Bishop Hall, Miss Gibbins and Professor Forster, both in England at the time, appointed Miss Winifred Hurrell, an experienced headmistress, as Acting Headmistress, effective from 1 January 1946 until Miss Gibbins's return.[52] Miss Hurrell left England for Hong Kong as soon as she could. Lack of transport after the war delayed her arrival until 14 March 1946. Soon she found that she was the Headmistress of DGS, rather than just Acting Head.

After the first School Council meeting, Miss Anderson left for Shanghai to be married to Dr Robert Symons. They departed shortly after for England, where Dr Symons was engaged in a practice in Wales, but they soon moved to London, where Mrs Symons taught in a private school for one term to qualify for a postgraduate course in education at Lincoln College, Oxford.[53] After her departure, Mr Young Saye, who was responsible for the DBS boys in the school, immediately became the Acting Headmaster, correspondent, teacher, clerk, bursar, and head gardener of DGS. Every day, he started at 8 am and worked ceaselessly in his many different capacities until bedtime. Mr Young Saye had been

---

49. "Diocesan Girls: School Observes the First Post-war Speech Day", *South China Morning Post*, 14 December 1946.
50. Symons, *Looking at the Stars*, 31.
51. "Diocesan Girls: School Observes the First Post-war Speech Day", *South China Morning Post*, 14 December 1946.
52. Minutes of School Council Meeting, 11 December 1945.
53. Symons, *Looking at the Stars*, 36.

supplementing the meagre salary of a teacher by private coaching, which increased his income by almost 80 per cent. Devoting too much time to his role as Acting Headmaster, a position for which he was not compensated, he lost his private coaching business, which he could ill afford because of his ailing wife. Even after the arrival of Miss Hurrell, the workload did not reduce because of the constant arrival of old students who wished to be readmitted. In the end, the school compensated him with a grant. When DBS reopened on 29 April 1946, he returned with all the senior boys to DBS while the younger ones remained at DGS.[54] His selfless and devoted service to DGS during these trying months deserves special commendation.

Miss Gibbins did not resume her position in Hong Kong because of her mother's continual ill health. With deep regret, she resigned from DGS and was appointed Headmistress of St Mary's School, Calne, an independent private boarding school in Wiltshire, England. Over the years, she remained closely connected with DGS, and on many occasions, she was asked by Bishop Hall to recruit teachers and to interview candidates on behalf of the school. She returned for the school's centenary celebration in 1960. At the invitation of Mrs Symons, on her retirement from St Mary's School, Calne, she became the Acting Headmistress of DGS during Mrs Symon's leave from October 1972 to May 1973.[55]

During the brief period when she headed DGS, Miss Gibbins added the 1940 extension to provide proper classrooms for all students and a laboratory. She introduced the teaching of the Chinese language to the curriculum and added mathematics, botany, and more academic aspects to other subjects, and improved the academic standards of the school. After being interned at the Stanley Camp, she repossessed the school from the Japanese immediately after Hong Kong's liberation and guarded the school from looting, thus enabling its reopening as soon as possible. Her courage and foresight inspired admiration and affection in many.

---

54. Fung and Chan-Yeung, *To Serve and to Lead*, 70.
55. Symons, *Looking at the Stars*, 69.

Chapter 5

Post-war Rehabilitation: 1946 to 1953

Miss Alice Winifred Hurrell arrived in Hong Kong in 1946 when the city was experiencing one of its most difficult periods and when most people were struggling for a living. Peace did not come to China after the Second World War. The civil war between the Chinese Communist Party and the Nationalist Party had begun just prior to the end of the war with Japan, and it ended with the establishment of the People's Republic of China (PRC) on 1 October 1949. The devastation of this war brought a massive influx of refugees into Hong Kong, which was only partially stopped when the border was closed in 1951. Throughout the 1950s and 1960s, thousands of refugees crossed the border illegally, risking their lives, further swelling the rising population, and overwhelming the city's provision of housing, medical services, and education.

To make things worse, the Korean War began in 1950, and the United Nations embargo imposed on North Korea destroyed the fragile entrepôt trade of Hong Kong, which was just recovering from the Second World War. With the loss of this important source of revenue, the government was unable to cope with the unprecedented refugee problem. It seems almost incredible that Hong Kong would emerge, as it has often been described, like "a phoenix rising from the ashes", but in the 1950s, Hong Kong began to re-engineer itself into a manufacturing centre using the wealth and technological know-how brought in by immigrants from the north and the constant supply of cheap labour provided by the refugees. By the late 1950s, the economy of Hong Kong was gradually improving.

The Education Scene in Hong Kong

Post-war Rehabilitation and Expansion: A Challenging Undertaking

During the Second World War, many schools suffered serious damage. It was a daunting task for the government to reopen them and to provide education for a war-torn generation. Mr Thomas Richmond Rowell, who was the first Principal of Northcote Training College and a senior member of the Hong Kong Teachers' Association before the war, became the first Director of Education after the war. During the lean years of rehabilitation, education often had to compete with other post-war social needs, such as improvements to sanitation, healthcare, housing, and social welfare, for the government's limited financial resources. Mr Rowell's difficulties were compounded because he had to heed the United Kingdom's Labour government's new policy that gave equal opportunity of education to all children.[1]

After the war had ended and schools reopened, total enrolment in all schools was under 50,000. The rapid rise in population after 1948 owing to the influx of refugees and the post-war baby boom resulted in an ever-growing demand for school places for young children. Beginning in 1949, as a result of the combined efforts of the government, missionary societies, voluntary agencies, public-minded individuals, and enterprising businessmen, the school system markedly expanded. There were four types of schools in Hong Kong: government schools, which were financed entirely by the government; grant schools, which received support from the government under a grant code; subsidised schools, which obtained a fixed percentage of their budgets from the government; and private schools, which received no government funding.

In the late 1940s and the early 1950s, many families in Hong Kong were poor and schooling was costly. Men and women toiled tirelessly to send their boys to school, and girls as young as seven would look after younger siblings at home and help with household chores while both parents went to work for long hours. By the late 1950s, Hong Kong was becoming a manufacturing centre and wages were improving, so families that could afford it were able to send their boys to university while their girls, after School Certificate Examination, would be expected to leave school and find work to support their younger brothers through school.

Revision of the 1941 Grant Code: An Attempt at Parity

DGS continued to be a grant school after the war when there were twenty-two grant schools. All new schools built after 1960 were governed by the Subsidy Code instead of the

---

1. Yee Wang Fung and Moira Chan-Yeung, *To Serve and to Lead: A History of Diocesan Boys' School* (Hong Kong: Hong Kong University Press, 2009), 68.

Grant Code. During the post-war years, the government had to rely on voluntary efforts, especially the grant schools, to provide education for a large proportion of children in Hong Kong. The disparity between the salaries of teachers in grant schools and those in government schools was a major problem that was not addressed by the 1941 Grant Code, and the grant schools had great difficulty in recruiting teachers. In November 1945, Mr Rowell, who understood this problem well, set out to amend the code.[2] His proposal revised the salary scales for grant schoolteachers, both local and overseas trained. In addition, the Grant Schools Provident Fund was set up for all permanent teaching staff, with participation being mandatory for all teachers of grant schools except for those of religious orders or congregations. DGS had already been sending monthly allowances to Miss Sawyer after her retirement because of the lack of a retirement fund. The Grant School Council (GSC), chaired by Bishop Hall, agreed in principle to the amended code but found the regulations too restrictive. Despite their different positions, the GSC and the Education Department were appreciative of each other's attempts to restore post-war education in Hong Kong, and they finally agreed in 1946 to the revision of the 1941 Grant Code.[3]

This revision again did not address the problem of disparity in salary between teachers in government schools and grant schools. There were also other issues, such as the schools' ability to collect *tong fai*, which were fees to defray the cost of repairs, equipment, sports, and library services. Bishop Hall proposed a block grant made on a per capita basis and the freedom of each school to charge *tong fai*, but this was not accepted by the government. Another problem related to school premises. Some grant schools owned their premises, so they had no rent to account for in their annual expenses, but the grounds needed repair. The government allowed a building depreciation fund to be set up and for a certain amount to be added to expenses for repair or rebuilding in the calculation of the deficiency grant each year. This money became an important source of funds, not only for repair, but also for future expansion of DGS and other grant schools that owned their premises. More amendments were made to the revised 1941 Grant Code in subsequent years.

To bring parity to government and grant schools, the government placed into the Grant Code a number of conditions that all schools were to obey: the number of teachers per class, the number of clerks or secretaries per school depending on the number of students, the percentage of staff recruited from overseas, and the age of teachers at the time of employment to be under 35 years. For those aged over 35, the years of experience after they had reached that age were not considered in the initial salary calculation. The government also proposed a common entrance examination to all grant schools, separately for boys and girls, believing that this would give the public equal opportunity for entry into these

---

2. Patricia P. K. Chiu, *A History of the Grant Schools Council* (Hong Kong: Grant Schools Council, 2013), 90.

3. Chiu, *A History of the Grant Schools Council*, 91–92.

public-aided schools. This proposal was considered impractical by GSC and was rejected, but the same proposal would return later.[4] Miss Hurrell, the Headmistress of DGS after the war, though not an executive member, was a member of the GSC as Headmistress of DGS. She objected to the common entrance examination because of the different composition of the student body in different grant schools; for example, the higher percentage of European and Eurasian students in DGS compared with only Chinese students in Heep Yunn School would mean that the standard of English and Chinese would be quite different in the two schools. She felt that it was important to have different types of schools in Hong Kong to serve a diverse population and that there should be some flexibility in education for the grant schools.[5] Miss Hurrell often discussed school policies with Mr Gerald Goodban, Headmaster of DBS, who succeeded Bishop Hall as Chairman of GSC after the Bishop stepped down.

As Hong Kong prospered and education expanded greatly, the Education Department began to standardise all schools to achieve uniformity. The GSC fought against the increasing restrictions to their freedom to make their own decisions and to innovate, which it felt endangered the schools' ethos and individuality, something that was important for the development of the students and the community.

DGS under Alice Winifred Hurrell (March 1946 to August 1951)

The day after her arrival in Hong Kong on 14 March 1946, Miss Hurrell became Headmistress of DGS; she worked tirelessly to rehabilitate the school until her retirement. Miss Hurrell was a highly qualified educator who gained the degrees of BA in English and French and MA (Hons) in French at the University of London. She then went to Université de Caen in France and received the Diplome d'Etudes en Langue Francaise. Following that, she took the Archbishop Lambert Diploma in Theology and received a licence to teach theology.[6] Before the Second World War, she was the Headmistress of the Girls' Side Ranelagh School in Bracknell, Berkshire, and a lecturer in the Education Department at Reading University.[7] She had a wealth of experience in teaching and had taught in boarding schools, co-educational schools, and government grammar schools.

Miss Hurrell, already 55 years of age (which was then the official retirement age in England and Hong Kong), was appointed for a term of three years by special arrangement. Although she had just retired in England, she remained as energetic as ever.[8] As a

---

4. Chiu, *A History of the Grant Schools Council*, 100.
5. Chiu, *A History of the Grant Schools Council*, 99.
6. "D.G.S. Principal Miss A. W. Hurrell Leaves Today by *RMS Canton*", *South China Morning Post*, 2 August 1951.
7. "Miss Hurrell. Headmistress of DGS Leaving on Retirement", *South China Morning Post*, 7 July 1951.
8. Bishop Hall, DGS Speech Day Address, 11 January 1966.

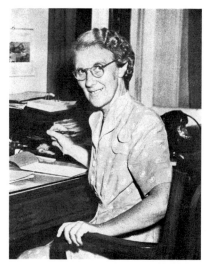

Figure 5.1: Miss Alice Winifred Hurrell (Headmistress 1946–1951). Source: School Archives.

拔萃書院

夏●里●露●新●任●院●長●

【本港訊】本港拔萃書院業已復課，限於目前環境，只能開設男女同校，該院院長，昨由夏里露女士接任。夏里露女士初由倫敦抵港，品學兼佳，獲博士名銜，會任倫敦女子高等學院教席云。

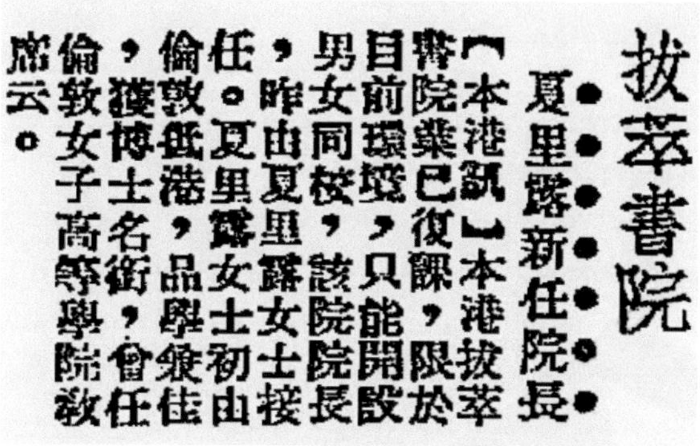

Figure 5.2: *The Kung Sheung Evening News*, 14 March 1946, announcing the arrival of Miss A. W. Hurrell from London. Source: *The Kung Sheung Evening News*, courtesy of Robert H. N. Ho Family Foundation.

grant school, DGS was governed by the Grant Code and constrained by a limited budget. Despite this, she guided the school successfully through the rehabilitation period and led the process of school expansion into the following decade. In all these endeavours, she was supported by a helpful and enthusiastic School Council. She retired as Headmistress of DGS in Hong Kong in 1951 when she turned 60, her term having been extended for another two years.

In 1948, Bishop Hall extensively advertised the position of Headmistress of DGS to succeed Miss Hurrell at the end of her three-year term. He was unsuccessful, but luckily, Miss Hurrell was physically robust enough to return for another two years after leave. Mrs Joyce Symons became Acting Headmistress for the second time for a few months while Miss Hurrell was away.[9] In 1949, Bishop Hall already had in mind Mrs Symons to be the next Headmistress of DGS on the retirement of Miss Hurrell. He believed the logical transition for the headship should be from a British headmistress to a Eurasian followed by a Chinese. At that point, Mrs Symons was unable to agree to Bishop Hall's invitation to succeed Miss Hurrell (see Chapter 6), so when he failed to find a replacement for Miss Hurrell upon her retirement in 1951, he asked Miss Molly Fisher to become the Acting Headmistress until a suitable candidate could be found.[10]

---

9. C. J. Symons, *Looking at the Stars: Memoirs by Catherine Joyce Symons* (Hong Kong: Pegasus Books, 1996), 41.
10. Bishop Hall to Director of Education, 27 June 1951, on Miss M. Fisher as Acting Headmistress of DGS.

Rehabilitation

The school had been emptied of all furniture, equipment, and furnishings by the time the war came to an end, so there were neither desks nor chairs. The day-to-day activities were carried out on tables, stools, and benches, borrowed from the RAF, or donated by other agencies. It was not until September 1947, two years after reopening, that the school was able to purchase a desk and a chair for each student.[11] The dormitories were also empty in the beginning, and the school had to rely on donations in kind, such as beds, sheets, and blankets or money from private citizens. It was not easy to get the school ready to receive boarders. Being a grant school, DGS received financial assistance to cover minor and major

Figure 5.3: Miss A.W. Hurrell and staff, 1947. Source: *The Quest* 1947, 8.
From left to right:
Back row: 1st Mr Lawrence Chan (translation/mathematics), 3rd Mr Pau Kwok Wan (Chinese), 4th Miss Sarah Abdullah (mathematics), 5th Mrs Lydia Moo Wong (English), 6th Mrs Grace So (geography)
Middle row: 3rd Miss B. T. Chiu, 6th Miss Margaret Mansfield (science)
Front row: 1st Miss P. Sinn (Chinese), 3rd Miss E. Allen (English), 5th Miss A. W. Hurrell (Headmistress), 6th Miss Molly Fisher (Acting Headmistress after Miss A. W. Hurrell retired), 7th Mrs C. M. Bird (English), 8th Miss Norah Edwards (music)
(The missing ones are teachers who could not be identified.)

---
11. Headmistress's Report, 15 June 1947.

Post-war Rehabilitation: 1946 to 1953   95

repairs, and the total amount given by the government came to $23,607—greatly relieving the school's financial burden.[12]

School enrolment rose rapidly after reopening as DGS began to receive former students (Table 5.1). DGS followed the custom of admitting a number of small boys under the age of 10 into the lower classes. At that time, DBS offered classes from Class 8 to Class 1. At the age of 10, boys usually left for DBS if they passed the entrance examination. The standard of Chinese in DGS was low because the school had been founded to teach English to Eurasian and European girls, and Chinese as a subject was only introduced to the curriculum in 1939. At the age of 10, if the boys did not pass the entrance examination for DBS, which had a higher standard of Chinese, it would be difficult for parents to find another school for them; so in 1949, the DGS School Council suggested to its counterpart at DBS that they should consider the possibility of organising a preparatory school for local boys because DGS would not be admitting boys after 1949.[13]

Table 5.1: Number of boys and girls in DGS, 1945 to 1946

Months	Boys	Girls	Total
December 1945	49	113	162
January 1946	92	154	246
February 1946	105	176	281
March 1946	106	179	285
April 1946	NA	NA	338
July 1946	NA	NA	304

Source: Interim Report Diocesan Girls' School December 1945 to March 1946; Headmistress's Report March–July 1946. Bishop's House Archive DGS 1946 General Files. NA: not available.

Although many students were successfully enrolled in the school after the war, it was more difficult to recruit expatriate teachers from England to teach in Hong Kong. Some of the pre-war expatriate teachers, who had been traumatised by internment during the Japanese Occupation, had no wish to return to Hong Kong; some had family responsibilities and others were hesitant because of Hong Kong's uncertain political future, with the PRC as its new neighbour. There were, of course, exceptions, such as the devoted Mr Gerald Goodban and Mr B. J. Monks of DBS.

Bishop Hall strongly believed in delivering a good bilingual education to students attending the Anglo-Chinese schools so that the graduates of these schools would better serve Hong Kong and take up the responsibility of bringing about peace and prosperity in

---

12. Director of Education to Director of Public Works Department. Major and Minor Repairs, Diocesan Girls' School, 9 October 1947, ED 2/8005/47, HKPRO HKRS156-1-280.

13. Minutes of School Committee Meeting, 14 June 1949.

the region through cross-cultural communication. It is better to learn English from a native English-speaking expatriate teacher, but it was difficult to find expatriate teachers who were willing to teach in a grant school in Hong Kong because of the lower pay than in government schools; in addition, females in any profession received lower pay (about 75 to 80 per cent) compared with their male counterparts in the same job. As can be seen, Bishop Hall had great difficulty in finding a successor to Miss Hurrell in 1951. The discrimination against teachers in grant schools and women was only to be addressed in the 1970s.

The Campus

The "Parthenon" Turned into a Boarding School

The boarding school had been an integral part of DGS. Since DGS comprised both a school and an orphanage, it had always accepted orphans and destitute children of European or Eurasian parentage as non-paying boarders, even after the word "orphanage" was dropped from the name of the school. In 1946, the school received fourteen girls for boarding from Rosary Hill, which also sent six boys to DBS. Rosary Hill, built at the foot of Mount Nicholson, was the Dominican House of Studies for the Far East. During the war, it opened its doors to dependents of prisoners of war, civil internees, and the British Red Cross, mostly Europeans and Eurasians, with the accommodation to be managed by the International Red Cross.[14] After the war, the International Red Cross could no longer keep these dependents at Rosary Hill, so it was only natural for orphans and those whose single parents could not support them that they would go to DGS and DBS because these schools had been orphanages before the war. In 1946, the school converted its play shed—the "Greek Temple" or the "Parthenon", as Mrs Symons referred to it—into a spacious dormitory to accommodate all the boarders, including the girls from Rosary Hill.[15]

During the post-war years, the Social Welfare Department provided an annual grant to partially support these children. Those whose fathers had belonged to the Hong Kong Volunteer Defence Corps and had died during the war or sacrificed their lives for the Allied cause could apply to the Hong Kong War Memorial Fund for support, but the amount given was disappointingly small.[16] The Welfare League, a Eurasian charity organisation, generously supported a few orphans each year.[17]

---

14. Vaudine England, "Zindell's Rosary Hill: Hong Kong's Forgotten War", *JRASHKB* 57 (2017): 35–66. Rosary Hill was a monastery, a massive building standing conspicuously on the slope of a hill above Happy Valley, visible from all parts of the harbour and Kowloon. It served as the training centre of missionaries coming from all parts of the world.

15. Minutes of School Council Meeting, 23 September 1946.

16. Headmistress's Report to the School Council, 21 April 1947.

17. S. M. Churn to Bishop Hall, 27 May 1948.

Figure 5.4: Opening of the new dormitory converted from the "Greek Temple", 1946. Source: School Archives.

A major problem for DGS was the high cost of running the boarding school. After the war, there was a considerable increase in the number of these children. Most of the time, the total cost of the non-paying boarders came to about half of the total budget of the boarding school. In 1947, when DGS had to come up with $40,000 for the new building for the Junior School, the cost of the non-paying boarders became a real problem. The school attempted to increase its fees in March 1948, but this proposal was rejected by the Education Department because of its mandate that all schools should increase their tuition fees simultaneously in September 1948. In the end, a joint appeal with DBS was organised under the name of Diocesan School and Orphanage, which was incorporated under an ordinance in 1892 and had the legal rights to the properties of DBS and later DGS, to raise funds for the orphans.[18] The appeal became an annual event until the schools each had their own ordinance in 1969.

Over the years, DGS benefited from dedicated expatriate staff, including those who lived in residence in the school. Resident staff were given free quarters in exchange for helping to supervise the boarders,[19] although their keen interest in the welfare of the boarders and the loving care they gave over the years could hardly be compensated for by free accommodation.

---

18. Minutes of School Council Meeting, 29 April 1948.
19. Headmistress's Report, 25 November 1946.

The School Chapel: A Retreat for Prayer and Quiet Reading

Christianity has always been the foundation of DGS and, under the tenure of all headmistresses, no line was drawn between the sacred and the secular. Miss Hurrell believed that all the school's work should be permeated by the Christian spirit; and the focal point for all was the school chapel.

In September 1945, when Miss Gibbins repossessed the school from the Japanese, she set apart a room on the top floor of the 1913 building for use as a chapel for daily evening prayers and Sunday evening services and as a retreat from noisy dormitories for prayer and quiet reading. Throughout 1946, the chapel had no chairs, but in 1947, alumnae and friends of the school subscribed benches. On 24 March 1947, a thanksgiving service was held in the chapel, with everyone seated. Alumnae and friends sent beautiful gifts, such as a blackwood table carved with grapes and vine leaves, a blackwood cross inlaid with silver, candlesticks, a prayer desk, and other items, from different parts of the world and all donated anonymously. The chapel was hallowed on Founders' Day, 1947, by Bishop Hall.[20]

Over the years, the school was closely associated with St Andrew's Church and St John's Cathedral. It was St Andrew's Church that provided the school with a priest to conduct Sunday service who gave addresses every week. The Dean and the Chaplain of the Cathedral responded to any requests for talks or discussions on religious topics.[21] On special occasions, such as Easter, Ascension Day, and Christmas, the school congregated

Figure 5.5: The School Chapel, 1951. Source: *The Quest* 1951, 17.

---

20. A. W. Hurrell, "The School Chapel", *The Quest* (1947): 16.
21. *The Quest* (1947): 7.

at the Cathedral. Every year saw a number of girls from the school being baptised or confirmed.[22]

A New Building for the Junior School

By July 1946, the total enrolment of the school had reached 358 students, exceeding the highest pre-war level of 340. As the population of Hong Kong climbed, more educational places were badly needed. Faced with overcrowding in the school and the lack of funds for any new building, Miss Hurrell considered an interim measure to increase space. In those days, Nissen huts were popular as they increased space almost instantly, even if only on a temporary basis. In 1947, a Nissen hut was received as a gift from Major Churn, a member of the School Council,[23] who continued to help the school on numerous occasions. This provided an assembly hall for the Junior School and a playroom for boarders, and one end was partitioned off to serve as the domestic science room. The school later acquired a second Nissen hut.

In 1947, the Education Department gave approval for the Junior (Primary) School to be separated from the Senior (Secondary) School, provided that suitable accommodation could be found. Such a move would improve the financial situation of DGS because the two schools could then apply separately for government funding, including capital building grants and government loans. The school planned to erect a Junior School building to accommodate 250 students and vacate the current occupied space so the Senior School could increase its students to 350. The September term of 1947 began with Miss Hurrell declaring that unusual arrangements were being made for the Junior School in preparation for the expansion of its premises. St Andrew's Church Hall was rented (for $500 per month) for the two kindergarten classes and two lower Junior School classes (Class 10 and Class 9). The rest of the classes remained on the Jordan Road campus.[24]

On 18 September 1947, the school celebrated its first Founders' Day after the war. This was a memorable and joyful occasion for the school and the old girls. Bishop Hall arrived at the school at 8 am to hallow the school chapel, as previously mentioned; this was followed by the celebration of Holy Communion. After the ceremony, Bishop Hall addressed the students during morning assembly and Mrs E. Matthew (previously Mrs Dunbar), an old girl, gave an interesting and amusing talk entitled "Memories of DGS".[25] In the afternoon, the Nissen hut was opened by Mrs Mabel Bronwyn Mardulyn, Major Churn's daughter

---

22. *The Quest* (1949): 20.
23. Minutes of School Council Meeting, 17 February 1947.
24. Headmistress's Report, 20 September 1947.
25. "A Glimpse of the D.G.S. in Days Gone By: Extracts from a Talk by Mrs. Dunbar on Founders' Day, 1947", *The Quest* (1950): 45–47.

and a DGS alumna. The Director of Education, Mr Rowell, toured the school the same afternoon and agreed to cover 50 per cent of the cost of building an eight-classroom Junior School on the school site with a government grant.

The observance of Founders' Day was discontinued after 1947. While no explanation can be found of this, it is quite possible that Miss Hurrell discovered that the history of DGS could be traced back to 1860, and it was therefore not appropriate to observe Founders' Day on 18 September, the anniversary of Bishop Hoare's death.

An eight-classroom building was required because the class structure of the Junior School in 1948 was as follows: one class each for KG2, KG3, KG4, Class 10, Class 9, and Class 8, and two classes of Class 7.[26] The new Junior School, built on the north-west corner of the playground, was meant to be semi-permanent, and to be replaced by a more permanent building at a later date.[27] The total cost of the building came to $89,991 and the government paid 50 per cent of this.[28] Mrs Lo Man Kam opened the Junior School on 28 April 1948, when the students who were in St Andrew's Church Hall moved into the new building. This released some of the space in the Senior School as well as in the Nissen hut. The hut was converted into a room for domestic science, outfitted with all the necessary equipment for the "modern" curriculum.

The building of the new Junior School unearthed a problem that both the school and the government had long forgotten. Readers will remember that the playground to the west of KIL 1281, the school site, was granted by the Recreation Ground Committee to the school in 1927, free of charge, to be used as a playground, and no building was allowed without the prior approval of the Public Works Department. The lease had been renewed every five years, with the last renewal date being 17 September 1936. The impending war and invasion by the Japanese in December 1941 resulted in the lapse of the lease without this being noticed by the government or school officials. Since that time, the lease had not been renewed, and in 1948, the Nissen huts and the new semi-permanent Junior School were erected on the site. This irregularity was discovered by the Crown Lands and Surveys Office of the Public Works Department in August 1949.[29] On being informed, Bishop Hall, as Chairman of the School Council, immediately wrote to the Colonial Secretary to lease the playground, not just as a playground but for future development of the school, which had by then expanded with the inclusion of a primary division and a kindergarten. The

---

26. Class structure of Junior School, *The Quest* (1949): 9–10.

27. Minutes of School Council Meeting, 20 September 1947.

28. L. G. Morgan, Director of Education, to the Headmistress of Diocesan Girls' School, 10 July 1948, Bishop's House Archive, DGS General File 1948.

29. Crown Lands and Surveys, Public Works Department, Hong Kong, to Chairman of the Committee of the Diocesan Girls' School, Re: Diocesan Girls' School Site, Jordan Road, Kowloon, 27 August 1949, Bishop's House Archive, DGS 1949 Minutes Files.

Figure 5.6: The new Junior School, 1948. Source: School Archives.

original site, KIL 1281, was far from adequate for a school that had plans for expansion.[30] In the end, the playground, allocated the lot number KIL 6329, was granted to DGS on a lease of seventy-five years (until 1987) starting from 7 June 1912, the same date that KIL 1281 was granted to the Diocesan Girls' School and Orphanage. This was a vital step that determined the growth of DGS on its current site.

Scholastic Activities

An Academic Stream and a Modern Stream

The school curriculum at this time was an academic one, designed to prepare students for a university education. It became obvious to Miss Hurrell that some of the students in the higher classes were not interested in or had difficulties with some of the academic subjects, particularly mathematics and science.[31] To deal with their choice of career, and to make

---

30. Bishop Hall to Colonial Secretary, Colonial Secretariat, Hong Kong, regarding Diocesan Girls' School site, Jordan Road, Kowloon, 11 October 1949.
31. Headmistress's Address, Speech Day, 18 November 1949.

the curriculum relevant to students, Miss Sawyer had introduced a commercial course in Class I in 1937, for those who, instead of going to university, wished to be prepared for a secretarial job after the School Certificate Examination. In the commercial course, the girls learned English, shorthand, typing, and business correspondence, as well as music and art.

In England, modern schools offered a curriculum for girls who were not interested in a university education. This emphasised domestic science and housecraft, such as cooking, laundry, and dressmaking. If a curriculum similar to this was to be introduced in DGS, it would require housecraft subjects to be initiated earlier. All students would take a basic course in housecraft from Class 6 to Class 4. In Class 3, however, students would be divided into two streams: academic and modern, because by then a girl's interests and abilities could be fairly assessed by herself and her teachers. The students in the academic stream would pursue academic subjects for matriculation and university entrance. The students in the modern stream would be prepared for commerce, nursing, social welfare, and similar careers. In the School Certificate Examination, modern students would take domestic science instead of laboratory science. They would be encouraged to take cultural subjects such as music, art, or handiwork, according to their skills. Students in the modern stream who passed the School Certificate Examination could stay on for Class I modern where they would be trained in secretarial or other vocational courses as well as housecraft.[32] Putting this modern curriculum in place required considerable resources, including the recruitment of an experienced teacher in relevant subjects and adequate space for domestic science laboratories and art and music rooms.

As 1950 approached, Miss Hurrell planned for the school expansion. She took into consideration the constructive speech given by Mr Rowell, the Director of Education, that encouraged DGS to establish a modern course, coinciding with her own plans, and this would require more space.[33] However, in the 1950s, government policy focused on the expansion of primary education, and obtaining a grant for secondary school expansion was not feasible. The school successfully found a solution to the problem. Instead of applying for an interest-free loan to build an extension, it requested a loan to replace the current unsatisfactory accommodation with something more suitable. For example, a domestic science laboratory was to replace a temporary kitchen; two classrooms were to replace two older rooms, one of which was an art room and the other of which had been condemned as a classroom by the education department because it was too dark; and a new staff room was required because the existing one was converted from a veranda that would have to be removed to give access to the new rooms.[34]

---

32. Headmistress's Address, Speech Day, 18 November 1949.
33. Headmistress's Address, Speech Day, 18 November 1949.
34. Director of Education to Financial Secretary, 26 July 1949, HKPRO, HKRS156-1-280.

Post-war Rehabilitation: 1946 to 1953

Figure 5.7: The 1950 Wing, later renamed Hurrell Wing. Source: School Archives.

The successful application for a government interest-free loan of $200,000 allowed the school to build a new wing,[35] which would provide a large room for cookery, laundry, and dressmaking and a room for a secretarial class. The building of 1950 wing enabled the school to accommodate the modern program and the Senior School was able to divide into two streams: academic and modern, from Class 3 upwards.

A Chinese Department

Even though Chinese was taught when the school reopened after the war, it was the weakest subject offered. In 1947, when Chinese students were required to take Chinese in the School Certificate and Matriculation Examinations, Miss Hurrell created a Chinese Department to raise the standard of Chinese language teaching. This followed examination requirements, the usual practice being the study of Chinese classics and learning how to structure compositions. The pupils in each class were divided into three levels, in descending order, according to their achievement in Chinese—A, B, and Special—and these were taught separately. At first, there were seven Chinese lessons a week, except in Class 4 which had eight. In Class 7, letter writing and penmanship were taught. In Class 4 and below, the Chinese subjects taught were reading, composition, and history; in Classes 1 to 3, the subjects were essays, composition, history, and translation. Modern Chinese and the Confucian Analects were added in Class 2. The teachers in the Chinese Department were

---

35. Director of Education to the Financial Secretary, 25 March 1950, Loan to Diocesan Girls' School, Sec. 15/661/46 ED, 2/2/8009/49, HKPRO, HKRS156-1-280.

faced with a number of difficulties: disparate abilities among students in the same class, the inadequacy of reference materials, and the syllabus of Chinese classics that most students found difficult to understand and irrelevant for everyday use.[36]

In 1948, Mr Lawrence S. L. Chan headed the Chinese Department. During that year, the Education Department and the University made the following changes to the Chinese curriculum: the discontinuation of teaching Chinese classics, the *Four Books*;[37] the adoption of specified Chinese textbooks for Classes 1 to 10 and kindergarten; and the inclusion of translation from Class 4 upwards. With the consent of the Headmistress, the Chinese Department declared that students who failed in Chinese would not be promoted to a higher class, and Chinese would be included in the entrance examination. Through the enforcement of these rules, the Department hoped that the standard of Chinese would improve.[38]

All schools were regularly inspected by the Education Department, and DGS had its first inspection in May 1950, following which a meeting was arranged at which teachers met the inspector and discussed with him the criticisms of their work and problems arising out of it. The school benefited a great deal from the inspection that was conducted in such a constructive and helpful way.[39]

School Life and Extracurricular Activities: An Enriched Programme

Infectious diseases were common after the war. Looking after a large number of boarders (up to eighty in 1949) living in close quarters was problematic. Immediately after the war, some of them were under-nourished and had poor resistance to infection. The school therefore appointed Dr A. W. Dawson to examine the boarders twice a year and day students once a year.[40] In addition, the school paid for boarders over the age of 12 to have a chest X-ray in order to exclude tuberculosis, the most common infectious disease after the war. The doctor also inspected the school. He found the general health of the students and the sanitation of the school buildings to be excellent. The dormitories were clean and the beds were kept tidy by students and not crowded together. The food supplied was of good quality and high calorific value.[41]

---

36. A. W. Hurrell, "The Work of the Chinese Department", *The Quest* (1947): 18.

37. *The Four Books* (四書, Sìshū) are Chinese classic texts illustrating the core value and belief systems in Confucianism.

38. "The Work of the Chinese Department", *The Quest* (1949): 24.

39. *The Quest* (1950): 18.

40. Minutes of School Council Meeting, 25 November 1946.

41. *The Quest* (1950): 18.

Post-war Rehabilitation: 1946 to 1953

It is unclear when the school house system was established, but the first documentation could be found in *The Quest* of 1947; the houses were named after colours: red, blue, green, and yellow.[42] In 1948/1949, the houses were named after former headmistresses instead: red changed to Smith, blue to Skipton, green to Sawyer, and yellow to Gibbins.[43] The aim of organising the school into houses was to integrate students across age divisions for sharing and mentoring purposes, whether in the academic realm or in music, sports, or other areas. In later years, house activities were confined to sports.

The prefect system was reinstated once the war was over. In 1947, there were seventeen prefects and one head girl. Until all the Form 6 boys returned to DBS, there was also one head boy. The prefects were nominated and elected by the student body to represent the school, and to enforce the school rules—which they helped to make.[44]

In line with the new ideas in education that started to be popular in Europe just before the war, Miss Hurrell introduced field trips and school visits in 1947. The girls visited the Royal Observatory, canneries to learn about industrial processes of canning, Yung Hwa (Hua) Film Studio to learn how films were made, and the Dairy Farm to learn about the pasteurisation of milk. Miss Hurrell also started to give career talks to prepare Class 1 girls for their future.

The school magazine, *The Quest*, was first issued in 1941. Although there was a record that a school magazine had been printed in April 1924, with another issue in October of the same year,[45] there was no mention of its name, and copies of either issue have not been found. After the war, the *Diocesan Schools Magazine* appeared in 1946, the first ever joint school magazine with DBS. Unfortunately, that issue has also not been located. *The Quest* was revived and published in 1947.[46] In 1949, it was revived again, this time in two volumes, one in English and one in Chinese, and was then issued annually until 1955. Since then, *The Quest* has appeared at intervals of two to three years, and in 1960, it was simply called *Quest*.

The annual bazaar continued to be an important event, raising money for the Orphans' Fund and other charitable organisations. It encouraged alumnae of the Diocesan Old Girls' Association (DOGA), parents, and students to make a concerted effort to create a fun-filled event that showcased creativity, originality, and cooperation. The annual event continued until 1967 when it was discontinued because of the riots that year; it was replaced by a mini-bazaar that has been held annually since 1970.[47]

---

42. "Sports Notes", *The Quest* (1947): 31.
43. "A Summary of House Points Gained and Lost", *The Quest* (1949): 30.
44. Annabelle Young, "Our Prefect System", *The Quest* (1947): 25.
45. "Diocesan Girls' School Prize Distribution", *South China Morning Post*, 28 February 1935.
46. Editorial, *The Quest* (1947): 1.
47. Headmistress's Report, January 1972.

Figure 5.8: The School Bazaar, 1948. Source: *The Quest* 1949, 9.

The cultural life of the school was enriched by music and drama. A programme was organised in which each class took turns in entertaining the school with music or for an invited guest to lecture on music during the last lesson period on Friday.[48] The school's musical tradition began with the joint appointment with DBS of Mr S. Gordon Hemery in April 1947. Mr Hemery came from a musical family in England and had studied at the Royal College of Music. He formed the Diocesan Schools' Choral Society with students from both schools and presented several successful concerts: arias from Puccini's *Tosca*, Handel's *Messiah*,[49] and Stainer's *Crucifixion* performed by the joint choirs of both schools. When Mr Hemery left Hong Kong after sixteen months to take up a lectureship in music at London University, Miss Norah M. Edwards took up the baton and continued to enhance the school's musical tradition. She organised concerts and also raised funds to purchase musical equipment.[50] The school presented Gilbert and Sullivan's opera *The Pirates of Penzance* with DBS on the radio in 1951 and on stage in 1952.[51] It was also honoured with first prize in the interschool drama competition of 1950 with a production of F. Sladen-Smith's comedy *The Invisible Duke*.

---

48. Headmistress's Report, 14 November 1947.
49. "Mr G. Hemery, Music Director at Diocesan Schools, Leaving Colony", *South China Morning Post*, 5 August 1950; *The Quest* (1951): 21.
50. "Schools' Concerts, Vocal, Instrumental, Music at DGS", *South China Morning Post*, 20 April 1951.
51. "Pirates of Penzance", *The Quest* (1951): 21; *South China Morning Post*, 8 December 1951.

Post-war Rehabilitation: 1946 to 1953   107

Figure 5.9: Junior School concert, 1947. Source: School Archives.

In sports, the school hockey team won all six matches it played in 1950: three against the University and three against King George V School. The tennis team lost to the University but gained enough experience to defeat the King George V team. Netball continued to be the most popular game, and the school team won all its matches except one. The school held its first inter-class gymnastic competition in March 1950.[52]

The Boys' and Girls' Club, which was re-established as a branch of the Hong Kong Boys' and Girls' Club, was founded by Bishop Hall before the war. Headed by the Headmistress, it was formally inaugurated on 7 November 1947. A qualified teacher was engaged to lead a group of volunteer Senior School students to teach (after regular school hours) street children who would otherwise have no schooling. The children, disparate in age and standards, were divided into grades and were taught language, basic knowledge, hygiene, current affairs, good manners and behaviour, and some geography.[53] DGS girls gained valuable experience in fundraising, running an educational club with a curriculum, and childcare. They also learned about giving service to the community.

The Second Kowloon Guide Company of the school was reactivated in February 1947 with thirty-two girl guides. The Second Kowloon Brownie Pack followed in March. In November, the Pack formed a guard of honour for Lady Grantham, wife of Governor

---

52. *The Quest* (1950): 18–19.
53. "The DGS Girls' Club", *The Quest* (1947): 30.

Alexander Grantham, as she arrived at the St Andrew's Garden Fête.[54] By the end of 1947, the Girl Guides and Brownies were back in full swing as in the pre-war days.

The First Parent Teacher Association in Anglo-Chinese Schools

Although parent teacher associations (PTAs) had existed all over the world since the beginning of the twentieth century, Hong Kong Anglo-Chinese schools did not have them. After spending many of her after-school hours in interviews with parents, who discussed their problems and sought her advice on the future of their children,[55] Miss Hurrell decided that a PTA for DGS would be beneficial as it would allow parents to communicate directly with teachers. She established it shortly before she left Hong Kong on 15 June 1951, and the first meeting was presided over by Dr Yeo Kok Cheang, who was the then Deputy Director of Medical and Health Services and a parent of a DGS student. The PTA had its first general meeting in October of the same year. Just like the DOGA, the PTA has contributed enormously to the development of the school over the years, and its achievements will be presented in depth in the second part of the book.[56]

Miss Hurrell's Dream

In her 1950 Speech Day address, Miss Hurrell spoke of her dream for the school. Despite the new wing, the Senior School was inadequate, lacking an assembly hall of appropriate size, a dining room, a gymnasium, and a swimming pool. Her desire was that the school should have the facilities that most secondary schools in England possessed. Recognising the difficulties in obtaining funding for the school's expansion, she wisely planned for the future growth to be carried out in stages as and when funds became available, with the hope that by 1959 her plan would have been executed, in time for the centenary celebrations.[57] The first part of the school expansion, the 1950 Wing, had been completed before her retirement. The rest of her dream would have to be realised by her successor.

Farewell to Miss Hurrell

Miss Hurrell retired in August 1951 and Miss M. Fisher became Acting Headmistress until March 1953 when she was replaced by Mrs C. Joyce Symons, Headmistress of the school.

---

54. "2nd Kowloon Guide Company and 2nd Kowloon Brownie Pack", *The Quest* (1947): 26.
55. "D.G.S. Principal Miss A.W. Hurrell Leaves Today by *RMS Canton*", *South China Morning Post*, 2 August 1951.
56. Ruth Mack, "The Parent Teacher Association" *The Quest* (1951): 15.
57. Headmistress's Address, Speech Day, 1950.

Post-war Rehabilitation: 1946 to 1953

During her relatively short period of five years as Headmistress of DGS, Miss Hurrell achieved the incredible feat of bringing the school successfully through the post-war rehabilitation period into a time of expansion, even taking it to a higher level of academic and cultural achievement. The student body almost doubled, rising from about 360 in 1946 to 618 in 1951. She expanded the Junior School, giving it a separate new building, and at the same time placed the day school and boarding school on a more sustainable financial footing. She introduced a modern programme to the school curriculum, with an extension being built for this purpose,[58] and she also started a programme to improve the school's standard of Chinese. Her school was the first to introduce educational visits for students and to create a PTA, ahead of other Anglo-Chinese schools in Hong Kong.

Miss Hurrell accomplished all the above after she turned 55, when most people in her generation would have been considering retirement. Her success was brought about by her boundless enthusiasm, energy, perseverance, efficiency, and a cheerful, charming personality that won the respect, loyalty, and admiration of her colleagues, the Director of Education, and the community. It was Miss Hurrell who created the new DGS motto: "Daily Giving Service—with a smile".[59] The school was extremely fortunate to have her as Headmistress, as she put new life and spirit into it after the war. She left behind a large number of affectionate friends, students, and their parents, who all wished her a long and happy retirement.[60] On 2 August 1951, she left Hong Kong on the *RMS Canton* for England.

Miss Hurrell returned to Hong Kong to teach in Chung Chi College from 1953 to 1955 at the request of Bishop Hall before she finally retired to England. In 1960, at the invitation of the school and the alumnae, she once again visited Hong Kong to take part in the joyous centenary celebrations.[61] In England, she did not live a retired and sheltered life, for it was not her nature to do so. She kept busy lecturing and attending conferences, and made it a point to attend the annual Hong Kong Diocesan Church Meeting in London where she looked forward to meeting people from Hong Kong. She passed away in March 1969, and a memorial service was held in the school chapel, conducted by Bishop John Gilbert Hyndley Baker (Bishop of Hong Kong and Macau 1966–1981).[62] The school also set up the Miss A. Winifred Hurrell Memorial Scholarship Fund in her honour.[63]

---

58. The Headmistress's Report, *The Quest* (1947): 5.

59. Headmistress's (Mrs Symons) Report, June 1969.

60. "Miss Hurrell, Headmistress of DGS Leaving on Retirement", *South China Morning Post*, 7 July 1951.

61. "Staff and Old Girls of DGS", *South China Morning Post*, 13 January 1960.

62. In 1951, following the establishment of the People's Republic of China, the Diocese of Hong Kong was separated from the Diocese of South China. The Diocese of Hong Kong and Macau remained in the Anglican Communion, while the Diocese of South China became part of Chung Hua Sheng Kung Hui.

63. Minutes of School Council Meeting, 17 June 1969.

Chapter 6

The Great Expansion: 1953 to 1985

Historical Background

1953 to 1970: From Poverty to Prosperity

When Mrs Catherine Joyce Symons became Headmistress of DGS in 1953, a ceasefire had occurred in Korea. The United Nations embargo had speeded the change in Hong Kong from a city that was dependent on entrepôt trade into a manufacturing centre. Among the large numbers of refugees from China, the entrepreneurial Shanghainese brought capital and technology, while the rest brought a seemingly endless supply of cheap labour. Within a few years, manufacturing industries such as textiles and clothing were blossoming. In the 1960s and 1970s, employment in industries grew at an annual average rate of 13 per cent. Wages began to edge up noticeably for skilled workers starting in 1957, followed by those of the semi-skilled.[1] By the late 1960s, Hong Kong was transformed into a regional manufacturing centre, and its gross domestic product (GDP) was rising at a rate of about 10 per cent per year.[2] In the meantime, the population in Hong Kong rose from 2 million in 1951 to 5 million in 1980, owing to the post-war baby boom and the influx of refugees, and this posed great challenges for all social services, including housing, education, and medical and health services. Even though wages had increased, poor housing, abominable

---

1. L. C. Chau, "Economic Growth and Income Distribution in Hong Kong", in *25 Years of Social and Economic Development in Hong Kong*, ed. Benjamin K. P. Leung and T. Wong (Hong Kong: Hong Kong University Press, 1994), 494.

2. *Hong Kong Annual Reports*, 1960–1970.

working conditions, and widespread corruption, especially in the police force, bred social discontent and unrest.

On the morning of 4 April 1966, a 27-year-old man began a hunger strike at the Star Ferry Terminal in Central District, protesting against a 5-cent increase in the ferry fare. He quickly drew a crowd of supporters and riots ensued. The subsequent Commission of Inquiry of Kowloon Disturbances reported that the causes of the riots were the underlying sense of insecurity and distrust of government among young people, compounded by economic recession, high unemployment, and a shortage of housing.[3] The Commission concluded that the excessive energy of young people contributed to the unrest and recommended that more activities should be provided to keep them occupied.

In the spring of 1967, the Cultural Revolution spilled across the border to Hong Kong. Leftist workers and students from "patriotic" schools orchestrated street demonstrations and planted both real and fake bombs to paralyse the city. For six months, violent protests and riots occupied the streets of Hong Kong. Public confidence in Hong Kong's future plummeted and many residents emigrated.[4] The 1966 and 1967 riots led people to question the legitimacy of the colonial government.[5] The government had remained conservative in its financial and economic policies, allocating less than 10 per cent of its budget to all social services combined, despite economic improvement since the late 1950s. This policy resulted in overcrowding and the proliferation of squatters' huts in many parts of Hong Kong,[6] tremendous congestion in hospitals and long queues in outpatient clinics, and a social welfare system funded largely by local and international volunteer agencies. Growing international hostility toward colonialism and local social discontent compelled the government to place resources on improving living and working conditions and social services.

1971 to 1985: Building up of "Hong Konger" Identity

Throughout the 1970s, the economy of Hong Kong continued to grow with its GDP rising at a remarkable annual rate of 18 per cent per year.[7] The booming economy of the 1970s enabled the reform-minded Governor Crawford Murray MacLehose to spend generously

---

3. Kowloon Disturbances 1966, Report of Commission of Enquiry, Hong Kong Government, J. R. Lee Acting Government Printers, 1967.

4. Kate Whitehead, "Witnesses to Anarchy: The 1967 Riots in Hong Kong, by Some of Those Caught Up in the Violence", *South China Morning Post*, 22 April 2017, accessed 15 May 2020, https://www.scmp.com/magazines/post-magazine/long-reads/article/2089195/witnesses-anarchy-1967-riots-hong-kong-some-those.

5. Ian Scott, *Political Change and the Crisis of Legitimacy* (Hong Kong: Oxford University Press, 1989), 236–239.

6. M. Castells, *The Shek Kip Mei Syndrome: Economic Development and Public Housing in Hong Kong* (London: Pions Ltd, 1990), 136.

7. Revenue and expenditure for each year obtained from Hong Kong Annual Reports of respective years, 1970–1980, Hong Kong Government.

on various public projects. In 1972, he announced the ambitious Ten Years Housing Programme to resettle 1.9 million people. New towns were established in remote sites in the New Territories and city slums were cleared. Infrastructural projects such as the first cross-harbour tunnel and the mass transit railway system were initiated, linking the new towns with the city. Medical and health services greatly expanded. Extra funding was allotted to social welfare.[8] Long-term plans were developed for education, medical and health services, and social welfare.[9] Established in 1974, the Independent Commission Against Corruption (ICAC) quickly won a reputation for probity. All these measures improved the quality of life and inspired confidence and social stability. It was during the MacLehose era that the people of Hong Kong developed their own identity and called themselves "Hong Kongers".

US President Richard Nixon's 1972 visit to Beijing signified China's emergence from isolation. In 1979, the People's Republic of China (PRC) initiated an open policy and economic reorientation and modernisation. Factories from Hong Kong began to move into South China for cheaper labour, while the city gradually transformed itself into a global service and financial centre, supported by a young and well-educated population. In 1984, the Sino-British Agreement was signed when Deng Xiaoping, the paramount leader of the PRC, devised a practical formula to preserve the spectacular success of Hong Kong based on an ingenious policy of "One Country, Two Systems", which was meant to last for fifty years following the handover of Hong Kong to the PRC in 1997 at the expiry of the lease of the New Territories.

Educational Development in Hong Kong: The Great Expansion

1951 to 1970: Expansion of Primary Education

In the 1950s, Hong Kong's Education Department (ED) grappled with two major problems—on the one hand, a predominantly young and rapidly growing population and, on the other hand, increasing pressure from the new Labour government in Britain to provide universal access to education for all children. The department implemented a policy of expansion of primary education and teacher training in order to rectify the short-comings of the system.[10]

Ambitious government school-building programmes were launched in the 1950s, and at their peak 45,000 primary school places were added each year. To accommodate the

---

8. *Hong Kong Annual Report*, 1968, 10.

9. Hong Kong Legislative Council Debates Official Report. In the session of the Legislative Council of Hong Kong which opened 17 October 1973 in the Twenty-Second Year of the Reign of her Majesty Queen Elizabeth II.

10. K. W. J. Topley, Secretary for Education, "The Hong Kong Education System", June 1981, Government Secretariat, Hong Kong Government.

ever-increasing numbers of school-age children but with only limited resources, each school building was to be bi-sessional (morning and afternoon sessions) or even tri-sessional (morning, afternoon, and evening sessions). The Grantham Training College,[11] and then the Sir Robert Black Training College,[12] were opened in 1951 and 1961 respectively to meet the large number of teachers required. The results of these tremendous efforts can be found in Table 6.1, which shows increases in enrolment at all levels of education in 1960 compared with 1950. At all levels of education, the percentage of boys enrolled were higher than those of girls in 1950 and 1960, even though the enrolment of girls had increased.

Table 6.1: Number and percentage of students enrolled in schools by gender and by level of education, 1950 and 1960

Educational Level		1950	1960
Primary	Total N	120,556	393,571
	Male N (%)	72,311 (60)	218,999 (55.6)
	Female N (%)	48,245 (40)	174,572 (44.4)
Secondary	Total N	26,498	74,115
	Male N (%)	17,255 (65)	45,052 (60.8)
	Female N (%)	9,243 (35)	29,061 (39.2)
Post-secondary	Total N	2,683*	11,987
	Male N (%)	2,112 (78.7)	9,020 (75.2)
	Female N (%)	571 (21.3)	2,967 (24.8)

Source: Hong Kong Government Census and Statistics Department 1947 to 1967; *post-secondary education in 1950 included adult education.

The policy of expanding primary education without commensurate expansion of secondary education created a serious bottleneck in Form 1, the first grade in the secondary school system. In 1955, the government began to use the Joint Primary 6 Examination, which had been introduced in 1949 to mark the completion of primary education, to select students to enter Form 1 for secondary education.[13] As the economy in Hong Kong grew, in 1965 the government published a White Paper on Education Policy that stated: "The final aim of any educational policy must be to provide every child with the best education which he or she is capable of absorbing, at a cost which the parents and the community can

---

11. Anthony Sweeting, *Educational History of Hong Kong 1941–2000, Visions and Revisions* (Hong Kong: Hong Kong University Press, 2004), 164.

12. Sweeting, *Educational History of Hong Kong 1941–2000*, 172.

13. Hung-kay Luk, *A History of Education in Hong Kong* (Hong Kong: Lord Wilson Heritage Trust, 2000), 72.

afford."[14] It proposed to increase the existing number of secondary places from 15 per cent to 20 per cent of the total number of primary students completing the primary course.

1971 to 1985: Expansion of Secondary and Tertiary Education

By 1971, the government finally had an adequate number of primary places for implementing compulsory, free six-year primary education for children aged 6 to 12. Further expansion in education after 1971 however, required more careful planning because of the rapid demographic, social, and economic developments in Hong Kong. The education policies of the 1970s, outlined in the White Papers of 1974 and 1978, were published after extensive consultation with the public in the form of Green Papers. Other factors that influenced education policies were the riots of 1966 and 1967, and pressure from activist groups such as the Education Action Group, which was founded by a few enthusiasts, the leader being a former DGS girl, Sansan Ching (1964 graduate), to campaign for or against specific education issues.[15]

The main aim of the 1974 White Paper on Secondary Education Over the Next Decade was to provide three years of free junior secondary education for all children in the 12–14 age group and sufficient places in senior secondary forms for at least 40 per cent of the 15–16 year group by 1979.[16] The target of nine years of compulsory, free general education consisted of six years in a primary school and three years in a secondary school. At the conclusion of nine years, there would be a form of selection by which 40 per cent of the 15–16 age groups would progress to senior secondary forms, with places provided in grammar and technical streams in the ratio of 6:4.[17] The government actually managed to implement this policy one year early, in 1978. The move was believed to be a response to the criticism of some European countries of Hong Kong's poor labour policy.[18] The expansion of secondary education resulted in a rapid increase in the percentage of full-time students aged 12–16 years, from 37 per cent in 1961 to 70 per cent in 1976, and the target of 100 per cent was finally reached in 1981, earlier than expected.[19]

Since the introduction of universal primary education (1971) and junior secondary education (1978), there were very few differences between the grant schools and other

---

14. Sweeting, *Education in Hong Kong 1941–2000*, 251.

15. Sweeting, *Education in Hong Kong 1941–2000*, 245–247.

16. White Paper, Secondary Education in Hong Kong over the Next Decade, tabled in the Legislative Council, 16 October 1975, Hong Kong Government, accessed 11 March 2022, https://www.eduhk.hk/cird/publications/edpolicy/02.pdf.

17. Topley, "Hong Kong Education System".

18. Yee Wang Fung, "Education", in *Hong Kong in Transition*, ed. Joseph Cheng (Hong Kong: Oxford University Press, 1986), 307.

19. Luk, *A History of Education in Hong Kong*, 73, 91.

subsidised schools. In 1973, The Grant Code and Subsidy Code were unified as the Code of Aid. All subsidised schools were regarded as "aided schools". But due to their distinguished history and alumni, the grant schools have established themselves as a tier of elite schools in Hong Kong and continued to be referred to as grant schools to preserve their former identities.[20]

With progressive improvement in the economy, the government turned to the next stage of education development. The 1978 White Paper on the Development of Senior Secondary and Tertiary Education focused on the provision of subsidised senior secondary places for about 60 per cent of the 15-year-old population in 1981, rising to more than 70 per cent by 1986. Teacher education was to be further strengthened, the school curriculum enriched, and the facilities and support services to schools improved.[21] During this period, five technical institutes were built and equipped, offering a wide range of disciplines. The Hong Kong Technical College became the nucleus of the Hong Kong Polytechnic, to provide 26,000 full-time and part-time places for students by the end of the 1970s. This period of accelerated educational expansion ended with the Organisation for Economic Cooperation and Development Education Panel visiting Hong Kong to conduct an overall review in 1981 to 1982; its report was published in November 1982. This culminated in the formation of the Education Commission in 1984 to oversee and coordinate the development of all sectors of education.

Growing Importance of the Chinese Language

Before the Second World War, there was no perceived demand for Hong Kong, a British colonial administrative region, to provide its own system of university education in the Chinese language. There were two types of secondary schools in Hong Kong: Anglo-Chinese secondary schools, which prepared students for higher education in the University of Hong Kong or universities in other parts of the British Commonwealth and the USA, and Chinese middle schools which prepared students for universities in China. This all changed with the establishment of the PRC in 1949 and the closing of the border in 1951. Many graduates from Chinese middle schools had no easy path to higher education, although some students found their way to universities in China.[22] In the late 1950s, the government approved the founding of post-secondary colleges that were staffed by teachers from universities in China. The colleges were organised around Chinese rather

---

20. The Hong Kong Education System, Hong Kong Education Department, 1981.
21. "The Development of Senior Secondary and Tertiary Education in Hong Kong", October 1978, Hong Kong Government, accessed 6 May 2020, https://www.eduhk.hk/cird/publications/edpolicy/04.pdf.
22. D. J. S. Crozier to Colonial Office, 26 May 1957, The Post-Secondary Colleges of Hong Kong, CO 1030/571, 286–289.

than British curricula. They received financial support from different sources: missionary organisations,[23] the Guomindang government in Taiwan, and the Hong Kong government. Of these, Chung Chi College, New Asia College, and United College were among the most reputable and well managed. These three post-secondary colleges formed the Chinese University of Hong Kong (CUHK) in 1963 after a great deal of preparatory work by these colleges and the government.[24]

The establishment of Chinese post-secondary colleges and the CUHK was accompanied by a growing awareness of the importance and a heightened demand for wider use of the Chinese language in Hong Kong when China was beginning to industrialise and open to the rest of the world. The riots of 1966 and 1967 led Governor David Trench to examine a number of socio-economic policies in Hong Kong and to set up a Chinese Language Committee in 1968. This was followed by a proposal from the student unions of HKU and the Chung Chi College to make Chinese one of the official languages.[25] These two student unions had, three years earlier in 1965, organised a conference on improving post-secondary education in Hong Kong when the above proposal was discussed in one of the symposia, and it received enthusiastic support.[26] All these concluded in the enactment of the Official Languages Ordinance in 1974 to include the Chinese language as the second official language in Hong Kong.[27]

Extracurricular Activities: Gaining Importance for Young People

When Murray MacLehose became governor in 1971, he paid special attention to the major finding of the Kowloon Disturbances Commission of Inquiry—young people's collective lack of belonging to the community.[28] He set up the Council for Recreation and Sport in 1973 to advise on how to expand facilities for recreation, maximise their use, increase supervision of the activities, and to advise the government on any special services and

---

23. Far East Department, Colonial Office, 2 November 1962, Hong Kong Post-Secondary Colleges, CO 1030/1094, 24–27.

24. A. N. H. Ng-Lun, *Quest for Excellence: A History of the Chinese University of Hong Kong* (Hong Kong: Chinese University Press of Hong Kong, 1994), xx.

25. 馮以浤，〈學運的歷史意義及評價〉，載香港專上學生聯會編，《香港學生運動回顧》（香港：廣角鏡出版社，1983），292–304. Yee Wang Fung, "Student Activism—A Force not to be Ignored," in *Hong Kong Student Activism in Retrospect*, ed. Hong Kong Federation of Students (Hong Kong: Wide Angle, 1983), 292–304.

26. Ibid.

27. Ping Chen, "Language Policy in Hong Kong during the Colonial Period before July 1, 1997", in *Language Planning and Language Policy: East Asian Perspectives*, eds. Ping Chen and Nanette Gottlieb (Cornwall: Curzon Press, 2001), 111–128.

28. Kowloon Disturbances 1966, Report of Commission of Enquiry, Hong Kong Government, J. R. Lee Acting Government Printers, 1967.

amenities necessary to meet the leisure-time needs of young people. Many country parks and reserves were opened in the 1970s for the citizens to enjoy.[29]

Facilities including the Queen Elizabeth Sports Centre, Hung Hom Sports Centre, Tsuen Wan Town Hall, Shatin Town Hall, Tuen Mun Town Hall, the Race Course in Shatin, and the Ocean Park were built so as to induce in people a sense of belonging to Hong Kong. In 1974 the Recreation and Sports Affairs Section was created under the ED, and in 1977 the Hong Kong Music Office was formed by the government. These organisations contributed greatly to the promotion and development of recreational and extracurricular activities (ECAs) for young people and students in Hong Kong.[30] In fact, many studies showed that ECAs improved educational achievement, self-confidence, leadership skills, and teamwork abilities and were vital for whole-person development in school children.[31] As a result, ECAs began to develop in secondary schools in Hong Kong in the 1970s. Further expansion took place after the 1983 conference, which was organised by the CUHK and the ED to review the benefits of ECAs in mass education and was widely attended by the education sector in Hong Kong. The conference resulted in the official recognition of ECAs as an informal school curriculum and the formation of the Hong Kong Extracurricular Activities Masters Association by a group of enthusiasts.[32]

Mrs Joyce Symons, the Headmistress of DGS, navigated the school through a period when Hong Kong underwent rapid transformation from a city with only entrepôt trade into a regional manufacturing centre and on its way to becoming a global financial centre, from a poverty-stricken society into a relatively affluent society, and from a city with a corrupt government to a clean and efficient one with an improved healthcare system and a relatively well-educated population—all within three decades. During this period, the school was expanded in response to the demands of the growing population. Mrs Symons complied with the ED's regulations, but she did more. Looking ahead to help her students to cope with the changing society, she enriched the school's provision of academic, cultural, and sports programmes to broaden their lives, and introduced teaching and learning strategies

---

29. Hong Kong Legislative Council, 17 October 1973, Official Report of Proceedings, 10, accessed 9 June 2020, https://www.legco.gov.hk/yr73-74/h731017.pdf.

30. 馮以浤，〈麥理浩年代的社經政策與課外活動的發展〉，載曾永康、黃毅英編，《香港學校課外活動發展史》（香港：香港城市大學出版社，2021），頁63–67。Yee Wang Fung, "The Socio-economic Policy and Development of Extracurricular Activities in MacLehose's Era", in *The History of Extracurricular Activities in Hong Kong Schools*, ed. Tsang Wing Hong and Wong Ngai Ying (Hong Kong: City University of Hong Kong Press, 2021), 63–77.

31. J. Eccles, "Extracurricular Activities and Adolescent Development", *Journal of Social Issues* 59 (2003): 865–889; Erin Morris, "Participation in Extracurricular Activities and Academic Performance: A Comprehensive Review", master's degree dissertation, Western Kentucky University, 2019.

32. 馮以浤，〈麥理浩年代的社經政策與課外活動的發展〉，頁76–77。Yee Wang Fung, "The Socio-economic Policy and Development of Extracurricular Activities in MacLehose's Era", 76–77.

to help them integrate their experience. She set the directions for future development of the school to provide the students with an all-round education.

A Headmistress in the Making: Mrs Catherine Joyce Symons before 1953

Mrs Catherine Joyce Symons (née Anderson) was the longest serving Headmistress in the history of DGS, with her administration spanning a period of thirty-two years. Born in 1918 in Shanghai with Eurasian parents, her heritage could be traced back to England, Scotland, Austria, Spain, America, and China. Being Eurasian, Joyce Anderson felt a lack of acceptance from both the Chinese and the Europeans, as racial discrimination was prevalent. She made a conscious effort to stand up for herself, even at a young age, to strive to do her best in all aspects of life, and to fight to be accepted on equal terms.[33] She began to attend DGS at the age of seven and was admitted to HKU with a King Edward VII Scholarship, the highest honour given to a new entrant that year. In 1939, she returned to teach in DGS where she discovered her love for the profession. She and her family fled to Macau during the Japanese Occupation.[34]

After Hong Kong's liberation from the Japanese, Joyce Anderson returned to DGS and reopened the school on 1 October 1945 on behalf of Miss Gibbins, who, as readers will recall from Chapter 4, had repossessed the school from the Japanese but was repatriated to England for recuperation. Joyce left Hong Kong for Shanghai in December that year to be married to Dr Robert Symons. They then departed for the UK where Joyce enriched her teaching experience in a private girls' school and took a postgraduate course in education.[35]

On returning to Hong Kong in 1948, Mrs Symons became the Acting Headmistress of DGS again, relieving Miss Hurrell when she was on leave in England. When Miss Hurrell resumed her position after six months of respite, Mrs Symons became a member of the DGS School Council. In 1949, Bishop Hall asked her to be the next Headmistress of DGS after Miss Hurrell's impending retirement. However, Mrs Symons declined his kind offer, revealing to him that she was suffering from a brain tumour, diagnosed by a specialist in London in 1947.[36] When the School Council failed to find a worthy successor to Miss Hurrell, it appointed Miss Molly Fisher to be the Acting Headmistress from August 1951.[37] But Bishop Hall had not given up the hope of appointing Mrs Symons as the next Headmistress, and in early 1953, his prayers were answered. Mrs Symons learned that her

---

33. C. J. Symons, *Looking at the Stars: Memoirs by Catherine Joyce Symons* (Hong Kong: Pegasus Books, 1996), vi.
34. Symons, *Looking at the Stars*, 27–30.
35. Symons, *Looking at the Stars*, 35–40.
36. C. J. Symons, "HKU, Macao and the DGS", in *Dispersal and Renewal*, ed. C. Matthews and O. Cheung (Hong Kong: Hong Kong University Press, 1998), 165.
37. Minutes of School Council Meeting, 9 July 1951.

brain tumour had stopped growing, and this life-changing news triggered her to re-evaluate her life. With her future appearing more stable, what path should she follow? Mrs Symons believed that God had spared her for a purpose. A devout Anglican, she prayed hard, and she found the answer.[38] She chose 1 April 1953 to take up her new position. Thus began her illustrious career as Headmistress of DGS for the next thirty-two years, during which DGS became one of the pre-eminent schools in Hong Kong with excellence in academic and extracurricular activities.

DGS under Mrs Catherine Joyce Symons (1953 to 1985)

When Mrs Symons became the Headmistress in 1953, the Senior School (Secondary School) had two classes each from Form 1 to Form 6 and the Junior School (Primary School) had eight classes: two classes of Primary 5 and 6 and one class each of Primary 1 to 4. There was also one kindergarten class and a boarding school with about fifty boarders.

In the 1950s, as the government expanded primary education, it also began to exert more control on all schools, including grant schools. Bishop Hall, Chairman of the Grant Schools Council, with most of the principals of these schools, fought hard for less government control so they were free to innovate and to provide the diversity in education that was beneficial to the community. Bishop Hall intended for the Anglican grant schools to develop their own ethos and individuality, and stressed the importance of bilingual education in the Anglo-Chinese schools. Mrs Symons fully subscribed to this view. She discussed each of her priorities with the Bishop, who chaired the DGS School Council,

Figure 6.1: Dr Catherine Joyce Symons (née Anderson) (Headmistress 1953–1985). Source: School Archives.

---

38. Symons, *Looking at the Stars*, 45, 46.

before involving the School Council and the staff. She spent her first term observing how the school operated before developing long-term plans, five-year plans, annual plans, and even a daily plan, for the improvement of DGS.[39]

In 1956, the school had a total enrolment of 772 with 34 teachers, giving a student-teacher ratio of 22.7:1, higher than the ratio in the pre-war era. It had a group of very loyal expatriate staff when Mrs Symons became Headmistress. They were Miss Margaret Mansfield, who had taught at the school for a few years before Mrs Symons's appointment and later served as a Deputy Headmistress; Mrs Inger Kvan, who became Mrs Symons's stalwart supporter; Mrs Nancy O'Connell, who taught drama; and Miss Marjorie Maneely, a retired music teacher from Scotland, who taught music. Among the local staff were Miss Ethel A. Allen, who taught Mrs Symons when she was ten years old, and the two Chans: "Big" Chan (Mr Lawrence S. L. Chan) taught mathematics and translations for years, and "Small" Chan (Mr Chan Yik Cham) was responsible for upgrading Chinese in DGS and inspiring many girls to improve their mother language. They remained devoted to the school until their retirement.

In 1973, the school administration was decentralised when four experienced senior teachers were appointed to head different departments: Mr Chan Yik Cham, Chinese; Mrs Katherine M. Mason, English, French, and music; Mrs Lam Yee Ling, science, mathematics, and domestic science; and Mrs Irene So, history, geography, economics, and public affairs. Mrs Inger Kvan became the Deputy Headmistress.[40] They coordinated syllabuses, chose the textbooks, checked examination questions, and made decisions on the use of the school library and library books. Each of the four departments had their own budget to purchase necessary equipment. The number of departments increased to seven in 1980. Decentralisation of administration relieved Mrs Symons from some of her day-to-day duties, and this certainly benefited the school, especially when her civic responsibilities increased as the decade progressed.

DGS has always been proud of its heritage as a multinational school. Teachers of all races had always shared one common room and one staffroom harmoniously.

In 1953, DGS was a grant school (both Senior and Junior). It obtained its income from three sources: tuition fees, which were surrendered to the ED in return for a grant for staff salaries, the maintenance of buildings, and some "approved expenditure"; school charge (*tong fai*), which covered expenditure that could not be partly or wholly recovered from the ED and also for differences in salary when the school employed a teacher with higher qualifications than those approved by the government; and boarding fees. The school fees for 1956/1957 are shown in Table 6.2.

---

39. Symons, *Looking at the Stars*, 47–48.
40. Minutes of School Council Meeting, 17 January 1974.

The Great Expansion: 1953 to 1985

Figure 6.2: Mrs C. J. Symons and staff, 1956. Source: *The Quest* 1956, 5.
From left to right:
Back row: Miss Yeung, Mrs Kong, Miss Seen, Miss Der, Miss Wong, Mrs Steven, Miss Carvalho, Miss Townend, Mrs Wong, Mrs O'Connell, Mrs Liang, Mrs Poole
Middle row: Mr Y. C. Chan, Mrs Thoresen, Mrs Cowie, Mrs Lee, Mrs Yau, Miss Brown, Miss Tillstone, Mrs Shaddock, Miss Abdullah, Miss Bird, Miss Burbidge, Mr Wong
Front row: Miss M. Swanston, Mrs Yu, Mrs Triggs, Miss Watt, Mr L. Chan, Mrs C. J. Symons, Mrs So, Miss Wilson, Miss Sinn, Mrs Mansfield, Miss Edwards

Table 6.2: DGS School fees 1956/1957

Class/Form	Tuition/ Government	*Tong fai* / School	Monthly Total	Annual Total
Primary 1 to 6	NA	NA	$21	$210
Form 1 to 2	$24	$12	$36	$360
Form 3 to 6	$24	$16	$40	$400

Source: Minutes of School Council Meeting 23 October 1956; NA = not available.

The school greatly expanded under Mrs Symons's headship, and the number of students grew from 622 in 1953 to 1,432 in 1985 (Figure 6.3).

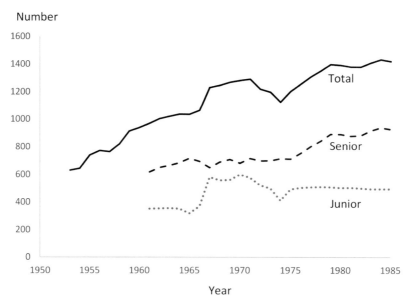

Figure 6.3: Enrolment of DGS, 1953 to 1985. Source: Minutes of School Council Meetings of respective years. Note: Data before 1960 is incomplete.

An Independent Institution: Incorporation and a New Constitution

The properties of DGS were vested with the Chairman of the Committee of the Diocesan School and Orphanage (DSO), an incorporated company, which also had legal rights over the properties of DBS since 1892. In 1969, the school gained a new ordinance, the Council of the Diocesan Girls' School Incorporation Ordinance (Chapter 1124), 1969,[41] which included the constitution established in 1968 for the DGS School Council.[42] The transfer of the properties, KIL 1281 and KIL 6329, from the Chairman of the Committee of the DSO to the Council of the Diocesan Girls' School also took place during the process.[43] Although on the surface nothing seemed to have changed, having this new ordinance signified the independence of DGS as an institution—no longer dependent on the Chairman of the Committee of the DSO. DBS also received its own ordinance through the same exercise.[44] In the 1968 constitution, the membership of the School Council was specified as follows:

---

41. Notes on subsequent action taken on paragraphs IV and V of the Conclusions, 11 August 1970, Bishop Baker to Sir C. Y. Kwan, 28 July 1969.
42. DGS draft constitution, 1969, BHA DGS Minutes File, 1961–1973, 142–144.
43. Lands Officer to Messrs C. Y. Kwan & Co., 21 October 1969.
44. Notes on subsequent action taken on paragraphs IV and V of the Conclusions, 11 August 1970, BHA DGS 1970 General Files.

The Bishop of Hong Kong or his nominee (chairman)

The Vicar of St Andrew's Church or his nominee

One lay representative each appointed by the Diocesan Synod and the Diocesan Conference

The Headmistress

The President of the Diocesan Old Girls' Association (DOGA)

The Chairman of the Parent Teacher Association (PTA)

The Honorary Treasurer

Members of the community (not more than four) appointed by the Bishop, of whom at least were two old girls of the school, one member of the Faculty of the HKU and/or one from the Faculty of the CUHK

Co-opted members by the School Council, not exceeding seven, could be appointed from time to time. The appointed bodies were asked to assign, if agreeable to them, appropriate existing members of the Council as their representatives to the School Council. The co-opted members were to serve a term of three years from the introduction of the new constitution.

Evolving Structure of Kindergarten and Junior School

Closure of Kindergarten

DGS had only one kindergarten class in 1953. In 1954, the Green hut (Figure 6.4) was built for the kindergarten children next to the Nissen huts. The year 1964 saw the last kindergarten class in DGS as a result of reorganisation. The Green hut was demolished to make way for a swimming pool.

A Six-Year Programme for the Junior School

After the Second World War, there were two types of schools in Hong Kong—Chinese schools and Anglo-Chinese schools. The Anglo-Chinese schools, of which DGS was one, followed the English tradition, offering Class 1 (highest) to Class 10 (lowest) and one year of kindergarten. When the Junior School was built in 1948, it had eight classrooms, two classes each of Class 7 to Class 10. In 1951, a major change occurred in the Anglo-Chinese grant schools whereby entry to Senior School would take place after six years in the primary school. Primary school education would be given greater attention so that well-rounded courses were provided, complete in themselves. All classes in primary schools were to be called "classes" while secondary school classes were to be called "forms".[45]

---

45. Patricia P. K. Chiu, *A History of the Grant Schools Council* (Hong Kong: Grant Schools Council, 2013), 111–112.

Figure 6.4: Nissen huts and Green hut (closest to Chi Wo Street), c. 1950. Source: School Archives.

In 1951, the Junior School operated in one session only with a total of eight classes. It had one class each of Primary 1 to 4 and two classes each of Primary 5 and Primary 6. DGS received girls from the Diocesan Preparatory School (DPS) into Primary 5 if they passed an entrance examination. DPS had one stream of children, boys and girls, from kindergarten to Primary 4. After Primary 4, DPS boys entered DBS and the girls DGS for Primary 5.[46]

In 1955, the ED announced that students from all schools—including grant schools and private schools—had to take part in the Joint Primary 6 Examination, which was used to select students for entrance to Form 1 in secondary schools. Grant schools with a primary section, such as DGS, were told to change the primary section to become a subsidised bi-sessional school or a private school. If the school became a subsidised bi-sessional school, it could choose one of two schemes. The first scheme (Scheme A) was that it could take part in the Joint Primary 6 Examination with the school retaining 65 per cent of its own pupils to enter Form 1 and the remaining 35 per cent competing with outsiders for places. The second scheme (Scheme B) was not taking part in the Joint Primary 6 Examination, with the school retaining 70 per cent of its own pupils and admitting 30 per cent newcomers into Form 1.

---

46. Mrs Symons to Bishop Hall, 25 June 1965.

The Great Expansion: 1953 to 1985 125

If the school were to go private, then it could remain as a single session school and there would be no need to enter the Joint Primary 6 Examination, though 30 per cent of Form 1 places had to be given to newcomers. If DGS Junior School were to become private, the interest-free loan of $40,000 from the government for the building of the Junior School in 1948 could be waived, and the land on which the Junior School stood and the hockey field should be held in the name of the Senior School; the Crown Rent for these properties would be met by the ED.[47]

The government's reasons for the proposed changes were to economise on expenditure on grant schools so that the savings could be spent on building more subsidised primary schools to meet the needs of the growing primary school population, and to ensure the best pupils from all primary schools had a fair chance of entry to a government secondary or a government-aided school.

Most of the grant schools objected to the proposals for reasons best expressed by Mr Gerald Goodban, Headmaster of DBS, in a draft memo to the Grant School Council: "Our objections to a huge Joint Primary 6 Examination are not due to any fears that our boys would not do well in it but that it will produce a uniformity quite fatal to the spirit on which the whole grant school system is run. The grant schools are not all alike."[48] In the end, most of the Anglican grant schools, including DGS, opted for the second option (Scheme B): not to enter the Joint Primary 6 Examination and to give 30 per cent of Form 1 places to the government for the successful candidates of the Joint Primary 6 Examination.[49]

In June 1955, the School Council formed a subcommittee to decide on an appropriate action in order to retain the distinct characteristics of the school and to remain a single session school. After a lengthy negotiation, the government allowed the Junior School to remain in the grant code until 1958 or 1959. However, starting in September 1956, DGS would have to admit outside students who passed the Joint Primary 6 Examination to 30 per cent of its Form 1 places. This certainly presented a problem to the school, which naturally wanted to retain all its Primary 6 students.

The Junior School Becoming a Private School

In October 1955, Mrs Symons recommended to the School Council that the Senior School should expand to have three instead of two classes in each form. She believed that DGS was founded to educate girls for a total duration of thirteen or fourteen years and not just six years. Since the Junior School had two classes of Primary 6 and the Senior School had to

---

47. Minutes of School Council Meeting, 24 May 1955.
48. Mr Gerald Goodban, draft memo, 31 March 1955, in Chiu, *A History of the Grant Schools Council*, 121.
49. Chiu, *A History of the Grant Schools Council*, 123.

offer 30 per cent of Form 1 places to pupils from other schools and, at the same time, keep two classes of students from the Junior School, the Senior School should expand to have three classes from Form 1 to Form 5.[50] For this expansion, a new school building would be necessary to replace the 1913 building. This would be the Centenary Building, marking the school's centenary in 1960. Mrs Symons' proposal was enthusiastically accepted by the School Council. When the school applied to the government for a building grant and an interest-free loan, the government approved the application on the condition that the Junior School would change into a subsidised school or a private school by 1959. After due consideration, the School Council chose the latter to preserve the school's character, allowing all the students in Primary 6 to be able to enter Form 1, unless she failed the regular school examination twice. In 1959, the Junior School became a private school. Without government subsidy, the monthly fees were raised from $21 to $60 for the first child in the family and from $21 to $30 for subsequent children. Despite the fee increase, all children remained at the school.

Failed Attempts of Junior School to Return to Subsidy Status

In 1965, the Junior School fell into deficit because of high inflation and the rise in teachers' salaries. The school reconsidered the situation of the Junior School, because by then there was less incentive for it to remain as a private school, the main reason being that the Joint Primary 6 Examination, renamed the Secondary School Entrance Examination (SSEE), was to be compulsory for all schools by 1968. There was also a concern that parents might feel there was nothing to be gained by paying a high fee when a spot could not be guaranteed in the Senior School. Moreover, the semi-permanent Junior School building, which was constructed with wood in 1948, was becoming increasingly expensive to repair and clearly needed to be rebuilt. The Junior School's expenditure would only continue to increase. The School Council reviewed its position on the status of the primary school and decided that the school should aim to maintain a bilingual, well-rounded education while providing students with the necessary skills to pass the SSEE; it could be either a private school or a partially subsidised school as long as these aims could be achieved.[51]

When the school applied to the ED in January 1966 for partial subsidy to the Junior School, requesting 50 per cent recurrent subsidy and a 25 per cent interest-free building

---

50. Diocesan Girls' School Council Subcommittee on Possible Primary School Changes, 1955; The Headmistress's Recommendations on Primary School Changes, 25 October 1955; Bishop Hall and Mrs Symons to Parents on the Change of Status of the Junior School, 9 March 1959.

51. Minutes of School Council Meeting, 29 April 1966.

The Great Expansion: 1953 to 1985   127

loan with a 25 per cent building grant for a new building, the government only approved a "recurrent subsidy" to the Junior School for the year 1966/1967.[52]

In 1967, the Junior School decided to expand to two classes per level from primary 1 to 4 which only had one class each so far. Four classes were temporarily accommodated in the Centenary Building as the number of boarders were reducing and some rooms were vacated.[53] In October 1971, the school applied to the ED for a capital subsidy for rebuilding the Junior School to accommodate 540 students and also to change its status into a fully subsidised school. After prolonged consideration, the ED denied the request to change status but agreed to grant an 80 per cent interest-free loan to the school for reprovisioning.[54] It also approved increases in fees, which had remained at $600 annually since 1959, to $1,500 annually starting in 1973.[55] With these changes, the Junior School building was finally rebuilt between 1974 to 1975.

In the early 1980s, inflation rose to above 10 per cent in Hong Kong, and the Junior School, being private, had to charge higher tuition fees. With a projected deficit of over $330,000 for the academic year 1980/1981, the ED approved DGS School Council's request for an increase in tuition fees from $1,700 per annum in 1980/1981 to $2,300 per annum in 1981/1982. Alarmed by the possible threat to long-term survival of the Junior School, the school began to negotiate with the ED to reinstate the Junior School as a fully subsidised school. There was also a lingering uneasiness among members of the School Council that the Junior School, being private, would lose its status as a feeder to the Senior School.[56] Thankfully, the ED affirmed that the feeder status of the Junior School would unlikely change since the feeder system and the financial system operated independently.[57] Finally, on 17 November 1981, the ED requested a meeting with Mrs Symons, Mrs Daphne Quay Ying Blomfield, the Headmistress of the Junior School, and two School Council members. The ED had decided not to change the status of the Junior School, because there were more than enough primary school places in Hong Kong, especially in the south Kowloon area, and the ED had turned down similar applications from other private schools.[58] The school could apply for an increase in fees each year and have a remission system for families that could not afford the fees. The decision was final, and the Junior School remains private up to the present. To a certain extent, this decision of ED influenced the change of the Senior

---

52. Mrs Symons to Director of Education, 18 January 1966; N. M. Ho for Director of Education to Mrs C. J. Symons, 8 August 1966.

53. Minutes of School Council Meeting, 29 June 1967.

54. Director of Education to Mrs Symons, 7 September 1973.

55. Director of Education to Mrs Symons, 7 September 1973.

56. Mrs Symons to Director of Education, 27 June 1981.

57. D. B. M. Board to Mrs Symons, 24 November 1981.

58. Discussion on the Status of Diocesan Girls' Junior School between Mrs Symons, Mrs Blomfield, and two members of the School Council with Mr DBM Board in his office, 17 November 1981.

School to Direct Subsidy Status (DSS) at a later stage. The regrettable consequence of high fees for Junior School was the reduction of students from less privileged families—a loss to the school as these students, who were usually very diligent and attentive, had traditionally been a significant asset to the school.

Diocesan Girls' Junior School (DGJS)

In 1975, the Junior School officially became known as the Diocesan Girls' Junior School (DGJS). In September, the Junior School welcomed Mrs Rachel Benton as the first headmistress in its history.

Thus far, the headmistress of DGS had been responsible for both the Senior and Junior schools. The appointment of a headmistress specifically for the Junior School was intended to reduce the heavy responsibilities of Mrs Symons, who would assume the role of supervisor of the Junior School while remaining Senior School Headmistress.[59] Mrs Benton worked only in the mornings, but when she retired, a full-time headmistress was appointed: Mrs Daphne Blomfield who was teaching geography and English in the primary and secondary sections of St Paul's Co-Educational College before she replaced Mrs Benton in 1978. It was Mrs Blomfield who initiated the "Big Sister Programme" in which each Primary

Figure 6.5: Mrs Rachel Benton, first Headmistress of the Junior School, with prefects of the Junior School (1975–1976). Source: *Quest* 1975–1976, 87.

---

59. Minutes of School Council Meeting, 4 July 1975.

6 student was paired to take care of a Primary 1 new girl for the first year. She also foresaw the future demand for Putonghua and introduced it to the curriculum at a time when it was not widely taught in Hong Kong. She encouraged participation in team competitions so that more students could be involved and would bond through cooperative efforts and shared goals.[60]

Evolving Structure of the Senior School

A Seven-Year Programme for the Senior School

Changes occurred in the upper forms of the Senior School very early on in Mrs Symons' tenure. In 1953, the ED announced that the matriculation course would henceforth comprise two years instead of one in order to increase the number of university places and to produce more graduates. During the second matriculation year, students would be taught the curriculum of first year university. The year 1953/1954 was the first year that secondary schools had two matriculation classes: Lower 6 Form and Upper 6 Form.[61] For the first time, the secondary schools offered seven years of education instead of six years.

Figure 6.6: Lady Grantham's visit to the school, 1952. Source: School Archives.

---

60. Mrs Daphne Blomfield, accessed 10 June 2020, http://www.doga.org.hk/index.php/110-interviews/headmistresses/161-mrs-daphne-blomfield.
61. *The Quest* (1953): 4–5.

From Two to Three and to Four Classes Per Form in the Senior School

In 1956, in response to the government's ruling that all grant schools with primary sections would have to take in "outside students" who passed the Joint Primary Examination to fill 30 per cent of Form 1 places, DGS expanded Form 1 from two classes to three classes to accommodate its own two classes of Primary 6 students and 30 per cent of "outside" students in Form 1. The Senior School had three classes for each form from then on.

In 1974, the government published the White Paper on Secondary Education intending to increase Junior secondary education and to provide nine years of free compulsory education. In 1976, it proposed the abolition of SSEE and introduced a new system of allocation of students, known as the Secondary School Placement Allocation System (SSPA). Under this system, parents of Primary 6 students chose the schools and the allocation was dependent on the student's position, in order of merit, among Primary 6 students from their own school. They were required to sit the Academic Aptitude Test—a two paper test for verbal and numerical reasoning that did not require any memorisation of facts. Unfortunately, this did not prevent schools from drilling the students to prepare them for the test. The results were used as a means of comparing standards among primary schools. The whole territory was divided into twenty-four "school nets" based on the location of primary schools. The converted marks of all students in a net were put into an order of merit and divided into five bands.[62] For grant schools with a feeder primary school such as DGS, the government recommended that by the summer of 1982, 15 per cent of Form 1 places would be discretionary places, and the remaining places would be divided equally, half to be filled through feeder allocation and half through general allocation. The proportion of places in Form 1 for "outside" students would be increased from 30 per cent to about 50 per cent.[63]

In September 1976, the school opened the fourth Form I class and began admitting 50 per cent of "outside" students to Form 1, while retaining its two classes of Primary 6 students — way ahead of the government's deadline of 1982 for such a requirement.[64] Despite the changes in the structure of the Senior School, it remained a grant school throughout, receiving subsidies from the government.

---

62. Sweeting, *Educational History of Hong Kong 1941–2000*, 268, 322–323.

63. Chapter III, A Proposed New Allocation System, Education Department Hong Kong, 19 January 1976; Minutes of School Council Meeting, 23 June 1978.

64. Minutes of School Council Meeting, 2 December 1974, 12 March 1976, and 1 November 1979.

Changing School Campus and Facilities

In 1953, the Senior School was housed in the 1913 main building, the 1940 Wing, and the 1950 Wing, and operated two classes each of Form 1 to Form 6. The increase in the number of classes necessitated expansion of the school campus with more buildings and better facilities.

Figure 6.7: DGS Jordan Road side in the 1950s. Source: School Archives.

The New Centenary Building

In 1955, when the School Council decided to increase the Senior School from two classes to three classes in each form, it was quite obvious that a new school building would be required. This would have the necessary classrooms and special rooms for teaching as well as an assembly hall, the construction of which would likely be supported by the government. However, the building of a gymnasium, a boarding school for 80 to 100 boarders, accommodation for about 15 teachers and expatriate staff, and a chapel for about 150 people would be the responsibility of the school.[65]

A Centenary Building Subcommittee was formed with the following members: Major Samuel M. Churn (Chair), Mrs Joyce Symons, Mr John Francis Grose, and Mr D. Benson. The cost of the Centenary Building, which would be supported by the government, was estimated by Messrs Palmer and Turner Architects to be $1.4 million, excluding the Junior School. The cost of building the gymnasium and the boarding school, not funded by

---

65. Minutes of School Council Meeting, 20 March 1956.

the government, would be another $0.5 million. The subcommittee decided to defer the rebuilding of the Junior School.[66]

In August 1956, the school applied to the government for financial support to replace the 1913 old school building.[67] The government offered the school a building grant of $515,000 and an interest-free loan of $312,000 repayable over ten years. But there was a condition attached: as noted previously, the Junior School had to change either to a subsidised or a private school by 1958 or 1959.[68] The rest of the funds would have to come from fundraising campaigns. A booklet was printed for this purpose, and permission was obtained from the ED for the campaign.[69]

The arrangement of the school during the period of construction was as follows: the boarding school moved to Heep Yunn School where space was available; the Senior School became bi-sessional in the 1940 Wing with Forms 1 to 3 in the morning and Forms 4 to 6 in the afternoon; the Headmistress's office, staffrooms, school office, domestic science laboratory, reference library, and the Upper 6 Form were located in the 1950 Wing. One Nissen hut was used for storing furniture and the other acted as a kitchen and dining room for boarders. The resident staff lived in rented premises.[70]

At the end of December 1957, after all the planning and preparations for the Centenary Building had been finalised, the old 1913 main building was set to be demolished. After the winter examination in 1957, Mrs Symons invited old girls back to the school to tell their personal stories about the old building. She allowed the girls to paint pictures on the walls of classrooms and corridors, after school hours, and offered the assembly hall to the prefects. To crown it all, the Head Prefect of that year and another girl produced a mural of a stained-glass window on the wall nearest the stage. This dose of nostalgia seemed to be shared equally by the old girls, current girls, and staff.[71]

Demolition of the 1913 block took place on 27 December 1957 with pile-driving commencing on 5 March 1958. The dedication of the site took place on 24 April 1958. The day before, the architect asked Mrs Symons to choose a spot for "the turning of the sod", the groundbreaking ceremony. She took her time to look around, and finally decided on the centre of the proscenium arch of the new stage in the huge 1,000-seat assembly hall. She told no one except the Rev. Owen V. Eva, vicar of St Andrew's Church. The following morning, she found that someone had beaten her to it. The builders' foreman had chosen

---

66. Minutes of School Council Meeting, 23 October 1956.

67. Mrs C. J. Symons to the Education Department, 10 August 1956.

68. Director of Education to Mrs C. J. Symons, 12 October 1956, regarding the application for Building Grant and Interest Free Loan.

69. Minutes of School Council Meeting, 22 January 1957.

70. Mrs C. J. Symons to Bishop Hall on reorganisation of DGS in 1958, 3 December 1957.

71. Symons, *Looking at the Stars*, 55.

Figure 6.8: Demolition of the 1913 main building in December 1957; (centre) mural of a stained-glass window painted on the wall of the Assembly Hall. Source: *Quest* 1960, 2.

that very place to offer libations to his gods with joss-stick, bright red candles, and even brighter red roast suckling pig! He had chosen the spot because of its good feng shui.[72] It seems that there is not much difference in geomancy between the East and the West after all.

During the construction period, the school was allowed to use the Boy Scouts headquarters just across Jordan Road once a week for a full assembly as well as their gymnasium and art and craft room. The school buildings, the Centenary Building, the gymnasium, and the assembly hall were finally completed after a full year (Plates 1 and 2). The total contributions to the Centenary Building Fund from donations amounted to $404,262. When the school moved in, $750,000 was still required to cover the total cost of construction.

The Speech Day on 20 February 1959 was chosen for the opening ceremony for the Centenary Building, officiated by Mr Douglas James Smyth Crozier, the Director of Education, amid great celebrations.[73] Regrettably, Major Churn, who had worked so hard

---

72. Symons, *Looking at the Stars*, 56.
73. Minutes of School Council meeting, 27 January 1959.

Figure 6.9: Aerial photo of DGS showing the Centenary building, assembly hall, and gymnasium in 1959. Source: School Archives.

chairing the Centenary Building Subcommittee and donated so generously to the school, was unable to attend the opening ceremony. On the same day, he only caught a glimpse of the new building in passing as he was driven to hospital in an ambulance; sadly, he passed away shortly afterwards at the age of 72. Major Churn, who was the Chairman of the Welfare League, a Eurasian charitable organisation, had donated regularly to support the orphans in DGS and DBS during the post-war years. The school dedicated a memorial tablet to honour him for his long-standing service. The unveiling of the tablet took place after evensong on 15 December 1959.[74]

Celebration of the School Centenary

In 1960, the school celebrated its centenary, with the Centenary Building having been recently completed. Mrs Symons invited the previous three surviving headmistresses—Miss Dorothy Sawyer, Miss Elizabeth Gibbins, and Miss Winifred Hurrell—to join the festivities from funds raised by DOGA members.

The centenary celebration took place on the annual Speech Day on 14 January 1960 with Sir Robert Brown Black, the Governor, and Lady Black attending. The commemorative plaque was unveiled by the Governor, and Lady Black presented the prizes and scholarships to the students. Mrs Symons then warmly welcomed the three previous headmistresses

---

74. Minutes of School Council Meeting, 28 July 1959.

The Great Expansion: 1953 to 1985   135

who had played pivotal roles in the school's development from 1925 to 1951. The convergence of the past, the present, and the future represented to her the school's legacy and its continuity. She made a speech in which she declared that she and the students had a moral responsibility to uphold DGS's heritage:

> Miss Sawyer, my teacher, Miss Gibbins, my headmistress when I first became a teacher in 1939 and Miss Hurrell, my ever-helpful adviser since 1953. Many of you in the hall tonight remember these ladies with gratitude and affection as I do. I know you are delighted to see them all today and to pay them homage for their tremendous work for the school. There are moments in life when only simple words will do . . . This is my only message to my girls this evening. We have inherited an old and revered school, we have been given magnificent buildings, but with them, we have been handed the future of this school. You have grown to admire and love these buildings, but you are the school. Remember our motto, "Daily Giving Service".[75]

In the evening, a Chinese-style dinner party was held in thanksgiving with many tables seating the headmistresses, the School Council members, teachers, school prefects, all the boarders, and all the non-teaching staff.[76] To many, having the past three headmistresses together was a historical event, and for Mrs Symons, it crowned her happiness.

The centenary year ended with a thanksgiving service in St John's Cathedral on 15 December 1960. Mr Crozier, the Director of Education, read the first lesson, the Reverend Eva officiated the service and read the second lesson, and the Dean of the Cathedral gave the sermon. Bishop Hall led special prayers of dedication and thanksgiving.

The Boarding School

The Centenary Building was planned with facilities for eighty to one hundred boarders. Before the war, schools with boarding facilities in Hong Kong were popular for expatriate children whose parents were in missionary or diplomatic services in China and for overseas Chinese children from British Malaya, Singapore, Annam (Vietnam), and Siam (Thailand), and even from China. There were also some local girls whose parents wanted them to have a boarding school education. DGS gave them a good English education and ensured regular hours of work, rest, and play. The boarding school enabled cross-cultural exchange in a casual way between students of different nationalities, and many lasting friendships developed in this multicultural community. After the Second World War, the school accommodated, over time, forty orphans or children of destitute mothers. Boarders reached the highest number of eighty in the early 1950s. After this, many missionaries and

---

75. Headmistress's Address, Speech Day, 14 January 1960.
76. "The Thanksgiving Dinner", Quest (1960): 21.

Figure 6.10: Centenary celebration in 1960 with four headmistresses present.
From left to right: Miss E. M. Gibbins, Miss H. D. Sawyer, Bishop R. O. Hall, Miss A. W. Hurrell, and Mrs C. J. Symons. Source: *Quest* 1960, 15.

diplomats left the PRC to return to their own countries, reducing the need for boarding for international students. Furthermore, the war orphans graduated and left the school one by one, and by 1969, only four of them were left. High boarding fees owing to the increased cost of living discouraged local families from sending their children to boarding schools.[77] By the late 1960s, the total number of boarders was reduced to around twenty. In 1971, the School Council felt that the excess space for dormitories could be better utilised and decided with much regret to close the boarding school after the summer term of 1972 to give way to the Sixth Form Centre.[78] However, the boarding school was only finally closed in 1973.

The Chapel of the Holy Spirit

The school chapel was essential for boarders and staff who were in residence. Evensong on weekdays and Sunday evening service took place there. When the new chapel, a

---

77. Minutes of School Council Meeting, 21 October 1969.
78. Minutes of School Council Meeting, 11 May 1971

remodelling of two classrooms and a veranda of the 1950 wing, was completed in 1959, Bishop Hall hallowed and named it the Chapel of the Holy Spirit.[79] On 24 April 1959, he led the procession of guests to the door of the new chapel, knocked on it three times with his staff, and said a special prayer of blessing when the chapel door was opened. The new chapel had a lofty ceiling and long windows, and a colour scheme of blue and white.

Improved Facilities

A number of facilities became available or were improved from the 1960s. In 1960, the school library held 4,167 books. In 1962, with the help of Dr Francis K. Pan of the School Council, who had experience with the Mencius Foundation Library, the layout and catalogue system were improved.[80] Senior girls volunteered to help in the library, and in so doing, learned about library work. Expansion occurred in 1963/1964 with funding from proceeds of the Annual School Bazaar. In the 1970s, the change in curriculum and in the methods of teaching encouraged the use of the library as an indispensable part of learning.

Although there was an indoor gymnasium in the Centenary plan, a swimming pool was not in the budget. In 1962, the PTA approached the School Council for permission to build one. In May 1964, the project was made possible by fundraising organised by the PTA, supported by Mr K. C. Pang, Mr Li Chi Ho, and many other parents.[81] A 25-metre swimming pool was completed in the following year, offering exercise and recreational opportunities to students and staff, and providing important training facilities for students (Plate 3).

In 1977, a new flyover was built on Gascoigne Road adjacent to the Centenary Building and the 1940 wing. This was to be part of the West Kowloon Corridor linking the city centre with the satellite towns in the New Territories. The loud construction and traffic noise made teaching in the classrooms impossible. The school installed air conditioning for the Senior School, so the windows could be kept shut, with an interest-free loan of $250,000 from the government. In 1984, after an expert found that even in the quieter classrooms in the Junior School the noise levels were above the upper range of acceptable environmental noise levels, Mr George Tong, a parent, underwrote the cost of air conditioning all rooms in the Junior School except the Junior Hall and the China Light and Power hut, which were not in the same building.[82] Air conditioning of the school buildings reduced the street noise and room temperature, and improved the environment for learning tremendously.

---

79. "The Diocesan Girls' School: Bishop Dedicates New Chapel of the Holy Spirit", *South China Morning Post*, 25 April 1959.
80. Minutes of School Council Meeting, 12 March 1963.
81. Minutes of School Council Meeting, 25 August 1964.
82. Headmistress's Report, Junior School, December 1984.

Facilities for teaching and learning were also improved in the Senior School. In 1975, when the Junior School classes moved into their own new building (see next section), five classrooms were vacated in the Centenary Building. Two of the five rooms were converted into a science laboratory for Forms 1 to 3. Other rooms were renovated for special use: an English Room, a Chinese Library, a French room, and a new visual aid room for Forms 1 to 5 that could also be used for committee meetings and lectures.[83] In 1981, the school received a donation from the estate of the late Miss Annie Chan of $1.1 million to build a Language Laboratory. This enabled the students to improve pronunciation and also allowed more interactive teaching.[84] In 1982, the school further received two generous donations, one of $10,000 for a computer room, and the other of $60,000 for building a hut for Junior School extracurricular activities.

A New Building for the Junior School

The Junior School building, a semi-permanent structure built in 1948, had reached an age that required expensive repair each year. In 1968, the school asked the ED for assistance in rebuilding,[85] but the request was not granted.[86]

On 6 October 1971, the school reapplied to the ED for a capital subsidy to allow rebuilding for the accommodation of 540 students, and also to change its status from private to a fully subsidised school for the reasons discussed earlier. The government considered DGS's request for almost two years, and then, on 7 September 1973, granted an 80 per cent interest-free loan to the school for reprovisioning but denied the change of status as discussed.[87]

When an interest-free loan of $975,720 was approved by the government in 1974, the school, with permission from the ED, organised an appeal for building funds.[88] The demolition of the old building took place in mid-August 1974, and the new building was completed before the academic year of 1975. The new Junior School building, designed by Messrs Palmer and Turner, had two blocks, each with six classrooms in two storeys, connected by a separate wing that consisted of a small administrative block and two other rooms.

The service of thanksgiving for and dedication of the new Junior School took place on 7 November 1975. After the service, Bishop Baker, who had succeeded Bishop Hall, unveiled a plaque to commemorate the new building. This was followed by the unveiling of a second

---

83. Headmistress's Report, November 1975.
84. Headmistress's Address, Speech Day, 6 November 1981.
85. Mrs Symons to Education Department, 29 July 1968.
86. D. B. M. Board for Director of Education to Mrs Symons, 16 August 1968.
87. Mrs Symons to Director of Education, 6 October 1971; Director of Education to Mrs. Symons, 7 September 1973.
88. Minutes of the Junior School Building Subcommittee Meeting, 9 April 1974.

The Blessing

Figure 6.11a: The Reverend R. K. Hyatt "turned the earth" for the first time and gave his blessing for the building of the Junior School, 7 February 1975. Source: *Quest* 1975–1976, 95.

Figure 6.11b: The Junior School completed in 1975. Source: School Archives.

plaque on the General Studies Centre by the President of the Welfare League. Lastly, Mrs Maria Fincher and Miss A. Chan, two alumnae, unveiled a plaque dedicated to the late Bishop Ronald Owen Hall, who had been the Chairman of the DGS School Council from 1932 to 1966 but had sadly passed away earlier in 1975 at his home in Oxford.[89]

DGS carried a debt of $1.2 million when the Junior School construction was completed. Starting in 1976, the school repaid the government $100,000 every year. In 1978, when the government announced compulsory free education for nine years, the school requested the government to cancel the interest-free loan in line with the new free education policy, but the government declined. It was only after the third request was made in 1981 that the remainder of the loan, standing at around $650,000, was cancelled.[90]

Scholastic Activities: Curriculum and Pedagogy

Compulsory SSEE and the Junior School Curriculum

The school provided a liberal education with instruction in English from Primary 1 onwards from its founding. The Chinese language was not taught in school until 1939, and the standard of Chinese among students was weak. During Miss Hurrell's tenure, the Junior School began to improve this aspect of the curriculum by adopting the syllabus and textbooks used by other grant schools, such as DBS and St Paul's Co-Educational College, and increasing the number of hours of instruction relating to Chinese subjects. The few Eurasian girls who did not wish to study Chinese learned French instead.

When the SSEE was applied to all students for entry to secondary schools, the Junior School modified its curriculum to equip students for this examination, placing greater emphasis on English, Chinese, and arithmetic, and giving each of the three subjects ten periods per week.[91] In 1966, Primary 6 students were asked to take the SSEE, but the results were not used for the allocation of places. Of the fifty-one students who took the examination, thirty-eight passed (74.5 per cent). The following year, the number increased to fifty-four out of sixty-four (84.4 per cent). In 1968, when the SSEE became operational for DGS, 88 per cent of the students passed. The results continued to improve, and in 1973 the pass rate reached 99.1 per cent.[92]

---

89. Programme of Events, Service of Thanksgiving and Dedication, 7 November 1975.
90. Minutes of School Council meeting, 21 November 1980.
91. Headmistress's Report, April 1966.
92. Headmistress's Reports of respective years.

Streaming in the Lower Forms

The admission of 30 per cent "outside" girls to Form 1 classes in 1956 posed a problem for English teaching.[93] The English of this intake was not up to par because it had been taught as a second language to these students in their primary school. After observing these students for a couple of years, the school decided to practise streaming so students could work at a speed that they were comfortable with; at the same time, this made teaching easier.

In September 1959, the students in each form were divided into three classes, X, Y, Z, in alphabetical order according to their surnames. English, Chinese, and mathematics were streamed into three levels: A, B, and C. The A stream would attempt to cover the whole syllabus, the B stream 80 per cent, and the C stream perhaps only 60 per cent. In Forms 1, 2, and 3, the gap would be closed by special coaching classes in these three subjects during the summer vacation, usually carried out by volunteer students from the Upper 6 Form. The rest of the subjects were not streamed. There was no student ranking, but grades were given on classwork and recorded in a special book for reference.[94] There were three examinations each year, but ranking was not given. In all three streamed subjects, a pass (a score of 50 per cent or higher) was necessary. In non-streamed subjects, failure in only one subject was allowed. Transfer from stream to stream was made annually after the summer examination unless there were cases of extreme misfit—when a teacher was able to immediately transfer a student.

Although the English of the "outside" girls was initially poor, the students gradually improved, and by the end of Form 3 their English was on par with the other students. Mrs Symons appreciated their presence as they brought a new element of diversity to the school. They were hardworking, polite, keen, tidy, and attentive, and their standards in Chinese and mathematics were high.

In September 1976, the school opened a fourth Form 1 class (X, Y, and Z were joined by U) to accommodate 50 per cent of "outside" students in Form 1 and to retain as many as possible of their own students from the two Primary 6 classes. Three years later, ED replaced SSEE with SSPA in allocating students. This new method of allocation resulted in students with even lower standards of English being assigned to the school. English teaching was slowed down because everything had to be repeated in Chinese. After the first term of 1979/1980, a major reorganisation took place, and instead of streaming, Form 1 had two classes of girls from its Junior School and two classes of "outside" girls.[95] The two groups were taught separately. The girls from the Junior School were in the U/X groups and the new girls were in the Y/Z groups. Because of the similarity in background of the

---

93. Minutes of School Council Meeting, 22 October 1957.
94. Minutes of School Council Meeting, 28 October 1958.
95. Minutes of School Council Meeting, 16 March 1979.

girls within each group, teaching and learning progress was made at optimal pace, with the teachers and girls in the Y/Z group making an effort to be on par with the other group in English.

This reorganisation proved to be an effective strategy for absorbing a large group of new students of disparate accomplishments into the same form. However, as the Junior School students and the "outside" girls came from different backgrounds, the couple of years when they were kept apart with less opportunities for the two groups of students to mingle and learn from each other inadvertently led to some perceived discrimination. An effort was made by the headmistresses, the teachers, PTA, and the student body to rectify the situation and to prevent such a problem over the next few years.

The 1978 White Paper also proposed that 60 per cent of the 15-year-old population should be provided with subsidised senior secondary places (Form 4 to Form 6) in 1981, but that Form 3 students had to pass the Junior Secondary Education Assessment (JSEA). During 1981, all 156 Form 3 students in DGS passed the JSEA and were promoted to Form 4. During 1984, the first batch of students with 50 per cent "outside" girls, who entered Form 1 by SSPA in 1979, took the School Certificate Examination. The pass rate was 96.4 per cent, not different from previous years, and this percentage was considered very high for a four-class school.[96] The high academic standard of DGS had been maintained.[97]

Curriculum of Lower and Upper 6 Forms

Before 1953, students from Form 4 onwards were divided into academic and modern streams. At the end of Form 5, the students took the School Certificate Examination. When they passed the examination, the students could choose Form 6 academic if they wished to enter HKU or Form 6 modern if they were aiming for nursing, social services, or secretarial work as career paths (see Chapter 5). A few left to continue their studies overseas.

The matriculation curriculum changed in the 1953/1954 academic year from one to two years— the Upper and the Lower 6 Forms. DGS was the first girls' school to develop an Upper 6 Form. At that time, neither DGS nor DBS had adequate facilities or teachers to develop first-year university courses for all the subjects. DBS boys who wished to take the subjects offered at DGS, such as advanced levels of biology, history, and Chinese, would go to DGS for their lessons, while DGS girls went to DBS for physics, chemistry, and geography.[98] Realising that this arrangement could not go on for long in view of the distance separating the two schools, DGS decided to have another laboratory for physics and chemistry

---

96. Headmistress's Report, Senior School, December 1981.
97. Headmistress's Report, 1984; Speech Day Booklet, November 1984, 28, 29.
98. Headmistress's Report, October 1954.

The Great Expansion: 1953 to 1985

and to renovate the biology laboratory.[99] The collaboration with DBS ended after 1957/1958 because DBS had completed the reorganisation of its own Upper 6 Form.

From the 1950s, women in Hong Kong gained more recognition in the family and in society because of the growing economic role they played. With improvement in household earnings, families were more willing to send their girls to schools and universities with the hope that they too would become professionals. In the 1960s, fewer and fewer girls joined the commercial course after passing the School Certificate Examination as they aspired to something more challenging. Students from wealthier families left for higher education abroad, but the Hong Kong School Certificate did not give them direct entry to universities overseas. In 1965, HKU announced that it would abolish the Ordinary Level Matriculation Examination in 1966. Girls who passed the School Certificate Examination in July 1965 might, if they wished to matriculate, study for the full two years. The school took this opportunity to replace the commercial course with a new course—the new Form 6 General, which DBS had established in 1962. This course would lead to ordinary level London General Certificate Examination (GCE-O) and enable students to enter UK schools for the advanced level matriculation or to take the College Entrance Examination Board for entry to US colleges and universities. The subjects included English, Chinese, French, religious knowledge, history, geography, English literature, dressmaking, human anatomy and physiology, British constitution, biology, chemistry, physics, and mathematics. DGS became the only school in Hong Kong to teach the GCE subjects.[100] In 1976, the curriculum was further developed to suit candidates for the Chinese University Matriculation Examination, which could be taken one year after the School Certificate Examination.[101]

Because the students in Upper 6 were older and more mature than students in other forms, the school created a Sixth Form Centre to provide for them not only the appropriate curriculum but also a physical space and environment that were conducive to learning and the exchange of ideas. It was located on the fifth and sixth floors of the Centenary Building where vacant dormitories had been renovated using donations from Major Churn's family. The sixth formers had a lounge in which to relax, reading cubicles for work, lecture rooms, classrooms with more adaptable furniture, and lockers instead of unwieldy desks.[102] The Sixth Form Centre was completed in October 1972.

---

99.   Minutes of School Council Meeting, 24 January 1956.

100. Headmistress's Report, November 1964.

101. Minutes of School Council meeting, 12 March 1976.

102. Minutes of School Council Meeting, 19 October 1971; "Concerning the Role and Functions of the Sixth Form", *Quest* (1973–1974): 110.

Figure 6.12: Miss E. M. Gibbins unveiling the plaque of the Sixth Form Centre, 1972. Source: *Quest* 1973–1974, 110.

A Broad Liberal Education

The school had always believed that students should have an education based on ethics and moral principles and not an economic or utilitarian education with the sole aim of promoting economic prosperity and individual wealth. Although specialisation began at Form 4 level, the school offered general arts (history and English literature) courses in Form 4 Academic, while general science courses were added to Form 4 Modern. Even though students might not be taking these subjects in the School Certificate Examination, they were still considered as important as any other.[103] The curriculum of Form 6 General reflected a broad liberal education. Two conferences were held every year with a panel of outside speakers on various topics including Christianity, Buddhism, Confucianism, Democracy, Communism, and other political theories.[104] Even though DGS is an Anglican school and embraces Christianity fully, it still feels it is important for students to know about other religious practices, the diversity of beliefs, and the need for tolerance and respect of individual rights.

---

103. Headmistress's Report, September 1959.
104. Minutes of School Council Meeting, 27 June 1969.

The Great Expansion: 1953 to 1985   145

From the 1970s, during the week before the break for Christmas each year, a series of special events took place. In addition to excursions, special seminars were organised. Mrs Symons usually gave a talk to Form 3, 4, 5, and 6 students on careers. Outside speakers were invited to give presentations on topics such as the population explosion, teenage problems, drugs, careers, and university education abroad. In 1975, for example, a seminar on drugs was held for Forms 4 to 6, followed by a discussion. The topics that were chosen helped students to understand the workings of a harmonious society, the environment, and the problems encountered by their generation.

Innovations: Sex, Political, and Religious Education

The ED had regulations and recommendations for the curriculum to ensure uniformity and a reasonable standard among schools. DGS followed these regulations, but at the same time, added some innovations to provide a broad liberal education for its students.

DGS was the first girls' school in Hong Kong to offer sex education. Mrs Symons foresaw the inevitable arrival of the sexual revolution in Hong Kong, accompanied by the risks of unwanted pregnancies and sexually transmitted diseases. In early 1967, she decided to introduce sex education after discussing the matter with parents in the PTA as well as with teachers and the girls themselves.[105] On the day of the first lesson, photographers and reporters arrived in the school in full force, raring for controversy; after all, this was the first girls' school in Hong Kong brave enough to put sex education on the curriculum. Mrs Symons was ridiculed by some sections of the community and condemned for giving girls sex education, which was seen by some as an act of "evil heresy". Many schools shied away from this natural and relevant education until years later.

The 1967 Communist-inspired riots in Hong Kong had a profound effect on Mrs Symons. After the incident, Mrs Symons was deeply sympathetic to the families that decided to take their daughters out of school and emigrate. The most pressing questions the students asked of themselves, their friends, their parents, and their teachers, were "Should I go away to study and settle?" or "Should I stay in Hong Kong?" These were prescient questions, and they were repeated in following generations of DGS girls and among students at other Hong Kong schools. Mrs Symons felt that the students should be more informed about the various types of government and political theories when making decisions about their future, so she introduced two courses on Education for Citizenship in 1969. These included lessons on civic responsibilities and political theories. In Forms 1, 2, and 3, teachers of Chinese subjects gave lessons on Civics and Citizenship, following the main Chinese textbooks that were used in government schools. In Forms 4, 5, and 6,

---

105. Headmistress's Report, April 1967.

teachers of scripture, history, economics, and public affairs were responsible for political theories. It was courageous of Mrs Symons to teach politics in the classroom without the support or assent of the government of the day. In 1974, she appointed Mr Mok Chiu Yu, a social and political activist, to teach economics, economics and public affairs, and government and public affairs, even though Mrs Symons was told by the Chief Justice that Mr Mok should not be allowed to register as a teacher. Mr Mok was popular among students, especially as a careers master; under his aegis, various professionals gave talks to the school, and he also supervised the students' careers committee. He served the school for fifteen years before he left to pursue his dream—to change the world through cultural activities in the community.[106]

Improvement in Pedagogy

Over the years, teaching methods at DGS had improved steadily in most subjects, in particular in Chinese, English, science, and geography, partly owing to curriculum reform, introduced by the Curriculum Development Committee of the ED, and partly as a result of innovations made by Mrs Symons and her staff.

Mrs Symons disliked rote memorisation as a method of learning; this was used frequently in the teaching of Chinese language subjects. Despite the efforts of Miss Hurrell to improve the standard of Chinese in the early 1950s, few students at DGS took ordinary level Chinese in Lower Form 6, because it was perceived to be too difficult or too dull, and it was hard to get good marks in matriculation examinations. All girls opted for lower level Chinese, as this would satisfy the requirement for matriculation. As the Chinese language became more important in Hong Kong, Mrs Symons invited Mr Chan Yik Cham, or "Small" Chan, to upgrade Chinese teaching. Mr Chan began by organising Chinese plays in the school, and the proceeds from the sale of tickets went toward the purchase of Chinese books for the library.[107] The first Chinese play, *The Last Rose of Summer* (曲終人杳), presented in the school on 8 and 9 July 1953, was a huge success.[108] Mr Chan was responsible for everything on the stage, as well as backstage, working as director, lighting manager, sound effects technician, scenery designer and builder, and renter of costumes. His enthusiasm was infectious and motivated the students.[109] He also formed the Chinese Literary Club and invited many outside speakers to highlight Chinese cultural interests. As a result of his efforts, more students became interested and took Ordinary level and Advanced level Chinese matriculation examinations. By the late 1970s and early 1980s,

---

106. Email communication from Mr Mok Chiu Yu, 14 November 2020.
107. Minutes of School Council Meeting, 27 October 1959.
108. Announcement of "The Last Rose of Summer", BHA DGS 1953 Minutes Files.
109. "Report on the Flowers of Martyrdom", *Quest* (1960): 35.

The Great Expansion: 1953 to 1985

there was no difference in the percentage of pass rates in Chinese and in English in the School Certificate Examination. Mrs Tang (née Ng) Hung Sang joined the school in 1965 and succeeded Mr Chan after his retirement in 1979 as head of the Chinese Department. Mrs Tang expanded his work by encouraging students to take part in competitions within the school in calligraphy, quizzes in Chinese history, and interschool (between schools) competitions in drama, as well as debates in Chinese.

English was the medium of instruction and used in all forms of communication in DGS. Students were encouraged to join the debating society to take part in interhouse (different houses within the school) and interschool debates, and to participate in drama competitions to improve their spoken English and diction. In the 1960s and 1970s, when there was growing awareness of the importance of the Chinese language, Mrs Symons had perpetuated the rule that only English was to be spoken at all times in the school. This, together with appointing expatriates to teach English and other subjects, maintained the excellent English of DGS graduates. Most Chinese parents in Hong Kong at that time, even though they were conscious of their origin, would go a long way to get their children into a school that used English as the medium of instruction, as fluency in English ensured a better future for their children both in Hong Kong and overseas.

The teaching of geography in the upper forms also changed in the 1970s. The syllabus was rearranged with added emphasis on the human impact on the environment. Visits to sites such as the container terminal, together with exhibitions and lectures at universities and polytechnics, and field work on land use, were also undertaken to give students first-hand experience of the topics they were studying.

Academic Performance

The academic standard of the school improved progressively after the Second World War. The percentage of DGS students who passed the Hong Kong Certificate of Education Examination had been consistently above 90 per cent over the years since 1954,[110] compared with the average pass rate of 50 to 60 per cent among all Hong Kong schools. Similarly, the percentage of students who passed the Hong Kong Advanced Level Matriculation Examination after 1960 was always above 80 per cent, more often above 90 per cent (Figure 6.13).

---

110. Minutes of School Council Meeting, 20 July 1954.

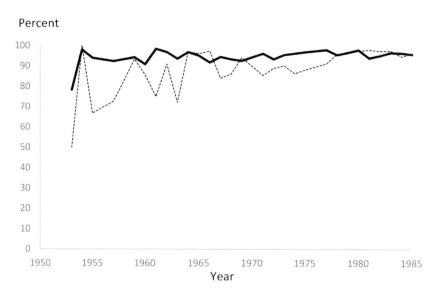

Figure 6.13: Percentage of students who passed HKCEE and HKALE, 1953 to 1985. Source: Minutes of School Council Meetings. Note: Solid black line=HKCEE, dotted line=HKALE.

School Life

Religious Activities: Morning Assembly, Student Christian Association

By tradition, the school had a morning assembly, a time for girls from Christian homes to stand quietly during prayers with girls from Buddhist, Muslim, and atheist or agnostic homes. All learned to respect the opinions of others and the Christian ideals of love, peace, service, compassion, thankfulness, justice, endurance, and humility that the school has always tried to impart. The service was brief and simple: introit, hymn, reading from a Bible passage, and sometimes comments from the Headmistress to reinforce a significant point, followed by notices. Many old girls, Christians and non-Christians alike, have valued the morning assembly when the whole school gathered together in fellowship.

Religious worship played an important role in school life, especially for the boarders and resident staff. In September 1953, Miss Nancy Wilson, who had served the school briefly earlier, returned to DGS from the Presbyterian Mission in New Zealand at the request of Mrs Symons to become the school "chaplain" and scripture teacher.[111] Her warm, enthusiastic, and loving personality led to the conversion of a number of girls. The Sunday evening service in the school chapel was usually led by the Vicar of St Andrew's Church or Christ Church. Established in 1954, the Student Christian Association had about eighty members

---

111. Minutes of School Council Meeting, 17 March 1953.

in the beginning. Two meetings were held each month, one with an outside speaker and the second allowing discussion among the members on certain topics. They held joint conferences with equivalent groups in other schools and helped to teach Sunday school at St Thomas's Church, and also gave pre-Christmas gifts to the children.[112] Retreats were organised from time to time depending on the needs of the students, usually in the Christian Research Centre at Tao Fung Shan.[113] Bishop Hall believed in education for education's sake. The school did not require any staff or students to become Anglicans, but there were always some girls who were baptised and confirmed during their years at DGS.

Health Programme

In November 1952, a mass chest X-ray examination was carried out by the government Tuberculosis Service for the first time in DGS when teachers, students, and non-teaching staff were asked to take part, and those with abnormalities were sent to one of the government chest clinics for further investigation.[114] In 1953, the government School Health Programme broadened its service to cover students other than those in government schools. Participants paid just $5 a year for medical examinations, including hospitalisation. During that year, 150 girls joined the School Health Programme, all receiving BCG vaccinations and typhoid immunisation. Eighty-six girls received dental treatment.[115] The School Health Programme changed its name over the years and is now called the Student Health Service.

Extracurricular Activities: Building a Strong Foundation

As early as 1947, Miss Hurrell initiated field trips for Class I students after their examinations in June. When she retired in 1951, the practice became less regular. In the 1970s, Mrs Symons reinstituted the practice so students could experience many aspects of life in Hong Kong. In 1977, for example, a total of forty-six visits were made by students, with pre-visit briefings and debriefings afterwards. The lower forms visited schools for handicapped children, hospitals, newspaper companies, Hong Kong Philharmonic Orchestra rehearsals, the Kadoorie Farm, and the airport. The upper forms toured banks, factories, the Independent Commission Against Corruption, Town Gas Centre, the *South China Morning Post*, the container terminal, a sewage treatment plant, Lai Chi Kok incinerator, and various open days and exhibitions on social work. Teachers and students found these

---

112. "Student Christian Association", *The Quest* (1954): 20.
113. "Retreat", *Quest* (1981–1982): 8.
114. Minutes of School Council Meeting, 8 December 1952.
115. "The Headmistress's Report", *The Quest* (1953): 5.

visits interesting and rewarding. In 1984, the number of school visits increased to fifty-five, spanning different forms and subjects.[116] Regular school visits as part of the curriculum in Hong Kong schools were only mandated after 1997. DGS was over twenty years ahead in learning through interactive experience.

The varieties of ECA during this period (1953 to 1985) are shown in Table 6.3.

Table 6.3: Extracurricular activities in DGS from 1953 to 1985 by period of commencement

Arts/Music	Sports	Academic	Hobbies	Services (social/school)	Religion
Before 1953					
Choirs	Tennis	Quiz	Gardening	Brownies	
Voice Solo	Hockey	Excursions	Needlework	Girl Guides	
Instrument Solos	Gymnastics	Publication*		Girls' Club	
Drama	Netball			Boys' Club	
1953–1985					
Chinese Choir	Fencing	Science	Home Economics	Citizens' Club	Student Christian Association
String Orchestra	Volleyball	English Debating Society	Bridge	Young Citizens' Club	Youth Fellowship
Percussion Band	Rounders				
Symphony Orchestra	Athletics	Chinese Literary		Red Cross	Retreats
Instrumental Classes (Western/Chinese)	Swimming	Creative Arts		Career Committee	
Art	Life-Saving	History			
Chinese Orchestra	Badminton	Astronomy			
Madrigal Group	Table Tennis	Conservancy			
Drama and debate	Cross Country	Current Affairs			
	Folk Dance	Putonghua			
	Bowling				

Source: *Quest* and Speech Day Booklets 1953 to 1985. Note: The Duke of Edinburgh's Award Scheme started in 1962/1963, not belonging to a single category in the table. *School magazine.

The school magazine, *The Quest Magazine of the Diocesan Girls' School* (*The Quest*) simplified to *Quest* in 1960, evolved over the years into a magazine centred on student life and

---

116. Headmistress's Report 1984, Minutes of School Council Meeting, 15 June 1984.

The Great Expansion: 1953 to 1985

activities with mostly students on the editorial committee and supervised by two to three teachers. In 1972, the Chinese section of *Quest* was given a Chinese name, 研幾, reflecting the increasing importance of Chinese in the school. In the 1970s and 1980s, the magazine became more complicated and departmentalised with members of the editorial committee assuming more direct roles in reporting school activities, such as clubs, sports, French, art, and photography, with representatives from each form increasing the size of the editorial committee.

The Duke of Edinburgh's Award Scheme (renamed Hong Kong Awards for Young People in April 1997) was offered for the first time in 1956.[117] This was designed to encourage teenagers to develop their talents and find new interests in their leisure. The emphasis was not on competition with others but on guiding young people to achieve a set of standards by their own efforts in four categories: design for living, interest, service, and adventure.

In 1959, the school had a new gymnasium and a new expatriate Physical Education (PE) teacher, Miss Helen Macgregor Paterson. Gymnastics and rounders teams were organised. Around the same time, training in athletics began with Mr Kennedy Skipton (an English teacher) on Tuesday afternoons at the King's Park and on Saturday morning at DBS with Mr James Lowcock,[118] enabling a few girls to enter the Interschool Athletics Competition. The school had a number of outstanding athletes over the years, including Susan Johnson in long jump,[119] and Pamela Baker in both high jump and long jump.[120] In 1963, the school came first in the interschool swimming and interschool life-saving gala, and was champion of both competitions for a number of years. DGS won the Omega Rose Bowl, which was awarded to the school with the highest points in athletics, swimming, badminton, table tennis, basketball, and volleyball, every year from 1966 to 1973, then again in 1975, 1977 to 1979, and 1981 to 1985.[121] During this period, the following girls received the Sportsgirl of the Year award: Pamela Baker, 1966; Barbara Winyard, 1967; Anne Mikel, 1968 and 1969; Kim Fenton, 1970; Susan Johnson, 1971; Diane U, 1973; Rita Bendall, 1975; Angela Lau, 1979; Krista Ma, 1981; Michele Rosario, 1982; Sandra Khoo, 1983; and Ingrid Lai, 1985.[122] In the early 1980s, the school began to employ professional coaches for the athletics team. Mr Tang Kun Loi first joined the school as a coach and later became one of the PE teachers, contributing to the mounting interest of students in sports and the success of the school

---

117. The Hong Kong Award for Young People, accessed 11 March 2022, https://www.ayp.org.hk/.

118. "Skipton House Report", *Quest* (1960): 31.

119. "Girls Set Four New Records", *South China Morning Post*, 23 March 1968.

120. "Diocesan Schools Reign Supreme", *South China Morning Post*, 2 April 1968.

121. Headmistress's Reports available from respective years from 1966 to 1985, *Quest* during that period, and BOCHK Bauhinia Bowl, accessed 9 December 2021, https://en.wikipedia.org/wiki/BOCHK_Bauhinia_Bowl. In 1984–1985, the award was shared with Heep Yunn School.

122. Headmistress's Reports 1966–1985, *Quest* during that period, and BOCHK Bauhinia Bowl; 1966 means for the academic year 1965–1966, 1967 means 1966–1967, and 1985 means 1984–1985.

Figure 6.14: The first Omega Rose Bowl Award presented to DGS, 1965/1966.
From left to right: Miss M. Williams, E. Sinn, Mr Campbell, P. Baker, Mrs C. J. Symons, Mrs M. Reeves.
Source: *Quest* 1966, 35.

in interschool competitions. He believed that during the tenure of Mrs Symons, the school built a strong foundation for sports development.[123]

When the Hong Kong Schools Music Festival began in 1949, the school participated in various categories of competitions every year. A string orchestra was formed in 1966 with help from the ED and a donation of $2,500 to purchase musical instruments.[124] At that time, there were fifty girls learning to play violin, six viola, and nine cello. These efforts came to fruition in 1970 when the school came second in the intermediate string orchestra category,[125] and then took first place in 1972 in both the senior and intermediate categories. A full symphony orchestra was formed in 1973, and a Chinese orchestra was established a little later. In 1973 and 1975, the Senior School Orchestra came first in the Music Festival.

---

123. Email communication from Mr K. L. Tang, 20 August 2020.
124. Headmistress's Report, November 1966.
125. "Results at a Glance", *South China Morning Post*, 15 March 1970.

Plate 1: The Centenary building built in 1959. Photograph taken in 2000 celebrating the 140th Anniversary. Source: School Archives.

Plate 2: The gymnasium built in 1959. Source: School Archives.

Plate 3: Swimming team in the swimming pool built in 1965. Source: School Archives.

Plate 4: Extension I building (right) and Extension II building (left) completed in 1993 and 1996 respectively. Source: School Archives.

Plate 5: The musical *The King and I* staged in Shatin Town Hall in 1996. Source: School Archives.

Plate 6: The 150th Anniversary Celebration Dinner held in the Hong Kong Convention & Exhibition Centre on 5 May 2010. Source: School Archives.

Plate 7: DGS family members honoured to serve as torchbearers in the Beijing 2008 Olympic Torch Relay in Hong Kong. Source: School Archives.

The school offered a number of concerts each year, including Christmas concerts, and also performed at services at St John's Cathedral[126] and during prize-giving ceremonies. During the 1950s and 1960s, DGS produced plays both in English and in Chinese, and entered interschool drama competitions. The play that won the competition was often repeated in the school and generated some funds both for the school and for charities. Drama became less popular after the 1970s because of the increasing number of ECAs and the long hours required after school for play rehearsals.

DGS and DBS often had joint teams competing together in categories such as mixed choirs and madrigal singing, in addition to joint musical productions. Over the years, in many families while the girls attended DGS, their brothers were attending DBS. Both schools enjoy the advantages of being single-sex schools where girls are free of the pressure to compete with boys in male-dominated subjects such as math and sciences, while boys can pursue traditional "feminine" interests such as music and poetry more easily. Yet, they provide plenty of opportunities for cooperation in extracurricular activities, where students can learn cooperation with members of the opposite sex as in co-educational schools.

In 1963, social services work became more organised after The Hon. Hugh David MacEwen Barton donated 200 shares of Jardine, Matheson and Co. Ltd towards the development of the DGS Citizens' Club. The School Council appointed a subcommittee to formulate regulations to govern this grant, which was to be given out for social projects.[127] By 1969, there were fifty-two girls who did voluntary work each week in a number of charitable organisations, helping out in various activities such as teaching boys and girls to read and write, feeding babies, helping disabled people, and translating letters into English.[128]

There were interschool competitions such as debates and essays to promote interschool cultural exchange and friendship. A series of joint school projects was organised in the 1970s, as shown in Table 6.4.

In the Junior School, ECAs took place throughout the academic year. In 1980, Chinese chess games were conducted for primary students during Wednesday lunchtimes, and different activities took place after school hours: ballet for beginners on Mondays, Brownies on Tuesdays, gymnastics on Wednesdays, and swimming and other sports training when required by the school.[129]

Since there were so many ECAs, the school emphasised to students that they were to choose responsibly. Once joined, each activity should be attended. Through these activities, students learned new skills, improved their self-esteem, built up discipline, and shared in the mutual obligation of working as a group.

---

126. Headmistress's Report, May 1962.
127. Minutes of School Council Meeting, 12 March 1963.
128. "Citizens' Club", *Quest* (1964): 19.
129. Junior School Headmistress's Report, November 1980.

Figure 6.15: Senior School Junior Choir, conducted by Mrs Poppy Crosby, winning in the Hong Kong Schools Music Festival, 1970. Source: School Archives.

Figure 6.16: The Chinese play "The Flowers of Martyrdom", 1959. Source: *Quest* 1960, 3.

Table 6.4: Examples of interschool competitions and joint school projects, 1953 to 1985*

Competitions	Joint School Projects
Hong Kong Schools Music Festival	Joint Schools Debate
Hong Kong Schools Speech Festival	Joint Schools Science Exhibition
Radio Hong Kong Quiz	Joint School Art Exhibition
Rediffusion Television Quiz	Hong Kong Schools' Joint Economics and Public Affairs Exhibition
Shell Essay Competition	
Omega Rose Bowl	
Interschool Swimming Competition	
Hong Kong Interschool Athletics Competition	
Royal Commonwealth Essay Competition	
SCMP Forum Essay Competition	
American University Club Speech Contest	
Interschool Olympiad	

Source: *Quest* from 1953 to 1985. *Projects were started in different years.

The End of an Era: Retirement of Dr Symons

Mrs Symons followed the school's motto of "Daily Giving Service" throughout her life. Her opportunity to serve Hong Kong arrived in 1966 when she was appointed a Justice of the Peace. In 1969, she was assigned by the government to the Urban Council where she joined committees on Recreation and Amenities, City Hall and Library, and Public Health, and helped improve various recreation amenities, gardens and parks, and a low-cost housing scheme.[130] Mrs Symons was appointed by Governor MacLehose to be a member of the Legislative Council on 5 July 1972.[131] While working with the Governor during that decade, she actively promoted the enactment of various legislation with progressive policies. It was in the battle against corruption that she personally valued and contributed most. She served on the two most important committees of the ICAC: the Advisory Committee on Corruption and the Operations Target Committee.[132] In 1978, she reached the pinnacle of her career in public service when she was appointed to the Executive Council on which

---

130. Symons, *Looking at the Stars*, 67.

131. Hong Kong Legislative Council, Official Report of Proceedings, 5 July 1972.

132. Annual Report by the Commissioner of the Independent Commission Against Corruption, 1974; prepared by J. Cater, CBE, JP, Commissioner of the ICAC, for submission to His Excellency Governor Sir Murray MacLehose in accordance with Section 17 of the ICAC Ordinance, 1974.

she served for two years, remaining afterwards on the Board of Education and the ICAC committees.[133]

This decade of public service to the community was also a period of intense education reforms and social change. The amount of time and energy demanded by her public service work was considerable, and inevitably diverted some of her attention from the school. This, at times, created problems over the matter of delegation of authority and decision making in her absence. But the strong management team helped to keep the school running. Her unwavering commitment to public service inspired future headmistresses, who attempted to emulate her.

The 1970s brought a series of personal losses as well as honours to Mrs Symons. She lost her husband in 1974, her spiritual mentor Bishop Hall in 1975, and her mother in 1979. In the same decade, Mrs Symons received numerous honours: Officer of the Most Excellent Order of the British Empire (OBE) in 1971, the degree of Doctor of Laws *honoris causa* from the University of Hong Kong for her outstanding public service,[134] and Commander of the Most Excellent Order of the British Empire (CBE) in 1978.

In 1977, before Mrs Symons reached the retirement age of 60 years, the School Council unanimously resolved to invite her to continue working until she reached 65.[135] The School Council also set up a special retirement fund for her. In 1981, two years before she turned 65, the staff members of DGS signed a petition addressed to the Chairman of the School Council asking for the extension of her service beyond 1983. The ED also expressed its pleasure to be able to grant the extension.[136] During 1983, the school celebrated Dr Symons' thirtieth anniversary as Headmistress of DGS. The highlight of this event was the performance of a choir made up of school staff members, which earned the most applause.

On 17 May 1984, Dr Symons, by then 66 years of age and getting tired, wrote to Bishop Peter Kong-kit Kwong (Bishop of Hong Kong and Macau 1981–1998, Archbishop and Primate of HKSKH 1998–2006),[137] who had succeeded Bishop Baker, that she wished to resign for health and personal reasons as Supervisor and Headmistress of DGS at the end of March 1985—a most difficult and heart-wrenching decision. She hoped that Bishop

---

133. Peter Bernard Harris, "Catherine Joyce Symons, 1978 Congregation. Doctor of Laws (honoris causa), The University of Hong Kong".

134. Harris, "Catherine Joyce Symons".

135. Minutes of School Council Meeting, 4 November 1977.

136. Director of Education to Bishop Peter Kwong, 26 March 1982.

137. In 1951, following the establishment of the People's Republic of China, the Diocese of Hong Kong and Macao became a detached diocese, which did not belong to any Province. In 1998 the Province of Hong Kong Sheng Kung Hui (consisting of the Diocese of Hong Kong Island, the Diocese of Eastern Kowloon, the Diocese of Western Kowloon, and the Missionary Area of Macau) was established. The Most Rev. Peter Kwong was elected the first Archbishop and Primate of the Province. He retired in 2006.

The Great Expansion: 1953 to 1985   157

Kwong and the School Council would find a suitable successor.[138] What remained was for the school to show their gratitude and to send her off to her retirement with a gala concert at the City Hall on 18 March 1985. At the end of the concert, representatives from the Junior School and the Senior School presented their souvenirs and speeches.

Most of the students discovered that, although an imposing figure, Dr Symons was warm and caring, and they had learned to revere and love her. After many farewell parties and dinners, she left for Surrey, England, where she made her new home. In retirement, she published her memoirs, entitled *Looking at the Stars: Memoirs of Catherine Joyce Symons*, and visited old girls in Canada in 1988. Between 1986 to 1999, she was invited several times to visit Hong Kong by old girls and Mrs Elim Lau, the new Headmistress, to talk to the students at assembly and in small groups, and to meet the prefects and the staff. Dr Symons passed away in Surrey on 11 June 2004 at the age of 85.

Dr Catherine Joyce Symons, as the head of DGS for thirty-two years, had a long and illustrious career in education and public service. She expanded the school and vastly improved its performance in academic and extracurricular activities. A gifted teacher and a visionary educationist, she contributed enormously to education not only for students in DGS but also for all students in Hong Kong. While pushing for compulsory free education for school-age children in Hong Kong, she also fought for the freedom to introduce novel programmes to suit the particular needs of students in her school. She believed that her school had a duty to try to inculcate a sense of values, based on the best elements in Christian, Chinese, and Western democratic culture, and to equip each student with intellectual honesty and critical thinking, so she could become an educated woman with innate toughness and poise, and a well-rounded person. To achieve these aims, teachers, she said, should teach their students to think, to assess, to deliberate, and to live unselfishly and walk with pride into the future.[139] She promoted a broad liberal education before specialisation, and pioneered the introduction of sex education and political education to the school. She encouraged extracurricular activities to build up the character of the students and to induce a sense of unity and belonging. She reminded her students always to be honest and fair and to fight for what was right; she also instilled in them a sense of responsibility to contribute in their own ways to the society they lived in, in keeping with the school motto of "Daily Giving Service".

The retirement of Dr Symons could be seen as the end of an era for DGS. Her dedicated tenure of thirty-two years provided a sense of stability and continuity, which was crucial in allowing DGS to grow in a rapidly changing society.

---

138. Dr Symons to Bishop Kwong, 17 May 1984.
139. Headmistress's Address, Speech Day, 21 November 1984.

Chapter 7

Consolidation and New Challenges: 1985 to 1999

Mrs Elim Lau (née Pong, 劉龐以琳) became Headmistress of DGS in April 1985. It was several months after the signing of the Sino-British Joint Declaration, according to which Hong Kong would cease to be a British Dependent Territory on 1 July 1997 and become a Special Administrative Region of the People's Republic of China under the "One Country, Two Systems" principle that would be maintained for the next fifty years. The majority of people accepted the joint declaration and looked forward to building a future in Hong Kong. Some, however, emigrated, mainly to the UK, Canada, USA, Australia, Singapore, and New Zealand.

When the Tiananmen Square incident erupted on 4 June 1989, people in Hong Kong reacted with anger, fear, and despair. Their confidence in Hong Kong's future was suddenly shaken. Many families began to migrate to other countries again. In 1990, the outflow of people was 62,000, reaching a peak of 66,000 in 1992.[1]

After the Tiananmen Square incident, the Chinese government concentrated on modernisation and industrialisation to improve the livelihood of its citizens. When China emerged as the "factory of the world", its gross domestic product (GDP) grew at a rate of 10 per cent or above each year. In the meantime, the people in Hong Kong regained their confidence in their future, appeased by the famous pragmatic saying, "It doesn't matter whether a cat is black or white, as long as it catches mice", and they started to rebuild society as the economy began to grow again.[2] At the time of the handover in 1997, the GDP

---

1. Government Information Report, "Hong Kong Population: Characteristics and Trends", accessed 19 March 2021, https://www.info.gov.hk/info/population/eng/pdf/report_eng.pdf.

2. Steve Tsang, *A Modern History of Hong Kong* (Hong Kong: Hong Kong University Press, 2006), 178–179.

per capita of Hong Kong exceeded that of Britain, but there was great disparity of wealth, which was enjoyed by only a small proportion of the population.[3]

The 1980s saw, for the first time, signs of an ageing population in Hong Kong as the number of residents below the age of 25 fell in comparison with the previous decade. The birth rate, which had started to decrease in the late 1950s, continued to drop during the 1980s.[4]

In the meantime, the population in Hong Kong became increasingly more educated. By 1996, 95 per cent of boys and 97 per cent of girls attended junior secondary school (12–16 age group) and close to 60 per cent of boys and 70 per cent of girls attended senior secondary school (17–18 age group), a higher proportion of girls than boys—a tremendous achievement for girls.[5] An equal proportion of boys (21.9 per cent) and girls (22 per cent) received matriculation or university education (19–24 age group). The increase in the number of girls receiving higher education took place because women were able to work outside their homes; this was partly brought about by the government permitting domestic workers from other Asian countries to work in Hong Kong from 1974. The growth of a well-educated population in Hong Kong accelerated its development into a financial centre in the 1990s.

Education in Hong Kong: From Increasing Quantity to Improvement in Quality

Expansion of Post-secondary Education

Following the decline of the school-aged population, the demand for the expansion of primary and secondary education abated in the 1980s and 1990s respectively. The government, driven on the one hand by an ever-increasing number of secondary school graduates and on the other by the shortage of highly educated and skilled workers in many areas as a result of "brain drain" through emigration, turned to expansion of tertiary education. In the early 1980s, there were only two universities in Hong Kong, Hong Kong University (HKU) and the Chinese University of Hong Kong (CUHK). By the mid-1990s, Hong Kong had ten degree-granting institutions, eight of which were under the University Grants Committee. The remaining two were the Open Learning Institute of Hong Kong (later renamed Open University of Hong Kong and at present the Metropolitan University of Hong Kong, although it will likely change its name again in the near future) and the

---

3. Ian Scott, *Political Change and Crisis of Legitimacy* (Hong Kong: Oxford University Press, 1989), 236–239.

4. Hong Kong Medical and Health Service Annual Reports, Crude birth rates, 1950–2000.

5. Grace C. L. Mak, "Women and Education", in *Women and Girls in Hong Kong: Current Situation and Future Challenges*, ed. Susanne Y. P. Choi and Fanny M. Cheung (Hong Kong: Hong Kong Institute of Asia-Pacific Studies, The Chinese University of Hong Kong, 2012), 24.

Hong Kong Academy of Performing Arts, providing young people a variety of choices in higher education.

Education Commission Reports

During this period, the government, following the world trend, turned to improving the quality of education by implementing the recommendations of the report published in 1982 by an international panel of visitors from the Organisation for Economic Cooperation and Development (OECD), also known as the Llewellyn Report.[6] The panel reviewed the status of education in Hong Kong after a prolonged period of education expansion at the request of the Education Department. One of the recommendations of the Report was to establish an Education Commission to coordinate the development of education at different levels and to give advice on education policy.[7] The Education Commission Reports (ECR) and the responses of DGS to the proposals of the ECRs will be discussed in the section entitled "Challenges of Education Reforms and Education Commission Reports".

Extracurricular Activities: Recognised Programme for Whole Body-and-Mind Development

Before the Second World War, the scope of extracurricular activities (ECAs) was limited. ECAs were usually found in Anglo-Chinese grant schools and a few Chinese schools such as Pui Ching Middle School. In particular, musical activities were rare until the establishment of the Hong Kong Schools Music Association in 1941. There were Boy Scouts, Girl Guides, Cubs, and Brownies. Most girls' schools, including DGS, focused on social services, such as running boys' and girls' clubs, teaching poor children to read and write, and offering them food. After the Second World War, the establishment of the Hong Kong Schools Music Festival in 1949 and the Hong Kong Interschool Sports Competitions in the 1950s helped popularise ECAs in schools, especially in the Anglo-Chinese schools. As discussed in Chapter 6, ECAs, which became regarded as essential to body-and-mind development of young people, were formally accepted in the 1980s as part of the education structure. A striking feature of education in Hong Kong in the 1980s was the proliferation of ECAs in schools, and this became an important factor when students were considered for awards, and even sometimes for admission to "elite" schools.

---

6. Anthony Sweeting, *Educational History of Hong Kong, 1941–2001: Visions and Revisions* (Hong Kong: Hong Kong University Press, 2004), 339.

7. Sweeting, *Education in Hong Kong, 1941 to 2001*, 366.

Consolidation and New Challenges: 1985 to 1999

During the decade and a half running up to the handover in 1997, the Education Department (ED) continued to work with enthusiasm to expand post-secondary education in Hong Kong and to bring about education reforms to improve the quality of education. ECAs continued to blossom in schools during this period. This chapter focuses on the responses of DGS to a number of challenges, such as the pending handover, reforms to improve the quality of education, and evolving demands on the school to place greater emphasis on sciences, computers, and information technology (IT), as it made its way through the transitional years.

DGS and DGJS Headmistresses, 1985 to 1999

To cope with the challenges of this period, the school was fortunate to have the leadership of Mrs Elim Lau, an alumna and the first Chinese Headmistress of the school, who was appointed to succeed Dr Symons in 1985.[8] Like Dr Symons, she completed her kindergarten, primary, and secondary schooling at DGS. After university education at HKU and postgraduate studies in education, she returned to DGS to teach for two years. She then moved to the Kowloon Chamber of Commerce English Secondary School to become a part-time geography teacher in order to devote more time to her children. In September 1977, she began teaching full-time in DBS in various capacities until September 1983, when she was appointed Dean of Students (Deputy Head) at DBS, a position she held till 31 March 1985.

When Mrs Elim Lau became Headmistress of DGS, Mrs Daphne Quay Ying Blomfield was the Headmistress of the Junior School. At the same time, Mrs Doris Ho (née Ko, 何高雪瑤), also an alumna and an Administrative Officer in the Hong Kong government, was appointed the supervisor of both the Senior and Junior schools.[9] Before DGS became a Direct Subsidy Scheme School, even though the Senior School and the Junior School were different institutions, they had been managed under the Constitution of DGS by the same School Council. Since matters concerning both schools were discussed during the same School Council meeting, it was appropriate for the school supervisor of the two schools to be the same person. The Headmistress of the Senior School was an ex-officio member of the School Council, but not the Headmistress of the Junior School. Administratively, the two schools were different: the Senior School was a grant school receiving subsidy from

---

8. Minutes of School Council Meeting, 10 December 1984.

9. Among grant schools, the principal and the supervisor could be the same person during Mrs Symons's era, but the principal must have had several years' experience as a principal first. However, in the Education Ordinance, 2005 (Cap. 279 Education Ordinance—Section 40AJ Supervisor), it was clearly stated that the principal could not be the supervisor of the school; Functions of Supervisor, Education Bureau, HKSAR, accessed 6 July 2020, https://www.edb.gov.hk/en/sch-admin/sbm/corner-imc-sch/delegation-function-sv.html.

Figure 7.1a: Senior School: Mrs Elim Lau (née Pong) (Headmistress 1985–1999). Source: Mrs Elim Lau.

Figure 7.1b: Junior School: Mrs Daphne Quay-Ying Blomfield (Headmistress 1978–1989). Source: Mrs Daphne Blomfield.

Figure 7.1c: Junior School: Mrs Rebecca Luen-Yuen Yip (née Lit) (Headmistress 1989–1999). Source: Mrs Rebecca Yip.

the government while the Junior School was a private school. The two headmistresses worked independently.

Mrs Daphne Blomfield, recruited by Dr Symons to head the Junior School in 1978, shared the same vision as Dr Symons: to keep the Junior School as a small family school in which students knew one another. Mrs Blomfield dedicated eleven years of her life to serving the school with creativity, patience, and generosity. She was succeeded by Mrs Rebecca Luen Yuen Yip (née Lit, 葉列鸞琬), an alumna and an Anglican, who had spent most of her school years at DGS as a boarder because her parents were Anglican missionaries in China. Mrs Yip regarded DGS as her home. She taught at the Junior School after her training as a teacher in 1958 but emigrated to Canada in 1969. On returning to Hong Kong, she resumed teaching in her alma mater in 1979. In 1982, she became the Headmistress of Heep Yunn Primary School, and in 1985, at the request of Dr Symons, she returned to teach at the Junior School. When Mrs Blomfield retired in 1989, Mrs Yip was appointed Headmistress of the Junior School.[10] Dr Symons, who looked after Mrs Yip throughout

---

10. Minutes of School Council Meeting, 16 March 1989.

Consolidation and New Challenges: 1985 to 1999

her school life, told her a cardinal rule about being a school headmistress when she was appointed at Heep Yunn Primary School: never accept a personal gift from anyone inside or outside the school.

Administration during the Transitional Years

Mrs Elim Lau's tenure as Headmistress of DGS was not at all easy, as she had to fill the shoes of her predecessor, Dr Symons, whom she admired and emulated. It was her personal mission to successfully lead the school into the new era—the handover in 1997—which she did splendidly.

Mrs Lau made the very wise decision at the beginning of her tenure to continue the policies laid down by her predecessors, as they had worked well. As she settled in, she introduced changes where she saw the need for them, while adhering to ED policies. However, in the decade leading up to 1997, a number of challenges arose: these included the problem of emigration of staff and students during the school year, the upkeep of the ageing school buildings, the demands of the ECR which were published every two years, and the emphasis on computerisation and the use of information technology (IT) in teaching.

During Mrs Lau's tenure, school enrolment increased from 926 in the Senior School and 494 in the Junior School in 1985 to 1,017 and 631 respectively in 1999. The increase was slightly greater in the Junior School because of the increase from two to three classes for each primary level in 1996. Despite the decrease in the primary school-age population in the 1980s, enrolment in DGS continued to rise steadily. In 1985/1986 the whole school had a teaching staff of sixty-eight, giving a student–teacher ratio of 20.8:1, the same as 1956.

In the 1970s, Mrs Symons had divided the teachers into four departments according to subjects. Each department was headed by a senior teacher and given an annual budget. With growing specialisation, Mrs Lau increased the number of departments in the school to nine: English and French; Chinese; mathematics; biology and general science; physics and chemistry; geography; history; economics, principles of accounts, sociology and psychology; and art, music, physical education, and home economics. In 1990, the number of departments was increased to thirteen showing the changing emphasis on different topics (see Chapter 15, Table 15.2). The heads of departments were responsible for the daily running of their departments, as well as teaching and learning activities.

After the Second World War, the school recruited expatriates to teach English, who formed about 50 per cent of the teaching staff. However, Figures 7.2 and 7.3 show that the teaching staff were almost all Chinese in the Senior and the Junior School in 1987 and 1989 respectively. In the 1970s, there was a progressive increase in Chinese graduates from HKU, and many took postgraduate teaching diplomas or a degree in education and became adept in using English for teaching. The demand for higher pay and living allowance deterred the

Figure 7.2: Mrs E. Lau and Senior School staff, 1987/1988. Source: *Quest* 1987–1989, 66.
From left to right:
Fifth row: Mr W. K. Lau, Miss J. Clark, Mrs E. Lee, Mrs E. Lung
Fourth row: Mrs C. Weng, Miss R. M. Griffiths, Mrs J. Oxley, Mr K. L. Tang, Mr H. Y. Leung, Mrs Y. W. Lau, Miss S. So, Miss L. Lau, Mrs H. Wickins, Mrs V. Chan
Third row: Mrs R. Wong, Miss M. C. Lau, Miss A. Wong, Miss I. Mok, Miss B. Lee, Mrs D. Chan, Mrs M. Tsui, Miss A. Chan, Mrs H. Tang, Mrs A. Lee
Second row: Mrs P. Hui, Mrs D. Lai, Mrs B. L. Donnan, Mrs C. Hung, Mrs R. Lee, Miss M. Nee, Miss K. Wong, Mrs A. Ma, Miss M. Lee, Mrs R. Pei, Mr R. Lau
Front row: Miss R. Keung, Mrs I. So, Mrs A. Hurst, Mr C. Y. Mok, Mrs Y. L. Lam, Mrs E. Lau, Mrs P. Kan, Mrs H. S. Tang, Mrs M. Chan, Mrs J. Chiu, Miss E. Lo
(Absent): Mrs K. Lamsam, Mrs T. Wong, Mrs D. Choy

engagement of expatriate teachers. In the 1980s, there was also a restriction on appointing expatriates to teach English in government and aided schools.

As a private school, the Junior School charged higher fees than the Senior School, a grant school. The annual fees of the Junior School increased from $1,500 in 1973/1974 to $8,150 in 1989/1990 owing to rises in teachers' salaries and inflation. The fees in the Senior School were lower. In 1989/1990, students in Forms 1 to 3 only had to pay *tong fai* of $40 annually because of free education in the junior secondary forms. Students in Forms 4 and 5 paid a total of $1,520 per year and students in Forms 6 to 7 paid $1,920 per year.[11]

---

11. Headmistress's Report, December 1989.

Figure 7.3: Mrs R. Yip and Junior School staff, 1989/1990. Source: *Quest* 1989–1990, 163.
From left to right:
Back row: Mrs M. Lo, Miss N. Chu, Mrs L. Fung, Miss N. Cheng, Mrs W. Wong, Mrs E. Tse, Mrs S. Yeung, Miss M. Tsao, Mrs Y. Chan, Mrs S. Kun, Miss I. Ng, Mrs Y. K. Tam
Front row: Mrs B. Wong, Mrs K. Watt, Mrs M. Leung, Mrs R. Yip, Miss O. L. Ma, Mrs C. Cheung, Mrs C. Yeung

One of the problems facing Hong Kong schools in the 1980s was the loss of students and teachers due to emigration. As the handover date approached, however, this lessened; instead, some of the emigrants returned to Hong Kong after having obtained residency status or citizenship of their adoptive countries. As it was difficult to fill vacancies in the middle of the year, the Junior School invariably lost some of its much-needed income.[12] When new teachers were appointed, Mrs Elim Lau paid special attention to them and helped them whenever necessary. During her tenure, she tidied up administrative details, and taught her staff to organise school functions properly so that the school ran efficiently.

---

12. Minutes of School Council Meeting, 13 June 1990.

Changes in the Campus

In March 1985, the Parent Teacher Association (PTA) suggested that each of the retired headmistresses should be commemorated by a building at the school, and the School Council concurred. The 1940 Wing, or the Science Wing/Block, was renamed the Gibbins Wing; the 1950 Wing, or the Domestic Science Wing/Block or Chapel Block, was renamed the Hurrell Wing; and the Centenary Wing, the Symons Block. Commemorative plaques were placed on a wall of each of the three blocks facing the front lawn and the garden area.[13]

By 1989, the Centenary Building, now thirty years old, was showing signs of wear and tear. Major and minor repair works were required in different parts of the Senior School buildings. The Junior School, even though it had only been built in 1975, also required restoration: part of the roof was infested with termites and needed the expertise of a pest control company. The Senior School had expanded from three to four classes per form at every level from Forms 1 to 5 in 1979, with the result that the Centenary Building, which was built in 1959 and designed to accommodate three classes per form, was now much too small. Despite the closure of the boarding school and conversion of the dormitories into the Form 6 Centre for Form 6 students, more laboratory space and special rooms were required for the growing number of students over the years. The changing emphasis on sciences, computers, and technology in the curriculum to adapt to the modern world necessitated new facilities and more space.

Extension Phase I

The plan for an extension began after a fire erupted on 24 November 1990 between the two huts (Edmund Cheung hut and China Light and Power hut) near the Chi Wo Street stone wall. They were used as an activity room for the Senior School students and as the Junior School library respectively.[14] Fortunately, there were no casualties. Both huts were steel-framed and approved by the government, but their contents were badly damaged. The School Council agreed in principle to build an extension to the school and asked the two headmistresses to find potential donors and to tackle the building plans.[15]

In 1991, the headmistresses came up with a proposal to erect a new five-storey building extension. Mrs Lau had spent considerable time and thought on the appropriate site for a new extension that could be used by both the Junior and Senior schools—and had decided on the site of the servants' quarters next to the Centenary Building. It would blend in with

---

13. Minutes of School Council Meeting, 11 March 1985.
14. The library hut was donated by China Light and Power Ltd and had been decorated delightfully by parents; the other hut was donated by the Cheung family as an activity room.
15. Minutes of School Council Meeting, 13 December 1990.

Consolidation and New Challenges: 1985 to 1999

the existing buildings and cause the least disturbance to daily activities during demolition and construction. The ground floor of the building would serve as a covered playground.[16]

The Building Committee was established with Mr H. Lok, Mr S. H. Cheung, Mrs Katherine Fok as members, and Mrs Doris Ho as the Chair. When the ED gave permission for an appeal for funds, the Building Extension Appeal Committee was formed under the honorary patronage of Sir Quo-wei Lee, and co-chaired by Mrs Ng Saw Kheng (Chairperson of the PTA) and Mrs Josephine Chang (President of the Diocesan Old Girls' Association, DOGA). One of the fundraising events was the in-house musical *Humbug* produced by Mrs Jean Valerie Oxley; another was a walkathon, organised by the Walkathon Organising Committee, co-chaired by Mrs Isabel Huen and two members of the DOGA General Committee. The walkathon took place on 18 October 1992 at the Royal Hong Kong Jockey Club in Shatin. It was a unique fundraising event and the first of its kind for a local school, with strong support from the Jockey Club and a special guest performance by Hong Kong movie actor Andy Lau and alumna singer Karen Mok (aka Karen Morris). The whole campaign raised a total of $12 million, the target having been $7 million. The construction began on 30 January 1993.[17]

The primary addition in the new extension to the Senior School was the student activity centre. DGS was the first aided school to have such a centre included in the list of rooms that were entitled to government subsidy for major repairs—an indication that the ED had officially recognised the importance of ECA. The new extension also offered the Junior School a modern library and a new computer room. Together with the new programmes for learning grammar, comprehension, creative writing, mathematical drills, and problem-solving, the Junior School became the first primary school in Hong Kong to use computers to assist learning.[18]

The Extension Phase I (Plate 4, Figure 7.4a, and 7.4b) was opened by Mrs Lavender Patten, the "First Lady" of Hong Kong, on 15 December 1993, the school Speech Day. In addressing the school, Mrs Patten praised it for its pioneering role in female education and urged the girls to be role models for the next generation.[19] After the opening ceremony, the donors were each presented with a key to unlock the door of the rooms that they had donated.

---

16. Minutes of School Council Meeting, 30 March 1991.

17. Minutes of School Council Meeting, 10 April 1992.

18. "A Dream Comes True", *Quest* (1992–1994): 236.

19. "Speech by Mrs Lavender Patten at the Building Extension Opening Ceremony of the Diocesan Girls' School", *Quest* (1992–1994), V.

Figure 7.4a: Extension Phase I completed in 1993. Source: School Archives.

Figure 7.4b: Mrs Patten at the opening ceremony of Extension I Building on 15 December 1993. Source: School Archives.
From left to right: Mr S. D. S. Bokhary, Hon Treasurer of the School Council, Mrs Doris Ho, Sir Quo-wei Lee, Mrs Patten, and Mrs Elim Lau

Extension Phase II

While the building of the Extension Phase I was ongoing, new cracks appeared on the walls of the assembly hall of the Junior School, the changing room, and the staff toilet as a result of the construction work. During heavy rain, morning assemblies were carried out under a canopy of colourful umbrellas.[20] Despite the pronouncement from the architect and the construction company that there was no immediate danger from the leak, the hall had to be repaired or rebuilt. The assembly hall had quite an interesting history. It had originated as the covered playground or "Greek Parthenon" for gymnastics in the 1930s and had been converted into a dormitory for boarders after the war. In 1959, it became the assembly hall for the Junior School when the boarders were relocated to the new Centenary Building.

The final decision to rebuild the hall stemmed from Mrs Yip's appeal for smaller classes in the Junior School. In 1993, there were forty to forty-two students in each class, presenting difficulties for teaching and for recruiting new teachers. In addition to having these large class sizes, the Junior School was a one-sessional, full-day school, while most teachers preferred a half-day school. To make the teaching positions more attractive, Mrs Yip suggested reducing class sizes, thus reducing the student–teacher ratio, and improving conditions of service such as introducing medical and hospital insurance. The School Council agreed with her and decided to increase each primary level to three classes, decreasing class size from forty-two to thirty-five students. Instead of repairing the Junior School hall, it was decided to redevelop the site with a five-storey classroom and function rooms block at an estimated cost of $26 million.

When the Extension Phase II fundraising committee approached the Royal Hong Kong Jockey Club Charities Trust, which had so far not given funds to any individual school, everyone was surprised when they agreed to donate $12 million to the project, provided that the school was responsible for the rest of the building funds. The school decided to accept the grant and that if the target of $26 million was not reached by fundraising, only three floors would be built for the Junior School, although the foundations would be able to support two extra floors at a later date.[21]

The generosity of parents, alumnae, and the public prevailed. In 1996, the total amount collected for the Extension Phase II reached $30 million (including the donation from the Royal Hong Kong Jockey Club).[22] The building was completed by the end of 1996, providing an assembly hall, more classrooms and special rooms for the Junior School expansion,

---

20. Mrs R. Yip, telephone interview by the author on 24 June 2020; Minutes of School Council Meeting, 30 March 1993.

21. Minutes of School Council Meeting, 17 November 1994.

22. Minutes of School Council Meeting, 25 March 1996.

Figure 7.5a: Junior School old school hall outside, c. 1980. Source: School Archives.

Figure 7.5b: Junior School old school hall inside, c. 1980. Source: School Archives.

Consolidation and New Challenges: 1985 to 1999

and much-needed laboratories for the Senior School.[23] An overhead walkway was constructed to connect the two building extensions, allowing science students easy access to the laboratories. The Extension Phase II (Plate 4, Figure 7.6a and 7.6b) was opened on 19 December 1996 by Mr Donald Tsang, the Financial Secretary.

With the completion of the two extensions, the Senior School began the process of renovating its older buildings and upgrading its facilities. A new general science laboratory for the junior secondary forms, an Information Technology Centre, and a second computer room in the Symons Block were added to cope with the growing number of science students,[24] and to allow the introduction of computer and IT courses in the lower secondary forms (see section on Scholastic Activities).

Up to 1994, only the rooms adjacent to Gascoigne Road were air-conditioned. In that year, thanks to the ED's Noise Abatement Programme, air conditioning was installed in the remaining rooms in the Centenary Building.[25]

Challenges from Reforms Proposed in Education Commission Reports (ECRs)

At the recommendation of the OECD Panel, the Education Commission was formed in 1984 to oversee and coordinate the development of all sectors of education. The Education Commission published a series of seven reports (Education Commission Reports ECR1–7) between 1984 and 1997, focusing on improving the quality rather than increasing the quantity of education. The ECR1-6, published between 1984 and 1996, formed the first wave of reforms and covered the following areas: language teaching and learning, teacher quality, private sector school improvements, curriculum development, teaching and learning conditions, and special education.[26] ECR7, published in 1997, is often considered to be the second wave of reforms to be implemented from 1997 to the 2000s, and will be discussed in Chapter 8. The ECRs were a challenge to all schools, and as the new Headmistress, Mrs Lau had to strike a balance between complying with the ECRs and maintaining the school's own policies and ethos.[27] Only those ECR proposals that affected the school are discussed below.

The second proposal of ECR1 (1984) was to improve the standard of Chinese and English languages in schools. While the English language had always been of a high standard in DGS, its Chinese instruction had also improved remarkably in the 1980s. By 1993, 99.5 per

---

23. "Building Extension, Phase II", *Quest* (1996–1998): 17.

24. "Foreword", *Quest* (1996–1998): 2.

25. Minutes of School Council Meeting, 27 June 1994.

26. Yin Cheong Cheng, "Hong Kong Educational Reforms in the Last Decade: Reform Syndrome and New Developments", *International Journal of Educational Management* 23, no. 1 (2009): 65–86.

27. Mrs E. Lau, email communication, 4 August 2020.

Figure 7.6a: Extension Phase II completed in 1996. Source: School Archives and *Quest* 1996–1998, 20.

Figure 7.6b: Opening ceremony of Extension Phase II by the Hon. Donald Tsang in 1996. Source: School Archives and *Quest* 1996–1998, 20.
From left to right: The Reverend J. Aldis, Mrs R. Yip, Mrs K. Fok, Mrs E. Lau, the Hon. D. Tsang, Bishop T. Soo, Mr A. Li, Mrs D. Ho, Mrs H. Yu, Mrs S. K. Ng, and Mrs J. Chang
Back: Lau Hynn Ming; Front: Pang Oi Ying

Figure 7.7a: Chemistry laboratory in Extension Phase II, late 1990s. Source: School Archives.

Figure 7.7b: Cookery class in Hurrell Wing, late 1990s. Source: School Archives.

Figure 7.7c: Library in Symons Block, late 1990s. Source: School Archives.

cent of the school's participants in the School Certificate Examinations passed English, and 68 per cent were awarded a distinction, while the respective numbers for Chinese were 98.5 per cent and 67 per cent.[28] ECR1 also established a clear policy for teaching to be carried out in Chinese, the mother tongue. The government recognised that some schools, such as the grant or aided schools, had been operating successfully with English teaching and allowed these schools to continue to teach in English if they wished to do so, provided that certain requirements were satisfied.[29] Over the years, DGS has consistently been allowed to use English as its medium of instruction.

ECR2, published in 1986, addressed the issue of sixth form education.[30] In 1984, CUHK started the Provisional Acceptance Scheme to take in Lower 6 students based on the results of their Hong Kong Certificate of Education Examination (HKCEE) and the Chinese University Higher-Level Examination taken after Lower Form 6. As a result, a number of students were siphoned off by CUHK, resulting in wastage of Upper Form 6 places. This affected many secondary schools. The ED created a new type of Form 6 curriculum as a self-contained course (Advanced Supplementary, AS) for students who might not wish to proceed to university. An AS Level Examination was to be taken at the end of the new curriculum.[31]

In 1992/1993, DGS closed the one-year Form 6 General class and opened another two-year Upper 6 Arts Class offering the new Advanced Level (AL) programme.[32] Form 6 students could take the AL subjects and/or AS subjects that the ED had created to broaden the sixth form curriculum. DGS offered Form 6 places to its own Form 5 girls who met the basic qualifications and to students who were not accepted by their own schools. As anticipated, the overall performance of the Upper 6 Form dropped. With more girls emigrating and some leaving after Lower Form 6 for early acceptance by CUHK, the school decided to close one of the Upper Form 6 classes after the academic year 1994/1995.[33]

ECR3 (1988) dealt with the future of private schools by introducing a new Direct Subsidy Scheme (DSS), which would enable private or aided schools that complied with relatively modest conditions to receive limited but direct financial assistance from the government;

---

28. Headmistress's Report 1992/1993, Speech Day Booklet, November 1993, 9 (results of English and Chinese language examinations).

29. Education Bureau, Hong Kong, "Why Should We Teach in the Mother Tongue?", accessed 12 March 2022, https://www.edb.gov.hk/en/edu-system/primary-secondary/applicable-to-secondary/moi/guidance-index. html#:~:text=With%20the%20use%20of%20Chinese,better%20cognitive%20and%20academic%20development.

30. Education Commission Report no. 2, Education Bureau, HKSAR, accessed 12 March 2022, https://www.e-c. edu.hk/doc/en/publications_and_related_documents/education_reports/ecr2_e.pdf

31. Yee Wang Fung and Moira Chan-Yeung, *To Serve and to Lead: A History of Diocesan Boys' School* (Hong Kong: Hong Kong University Press, 2009), 125.

32. Headmistress's Report, 1993/1994, Speech Day Booklet, 15 November 1994, 8, 9.

33. Headmistress's Report, 1994/1995, Speech Day Booklet, 16 November 1995, 7.

Consolidation and New Challenges: 1985 to 1999

in return, they could maintain some control over their students and their curricula.[34] DGS decided not to join the DSS scheme at that time because the school was able to achieve its aim with the resources available.[35]

ECR4 (1990), which focused on curriculum development, attainment targets and related assessments, and language in education, received considerable public support.[36] The ED held seminars for teachers to familiarise themselves with the implementation of the Targets and Target-Related Assessment Programme and the Target Oriented Curriculum (TOC) Programme.[37] The school, both Junior and Senior, was closed for three days to allow teachers to attend the seminars in January 1993. Mrs R. Yip, who attended, reported to the School Council that the school had already been practising what the ED recommended. The school decided to adopt the full TOC spirit in teaching and learning, but the format of lessons would not rigidly conform to the ED's TOC.[38]

ECR5 (1992) was devoted to upgrading the teaching profession. It recommended combining the Colleges of Education and the Institute of Language Education to form a new Institute of Education, which would offer courses at degree level.[39] This report had the support of schools and teachers, including those from DGS, because more qualified teachers would be created at a time when many teachers were leaving Hong Kong. Students would also have a wider choice of subjects and better support services.

The School Management Initiative (SMI), proposed by ECR5, was to allow participation in decision-making by all concerned parties, including principals, school management committees, parents, and representatives of teachers and students. The DGS School Council decided not to participate, because over the years the school had always invited a senior staff representative to attend the first School Council meeting of each academic year to reflect the opinions and requests of the department heads and to report on their expenses and budget for the past year;[40] it was already practising what the SMI was initiating.

---

34. Education Commission Report no. 3, Education Bureau, HKSAR, accessed 12 March 2022, https://www.e-c. edu.hk/doc/en/publications_and_related_documents/education_reports/ecr3_e.pdf.

35. Minutes of School Council Meeting, 13 June 1990.

36. Education Commission Report no. 4, Education Bureau, HKSAR, accessed 12 March 2022, https://www.edb. gov.hk/attachment/en/curriculum-development/major-level-of-edu/gifted/guidelines-on-school-based-gifted-development-programmes/ecr4_e.pdf.

37. Minutes of School Council Meeting, 7 December 1992, on Information Paper Target Oriented Curriculum, Paper No. CB (2)1063/98-99(03).

38. Minutes of School Council Meeting, 1 December 1997.

39. Education Commission Report no. 5, Education Bureau, HKSAR, accessed 12 March 2022, https://www.e-c. edu.hk/doc/en/publications_and_related_documents/education_reports/ecr5_e.pdf.

40. Minutes of School Council Meeting, 28 June 1991.

ECR6 (1995) again focused on the language of instruction.[41] Approval was given to DGS to use English for teaching all academic subjects for the academic year of 1998/1999 and future Form 1 intake. The school, however, requested the use of Chinese in the teaching of non-academic subjects such as art, home economics, and physical education in anticipation of the difficulty of recruiting new teachers of non-academic cultural subjects. In addition, the ED also recommended the benchmarking of teachers and testing their language proficiency, starting with language teachers. This proposal upset many teachers in Hong Kong but not those at DGS.[42]

Towards the end of the twentieth century, the ED, recognising the power of IT in widening opportunities for learning, began to adopt its use in schools. The ED published a consultation document entitled "Information Technology for Learning in the New Era. Five Year Strategy (1998/99 to 2002/03)" and provided substantial resources, including software, and professional development for teachers to facilitate the use of IT in teaching.[43] DGS incorporated the new programme with enthusiasm.

Scholastic Activities: Curriculum, Computers, and Information Technology in Teaching

During this period, the school focused on curriculum changes and on the teaching of IT and computerisation.

In the academic year 1994/1995, the school saw two changes in the curriculum. First, science subjects were offered to two of the four Form 4 classes instead of one.[44] More science-related job opportunities and science programmes opened up at the tertiary level, requiring more science-trained graduates from secondary schools. Science subjects were also made more interesting by curriculum reforms initiated by the Curriculum Development Institute, which was formed in 1992.[45] The school recommended some girls to join the elite programmes, such as the Science Enhancement Programmes co-organised by the ED and the Chinese University of Hong Kong for Form 3 and 4 students.[46]

---

41. Education Commission Report no. 6, Education Bureau, HKSAR, accessed 12 March 2022, https://www.e-c.edu.hk/doc/en/publications_and_related_documents/education_reports/ecr6_e.pdf.

42. Minutes of School Council Meeting, 24 March 1997.

43. John Pearson, "Information Technology in Education: Policy and Provision in Hong Kong Schools", *Journal of Information Technology for Teacher Education* 10 (2001): 279–290.

44. Headmistress's Report 1995–1996, Speech Day Booklet, 1996, 7.

45. "Information Paper—Curriculum Development Institute", Panel on Education Paper, 17 October 1997, Legislative Council, HKSAR, accessed 19 March 2021, https://www.legco.gov.hk/yr97-98/english/panels/ed/papers/ed1710-6.htm.

46. Dr Thomas Man, email communication, 12 August 2020.

Second, computer literacy was implemented in Form 1. The use of computers in teaching in the Junior School had begun earlier, when a new computer room was added in the Extension Phase I in 1993 and a new system was installed for computer-assisted teaching, which the students enjoyed immensely.[47] In 1999, the computer laboratory was further upgraded into a Multimedia Learning Centre (MMLC) with new hardware that would adopt the Computer Mastery Programmes from Futurekids. This programme included computer-assisted English and mathematics programmes, computer sciences, and other educational components.

The Senior School acquired a new computer system funded by the ED in 1987, and a classroom was renovated into a computer laboratory.[48] More development of IT in the Senior School occurred in 1997 when DGS applied to the ED to open an AS Computer Application Course for Form 6. The ED approved an additional teacher for DGS and offered six new computers, while the DOGA donated funds for additional computers and for changing one of the old laboratories into the second computer room.[49] Under the Hong Kong Cyber Campus Project of the CUHK, a dial-up router was set up in one of the two computer rooms to enable simultaneous access to the internet by the computers in that room through a single telephone line. By September 1998, the school's computer department was able to expand and offered the AS Computer Applications Course to Upper 6.[50]

In 1999, DGS was included in the second batch of schools for the implementation of the MMLC project under the auspices of the ED, which provided basic funding to meet the standard provisions, but the school had to provide approximately $550,000 for the purchase of additional computers, software, and furniture for the effective use of an MMLC.[51] An IT team of eight members was formed to be responsible for the purchase and allocation of computers, training of the staff, internet access for the school, computerisation of the library, and establishment of the MMLC.

In both the Senior and Junior schools, the staff were given about fifty hours of Professional Development Training to equip them with the skills to teach the Computer Mastery Programme.[52] These steps enabled the school to enter the new technological age before the new millennium.

---

47. Minutes of School Council Meeting, 28 March 1995.
48. Minutes of School Council Meeting, 10 December 1987.
49. Minutes of School Council Meeting, 24 June 1997.
50. Minutes of School Council Meeting, 15 December 1998.
51. Minutes of School Council Meeting, 3 July 1999.
52. Minutes of School Council Meeting, 3 July 1999.

Figure 7.8: One of the computer rooms, c. 1998. Source: School Archives.

Academic Performance

In terms of teaching, Mrs Lau strongly believed in the policy of rotation of teachers so that the students were taught by a different teacher each year in each subject and that they would be able to experience and benefit from a variety of teaching styles and expertise.[53] The Chinese Department, after the retirement of Mr Chan Yik Cham, was headed by Mrs Tang Hung Sang, a passionate and able language teacher. She, along with Mrs Lee (née Poon) Kit Ming, nurtured the Chinese Drama Club and stimulated the students' interest in Chinese. The school also opened up more streams for Chinese so that students needing more help with the language were able to learn from more experienced teachers in smaller classes.

Despite the changes in the curriculum, with emphasis on science, computers, and IT, the students' performance in public examinations was outstanding. The pass rate each year was consistently above 95 per cent in the HKCEE. The numbers of students scoring As and Bs (A being highest and F indicating failure; results below F were designated as U or

---

53. Mrs E. Lau, email communication, 11 August 2020.

Consolidation and New Challenges: 1985 to 1999   179

unclassified) increased rapidly after 1991.[54] The maximum number of subjects a student could take in the HKCEE was ten. There were a number of high achievers in DGS each year, scoring over eight As and sometimes even ten. During the period 1990–1999, six DGS girls scored straight As in all ten subjects in the HKCEE.[55] The performance of DGS students in the Hong Kong Advanced Level Examinations (HKALE) was just as noteworthy, with a pass rate invariably above 90 per cent and many distinctions and credits.

The high academic standing resulted in numerous prestigious local and overseas scholarships being awarded to DGS students, including the Jardine Scholarship, the UK/Hong Kong Scholarship, the Sir Edward Youde Memorial Award for Overseas Studies, the Sino-British Fellowship Trust Scholarship, and others for studies in overseas universities such as Oxford, Cambridge, Yale, and Harvard.[56]

School Life

The Rhythm of School Routine

School events followed an annual pattern. The first term of the new school year commenced on the first day of September if it was not a public holiday, and the second term began on the first working day after New Year's Day each year. The interhouse swimming gala was held in September, while the interhouse athletics meet occurred in November. Intensive training usually took place between the interhouse and interschool competitions. The interhouse competitions prepared students for the tougher interschool sports events later in the school year, in October, November, and March.

The Hong Kong Schools Speech Festival ran from November to December and the Hong Kong Schools Music Festival from February to March. The winners of the Hong Kong Schools Music Festival proudly presented an Easter Concert to their parents and teachers before the end of the second term. The third term began after the Easter holidays. During this term, students were preoccupied with their academic work and examinations. Form 5 students took the HKCEE and Upper 6 students sat for the HKALE. The lower

---

54. Since 1966, the results of the Hong Kong School Certificate Examination were graded from A to H. Grades below F were considered failures, while grade A was considered passed with distinction and B and C as passed with credit. From 1968 to 1984, the results were classified as A(1), B(2), C(3), D(4), F(5), G(6), and H(7), A(1) being the highest and H(7) the lowest. From 1985, grades below F were not recorded. From 1991, each grade was divided into two subgrades: A(01), A(02); B(01), B(02), etc. By 2002, all subgrades were abolished and the grading of A(a), B(b), C(c), D(d), E(e), and F(f) were used. From 2002, the results were graded as 5* (Five*), 5 (Five), 4 (Four), 3 (Three), 2 (Two), 1 (One), 5 (Five) being the highest and 1 (One) being the lowest. The outstanding performers were graded 5* (Five*). The HKCEE was abolished after 2011.

55. Headmistress's Reports, Speech Day Booklets from 1985/1986 to 1998/1999.

56. Minutes of School Council Meeting, 24 June 1997.

forms had school examinations in June, followed by a series of ECAs such as educational visits, career days, and other activities until the school year completed around mid-July. In late July, Upper 6 students returned to the school for the results of their examinations, while Form 5 students returned in early August to apply for admission to Form 6, pending their examination results.

130th Anniversary Celebration

The most memorable year during this period was the one-hundred-and-thirtieth anniversary of DGS in 1990, which was celebrated with several events throughout the year. Festivities began on the Speech Day of the year 1988/1989 on 5 January 1990. The Secretary for Education and Manpower, Mr Yeung Kai-yin, a former DGS student in the Primary School when boys were admitted in the 1940s, officiated at the switching on of lights ceremony. The Senior School assembly hall was immediately made resplendent with a flood of coloured bulbs, decorating a huge display board, to celebrate the occasion.

On 4 July, Form 3 students put on the musical *Tom Sawyer*. Mrs Jean Oxley, the music teacher, with amazing stamina, trained the one hundred teenagers to sing in unison.[57] Speech Day of 1989/1990 academic year took place on 20 November 1990, attended by Mr Li Yuet Ting, the Director of Education, as special guest, and he handed out the awards and certificates. Noting the numerous awards, scholastic and extracurricular, he commended the school on its successful and well-rounded education and encouraged the school and its students to uphold the tradition.[58]

It was during the Open Days of 18 and 19 December 1990 that the parents and guests fully appreciated the many facets of DGS school life:[59] in addition to its academic excellence, the school had expanded its energy and potential for sports, music, debate, and other ECAs. During the opening ceremony, over 900 DGS students assembled along the balconies of the main block and the Gibbins Wing in their school uniform of blue shirts, grey skirt or tunics, and the signature red ties, and with bright smiles on their faces welcomed Lady Wilson, who was greeted warmly by Bishop Peter Kwong, Mrs Doris Ho, Mrs Elim Lau, and Dr Joyce Symons, who flew in from London to join the ceremony, along with Mrs Rebecca Yip and other distinguished guests. The "Te Deum" then rang out from the balconies and in the front lawn. Lady Wilson and the official party toured the school and enjoyed performances by the Junior School Choir and the Chinese Orchestra in the Junior School Hall, followed by an outdoor gymnastics display, demonstrations of fencing indoors, and

---

57. *Quest* (1990–1991): 2, 3.
58. *Quest* (1990–1991): 4.
59. *Quest* (1990–1991): 6, 7.

Red Cross and Girl Guides parades in the field. The highlight of the day was when a giant DGS 130th anniversary six-layer cake decorated with icing and yellow roses appeared, and Mrs Lau invited Lady Wilson and Dr Symons to cut it. Festivities resumed on the second Open Day, when parents and guests enjoyed a fashion show and performances from the Dance Club and Drama Club with displays of musical and other talents from the school.

The school also put on an exhibition during the two Open Days with a theme of "Into the 90s", emphasising environmental issues in every major section and thus reflecting the social awareness of the students. The exhibition, with participation by both the Senior and the Junior schools, consisted of the following sections: English, Chinese, science, social science, the humanities, the arts, home economics, and ECA.[60]

The year ended with a simple but moving Thanksgiving Service on 20 December 1990 at St John's Cathedral. After the introit, a procession of alumnae representatives of the decades 1920–1980, followed by girls representing each class from Primary 1 to Upper 6, appeared from the west door and walked slowly to the steps of the altar. At the altar, each representative placed a single yellow rose (chosen because the school was housed in Rose Villa in 1899) on a model of a tree and then proceeded to her seat—the past and

Figure 7.9: Lady Wilson's (wife of Governor Lord Wilson) visit to the school for the 130th Anniversary celebration. Source: *Quest* 1990–1991, 8–9.

---

60. *Quest* (1990–1991): 12–19.

Figure 7.10: Lady Wilson (centre) and Dr C. J. Symons (right) cutting the cake at the DGS 130th Anniversary on 18 December 1990 with Mrs E. Lau (left). Source: *Looking at the Stars*, opposite 59.

the present together in continuity. The old school hymn "Blest Are the Pure in Heart" was sung, followed by the reading of the lessons by the headmistresses. Dr Symons led the congregation in a beautiful prayer of dedication after the Bishop Peter Kwong's memorable and thought-provoking sermon. The service and the anniversary celebrations ended with prayers for the school, an emotional rendition of the school hymn, and blessings from the Bishop.[61]

Preparation for the Handover

When the 1997 handover drew near, the school considered its stance in relation to the celebrations. It decided to remain apolitical as an educational institution before the handover and gave the following directive: any request or visit from any institution in China should be referred to the ED. The interests of DGS students should come first, and proposed activities were not to interfere with students' schoolwork or examinations, the school's reputation should not be affected, and parental consent must be sought.[62] To equip the students for changes after the handover, DGS launched a programme on civic education about China.

---

61. *Quest* (1990–1991): 24.
62. Minutes of School Council Meeting, 24 March 1997.

Figure 7.11: Thanksgiving Service for the 130th Anniversary, 20 December 1990, at St John's Cathedral.
Back row: Mrs D. Ho, Mrs D. Blomfield, Mr S. D. S. Bokhary, Mrs K. Fok, Mrs G. Mok
Front row: Bishop P. Kwong, Dr C. J. Symons, Mrs E. Lau, Mrs M. Fincher, Mrs R. Yip, the Reverend Hanson
Source: *Quest* 1990–1991, 24.

A staff visit to a few middle schools in Shenzhen was carried out on 7 December 1997, and a programme called China Week was held in February 1998, when prominent leaders were invited to introduce China's education system and culture. On 8 April 1998, forty-two girls and six teachers visited Shenzhen Middle School where friendly debates and badminton and table tennis matches took place.[63] Similar visits continued in later years.

Proliferation of Extracurricular Activities

In the 1980s, the ED promoted ECAs because of their educational value and importance to students' personal development. Mrs Lau was able to assign some rooms for ECAs when the school extensions were built. During this period, the school underwent rapid growth in sports, providing equipment and facilities in the school, renting external facilities, and promoting new sports.[64] In addition, Mrs Lau emphasised that students should try their best according to their ability, and refrain from creating a highly competitive and adversarial atmosphere, so that the students could truly enjoy themselves and form long-lasting friendships with one another.[65] She paid special attention to those who were excelling in sports or music but falling behind in their academic work. She helped and encouraged them to achieve a good academic standing, which assured these students a brighter future.

In 1989, there were over forty different ECAs at DGS. Each of the activities had one or two teachers in charge. An ECA Committee, consisting of students and teachers, was formed to strengthen intra-school communications, promote efficient management of clubs and teams, and at the same time, provide leadership training for students on the committee.

In sports, DGS girls excelled in swimming and in life-saving, taking championships in swimming in fourteen successive years and achieving a Grand Slam in all grades in inter-school swimming competitions many times during those years. As life-saving guards, the girls performed just as brilliantly, also taking championships. Robyn Lamsam created excitement in the whole school on 11 March 1992 by setting a new Hong Kong record in 50-metre freestyle with a time of 25.78 sec. At 14, she became Hong Kong's youngest athlete to be selected to compete in the Summer Olympics at Barcelona in July 1992.[66] Robyn went on to win many awards and honours.

DGS students appeared to be particularly skilful in orienteering, taking the championship in interschool open competitions for eight years in a row from 1998/1999. DGS students represented Hong Kong in several sports at international level, such as the

---

63. *Quest* (1996–1998): 22.
64. Mr Tang Kun Loi, email communication, 20 August 2020.
65. "School Focus. Diocesan Girls' School", *South China Morning Post*, 26 January 1986.
66. "Barcelona Bound: Hong Kong's Representatives at the 25 Olympiad", *South China Morning Post*, 7 July 1992.

Consolidation and New Challenges: 1985 to 1999 185

Figure 7.12: Robyn Lamsam winning Hong Kong's first individual Asian Games medal in swimming at the 1994 Hiroshima Asian Games. Source: Kim Lamsam.

Asia-Pacific Orienteering Championships, the Asian Games in Japan, the Interport Athletics Competition in China, and the World Youth/Cadet Fencing Championships in Belgium and Indonesia, as well as many others over the years. Their excellent results relied not only on personal determination and hard work but also on the support from their families, teammates, their sports teachers, Miss Jill Clark, Mrs Paulina Hui, and Mr Tang Kun Loi, and the school.

In music, DGS girls won many awards in solo piano, singing, and instruments during the Hong Kong Schools Music Festival. Musical activities flourished because of the rich musical atmosphere in the school bolstered by the continual achievements in local competitions. There were many in-house musical activities, such as annual Form 3 musicals and performances during speech days. More choirs were established in which all girls could participate without auditioning. The school provided popular lessons for learning musical instruments, both Western and Chinese, on Saturday mornings.[67]

One of the most significant milestones in this period was the formal re-establishment of mixed choirs for DGS and DBS, which were conducted by a music teacher from DBS.

---

67. Mrs Oxley, Speech Day Booklet, 16 November 1988, 17.

Figure 7.13: Madrigal and Quick Study with DBS, champion in both competitions, 1994. Source: Dr Nicholas Chan.

Although the schools cooperated every year in highly successful Madrigal and SATB Quick Study teams, the mixed choirs lay dormant from 1984 to 1998. In 1998, a Junior Mixed Choir for girls and boys in Forms 1 to 3 of the two schools was formed, going on to win the title of Best Junior Choir in the Hong Kong Schools Music Festival in 2000.[68]

The music highlight of 1996 was the production of *The King and I*—the first musical production held at a public venue in the history of DGS.[69] This featured DGS's own singers and orchestra; the students made their own costumes and props as well as managing the lighting and backstage technicalities, to an extent that few schools had previously achieved. Girls from both the Senior and Junior schools participated, and teachers and parents supported the endeavour. This fundraising extravaganza was presented to high acclaim on 27 and 28 June at the Sha Tin Town Hall (Plate 5).

The ECA Committee kept a record of the activities of all school clubs. A number of new clubs were added between 1985 and 1999 to the already long list (Table 7.1). The ideas for initiating these clubs came from the students, the teachers, or the Headmistress, who often subsidised some of the club celebrations herself.[70] Some of the clubs provided services to the school, the Library Committee and the Careers Committee being the prime examples. The club with the highest number of participants was the Citizens' Club, with a membership of 300. This provided a large variety of community service and voluntary work opportunities for its members, including selling flags, teaching children to read and write, and helping the blind, the elderly, and the disabled. The Mathematics and Computer Club topped all the clubs in popularity, with the computer section more vibrant than the

---

68. *Quest* (1999/2000): 47, 52, 58.
69. "The King and I", *Quest* (1996–1998): 2.
70. Mrs E. Lau, email communication, 4 August 2020.

Consolidation and New Challenges: 1985 to 1999

mathematics section. In 1998, it was split into two clubs. The Audiovisual Team charmed its members because of its special lighting effects, and all members had a chance to take a training course to learn appropriate techniques.[71]

Table 7.1: New ECA added to the school between 1985 and 1999

Arts/Music	Sports	Academic	Hobbies	Services (social, school)
Music Club	Basketball Team	Society of Communications	Reading Club	Zonta Z[+] Club
Mixed Choirs	Orienteering Team	English Club	Philatelic Club	Library Team
Wind Band		Mathematics and Computer Club*	Photography Club	Audio-visual Team
		Model United Nations		Counselling Team
		Chinese Debating Society		Newspaper Service Committee
				ECA Student Committee
				Health Education Group

Source: *Quest* and Speech Day booklets between 1985 and 1999. [+]Social Service Club.
*Later expanded to Mathematics Club and Computer Club during this period.

The Model United Nations was formed in 1989. Participating students were required to conduct research and to learn to think critically. Throughout the process, they acquired skills in debating, communication, and public speaking. The Careers Committee, also run by students, managed the Careers Library, organised talks and visits, and acted as a vital link between careers teachers and students. Many representatives from overseas tertiary and secondary institutions were received. Some visitors gave talks to students to provide an overall view of their institution and their research. The Careers Committee also helped many students in their application for scholarships and further studies in Hong Kong or abroad.

Educational visits remained an important part of ECA. Most of them were arranged at the request of subject teachers to supplement their classroom teaching: such visits were informative for both teachers and students, and made learning more interesting.

71. "Survey", *Quest* (1990–1991): 90–91.

Religious activities flourished in the school. The Rev. John Menear of St Andrew's Church was responsible for Friday morning assemblies while the Rev. G. Gillard led the fortnightly Wednesday lunchtime Holy Communion service. In 1983, student-led assemblies began, with each class taking turns once a year to present their thoughts and reflections on a topic within an overall theme, in place of the traditional assemblies led by the Headmistress or staff from DGS or St Andrew's Church. The Youth Fellowship grew under the capable and dedicated leadership of senior students. During the Advent season, the Fellowship invited staff and the rest of the school to join them in carols, prayers, and meditation in the Chapel. Every December, either a retreat was organised at Tao Fung Shan, or a two-day religious and political conference was held, with outside speakers being invited to share their faith and their political beliefs. The Youth Fellowship also collected funds for various charities, such as Oxfam, homes for the elderly, shelters for the homeless, Project ORBIS (for eyes), and Project Hope.[72]

In addition to the usual pastoral care, a counselling and guidance team was established around 1986, in line with the policy of the ED to strengthen the supportive function of teachers, so students could be helped to cope with academic, emotional, or social problems they might encounter.[73]

The Junior School had always been active in ECA. When Mrs Yip took over, she enthusiastically encouraged more students to participate. In sports, the Junior School was awarded the Best Primary School Overall Sports Achievements Gold Cup for eleven years in a row, and the Sportsgirl-of-the-Year went to one of its students for seven consecutive years from 1988. The Junior School participated in interschool competitions in various sports as well as the Hong Kong Schools Music Festival and Hong Kong Schools Speech Festival, and did well in many categories. The students also joined the Royal Commonwealth Society Essay Competition, Hong Kong Youth Cultural and Art Competition, and Chinese Calligraphy Competitions. In 1995, Primary 6 students took part in a five-day camp organised by Outward Bound School, during which interpersonal skills and technical skills for wilderness journeys were taught. The technical skills included how to pack appropriately, to navigate, to cook meals, and to wash up. The feedback from parents was positive. There were a number of other ECAs including the Brownies, Indoor Games Club, Gardening Club, two Chinese Book Clubs for Primary 1 to 6, and two English Book Clubs for Primary 4 to 6 students.[74]

---

72. Mrs A. Hurst, "Religious Activities", Speech Day Booklet, 1985, 20.

73. Mrs A. Hurst and Miss E. Lo, "Counselling and Guidance", Speech Day Booklet, 18 November 1987, 23.

74. Minutes of School Council Meeting, 26 June 1995.

Competitions and Awards

In addition to the usual interschool competitions in sports, music, speech, debates, and drama during this period, there were added competitions in writing, mathematics, science, and computers/IT. The winners of these competitions often received generous awards and scholarships. The growing affluence of Hong Kong in the 1980s had resulted in many families' willingness to establish a large number of awards and scholarships that recognised outstanding students.

The more well-established and prestigious local awards that DGS students frequently won were the *South China Morning Post*'s Student-of-the-Year and its awards in various categories such as Music, Sports, Visual Art, Mathematics and Science, Linguistics, the Best Devotion to the School, and the Most Improved Student. There were also the Omega Rose Bowl Sportsperson-of-the-Year, the Hong Kong Sports Development Board Elite Scholarships, the Community Youth Club (CYC) Outstanding Member Award, and the Hong Kong Outstanding Students of the Year Awards, donated by the Lion and Globe Educational Trust.

Many of these awards demanded excellence in academic work and in ECAs such as music, sports, or community services, and were awarded to well-rounded, socially mature, and community-minded individuals. For the *South China Morning Post* awards, the candidates were nominated by various schools and shortlisted by a panel of judges; the shortlisted finalists were selected and interviewed, and a winner was chosen.[75] According to Mrs Elim Lau, the awards to DGS girls came as the result of a deliberate team effort, often involving initiatives from students, parents, and teachers. The students with potential were sometimes identified years prior to their eligibility, and the school would observe and offer encouragement and guidance, matching them with leadership opportunities to further their growth.[76] A good number of DGS girls won such awards (Table 7.2).

Retirement of Mrs Rebecca Yip and Mrs Elim Lau

In 1998, Mrs Rebecca Yip submitted her resignation, intending to retire in 1999 as her husband was also retiring. The recruitment exercise to replace her was disappointing: Mrs Yip had set such a high standard as the Junior School Headmistress that finding someone to replace her was naturally difficult.[77] In the end, the school was able to find an excellent successor, Mrs Emily Dai, another alumna who went to HKU and took postgraduate certif-

---

75. "The Student of the Year Eligibility", *South China Morning Post*, accessed 7 July 2020, https://studentoftheyear. hk/assessment-criteria.

76. Mrs E. Lau, email communication, 4 August 2020.

77. Minutes of School Council Meeting, 19 June 1998.

Table 7.2: Number of DGS students receiving prestigious awards, 1984/1985 to 1998/1999

Award	Number
SCMP Student of the Year	6*
SCMP Musician of the Year	4
SCMP Sportsperson of the Year	5**
SCMP Visual Artist of the Year	1
Hong Kong Outstanding Student of the Year by Lion and Globe Education Trust	17***

Source: Speech Day booklets from 1985 to 1999; * one girl from DGS in each successive year from 1994/1995 to 1997/1998; ** one girl won the same award in three consecutive years; *** former name "Outstanding Female Students of the Year in HK"; at least one DGS girl in 13 consecutive years from 1984/1985 to 1997/1998.

icate courses in education. She had served in the ED for over fifteen years, and gained vast experience in teaching and in administration locally and overseas before being appointed to head the Junior School.

In March 1994, Mrs Elim Lau, wishing to retire, submitted her resignation.[78] The School Council formed a selection committee to search for a new Head to lead the school through the period of the 1997 handover. From the five candidates, the School Council found Mrs Stella Lai Kuen Lau (née Kun), an exceptional candidate, best suited for the job. An alumna of DGS, Stella read sociology at the University of Waterloo in Canada. After graduation, she taught briefly at the Hong Kong Christian College, then worked as a community relations officer at the Independent Commission Against Corruption and as a language instructor at the Ministry of Defence Chinese Language School in the UK until the mid-1980s, when she moved with her family to live in Switzerland. On returning to Hong Kong in 1990, she joined the staff of her alma mater to teach psychology. Mrs Elim Lau was so impressed with Stella's outstanding work that she promoted her in 1993 to become a Senior Graduate Mistress and Head of Counselling after she received part-time postgraduate training from the CUHK. Following her interview, the School Council sought the approval of Bishop Peter Kwong for the appointment of Mrs Stella Lau to be the next Headmistress of DGS.[79] However, the Bishop pointed out that this appointment would not obtain the ED's approval, as she did not meet their criteria because of her short teaching experience as well as the few years in which she had been a Senior Graduate Mistress. Finally, the Bishop was successful in persuading Mrs Elim Lau to stay on.

---

78. Elim Lau to Archbishop Peter Kwong, Elim Lau to Mrs Doris Ho, 14 March 1994.

79. DGS Selection Interview, 4 June 1994, BHA, DGS Minutes File, 1994.

Four years passed quickly. In March 1999, Mrs Elim Lau informed Bishop Thomas Soo (Bishop of the Diocese of Western Kowloon 1998–2011)[80] that she was determined to retire on 31 August 1999 so that the 140th anniversary celebration and the ED's ECR 7 related reforms in the new millennium, both projects she had already begun to work on, would begin with the appointment of a new Headmistress. Following an open recruitment exercise and after deliberation by the School Council, Mrs Stella Lau was appointed.

During her tenure and retirement years, Mrs Elim Lau devoted herself to public service just as her predecessor had done. She was appointed a Justice of the Peace in 1992 and served on a number of government committees and councils, including the Hong Kong Examination Authority, the School Examination Board (as Chairperson), the Hong Kong Jockey Club Music and Dance Fund (as a trustee), the Hong Kong Schools Drama Council, the former Language Fund Advisory Committee, the Standing Committee on Language Education and Research Committee, and many others. As Headmistress of DGS, she was a member of the Yau Tsim Mong District School Principals Committee and served on the executive committee of the District's Youth Club.[81] She was appointed Member of the Most Excellent Order of the British Empire (MBE) in 1997.

The year 1999 marked the end of another era for DGS as both headmistresses, Mrs Elim Lau and Mrs Rebecca Yip, retired. During their tenure, both had upheld the school's rich culture and tradition, greatly expanded ECA, and overseen excellence in both scholastic and extracurricular activities. Both were devout Christians and caring leaders who shared with the school community love, peace, compassion, and tolerance, ensuring a spirit of cooperation and mutual respect in the school and beyond. They devoted much time to their students and greatly influenced the future development of many graduates. Under their loving and judicious guidance, the school continued to grow as one of the leading schools in Hong Kong, with its graduates much sought after by both local and prestigious overseas universities and colleges.

---

80. In 1951, following the establishment of the People's Republic of China, the Diocese of Hong Kong and Macao became a detached diocese, which did not belong to any Province. In 1998 the Province of Hong Kong Sheng Kung Hui (consisting of the Diocese of Hong Kong Island, the Diocese of Eastern Kowloon, the Diocese of Western Kowloon, and the Missionary Area of Macau) was established. Bishop Thomas Soo was Bishop of the Diocese of Western Hong Kong where DGS is located.

81. "An Interview with the Headmistress, Mrs. Elim Lau", *Quest* (1996–1998): 12–16.

Chapter 8

The Turbulent Modern Era: 1999 to 2019

The first two decades of the twenty-first century were far from peaceful in Hong Kong. Although the return of sovereignty of Hong Kong to China in July 1997 went smoothly, the city was dogged by a series of economic downturns, outbreaks of epidemics, and political upheavals. All these challenges affected the school's operation.

The Asian financial crisis began soon after July 1997 in Thailand, wreaking havoc in the Asian markets. Although Hong Kong came out relatively unscathed, its economy took time to recover. In 2008, the financial crisis caused by the bursting of the housing bubble in the United States sent shock waves through the global financial markets with widespread, devastating effects. Hong Kong was no exception and was plunged into recession for more than a year, only starting to show signs of recovery by the end of 2009.

Since 1997, Hong Kong has faced several outbreaks of emerging infectious diseases. In December 1997, Avian Influenza (H5N1) hit Hong Kong. In 2003, a mysterious and serious pneumonia known as severe acute respiratory syndrome (SARS) began in South China and spread to Hong Kong, affecting thousands and killing 300 people. The financial loss owing to SARS was estimated to be around $40 billion in Hong Kong alone.[1] In 2009, the swine flu (H1N1) epidemic, originating in the United States, arrived in Hong Kong.[2] Having learned its lesson from SARS, Hong Kong was well prepared. Although some schools where students had the disease were closed, the virus caused only a mild illness. The epidemic ended without seriously affecting the economy or school activities.

---

1. Moira Chan-Yeung, *A Medical History of Hong Kong 1942–2015* (Hong Kong: The Chinese University of Hong Kong Press, 2019), 154–163.

2. Chan-Yeung, *A Medical History of Hong Kong*, 164–166.

During the past two decades, political unrest has grown in Hong Kong as the people have begun to fear that they will lose the freedom and high degree of autonomy that were promised by the Sino-British Agreement under "One Country, Two Systems" and the Basic Law. Peaceful demonstrations demanding universal suffrage for election of members of the Legislative Council and the Chief Executive have been a consistent theme and a regular occurrence. In 2019, fuelled by the strong antipathy created by a widening wealth gap, the growing population below the poverty line, and unrealistically high real estate prices, the government's proposal for the Extradition Bill set off a series of events: a sit-in at the government headquarters on 15 March 2019, massive peaceful demonstrations, and finally ugly violence that caught the world's attention. The protests and violence persisted throughout the long, hot summer of 2019. When the school opened in September 2019, it entered its one-hundred-and-sixtieth year in a completely different era, facing much greater challenges than ever before.

Educational Development and Reforms

Despite the recurrent political turmoil, educational reforms in Hong Kong did not slow down. The second wave followed the international movement towards marketisation, accountability, and quality improvement in education. It began with the publication in 1997 of the Education Commission Report no. 7 (ECR7) entitled "Quality of Education",[3] and the reforms proposed were implemented soon afterwards. In addition, the Education Department (ED) published a number of other proposals from 1999 to 2002, such as the curriculum development proposals to be implemented simultaneously, intending to reach the targets in a very short period of time.

In 2003, the Advisory Committee on Teacher Education and Qualifications proposed that teachers be required to pursue professional development activities for no less than 150 hours during the three-year period between 2003 and 2006. The cycle of 150 hours every three years became the standard in the future. The government organised courses, seminars, and workshops so that teachers could obtain the necessary knowledge and skills to implement planned changes. These included school-based curriculum, school-based assessment, new curriculum subjects, School Management Initiatives, school self-evaluation, language proficiency for English medium for instruction, Putonghua (PTH) teaching, use of IT in teaching, learning, and management, and a number of other activities, all in addition to ongoing teaching. The seemingly endless increase in professional development activities and training soon became a serious burden. Overloaded with stress

---

3. Education Commission Report no. 7, Handbook on Education Policy in Hong Kong, accessed 26 September 2020, https://www.eduhk.hk/cird/publications/edpolicy/27.pdf.

and fatigue, some teachers resigned.[4] The Hong Kong Institute of Education organised a number of staff development days that included conferences and workshops. One of them was on "Teacher Burn Out",[5] but this regrettably failed to prevent two teachers committing suicide in the territory.[6]

As a result of the downward spiral in Hong Kong's birth rate, the reduction in the number of classes, and laying off of teachers, and even closure of primary schools, mounting pressure was created on teachers and schools, culminating in a protest by those involved in the teaching profession at the beginning of 2006.[7] Realising the serious repercussions the reforms had on the mental health of teachers, the government established a committee to study the work pressure on teachers, to investigate the causes, and to recommend the solutions. In 2007, the Secretary for Education was replaced. The new Secretary began to implement policies to improve the working conditions of the teachers, such as smaller classes, increasing salaries, establishing vice principal posts at primary schools, and slowing the speed of education reforms.[8] In the year 2008/2009, the government finally granted twelve years of free education to all school-age children.

The most drastic change to secondary schools was the implementation of the New Senior Secondary Curriculum (NSS) in 2011/2012, reducing secondary education from seven years to six years to be in line with Chinese and US secondary schools. The examinations, the Hong Kong Certificate of Education Examination (HKCEE), and the Hong Kong Advanced Level Examinations (HKALE), which were taken at the end of Forms 5 and Upper 6 respectively, were replaced by the Hong Kong Diploma of Secondary Education (HKDSE) examination at the end of six years of secondary education. University education became four years instead of three. Consistent with advances in education internationally, liberal studies and science, technology, engineering, and mathematics (STEM) programmes were introduced, as were the other learning experiences (OLE).

Education reforms during this period greatly impacted on the development of DGS in many aspects, including the physical, financial, and administrative structure of the school, the curriculum, and teaching and learning methods. However, the school embraced these changes readily, as can be seen in the following pages. It continued to expand during these

---

4. Yin Cheong Cheng, "Hong Kong Educational Reforms in the Last Decade: Reform Syndrome and New Developments", *International Journal of Educational Management* 23, no. 1 (2009): 75–76.

5. Cheng, "Hong Kong Educational Reforms in the Last Decade", 76.

6. "Teachers Protest following Stress-Related Suicides", *Education International*, 23 January 2006, accessed 28 June 2020, https://www.ei-ie.org/en/detail/54/hong-kong-teachers-protest-following-stress-related-suicides.

7. A. S. Yeung and W. P. Liu, "Workload and Psychological Well-being of Hong Kong Teachers", paper presented at the Australian Association for Research in Education, Fremantle, November 2007, accessed 29 September 2020, https://www.aare.edu.au/data/publications/2007/yeu07421.pdf.

8. Cheng, "Hong Kong Educational Reforms in the Last Decade", 81–82.

The Turbulent Modern Era: 1999 to 2019

challenging times, growing significantly in campus size and in pedagogical capacity, and it offered a world of new opportunities to its girls.

DGS and DGJS Headmistresses, 1999 to 2020

Mrs Emily Tin Mei Dai (née Ho, 戴何天美) became Junior School Headmistress in April 1999, and Mrs Stella Lai Kuen Lau (née Kun 劉靳麗娟), became Senior School Headmistress in September of the same year. When Mrs Dai retired after eighteen years of service, she was succeeded by Mrs Annie On Lai Lee (née Lee, 李李安麗), who had been a Deputy Headmistress of the Senior School.[9] Mrs Doris Ho remained the Supervisor of both the Senior and Junior schools for the next two decades, providing the necessary continuity.

Mrs Dai summarised her mission for the Junior School as follows:

> providing a holistic education based on Christian principles by nurturing spiritual, intellectual, emotional and physical well-being of our students and offering an integrated approach to learning to cultivate a spirit of intellectual enquiry and creativity, organizing a wide range of other learning experiences to acquire life, social and

Figure: 8.1a: Senior School: Mrs Stella Lai Kuen Lau (née Kun) (Headmistress 1999–present). Source: Mrs Stella Lau.

Figure 8.1b: Junior School: Mrs Emily Tin Mei Dai (née Ho) (Headmistress 1999–2016). Source: Mrs Emily Dai.

Figure 8.1c: Junior School: Mrs Annie On-lai Lee (née Lee) (Headmistress 2017–present). Source: Mrs Annie Lee.

---

9. Minutes of School Council Meeting, 22 March 2016 and 12 October 2016.

communication skills and promoting in students an awareness to serve as confident and responsible members of the global community.[10]

Mrs Lau said in an interview: "Education in post-1997 is very much learning with technology which, alongside the introduction of skills, also connects people with the outside world . . . It needs to be better provided for in terms of technological hardware and go more international." She endeavoured to help her students acquire a global mindset that prepared them for lifelong learning in the future wherever they go: "Our students should also be led to find their place in China through understanding China and acquiring their national identity."[11]

Their vision and mission for the school can be seen in the subsequent development of the school during this period. Under their able leadership, the school underwent remarkable changes, including the conversion of the Senior School from a grant school to a Direct Subsidy Scheme (DSS) school and dramatic changes to the campus under the School Improvement Plan (SIP) and the redevelopment project, which accommodated more students and provided more facilities for learning.

Teachers and Students

In 2000/2001, the school enrolment was 1,652 with 1,011 in the Senior School and 641 in the Junior School. Despite a fall in the school-age population in Hong Kong, the total enrolment increased gradually, with the rise mostly in the Junior School. In 2018/2019, total enrolment reached 2,044, the highest in the history of the school, with 1,157 students in the Senior School and 887 in the Junior School (Figure 8.2).

In 2000/2001, the school had ninety teachers, fifty-eight in the Senior School and thirty-two in the Junior School, and the student–teacher ratio for the whole school was 18.3:1. The student–teacher ratio of the Senior School, a grant school, was 19.1:1, the same as previous years, while the ratio of the Junior School, a private school, was reduced to 19.3:1 from 24.6:1 in 1986/1987. In 2000/2001, women dominated the teaching staff in the Senior School, accounting for 80 per cent. Being a girls' school with emphasis on the liberal arts, such a gender distribution is to be expected. Since the 1990s, more DGS girls have become interested in science subjects, and the number of science classes has increased from one to two (out of four classes per form). The percentage of male staff increased only to 29 per cent by 2018 as more women acquired Bachelor of Science degrees, and they became competent science teachers. With the handover in 1997 and the political situation uncertain, the percentage of expatriate teachers continued to drop, and accounted for only 3.5 per

---

10. Mrs Emily Dai, email communication, 18 August 2020.
11. Mrs Stella Lau, email communication, 17 August 2020.

The Turbulent Modern Era: 1999 to 2019

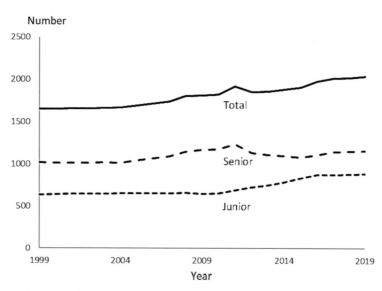

Figure 8.2: Enrolment in DGS, 1999 to 2019. Source: Data from *Quest* or Speech Day Booklets of respective years.

cent of the teaching staff in 2000/2001. As the 2000s wore on, and the political situation appeared to be stable, more expatriates joined the teaching staff, reaching 13 per cent in 2018. In the Junior School, there were no male teachers and no expatriate staff in 2000/2001. The gender, ethnicity, and qualifications of the teaching staff over the years can be found in Chapter 15, Figures 15.2 and 15.3.

In 2000, Mrs Lau increased the number of departments in the Senior School to seventeen, separating computer studies and information technology (IT) from mathematics, dividing science subjects into physics and chemistry, and giving art a separate department to encourage the further development of these subjects. In 2019, with better resources, Mrs Lau further increased the number of departments to nineteen, adding new subjects of growing importance, such as business and international studies, technology and living, and psychology, and at the same time, she encouraged interest in science earlier in school by introducing a junior science department. The nineteen departments are listed in Chapter 15, Table 15.2.

By 2019, the Junior School had formed a department for each subject: Chinese, English, mathematics, general studies I (English), general studies II (Chinese), music, art, IT, Putonghua, and scripture.

The responsibilities of a department head are numerous, with the main focus on the daily running of the department and any matters related to teaching and learning activities. These include overseeing the implementation of subject syllabuses, monitoring curriculum changes as instructed by the Curriculum Development Institute and Hong

Kong Examination Assessment and Authority, advising the school on developments in the subject and the choice of curriculum, the deployment of teachers, annual assessment of teachers, encouraging colleagues in the department to take part in professional development, to plan expenditure, control and allocation of funds and resources, and to put together a budget for the operation of the department for the school's approval. The head of a department could also be a teacher in charge of the extracurricular activities (ECA) teams, besides the Curriculum and Studies Team, and is also responsible for communicating with other departments. The decentralisation of duties enables the Headmistress to explore more broadly the school's future developments by establishing connections with the local community and the world at large, to ensure a bright future for her students wherever they will be.

Figure 8.3: Mrs S. Lau and Senior School staff, 2001/2002. Source: *Quest* 2001–2002, 8.
From left to right:
Fourth row: Mr C. T. Fung, Mr S. Chu, Mr J. Oddie, Dr T.W. Leung, Mr M. W. Or, Mr S. Mok, Mr J. Ng, Mr K. L. Tang, Mrs Y. T. To, Mrs W. Chiu, Mrs H. Au, Mrs L. Tang, Mrs K. Y. Lam, Mrs A. Lo, Ms K. Soong, Ms J. E. Howard, Miss C. Wong
Third row: Miss A. Leung, Mrs M. Law, Miss K. Suthiphongchai, Miss K. Leung, Miss I. Cheung, Miss Y. Leung, Mrs P. S. Tong, Miss S. Ko, Mrs P. Lee, Mrs A. Chan, Miss K. M. Tsui, Mrs K. M. Lee, Mrs L. Yip, Mrs R. Santos, Miss C. Ho
Second row: Miss D. Wong, Mrs A. Wong, Mrs J. Chan, Mrs S. P. Sum, Mrs C. Chan, Miss M. Ng, Miss S. Y. Fang, Miss B. Lee, Miss C. Ng, Mrs C. Chiu, Mrs A. Cheng, Mrs L. Wong, Mrs J. Ng, Mrs P. Kam
Front row: Mrs M. Fong, Mr N. B. Wong, Mrs K. L. Shing, Mr S. K. Lam, Mrs J. Chiu, Mr T. Man, Mrs S. Lau, Mrs A. Lee, Mr M. H. Au, Mrs A. Leung, Mrs C. P. Ho, Mrs P. Hui. Absent: Mrs L. Grady

The Turbulent Modern Era: 1999 to 2019

Figure 8.4: Mrs E. Dai and Junior School staff, 2001/2002. Source: *Quest* 2001–2002, 182.
Front left to right:
Third row: Miss M. Lam, Mrs L. Chan, Miss K. Li, Miss K. L. Shing, Miss T. W. Tang, Miss A. Koo, Mrs V. Ng, Miss K. N. Chou, Miss A. Cheung, Miss S. H. Wong, Miss E. Poon
Second row: Mr O. Lee, Miss W. Cheung, Mrs C. K. Chung, Miss L. Leung, Miss H. K. Lee, Mrs J. Holdefer, Miss P. Wong, Miss L. Wong, Mrs T. Fung, Mrs P. Lee, Miss L. Cheng, Mrs J. Taylor
Front row: Mrs W. K. Lo, Mrs C. Fan, Mrs C. Cheung, Mrs N. Yau, Miss O. L. Ma, Mrs E. Dai, Mrs M. Leung, Mrs K. Watt, Mrs C. Yeung, Mrs L. Fung, Mrs C. Chiang

The Senior School Turning into a Direct Subsidy Scheme School

As mentioned earlier, DGS did not join the Direct Subsidy Scheme (DSS) when it was initially proposed in ECR3 in 1991. In December 2001, the government again invited schools to join the DSS.[12] Under this scheme, schools were allowed to collect school fees in addition to the subsidy from the government, and were free to decide on their entrance requirements and design their own curriculum, although the curriculum had to meet the standards for local examinations. At around that time, the ED abolished the Academic Aptitude Test (AAT), which had been used to classify students into five bands for placement in secondary schools. Instead, the students were divided into three bands for allocation purposes, based on the performance in AAT by the students in their schools over the past three years. With fewer categories, the students' scholastic abilities varied widely within each band, making teaching more difficult because of the diverse academic strengths and weaknesses of students in the same class. This compulsory allocation process made it less attractive for a secondary school to remain as a grant school.[13]

---

12. From Director of Education to Supervisor/Heads of all Secondary Schools and Primary Schools, Circular Memorandum no. 210/2001, 28 June 2001, Re: Direct Subsidy Scheme (DSS).
13. Cheng, "Hong Kong Educational Reforms in the Last Decade", 71.

At the same time, the ED indicated that the "through-train" mode would allow a primary school to transfer its graduates directly to its linked secondary school without going through the central allocation process, but only schools that satisfied certain conditions laid down by the ED could be linked: the primary and secondary schools should have similar philosophies and aspirations for education; the number of Secondary 1 places (first year secondary school) in the school must exceed the number of Primary 6 graduates of the linked primary school; and the primary and secondary schools must have the same mode of financing to ensure consistency in admission criteria, although a private primary school could be linked to a secondary school that was either a private or a DSS school.[14]

In 2001, DGS Senior and Junior schools satisfied only the first two requirements. To be fully qualified for the through-train mode, the two schools were either to be a private school or a DSS school as stipulated in the third requirement. The Senior School was at that time a grant school and the Junior School a private school. The only way for them to be linked was for the Senior School to change to DSS status or to become a private school since the Junior School had attempted on several previous occasions to change its status back to a subsidized school without success (Chapter 6).[15] After lengthy discussions and serious planning, DGS decided to join the DSS. This change would provide opportunities for the school to introduce its own curriculum and set its own student admissions criteria and tuition fees, while at the same time receiving a subsidy from the government, enabling it to employ more teachers and to upgrade its facilities to enrich school life—conditions that the grant schools had been fighting for in the past. This would also provide an opportunity for the school to expand.[16]

A consultation session with the Parent Teacher Association (PTA) was held on 11 June 2004, when over 650 parents and representatives from the Education and Manpower Bureau (EMB, the new name for the ED from 2003) attended the meeting. The consultation session was very cordial, and there was unanimous support for the decision to join the DSS. By then, St Paul's College, St Paul's Coeducational College, and DBS had already made this change. The parents who did not come to the meeting were fully informed of the outcome in a letter dated 24 June 2004 from the supervisor of the school.[17] As a DSS school, DGS's annual tuition fee was $38,000 payable in ten equal instalments. Some DSS schools were criticised for raising school fees despite the economic downturn and for benefiting the private education sector and well-off students at the expense of the public sector. The

---

14. Appendix 1: "Through-Train Mode", Education Bureau, accessed 29 September 2020, https://www.edb.gov.hk/en/edu-system/primary-secondary/applicable-to-primary-secondary/through-train/index.html.

15. Minutes of School Council Meeting, 7 May 2001.

16. Diocesan Girls' School, Participation in the Direct Subsidy Scheme and School Expansion Plan, 2001, attached to Minutes of School Council File, 7 May 2001.

17. Minutes of School Council Meeting, 26 July 2004.

fees at DGS were below the general level charged by comparable schools and matched the hopes of most stakeholders. The parents and staff were relieved, while the public welcomed the decision as admission was territory-wide. A fee remission programme was available for financially disadvantaged students.

The School Council had deliberated at great lengths over the effect of the school's conversion to DSS status, as it might put some students at a disadvantage. DGS historically was a school for underprivileged young girls, with a mission to provide an education of excellence based on the Christian faith to girls of all sectors. Before the conversion, about 50 per cent of students in Form 1 came from "outside" schools, some of whom might have had less privileged backgrounds. As a DSS school, DGS was obliged to reserve no less than 10 per cent of total school fees for fee remission. A brief study of the fee remission programme shows that the reserved funds were fully utilised. From 2005 to 2019, there were altogether 454 applications for fee remission—twenty-five to fifty per year—and all were approved. Between 2005 and 2013, the total amount spent was less than 50 per cent of the reserved funds for fee remission, and the school decided to use the rest of the funds on scholarships. From 2013, the amount spent on fee remission increased, and together with scholarships reached 90–100 per cent, with two years exceeding 100 per cent. The school also offered scholarships from a number of donors. However, it is unclear to what extent the school lost potentially bright and gifted students because its DSS status may have dissuaded less privileged families from sending their daughters there.

The target date for conversion of the Senior School to DSS and the through-train arrangement with the Junior School was September 2005.[18] The School Council, incorporated under Ordinance as the sponsoring body of the school, entered into contract with the government to set up the DSS structure. A School Management Committee (SMC) was required to be formed which would enter into a service agreement with the government.[19] A DSS subsidy would be granted by the government to the SMC every year, calculated on the number of student intake; in return, the SMC was responsible for the submission of annual school reports, education plans, and account statements to the Education and Manpower Bureau (EMB), which would review the performance of the school periodically. The school sponsoring body remained in charge of the oversight of the school's mission.

Students who were admitted before 2005 followed the old fee schedule until their graduation, but new students admitted after 2005 had to pay school fees at $38,000 per year for all forms. Table 8.1 shows the Senior School fees before the changeover to the DSS and the fees during the transition years. This includes the classes where the government provided free education up to nine years (Primary 1 to 6 and Forms 1 to 3), starting 1998/1999. The fees of the Senior School have not increased since 2005.

---

18. Minutes of School Council Meeting, 28 April 2004.
19. Minutes of School Council Meeting, 14 September 2005.

Table 8.1: Senior School fees (HKD) before and during the transition years to DSS

Year	Form 1	Form 2	Form 3	Form 4	Form 5	Form 6	Form 7[+]
2004–2005	0	0	180	5,340	5,340	9,040	9,040
2005–2006	38,000	0	180	5,340	5,340	9,040	9,040
2006–2007	38,000	38,000	180	5,340	5,340	9,040	9,040
2007–2008	38,000	38,000	38,000	6,310	6,310	10,160	10,160
2008–2009	38,000	38,000	38,000	38,000	290[*]	290[*]	290[*]
2009–2010	38,000	38,000	38,000	38,000	38,000	290[*]	290[*]
2010–2011	38,000	38,000	38,000	38,000	38,000	38,000	290[*]
2011–2012	38,000	38,000	38,000	38,000	38,000	38,000	38,000

Source: School Archives. Note: Form 4 and above paid school fees from 2004/2005 to 2007/2008; [*]from 2008/2009, free education for Form 4 upwards began and students from these forms only paid *tong fai*; [+] Upper Six.

Under the DSS, any surplus funds from DGS are ploughed back into the school via the SMC, and used for appointment of more teachers with better qualifications, for professional development of the staff, and subsidies to students so they can attend exchange programmes outside Hong Kong.

The Junior School, being a private school directly operated by the School Council, charged $29,000 per year in 1998/1999. The fees rose almost every year, reaching $67,000 in 2018/2019, partly owing to an increase in teachers' salaries and the growing number of teachers, and partly due to inflation.

Relationship with Hong Kong Sheng Kung Hui

As readers will recall, in 1969 the school was incorporated as a legal entity by the Council of the Diocesan Girls' School Ordinance (Chapter 1124), with full power to manage, administer, and operate the school. From its early days as a girls' school and orphanage, the school has always maintained a close relationship with the Anglican Church of Hong Kong (Hong Kong Sheng Kung Hui from 1998 onwards), with the Bishop or his representative being the Chairman of the School Council, and the Vicar of St Andrew's Church also serving on the school's board. Accordingly, DGS benefits from the Christian guidance and ministry of the Church, and its students, in turn, serve the Church through choral singing and other activities.

During Archbishop Peter Kwong's tenure, there was a conscious effort to draw a line between the liabilities of the Church and Anglican grant schools. The Anglican (Hong Kong) Secondary Schools Council Limited (or the Anglican Council) was formed to coordinate the group of Sheng Kung Hui schools (Category A) and schools affiliated with HKSKH (Category B) to contribute to Christian education in Hong Kong. DGS belonged to Category B and was invited to join the Anglican Council as an Affiliated Member in 2006.[20]

The School Campus

School Improvement Plan or Extension Phase III

In 2001, the ED, under the School Improvement Plan (SIP), scheduled to upgrade about 800 schools to "Y2K or Year 2000 standard", appropriate for the new millennium, by 2005. DGS was placed in the final phase of the programme. Following a visit to the school to assess its facilities, the ED sent several proposals to the school, and DGS elected to demolish the old gymnasium block and replace it with a building equipped with up-to-date facilities.[21]

While the government would pay for the construction of the building, it provided only Y2K standard facilities; the school would have to upgrade them for other uses. The SIP building,[22] which was finally completed in 2005, incorporated the school campus's signature blue and grey colours with the horizontal building lines of the Extension Phase I. Thus, it integrated very well with the rest of the buildings in the campus. While inconspicuous from the outside, the building boasted many modern facilities: a mini-theatre, a computer learning centre, a liberal studies room, language rooms, a dance/drama studio with stage lighting and professional stage equipment, a multipurpose air-conditioned gymnasium for various sports, a rooftop tennis court, a music room, and four music practice rooms. Completed in 2005, this was the best one-hundred-and-forty-fifth anniversary present the school could have.

School Redevelopment Project: An Ambitious Undertaking

The conversion to DSS enabled DGS not only to redevelop the whole campus but also to obtain partial funding from the government.[23] However, the question arose as where to locate the redeveloped school. The school, standing on 1 Jordan Road since 1913, had deep roots there. Until the Second World War, the neighbourhood was quiet, but with the population explosion after the war, it became much more crowded. The advantage of having an MTR station at Jordan Road, while offering convenient transportation to staff and

---

20. Minutes of School Council Meeting, 29 August 2006.
21. "The School Improvement Project", *Quest* (2003–2004): 24.
22. "The School Improvement Project", *Quest* (2005–2006): 39.
23. Minutes of School Council Meeting, 28 April 2004, Annex C.

Figure 8.5a: School Improvement Plan or Extension Phase III. Source: *Quest* 2005–2006, 37.

Figure 8.5b: Bird's-eye view of the school, 2009. Source: School Archives.

students, was offset by increasing congestion in the area along Chi Wo Street. In addition, being located between two major roads, Jordan Road and Gascoigne Road—the latter having a flyover leading to the West Kowloon Corridor—meant air and noise pollution.[24] Another issue was size: would the present site be big enough to accommodate both schools after their expansion? Extensive discussion on the pros and cons of the matter showed how difficult it was to make a decision.

Mrs Stella Lau tried hard to identify new and suitable land for redevelopment, but to no avail. When DGS was told by EMB that it believed the size of the Jordan Road site was adequate for a 24-classroom primary school and a 36-classroom senior school, and therefore was not prepared to increase the land allotment to DGS, the incentive to relocate the school diminished. In the end, it was decided to rebuild the school in situ.[25]

The initial plan in 2006 was to demolish the Gibbins Wing, the Hurrell Wing with the Chapel, the Symons Block, the swimming pool, and the 1975 Junior School; this would cost $380 million. Further discussion centred around whether it would be better to demolish all buildings except the SIP building, which had only recently been completed. There were good reasons to demolish the Phase I and II extensions, which were completed in 1993 and 1996 respectively, because extensive renovation of these buildings would be required to integrate them with the rest of the redeveloped plan, and they would be more difficult to maintain in the future when all the new buildings were in place. The School Council expanded the school building subcommittee, led by Mr Marco Wu, from six members to twelve and set up a redevelopment project office in April 2007.[26] Despite the higher cost involved, the School Council, after careful deliberation and evaluation, finally decided to demolish all the buildings except the SIP building.[27]

After competitive tendering from six architectural firms, the building subcommittee, supported by the School Council, appointed Palmer and Turner, who had designed the Junior School in the 1970s, as the main architect, Rider Levett Bucknall Ltd as the quantity surveyor, and Penta Ocean Construction Co Ltd as the main contractor. The design that was approved by the School Council involved a budget of $630–640 million. The government agreed to provide the Senior School with $208.6 million and the Junior School with $175.8 million, a total of $371.6 million for the redevelopment project. The school would have to raise the rest of the funds.[28]

In 2008, donations pledged for the redevelopment plan amounted to around $180 million, $100 million short of the target. More fundraising activities were organised by

---

24. "Girls' School Pollution to Get an Airing", *South China Morning Post*, 18 December 1994.
25. Minutes of School Council Meeting, 13 December 2006.
26. Minutes of School Council Meeting, 13 December 2006.
27. Minutes of School Council Meeting, 6 November 2007.
28. Minutes of School Council Meeting, 23 March 2009.

the PTA and the Diocesan Old Girls' Association.[29] By February 2010, the Fundraising Committee, led by Mr Kenneth Ting, had raised another $80 million, making a total of $260 million including pledges.[30] Despite the economic downturn during this period, the amount pledged showed the remarkable support and the generosity of the parents, alumnae, and friends of DGS. The foundation stone laying ceremony took place on 22 April 2010, and the school requested two "hotel schools" from the Education Bureau (EDB, the EMB having changed its name in 2008, with the removal of Manpower to another bureau) to accommodate the school during the period of redevelopment.

Farewell and Time Capsule Ceremony

On 26 March 2009, the DGS family gathered at the Jordan Road campus to bid farewell to the old buildings in a ceremony presided over by Bishop Thomas Soo. As the choir, drawn from alumnae, with Senior and Junior School students, led the congregation in singing the "Te Deum", the drizzle stopped and the sun shone—a very auspicious day, indeed, for closing the campus. A ceremony followed in which fourteen items from the Junior and Senior schools, representing different aspects of life at the old campus and fond memories, were put into a time capsule in the shape of the Centenary Hall and sealed. The ceremony culminated in the congregation singing the school hymn; many were touched by the lyrics, and tears welled up. The ceremony ended with a familiar closing hymn, "Lord Dismiss Us with Thy Blessing".[31]

The school relocated to its hotel school locations over the Easter holidays of 2009.[32] The students knew little about what new experiences would await them upon their return.

The "Hotel Schools"

The EDB arranged for the Junior School to decamp to a public housing estate at Tseung Kwan O for the three-year rebuilding period. The facilities in this hotel school were found to be adequate, with seating capacity for 400 students, a basketball court, a covered playground, two multimedia learning centres, a big library, and several special rooms. The whole school was networked, with computer outlets in each room. The Headmaster of the previous decanted school agreed to leave behind hardware and fixtures for the Junior School.[33] The hotel school was only a twenty-minute drive from the Jordan Road campus.

---

29. Minutes of School Council Meeting, 23 November 2009.
30. Minutes of School Council Meeting, 24 February 2010.
31. "Farewell Service and Time Capsule Ceremony", *Quest* (2009–2010): 40.
32. Minutes of School Council Meeting, 23 March 2009.
33. Minutes of School Council Meeting, 4 January 2007.

The Turbulent Modern Era: 1999 to 2019

To avoid adding to heavy traffic during peak hours in the area, the new school hours began early at 8:10 am and ended early at 3:10 pm, and most students used the school bus services. When almost 900 parents toured the temporary school at the Parents' House-Warming Party on 30 April 2009, they were pleased with the set-up.[34] The Junior School students adjusted well to their new environment.

The Senior School was housed at Tack Ching Girls' School in Sham Shui Po. Owing to a delay in the rebuilding of Pooi To Middle School, the previous tenant of the premises, DGS decanting was postponed until the Easter holidays of 2009 instead of September 2008.[35] Both hotel schools required minor renovations and upgrades to security measures. The Junior School spent about $1.5 million on these renovations. As for the Tack Ching campus, the Architectural Service Department and EDB worked closely with the school to provide basic facilities within the limited time.

The transition of the Senior School to its hotel school went smoothly. The small and compact campus brought the students closer, enhancing their sense of belonging. The morning assembly was carried out in the basketball court in good weather; when it rained, the morning assembly moved to the hall for junior form girls. The school also had a small chapel on the seventh floor.[36] To compensate for the lack of space for ECA, the premises of nearby SKH Kei Fook Primary School were rented for after-school activities, such as basketball, table tennis, badminton, and Chinese orchestra practice. Whole-school annual activities such as Speech Day, mini-bazaar, and educational visits continued. The comprehensive school review conducted by the EDB went ahead as scheduled. In general, school life continued more or less as usual on the temporary school premises.[37]

When the students returned to the new campus in September 2011, they were surprised and delighted with the spacious buildings and the state-of-the-art facilities, especially the computer network and IT services.[38]

The New Campus

Reconstruction took twenty-eight months. With its main structures laid out in the plan of a cross, the redeveloped campus is expansive with buildings occupying most of the plot except for the entrance area (Plate 8a and b, Plate 9, Plate 10). The architect managed to maximise the utility of the land for building by introducing podiums with atriums and balconies at different levels. Alumnae would be unable to recognise it as their old school

---

34. Minutes of School Council meeting, 22 May 2009.
35. Minutes of School Council Meeting, 5 July 2007.
36. "Our New Home, 101 Castle Peak Road", *Quest* (2009–2010): 29.
37. Minutes of School Council Meeting, 22 May 2009.
38. Minutes of School Council Meeting, 24 February 2010.

Figure 8.6a: "Hotel school" in Sham Shui Po, c. 2009. Source: School Archives.

Figure 8.6b: Morning assembly at the Sham Shui Po "hotel school" campus, girls seated on their own beach stools.

from the street, except for the blue and grey colour of the buildings and the large school crest on the wall of the building where the Symons Block used to be. The Senior School has doubled in size, allowing additional classrooms for more students and more facilities for science and technology, for teaching of languages, and for ECAs. Likewise, the Junior School has tripled its usable area.

The familiar field on which alumnae played or relaxed in their old school days has been replaced by verdant grass strips situated at DOGA Place opposite the DGS Plaza. The sports field is now 13 metres above ground, and walled in from Chi Wo Street and Jordan Road. A three-laned, 176-metre non-standard track surrounds the sports field, which is made of artificial turf that has replaced the previous high-maintenance lawn. The sports field comprises areas for high jump, long jump, discus, shot put, javelin, hockey, handball, rugby, and golf. The swimming pool has six 25-metre lanes equipped with FINA standard competition diving platform (Plate 11). The well-stocked library is equipped with state-of-the-art computers for research and offers a peaceful ambience. The 200-seat chapel, heralded by a piece of DGS history, the 1959 brass bell, is open to all who seek spiritual guidance. Thus, the loss of the lawn has been fully compensated for by the space and the state-of-the-art facilities.[39]

The move back to 1 Jordan Road was particularly exciting for the Junior School girls, who experienced a fine mixture of novelty and nostalgia. The girls were delighted that their favourite old garden—the Middle Garden—the playground with swings, and the reading castle were still present, but had been given a new look. The Middle Garden is now surrounded by the school building, and this is where the playground equipment of the former Corner Garden can be found. The Environmental and Gardening Club has turned the Middle Garden into their harvest backyard, with members promoting green practices to their fellow schoolmates.

The Gascoigne Road entrance to the Junior School has a landscaped courtyard facing the two-storey library, a favourite place for the girls, the Assembly Hall, and the Performing Arts Centre (Plate 10). The main building has dedicated rooms on the ground level, such as the Chinese Culture Room and the PTA room, where parents spend countless hours planning activities and making important decisions for the benefit of the school and students. The well-equipped gymnasium is on Level 2, while the Modern Science Centre with fully equipped workstations and the Student Activity Centre are located on Level 8.[40]

The hard work and dedication of the headmistresses, the school supervisor, members of the School Building Subcommittee, and members of the Fundraising Campaign

---

39. "The Campus", *Quest* (2011–2012): 11–38.
40. Headmistress's (DGJS) Report of 2011/2012.

Figure 8.7: Old school bell in the redeveloped campus. Source: School Archives.

Figure 8.8a: Senior School library. Source: School Archives.

Figure 8.8b: DGS Plaza. Source: School Archives.

The Turbulent Modern Era: 1999 to 2019   211

Figure 8.9: Junior School playground and basketball court. Source: School Archives.

Committee should be recorded with appreciation here. The redevelopment of DGS was a daunting undertaking.

The redeveloped campus, completed on schedule, was ready for occupation in September for the new academic year 2011/2012. The opening ceremony took place on Speech Day, 17 January 2013, when the school also celebrated its one-hundred-and-fifty-third anniversary.[41] The ceremony was officiated by the Most Reverend Dr Paul Kwong, Archbishop and Primate of the HKSKH (Archbishop 2007 to 2020) (Figure 8.10).[42]

A New Administrative Structure and a New Management

After the Education (Amendment) Ordinance was enacted in 2004, the DGS School Council duly formed the Diocesan Girls' School Management Committee Limited (DGSMC), a company limited by guarantee, and signed a management agreement with DGSMC over the supervision and administration of DGS. DGSMC, in turn, signed an agreement with the government to manage and operate DGS. The purpose of the SMC

---

41. Headmistress's Report for 2011/2012 Speech Day Booklet, 17 January 2013.
42. *Quest* (2013–2014): 33–34.

Figure 8.10: Opening ceremony of the redeveloped campus on 17 January 2013 by Archbishop Dr Paul Kwong. Source: School Archives.

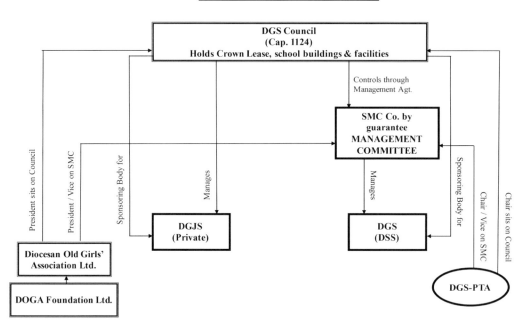

Figure 8.11: DGS administrative group structure. Source: School Archives.

was to decentralise and transfer some decision-making processes from the EDB to individual schools in matters related to school finance, human resources, and curriculum design, among others. However, in return, schools had to satisfy government regulatory requirements, such as limiting the maximum number of managers from the sponsoring body to sixty per cent of the SMC board, with the balance being represented by respectable citizens from the community in order to provide additional input to the school.

The DGS School Council had been managing both schools after 1947, following the ED's approval for the Junior School to be separated from the Senior School. However, with the conversion of the Senior School to DSS in 2005, the DGSMC managed the Senior School while the School Council continued to manage the Junior School.[43] Some members of the School Council became ex-officio members of the DGSMC. Mrs Doris Ho remained the Supervisor of both schools. The administrative structure of DGS is shown in Figure 8.11.

In 2019, the membership of the School Council was as follows:

Chairman: The Rt Rev. Andrew Chan

Vice-Chairman: The Rev. Alex McCoy

Members: Mrs Doris Ho (Supervisor)

Mrs Stella Lau (Headmistress, Senior School)

Mrs Annie Lee (Headmistress, Junior School)

Mrs Josephine Chang (Hon. Treasurer)

Mrs Sheilah Chatjaval

Mr Ronnie Cheng

Ms Stephanie Cheung

Mrs Yvette Ho

Prof. Arthur Li

Mr Hardy Lok

Mrs Ng Saw Kheng

Mrs Susanna Wong

Mr Marco Wu

Ms Benita Yu

The Hon. Madam Justice Yuen, JA

Ms Yvonne Chan (President, DOGA Ltd.)

Mrs Sherlynn Chan Wong (Chairperson PTA)

---

43. Minutes of School Council Meeting, 16 July 2009.

The Junior School Headmistress became a full member of the School Council in 2005. When DGS switched to DSS mode, the Junior School Headmistress was also invited to become a member of the DGSMC.

In addition, the EDB required the school to set up at least four subcommittees under the DGSMC in Finance, Development, IT, and Legal. The DGSMC members were to serve as heads of these subcommittees. The DGSMC monitored the work of the different subcommittees and served as checks and balances on the work of the school. The different subcommittees meetings were held on an ad hoc basis to allow flexibility. The School Council and DGSMC conducted regular quarterly meetings, with additional meetings held as necessary. The terms of service of the School Council and DGSMC members ranged from three to six years; both could be renewed.

The new DSS status and the management of a much larger complex required new administration strategies. The Senior and Junior schools, financed differently, had to be separately managed.[44] To cope with this, the school had an administrative team for the first time.[45] Dr Thomas Man, the former vice principal of the Senior School, who understood the internal operation of the school well, was appointed as head and coordinator of the administrative unit in September 2011. The administrative unit was responsible for the operation of six different offices: a school office responsible for janitorial services; an accounts office; a development and public relations office; a facility management office; a technical support office; and a maintenance and repair office. More non-teaching staff were employed to ensure that the school ran smoothly.[46]

Communication in the New Campus

IT is vital to have good communication in the expanded campus. Fortunately, this was planned for by DGS early. Even before the new millennium, the school had participated in the first five years (1998–2003) of IT in the ED's Education Project. During these five years, DGS developed its intranet system with a local area network linking most parts of the campus. The school had two multimedia learning centres, two computer rooms, and projection facilities mounted in all laboratories, classrooms, and dedicated rooms. The IT Department had a supporting team and a coordinating team for maintaining the day-to-day administration as well as applying IT in teaching and learning.[47] In 2000, the IT Department received $474,000 from the ED's Quality Education Fund to set up a web-based ECA information system to automate management and dissemination of ECA

---

44. Minutes of School Council Meeting, 1 February 2011.
45. Minutes of School Council Meeting, 1 February 2011.
46. Dr Thomas Man, email communication, 12 August 2020.
47. C. P. Ho, IT in Education, Report for 2000.

The Turbulent Modern Era: 1999 to 2019

activities. Following this, the IT Department wisely concentrated on the development of eClass and virtual classroom systems for most academic subjects, which proved to be vital when the COVID-19 pandemic broke out.

In the redeveloped campus, all buildings were connected to the school network via optic fibre backbone and wireless local area network. The day-to-day administration and the library were all computerised. All the classrooms and special-use rooms were covered by a Wi-Fi network. In addition, a video conferencing system was installed in the Modern Language Centre and in the Chinese Cultural Centre.[48] The campus had TV sets outside halls and along corridors, projectors and audiovisual systems in halls, and video-conferencing facilities in various rooms.[49]

The total budget for IT infrastructure for the new campus was $8 million, and every year there was a budget earmarked for upgrading the facilities. The IT Department became the nerve system of the DGS campus, allowing the school to operate smoothly and effectively.

School Expansion and Primary 1 Admission

The redeveloped campus enabled the school to expand. Previously, the Junior School had eighteen classes, three classes per level. In the school year 2011/2012, the first year of operation in the redeveloped school campus, the Junior School began to recruit four instead of three classes in Primary 1. By 2016/2017, the Junior School operated at full size with twenty-four classes.[50] The Senior School had already begun to expand from four to five classes starting in Form 1 in 2005, and by 2011/2012, the Senior School had five classes per form. The plan was to increase further to six classes per form when space became available on the redeveloped campus.[51] However, with the progressive reduction in student population in Hong Kong, this expansion plan was put on hold in 2011/2012. On this occasion, the increase of four to five classes per form did not affect students in Form 1 academically as before. The new girls were selected based on their primary school record and a face-to-face interview by the Headmistress.

Admission to DGS is much sought after. When the Junior school had three classes in Primary 1, there were consistently over 2,000 applicants for about 110 places. As every girl had to be interviewed, it usually took about forty-five days to complete the admission interviews. For the school year 2009/2010, Mrs Emily Dai proposed a different set-up for Primary 1 admission. Parents were encouraged to download the application form from the school website and return the completed forms by registered mail. In October 2009,

---

48. Headmistress's Report for 2011–2012 Speech Day Booklet, 17 January 2013.
49. Minutes of School Council Meeting, 24 February 2010.
50. Mrs Emily Dai, email communication, 29 March 2021.
51. Minutes of School Council Meeting, 28 April 2004, Annex C.

the first round of interviews was carried out with the girls in groups and all the primary school teachers taking part. These group interviews were completed smoothly in two days. Between 500 and 600 candidates were selected for the second round of interviews. These were conducted by Mrs Dai, the Headmistress, and a senior teacher individually with each girl, starting in November. A committee then vetted the recommended list and made appropriate decisions before releasing the results.[52] This format reduced the number of days for interviews by about two-thirds and has been practised since.

Quality of Education: Staff Development, Quality Assurance, External Review

The ED proposed a number of educational reforms at the turn of the century to improve the quality of education, especially the quality of teachers. By 1999, there were still a number of teachers in the Junior School who were non-degree holders and were referred to as certificated mistresses. Dedicated and excellent teachers, many of them took bachelor/master's degree courses to upgrade their qualifications as university-graduate teachers,[53] even before the ED changed its regulation requiring all teachers to hold a bachelor's degree by 2004.[54]

When DGS became a DSS school, more funds became available. One result was that the terms of employment for teachers improved. To attract better qualified teachers, DGS offered a better salary package with medical insurance coverage. More teachers were employed so that each class could be divided into smaller groups and students received more individualised attention.[55] The increase in the number of teachers resulted in a reduction of the student–teacher ratio in the Senior School[56] from 17.4:1 in 2000/2001 to 11.2:1 in 2018/2019.

The school spent the bulk of its income on staff salaries and benefits, hoping to recruit and to retain quality and experienced teachers, many of whom had postgraduate qualifications and training.[57] Development days were organised, as required by the ED, for teachers to learn new areas of development such as IT in Education, or to improve their skills in teaching as in the STEM programmes. Teachers attended conferences organised by the Institute of Education or some other institutions through exchange programmes in the city

---

52. Minutes of School Council Meeting, 10 September 2009; Minutes of School Council Meeting, 23 November 2009.

53. Mrs Emily Dai, email communication, 18 August 2020.

54. "Hong Kong: Teacher and Principal Quality", Centre on International Education Benchmarking, accessed 2 April 2021, https://ncee.org/what-we-do/center-on-international-education-benchmarking/top-performing-countries/hong-kong-overview/hong-kong-teacher-and-principal-quality/.

55. Minutes of School Council Meeting, 22 June 2015.

56. Mr S. K. Lam, email communication, 16 September 2020.

57. Minutes of School Council Meeting, 13 March 2013.

The Turbulent Modern Era: 1999 to 2019

or overseas. These teachers then shared their experience with their colleagues.[58] In 2010, the school arranged for teachers in both the Senior and Junior schools to visit the Expo 2010 in Shanghai as part of their staff development programme.[59]

Echoing the international trend of educational quality assurance in the 1990s and the proposals in ECR7, the ED established a Quality Assurance Programme in 1997 to develop a system of performance indicators for reviewing schools. All aided and DSS schools were required to conduct self-evaluations and report them annually, along with their achievements and follow-up actions in the school reports that should be endorsed by the school management committees. From 2004, EMB started school reviews once every four years to validate the schools' self-evaluation.[60]

DGS had its first comprehensive review in 2010, the sixth year of DSS operation. The EDB found that, in general, the school performed well in areas related to student support and received tremendous support from parents. DGS student performance was excellent, but two areas of concern were identified: while teamwork contributed to the success in the school, there was an age gap among the teachers, and it was recommended that the school should make careful succession plans to pave the way for prospective leaders; while the school performed well academically in many areas and also scored high in music competitions in groups or in solos, it did not perform as well in the academic study of music. In response, the school directed resources and attention to building a comprehensive music programme for students who wished to study music academically.[61]

Quality of Education: New Curriculum and Pedagogy

New Senior Secondary Curriculum (NSS) and GCE A-Level Curriculum

In 2004, the EMB proposed to change the senior secondary education and university education from the existing British system of 3+2+2+3 (three years of junior secondary, two years of senior secondary, two years of matriculation, and three years of university) to a new academic structure of 3+3+4 (three years of junior secondary, three years of senior secondary, and four years of university), which is more aligned with the Chinese and US higher education systems. The Primary 5 students of the 2004/2005 school year would be the first cohort to enter this new academic structure. Students would have six years of secondary education with the NSS curriculum, including four core subjects: Chinese language, English language, mathematics, and liberal studies; and two to three additional

---

58. Minutes of School Council Meeting, 20 March 2019.
59. Minutes of School Council Meeting, 3 November 2010.
60. Cheng, "Hong Kong Educational Reforms in the Last Decade", 72.
61. Minutes of School Council Meeting, 27 September 2011.

subjects from twenty NSS elective subjects (Category A) or applied learning courses (Category B) according to their interests. Students could also take other languages (French, German, Japanese, Spanish, Hindu, or Urdu) as elective subjects (Category C). Students also had to acquire OLE for whole-person development. These included moral and civic education, community service, aesthetic development, physical development, and career-related experiences.[62] The NSS curriculum was first implemented in 2009/2010 for Form 4 students or Secondary 4 students—at the same time, classes in the Senior School were no longer called Form 1–6 but Secondary 1–6.

The aim of introducing liberal studies and making it compulsory was to ensure that all students developed an understanding of the major issues confronting society in the twenty-first century and that the students were equipped with the critical thinking skills they needed in order to make informed, critical judgements about these issues. The areas of study included self and personal development; society and culture; science, technology, and the environment; and independent enquiry in which the students were to conduct their own research into a problem of their choice in areas such as education, religion, sports, art, media, and information and communication technology (ICT). Thus, the subjects contained elements of science, humanities, and liberal arts, and ensured that all students would have some degree of breadth in their senior secondary studies.

In 2012, the HKDSE was introduced to assess students at the end of six years of secondary education, abolishing and replacing the HKCEE, which was conducted at the end of five years of the old secondary education system. In the HKDSE, the results of Category A subjects were classified into five levels, 1 to 5, with 5 being the highest and 1 the lowest. The level 5 candidates with the best performance were awarded a 5**, and the next top group of candidates were awarded a 5*. Performance below level 1 was designated as "Unclassified" and was not reported on the certificate.[63] Britain's Universities and Colleges Admission Services, after an in-depth study of Hong Kong's new secondary curriculum, considered HKDSE equivalent to the UK's GCE A-level. The HKDSE was also found to be equivalent to the Australian Secondary Certificate of Education, and a high school diploma from a university preparatory programme in the USA.[64]

The year 2012/2013 was called the year of "Double Cohort". During that year, two groups of students entered university: the last batch of Upper 6 students who had passed the HKALE, which was abolished after 2012, and the first to pass the HKDSE.[65] Judging from

---

62. Cheng, "Hong Kong Educational Reforms in the Last Decade", 70.

63. Hong Kong Examination and Assessment Authority, accessed 15 July 2020, http://www.hkeaa.edu.hk/en/hkdse/introduction/.

64. WENR, Secondary Education in Hong Kong, accessed 15 July 2020, https://wenr.wes.org/2013/01/wenr-januaryfebruary-2013-hong-kong-secondary-education.

65. Minutes of School Council Meeting, 17 August 2011.

the results of the HKDSE, the assessment of universities overseas, and the popularity of the OLE programme, as discussed later, the implementation of the NSS curriculum in DGS has been highly successful.

In the past, only the GCE O-level programme was offered at DGS.[66] In 2015/2016, the school began to offer an alternative two-year GCE A-level curriculum in chemistry, biology, mathematics, geography, economics, history, and psychology. In 2017, Chinese (GCSE, General Certificate of Secondary Education, UK, first language paper) and English (academic paper for the International English Language Testing System, or IELTS) languages were also included in the programme after consultation with the relevant examination boards. These programmes are for some DGS girls with an English-speaking background who wish to continue their post-secondary education in universities in Hong Kong rather than overseas.

Amidst all the changes to the curriculum, in the Senior School there was a gradual shift in emphasis from liberal arts to more science-oriented programmes from the 1990s, and this change accelerated after the turn of the millennium. In 2017/2018, the majority of competitions in which DGS participated were in mathematics, science, computer science, and technology, reflecting the world trend and the schools' emphasis in this direction.[67]

New Pedagogy in the Senior School

With an increased number of teachers, the school streamed students in junior forms into sets for English, Chinese, mathematics, and liberal studies. Students were also streamed into PTH and Cantonese sets for Chinese language lessons; the Cantonese group also learned PTH but not as intensively as the PTH group.

The new millennium brought in many changes in the school curriculum and also new methods of teaching and learning to cope with the rapid advances in science and technology globally. In 2000, a Science Committee was set up at DGS among the science teachers of all four departments (science, biology, physics, and chemistry) to discuss a number of issues, such as classroom management of new initiatives in their fields and interdisciplinary joint ventures, but the emphasis was on teaching techniques. The teachers participated in the Professional Collaborative Project organised by the ED from 2001 to 2004 in which teachers shared their teaching practices such as Pedagogy for Scientific Investigations with educators and teachers from other schools in Hong Kong, and in the Staff Exchange Programme of 2004/2005 when science teachers from Jiading No. 2 High School Shanghai visited DGS. The science teachers tried out new initiatives, for example, in the

---

66. Minutes of School Council Meeting, 15 September 2015.
67. "Achievements 2016–2018", *Quest* (2016–2018): 280–294.

use of IT in teaching, which resulted in virtual classes, vital for teaching during the subsequent COVID-19 pandemic.[68] In 2006/2007, the science teachers organised the Science and Maths Fair jointly with the Junior School, and invited participants from schools in mainland China and Australia with overwhelming success. These exhibitions were carried out with the purpose of enhancing the students' learning of how to put into practice the knowledge they had gained.[69]

In 2015, the EDB published its "Report on Promotion of STEM Education-Unleashing Potential in Innovation" and introduced the STEM programme. Both the Senior and the Junior schools embraced the programme enthusiastically. Using this approach, students were encouraged to develop the following skills: problem solving, critical and independent thinking, creativity, motivation and initiative, effective communication, IT and computer literacy, and teamwork. With these attributes, students became lifelong learners, adaptable to the modern, constantly changing world. The EDB also renewed the curricula of key learning areas in science, technology, and mathematics, and provided learning and teaching resources for schools. In 2019, a whole-school Innovation and Technology Project was held, when other learning programs (OLP) were launched in conjunction with the Chinese University and the Hong Kong University of Science and Technology, to equip girls with knowledge about opportunities in STEM. Concepts such as human-centred design thinking, application of cutting-edge technologies in artificial intelligence, big data and cloud computing were introduced.[70] Teachers also participated in an online STEM course offered by Harvard Graduate School of Education.[71]

One can see that at DGS learning academic subjects is no longer dependent on classroom teaching. It can take place in multiple formats and in different settings as discussed above. However, following the old tradition, local educational visits are still carried out, usually during the week after school examination in December and/or in June each year. In the 2000s, educational visits extended to regional and international destinations.

The new curriculum and new pedagogy have not affected the excellent results in public examinations by DGS students. The pass rates were close to 100 per cent for HKCEE and over 95 per cent for HKALE. When these two examinations were abolished and replaced by the HKDSE in 2012, the performance of the students remained remarkable. Many students also took the IELTS, which is accepted by more than 10,000 organisations in over 140 countries where English is the main second language.[72] DGS students achieved

---

68. Dr Thomas Man, email communication, 12 August 2020.

69. Minutes of School Council Meeting, 30 August 2010; Minutes of School Council Meeting, 19 June 2013.

70. DGS at Cutting Edge. *DGS Kaleidoscope*. Newsletter No 24, January 2020, accessed on 22 March 2022, https://www.dgs.edu.hk/development/news/vol24/01%20DGS%20Vol24_DGS.pdf

71. Minutes of School Council Meeting, 2 July 2019.

72. "What is IELTS?", accessed 24 July 2020, https://www.ielts.org/.

exceptional results in this examination. Some won scholarships to study locally or overseas in prestigious universities as in previous years.

New Pedagogy in the Junior School

The Junior School curriculum aimed to equip the students with three literacy skills: English, Chinese, and ICT. In English, drama was introduced early to all Primary 4 and 5 students during oral lessons to enhance English eloquence and confidence when performing to a large audience. In Chinese, the learning of Putonghua was started at an early age, and teachers with native PTH proficiency were employed to teach PTH and the Chinese language. In September 2006, a PTH stream in the study of Chinese language was introduced in the upper primary levels. For the Cantonese stream, although the Chinese lessons were conducted generally in Cantonese, the girls were taught to read the Chinese text and the vocabulary in the textbook in both PTH and Cantonese during Chinese lessons. PTH days, PTH club, and PTH drama classes were organised, and students were encouraged to participate in the PTH section of the Hong Kong Schools Speech Festival.[73] As a result, the girls become proficient in PTH early. The goal in ICT literacy was to facilitate students to practise and apply IT skills in meaningful and relevant activity-based projects.[74]

In 2004/2005, Junior School students were encouraged to use enquiry and an investigative approach in learning the General Studies Curriculum and in project work to increase their problem-solving skills. Thus, they learned how to search for information, form hypotheses, design experiment procedures, document their experimental journey, and present their work. Since the 2007/2008 school year, this student-centred investigative learning approach was used in Primary 5 and 6, with students completing project work by applying these scientific methods and processes. In 2009/2010, the teachers organised a science fair for Primary 6 girls to present their science research projects in different small booths in the Junior Hall. To enhance learning both inside and outside the classroom, the school formed partnerships with the PTA, outside organisations, and local universities to encourage students to venture beyond the confines of formal classroom teaching. For example, a special three-day "Creative Thinking and Expression Skills Day Camp" was organised at Hong Kong University of Science and Technology (HKUST)—an interdisciplinary development project to promote creativity through hands-on and minds-on learning experiences to cultivate positive values and attitudes towards environmental issues. The students attended field trips, creative thinking workshops, and creative expression workshops on the HKUST campus. They practised communication and expressed

---

73. Email communication with Mrs Emily Dai, 18 August 2020.
74. Headmistress's Report, Junior School 1999/2000, Speech Day Booklet, January 2000, 74.

their ideas on environmental issues creatively through English and PTH drama enactment, English debate, web page design, video production, and animation.[75]

The Junior School participated in a number of programmes organised by the EMB and professional bodies, such as the Chinese Language Creative Writing Programme organised by the Gifted Education Section, EMB. Students who had taken part in the project showed remarkable improvement in poetry writing and creative writing skills. The following awards were presented to DGS students for outstanding performance: Hong Kong Budding Poets (English) Award, Hong Kong Budding Poets (Chinese) Award, Hong Kong Budding Scientists Award, among others.

After the abolition of the AAT in 2000, the ED launched the Territory-Wide System Assessment to assess Primary 3 and Primary 6 students in three core subjects: English language, Chinese language, and mathematics. The Junior School students performed remarkably well in all three areas. The results of pre-S1 Hong Kong Attainment Tests for Primary 6 students were just as outstanding.[76]

School Life in the Modern Era

New Features in School Routine

School life changed after the handover in 1997. Since 2003, the school has held flag-raising ceremonies twice a year: to celebrate the establishment of the Special Administrative Region on 1 July and the National Day on 1 October. During these occasions, the students sing the national anthem followed by a short speech from the Headmistress or a senior volunteer student.

The old tradition of holding assembly each morning remains unchanged in both the Junior School and the Senior School. The pastors and religious staff from St Andrew's Church lead the morning assembly in both schools once a week. In the Junior School, Christian teachers, scripture teachers, old girls, and parents are invited to share their faith during assembly.[77]

In winter, school starts at 8:10 am and finishes at 3:40 pm, and in the summer at 7:55 am and 1:20 pm respectively. In the winter session, there are seven lessons during the day from Monday to Friday, with a break at 10:55 am lasting for twenty minutes and lunch at 12:55 pm lasting for one hour and five minutes. In the summer, there are two breaks, each lasting

---

75. Headmistress's Report, Junior School, 2009/2010, Speech Day Booklet, 2010, and email communication with Mrs Emily Dai on 18 August 2020.

76. Mrs Emily Dai, email communication, 18 August 2020; Government Assessments 2000/2001 and 2004/2005, 18 August 2020.

77. Mrs Emily Dai, email communication, 18 August 2020.

for fifteen minutes, with no lunch break. The HKDSE usually commences near the end of March and applications for the Joint University Programmes Admissions System also take place in the same month.

More trips have been organised for students. The school has formed links with mainland schools in Beijing, Tianjin, Shanghai, and Guangzhou.[78] Initially, there were three sister schools on the Mainland; this number gradually increased to twelve. The school has also followed the globalisation trend and has developed connections with sixteen schools in Singapore, Korea, Japan, India, Australia, and the USA.

Every year, some DGS girls visit sister schools on the Mainland or in other cities around the globe; in return, the school has received students from sister schools elsewhere. DGS subsidises students to take part in these educational trips using funds raised from donations. One of the student groups in the exchange programme attended an intensive course in Japanese during the exchange, and subsequently all students in that group who took the HKDSE were awarded distinctions in Japanese.[79] Every student, irrespective of her school results, is entitled to take part in extra learning opportunities. If she aspires to the

Figure 8.12: Hangzhou Foreign Language School students joining the morning assembly, 4 October 2018. Source: School Archives.

---

78. Minutes of School Council Meeting, 27 October 2004.
79. Minutes of School Council Meeting, 11 October 2013.

opportunity, the school supports her in providing coaching or other forms of support. From 2015/2016 to 2018/2019, around 550 to 750 students each year travelled outside Hong Kong supported by the school to take part in special learning activities, such as world debates or science forums, or national and international competitions in sports or music.[80]

The SARS Epidemic

The epidemics that battered the world and changed the way of life for many also affected DGS school life. During the SARS outbreak in 2003, the school was completely closed from 29 March to 12 May 2003, and this was extended to 19 May 2003 for the Junior School and Forms 1 to 3 in the Senior School. During closure, only notices to parents and homework instructions were uploaded to the school homepage. Teachers communicated with students through email and virtual classrooms via the school intranet, but virtual lessons were not possible.[81] When students returned to school, new measures were introduced for infection prevention. They had their temperature checked before they entered their classrooms and wore masks in the school throughout the day, except during meal times. There were also reminders to wash hands and use hand sanitiser.

After the SARS epidemic, the teachers and the IT Department began to develop eClass virtual classrooms so that teaching could be conducted through the internet if necessary. Teaching materials, revision exercises, and quizzes were regularly uploaded so that students could access these resources at home. Students submitted their assignments and projects via the eClass virtual classrooms.

In 2016, DGS began to implement a one-student-one-iPad policy, and school-based teaching materials were gradually migrated from eClass virtual classrooms to iTunes U courses for easy access.[82] Students were allowed to keep and use their iPad at all times to facilitate teaching and learning but had to return them when they left school. Within a short time, students were using iPads frequently for searching for information online, reading teaching materials, and submitting homework. In 2017, the school began to use Google classrooms. All these systems prepared teachers and students well for the use of virtual lessons in case any future epidemics should require school closure.

---

80. Mrs Stella Lau, email communication, 17 August 2020.
81. IT in Education, Report for 2003.
82. IT in Education, Report for 2016.

Other Learning Experience and Extracurricular Activities

With the education reforms promoted by the EDB, ECAs were complemented by a new concept, other learning experiences (OLEs). This is considered part of the secondary school teaching curriculum, and ECA is the means by which students acquire various learning experiences. There are five areas under the OLEs: moral and civic education, community service, career-related experiences, aesthetic development, and physical development. As a result, there were changes in the school calendar too. In 2008/2009, the school organised fourteen OLE days spreading throughout the school year when ECAs could be carried out during class time. To allow for this change, the school renamed the ECA team the OLE team. This change improved the quality of school life as students no longer needed to conduct ECAs only at lunchtime or after school hours. The school recommended that each student should join at least two ECAs.[83] The OLE programmes were well planned. They consisted of workshops organised by local agencies and courses offered by local universities, in programmes such as magazine writing and layout, photojournalism, production of documentary films, a photography club, and a computer club. The OLE offered students a wide exposure to other interests that might lead to more career opportunities.

During the tenure of Mrs Stella Lau and Mrs Emily Dai and later Mrs Annie Lee, the school's ECAs reached a peak. The school was actively engaged in arranging students to attend exchange programmes, national and international competitions in academic subjects such as mathematics and science and IT, and in other ECAs such as music and sports.

ECAs in the Senior School

DGS had kept the interschool swimming championships for thirty-four years from 1985. After Robyn Lamsam, DGS had other champion swimmers: Sherry Tsai who won the Hong Kong's Best Swimmer Award four years in a row (1998–2001) and at one time held fourteen Hong Kong records[84] and Rosanna Hang Yu Sze who won a total of one silver and eight bronze relay medals at the Asian Games of 2006, 2010, 2014, 2018. To encourage elite athletes to attain their sport and academic goals, the school has increasingly provided resources to support them. After producing several Olympians over the years, DGS was awarded a Women and Sport Achievement Diploma from the International Olympics

---

83. Minutes of School Council Meeting, 28 August 2008.
84. "A Born Fighter", *Quest* (2009–2010): 26; Sherry Tsai, accessed 5 July 2021, https://en.wikipedia.org/wiki/Sherry_Tsai.

Committee in 2019, in recognition of its outstanding contribution towards promoting the development of sports for women and girls through the years.[85]

The school stimulated students to take on new sports such as archery, indoor rowing, handball, and dragon boat rowing, enabling the school to capture the Rising Star Award for ten years running since 2009. It also provided students with coaches and opportunities to attend the Beijing Olympics and Guangzhou Asian Games. More than fifty students represented Hong Kong in international competitions every year in different disciplines including swimming and athletics.[86] More about sports activities can be found in Chapter 13.

The symphony orchestra had improved its performance, winning more firsts and seconds than in previous years in the Hong Kong Schools Music Festival, as did the string and the Chinese orchestras. DGS senior choir often won first or second places in competitions, either in Chinese or in foreign languages, and were frequently awarded Best Girls' Choir of the year. The senior mixed choirs (with DBS), under the guidance of Mr Ronnie Cheng, often achieved remarkable results, capturing the Best Mixed Voice Choir on many occasions over the years. The senior mixed choir was invited to sing the national anthem at the flag-raising ceremony to celebrate the fifty-second anniversary of the founding of the People's Republic of China at the Hong Kong Convention and Exhibition Centre in 2001, and many years thereafter.[87]

During this period, for the first time, DGS choirs ventured outside Hong Kong to compete internationally. The senior mixed choir (with DBS) won gold medals in the biennial World Choir Games on almost every occasion after 2008, as did the DGS senior choir. Both choirs were twice crowned world champions after 2010.

In 2001, a survey was carried out in the Junior School on students' interest in music. Of the 640 students, 591 (92.3 per cent) were learning to play at least one musical instrument; of the latter group, 388 were learning to play two.[88] It is not surprising that DGS had seven choirs, two madrigal and quick study groups (with DBS), a string orchestra, a symphony orchestra, a school band, and a Chinese orchestra at that time. The school also ran nineteen classes for Western and Chinese instruments.[89]

The most significant musical events were the large-scale musicals put on by the school, often involving a large number of students. The musical *The DGS Girl*, produced in September 2005 to commemorate the one-hundred-and-forty-fifth Anniversary of DGS, was a brave venture. Staging musicals had been a long tradition at DGS, with *The Pirates*

---

85. *Kaleidoscope* Newsletter No 23, 2019, accessed on 24 March 2022 https://www.dgs.edu.hk/development/news/vol23/01%20DGS%20Vol23_DGS.pdf

86. Mr K. L. Tang, email communication, 20 August 2020.

87. *Quest* (2001–2002): 110.

88. Minutes of School Council Meeting, 7 May 2001.

89. "Musical Activities", *Quest* (2001–2002): 107–110.

The Turbulent Modern Era: 1999 to 2019

Figure 8.13: Tshwane World Choir Game in South Africa. DGS Choir, DBS Choir, and DGS/DBS Mixed Choir winning the championships in all three categories, July 2018. Source: Mr Ryan Chui.

of Penzance (performed in collaboration with DBS) and *Iolanthe* in the 1950s, *The King and I* in 1996, *The Wizard of Oz* in 2000, and *House of Wonders* in 2013; but *The DGS Girl* (Plate 13) was in a class on its own. The whole production was carried out by DGS girls, starting with research into the school's history, followed by writing of the script, adapting the music, composing the lyrics, and the actual performance. They then auditioned the main roles. Rehearsals began early during the Chinese New Year holidays and continued into the summer, becoming more and more intense as September approached. The girls took charge of props, lighting, costumes, and makeup, and performed in the orchestra under the guidance of Mrs Kit Ming Lee, Mrs Helen Wai Yi Au, Ms Synthia Ko, and other teachers. In total, 700 students were involved in producing this original musical, which won public acclaim. The *South China Morning Post* described it as "the most ambitious musical embarked on by any school in Hong Kong".[90] Such a huge project, taking months to implement and involving so many students, required commitment and dedication. Moreover, the students had to learn how to get along with each other. The project also enabled the students to discover their talents and build their confidence.

---

90. "The DGS Girl", *Quest* (2005–2006): 16–20.

The publication of the school magazine, *Quest*, inaugurated in 1941, continues to be one of the important ECAs. It is published once every two years, with an English and a Chinese volume each time. There are two teams responsible for the English publication: the editorial team of ten to sixteen students and three to four teachers, the art team of sixteen to twenty-six students and the visual arts teacher. Two students act as editors-in-chief. The Chinese publication comprises an editorial team of twelve students and six teachers.

A newsletter, *Kaleidoscope*, is printed twice a year to keep stakeholders informed of what is happening in the school. The English teachers of the Senior and Junior schools, members of the PTA and DOGA, together with Ms Shirley Ping of the School Development Office, are responsible for its production. It includes news of the school and initially included an account of the redevelopment. The first issue of *Kaleidoscope* was printed in January 2008, and it continued publication even after the redevelopment was completed. It consists of sixteen to twenty pages and 3,000 copies are printed per issue, while a digital copy is available on the school website. With many attractive pictures, it is enthusiastically welcomed by readers.[91]

Another publication, the *VA Magazine*, showcasing Form 5A students, has been published every December since 1993. It was started by Mrs Carolyn Weng, an English teacher, as part of the class journalism project. Highly successful for being fun and vibrant, the *VA Magazine* tradition continued even after Mrs Weng left. The magazine has 150–160 pages per issue and 800–1,000 copies are being printed each year. The magazines are sold during the mini-bazaar by the VA girls almost at cost. In line with inflation, the total price has risen from $40 in the 1990s to $70 today. The school pays for the printing, and the proceeds of the sale are returned to the school magazine account. Any profit made is donated to charities selected by the students.[92]

In the Senior School, more clubs of diverse interest have been started, and they continue to flourish. The clubs in 2018 are listed in Table 8.2.

Information on the activities and events of each of the ECAs was computerised for easy management and dissemination.[93] Sixteen workstations were placed at different locations throughout the campus, twelve of them acting as information kiosks. Daily ECA announcements were displayed on a large plasma display screen outside the school hall. The automated system allowed venues to be booked for meetings and training; rehearsal schedules, scripts, lyrics, and music files to be uploaded; and for documents and attendance records to be submitted.[94]

---

91. Ms Shirley Ping, School Development Office, email communication, 18 September 2020.
92. Mr Joe Oddie, email communication, 18 September 2020.
93. IT in Education, Report for 2000–2001.
94. IT in Education, Report for 2003.

Table 8.2: Clubs/teams/committees/groups in the Senior School in 2018

Arts/Music	Sports	Academic	Hobbies	Social Services / Others
Chinese Orchestra	Archery	Business Enterprise	Bridge	Audio-visual
Concert Band	Athletics	Chinese Debating	Chess	Careers
Dance	Badminton	Chinese Literary	Food Technology	Citizens'
Drama Ensemble	Basketball	Classics	Image Design	Counselling
Instrumental Classes (Western & Chinese)	Beach Volleyball	Computer	Pet	Girl Guides
Instrumental Ensemble	Bowling	Conservancy	Photography	Health Education
Madrigal	Cross Country	Current Affairs		Hospitality
School Choirs	Dance	DGS Programming		Library
String Orchestra	Dodgeball	Electronics & Robotics		Media Production
Symphony Orchestra	Dragon Boat	English Debating		Overseas and Local Exchange Organising Committee
Visual Arts	Fencing	Humanities		Red Cross
	Handball	International cultures		School Cheering
	Hockey	Mathematics		Youth Fellowship
	Indoor Rowing	Model United Nations		The Hong Kong Award for Young People
	Life Saving	Psychology		
	Netball	Reading		
	Orienteering	Science		
	Rugby Sevens			
	Squash			
	Swimming			
	Table Tennis			
	Tennis			
	Volleyball			

Source: *Quest* and Speech Day Booklets 2016 to 2018 and school circulars.

Figure 8.14: Five S2 girls developed a mobile app named Dementia Care Companion and won the Grand Prize in the Technovation Challenge, the world's largest STEM competition for girls between ages 10 and 18, at Google's headquarters in the Silicon Valley, USA, in 2017. Source: School Archives.

ECAs in the Junior School

During the tenure of Mrs Emily Dai and later Mrs Annie Lee, ECAs greatly expanded in the Junior School. Exchange visits were carried out in the Junior School, but these were limited to upper primary students.[95] Parents often helped out on these trips, and without their help, it would have been much more difficult to organise them.

In sports, the Junior School was awarded the Gold Cup for outstanding overall sports achievement in the Kowloon West District in 2018, and also a special Gold Cup for being the overall champion for the twenty-ninth year running.[96] Throughout the year, interested students were given training in athletics, swimming, badminton, netball, volleyball, table tennis, and basketball. The Junior School musicians performed equally well that year: the Junior choir came first both in singing in Chinese and in a foreign language, as did the symphony orchestra and string orchestra.[97] Classes were offered for every instrument used

---

95. Minutes of School Council Meeting, 14 December 2012.
96. *Quest* (2016–2018): 294.
97. *Quest* (2016–2018): 293.

The Turbulent Modern Era: 1999 to 2019   231

Figure 8.15: DGJS Chinese Orchestra rehearsal. Source: School Archives.

in both Western and Chinese orchestras and, as in the Senior School, these classes were held on Saturday mornings.

The Junior School also had a number of clubs, including the Brownies, Red Cross, Drama Club, English Book Club, Chinese Book Club, Computer Club, Dance Club, Debating Team, Environment and Gardening Club, Healthy Little Chef Club, Internet Club, Putonghua Club, Visual Art Club, Indoor Activities Club, and Mathematics Olympiad Club.[98] The Junior girls often participated in the large-scale musicals along with the Senior girls.

Looking Forward to a New Era

Mrs Dai spent thirty-two years of her life in DGS, fourteen years as a student, and eighteen years as Headmistress of the Junior School. Following in the footsteps of her role model, Mrs Symons, she improved the curriculum and ensured not only intellectual and physical development but also spiritual well-being of the students. When Mrs Dai retired in 2016, she was praised by her colleagues as an accomplished educationalist. Mrs Dai was succeeded

---

98. *Quest* (2016–2018): 189–215.

by Mrs Annie Lee. Aided by the whole team of dedicated teaching staff, the two Junior School headmistresses elevated the reputation of the Junior School through excellence in academic work and ECAs.

Mrs Stella Lau is a progressive, forward-looking, energetic, and highly efficient and effective individual, who has spared no effort to provide the very best, whether in facilities or in opportunities, and the most advanced knowledge to her students. She has travelled to various prestigious schools in China and in many other parts of the world to foster national and international connections and to open up opportunities for student and teacher exchanges.[99] She often speaks of the "five pillars" of education at DGS: pursuit of knowledge, music making for aesthetic enjoyment, sports for health, generous service to others in line with DGS's motto of "Daily Giving Service", and spiritual growth, acknowledging God's blessing and grace through Christianity.

Changing into a DSS school enabled the redevelopment of the whole campus, resulting in improved school facilities, expanded staff recruitment, and increased opportunities for professional development. At the same time, the students enjoyed better learning opportunities in both academic and extracurricular activities. Mrs Lau encouraged IT development, which proved to be indispensable to school administration, management, and teaching, especially during periods of school closure owing to epidemics or pandemics.

Like her predecessors, Mrs Stella Lau has been actively involved in public service, serving on a number of committees such as the Chairperson of the Women's Commission of the HKSAR government from 2012 to 2018, and Chair of the Board of the Hong Kong Schools Sports Federation since 2009. She has also served on other advisory committees, including the Sports Commission and the University Grants Committee. In 2017, Mrs Lau was awarded the Silver Bauhinia Star in recognition of her distinguished public service and her valuable contribution towards the promotion of well-being of women in Hong Kong.

Toward the end of the second decade, drastic political changes were in the wind that may completely alter the fabric of Hong Kong society. The School Council, the school supervisor, the headmistresses of DGS, and the entire team of dedicated and inspiring teachers have guided the school successfully through the turbulent first two decades of the twenty-first century, and their collective wisdom will certainly hold firm to the school's mission to provide a first-rate, all-round, liberal, Christian education for girls. With their leadership and the support of the girls, the parents, and the community, the school can sail forth bravely into a bright future.

---

99. Minutes of School Council Meeting, 21 January 2003.

Plate 8: Aerial photograph of the redeveloped camps completed in 2011 and the Boarding House completed in 2020. Source: School Archives.

Plate 8a: Facing Jordan Road showing the Senior School buildings. Source: School Archives.

Plate 8b: Facing Gascoigne Road showing the Junior School buildings. Source: School Archives.

Plate 9: DGS main gate, Jordan Road entrance. Source: School Archives.

Plate 10: The Junior School gate, Gascoigne Road entrance. Source: School Archives.

Plate 11: Upper panel: auditorium (left) and swimming pool (right); Middle panel: Junior School assembly hall (left) and Junior School library (right); Lower panel: track & field. Source: School Archives.

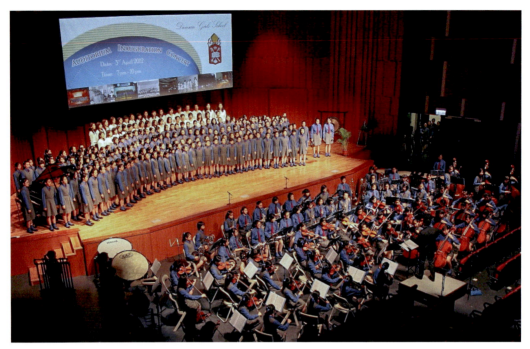

Plate 12: DGS Auditorium Inaugural Concert, 3 April 2012. Source: School Archives.

Plate 13: *The DGS Girl*, an original musical, performed in Shatin Town Hall on 2–4 September 2005 to celebrate the school's 145th Anniversary. Source: School Archives.

Chapter 9

"We Reap What They Have Sown"

This chapter briefly summarises the school's history and delineates the results of its education and nurturing programmes by examining the qualities of its graduates and their contributions to the community, locally and abroad—to examine the outcome of the seed sown by one of the missionaries during the nineteenth century in Hong Kong.

Mrs Lydia Smith, the wife of the first Bishop of Victoria and China, founded the Diocesan Native Training School in 1860 to teach Chinese girls Christianity and English, with the ultimate aim of enabling them as potential marriage partners of Chinese pastors to spread the gospel. Because of cultural and social differences, this first foundation did not survive long; however, the Church changed it into a co-educational institution for orphans of European and Eurasian extraction. Subsequently, the campus was turned into a boys' school, with no girls, owing to pressure from the business community to produce more boys with bilingual skills for commerce. Yet, its chequered beginning aside, the girls' school flourished after it was re-established as the Diocesan Girls' School in 1899 at another location.

During its 160-year history, DGS has evolved in line with social, cultural, economic, and political changes in Hong Kong and has responded well to the needs of the local community during each stage of the city's transition. After the Second World War, Hong Kong developed from a small town to become a regional manufacturing centre and, finally, a global financial hub. The school also evolved from a relatively small multinational school with 340 Chinese, European, and Eurasian girls before the Second World War to one with an enrolment of over 2,000 mostly Chinese girls today.

Despite changes in the curriculum, the education system, and numerous reforms brought forward by the Education Department, the school prospered, not only successfully implementing all the modifications but also introducing innovative programmes to its students. As the school's original mission was to teach girls English, all subjects were taught in the English language until 1939 when the teaching of Chinese was introduced for Chinese girls. The growing importance of China after the establishment of the People's Republic of China in 1949, and the emphasis on bilingual education from Bishop Hall of the Anglican Church, led to progressive improvement in Chinese teaching and in students' academic performance in Chinese subjects. At present, DGS girls are equally proficient in Chinese and English. The school has also developed in recent decades from one that provides a mainly liberal arts education to one with equal emphasis on arts and sciences and computer and information technology, in line with the needs and advances of the modern world.

In keeping with its mandate to provide an all-round education, the school has vastly expanded its extracurricular activities. While initially, before the Second World War, it offered certain social services, such as a boys' and girls' club to teach reading and writing to children without schooling, it now offers a great variety of extracurricular activities in music, sports, field visits, and different kinds of clubs covering interests in a range of academic topics and hobbies.

As the school expanded with the increase of population in Hong Kong, the school campus progressively enlarged to accommodate more students. Since the school adopted the Direct Subsidy Scheme (DSS), it has redeveloped its campus and increased the usable space two to three times to accommodate the vastly expanded scholastic and extracurricular activities. The campus is well supported by information technology for teaching and for communication. Its DSS status has also allowed it to have a larger and even better qualified staff, which has ample opportunities for professional development, and has given students exposure to competitions in STEM, music or sports and exchange programmes in both national and international arenas.

Since the beginning of the twenty-first century, the proportion of young women in institutes of higher education in Hong Kong has exceeded that of young men. During the evolution of female education, DGS has played a significant and pioneering role in educating girls, especially in English. Despite the multiple challenges the school has faced and its metamorphosis to adapt to the needs of society, it maintains its ethos and mission of providing an all-round education for girls based on Christian principles.

At present, the school is one of the elite schools in Hong Kong, known for its excellence in providing a well-rounded education and is therefore much sought after by parents for their daughters. The achievement of the school over the years can be attributed to the hard work and dedication of many people: the headmistresses, Miss Elizabeth Skipton, Miss Catherine Ferguson, Miss Dorothy Sawyer, Miss Elizabeth Gibbins, Miss Winifred Hurrell, Mrs Joyce Symons, Mrs Elim Lau, and Mrs Stella Lau; and in the Junior School, Mrs

Rachel Benton, Mrs Daphne Blomfield, Mrs Rebecca Yip, Mrs Emily Dai, and Mrs Annie Lee; as well as the devoted staff and, of course, the students themselves over the years. Behind the scenes is the School Council. Among its members, the School Supervisor, Mrs Doris Ho, and the Honorary Treasurer, Mr S. D. S. Bokhary, deserve special mention. Mrs Doris Ho's wise counsel and leadership since 1985 have ensured that the school has adhered firmly to its original mission. Mr Bokhary, who served on the School Council from 1965 to 2011, spent countless hours helping the school balance its books, looking after its investments, and safeguarding its financial well-being. The strong and generous support of the parents and old girls, individually or through the Parent Teacher Association (PTA) and the Diocesan Old Girls' Association (DOGA), all contributed to the continual success of the school. These individuals, in fact, practised "love in action" according to the teaching of Christianity.

Qualities Nurtured in DGS Girls

What kinds of students did DGS produce over the years? It seems that the school has nurtured a large number of intelligent, talented, and hard-working young women with divergent skills, as shown by the following comments from a number of people who are not connected to DGS: "from good families, educated, well-mannered, excellent in English and in debates, arrogant"; "elegant, determined and demanding"; "outgoing, smart, and active"; "dignified, assertive, poised, pursuers of perfection"; "resourceful, independent"; "competitive".

The comments from DGS teachers are quite revealing about the nature of their students. In general, they are regarded as talented, creative, determined, and they work very hard to achieve their aims, as indicated by the following comments:

> They are to me highly competent, efficient, and talented. . . able to appreciate different talents and learn to collaborate with others. . . They can be focused on excelling.

> They are outstanding. They sometimes cannot appreciate the fact that simple tasks in their eyes can be difficult in others' hands. . . Many DGS girls endeavour to be perfect, which is not possible in human terms.

> They are motivated and self-driven students with a strong sense of belonging.[1]

The following comments were collected by members of DOGA from a number of DGS graduates over the years to show how the students perceived themselves and how the school had prepared them for their future:

---

1. Comments from responses of teachers, current and former, to the author's questionnaire.

1930s The all-round education that DGS provides is a good model... teaching students to be independent... Studying at the DGS, our lives were strict and our work orderly. This formed a good basis of my life and work hereafter. Our teachers expected the best of us and tried to draw out the potential of each student.

1960s In the class, you would find diverse and colourful personalities, whether they were liberalists, leftists, idealists or even rebels. DGS was extremely tolerant of their diversity and personality and gave them space to explore different ideas... Through these activities [ECAs], the girls learnt how to build up their organisational skill, self-confidence and independence, characteristics of DGS girls which are helpful for them in many aspects throughout life.

1970s ... a high level of language and other skills ... a sense of self-confidence ... The Bible Knowledge from the Religious Studies classes was the most valuable ... it was the Bible reading that provoked a lot of thought and reflection.

1980s ... the motto "Daily Giving Service" ... good language and communication skills, a fairly open and inquisitive mind, and a somewhat grounded personality ... having the courage to speak from the heart, both positively and negatively ... not shying away from failure and being bold in attempting to solve difficult problems ... always striving to do better.

1990s Education at DGS cultivates independence, a strong sense of responsibility and principles in its students and nurtures the 'steel' underlying the varying and diverse characters of DGS girls.[2]

What nurtured these qualities in DGS girls? First, the school is known to give an all-round education. Its scholastic programme facilitated academic excellence and development of diverse skills, and its extracurricular activities cultivated a sense of responsibility, self-identity, confidence, and self-esteem.

Secondly, the school's highly tolerant attitude and its respect for divergent views allows students to explore, develop, grow, and mature at their own pace during the formative years of their lives. Such a progressive, liberal, and supportive attitude applies equally to the teaching staff. Most of the teachers feel that the school is highly supportive of their endeavours and that they have a rewarding career and are therefore loyal to the school.

Finally, the Christian principles of love, honesty, fairness, forgiveness, and a spirit of giving that are encouraged during the morning assemblies with brief scripture readings and addresses from the headmistresses, clergy from St Andrew's Church, and religious studies teachers helped many students in their personal growth even after graduation. Among DGS graduates who are not Christians, many remember these lessons long after they left school.

---

2. From interviews carried out by members of the DOGA over a period of time. http://www.doga.org.hk/index. php/doga-news/conversations/old-girls-profiles/109-interview

Work and Career of Graduates after DGS

To give an idea of some of the contributions of DGS graduates, we sought information about their careers and lives over the years. As there are no archives listing DGS graduates before 1999, chosen professions after graduation can only be studied indirectly, from the records of local universities and from information furnished by graduates.

We have well-documented career histories of two graduates before 1900 from other sources. Lydia Leung, a graduate of Diocesan Native Female Training School (DNFTS), married a Chinese catechist in 1864. She realised the ultimate purpose for which DNFTS was created. In Foochow, where she lived with her husband, she established a girls' school to teach reading and writing. Her successful venture was well publicised in the *Female Missionary Intelligencer* (see Chapter 1). Another graduate, Doris Hazeland, a Eurasian girl, was from the Diocesan Home and Orphanage (DHO). She was the younger sister of Frank Hazeland, an assistant master to Mr William Arthur at the DHO. Doris was enrolled there in 1873. After leaving school, she taught in the Church Missionary Society High School and was transferred to St Stephen's Girls' School when the former school closed its doors in 1919. Doris taught English and needlework. She died in 1942 in the school as a patient when the school was converted into a relief hospital during the Second World War and was remembered as a kind lady who never failed to show tenderness to children.[3]

The career paths of most DGS graduates up to the Second World War largely reflected the position of Eurasian women in Hong Kong, who made up a large percentage of DGS students at that time.[4] Graduates became nurses, teachers, stenographers, or bookkeepers in large commercial or trading firms owing to their high standard of English.[5] Those who came from good families in Hong Kong married into prestigious families. Very few received a university education. However, by the end of the 1930s, the numbers attending university increased considerably. DGS was producing more Arts graduates at Hong Kong University (HKU) than any other girls' school in Hong Kong, and most of them entered the education profession. Irene Cheng and Catherine Joyce Symons are excellent examples. A few DGS graduates entered medicine and became doctors, such as Eva Ho Tung.

After the war, the school published *The Quest* (renamed *Quest* after 1960) regularly, and a section on old girls was included. In recent decades, the school has kept more archival material, enabling us to have a better idea of the direction of the career choices of alumnae. In the 1950s, the average number of students who sat the Hong Kong Certificate of Education Examination (HKCEE) each year was 60, and this increased to 150 in the first

---

3. Kathleen E. Barker, *Change and Continuity: A History of St. Stephen's Girls' College, Hong Kong, 1906–1996* (Hong Kong: Hong Kong University Press, 1996), 34, 40, 128.

4. C. J. Symons, *Looking at the Stars: Memoirs by Catherine Joyce Symons* (Hong Kong: Pegasus Books, 1996), vi.

5. Symons, *Looking at the Stars*, 95.

decade of this millennium; the pass rate of DGS students fluctuated between 85 and 90 per cent. The average number of DGS matriculants each year increased from around fourteen during the 1950s to about seventy-eight during the first decade of the twenty-first century (see Figures 9.1 and 9.2).

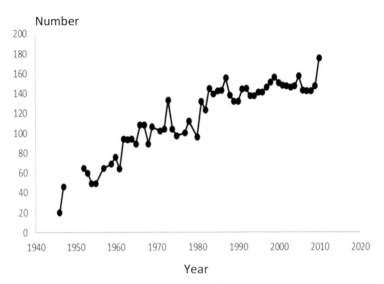

Figure 9.1: Number of students who sat the HKSCE/HKCEE, 1946–2012. Source: School Archives, prepared by Dr Alice Cheung.

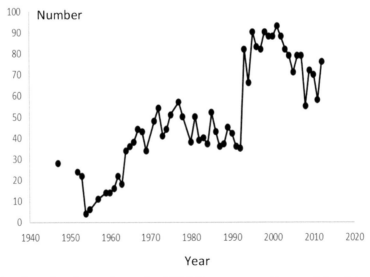

Figure 9.2: Number of students who sat the HKALE, 1946–2012. Source: School Archives, prepared by Dr Alice Cheung.

"We Reap What They Have Sown"

Following the initiative of Miss Gibbins (Headmistress, 1939–1945) to introduce Chinese, botany and mathematics in the DGS curriculum, and to upgrade subject standards in English literature, history, and geography,[6] more DGS graduates entered higher education in the 1950s. By then, HKU had faculties in science in addition to arts, medicine, and engineering; a department of architecture was also established. In the 1950–1951 school magazine, Miss Hurrell reported that there were sixty-seven DGS alumni at HKU, sixty girls and seven boys, the latter originally from DBS but graduating before it was ready to reopen after the war. Of the sixty female graduates, thirty-six (60 per cent) were in arts, fifteen (25 per cent) in medicine, five (8.3 per cent) in architecture, and four (6.6 per cent) in science; of the seven male graduates, six were studying medicine and one the arts. When the government introduced a bursary scheme for prospective teachers in the mid-1950s, more students entered HKU to become teachers with a university degree.

Miss Hurrell emphasised the importance of female education as well as the need for women to become teachers.[7] Even today, the necessity prevails. While DGS graduates pursue their further studies in a diverse range of fields, the school is blessed with girls who are passionate in taking up this responsibility. According to the current list of teachers in the Senior and the Junior schools, there are respectively eleven (11.2 per cent) and thirteen (22.4 per cent) old girls serving, passing on knowledge and traditions of the school to the younger generation.

By the mid-1960s, DGS students were graduating from almost every faculty, including medicine and engineering, whether from HKU or other universities abroad.[8] In 1963, Mrs Symons reported that of the fifty-eight girls who had left school, 19 per cent entered HKU and 43 per cent left for the UK, Canada, or the USA; 10.3 per cent were admitted to teacher training colleges and 5.2 per cent to nursing schools; while 5.6 per cent became secretaries in big corporations. Following the establishment of additional faculties at HKU in social science (1967) and law (1969), and faculties of arts, science, and social science at the Chinese University of Hong Kong (CUHK) in 1963, and business administration in the 1970s, the choices in local tertiary education increased. This, no doubt, contributed to the increase in the number of graduates who built their careers in the fields of government, law, and finance in the 1970s.

Since the mid-1980s, there has been a further climb in numbers of DGS graduates entering local universities, as a result of the continued expansion of faculties at HKU and CUHK, as well as the Hong Kong Polytechnic, Baptist College, City Polytechnic of Hong Kong (which became universities in 1994), and the Hong Kong University of Science and

---

6. Symons, *Looking at the Stars*, 87.

7. "Miss Hurrell's Address on Speech Day, 4 Dec. 1953", *Quest* (1953): 13–14.

8. Symons, *Looking at the Stars*, 87.

Technology (1991). These opened up more opportunities for students to enter a wide range of professions hitherto unavailable in Hong Kong, from information technology, education, and marketing to social work and various paramedical professions. Since the turn of the twenty-first century, the gap between male and female enrolment in post-secondary education gradually narrowed. Female enrolment has comfortably overtaken male enrolment, being 53.7 per cent and 46.3 per cent respectively in 2014 in University Grants Committee-funded programmes in Hong Kong. While women have traditionally dominated in the arts, the social sciences, and other humanities programmes, more of them have found their way into medicine, science, and engineering.

DGS has kept a record of all students who sat the HKCEE, the Hong Kong Advanced Level Examinations (HKALE) since 1998, and after 2012, the Hong Kong Diploma of Secondary Education (HKDSE) and the universities and faculties they were admitted to. The majority of DGS graduates entered local universities. With the increasing new programmes introduced by local universities in response to the changing world, the range of programmes taken by the girls varied widely. Table 9.1 shows examples of local university programmes that graduates were admitted to since the millennium.

A number of students went overseas to pursue higher education. Table 9.2 shows the number and destination of these graduates between 2012 and 2019 after the HKDSE was introduced, while Table 9.3 shows examples of overseas institutions they entered.

Contributions of DGS Graduates to Society

Ever since the school was founded, it has been generously supported by the taxpayers of Hong Kong, various individuals in the community, and particularly parents and old girls, who have never failed to donate to the school when needed. In return, DGS graduates are found serving in all sectors of society and in different professions. The following list, compiled after consultation with a number of old girls, shows examples of some of the areas in which some graduates have made their mark. It is very likely that there are many more DGS girls not on the list here, who have served and are serving the community in many other distinguished ways that we have lost touch with.

The alumnae's married names and years of graduation are in parentheses.

In Education

Irene Ho Tung, 何奇姿 (Cheng, 1917), was admitted to HKU in 1921, three years after she passed her matriculation examination in 1918. She was the first female Chinese graduate of HKU and served as the first female Inspector of Schools in Hong Kong after the war. After retirement from the government, she became the Principal of the Confucian Tai Shing

Table 9.1: Degree programmes DGS graduates pursue in local universities

Year 2000 after HKALE	Year 2019 after HKDSE and GCE A-Level	
Arts	Arts	Journalism
Architectural Studies	Actuarial Science	Journalism and Communication
Business	Biomedical Engineering	Law
Chinese	Biomedical Sciences	Management
Cognitive Science	Building Science and Technology	Medical Laboratory Science
Dental Surgery		Medicine
Economics	Building Services Engineering	Medicine (Global Physician-Leadership Stream)
Engineering	Business Administration and Juris Doctor (double degree)	
Finance		Nursing
Food and Nutritional Science	Business Administration and Management	Occupational Therapy
Government and Laws		Pharmacy
Government and Public Admin.	Creative Advertising and Media Design	Philosophy
Hotel Management	Criminology and Sociology	Physical Education, Exercise Science and Health
Journalism and Communication	Dental Surgery	Physical Education and Recreation Management
Language Education	Data Science	
Law	Data Science and Business Intelligence	Physiotherapy
Medicine		Property Management
Physics	English	Public Health
Physiotherapy	Engineering	Public Policy and Politics
Professional Accountancy	Financial Technology	Quantitative Finance
Psychology	Global Business	Risk Management and Business Intelligence
Public and Social Admin.	Global Economics and Finance	
Science	Global Studies	Science
Social Work	Government and Public Admin.	Social and Behavioural Sciences
Sociology	Government and Laws	Social Sciences
Speech and Hearing Science	Hotel Management	Speech and Hearing Sciences
Translation	Information Systems Engineering	Theoretical Physics

Source: School Archives. Note: Table prepared by DGS Careers Team.

Table 9.2: Number and destination of graduates attending universities outside Hong Kong

Country	2012	2013	2014	2015	2016	2017	2018	2019
Australia	2	4	2	2	3	6	3	3
Canada	5	1	3	3	3	7	5	2
China	0	2	3	0	1	1	3	1
Germany	0	0	0	0	1	0	0	0
Japan	1	0	0	0	0	0	1	0
Singapore	0	1	0	0	0	0	1	0
Switzerland	1	1	0	1	1	1	0	1
UK	20	21	17	21	19	24	17	19
USA	22	16	15	10	12	9	5	8
Total:	51	46	40	37	40	48	35	34

Source: School Archives. Note: Table prepared by DGS Careers Team.

Table 9.3: Overseas universities where DGS graduates pursue their studies, 2012–2019

Country	Examples of Universities
UK	University of Cambridge, University of Oxford, London School of Economics, Imperial College London, University of St Andrews, University College London, University of Warwick, University of Leeds
USA	Massachusetts Institute of Technology, Cornell University, UC Berkeley, University of Pennsylvania, Johns Hopkins University, Princeton University, University of Michigan, UCLA
Canada	University of Toronto, University of British Columbia, McGill University, University of Alberta
Australia	University of New South Wales, University of Sydney, University of Melbourne, University of Adelaide, University of Queensland
China	Tsinghua University, Peking University, Zhejiang University, Beijing Normal University
Switzerland	École hôtelière de Lausanne, Les Roches International School of Hotel Management
Singapore	National University of Singapore
Taiwan	Chinese Culture University
Japan	Keio University
Germany	Hochschule für Musik Freiburg

Source: School Archives. Note: Table prepared by DGS Careers Team.

School in Wong Tai Sin. After moving to the USA, she started a weekend school where Chinese children could learn Chinese, and she lectured at the University of California San Diego. Her public service included serving on the executive board of the World Federation for Mental Health.

Catherine Joyce Anderson (Symons, 1934), Rebecca Luen Yuen Lit, 列鸞琬 (Yip, 1955), Elim Pong, 龐以琳 (Lau, 1958), Stella Lai Kuen Kun, 靳麗娟 (Lau, 1972), and Emily Tin Mei Ho, 何天美 (Dai, 1974), all served as Headmistresses of the Senior and Junior schools. Their contributions to the school and to the community are described in detail in Chapters 6–8.

Doris Ko, 高雪瑤 (Ho, 1957), was the long-serving and dedicated school supervisor on whose wise counsel the school has depended for the past thirty-six years. Doris graduated from Leeds University, majoring in English, and obtained a Postgraduate Certificate in Education from the London Institute of Education, London University. She taught in a comprehensive school in London before returning to teach in St Paul's Co-educational College and then DBS, before joining the Hong Kong government, serving in a number of departments as an administrative officer, and retiring as Deputy Secretary for Health and Welfare. On retirement, she joined the Hong Kong Jockey Club and headed the Charities Department for seven years. She was appointed Justice of the Peace in 1997.

Faith Ko, 高文蘊 (1956), was the founding principal of Kowloon True Light Girls' College for twenty-five years (1973–1998). She served the school with great dedication and love. No one would imagine that after graduation from HKU, Faith would join the police force as an inspector for a few years before turning to education.

In Academia and/or Arts

Chiu Yee Ha, 趙綺霞 (1955), a talented pianist, graduated from the Royal College of Music in London and the Juilliard School of Music in New York after studying with a number of distinguished artists. She performed with the London Philharmonic Orchestra at the historic inauguration of the first concert hall in Hong Kong. She became a concerto artist with a number of orchestras, including the Hong Kong Philharmonic and the Vienna Symphony under Christopher Eschenbach. She also appeared in solo or chamber music recitals in many parts of the world. She has taught at Juilliard and Duquesne University. The Hong Kong Schools Music Festival has a trophy named in her honour. Chiu Yee Ha is on the celebrated roster as a Steinway Artist. She resides in Pittsburgh, Pennsylvania, USA.

Jane Chui Chun Lai, 黎翠珍 (1956), an HKU graduate who also studied at Bristol University. She taught English Literature and Translation at HKU and at the Hong Kong Baptist University (BU). She was Dean of the Faculty of Arts at BU and retired as Emeritus Professor and an Honorary Fellow of the Hong Kong Translation Society. A founding member of the Seals Theatre Company, the Hong Kong Federation of Drama Societies, and the International Association of Theatre Critics (Hong Kong), she has a long association with the Hong Kong theatre scene, mainly in the translation of plays for performance. She is co-editor of *The Oxford Anthology of Contemporary Chinese Drama* and has published in both English and Chinese languages.

Elizabeth Yuk Yee Sinn, 冼玉儀 (1966), an outstanding historian of modern China and Hong Kong, is well recognised locally and abroad, and has published many books and articles in these areas. She was the Deputy Director of the Centre of Asian Studies (HKU), and is currently Honorary Professor at the Hong Kong Institute for the Humanities and Social Sciences. Outside the university, she served as a member of the Humanities Panel of the HK Research Grants Council, the Antiquities Advisory Board, and as the vice-president of the Royal Asiatic Society (Hong Kong Branch). She is an honorary advisor to the Hong Kong Museum of History and led the Hong Kong Memory Project to produce an online platform for materials on Hong Kong's history, culture, and heritage from 2006 to 2013. The Chinese edition of her book *Pacific Crossing: California Gold, Chinese Migration, and the Making of Hong Kong* won the 2021 KOPUS (Korean Publishers Society) Best Asian Books of the Year Award.

Jenny Fong Suk So, 蘇芳淑 (1966), daughter of Mrs Grace So, DGS teacher from 1946 to 1968, received a BA, MA, and DPhil from Harvard University. Jenny became the Senior Curator of Chinese Art at the Freer Gallery of Art and Arthur M. Sackler Gallery of the Smithsonian Institution, Washington, DC. She joined the Department of Fine Arts, CUHK, in 2001 and became Chair of the Department (2001–2008), the Director of the Institute of Chinese Studies (2002–2011), and the Director of the Art Museum (2013–2015). She is currently Adjunct Professor of Fine Arts, CUHK. Her research focuses on art and archaeology from the prehistoric period through the Bronze Age, and culture and artistic exchanges between China and its neighbours over the ages. She is a world-renowned expert on ancient Chinese jades, Chinese art in Hong Kong, and ancient Chinese gold and artistic cultural exchange.

Li Wai Yee, 李惠儀 (1977), after receiving a BA from HKU and a PhD from Princeton University in 1987, became an associate professor of Princeton from 1996 to 2000 and Professor of Chinese Literature at the Fairbank Centre for Chinese Studies since 2000. She has taught courses on Ming-Qing culture, early Chinese thought and historiography, gender and sexuality, and premodern fiction and drama. Her research spans topics ranging from early Chinese thought and narrative to late imperial Chinese literature and culture, and she has published extensively in this area. She is co-editor of *The Oxford Handbook of Classical Chinese Literature* and has received fellowships or grants from the Harvard Society of Fellows, the Chiang Ching-kuo Foundation, ACLS, Radcliffe Institute of Advanced

Study, and the American Academy in Berlin. In July 2014, she was elected by Academia Sinica to its List of Academicians.

Mary Jean Chan, 陳瓊瑪 (2007), an award-winning poet, graduated with a BA (Political Science) from Swarthmore College and a MPhil (International Development) from the University of Oxford (2014). Mary Jean also completed an MA and a PhD in Creative Writing from Royal Holloway, University of London (2019). Currently a Senior Lecturer in Creative Writing (Poetry) at Oxford Brookes University and a supervisor on the MSt in Creative Writing at the University of Oxford, Mary Jean's debut poetry collection, *Flèche* (Faber & Faber, 2019), won the 2019 Costa Book Award for poetry and was named Book of the Year in *The Guardian*, the *Irish Times*, and *The White Review*. In 2020, it was short-listed for multiple literary prizes, including the International Dylan Thomas Prize, the John Pollard Foundation International Poetry Prize, the Jhalak Prize, and the Seamus Heaney Centre First Collection Poetry Prize.

In Public Services

Frances Sing Wong, 黃星 (1940), was recruited by Gong Peng, Chou En-Lai's secretary and interpreter, into the Information Department, Chinese Foreign Service, People's Republic of China in the early 1950s. She wrote two books about her personal experience: *China Bound and Unbound: History in the Making*, 2010, and *The Lost Schools*, 2018. During the seventieth anniversary of the People's Republic of China, she received two commemorative medals issued by the Central Committee of the Chinese Party in recognition of her contributions to the diplomatic cause of China, to resisting US aggression, and to providing aid in Korea as a Chinese People's Volunteer.

Elizabeth Chi-lien Chien, 錢其濂 (Wong, 1954), a graduate of HKU, joined the civil service in May 1969. She held appointments in the Social Welfare Department, Music Office, Finance, Home Affairs, Lands and Works, and the Municipal Services. She retired from the post of Secretary for Health and Welfare in September 1994. In 1994, she brought to the forefront the necessity of much-needed healthcare reforms. Elizabeth greatly strengthened the professional team of the Music Office and was deeply involved in the preparation and policy development for the establishment of the Hong Kong Academy for Performing Arts. After her retirement, she wrote the book *Thanks for the Memories*.

Katherine Shiu-ching Lo, 羅兆貞 (Fok, 1957), joined the Hong Kong government as an Administrative Officer in September after graduation from HKU. After serving in various positions in the government, she was promoted to Commissioner for Labour from 1992 to 1994 and became the Secretary for Health and Welfare from 1994 to 1999. During her tenure as an administrative officer, she was appointed to the Legislative Council and the

Standing Committee on Civil Service Salaries and Conditions of Service. She also served as the Director of the Community Relations Department of the ICAC from 1983 to 1987.

Sarah Mary Sau-tung Liao, 廖秀冬 (1968), obtained her BSc, MSc, and PhD from HKU and MSc in Analytical Chemistry from the University of Birmingham, UK. Upon returning to Hong Kong, she researched into workplace health and safety and environmental pollution for fifteen years, both locally and in the Pearl River Delta. In the ensuing fifteen years, she worked from her own consulting firm to solve workplace and environmental pollution problems for the government, private sector, and community. She retired in 2007 after working as Secretary for the Environment, Transport, and Works and was the environmental expert for the Beijing government's bid for hosting the 2008 Olympics. Since retirement, she has been helping the disadvantaged in the community and advising various boards of trustees and councils on environmental sustainability issues. Sarah is a Fellow of Royal Society of Chemistry, a Justice of the Peace, and a recipient of an MBE and Gold Bauhinia Star.

Eva Cheng, 鄭汝樺 (1978), has served in various Hong Kong government departments, including Deputy Head of the Central Policy Unit, Deputy Director of Administration (1997), Deputy Secretary for Information Technology and Broadcasting (Commerce Industry and Technology) (1998–2003), Commissioner for Tourism (2003–2006), and Permanent Secretary for Economic Development (2006–2007). She was also at one time the Secretary for Transport and Housing and the Chair of the Hong Kong Housing Authority. Her services were recognised by the Gold Bauhinia Star award.

In Health and Medicine

Rebecca Ho Wai Chan, 陳可慰 (Chung, 1938), trained at the Queen Mary Hospital and was a nurse with the Flying Tigers in the US Army, both at or near Kunming Airport during the Second World War. In 1943–1944, she flew over the Himalayas between Calcutta and Chongqing about fifty times serving as a nurse, at the risk of losing her own life. After the war, she became the Sister Tutor-in-Charge of the nursing school at the Tung Wah Group of Hospitals from 1964 to 1975. She was appointed a member of the Hong Kong Nursing Board and the Midwives Board, and was later elected President of the Hong Kong Association of Nurses and Midwives.

Moira Mo Wah Chan, 陳慕華 (Yeung, 1955), an HKU alumna, became Professor of Medicine at the University of British Columbia (UBC) in 1982, Emeritus Professor of Medicine of UBC in 2004, and Hon. Clinical Professor of Medicine at HKU at present. She served on or chaired a number of research grants and advisory committees, including the Medical Research Council and Health and Welfare of Canada, the Pulmonary Disease Advisory Committee of National Institute of Health (USA), the International

Union Against Tuberculosis and Lung Disease, and the World Health Organization. Her contributions in the field of occupational asthma and occupational lung diseases were recognised by several awards, including the prestigious Distinguished Achievement Award from the American Thoracic Society. After retirement, she published several medical and non-medical history books.

Vivian Chi-woon Taam, 譚智媛 (Wong, 1962), is an alumna of HKU and a College Fellow of three disciplines: obstetrics and gynaecology, internal medicine, and public health. She identified the route of transmission of hepatitis B from mother to baby, and laid the foundation for the prevention of liver cancer. As the Hospital Chief Executive of Queen Mary Hospital, she pioneered a number of quality improvement programmes, including the Institutional Review Board for clinical research. As the Public Health Specialist for the World Bank and Chair of the Safe Motherhood Initiative of the International Federation of Obstetrics and Gynaecology, she steered planning policies to prevent maternal deaths in developing countries. Dr Wong plays a crucial role in building a tripartite model of modernisation and collaboration for Chinese Medicine and in promoting the integration of Chinese and Western medicine at present.

Karen Siu Ling Lam, 林小玲 (1969), is Chair Professor in Medicine, Clinical Director of the State Key Lab of Pharmaceutical Biotechnology, Academic Lead of the Clinical Trial Centre, and Director of Clinical Operations, HKU Health System, at HKU. She founded the K. K. Leung Diabetes Centre, Queen Mary Hospital, in 1994. She was the Department Head and Chief of Endocrinology and Metabolism at the University Department of Medicine, the Founding President of Diabetes Hong Kong, a past President of the Hong Kong Society of Endocrinology, Metabolism and Reproduction, and a past Chair of Advanced Internal Medicine and Endocrinology, Diabetes & Metabolism specialty boards, of the Hong Kong College of Physicians. She currently serves as an associate editor or editorial board member of several international peer-reviewed journals in diabetes and endocrinology.

In Science and Research

Virginia Man-yee Lee, 李文渝 (1962), obtained a PhD in Biochemistry from the University of California at San Francisco (1973). Her research focused on Alzheimer's disease, Parkinson's disease, frontotemporal lobar degeneration, and other disorders. She is currently the John H. Ware Third Endowed Professor in Alzheimer's Research, Professor at the Perelman School of Medicine University of Pennsylvania, Director at the Center for Neurodegenerative Disease Research, and Co-director at the Marian S. Ware Center for Alzheimer's Drug Discovery Programme. She received the Lifetime Achievement

Award in Alzheimer's Disease Research from the Alzheimer's Association (2009) and a Breakthrough Prize in Life Sciences (2019).

Vivian Wing-Wah Yam, 任詠華 (1980), was elected a member of the Chinese Academy of Sciences in 2001, the youngest ever elected member. She graduated from HKU with a BSc in Chemistry, first class honours in 1985, and a PhD in 1988. In 1990, she rejoined HKU and has been a Chair Professor in Chemistry since 1999. Her research focuses on molecular functional materials, especially luminescent materials for energy-efficient organic light emitting diodes. This has enabled much more efficient displays in mobile phones and laptops. During her years of studying and lecturing, Vivian received numerous awards and scholarships, including the L'Oréal-UNESCO For Women in Science Award in 2011 and the Croucher Senior Research Fellowship in 2000.

Helen Mei Ling Meng, 蒙美玲 (1983), is a trailblazer in the field of Artificial Intelligence and a researcher in multilingual speech and language processing, multimodal human-computer interaction, and big data decision analytics. She received SB, SM, and PhD degrees in Electrical Engineering and Computer Science from the Massachusetts Institute of Technology. She is presently Patrick Huen Wing Ming Chair Professor of the Department of Systems Engineering and Engineering Management at CUHK. She develops exciting speech and language technologies for graceful and personalised human-machine communication, with applications in computer-aided language learning, assistive technologies for users with communicative impairments, and automatic detection of cognitive impairments.

In Social Work

Lucy Man Fai Ching, 程文輝 (1954), lost her eyesight at just six months of age. She learnt both English and Cantonese Braille. Instead of going to a special school, Lucy attended DGS. After graduation, she attended the Perkins Institute for the Blind in Boston (1956). In 1959, the Social Welfare Department in Hong Kong employed her to help the handicapped. She became the Department's first blind social worker. In recognition of her contributions to the handicapped, Lucy received an MBE in 1975 and was awarded the HKU Honorary Degree of Doctor of Social Science in 1992 and a Hong Kong Baptist University Honorary Doctor of Law in 1997. Her book, *One of the Lucky Ones*, was translated into several languages, including Braille, and made into a film.

In Environmental Protection

Man Si Wai, 文思慧 (1971), was a leader of the Hong Kong Green Movement and a graduate of CUHK. She obtained MA and PhD (1983) at the University of Western Ontario in History and Philosophy of Science. She began her teaching career at Lingnan University before moving to CUHK. In 1986, she championed the movement against the building of a nuclear power plant at Daya Bay, and secured signatures from about one million residents against this proposal. She was at one time the chair of the Hong Kong Philosophy Society. A prolific writer and a stimulating speaker, Si Wai published many books and articles on the environment and ecology, science and technology, and gave many lectures on democracy, human rights, social values, and ethics. After retirement in 2002, she opened an organic farm in Tai Po and continued to be active in the Green Movement.

In Business

Solina Hoi-shuen Chau, 周凱旋 (1978), co-founded Horizons Ventures in 2005 and sees disruptive-technology start-ups as a path to the "new normal" that will reframe our thinking and transform our lives. Horizons' string of notable early-stage investments include Zoom, Impossible Foods, Spotify, Siri, and DeepMind. Since 1996, through her H. S. Chau Foundation, more than $1.5 billion were put to work in support of education and women's causes around the world. Ms Chau also serves as a director of the Li Ka Shing Foundation. Four winning attitudes from Solina are: Be more, seem less; Keep a grateful heart; Be the positive difference; 1 Corinthians 13.

In Entertainment

Karen Man Wai Morris, 莫文蔚 (1987) is a talented artist in the entertainment industry. Since 1993, Karen has had more than twenty CD releases to her name and has starred in over thirty movies. She has received numerous awards, ranging from local to international, from the entertainment industry. In addition to her work in showbiz, Karen is actively involved with various social/charitable organisations in the Greater China Region and serves as an ambassador for the United Nations Children's Fund (UNICEF), the Society for the Prevention of Cruelty to Animals, and Animals Asia.

In Spiritual Matters

As the world moves toward science and technology and becomes increasingly materialistic, three exceptional DGS graduates gallantly defied such a trend and turned to care for the spiritual needs of people, fulfilling the dream of the founder of DGS, Mrs Lydia Smith, and the Female Education Society (FES) after 160 years.

Joyce Hoi-yan Wong, 黃凱欣 (1993), a medical graduate of the University of Edinburgh, is a missionary doctor and recipient of Compassion Award (2020). In 2006, she and her husband Henri Samoutou developed a non-profit eye centre in Bongolo, Gabon. In 2012, they founded New Sight Eye Care and moved with their three children to Impfondo to pioneer the charity's first eye centre in the Republic of Congo. They opened a second eye centre in Ouesso, Congo, in 2019 and are constructing a hospital to extend services to the region. In 2018, the Samoutous established Project Two Front Teeth, aimed at inspiring children to lead social change with creativity. An inspirational speaker known for her sincerity, Joyce has been regularly invited to speak to audiences, such as at TEDx.

Winnie Wan Yi Fung, 馮韻兒 (1998), obtained her PhD in Business Economics at Harvard University; she then taught economics at Wheaton College. At present, she is an associate professor and academic head at Lumina College, a Christian higher education institution in Hong Kong. She oversees the MA programme that combines faith with learning and helps students to "study God's world in light of God's word", seeking to cultivate a "biblically based, deep-structure and macro-perspective" that allows students to lead well in an ever-changing world.

Gina Ching-wan Yuen, 袁青雲 (1999), was one of the 10A scorers in the Hong Kong Certificate of Education Examination. After pursuing her graduate and postgraduate studies in Information Engineering at the CUHK, she worked in Morgan Stanley Asia Ltd (HK) for two years. She then left for the London School of Economics to study Finance and Economics, and upon her return joined the Hong Kong Monetary Authority as a manager. In 2012, Gina and her husband responded to God's calling and entered full-time seminary. She has been serving as an ordained preacher in the Chinese Rhenish Church Hong Kong since graduation.

In recent years, there have been several young DGS graduates who are being recognised for their contributions to public service and society, such as Dr Janice Wing Hang Tsang, 曾詠恆 (1992), who founded the Hong Kong Women Doctors Association and brought the Hong Kong breast cancer research group into the international arena. She was awarded the Hong Kong Outstanding Persons Award in 2014. Dr Emmy Yuen Mei Li, 李琬微 (1997), won the Hong Kong Humanity Award for her Cataract Free Zone initiative of Project Vision in Hainan where over 30,000 cataract surgeries were carried out on rural Chinese villagers and more than ten mainland doctors were trained in the technique of cataract surgery in one year. One can envisage that these young people will one day rise to prominence because of their service to the community.

In addition, there are countless DGS graduates who are serving and contributing to society in many aspects of life, locally and overseas, especially those who are selflessly caring for their families, the sick, the disabled, and the elderly with love and dedication, adhering to the school motto of "Daily Giving Service". To them we pay our tribute and respect.

Frances Wong, a 1940 graduate, summarised in her book *The Lost Schools* what DGS had taught her in twelve years: "To seek the truth, be a good citizen, obey the Ten

Commandments, work for humanity and do service, be contented, gain happiness by helping others, and enjoy life". These simple guidelines of serving others have over the years been shared by generations of students, helping them to find meaning and worth in life, not only for themselves but for their families and communities. Despite changes in society, changes in attitudes, and more enlightened education, these simple guidelines remain true and are still shared by DGS students and graduates in this complex modern world. It is hoped that DGS alumnae will be good citizens, and serve better in more diverse capacities and more effectively, and keep faith with God, with their fellow human beings, and with themselves.

Keeping Our Legacy Alive

The school reached the venerable age of 160 years in 2019/2020, but far from being ancient and fossilised, it has demonstrated its remarkable ability to innovate, adapting to the needs of this rapidly changing city. While this quality is applauded, it is equally desirable that some of its features remain unchanged.

DGS began in 1860 as a school for educating upper-class Chinese girls. This school survived only for a short time, and it was soon changed to a co-educational orphanage for orphans and children of impoverished parents. When it was re-established as a girls' school in 1899, the policy of taking in less privileged children persisted. It was only in the late 1910s that girls from upper-class families attended the school. Since then, the school has had an "open door" policy for girls whatever their family's circumstances. When the school switched to DSS status, the required school fees, though lower than those of private schools, may still be a hindrance to the less privileged, and the school fee remission programme may not be adequate to counter that consideration. The school has been alerted to that possibility and has tried to alleviate it by additional measures. It is hoped that efforts will continue to be made to preserve the tradition of serving girls from all walks of life.

While the school initially provided an English-only education, Chinese was introduced into the curriculum in 1939 by Miss Gibbins, who believed that all students growing up in Hong Kong, irrespective of ancestry, should learn Chinese, because they would invariably encounter two of the world's dominant cultures, Chinese and English, to be able to contribute in a special way toward international cooperation and peace. With the sociopolitical changes in Hong Kong after 2019, there will be more emphasis on Chinese language. The school's mission of producing young people, who are bilingual and understand the two civilisations, is even more pressing now than before.

The school was founded as a Christian school by the wife of a missionary who believed in "love in action" by providing education for girls. Her work has been perpetuated by other female Christians equally enthusiastic in their desire to serve the community by improving the education of women in Hong Kong. Christian values have always been the foundation of DGS, guiding its work in educating and nurturing its students. May the school be a place where these values will always be nurtured and celebrated—the values of love, compassion, mutual respect, acceptance, thankfulness, peace, and where action is guided by the motto "Daily Giving Service".

Part II

An Interlude: Metamorphosis in Bricks and Mortar

Vanessa Leung (1986)

An Interlude: Metamorphosis in Bricks and Mortar   255

All of the activities that have taken place at DGS over the last 110 years have been conditioned to some extent by the physical surroundings in which the DGS education was delivered. In order to understand the changing nature of that education, and the girls and teachers who participated in it, it is necessary to consider the school premises and the changes that have taken place over the last century.

Figure I.1: DGS premises during different periods. Drawn by Vanessa Leung (1986).

The Campus

1913–1928

- In 1913, DGS moved to its new quarters in Kowloon at 1 Jordan Road, its present site.
- The school added an extension in 1918 to cope with increasing enrolment.
- In 1928 a covered playground in a "Greek Temple" style was constructed for use for school activities.

Figure I.2: DGS, 1913. Source: Mr Bob Tatz, old boy of DGS.

Figure I.3: DGS with extension, 1918. Source: The National Archives, UK.

Figure I.4: The covered playground, 1928. Source: School Archives.

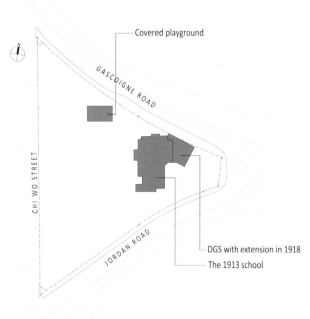

Ground plan I.1: Campus development map 1913–1928. Source: Drawn by Vanessa Leung.

An Interlude: Metamorphosis in Bricks and Mortar

1940

- In 1940, the school was able to add the 1940 Wing, renamed later as the Gibbins Wing, consisting of seven classrooms, a science laboratory, and an art room.

Figure I.6: The Gibbins Wing, 1940. Source: School Archives.

Ground plan I.2: Campus development map 1940–1941. Source: Drawn by Vanessa Leung.

Figure I.5: DGS, 1940. Source: School Archives.

1946–1954

- In 1946, expansion began with the conversion of a large dormitory from the covered playground, the "Greek Temple" building. Two Nissen huts were opened for classes in needlework and cookery.
- By 1948, the new Junior School building was completed.
- 1950 marked the 90th Anniversary of DGS and the 1950 Wing, renamed later as the Hurrell Wing, was built in commemoration.
- In 1954, a kindergarten was set up in the Green hut in the corner of the field, next to the Nissen huts.

Figure I.7: The dormitory, 1947. Source: *The Quest* 1947.

Figure I.8: Junior School building, 1948. Source: School Archives.

Figure I.9: The Hurrell Wing, 1950. Source: *The Quest* 1950.

Figure I.10: The Nissen huts and Green hut. Source: School Archives.

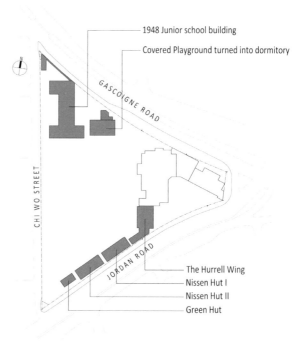

Ground plan I.3: Campus development map 1946–1954. Source: Drawn by Vanessa Leung.

An Interlude: Metamorphosis in Bricks and Mortar

1957–1965

- 1957 Christmas was celebrated for the last time in the 1913 hall before most of the school was demolished. The Centenary Building and Assembly Hall were completed in 1959.
- The new Gym Block was built thanks to a donation from the Hong Kong Royal Jockey Club.
- On 24th April 1959, Bishop Hall hallowed the newly built Chapel of the Holy Spirit on the ground floor of the Hurrell Wing.
- The 25m swimming pool, a gift from the PTA to the school, was built on the former site of the kindergarten. The pool was opened on 9 July 1965.

Figure I.11: Aerial view of the school in 1959. Source: School Archives.

Figure I.12: The Centenary buildings, 1959. Source: School Archives.

Figure I.13: The swimming pool, 1965. Source: School Archives.

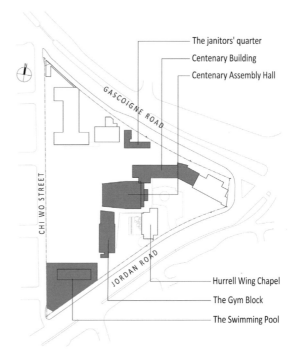

Ground plan I.4: Campus development map 1957–1965. Source: Drawn by Vanessa Leung.

1974–1984

- The Junior School, built in 1948, was demolished in 1974. The Junior School pupils came over to the Senior School for a year to allow for the development of the new buildings with 12 classrooms and 2 additional rooms. The rebuilding of the Junior School was completed in 1975. The dormitory in the covered playground building was turned into the Junior School assembly hall. In 1984, an extra floor comprising a music room and a conference room was added to the Junior School.
- The Edmund Cheung hut and the China Light and Power hut were completed in 1982 providing PE storage areas and multi-purpose areas.

Figure I.14: Edmund Cheung and the China Light and Power huts. Source: School Archives.

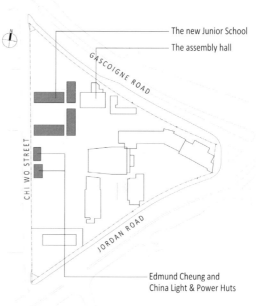

Ground plan I.5: Campus development map 1974–1984. Source: Drawn by Vanessa Leung.

Figure I.15: Junior School building, 1975. Source: School Archives.

An Interlude: Metamorphosis in Bricks and Mortar 261

1992–2001

Figure I.16: Extension Phase I, 1993. Source: School Archives.

- In 1992 the janitors' quarters were demolished to make way for the Extension Phase I, which was completed in 1993, with the Junior School occupying the 1st and 2nd Floors and the Senior School occupying the 3rd to 6th Floors.
- In 1995, the Junior School assembly hall was demolished to make way for Extension Phase II, completed in December 1996.
- In 2000, the School Crest was mounted on the façade of the Centenary Assembly Hall to commemorate the anniversary of the school. A 45m synthetic athletic track and a new long jump pitch were constructed with the school council's approval.
- DOGA Place was built as a gift from DOGA in 2001 to provide extra venues for students to hold meetings and informal discussions.

Figure I.17: Extension Phase II, 1996. Source: Janine Cheung (DGS, 1992).

Figure I.18: School Crest, 2000. Source: Janine Cheung (DGS, 1992).

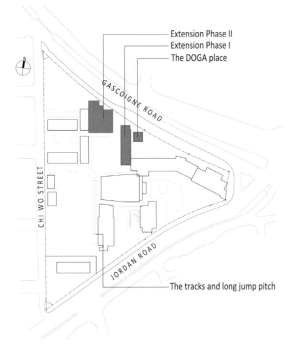

Figure I.19: DOGA Place, 2001. Source: School Archives.

Ground plan I.6: Campus development map 1992–2001. Source: Drawn by Vanessa Leung.

2003–2005

- The Gym Block was demolished in 2003 to make way for the new School Improvement Project (SIP) or Extension Phase III building which was opened in 2005. The new block provided a brand-new gym, a new student activities centre, language laboratories, a liberal studies room, a music room, three music practice rooms, a computer-assisted learning room, a Chinese orchestra room, new changing rooms, a rooftop tennis court, a covered playground, and a new tuck shop.

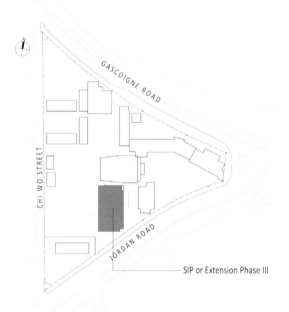

Ground plan I.7: Campus development map 2003–2006. Source: Drawn by Vanessa Leung.

Figure I.20: SIP building or Extension Phase III, 2005. Source: Janine Cheung (DGS, 1992).

Figure I.21: Aerial view of campus in 2009. Source: School Archives.

An Interlude: Metamorphosis in Bricks and Mortar 263

2009–2011

- A major redevelopment of the school took place at the beginning of Easter 2009 to provide a setting fit to take DGS and its students into the future. The construction work was completed in the summer of 2011. The Jordan Road campus was given an entirely new image. The majority of the school buildings were demolished and rebuilt apart from the SIP or Extension Phase III which was renovated.

Figure I.22: Junior School, 2011.
Source: Elaine Chan (DGS, 1992).

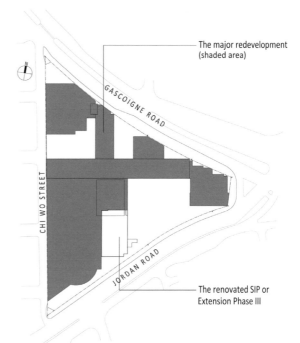

Ground plan I.8: Campus development map 2008–2011. Source: Drawn by Vanessa Leung.

Figure I.23: Aerial view of campus in 2021. Source: School Archives.

Part III

Various Aspects

Editors: Amy Ng (1991) and Moira M. W. Chan-Yeung (1955)

Chapter 10

Spiritual Life at DGS

Wun Tsz Sum (2007)

The Christian faith has always been the foundation of life at DGS, pervading the culture and directing the work of the school. Founded by faithful servants of God with a desire to improve the education of women in Hong Kong, the school has maintained a God-centred vision and mission, passed down for over a century and manifested in various forms through the school's religious activities.

The centrality of faith had been affirmed since the days of the Diocesan Home and Orphanage in the Institution Rules (as approved 18 January 1870 and revised 11 April 1870), where it is stated:

> That the objects of the Institution be to receive orphan children . . . and to board, clothe and instruct them with a view to industrial life and the Christian faith according to the teaching of the Church of England.[1]

To date, religious education is still a key element of DGS education, with one of the aspects of the school's mission being "to promote a holistic development based on Christian principles and sound moral values",[2] and described in the "School Profile" of the school's website as one of the five pillars of DGS education, alongside academic pursuit, stamina for sports, aesthetic appreciation, and generosity in social service:

> The fifth and final pillar . . . is spiritual nurturing that can be condensed into honouring God and people. Guided by Christian tenets and practices shared during morning assemblies, [religious knowledge] lessons and gospel camps, girls are brought into a closer relationship with God. It is our belief that through the wisdom of God's words,

---

1. Diocesan Home and Orphanage: Rules as approved 18 January 1870 and revised 11 April 1870, BHA.
2. DGS School Prospectus, 2019–2020.

girls will see the light and truth of His presence and conduct life in a way that is clear, productive and ultimately satisfying.[3]

This spiritual perspective, apart from teaching and learning, is also evident in how, at each milestone of the school's development, the school community has turned to God in remembrance and gratitude for His sustained grace to the school. Special thanksgiving services were held to commemorate the school's centenary in 1960 as well as every decade from the one-hundred-and-thirtieth anniversary in 1990 onwards, when the whole school community gathered together in praise of God's continued blessings upon the school. The very first chapel at the school was hallowed by Bishop R. O. Hall in 1947,[4] who also returned to dedicate the Chapel of the Holy Spirit, rebuilt as part of the centenary buildings, on 24 April 1959.[5] A dedication of the present-day Chapel of the Holy Spirit by Archbishop Dr Paul Kwong took place on 5 June 2020 as part of the one-hundred-and-sixtieth Anniversary Thanksgiving Service.

The rest of this chapter will explore the development of Christian life at DGS from its early days, and how spiritual nurturing throughout the years has shaped students' faith as well as values and character.

Early Development of Christian Life: The First Century of Growth (1860 to 1960s)

Beyond the Christian roots of DGS, including missionary organisations such as the Society for Promotion of Female Education in the Far East, which was supported by the London Missionary Society and the Church Mission Society, the running of the school over its first century was marked by close relationships between the school and the Anglican Church of Hong Kong, otherwise known as the Sheng Kung Hui (SKH). As former Headmistress Dr C. J. Symons wrote in the *South China Morning Post* in 1979:

> The "blueprint" of our school policy stems from the "social contract" of cooperation between Anglican-aided schools and the Government which our late Bishop, the Right Reverend R.O. Hall, had evolved as policy.[6]

In selecting the leadership of the school, it is evident that Christian faith has always been a significant consideration. In correspondence on finding a suitable candidate to replace Miss Hurrell after her retirement as Headmistress of DGS, Bishop R. O. Hall, then Chairman of the School Council, described "the central point of the work of the head of a Christian School" as a "pastoral one", saying elsewhere that the school needed "the kind of

---

3. DGS official website, www.dgs.edu.hk, accessed 29 December 2020.
4. A. W. Hurrell, "Headmistress's Report", *The Quest* (1947): 7.
5. "Headmistress's Report", *Quest* (1960): 10.
6. C. J. Symons, "Blueprint of DGS Policy Outlined", *South China Morning Post*, 15 March 1979.

Spiritual Life at DGS

woman who, had she been a man, would have been a priest and yet is essentially a teacher by profession".[7] Indeed, past headmistresses developed friendships with Bishop Hall based on their mutual faith in Christ, and all the headmistresses of DGS to date have held strong Christian values, prioritising the continuation of spiritual nurturing in the school.

Beyond the school's leadership, impacts of the close-knit relationship with the Anglican Church pervade many of its activities. Since DGS moved into its present site at 1 Jordan Road in 1913, the school has found, in St Andrew's Church, an Anglican church located in Tsim Sha Tsui, a steadfast partner and great supporter in the development of the school's religious life. Vicars of the church made up for the lack of staff at the school by taking up the teaching of scripture as well as English literature for senior classes.[8] With the expansion of the school, kindergarten and lower primary classes also temporarily used the hall and various rooms at St Andrew's for a brief while in 1947.[9]

Before the boarding school was closed down in 1973, a rich spiritual life was observed among boarders, often with the support of the clergy at St Andrew's and other SKH churches. There were daily evening prayers and Sunday Evensong services (later moved to Wednesdays) held in the School Chapel, and the occasional "launch picnic" and swimming parties on Saturday afternoons led faithfully by the School Chaplain and Vicar of St Andrew's Rev. J. H. Ogilvie, who also served as a member of the School Council between 1946 and 1955. Boarders also regularly attended services at St Andrew's on Sunday mornings.[10]

Daily morning assemblies, although in existence for a long time, were first recorded in 1953, with the whole school coming together to begin each day with worship through a hymn, Bible reading, a short message given by the Vicar of St Andrew's, the Headmistress, or teachers, followed by prayers.[11] Form chapel services began in the 1960s as well.[12] There was the occasional Holy Communion led by clergy from St Andrew's and Christ Church, and special services were also held at the school for Advent and Lent, such as the Christmas Carol Service and Maundy Thursday service, and Ascension Day service for senior girls at St John's Cathedral. Among students who attended evolved a greater interest in Christianity. Baptisms in the School Chapel and at St Andrew's or St John's Cathedral, and confirmations in various Anglican churches were held regularly for girls. In 1941, the school also saw the setting up of a religious discussion group, which invited internal and

---

7. Letters from R. O. Hall, Bishop's House Archive.
8. "A Glimpse of the D.G.S. in Days Gone By: Extracts from a Talk by Mrs. Dunbar on Founders' Day 1947", *The Quest* (1950): 47.
9. A. W. Hurrell, "Headmistress's Report", *The Quest* (1947): 4.
10. "A Glimpse of the D.G.S. in Days Gone By", 46; Elaine Tsien, "Padre Ogilvie", *The Quest* (1952): 16–17.
11. "Headmistress's Report", *The Quest* (1953): 6.
12. Speech Day Booklet, January 1963, 5.

Figure 10.1: DGS Baptismal Register. Source: School Archives.

external Christian speakers to give talks.[13] This culminated in the establishment of the Student Christian Association in January 1954, which continued to hold meetings once or twice a month for several years, and joint school activities such as the SKH Student Leaders' Conference.[14]

The 1960s and 1970s saw the rapid development of the school with the new centenary buildings, including the Centenary Hall and new Chapel, and the post-war years ushering in a greater sense of stability. The closing of the boarding school in 1973, a larger student population, and a greater variety of extracurricular clubs and activities meant more choices in how students could spend their time, and interest in spiritual activities appeared to have waned. However, a revival came soon afterwards when a weekly discussion group in the 1970s blossomed into the Youth Fellowship, established in October 1974.[15]

Development of Christian Curriculum and Activities: 1960s and Beyond

Spiritual nurturing at DGS has continued to evolve since the 1960s, the second century of the school's history, with long-standing traditions being upheld and adaptations being made to the religious education curriculum and other school-led activities to suit the needs of the girls. A holistic approach to the fostering of Christian faith and values was also supported by the student-led Youth Fellowship as well as family support based on Christian principles.

---

13. E. M. Gibbins, "D.G.S. Notes", *The Quest* (1941): 3.
14. "Extra-Curricular Activities", *The Quest* (1954): 6–7; Kathleen Wong and Elaine Tsien, "Student Christian Association", *The Quest* (1954): 20–21.
15. Barbara Cole and Yvonne Keh, "Youth Fellowship", *Quest* (1975–1976): 9.

Daily Morning Assembly

Morning assembly for the whole school has continued to be at the heart of DGS school life to this day, and continued even when the rebuilding of the school campus meant that the school had to use a much smaller "hotel school" campus and students had to sit on folding stools in the basketball court for assembly.[16] The hymn book used daily, which consists of both order of services and prayers as well as hymns, was first prepared in 1956 and underwent revisions in 1982.[17] The support of St Andrew's Church in this tradition of whole-school assemblies has remained steadfast, with the Vicar and staff coming in to lead one morning each week. Christian teachers also volunteer to share from the Bible and their personal faith experience, and the number of such staff on rotation to take morning assembly has grown to almost twenty. This has contributed to the vibrancy of spiritual life as the school is nurtured by the teaching of God's Word each day.

In 1983, student-led assemblies began,[18] with each class taking turns once a year to present their thoughts and reflections on a topic within an overall theme in lieu of assemblies led by staff of DGS or St Andrew's Church. These yearly themes covered topics such as "Outstanding Christians—Models For Us" (1985/1986), "Christian Perspectives on Various Social Issues" (1989/1990), "Appreciation" (1997/1998), "Developing Noble Characters" (2001/2002), and "Encounters with Jesus: Knowing God through Jesus Christ" (2018/2019). The form services in the Chapel led by various members of the clergy, which can be traced back to the 1960s, have also evolved. Today, the format of whole-school assemblies is adjusted when the school operates under the summer timetable, with chapel assemblies held for a different form each morning, while other classes conduct assembly in their own classrooms. The efforts by teachers and students alike to keep this tradition of daily morning assembly alive speak of the firm Christian foundation on which DGS education stands.

Christian Curriculum and Student Support

The formal religious education curriculum has also been adapted throughout the years. In a meeting of the members of the Victoria Diocesan Association in the 1920s, it was reported by then Headmistress Miss Sawyer that all students received a scripture lesson every

---

16. Speech Day Booklet, Religious Knowledge departmental report, December 2009.

17. *The Prayers and Hymns*, Diocesan Girls' School, Speech Day Booklets, November 1956, 10; November 1983, 17.

18. Speech Day Booklet, November 1983, 17.

Figure 10.2: Last morning assembly in the Centenary Hall before the redevelopment project in 2009. Source: School Archives.

Figure 10.3: The chapel in the new redeveloped campus in 2014. Source: School Archives.

morning,[19] and scripture prizes being awarded at Speech Day can be traced back to 1925.[20] The curriculum has evolved since then under the headship of Dr C. J. Symons and beyond, and a wide range of topics were introduced to cater to the sociocultural, educational, and spiritual needs of the times, including discussions on comparative religion and the relevance of the Christian faith to social issues.[21] With the importance of religious studies being acknowledged by the Curriculum Development Council in Hong Kong and made an official subject for the Hong Kong Certificate of Education Examinations (HKCEE), the school decided that all students should sit the subject in their Form 5 year, leading to a revision of the syllabus across all forms in 1993/1994.[22] After the abolishment of the HKCEE in 2010, owing to the introduction of the Hong Kong Diploma of Secondary Education Examination, DGS students were no longer required to sit the public examinations for the new Ethics and Religious Studies subject. However, Religious Education has continued to be a compulsory subject for all girls to this day, utilising a school-based curriculum. In particular, weekly Bible study groups spanning five to six weeks have been arranged for Secondary 1 students during their Religious Education lessons since 2009/2010, with Christian teachers volunteering to lead these sessions.[23] This further developed into the split-class mode of teaching for Secondary 1 in 2011/2012, enabling smaller classes and more effective pastoral care.[24] The support of Christian teachers at DGS goes beyond classroom teaching and learning, with the Counselling and Guidance Team set up in 1986/1987 by then Religious Knowledge head Mrs A. Hurst.[25] It has continued to foster both the intellectual and emotional growth of students in God's love and through the guidance of His Word ever since.

Christian Activities beyond the Curriculum

Aside from morning assembly and the formal curriculum, spiritual nurturing at DGS has been supplemented by other activities as well. Student retreats and related excursions that began in the 1950s, such as visits to St Christopher's Home and St Andrew's Church, and Christian conferences at Tao Fung Shan in Shatin, became regular retreats separately for

---

19. "Victoria Diocesan Association: 'At Home' at Helena May Institute, Review of the Work", *South China Morning Post*, 29 April 1926.

20. "Diocesan Girls' School, Prize Distribution, The Bishop's Remarks", *South China Morning Post*, 28 February 1925.

21. Speech Day Booklets, January 1980, 9; January 1981, 8–9; November 1986, 15.

22. Speech Day Booklet, November 1993, 23–24.

23. Speech Day Booklet, Religious Knowledge departmental report, December 2009.

24. Speech Day Booklet, January 2013, 99.

25. Speech Day Booklet, November 1987, 23.

senior and junior form girls in the late 1960s.²⁶ By the 1980s, retreats were open to senior form girls only, and owing to oversubscription,²⁷ eventually became a one-day retreat for Form 6 students, an arrangement that continued fairly regularly for all students of the form until the introduction of the New Senior Secondary curriculum in 2011/2012 by the Education Bureau. Two-day overnight Gospel Camps for junior form girls have been organised since 2009/2010, as well as one-day retreats led by Christian old girls for Secondary 5 girls. Holy Communion services led by St Andrew's have been adjusted from a fortnightly event in the 1970s to annual events, open to Christian girls and teachers on the last day of term before the Easter holidays. Special services to celebrate Christmas and Easter at the end of the school terms are also held for the whole school.

The Youth Fellowship set up in 1974 has thrived to this day, and from monthly or fortnightly meetings led by teachers has evolved into today's weekly lunch meeting led by Christian students on the committee and consisting of around fifty members. Activities include games, pizza lunches, worship through hymns and praise songs, small group Bible studies, discipleship discussion sessions, and special prayer meetings for senior students taking public examinations. These activities are open to all students, and have attracted girls

Figure 10.4: Retreat of Secondary 5 students at St Andrew's Church in 2019. Source: School Archives.

---

26. Patsy Bush, "A Visit to St. Christopher's", *The Quest* (1953): 22; Janet Huang and Janet Cunningham, "A Conference at Shatin", *The Quest* (1954): 49; Lily Tong, "A Visit to St. Andrew's Church", *The Quest* (1954): 60; DGS Speech Day Booklet, November 1968.
27. Speech Day Booklet, November 1982, 9.

Spiritual Life at DGS

Figure 10.5: Gospel Camp of Secondary 2 students in 2014. Source: School Archives.

from all faith backgrounds to gather, amid their busy schedules, for a sense of camaraderie and to learn more about the Christian faith during Monday lunchtimes. The Fellowship has also faithfully continued to lead the annual Gospel Week since the first event in February 1994.[28] This began as special lunchtime activities, and in recent years the student committee members have used various creative means such as original skits, mimes, worship, dance, and videos to present the Gospel message to fellow schoolmates during the week's assemblies. Week-long crusades led by the Youth Fellowship in the early 1990s have also evolved into evangelistic meetings as the highlight of the Gospel Week and were first held in 1996, with Christian speakers ranging from old girls to public figures, scholars, and pastors of different churches and denominations other than Sheng Kung Hui, delivering the Good News and inviting students' decisions of faith.[29] Occasionally, such evangelistic meetings took place outside school, sometimes led by overseas speakers such as Nick Vujicic, Australian-American Christian motivational speaker who was born without arms and legs, and German Paralympics champion Rainer Schmidt, in 2009; as well as a session by Will Graham, grandson of the renowned evangelist Billy Graham, which took place at the Hong Kong Stadium as part of the Franklin Graham Festival in 2007.[30] The various

---

28. Speech Day Booklet, November 1994, 25.
29. Speech Day Booklets, November 1992, 19; November 1996, 27.
30. Departmental Report of Religious Knowledge, 2009–2010; Minutes of the Religious Knowledge Department, 2008–2009.

Figure 10.6: Christmas carol singing in the mid-1990s with Youth Fellowship committee. Source: School Archives.

activities organised by the school and by fellow students have helped provide opportunities for girls to explore their faith, commit to, and deepen their relationship with God.

Family Support from a Christian Perspective

Beyond students' needs, the school has sought to support students' growth through ministering spiritually to their families as well. Working with the Parent Teacher Association, various seminars and gatherings were held to this end, aiming to foster better family relationships and equip parents from a Christian perspective. These have included, among many others, a mother and daughter retreat held in January 2013. In April and May 2013, St Andrew's Church hosted a five-week parenting course for DGS parents, to be followed by a parenting seminar led by Bishop Andrew Chan, Chairman of the School Council, in October 2013; fatherhood talks given by Dr Dave Currie, a family counsellor based in Canada, and Dr Hugo S. K. Chan, lay church leader and national director of Full Gospel Business Men's Fellowship in Hong Kong, in January and June 2015 respectively; and

Spiritual Life at DGS

a seminar on resilience and character-building given by Dr Choi Yuen Wan, founder of Christian youth organisation Breakthrough in October 2015. The positive reception of these sessions led to more regular meetings for parents, including a Christian mothers' Bible study group held every other week in collaboration with St Andrew's Church that began in January 2015, and multi-session breakfast gatherings for fathers led by Christian clinical psychologist Dr Lawrence Chen starting in March 2017, which have been well received by parents.[31]

The varied aspects of spiritual nurturing, from the daily faithful teaching of God's Word to the opportunity to experience the joys of Christian fellowship, are evidence of the school's dedication to building up students in their faith and Christlike character, so each one will flourish in life.

Christian Faith Lived Out through Service

Aside from fostering students' personal relationship with Christ, spiritual nurturing at DGS also aims to educate students to live out the school motto: "Daily Giving Service". As former Headmistress Mrs Elim Lau once explained:

> The D.G.S. spirit is the Christian spirit, one of love and loyalty. The essence is the willingness to serve the school with a sense of purpose and value. It is from this that we derived our school motto: "Daily Giving Service" . . . It is through our concern and service to others that we can put the school motto into action. At school, our girls offer service to God by attending assembly every day. They should also contribute unselfishly to the school by helping in the library or going to rehearsals and training and the like. At home, our girls should be responsible and helpful daughters who are always willing to assist with the housework. Serving the public by participating in voluntary work is another way of realising the school motto.[32]

The beginnings of social service can be traced back to the setting up of the DGS Girls' Club (also named the Yau Kwong Tuen), which first opened in February 1940 and resumed after the war in 1947. Students regularly took turns to help out as volunteer teachers in after-school classes for underprivileged children, who were provided with an evening meal, games, and homework assistance.[33] By 1951, there were over forty boys and girls joining these classes three times a week, and an additional Sunday School was set up, with DGS girls leading simple services to share the Christian faith with almost thirty children under the guidance

---

31. *Kaleidoscope* 12: 15; 13: 12; 15: 15; 18: 9.

32. Jane Ng, Vivian Au, Mary Chan, and Vivian Lau, "Interview with Mrs. Elim Lau", *Quest* (1985–1986): 1.

33. Elaine Ho, "The D.G.S. Girls' Club (Yau Kwong Tuen)", *The Quest* (1941): 15; Elise Wong, translated by Sylvia Hui; "The D.G.S. Girls' Club", *The Quest* (1947): 30–31.

of a scripture teacher.[34] Some members of the early Student Christian Association also helped out at the St Thomas's Club and Sunday School, a similar programme run by DBS.[35] These initial efforts paved the way for the birth of the Citizens' Club in 1963, which aimed in part "to interpret our School Motto 'Daily Giving Service' in a positive manner", and began with seven service programmes.[36] This number has grown to today's eleven regular services being run every day of the week, as well as various service projects in school and during long school holidays, involving over 200 student members and serving people from all walks of life and of various needs, ages, and nationalities. The current range includes tuition classes for children from low-income families and ethnic minority children, interest classes for the elderly, and programmes for those with disabilities.[37]

Besides the regular services of the Citizens' Club, the Youth Fellowship also organised outreach visits, in particular in the 1980s, including to elderly centres, a home for children with mental disabilities, and a Christian drug rehabilitation centre.[38] From 2006 to 2008, a series of service trips to a village school in Qingyuan, Guangdong, was also organised by the school in collaboration with a local Hong Kong church, during which groups of Form 3 students had the opportunity to teach their counterparts English vocabulary and pronunciation and be immersed in a Christian environment, under the guidance of the Reverend Kun and his family, to reflect on the meaning of service to others out of Christ's love for all.[39]

Apart from voluntary work, students have been encouraged to consider those less fortunate both in and beyond Hong Kong through religious activities. Since the 1950s, Lent offerings have been collected and donated to local and overseas charitable organisations, a practice that has continued to this day.[40] The Youth Fellowship also started holding the annual Famine Lunch activity in 1983, initially to raise money to aid famine relief in Ethiopia, whereby participants take a simple lunch to have a taste of what it feels like to go hungry, and raise money for those in impoverished conditions.[41] The Harvest Festival, which began in 1989, has remained a much-loved event: dried and tinned foods are donated to Christian organisations serving the poor in Hong Kong and abroad.[42] More recently, since 2015, a Christmas gift donation to SKH elderly homes, organised by St Andrew's Church, has involved student volunteers in helping to wrap hundreds of gift packages,

---

34. Alice Lam, "Our New Sunday School", *The Quest* (1951): 13–14.
35. Kathleen Wong and Elain Tsien, "Student Christian Association", *The Quest* (1954): 21.
36. Patricia Yeung, "The D.G.S. Citizens' Club", *Quest* (1964): 18–19.
37. Departmental Report of Service Team, 2019–2020.
38. Speech Day Booklet, November 1983, 17.
39. *Kaleidoscope* 1: 4.
40. Speech Day Booklet, November 1956, 9.
41. Speech Day Booklet, November 1983, 17.
42. Speech Day Booklet, January 1990, 15.

which include daily necessities and simple snacks. Through simple acts of service, students are guided to look beyond themselves to emulate the heart of Christian giving.

Beyond these various services offered to the community at large, and to which DGS as a school is committed, several graduates have made it their life commitment to serve in full-time Christian ministry in different domains, including Joyce H. Y. Wong, Winnie Wan Yi Fung, and Gina Ching-wan Yuen (see Chapter 9). They are a testament to the lasting impact of Christian education at the school.

Conclusion

The Christian faith at DGS is not a mere tradition or list of programmes; it is a source of purpose that drives all educational activities, and it is a source of strength for all staff and students alike who serve both inside and outside the school campus. It may be that not all who enter the gates of DGS come with a personal relationship with Christ, but through the spiritual nurturing during their time at the school, perhaps each may one day leave with a greater sense of God's presence and direction in their lives. As DGS carries forward the baton of a Christian school yielded to Christ, God willing, generations of DGS girls will continue to be raised up to be those who serve God and others, for the benefit of society and the glory of His Kingdom.

Chapter 11

Scholastic Activities

Janice Tsang (1992)

This chapter gives an overview of the scholastic activities of DGS since the time when it was first established as the Diocesan Native Female Training School (DNFTS), when girls were trained to be wives of graduates of St Paul's College until today, when DGS has evolved to become a prestigious school offering holistic girls' education in Hong Kong, preparing women leaders of tomorrow. The curriculum and pedagogy of the school have also undergone a series of transformations, with the objectives of the teaching and learning being constantly reviewed and redefined in response to curriculum changes, education reform, changes in society and the world at large, while upkeeping the vision, mission, and tradition of the school.

The scholastic activities of DGS are divided into five periods according to the tenure of the headmistresses, and not according to the education system.

The Early Years, 1860–1892

The school was initially inaugurated as the DNFTS in 1860 for Chinese girls. It closed down in 1869 and became a co-educational institution for the reasons described in Chapter 1. The co-educational Diocesan Home and Orphanage (DHO) accepted boys and girls in the beginning for boarding. Later, it only accepted day girls, and in 1892, it ceased to accept any more girls.

Scholastic Activities

Aims

The purpose of the DNFTS was "to introduce among a somewhat superior class of native females the blessings of Christianity and religious training," as stated in its first annual report.[1] The students were prepared either to become wives of graduates from St Paul's College who would become clergy, or school mistresses.[2]

Curriculum

From the beginning of the DNFTS, Christian values were the main focus of its education, and there was no formal curriculum. At that time, the three main "subjects" were "Christian values", "English language", and "basic life skills", including both social and daily life skills. Students were trained to be socially well-behaved young ladies through Christian conduct and etiquette. They learnt the English language through direct interactions with the mistress and through reading the Bible, which was their main "textbook". Students were obliged to attend Sunday School at St John's Cathedral. In 1863, when Miss M. A. W. Eaton took over as Superintendent, the curriculum was expanded to include English reading, writing, geography, and needlework, in addition to religious and moral education. There were no official textbooks apart from the Bible. The schoolmistress served more as a motherly matron and a mentor. At the beginning of 1866, Miss M. J. Oxlad was appointed to serve as both teacher and matron while the school was renamed the Diocesan Female School, but scripture and preparing students for baptism still formed the backbone of teaching and learning.

When the DHO was inaugurated in 1870, there were more boys than girls because young men who were bilingual were greatly needed in the business sector. There were only three teaching staff: Mr W. M. B. Arthur, the Headmaster; his wife, the matron; and a Chinese teacher. Mr Arthur probably followed the curriculum of Miss Eaton, concentrating on reading, spelling, writing English, and simple mental arithmetic. In 1878, when the learning of English was declared important by the Education Conference in Hong Kong, students were given five hours of compulsory English lessons with two-and-a-half hours of optional Chinese study each day.

Student Achievements

The DNFTS was an institution with the aim to prepare girls as marriage partners for graduates of St Paul's College who would be going into ministry to spread Christianity to the

---

1. Entry 2950, Minutes of Committee of FES, 11 March 1858.
2. C. T. Smith, *Chinese Christians: Elites, Middlemen, and the Church of Hong Kong* (Hong Kong: Oxford University Press, 2005), 207–208.

inhabitants in China. It was considered a great success when a DNFTS graduate married a minister who had graduated from St Paul's.[3] When the DHO was established and became a grant-in-aid school in 1873, the examination results of students were used to assess its achievements.

Developmental Years, 1898–1941

In the early twentieth century in the Western world, more opportunities became available for young women to become teachers as young men took up medicine, engineering, and business as their careers, leaving education of the next generation to women. In male-dominated societies, schools and universities began to open up for women. In Hong Kong, in 1898, the Anglican Church re-established the school for girls as the Diocesan Girls' School and Orphanage, and in 1900 it was renamed the Diocesan Girls' School (DGS). The school was initially for European and Eurasian girls, and all subjects were taught in English. Chinese girls were admitted in 1922. During this period, the school was successively under the headship of Miss Elizabeth D. Skipton (1899–1921), Miss Catherine A. Ferguson (1921–1924), Miss H. Dorothy Sawyer (1925–1938), and Miss Elizabeth M. Gibbins (1939–1941, 1945).

Aims

The aim of re-establishing a girls' school in Hong Kong was described by the Bishop of Victoria:

> That it is desirable to establish in Hongkong a boarding and day School for girls, more especially for Eurasian children, such school to aim at giving a liberal education according to the doctrines of the Church of England, and that this meeting pledges itself to do all it can in support of that scheme.[4]

Curriculum

Under the headship of Miss Skipton, there was no formal curriculum or pedagogy. In the beginning, there were very few textbooks except for the *Royal Reader*. The normal school day started with a half-hour of scripture for all classes; this was taught by Anglican clergy. Once DGS had joined the grant-in-aid scheme in 1900, it was able to expand, and

---

3. *Female Missionary Intelligence* (1 August 1864): 159–160.

4. Diocesan Girls' School and Orphanage Under the Patronage of Her Excellency Lady Blake, Hong Kong, March 1899, Hong Kong Public Record Office (HKPRO), HKMS94-1-06.

its curriculum was extended to include English (composition, grammar, and dictation), history, geography, arithmetic, needlework, and singing. The teaching content of history and geography was limited to places within the British Empire, with no reference to the local context. At that time, girls were not allowed to attend the University of Hong Kong (HKU), the only university in the territory at the time. Girls who made it to Class 1 generally completed their education at the end of secondary school. The school prepared them for the Oxford Local Examination, and the results of the examination marked the girls' achievements.

Miss Sawyer operated DGS along the lines of an English school. Even though its teaching faculty had expanded, few teachers possessed a university degree. Students in the lower classes were taught Bible studies, English, history, and geography. The subjects in senior forms were more diverse, including French, algebra, geometry, and trigonometry, which were available for those who were interested. There was no science in DGS except domestic science. The students of Class 1 sat for the Hong Kong Senior Local Examination (matriculation examination), while students of Class 2 took the Hong Kong Junior Local Examination (certificate examination) at the end of the academic year. In 1937, Miss Sawyer introduced a commercial course for students after the Hong Kong Junior Local Examination to teach them secretarial skills before leaving school.

The curriculum became more academic under the headship of Miss Gibbins, who introduced botany, then biology and full mathematics to the curriculum, and brought a more academic approach to the study of English literature, history, and geography. She introduced Chinese studies to the school in 1939 as this became a compulsory subject for all Chinese girls. The school completed an extension in 1940 to provide more classrooms and a science laboratory.

During this period, the teaching method was basically unidirectional, with teachers serving as the knowledge source, transferring knowledge to the students.

Student Achievements

Under the headship of Miss Skipton and Miss Sawyer, the school curriculum had shifted gradually from a single track to train homemakers to a dual track, with one stream for vocational training and an academic stream to prepare girls for university education. With the benefit of the more structured curriculum, two students, Irene and Eva Ho Tung, were permitted to enter HKU in 1921 and 1922, breaking the tradition of no Chinese females in the university. University education became feasible for upper-class local girls in Hong Kong. The few who were graduates of HKU before the Second World War became professionals, mostly in education, and a few in medicine.

The Post-war Years, 1945–1985

Aims

This period was under the headship of Miss A. Winifred Hurrell (1946–1951) and Mrs C. Joyce Symons (1953–1985). The headmistresses kept the aim of the school "to provide a broad liberal education based on Christian principles". Mrs Symons also placed emphasis on physical and spiritual growth in addition to academic progress.

Curriculum

Miss Hurrell efficiently rehabilitated the school after the war. At the time there were few families who could afford to send their daughters to the university, and girls were rather anxious that they should join the workforce after graduation to help support the family. Miss Hurrell divided the students after Form 3 into two streams: an academic stream to prepare students for the university and a "modern" stream to prepare students for secretarial work or for vocational training to become teachers and nurses. Despite the very tight budget, Miss Hurrell had the 1950 wing built to provide facilities for the modern stream.

Miss Hurrell established a Chinese Department in 1947 to improve the standard of this language, which had only been introduced to the school in 1939. After the war, the Education

Figure 11.1: The 1950/1951 matriculation class. Source: *The Quest* 1950, II.

Scholastic Activities

Figure 11.2: The commercial class at work. Source: *The Quest* 1950, III.

Department and HKU changed the Chinese curriculum, abandoned the use of the classical Chinese texts, the *Four Books*, and adopted specified Chinese textbooks for Classes 1 to 10 and the kindergarten. Translation was introduced in Class 4. Miss Hurrell introduced the concept of field trips to DGS, and students visited various places in Hong Kong, such as canneries, film studios, and the Royal Observatory, so that students could put into context what they had learned in the classroom. Miss Hurrell believed that teachers should work together with parents in the education of their children and established the Parent Teacher Association.

Educational needs continued to change as Hong Kong evolved from a city based on entrepôt trade to a regional manufacturing centre in the late 1950s and 1960s; by the 1980s, it was further transforming into a financial centre, requiring better educated young people. To prepare for expansion, Mrs Symons had the Centenary Block, assembly hall, and a gymnasium built to replace the 1913 block. In the new building, she established a well-equipped library, language laboratories, and science laboratories.

In 1953, the Education Department (ED) announced that the matriculation course would comprise two years instead of one year. DGS was the first girls' school to develop the Upper Six curriculum, which was equivalent to a first-year university curriculum—a daunting undertaking as it was difficult to find the necessary teachers.

During the 1960s, fewer and fewer students enrolled in the commercial stream. In 1966, when the government discontinued the Ordinary Level Matriculation Examination after Lower Form 6, Mrs Symons cancelled the commercial course and prepared all her students for higher education. She introduced a Form 6 General course to teach the ordinary level London General Certificate Examination (GCE-O) curriculum so that students were able to continue GCE-A (advanced) level in the UK and Commonwealth countries or further their education in US colleges and universities.

Students had to decide by Form 4 whether they wished to pursue science or arts subjects. However, the school required them, irrespective of their specialisation, to take general arts (history and English literature) and general science courses after Form 3, so they received a broader education up to Form 5. In addition, Mrs Symons followed all the regulations and the curriculum requirements that were introduced by the ED to ensure all schools would reach a certain standard during the era of mass education. In addition, she also initiated new programmes such as sex education (in 1967) and religious and political theories (in 1969). A sixth form curriculum was developed to give the students a broad liberal education.[5]

The Senior School received the first batch of "outside students" in 1956 from the Secondary School Entrance Examination. Because of the somewhat lower standard in English of the "outside girls", who mostly came from Chinese primary schools, Mrs Symons introduced streaming, a long-established strategy, but one that had not been previously used in the school. Students were streamed according to their level of competence in English, Chinese, and mathematics and were taught at different paces. The class with the subjects taught more slowly during term time received lessons during the summer holidays to catch up with other classes.

Rote learning by memorisation has been used in China since ancient times. Mrs Symons discouraged this mode of learning and introduced several other pedagogies. Instead of regular classroom teaching, talks, seminars, and conferences were introduced.[6] Broader topics such as social problems and environmental issues were offered, and teachers, including Mrs Symons herself, served as facilitators for the exchange of ideas. The school provided the space for the Sixth Form Centre with seminar rooms, meeting rooms, and a lounge to enhance exchange of ideas between students and between students and teachers. This enabled students to take a more active role in learning rather than just being passive recipients of knowledge. Science subjects such as physics, chemistry, and biology were

---

5. Headmistress's Report on the School, June 1970.
6. C. J. Symons, *Looking at the Stars: Memoirs by Catherine Joyce Symons* (Hong Kong: Pegasus Books, 1996), 58.

Figure 11.3: Lady Grantham visiting the cookery class, 1952. Source: *The Quest* 1953, 12.

Figure 11.4: Form IV science students in the chemistry laboratory, 1960. Source: *Quest* 1960, 25.

accompanied by laboratory experiments, as required by the ED, so that students could form hypotheses, design and perform experiments, and observe results before drawing conclusions.[7]

Student Achievements

Under the baton of Miss Hurrell, the school recovered gradually from the Second World War. In 1948, students from the academic stream and from the commercial stream achieved excellent examination results. Of the twenty-six students who passed the Hong Kong Matriculation Examination, four achieved distinctions in one or two subjects; of these, twenty-one also sat for the GCE (London University Matriculation Certificate) and passed. The modern stream who took the Pitman's Commercial Examination passed with excellent results (Figure 11.5).[8]

Mrs Symons created a new culture of continuous assessment in school, using grades rather than ranking. Only marks and grades were shown on the report cards. Subjects scored eighty marks or above, or A, were commended by a red mark, in contrast to the traditional convention that only failures would be marked red. Thus, the red marks indicated outstanding academic achievement, a tradition continued to this day.

The academic achievements of the girls continued to grow, as reflected in the results of public examinations, which high percentages of girls passed. The number of distinctions obtained in the Hong Kong Certificate of Education Examination (HKCEE) continued to rise, and in 1981, there were two students who each achieved distinctions in six subjects.[9] Wilma Komala (1972 graduate) was elected one of the six finalists in the Hong Kong Youth of the Year Contest, sponsored by the Lions International District 303,[10] while Dora Fung of Upper Six Arts in 1970 was awarded the Miss Computer '70 award.[11]

The all-round education had started to come to maturity. More girls completed tertiary education, be it locally or overseas, and more women university graduates became leaders of Hong Kong's fast-moving society. In 1978, an exhibition entitled "Change and Challenge" was organised when DGS celebrated its centenary as a grant school, which was officially opened by Governor Sir Murray MacLehose. The exhibition portrayed the many facets of DGS's school life and academic pursuits.[12]

---

7. Minutes of School Council Meeting, 26 July 1960.
8. Speech Day Booklet, 10 December 1948.
9. Headmistress's Report, 1980–1981.
10. "Hong Kong Youth of the Year Contest", Quest (1971–1972): 16.
11. Headmistress's Report, March 1978.
12. Quest (2009–2010): 17–18.

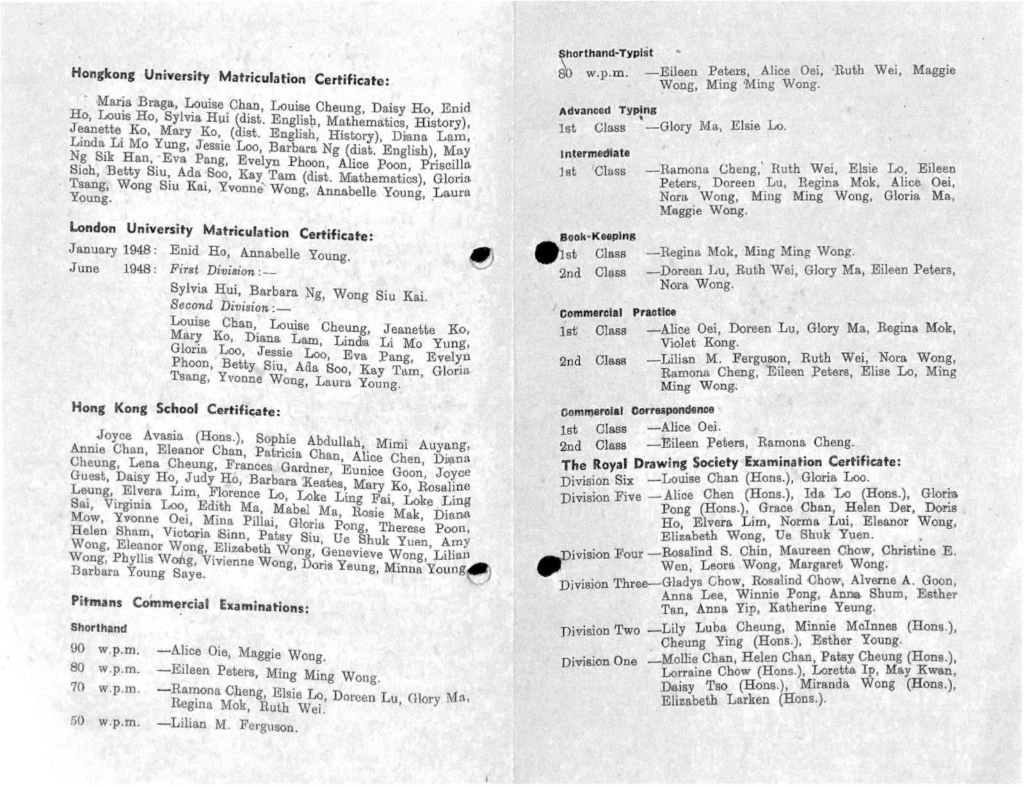

Hongkong University Matriculation Certificate:

Maria Braga, Louise Chan, Louise Cheung, Daisy Ho, Enid Ho, Louis Ho, Sylvia Hui (dist. English, Mathematics, History), Jeanette Ko, Mary Ko, (dist. English, History), Diana Lam, Linda Li Mo Yung, Jessie Loo, Barbara Ng (dist. English), May Ng Sik Han, Eva Pang, Evelyn Phoon, Alice Poon, Priscilla Sich, Betty Siu, Ada Soo, Kay Tam (dist. Mathematics), Gloria Tsang, Wong Siu Kai, Yvonne Wong, Annabelle Young, Laura Young.

London University Matriculation Certificate:

January 1948: Enid Ho, Annabelle Young.

June 1948: *First Division*:—

Sylvia Hui, Barbara Ng, Wong Siu Kai.

Second Division:—

Louise Chan, Louise Cheung, Jeanette Ko, Mary Ko, Diana Lam, Linda Li Mo Yung, Gloria Loo, Jessie Loo, Eva Pang, Evelyn Phoon, Betty Siu, Ada Soo, Kay Tam, Gloria Tsang, Yvonne Wong, Laura Young.

Hong Kong School Certificate:

Joyce Avasia (Hons.), Sophie Abdullah, Mimi Auyang, Annie Chan, Eleanor Chan, Patricia Chan, Alice Chen, Diana Cheung, Lena Cheung, Frances Gardner, Eunice Goon, Joyce Guest, Daisy Ho, Judy Ho, Barbara Keates, Mary Ko, Rosaline Leung, Elvera Lim, Florence Lo, Loke Ling Fai, Loke Ling Sai, Virginia Loo, Edith Ma, Mabel Ma, Rosie Mak, Diana Mow, Yvonne Oei, Mina Pillai, Gloria Pong, Therese Poon, Helen Sham, Victoria Sinn, Patsy Siu, Ue Shuk Yuen, Amy Wong, Eleanor Wong, Elizabeth Wong, Genevieve Wong, Lilian Wong, Phyllis Wong, Vivienne Wong, Doris Yeung, Minna Young, Barbara Young Saye.

Pitmans Commercial Examinations:

Shorthand

90 w.p.m. —Alice Oie, Maggie Wong.

80 w.p.m. —Eileen Peters, Ming Ming Wong.

70 w.p.m. —Ramona Cheng, Elsie Lo, Doreen Lu, Glory Ma, Regina Mok, Ruth Wei.

50 w.p.m. —Lilian M. Ferguson.

Shorthand-Typist

80 w.p.m. —Eileen Peters, Alice Oei, Ruth Wei, Maggie Wong, Ming Ming Wong.

Advanced Typing

1st Class —Glory Ma, Elsie Lo.

Intermediate

1st Class —Ramona Cheng, Ruth Wei, Elsie Lo, Eileen Peters, Doreen Lu, Regina Mok, Alice Oei, Nora Wong, Ming Ming Wong, Gloria Ma, Maggie Wong.

Book-Keeping

1st Class —Regina Mok, Ming Ming Wong.

2nd Class —Doreen Lu, Ruth Wei, Glory Ma, Eileen Peters, Nora Wong.

Commercial Practice

1st Class —Alice Oei, Doreen Lu, Glory Ma, Regina Mok, Violet Kong.

2nd Class —Lilian M. Ferguson, Ruth Wei, Nora Wong, Ramona Cheng, Eileen Peters, Elise Lo, Ming Ming Wong.

Commercial Correspondence

1st Class —Alice Oei.

2nd Class —Eileen Peters, Ramona Cheng.

The Royal Drawing Society Examination Certificate:

Division Six —Louise Chan (Hons.), Gloria Loo.

Division Five —Alice Chen (Hons.), Ida Lo (Hons.), Gloria Pong (Hons.), Grace Chan, Helen Der, Doris Ho, Elvera Lim, Norma Lui, Eleanor Wong, Elizabeth Wong, Ue Shuk Yuen.

Division Four —Rosalind S. Chin, Maureen Chow, Christine E. Wen, Leora Wong, Margaret Wong.

Division Three—Gladys Chow, Rosalind Chow, Alverne A. Goon, Anna Lee, Winnie Pong, Anna Shum, Esther Tan, Anna Yip, Katherine Yeung.

Division Two —Lily Luba Cheung, Minnie McInnes (Hons.), Cheung Ying (Hons.), Esther Young.

Division One —Mollie Chan, Helen Chan, Patsy Cheung (Hons.), Lorraine Chow (Hons.), Loretta Ip, May Kwan, Daisy Tso (Hons.), Miranda Wong (Hons.), Elizabeth Larken (Hons.).

Figure 11.5: Results of various examinations of DGS students, 1948. Source: DGS Speech Day Booklet 1948, 5–6.

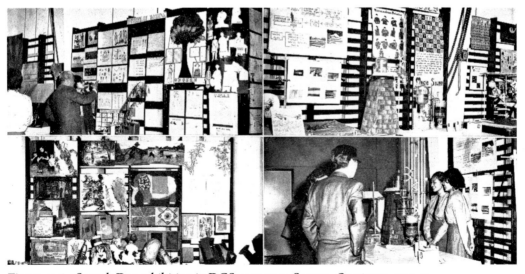

Figure 11.6: Speech Day exhibition in DGS, 1971-1972. Source: *Quest* 1971–1972, 7.

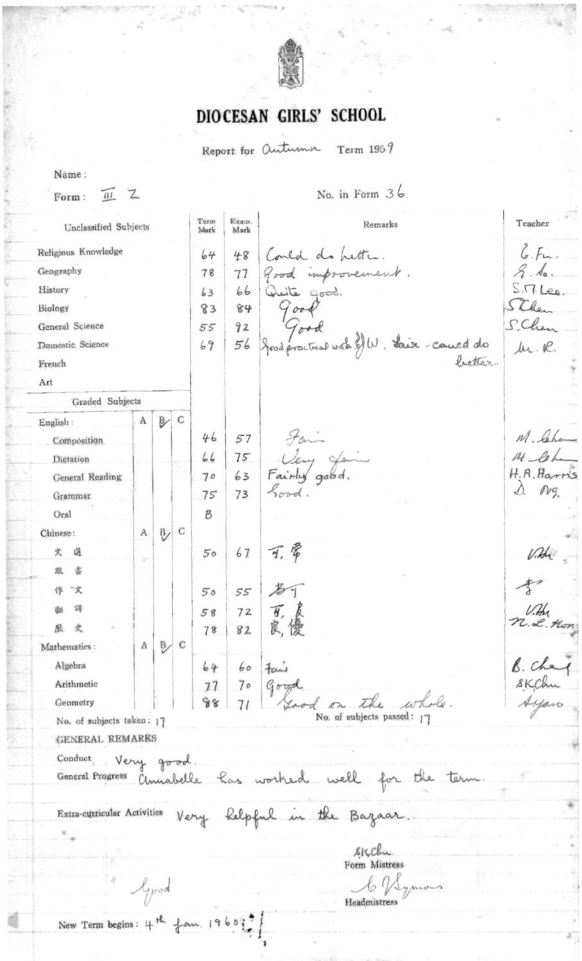

DIOCESAN GIRLS' SCHOOL

Report for Autumn Term 1959

Name:

Form: III Z

No. in Form 36

Unclassified Subjects				Term Mark	Exam. Mark	Remarks	Teacher
Religious Knowledge				64	48	Could do better.	C. Fu.
Geography				78	77	Good improvement.	[illegible]
History				63	66	Quite good.	S.T. Lee.
Biology				83	84	Good	S. Chen
General Science				55	92	Good	S. Chen
Domestic Science				69	56	Good practical work. [illegible] W. fair - could do better.	M. R.
French							
Art							
Graded Subjects							
English:	A	B ✓	C				
Composition				46	57	Fair	M. Chan
Dictation				66	75	Very fair	M. Chan
General Reading				70	63	Fairly good.	H.A. Harris
Grammar				75	73	Good.	D. Ng.
Oral				B			
Chinese:	A	B ✓	C				
文選				50	67	[illegible]	V. [illegible]
默書							
作文				50	55	尚可	[illegible]
翻譯				58	72	可, 良	V. [illegible]
歷史				78	82	良, 優	N. L. Hon
Mathematics:	A	B ✓	C				
Algebra				64	60	Fair	B. Chan
Arithmetic				77	70	Good	S.K. Chu
Geometry				88	71	Good on the whole.	A. Yau

No. of subjects taken: 17   No. of subjects passed: 17

GENERAL REMARKS

Conduct: Very good.

General Progress: Annabelle has worked well for the term.

Extra-curricular Activities: Very helpful in the Bazaar.

S.K. Chu
Form Mistress

Good

C. J. Symons
Headmistress

New Term begins: 4th Jan. 1960

Figure 11.7a: Student's report: Autumn, 1959. Source: An anonymous old girl.

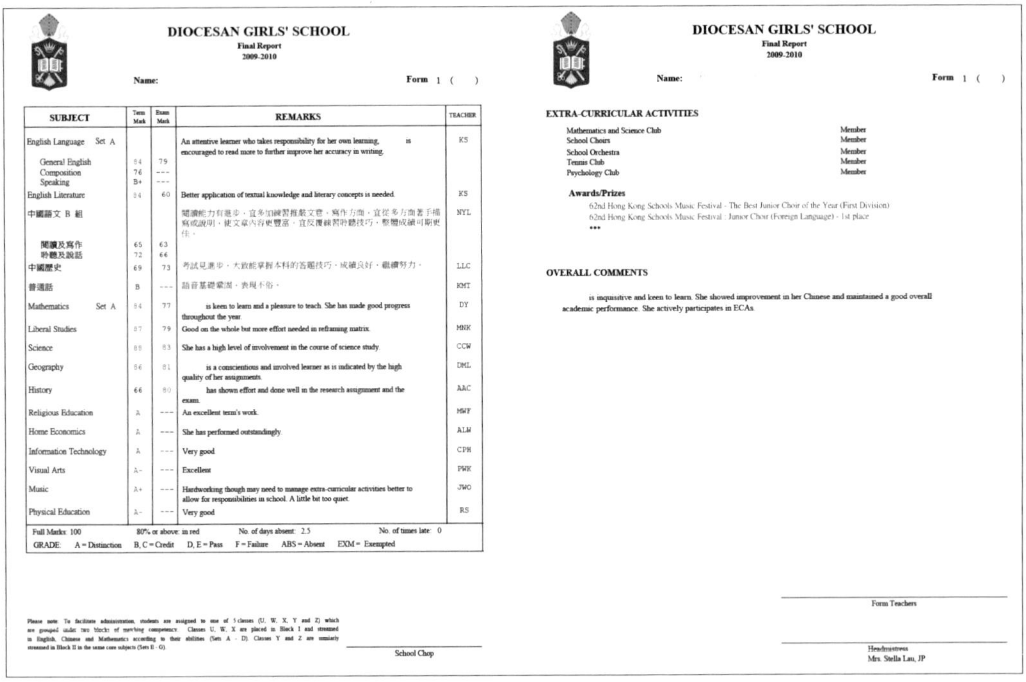

DIOCESAN GIRLS' SCHOOL
Final Report
2009-2010

Name: Form 1 ( )

SUBJECT	Term Mark	Exam Mark	REMARKS	TEACHER
English Language Set A			An attentive learner who takes responsibility for her own learning. is encouraged to read more to further improve her accuracy in writing.	KS
General English	84	79		
Composition	76	---		
Speaking	B+	---		
English Literature	84	60	Better application of textual knowledge and literary concepts is needed.	KS
中國語文 B 組			閱讀能力有進步，宜多加練習推敲文意。寫作方面，宜從多方面著手描寫或說明，使文章內容更豐富。宜反覆練習聆聽技巧，整體成績可期更佳。	NYL
閱讀及寫作	65	63		
聆聽及說話	72	66		
中國歷史	69	73	考試見進步，大致能掌握本科的答題技巧，成績良好，繼續努力。	LLC
普通話	B	---	語音基礎鞏固，表現不俗。	KMT
Mathematics Set A	84	77	is keen to learn and a pleasure to teach. She has made good progress throughout the year.	DY
Liberal Studies	87	79	Good on the whole but more effort needed in reframing matrix.	MNK
Science	88	83	She has a high level of involvement in the course of science study.	CCW
Geography	86	81	is a conscientious and involved learner as is indicated by the high quality of her assignments.	DML
History	66	80	has shown effort and done well in the research assignment and the exam.	AAC
Religious Education	A	---	An excellent term's work.	MWF
Home Economics	A	---	She has performed outstandingly.	ALW
Information Technology	A	---	Very good	CPH
Visual Arts	A-	---	Excellent	PWK
Music	A+	---	Hardworking though may need to manage extra-curricular activities better to allow for responsibilities in school. A little bit too quiet.	JWO
Physical Education	A-	---	Very good	RS

Full Marks: 100   80% or above: in red   No. of days absent: 2.5   No. of times late: 0

GRADE: A = Distinction B, C = Credit D, E = Pass F = Failure ABS = Absent EXM = Exempted

Please note: To facilitate administration, students are assigned to one of 5 classes (U, W, X, Y and Z) which are grouped under two blocks of matching competency. Classes U, W, X are placed in Block I and streamed in English, Chinese and Mathematics according to their abilities (Sets A - D). Classes Y and Z are similarly streamed in Block II in the same core subjects (Sets E - G).

School Chop

DIOCESAN GIRLS' SCHOOL
Final Report
2009-2010

Name: Form 1 ( )

EXTRA-CURRICULAR ACTIVITIES

Mathematics and Science Club	Member
School Choirs	Member
School Orchestra	Member
Tennis Club	Member
Psychology Club	Member

Awards/Prizes

62nd Hong Kong Schools Music Festival - The Best Junior Choir of the Year (First Division)
62nd Hong Kong Schools Music Festival : Junior Choir (Foreign Language) - 1st place
•••

OVERALL COMMENTS

is inquisitive and keen to learn. She showed improvement in her Chinese and maintained a good overall academic performance. She actively participates in ECAs.

Form Teachers

Headmistress
Mrs. Stella Lau, JP

Figure 11.7b: Student's report: Final, 2009–2010. Source: An anonymous old girl. Note: The red marks which indicate scores over 80 per cent cannot be seen in the black and white photograph.

Towards the New Millennium, 1985–1999

Aims

In 1985, Dr Symons retired, and Mrs Elim Lau took over the headship. The school's aim to provide a well-rounded education remained unchanged, and the DGS spirit of Christian love and loyalty with willingness to serve continued to be valued. In the 1990s, there was an increasing demand from girls to study science, and Mrs Lau increased the number of science classes from one to two accordingly.

Curriculum

Up to the 1980s, there was only one science class in each form at DGS. Form 3 students who wished to pursue science subjects in Form 4 were obliged to attend a special science class for a few weeks during the summer holiday. Tests were conducted at the end of the course, and only those who scored in the top forty would be accepted into Form 4 science class. In the academic year 1994/1995, one of the four Form 4 classes was transformed into a "mixed stream" where students could choose almost any elective subjects from both the arts and the science streams. In the academic year 1995/1996, the school changed this mixed stream class into a science class. The expansion of the science stream resulted in more girls entering the medical and paramedical fields.

Computer and IT facilities were developed in the school, and computer courses were offered in Form 1 in 1994/1995 to meet the demands of the new millennium. Students could choose either geography or computing for the HKCEE.[13] Further improvement in facilities allowed the school to offer the AS Computer Application Course in Lower Form 6 in 1997 and Upper Form 6 in 1998.

The maximum number of subjects to be taken in HKCEE by each student was increased from nine to ten. This additional subject could be music or religious studies. With Mrs Elim Lau's support, Mrs Aileen Hurst, head of religious knowledge, offered extra tutorials after school and during school holidays for students who opted to take religious studies as the tenth subject for the HKCEE. It was an open book examination and students were allowed to bring in the Bible. Rigid memorisation was not important, while a critical understanding of the topics was expected.

Group projects and assignments with more open-ended questions were given emphasis, and gone were the days of "spoon-feeding" to help students to score high marks in major examinations, with heavy reliance on textbook knowledge, rather than for the students to fully understand the essence of the subjects. Field trips increased in number, and were

---

13. "Foreword", *Quest* (1996–1998): 2.

usually carried out at the end of term around Christmas and New Year and at the end of the school year, in June or early July.

Student Achievements

The girls consistently achieved academic excellence. DGS celebrated its one-hundred-and-thirtieth anniversary in the year 1989/1990. It was also a year of outstanding scholastic achievements. Amy Chan (1990 graduate) attained ten distinctions in her HKCEE, becoming the first girl in Hong Kong to score straight As in all ten subjects (Figure 11.8). In the same year, Jennifer Tsang (1988 graduate) attained four As in the Hong Kong Advanced Level Examination (HKALE).[14] Following in their footsteps, Maria Chan (1991 graduate) scored ten straight As in the HKCEE, and Vivian Ling (1989 graduate) scored four As in the HKALE. Maria was awarded the coveted Jardine Scholarship while Vivian was also awarded a scholarship and offered a place at Oxford University.[15] During the period of 1990–1999, six DGS girls scored straight As in all ten subjects. Numerous prestigious local and overseas scholarships were awarded to DGS girls, including the Hong Kong Outstanding Young Student Award, the Yau Tsim Mong Outstanding Student Award, and scholarships to Oxbridge and the Ivy League universities.

The New Era, Redevelopment and Beyond, 2000–2019

Aims

Mrs Stella Lau took up her headship of the Senior School at the dawn of the twenty-first century after the retirement of Mrs Elim Lau. The school maintained its aim to provide a holistic and integrated education based on Christian values so that girls became well-rounded, knowledgeable, and compassionate women.

Curriculum

In accordance with the Education Bureau's education reform in 2008/2009, the New Senior Secondary (NSS) Curriculum came into effect in 2009/2010 at Secondary 4 level. The school established a Curriculum and Studies Team consisting of teachers across different subjects to collaborate in designing, implementing, and evaluating the school curriculum.[16]

---

14. The Headmistress's Report, Speech Day Booklet, 1990.
15. The Headmistress's Report, Speech Day Booklet, 1991, 7–9.
16. DGS Curriculum and Studies Team Protocol, 2019.

香港中學會考證書
HONG KONG CERTIFICATE OF EDUCATION EXAMINATION

茲證明
This is to certify that

陳可盈
CHAN HO YING AMY

參加一九九〇年香港中學會考，成績如下：
sat the 1990 Hong Kong Certificate of Education Examination and achieved the following results:

科目 Subject	等級 Grade	備註 Remarks
中國語文 CHINESE LANGUAGE	A(1)	O
英國語文（課程乙）ENGLISH LANGUAGE (SYLLABUS B)†	A(1)	O
經濟 ECONOMICS	A(1)	O
宗教 RELIGIOUS STUDIES	A(1)	O
生物 BIOLOGY	A(1)	O
化學 CHEMISTRY	A(1)	O
物理 PHYSICS	A(1)	O
數學 MATHEMATICS	A(1)	O
附加數學 ADDITIONAL MATHEMATICS	A(1)	O
電腦科 COMPUTER STUDIES	A(1)	O

考獲各等級的科數 Number of subjects within each grade
A 拾 10　B　　C　　D　　E　　F　　總數 Total 拾 TEN
TEN **********　**********　**********　**********　**********　**********

†英語科科試對象 English Language Profile of Results
讀寫 Reading/Writing Skills A(1)　聽力表達 Listening/Speaking Skills A(1)

Date of Birth ▬▬ Sex 女 F H.K. Identity Card No. ▬▬ Candidate No. ▬▬

W. C. Chan
陳永燊 W. C. Chan
香港考試局秘書
Secretary, Hong Kong Examinations Authority

註釋見背頁
Explanatory Notes
are printed overleaf

Figure 11.8a: Amy Chan's HKCEE Certificate 1990 listing the ten subjects. Source: Amy Chan.

Figure 11.8b: Amy Chan, DGS class of 1990, broke Hong Kong and DGS records as the first female student scoring 10 straight 'As' at the HKCEE in 1990. Source: Amy Chan.

Interdisciplinary learning became increasingly important and there was more collaboration between teachers of different subjects to enhance student learning. In 2008, a whole-school project was conducted, with all girls formed into different groups, each under the supervision of a teacher, including Mrs Lau, to research on the socio-political, economic, cultural, environmental, and technological changes in relation to China's 30 years of Reform and Opening up. While Liberal Studies teachers helped develop students' research skills in doing projects, they collaborated with English teachers who would teach girls the language and styles used in report writing, and Chinese teachers would teach girls the formal way to write minutes for their project group meetings. Other subject teachers supervised the different groups based on their expertise and interests.

A Science Committee was set up to provide a platform for all science teachers from four departments (science, biology, physics, and chemistry) to share their ideas and to enhance the quality of teaching and learning. The Science Committee developed pedagogy for scientific investigation using IT in teaching.

The major change brought about by the change in academic structure was the revision of a seven-year to six-year secondary education, with students sitting the Hong Kong Diploma of Secondary Education Examination (HKDSE) at the end of Secondary 6. This new HKDSE curriculum started in Secondary 4. On top of the four core subjects, most students could choose three electives. The old concept of science and arts streams was fading out, and the school offered more flexible options for senior students. Students were free to decide on any combination of electives that the school offered. There were also major curriculum renewals in the junior secondary curriculum, which involved the strengthening of values education, the promoting of STEM education (science, technology, engineering, and mathematics), and the fostering of an entrepreneurial spirit.

In 2015/2016, the school offered a two-year alternative curriculum: GCE A-Levels, offering several subjects, but not languages. The following year, both Chinese and English languages were added. This route provided girls who were weaker in Chinese, and might fail to meet the minimum requirement of level 3 in HKDSE but did very well in other subjects, with a better chance of admission to local universities.[17]

To improve the quality of education, a number of reforms regarding the qualification and continuous education requirement for teachers were made. Like students, teachers became lifelong learners in order to equip themselves as better teaching agents and facilitators.

The changeover to the Direct Subsidy Scheme in 2005 enabled the school to decide on its own curriculum and pedagogy, and to further increase the size of the teaching staff. The increased number of teachers made small group teaching possible.

---

17. "Implementing the Alternative Curriculum: A Levels", *Quest* (2016–2018): 25–26.

Figure 11.9: Excerpt from the list of major awards & scholarships, 2016–2017. Source: *Quest* 2016–2018, 27.

Learning and teaching changed from teacher-centred to more student-centred, as well as extended from inside the classroom to the outside. More outside classroom experiential learning was introduced, e.g. girls participated in the JA Company programme and attended seminars at the Hong Kong University of Science and Technology. Other Learning Programmes such as fashion design, Chinese Medicine, coffee brewing, as well as career-related programmes such as job-shadowing were organised.

Since the start of the new millennium, the school has also established an exchange programme with schools in mainland China, Australia, New Zealand, and the USA, ready for new challenges and opportunities in the new era. Both the teachers and students learned together and exchanged their learning experiences.

Student Achievements

The track record of outstanding results in public examinations continued during this period. DGS girls received good offers from various local and overseas prestigious tertiary institutions. The list of honours of DGS girls grew, locally and internationally.

Summary

Since its beginning in 1860 as the DNFTS to train women to be wives of clergy and schoolmistresses, DGS has undergone a dramatic transformation, from a school without a formal curriculum to one which offers a holistic education experience; becoming one of the most prestigious schools in Hong Kong with graduates who have achieved considerable professional success.

Chapter 12

Musical Life

Grace Chiang (1999)

The development of music in DGS can be divided into three stages:[1] the pre-Second World War era, the decades between 1945 and 1999, and the years since 2000. At first, music and singing were considered to be an "entertainment", and only after the Second World War do we see the beginnings of a formal curriculum and established ensembles, performances, and local competitions. By the twenty-first century, music encompassed structured teaching and activities, supported by overseas exposure and coaching by professional musicians.

Pre–Second World War Teaching and Performing

Humble Beginnings

Given the importance placed on music literacy and instrumental playing in the upbringing of a Victorian lady, it is no surprise that the earliest traces of music in DGS all pertain to piano playing and singing classes, while choral singing and singing games presented at the prize presentations were termed "entertainment".

Documentation of school music learning and activities are scarce prior to the Second World War. In the first few decades of the Diocesan establishment, the student population

---

1. Besides referring to *The Quest* (after 1960, the school magazine is called *Quest*) and various Speech Day Booklets, which focus mostly on awards and competitions, to provide a more comprehensive account of music in DGS, the current chapter takes reference from news articles, memoirs of old girls, and accounts by former music teachers. Pre-war records kept by the school were mostly destroyed during the Japanese Occupation.

was small and did not warrant a teacher solely dedicated to the teaching of music.[2] For instance, according to Reverend Featherstone, there were no separate music or singing lessons at the Diocesan Home and Orphanage (DHO) in 1871, except for an entry that reads "Preparing Evening Lessons",[3] which might have involved hymn singing and scripture reading.

Nevertheless, there were hints of music in school; at the 1885 DHO prize presentation, a special music prize was awarded to N. Orley.[4] These annual prize presentations also provide a glimpse into music activities at the time. One of the early song performances took place at the 1909 prize presentation,[5] and in 1910 the programme comprised the following: "a recitation by seven children addressing a welcome to her Ladyship [Lady Lugard]. There were two kindergarten songs and one by the older girls."[6] This was both entertainment and a showcase of students' abilities, and this practice continued well into the 1990s.

Hymn Singing

Any discussion of music in DGS cannot disregard hymn singing; by the 1900s, younger children learnt hymns during morning prayers,[7] and daily congregational singing at morning assemblies formed an iconic part of school life. In the first decades of the twentieth century, separate hymn and prayer books were used,[8] and the school hymn at the time was "Blest Are the Pure in Heart".[9]

Incidentally, the first mention of singing the "school hymn" was at the 1928 prize presentation[10] but without clear indication of the words sung. The current text of the school hymn, "Our Father, by Whose Servants", was written in 1920 by George Wallace Briggs (1875–1959)[11] and published under two different tunes in *Songs of Praise* (1931), neither of which is used by DGS. The Gosterwood hymn tune used for the current school hymn is an English traditional melody collected and harmonised by composer Ralph Vaughan

---

2. For instance, as E. J. Eitel outlined in his education report (1902), as per the 1879 Code and the 1893 revised code "New Code of Regulations for Educational Grants-in-Aid", there was no requirement for music or arts education, only the provision of needlework class in girls' schools.

3. W. E. Featherstone, *The Diocesan Boys School and Orphanage. The History and Records, 1969 to 1929*, 122.

4. *The China Mail*, 30 January 1885, "Nelly Orley received the prize for Needlework in the previous year", *The China Mail*, 24 January 1884, 2.

5. *South China Morning Post*, 23 July 1909.

6. *Hong Kong Daily Press*, 18 November 1910.

7. "A Glimpse of the D. G. S. In Days Gone By", *The Quest* (1950): 46.

8. Symons, *Looking at the Stars*, 14.

9. "Service of Thanksgiving", *Quest* (1990–1991): 24.

10. *South China Morning Post*, 2 March 1928.

11. Briggs wrote the hymn for Loughborough Grammar School in 1920 when he was Rector of Loughborough. The text appears in *Prayers and Hymns for Use in Schools* (1928) as "Loughborough School Hymn".

Williams in 1906. The text and music were never published as one piece, and to this day it is uncertain who combined the two; what is clear is that the current version of the text has been in use at least since 1941.[12]

Engaging Musical Talent

As for classroom music, since there was no formal music curriculum until the 1960s, much of the music learning relied on talent among the teaching staff. Regular singing lessons have been around since the 1910s, and at the time, it was not unusual for teachers at kindergarten and primary levels to teach singing; but as student enrolment expanded over the years, it became necessary to engage a separate teacher who had the necessary training and experience to conduct music lessons.

The school was blessed with a constant stream of music teachers for over a century. From the early days at Jordan Road, optional piano lessons were offered to students as well as members of the public who were interested. As early as 1917, Prof. Emilio Danenberg, who also donated the Music Improvement Prize in 1920, taught piano and singing at DGS.[13] The prize appeared again in 1924 as "Prize for Theory of Music", which was awarded to students under the care of Miss D. Stone.[14]

The arrival of Miss Sawyer in 1925 coincided with a period of greater musical activity. Help was sought from the church for an additional singing and music teacher. Mr Frederick Mason, organist and choirmaster of St John's Cathedral (also part-time singing and music teacher at DBS),[15] briefly taught singing at DGS.[16] Mr Rupert Baldwin, organist and choirmaster of St Andrew's Church,[17] joined the staff at DGS in 1926 and remained for eleven years.

With the introduction of the Trinity College of Music local examinations in the late 1920s, music became a recurring subject award at the annual prize presentations as students studied under Mr Baldwin and Miss Stone. In 1929, DGS entered ten students in the first cohort of Trinity examinations for piano performance, and the next year for both practical and theory examinations.[18] Subsequently, the Music Prize was featured intermittently until the outbreak of the war.

---

12. E. M. Gibbins, "D. O. G. A.", *The Quest* (1941): 3.

13. *South China Morning Post*, 12 September 1917, 20 February 1919, 14 March 1919, 15 March 1919, 18 February 1920.

14. *South China Morning Post*, 8 March 1924.

15. Featherstone, *The Diocesan Boys School and Orphanage*, 136.

16. *The China Mail*, 15 March 1926.

17. Mr Baldwin left DGS in 1937 to join Ying Wa College in 1938, and subsequently composed the current Ying Wa School Song.

18. *South China Morning Post*, 17 February 1930; *South China Morning Post*, 9 February 1931.

Two performances during this period particularly embodied the school motto, "Daily Giving Service". In November 1925, students performed on campus to raise funds for charity, and in February 1937, girls gave a concert at St Andrew's Church Hall, with the proceeds going to the Ministering Children's League.[19]

Hong Kong Schools' Musical Association

Despite the evacuation order of July 1940, music activities became more diverse owing to the establishment of the Hong Kong Schools' Musical Association (HKSMA) that same year.[20] This was a significant development for music education in Hong Kong, and far more influential than the founding members had envisaged. It aimed to provide students with quality concerts, talks, joint ensembles, and performance opportunities at a minimal subscription fee.[21] The first executive committee of HKSMA was chaired by Mr G. A. Goodban (DBS), with Miss B. T. Chiu (DGS), Brother Cassian (La Salle College), and Mr J. R. M. Smith, organist of St John's Cathedral, as committee members.[22] Over the course of the year, several concerts and a talk were organised, and student response was enthusiastic—among the 1,200 members of the association, 100 students and 11 staff members were from DGS.[23] The year's events concluded with a members' concert in which DGS choir and pianists contributed several items.[24] However, with the exception of the November 1941 Beethoven concert, further activities of the association were suspended as a result of the war, only to be revived in 1947.[25]

Post–Second World War to 1999: Teaching and Performing

Post-war Rebuilding

When the school reopened after the war, music-making was initially kept to a minimum. Mr Geoffrey Dibbs, organist and choirmaster of St Andrew's, taught singing until he returned to England to be demobilised.[26] Girls also joined the St Andrew's Choir as treble

---

19. *Hong Kong Daily Press*, 6 February 1937; *South China Morning Post*, 20 November 1925.

20. *South China Morning Post*, 10 January 1941; the association now known as the Hong Kong Schools Music and Speech Association (HKSMSA).

21. Student subscription was $1 per year, while teachers could join for $2.

22. *South China Morning Post*, 10 January 1941.

23. Phoebe Lee, "The Hong Kong Schools' Musical Association", *The Quest* (1941): 14–15.

24. *South China Morning Post*, 24 April 1941.

25. *South China Morning Post*, 12 November 1941.

26. M. Fisher, "Staff Diary", *The Quest* (1947): 12.

Table 12.1: DGS music teachers (c. 1920 to present)

Name	Years	Remarks
Prof. Emilio F. X. Danenberg	1917–1920?	Singing; Piano
Miss D. Stone	1923–1939?	Music Theory; Piano
Mr Frederick Mason	1926	Singing (O&C – St John's Cathedral)
Mr Rupert Baldwin	1926–1937	1925 PT instructor; Singing; Piano (O&C – St Andrew's Church)
Miss Shem	1937–?	Singing
Mr Geoffrey Dibbs	1946?–1947	Singing (O&C – St Andrew's Church)
Miss Caroline Braga	1947–1948	Piano
Mr Francis Wah Yiu Chung 鍾華耀	1947–1948	Singing
Miss Maple Quon	1948–1949	Music Theory; Piano; Music Appreciation
Mr S. Gordon Hemery	1949–1950	Singing; Director of Music for DGS and DBS (O&C – St Andrew's Church)
Miss Norah Mary Edwards 聞慧中	1950–1962	Initially shared between DGS and DBS
Miss Phoebe Wei	1954	Substitute; Edwards on furlough
Miss Amy Lo	1962–1963	
Miss Marjorie S. Maneely	1963–1967	
Mrs Jane Shen* (née Yuen) 沈袁經楣	1967–1968	
Mrs Poppy Crosby	1968–1981	1968 seconded from DGJS
Mrs Christine Mar (née Chu)	1970–1971	Substitute; Crosby on furlough
Mrs Christina Chiang* (née Chan) 蔣陳紅梅	1972–1982 1993–2018	1972–1982 and 1993–1996 PT F.1–2 classes; Chinese Choir; 2011–2014 as Music Director
Mrs Jean Valerie Oxley	1981–1997	1978: substitute; Crosby on leave
Ms Nancy Cheng* 鄭朗思	1984–1986 1988–1993	PT F.1–2 classes; Chinese Choir
Mrs Susanne Cheung	1996–1998	PT F.1–2 classes; Chinese Choir
Mrs Synthia Chan (née Ko) 陳高德儀	1997–2006	
Ms Cindy Wong 王家芝	1998–2000	PT F.1–2 classes; Chinese Choir
Ms Karen Soong* 宋加恩	2000–2004	PT F.1–2 classes; Chinese Choir
Mrs Agatha Tang (née Tsui) 鄧崔慧儀	2005–2009	PT F.1–2 classes; Folk Church Choir/ Chinese Choir
Miss Maggie Chan 陳漫玲	2006–2007	
Miss Patricia Lam 林家怡	2007–2008	
Ms Jacqueline Leung 梁維芝	2008–2009	
Ms Jenny Wong* 王菁儀	2009–2011	
Miss Grace Chiang* 蔣頌恩	2011–present	
Ms Dorothy Hui* 許加樂	2012–present	

Source: *Quest*, Speech Day Booklets, *The China Mail*, *South China Morning Post*.

Note: PT = Part-time; * = Old Girl; O&C = Organist and Choirmaster; ? = year uncertain.

Table 12.2: Junior School music teachers (c. 1920 to present)

Name	Years (Remarks)
Miss E. K. Walters	1920–1933; 1947–1949 (Kindergarten mainly; Singing)
Mrs Jane Shen* (née Yuen) 沈袁經楣	1956–1967
Miss T. Loh	1967–1968
Mrs Christine Mar (née Chu)	1968–1970
Mrs Christine Sin (née Yeung)	1970–1972; 1980–1981 PT**
Mrs Christina Chiang* (née Chan) 蔣陳紅梅	1972–1982; 1993–2018 (2011–2014 Music Director, 2014–2018 PT)
Miss Emily Chung	1981–1983
Mrs Susan Digby	1982–1985 (1982–1983 PT)
Mrs Agatha Tang (née Tsui) 鄧崔慧儀	1983–1991; 1992–1993
Ms Nancy Cheng* 鄭朗思	1984–1986; 1988–1993
Miss Clara Poon	1987
Miss C. Lo (Hau Yee)	1987–1988
Miss Angela To	1991–1992
Miss Lee Hung-kun 李洪瑾	1993–2002
Mrs April Nam (née Liu) 南廖海英	2002–2016 (2013–2016 PT)
Miss Dorothy Fok 霍曉彤	2011–2012
Miss Kylie Ng 伍倩彤	2012–2018
Mrs Winnie Fung 馮蘇錦兒	2012–2018
Mr Kelvin Lau 劉灝顯	2017–present
Ms Yuri Imamura 今村有里	2017–present
Ms Eunice Suen 孫嬿善	2018–present
Mr Joshua Ng 吳清華	2018–present

Source: *Quest*, Speech Day Booklets, *South China Morning Post*.
Note: PT = Part-time; * = Old Girl; ** Taught another subject 1975–1980.

and alto voices, and took part in their carol service.[27] There was an increase in activities in 1947, including a gramophone concert and a student piano recital.[28] In the autumn, a new Nissen hut was opened to be used as both gymnasium and music room,[29] and the HKSMA was revived with over one hundred DGS members.[30] Soon afterwards, a new grand piano

27. A. W. Hurrell, "Church Life", *The Quest* (1947): 15; *South China Morning Post*, 25 December 1946.
28. B. T. Chiu, "School Calendar 1947–48", *The Quest* (1947): 8–11.
29. *South China Morning Post*, 19 September 1947.
30. Grace Lo, "The Hong Kong Schools' Musical Association", *The Quest* (1947): 43.

was acquired with funds raised from concerts by Miss Caroline Braga,[31] and by 1948, there was a choir in the Senior School[32] and the first percussion band in the Junior School.[33]

Music in DGS truly flourished from 1949 onwards. The Associated Board of Royal Schools of Music began conducting local examinations in December 1948.[34] The music subject prize was reinstated in 1949, and from 1982 onwards it was regularly awarded. On 8 and 9 April 1949, the first ever Schools Music Festival competitions were held at DGS.[35] Most significantly, in April 1949, Mr Gordon Hemery was engaged from England as Director of Music for both DGS and DBS.[36] Like Baldwin and Dibbs before him, Mr Hemery was organist and choirmaster of St Andrew's, hence DGS's continued involvement with the church choir. Despite his short tenure, Mr Hemery established the joint Diocesan Schools' Choral Society in September 1949,[37] and the mixed choir made its debut on 29 March 1950, performing John Stainer's oratorio *The Crucifixion*.[38]

Miss Norah Edwards, a missionary from New Zealand,[39] joined DGS in 1950. She led the newly formed Senior and Intermediate choirs to compete in the 1951 Music Festival, along with the mixed choir, and the Junior School percussion band and choir.[40] Over the next few decades, competitions provided a strong incentive for schools and students alike to partake in various music and elocution activities (speech contests were introduced to the Music Festival from 1950), and naturally, talent was discovered along the way.[41]

---

31. *South China Morning Post*, 6 March 1948; A. W. Hurrell, "Headmistress's Report", *The Quest* (1949): 15. Also performing at the 12 March 1948 concert were John Braga, Tamara Brown, Marion Ahwee (DGS old girl), and Donald Fraser. The Scottish Donald James Fraser arrived in Hong Kong in 1947 and taught briefly at Queen's College and Northcote College of Education. He became organist of St John's Cathedral in 1949, and by 1950, he was Master of Music of the Education Department (ED). Fraser was instrumental in organising the first Schools Music Festival and the establishment of the ED Music Section in 1952. Two other concerts were held in 1949 to supplement the funds.

32. Joyce Avasia, "Speech Day", *The Quest* (1948): 20.

33. "Junior School Concert", *The Quest* (1948): 13.

34. *The China Mail*, 23 April 1949.

35. *South China Morning Post*, 8, 9 April 1949. The first competition was in the following categories: vocal solos for soprano, treble, tenor, and baritone; instrumental solos for piano, violin, cello, and other instruments; and a class for ensemble.

36. A. W. Hurrell, "Headmistress's Report", *The Quest* (1949): 14.

37. Maureen Lyen, "Diocesan Schools' Choral Society", *The Quest* (1949): 21. The Choral Society began rehearsing on 3 October 1949 and met on alternate weeks at either school.

38. *South China Morning Post*, 28, 29, 30 March 1950.

39. Yuan, Sylvia Yang, "'Kiwis' in the Middle Kingdom—A Sociological Interpretation of the History of New Zealand Missionaries in China from 1877 to 1953 and Beyond", PhD dissertation, Massey University, Albany, 2013, 409.

40. M. Fisher, "Headmistress's Report", *The Quest* (1951): 5–6. The Senior Choir won the Challenge Shield in 1951, while the Choral Society got its first taste of victory in 1954, the same year the Chinese choral classes were introduced.

41. The competitions soon overshadowed the HKSMA concerts for members, which were held until 1959.

Figure 12.1: Diocesan Schools' Choral Society concert at DGS, 19 April 1951. Source: School Archives.

Under Miss Edwards' tutelage, students served as pianists for morning and chapel services, and by 1956 the school had compiled a new DGS Hymn and Prayer Book.[42] Girls had a diverse music life of competitions, charitable concerts, and acclaimed performances, particularly the productions in collaboration with Mrs Nancy O'Connell—the 1952 Gilbert and Sullivan opera *The Pirates of Penzance* (a joint effort with DBS),[43] the 1956 Mozart adaptation *Papageno* (as part of the second Hong Kong Arts Festival),[44] and the 1959 Purcell opera *Dido and Aeneas*.[45] In celebration of the centenary year, the school gave three public performances of *Dido* from 14 to 16 April 1959 at the newly unveiled Centenary Hall, with an all-female cast of over 150 singers and dancers, accompanied by student pianists.[46]

The opening of the new hall also had greater implications for the performing arts in Hong Kong. Prior to the completion of the City Hall in Central in 1962, there was a general lack of performance venues, and school halls had long been alternative spaces to host public concerts, including those featuring world-class musicians. For instance, in April 1961, the Music Society of Hong Kong presented internationally renowned pianist Joerg Demus at the DGS Centenary Hall.[47]

---

42. "Music", *The Quest* (1950–1951): 27.
43. The operetta was performed on 22, 23, 25, and 26 February 1952 at DBS Hall after months of preparation and delay owing to the death of King George VI; *South China Morning Post*, 18 December 1951; 20 January; 9 and 23 February 1952.
44. *South China Morning Post*, 18 February and 5 March 1956. The lead was played by old girl Jane Yuen, who joined the DGS music staff later that year. The performance proceeds also contributed to the centenary building fund.
45. Speech Day Booklet, 10 January 1960; the opera was also produced to celebrate the tri-centenary of English composer Henry Purcell.
46. *South China Morning Post*, 18 April 1959. The opera ran from 14 to 16 April, with the DBS orchestra conducted by Mr Henry Li performing overtures as guests.
47. *South China Morning Post*, 11 April 1961; this was probably Demus's Hong Kong debut, as part of his first Asian tour.

1960s–1970s: Instrumental Development

Into the 1960s, Miss Marjorie Maneely and Mrs Jane Shen continued the good work of Miss Edwards; by then, girls' choirs had expanded into Junior, Intermediate, and Senior groups, often reaping outstanding results at the Music Festival competitions.[48] DGS continued to produce a growing number of musicians, some of whom won scholarships to study at conservatoires in the United Kingdom.[49] By the mid-1960s, the music section of the Education Department began to support schools to organise instrumental classes, and from September 1965, violin, viola, and cello lessons were offered on campus every Saturday morning.[50] With the help of Miss Margaret Money, these classes grew into a String Orchestra by autumn 1966.[51] The newly formed orchestra participated in the 1968 Music Festival and came third in the Intermediate class,[52] and in the following year, under the coaching of Miss Money and Mr John Cheng, came first.[53] Besides active participation in the Festival, DGS continued to serve the wider community through music, raising funds for the Community Chest and other service groups at the joint DGS–DBS Christmas Revue of December 1968.[54]

Mrs Poppy Crosby and Mrs Christina Chiang took over the helm in the 1970s, a decade that saw the establishment of the Recorder Ensemble and the Symphony Orchestra.[55] The choirs and orchestra performed regularly and were involved in the many productions produced by Mrs O'Connell and Mr Y. C. Chan, while maintaining a presence at the Festival competitions. At the 1973 Music Festival, the Symphony Orchestra competed in the Senior category for the first time and came first.[56] Concurrently, the number of instrumental classes in school increased, while lessons remained free of charge for students.[57] Instrumentalists continued to hone their skills, and several outstanding musicians were selected to join the new Hong Kong Youth Orchestra,[58] including Margaret Lynn, who was part of the Hong Kong delegation to the International Festival of Youth Orchestras at

---

48. *South China Morning Post*, 24 March 1963, 28 March 1965; Speech Day Booklets of 1965–1968; *Quest* (1964–1968).

49. Patsy Toh, Chiu Yee-ha, and Sheila Lai were among the first DGS pianists to have competed at the Music Festival and proceeded to pursue professional studies abroad.

50. Speech Day Booklet, January 1967, 13.

51. Speech Day Booklet, December 1967, 13.

52. Speech Day Booklet, November 1968, 12.

53. Pamela Yew, "Music Festival '69'", *Quest* (1970): 62.

54. Speech Day Booklet, November 1969, 7.

55. Speech Day Booklet, December 1970, 10.

56. Speech Day Booklet, December 1970; 香港工商日報, 8 April 1973.

57. Angela Ting, "The School Orchestra", *Quest* (1973–1974): 21. Students benefited from a stream of dedicated instrumental coaches in the 1970s, well into the new millennium.

58. Speech Day Booklet, January 1967, 13; October 1975, 6.

Figure 12.2: Miss Maneely and the Intermediate Choir, winner of two trophies in 1967. Source: School Archives.

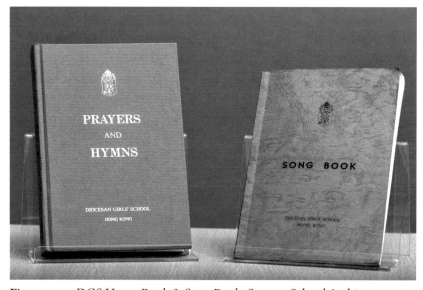

Figure 12.3: DGS Hymn Book & Song Book. Source: School Archives.

Aberdeen, Scotland, in 1973.[59] In 1974, the annual Music Festival was split into two competitions, with a Music Festival held in the spring and a Speech Festival in the autumn. Since then, both Senior and Junior schools maintained a strong presence in the solo speech and choral speaking contests, as well as the various musical competitions, with outstanding results. By the late 1970s, the Junior School also benefited from the Music Administration Office Scheme and held three weekly string classes on campus.[60]

Music lessons became more structured; music teachers trained at the Colleges of Education were instrumental in building a school-based curriculum.[61] Lessons covered a wide range of songs, many of which were included in the Song Book that was first published in 1975 and used until the early 1990s. Recorder playing was also introduced in Upper Primary classes during this time.

1980s and 1990s: Establishing Traditions

With Mrs Jean Oxley, Mrs Agatha Tang, and Ms Nancy Cheng joining in the 1980s, several developments took place in the academic and performance aspects of music. The introduction of a music syllabus for secondary schools as well as the government Centralised Scheme for music training in the 1980s meant that girls interested in taking music as an elective for the public exams (Hong Kong Certificate of Education Examination and Hong Kong Advanced Level Examination) had an alternative to the London General Certificate of Education. Meanwhile, classroom music expanded from singing to learning about Western composers and repertoires in parallel with activities such as class band and hymn singing. A music society was formed in 1985 as an interest club, conducting general meetings until the mid-1990s.[62]

In terms of performance, the strong choral tradition continued in both Senior and Junior schools, each with their own Junior, Intermediate, and Senior choirs, competing at the Music Festival as well as appearing in the school Christmas and festival concerts,[63] various church occasions, and local performances.[64] A new choral ensemble formed with DBS

---

59. Margaret Lynn, "International Festival of Youth Orchestras", *Quest* (1973–1974): 22.

60. Speech Day Booklet, January 1980, 28. The Music Administration Office (now known as Music Office) was established in 1977, taking over the instrumental classes offered by the ED music section and HKSMSA at schools across town, as well as managing the Hong Kong Youth Symphony Orchestra (est. 1978).

61. The ED curriculum for Junior School music was first released in 1968, with revisions in 1976 and 1987. The syllabus for Forms 1–3 music was only announced in 1983, Forms 4–5 guide in 1987, and Forms 6–7 in 1992.

62. Jeanne Park, "Music Society", *Quest* (1985–1986): 35.

63. The Christmas, Easter, and year-end Farewell Concerts became a staple in Junior School music life.

64. The Senior Choir was invited to sing at St John's Cathedral 1983 Christmas lunchtime concert; their performance of Britten's *A Ceremony of Carols* was recorded and broadcasted by RTHK Radio 4. DGJS choristers were invited to sing under the baton of Sir David Willcocks at HKAPA in November 1989.

Table 12.3a: Years of establishment of different music groups in the Senior School

Senior School	Year Est.
Senior Choir	1948
Diocesan Schools' Choral Society	1949
Intermediate Choir	1950
Junior Choir	1951
Instrumental Classes	1965
String Orchestra	1966
Symphony Orchestra	1971
Recorder Ensemble*	1971
Chinese Instrumental Classes	1981
Madrigal Group (& Quick Study)	1982
Chinese Orchestra	1984
Instrumental Ensembles	1988
Chinese Choir*	1993
Junior Mixed Choir	1998
Senior Mixed Choir	1999
Concert Band	2001
Guzheng Ensemble	2004
Folk Church Choir*	2006
Church Music Choir*	2011

Source: Speech Day Booklets, *Quest, South China Morning Post.*
Note: * Discontinued.

entered the madrigal and quick study competitions of the 1982 Music Festival,[65] marking a renewed collaboration between the two schools. Towards the final year of Mrs Elim Lau's tenure, the Junior Mixed Choir with DBS was established in 1998, one year prior to the revival of the Diocesan Schools' Choral Society (i.e., Senior Mixed Choir), the source of many new experiences in the following decades.

On the instrumental side, Mrs Oxley took over the baton for the School Orchestra, which continued to grow in size. Another new venture was Chinese music; Chinese instrumental classes began in November 1981,[66] leading to a new Chinese Music Club (1983)

---

65. The madrigal group, formed by four girls and four boys from the two Diocesan Schools, is a reiteration of the mixed voice quartet competitions of the 1960s. The group later expanded from eight to twelve singers and divided into two separate teams after 2000.

66. 〈中樂組報告〉,《研幾》1981–1982, 7. The first classes were taught by musicians of the Wang Kwong Chinese Orchestra 宏光國樂團.

Musical Life 309

Table 12.3b: Years of establishment of different music groups in the Junior School

Junior School	Year Est.
Junior Percussion Band*	1948
School Choir	1952
Junior Choir	1952
Senior Percussion Band*	1954
Intermediate Choir	1960
Senior Choir	1960
Instrumental Classes	1978
Recorder Ensemble / Recorder Band*	1985
School Orchestra*	1991
String Orchestra	1998
Chinese Instrumental Classes	1999
Junior Percussion Band	2000
Senior Percussion Band	2000
Melodica Ensemble / Melodica Band*	2001
Junior String Group	2005
Wind Band	2006
Church Music Choir*	2007
Symphony Orchestra	2007
Brass Ensemble	2009
Hymn Singing Group*	2013
Speech Choir*	2015
Chinese Music Ensemble	2017

Source: Speech Day Booklets, *Quest, South China Morning Post.*

Note: *Discontinued.

and subsequently the first Chinese Orchestra conducted by Mr Yu Chiu For.[67] The Junior School, after years of preparation, finally formed a Symphony Orchestra in 1991.

From 1982, students produced musicals every year during the summer term.[68] Dr Symons' farewell concert took place on 18 March 1985 at Hong Kong City Hall[69] and

---

67. 〈中樂社〉,《研幾》1983–1984, 7; 〈中樂團〉,《研幾》1985–1986, 7. DGS Chinese Orchestra came first in the 1989 Music Festival (Intermediate class), and gave a joint performance with the DBS and Wah Yan Kowloon College Chinese orchestras that summer (source: 〈中樂團〉,《研幾》1989–1990, 9). Subsequent conductors include Mr Lee Tse Ko and Mr Chen Kwok Fai.

68. Summer-term musicals are class-based, with performances ranging from Gilbert and Sullivan's *Trial by Jury* (1983 joint production with DBS), an abridged version of *The King and I* (1984), and extracts from *Cats* (1985).

69. Sunita Mulchandani, "A Farewell Concert for Dr. C. J. Symons", *Quest* (1985–1986): 5.

Figure 12.4: Junior School Symphony Orchestra debut conducted by Ms Nancy Cheng at Christmas Concert, 1991. Source: Ms Nancy Cheng.

Figure 12.5: The first DGS Chinese Orchestra performing at 1984 Speech Day. Source: School Archives.

included a fully staged second act of *The Pirates of Penzance*[70] as well as the Junior School's production of *Theseus and the Minotaur*.[71] Musicals thus became the natural choice when the time came to celebrate the school's one hundred and thirtieth anniversary, as well as to raise funds for the new extension buildings, with acclaimed performances of *Tom Sawyer* (1990), *Humbug* (1991), and a full-scale production of *The King and I* in June 1996.

Into the New Millennium

Learning, Performing, and Serving

The School's Music Department made great strides in the twenty-first century, with choirs and orchestras growing in range and skill, the introduction of new ensembles, a larger faculty, a significant increase of local and overseas exposure, and more systematic learning of music in school.

In 2011, the school promoted Mrs Christina Chiang to become the first Music Director, and in 2014, engaged Mr Leung Kin Fung to serve as Performing Arts Director. The number of full-time music teachers in both divisions also increased, allowing better support for students and a greater number of ensembles in school.

In terms of classroom music, the school-based curriculum expanded to one encompassing music history, Chinese music, world music, student ensembles, singing, and music composition, making full use of the school's information technology resources. Senior form students have the option to take music as an elective for the Hong Kong Diploma of Secondary Education Examination whereby a three-year programme with network partner schools—Maryknoll Convent School, La Salle College, and DBS—prepares them for public examination as they balance the study of critical listening and creative expression with musical performances. The Junior School music lessons cover the basic rudiments of music and recorder playing alongside classroom singing and class choirs.

Beyond the classroom, musicians have a very vibrant musical life. With an increased number of instrumentalists, the Senior School established the Concert Band (2000)[72] and the Guzheng Ensemble (2003),[73] while the Junior School acquired support from the Quality Education Fund to start new Senior and Junior Percussion Bands in 2000. To further encourage musical talent, DGS introduced the Music Exhibition scholarships

---

70. Speech Day Booklet, November 1985, 14.

71. Speech Day Booklet, November 1985, 40.

72. The first wind band appeared briefly in 1992/1993. The Symphonic Band, now renamed the Concert Band, was established in April 2000 and has about sixty members.

73. The first instructor of the Guzheng Ensemble was Miss Qin Yifeng, and the group is now led by Mr Chu Wai Hung.

after turning into a Direct Subsidy Scheme school, and in 2014, added the awards DGS Vocalists and Instrumentalists of the Year, and Entrance Scholarships for Music. The school engaged external conductors, such as Mr Kwok Hang Kei and Mr Cheung Hiu-fai, for the Chinese Orchestra; Messrs Philip Lee, Amos Lee, and Victor Tam for the Concert Band; and Ms Cindy Chen who coached the String Orchestra. Girls also benefited from sharing the talents of DBS music teachers who conducted the mixed choirs, namely Mr Ronnie Cheng, Mr Samuel Pang, and Mr Felix Shuen. In the Junior School, long-serving conductors include Ms Choi Suk-fan, Mr Elton Lee, and Mr Chiu Kai-keung.

In the new millennium, music activities in a typical year include instrumental classes, training camps during the holidays, competitions, concerts in spring and summer, and other performances. Since 2002, the Senior Mixed Choir has been regularly invited by the Home Affairs Bureau to sing the National Anthem at the Special Administrative Region anniversaries and National Day flag-raising ceremonies. Girls are also invited to perform at the Government House Open Day and National Day celebration concerts, fulfilling their civic duties. DGS is also a frequent guest at the DBS Homecoming Concerts, and occasionally there have been special collaborations with artists, such as dancer Mui Cheuk-yin, Russian pianist Ilya Itin, and the Yat Po Singers, as well as joint performances with the Shenzhen Lily Choir and the Hong Kong Chinese Orchestra. In addition, girls are heavily involved in the anniversary productions, including *The Wizard of Oz* (2000), *The DGS Girl* (2005), 150 Gala Dinner performance (2010), and *The House of Wonders* (2013).

Other activities include the annual DGS Concerto Competition (since 2014), exchanges with schools from Taiwan and Singapore, and outreach concerts on campus by local arts bodies, as well as the Cornell Glee Club and Cambridge Queens College Choir. Students have also benefited from masterclasses by international conductors including Ko Matsushita and Marin Alsop. However, none of this would be meaningful without giving back to the community. Girls served at the various occasions of the Sir Edward Youde Scholars Association and the Zonta Club, Hong Kong Sheng Kung Hui anniversary services, and sharing sessions at the Queen Elizabeth Hospital.

DGS has continued to excel in local competitions, garnering numerous first places and Best Choir accolades at the annual Music Festival, Hong Kong Youth Music Interflows,[74] and other events such as the Hong Kong International Youth and Children's Choir Festival (2006) and Winter Band Festival (2018).

In 2002, under the baton of Ms Synthia Ko, the School Choir competed for the first time at the biennial World Choir Games held at Busan, Korea. Since then, DGS has taken part

---

74. Since the 1990s, the Hong Kong Youth Music Interflows has been an annual event for local secondary and primary school symphony orchestras, string orchestras, concert bands, and Chinese orchestras to compete in their respective categories.

Musical Life

in other overseas competitions and frequently reaped outstanding results, most notably capturing World Champion titles in 2010 and 2018, as well as the Grand Prix Champion in 2016. The instrumentalists were also invited by the Education Bureau to represent Hong Kong at the National Arts Showcase of Primary and Secondary School Students, winning first prize at the Tsingdao (2016) and Suzhou (2019) showcases. A summary of the results appears in Table 12.4.

Furthermore, the school actively sought out opportunities for students to gain overseas exposure, participating in festivals in Macau, Guangzhou, Shenzhen, Taipei, and Tainan. DGS was also invited by the Hong Kong government to perform at the 2016 Kagoshima Prefecture Wind Festival, and at concerts in Wuhan and Changsha to commemorate the opening of the High Speed Rail in 2018. The Junior School choir also took part in the 2016 International Children's Choir Festival held in the United Kingdom, bridging cultures with music.

Beyond Jordan Road

Over the years, many graduates have chosen to study music at the tertiary level. Besides enrolling in local university music programmes and the Hong Kong Academy for Performing Arts (HKAPA), girls have also entered world-renowned institutions including the Juilliard School, Peabody Institute, Oberlin Conservatory, Eastman School of Music,

Figure 12.6: DGS Symphony Orchestra conducted by Mr Leung Kin Fung at Shenzhen Concert Hall, 2017. Source: School Archives.

Table 12.4a: Senior School's participation in international choral competitions

Month / Year	Competition	Results (Conductor)	
		DGS Choir	DSCS Choir with DBS
Oct 2002	Busan, Korea 2nd Choir Olympics	Gold Medal (Ms Synthia Ko)	Silver Medal (Mr Ronnie Cheng)
Jul 2006	Xiamen, China 4th World Choir Games	Silver Medal (Ms Synthia Ko)	–
Jul 2007	Wernigerode, Germany 5th International Johannes Brahms Choir Festival and Competition	–	Gold Diploma (Mr Ronnie Cheng)
Jul 2008	Graz, Austria 5th World Choir Games	Silver Medal (Mr Ronnie Cheng)	Gold Medal (Mr Ronnie Cheng)
Jul 2010	Shaoxing, China 6th World Choir Games	Gold Medal and Category Champion (Ms Jenny Wong)	Gold Medal and Category Champion (Mr Ronnie Cheng)
Jul 2011	Wernigerode, Germany 7th International Johannes Brahms Choir Festival and Competition	Gold Diploma and Category Winner (Ms Jenny Wong)	Gold Diploma, Category Winner, and Johannes Brahms Grand Prize Winner (Mr Ronnie Cheng)
Jul 2012	Cincinnati, USA 7th World Choir Games	Gold Medal (Miss Grace Chiang)	Gold Medal (Mr Ronnie Cheng)
Jul 2014	Riga, Latvia 8th World Choir Games	Gold Medal (Miss Grace Chiang)	Gold Medal (Mr Felix Shuen)
Aug 2016	3rd Singapore International Choral Festival	Gold Diplomas, Special Conductor Prize, and Grand Prix Champion (Miss Grace Chiang)	–
Jul 2018	Tshwane, South Africa 10th World Choir Games	Gold Medal and Category Champion (Ms Dorothy Hui)	Gold Medal and Category Champion (Mr Felix Shuen)

Source: Speech Day Booklets, *Quest*, Music Departmental Reports. DSCS—Diocesan Schools Choral Society.

Table 12.4b: Junior School's participation in international choral competitions

Month / Year	Competition	Results (Conductor)
Jul 2008	Llangollen International Musical Eisteddfod	Junior Children's Choirs – First Place (Mrs Christina Chiang)
Jul 2012	Cincinnati, USA 7th World Choir Games	Young Children's Choirs – Gold Medal (Mrs Christina Chiang)
Jul 2014	Riga, Latvia 8th World Choir Games	Young Children's Choirs – Gold Medal (Mrs Christina Chiang)
Jul 2018	Tokyo, Japan 1st Tokyo International Choir Competition	Children's Choir – Silver Prize (Miss Kylie Ng)

Source: Speech Day Booklets, *Quest*.

Table 12.5: Results of Senior School's participation in national instrumental competitions

Month/Year	Ensemble/Competition	Results
Aug 2005	Chinese Orchestra (with DBS Chinese Orchestra): 北京第三屆全國青少年民樂團隊北京邀請賽	2 First Level Prizes, 1 Second Level Prize
Aug 2007	Chinese Orchestra (with DBS Chinese Orchestra): 北京第四屆全國青少年民樂團隊北京邀請賽	3 First Level Prizes
Feb 2015	Guzheng Ensemble: 「青樂杯」首屆兩岸三地青少年古箏比賽	Silver Prize
Feb 2016	Guzheng Ensemble: 「青樂杯」第二屆兩岸三地青少年古箏比賽	Gold Prize
Apr 2016	String Quartet: 5th National Arts Showcase of Primary & Secondary School Students 全國第五屆中小學生藝術展演活動	First Level Prize
Apr 2019	Symphony Orchestra: 6th National Arts Showcase of Primary & Secondary School Students 全國第六屆中小學生藝術展演活動	First Level Prize

Source: Speech Day Booklets, *Quest*, Music Departmental Reports.

New England Conservatory of Music, Columbia University, Rice University, and Indiana University Bloomington in the USA; the Royal College of Music, the Royal Academy of Music, and University of Cambridge in the UK; and the Conservatoire de Paris in France.

Among those who have pursued a professional career, many have gained an international standing in their respective areas, such as pianist Chiu Yee-ha, 趙綺霞 (Class of 1955; Steinway artist who previously taught at The Juilliard School and Duquesne University); Margaret Lynn, 林敏柔 (Class of 1973; former Associate Dean of Music, HKAPA); Dr Joanna C. Lee, 李正欣 (Class of 1980; musicologist and international arts consultant); Margaret Yang, 楊惠 (Class of 1981; CEO, Hong Kong Sinfonietta); and Dr Jenny Wong, 王菁儀 (Class of 2004; Associate Artistic Director, Los Angeles Master Chorale).

From the humble beginnings of a handful of pianists and singers, DGS music has grown into an established department that boasts hundreds of members each year. The school has had the honour of nurturing countless talents that have walked through the Jordan Road gates. Generations of DGS musicians have continued in the steps of their elder comrades, dedicating their time and gifts to serving the community both locally and overseas, as performers, composers, academics, art administrators, music therapists, and educators.

Chapter 13

Sports

Robyn Lamsam (1994)

Throughout its history, DGS has been renowned for cultivating a unique environment of excellence, hand in hand with the school's emphasis on the all-round development of each individual student. Much of the school's strong reputation stems from its long-standing and successful sporting heritage that has produced outstanding athletes and stellar sporting achievements. From rudimentary beginnings, guided by the firm hands of forward-thinking and inspirational leadership, the physical education (PE) curriculum and sporting programmes have developed exponentially. DGS girls have gone on to represent the school and Hong Kong, winning multiple accolades at all levels of domestic and international sporting competitions including the Olympics, Asian Games, and World Championships.

During the nineteenth century, girls were discouraged from being active, and there were very few opportunities, if any, for them to take part in sports or other extracurricular activities. In 1913, however, the newly built DGS campus at 1 Jordan Road boasted coveted facilities including a tennis court and a playing field, which allowed more girls to take up sports at school, an uncommon privilege at the time. As the Hong Kong government began to promote physical exercise for the sake of the overall health and well-being of students,[1] the school grounds were simultaneously expanded. In 1929, DGS employed its first PE mistress to focus on the school's PE programme which mostly consisted of drills that took place on the newly built covered playground.[2] At a time when most Chinese girls were discouraged from playing sports for fear of neglecting their academic studies, DGS was one of the first

---

1. W. T. Featherstone, *The Diocesan Boys' School and Orphanage: The History and Records, 1969 to 1929*, 41.
2. "New Pavilion. Diocesan Girls' School Building Opened", *South China Morning Post*, 13 December 1928.

Figure 13.1: Rope climbing in the old gymnasium, 1955. Source: *The Quest* 1955, 20.

progressive girls' schools to actively promote them.[3] Gymnastics with small apparatuses including vaults and benches, ropes, softball, rounders, and various forms of Scandinavian, English, and Scottish folk dancing were later incorporated into the curriculum.

Given the influence of the early expatriate PE mistresses, tennis, hockey, and netball are the sports teams with the longest histories at DGS. During Miss Ferguson's tenure, six classes competed for the Lady Ho Tung Challenge Cup in tennis.[4] After the Second World War, rehabilitation of the tennis courts fuelled greater interest in the sport, which led to the institution of the Grace Lo Tennis Cup in 1949.[5] The following year, thirty-two girls took part in the school's first tennis championship in which Margaret Elena (Mussie) Fincher was the Champion in Singles and in Doubles, partnering Margaret Fernanda (Nana) de Carvalho.[6] In 1980, only five years after the establishment of its official tennis team, DGS prevailed in its first interschool championship, and has since won a record thirty-one overall championships. Several DGS tennis players have also represented Hong Kong at the Fed Cup Level, and have triumphed at numerous CRC Hong Kong Open Championships.

DGS has always been very fortunate to have its own playing field, and by the 1930s, school sports days and interschool hockey matches for the Brawn Cup were organised on school grounds.[7] In 1941, led by Captain Eva Churn, the DGS hockey team competed in the Ladies League against some of the strongest professional clubs in the territory.[8] DGS girls upheld the school's strong hockey tradition in the late 1960s, with Barbara Winyard and

---

3. *The Quest* (1941): 10.
4. "Diocesan Girls' School Annual Prize Giving", *South China Morning Post*, 8 March 1924.
5. Speech Day Booklet, 1949, 6.
6. *The Quest* (1950): 18.
7. "School Sports: Diocesan Girls' School Annual Meeting List of Winners", *South China Morning Post*, 10 April 1936; "Brawn Cup Matches", *South China Morning Post*, 10 February 1936.
8. *The Quest* (1940–1941): 19.

Kim Fenton the only schoolgirls selected for the Colony XI to play international matches against the Australian National Team. They were later joined by Pamela Baker against the Japanese National XI Hagaromo Team. In 1969, the DGS Team A XI won the Hong Kong Ladies' League Seven-A-Side Tournament and Gremlin's Cup.[9] Unfortunately, despite efforts to promote the sport and continued participation in the Hong Kong School Sports Federation (HKSSF) League, interest in hockey appears to have waned considerably.

Netball was always one of the most popular ball games at DGS. It was taught in PE lessons so that girls of all abilities were able to master the rules of the game. By 1941, in addition to interhouse and interclass competitions, the school had a flourishing interschool netball team captained by Patricia Kotewall, which won the Silver Cup and Joint School Knockout Tournament.[10] Today, interest in the sport holds steady in both the Senior and Junior schools, as well as amongst old girls. The Diocesan Old Girls' Association (DOGA) Netball Team was established in 2000 and has since competed in the Hong Kong Ladies Open League for twenty consecutive years, winning three championships. For the past two decades, the DOGA has also hosted the popular annual alumni netball tournament.[11]

The House System

Upon entry into the Junior School or the Senior School, every student was assigned to a house, which gave them a strong sense of identity and solidarity. Initially, the four houses were designated according to colour: Green, Blue, Red, and Yellow.[12] The houses were later renamed after the school's headmistresses—Smith for Red, Skipton for Blue, Sawyer for Green, and Gibbins for Yellow.[13] Then in 1960, Smith House was renamed Hurrell House.[14] As the number of DGS students increased, the school eventually unveiled its fifth house, Symons, in 1987.[15] As house activities played an integral part in school life, girls had a feeling of purpose when called upon to compete as representatives of their houses. Students were encouraged to take part in all interhouse activities, not only with the goal of winning championships and accolades, but also to reinforce house spirit, cultivate sportsmanship, and embrace the underlying notion that every individual's participation was for the overall benefit of the house.

---

9. Speech Day Booklet, 1969, 8; *Quest* (1968), 19.
10. *The Quest* (1941): 20.
11. Personal communication with Anna Wong, January 2021.
12. *The Quest* (1947): 31.
13. *The Quest* (1949): 30.
14. "Hurrell House Report", *Quest* (1960): 29.
15. "Symons House Report", *Quest* (1987–1988): 48.

Figure 13.2a: Hockey A or First XI Team, 1941. Source: *The Quest* 1941, 25.

Figure 13.2b: Barbara Winyard (1965), Pamela Baker (1967), and Kim Fenton (1968), representing the Hong Kong Team against the Japanese National XI Hagoromo Team. Source: *Quest* 1968, 19.

Figure 13.3: DOGA vs DGS Netball Team, annual end-of-term match in school, 2003. Source: Anna Wong.

Sports 321

In the mid-twentieth century, interhouse sports were held in May at the beginning of the summer term: two contestants from each House were selected to participate in each event, including Flat Race, High Jump, Long Jump, and Potato and Spoon Race.[16] In 1948, the Diocesan Old Girls' Association sponsored the House Challenge Shield for netball and the House Challenge Shield for hockey.[17] The following year, the Youngsaye Senior House Cup for All-Round Efficiency, previously known as the House Challenge Cup for All-Round Efficiency, was established, and by the early 1960s, interhouse competitions were firmly positioned in the school calendar.[18] In 1987, to stimulate enthusiasm and greater competition between the houses, the school implemented a complete overhaul of the entire house system to include the introduction of a wide array of new competitions, the formation of house committees, the production of House T-shirts, slogans, and songs, as well as annual house meetings.[19] Today, there are thirteen interhouse competitions encompassing sports, debating, drama, and even a much-coveted cheering award. The interhouse swimming gala is held in September while the interhouse athletics meet takes place in November each year. Students undergo intensive training after the interhouse events in preparation for the more challenging interschool sports competitions later in the year.

PE Teachers

As part of the school's focus on an all-round education, fully trained physical training mistresses were originally hired from England and tasked with the organisation of physical training and games. The earlier sports mistresses were: Miss Phyllis Ward, Miss Helen Patterson, Miss Lorna McGarvey, Mrs Monica Reeve, Mrs B. Renard, and Miss Sue Sowerbutts. Subsequent PE teachers had diverse approaches and attitudes towards sports and PE, but their devotion, enthusiasm, and expertise certainly paved the way for DGS's later sporting successes. Miss Molly Williams (1965–1976) believed that PE was crucial for building up one's character, and that mental strength and the right attitude would enable students to overcome all other difficulties later in life.[20] In 1975, Miss Jill Clark arrived at DGS where she remained as Head of the PE Department for the next two decades. Miss Clark's approach was to encourage enjoyment of sports for all students, and to create a more relaxed atmosphere during PE lessons as a contrast with academic pressures.[21] "Physical education is not just about competing at the interschool level or even at the interhouse

---

16. "Sports Notes", *The Quest* (1947): 32.
17. "Prize List", Speech Day Booklet, 1948.
18. "Prize List", Speech Day Booklet, 1949, 9.
19. "Interhouse Activities", *Quest* (1989–1990): 56.
20. "Interview with Miss Williams", *Quest* (1975–1976): 30.
21. *Quest* (1977–1978): 21.

level. The aim is to promote fitness among all students and knowledge of a healthy life-style, as well as introducing them to sports which they can enjoy after leaving DGS. I hope that students can understand the underlying lesson that hard work and fitness are needed to earn success in all aspects of our lives."[22] In 1978, Mrs Paulina Hui (née Lun) was the school's first local Chinese PE teacher, hired to bridge the gap with students from Chinese-speaking primary schools. During her incredible forty-two-year tenure, Mrs Hui had a particularly strong impact on the school's swimming and life-saving teams, spearheading them to thirty-five and twenty-five Interschool Overall Championships respectively.[23] Another PE teacher with a long history was Mr Tang Kun Loi, who was originally brought in as the school's athletics coach. From 1982 until 2018, Mr Tang led the school athletics team to fifteen overall championships and introduced some less vigorous sports such as archery, tenpin bowling, golf, and indoor rowing to encourage participation by students who were generally less active. Interest in tenpin bowling and indoor rowing quickly gained momentum, with both teams winning overall championships at their first interschool competitions in 2009.[24] Current PE mistress Mrs Rosa Santos has witnessed a dramatic transformation of DGS sports since her arrival in 1989: from the Volleyball Team's promotion to Division 1 in 2003 to winning its first overall championship in 2017; the Cross-Country team's thirteen Interschool Overall Championships; not to mention the incorporation of "modern" sports into the DGS sports curriculum such as dragon boat racing, dodgeball, rugby sevens, handball, and beach volleyball, several of which have already achieved promising results in a relatively short period of time.[25]

Swimming

With thirty-five HKSSF Interschool Division 1 Overall Championships, including an incredible twenty-six Grand Slams, swimming is arguably DGS's most successful sport at both domestic and international levels. The seeds of DGS's swimming legacy were possibly sown in 1965 when parents of the school gave DGS its own swimming pool.[26] Not only did having a 25-metre pool on school grounds facilitate training sessions for the swimming team, the incorporation of swimming into the PE curriculum resulted in an exponential increase in the number of students who learned how to swim.[27] At the time, approximately 75 per cent of DGS students could not swim, owing to the limited access to swimming

---

22. Personal communication with Miss Jill Clark, October 2020.
23. Personal communication with Mrs Paulina Hui, September 2020.
24. Personal communication with Mr Tang Kun Loi, September 2020.
25. Personal communication with Mrs Rosa Santos, January 2021.
26. Speech Day Booklet, 1966, 10.
27. *Quest* (1975–1976): 23.

pools around Hong Kong and the fact that the government had not yet started constructing many public swimming pools. For safety reasons, Miss Molly Williams initiated the White Cap System, whereby students who could not swim one length confidently would have to wear a white cap so that the lifeguards could easily spot any potential problems.[28] To qualify for a coloured cap, students were required to swim 50 metres freestyle and be proficient at a second stroke. As the school expanded, there was a significant increase in weak and non-swimmers, so to relieve the pressure at the shallow end, Miss Jill Clark moderated the criteria for coloured caps to swimming 50 metres of any stroke, 25 metres of freestyle or backstroke, and being able to tread water.[29] The White Cap System remains in place to this day.

Since the 1960s, DGS has had a multitude of exceptional swimmers, many of whom have represented Hong Kong internationally. This began with the remarkable Bendall sisters—Ruby, Rita, and Marlene—who together with Diane U were selected for the Hong Kong Schools' Swim Team to compete in a triangular series in Bangkok, Singapore, and Jakarta.[30] Since then, more than thirty DGS girls have competed at the highest level, with eight swimmers representing Hong Kong at the Olympic Games and twenty-six at the Asian Games, winning a total of one silver medal and eleven bronze medals.

In 1992, Robyn Lamsam was the school's first Olympian and Hong Kong's youngest representative at the Barcelona Olympic Games. She went on to win Hong Kong's first individual Asian Games swimming medal at the 1994 Hiroshima Asian Games. She was a two-time winner of the Omega Sportsgirl of the Year and the only three-time winner of the SCMP Sportsman of the Year Award. In 1996, she was awarded the Badge of Honour from Queen Elizabeth II—Hong Kong's only schoolgirl to have received that honour. Another notable DGS swimmer was Sherry Tsai, three-time Olympian, three-time Omega Sportsgirl of the Year, and recipient of the 2014 Junior Chamber International Hong Kong Ten Outstanding Young Persons Award.[31] The swimmer with the longest international career is Rosanna Hang Yu Sze, who competed at three Olympic Games, a record seven World Championships, and four Asian Games, with a total of one silver and eight bronze Asian Games relay medals to her name.[32]

---

28. Personal communication with Mark Williams, 8 March 2021.
29. Personal communication with Jill Clark, 9 March 2021.
30. Personal communication with Rita Bendall, 31 January 2021.
31. "Past HK TOYP Awardees", accessed 21 January 2021, http://toyp1.jcihk.org/en/past-hk-toyp-awardees/.
32. Personal correspondence with Rosanna Hang Yu Sze, 2 February 2021.

Figure 13.4a: Robyn Lamsam (1994) receiving the Badge of Honour from Governor Chris Patten, 1996. Source: Kim Lamsam.

Figure 13.4b: Sherry Tsai (2000), flag bearer for Hong Kong at the 2004 Athens Olympic Games. Source: unknown.

Figure 13.5: Interschool Swimming 31st consecutive Overall Champion, 2018. Mrs Paulina Hui with the team, before retiring from her 42 years of service at DGS. Source: School Archives.

Athletics

Before 1960, DGS had limited athletic activities. Athletics training began in earnest in 1959 when Mr James Lowcock, a teacher at DBS (later Headmaster), and Mr Kennedy Skipton (English teacher at DGS) enabled a few girls to enter the school's first interschool athletics competition. The school won its first Overall Championship, the Princess Margaret Shield, in 1965, bolstered by Hong Kong's record holder and champion Pamela Baker, who later represented Hong Kong at the 1966 Asian Games in Bangkok where she tied fourth in the high jump.[33] The school's champion A and B Grade relay teams were also invited to run at the Youth Rally held in honour of HRH Princess Margaret and the Earl of Snowdon at Government Stadium.[34] The DGS Athletics Team resumed its winning ways in 2001, and since 2006 has won the Interschool Division 1 Overall Championships thirteen consecutive times, including four Grand Slams. Over the years, more than one hundred DGS athletes have represented Hong Kong at international competitions and have broken multiple national records.

Figure 13.6: Pamela Baker (1967) receiving the B Grade Champions Trophy from HRH Princess Margaret at youth rally held in honour of Princess Margaret and the Earl of Snowden, 1965. Source: *Quest* 1966, 35.

Figure 13.7: DGS winning Interschool Athletics Grand Slam, 2018. Source: School Archives.

---

33. *Quest* (1968): 22.
34. "Sports Report", *Quest* (1966): 29.

International Sporting Achievements

DGS girls have also won medals on the international stage in several other disciplines, including life-saving, table tennis, and fencing. Since its first overall championship in 1972, the school's Life-saving Team has won that accolade a remarkable twenty-five times. Winnie Wong was also crowned World Champion in Line Throw at the 2016 and 2018 Life-saving World Championships and triumphed in the same event at the 2017 Commonwealth Festival of Life-saving in 2017. At the same event in 2019, Dolphin Chan won silver medals in the 100 metres Manikin Carry with Fins and the 200 metres Super Life-saver. In table tennis, Lee Ho Ching won a mixed doubles silver medal and women's doubles bronze medal at the 2014 Incheon Asian Games, followed by another bronze medal in mixed doubles at the 2018 Asian Games in Jakarta. Finally, in addition to fifteen Interschool Overall Championships, DGS Fencing Team members have won six Asian Games bronze medals in team events, as well as Liu Yan Wai's individual Foil bronze medal at the 2018 Jakarta Asian Games.

Figure 13.8a: Lee Ho Ching (2009) won Mixed Doubles Silver and Women's Bronze at the 2014 Incheon Asian Games in table tennis. Source: Brian Ching.

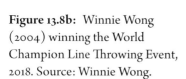

Figure 13.8b: Winnie Wong (2004) winning the World Champion Line Throwing Event, 2018. Source: Winnie Wong.

Development of School Sports in Hong Kong

The first interschool competition in athletics reported in the "Retrospective Highlights of the Development of Schools Sports in Hong Kong" recorded by the Hong Kong Schools Sports Association was between St Joseph's College and St Paul's College in 1877. Later that year, Hong Kong's first interschool athletics meet took place in Happy Valley. This led to the formation of the Interschool Sports Committee, which was responsible for organising interschool competitions until 1951, when the Hong Kong School Sports Association (HKSSA) was formally inaugurated on 15 February 1951 with a membership of only forty-six schools. Three years later, on 4 September 1954, interschool sports in Hong Kong developed further with the establishment of the New Territories Schools Sports Association (NTSSA), which included four district branches and an additional eighty-one member schools.[35] This coincided with increasing interest in sports within the general population and the formation of the Amateur Sports Federation of Hong Kong in 1949/1950, which became recognised as an Olympic Committee in 1951. Funding from the Hong Kong government increased accordingly with the Urban Council providing numerous sports halls, pools, courts, and playing fields for community use.[36] The Hong Kong Schools Sports Council (HKSSC) was launched in 1974 to offer support to the HKSSA and NTSSA, and to assume responsibility for organising the Interport and International competitions. Eventually, the HKSSA, NTSSA, and HKSSC were formally dissolved on 31 August 1997, and the three organisations were merged to form the Hong Kong Schools Sports Federation (HKSSF) with the intention of streamlining all interschool sports activities. The Federation was further subdivided into the Secondary School Sports Council and Primary School Sports Council, and the External Sports Committee which oversees the Jing Ying, Interport and International School sports competitions. There is also a collaborative feeder system in place with Hong Kong's National Sports Associations (NSAs) and the Hong Kong Sports Institute (HKSI), whereby athletes identified as having potential are given access to quality coaching and training facilities, and provided with opportunities to prepare for competitions on a national level as a part-time or full-time athlete. In addition to overseeing all school sports, the objectives of the HKSSF are to enhance and to raise the calibre of interschool sports, to work closely with NSAs and the HKSI in the selection of Hong Kong representation at Interport, Asian, and World competitions, as well as to foster sportsmanship and friendly rivalry among member schools.[37]

---

35. Notes by Jimmy (James) Lowcock on the Development of Interschool Sports in Hong Kong, supplied by William Ko.

36. "The Amateur Sports Federation & Olympic Committee of Hong Kong", in *The Quest for Gold, Fifty Years of Amateur Sports in Hong Kong, 1947–1997*, ed. S. F. Lam and Julian W. Chang (Hong Kong: Hong Kong University Press, 2005), 63–64.

37. Hong Kong School Sports Federation, accessed 17 December 2020, http://hkssf-hk.org.hk/hkssf_member.htm.

Table 13.1: Number of times DGS won overall championships and Grand Slams in interschool competitions from 1960 to 2019

	Overall Championship	Grand Slam
Archery	0	0
Athletics	15	4
Badminton	12	3
Basketball	2	1
Beach Volleyball	0	N/A
CrossCountry	13	2
Dodgeball	2	N/A
Dragon Boat	3	N/A
Fencing	15	1
Handball	0	N/A
Hockey	0	N/A
Indoor Rowing	8	5
LifeSaving	25	14
Netball	0	N/A
Orienteering	18	9
Rugby Sevens	0	N/A
Squash	3	N/A
Swimming	35	26
Table Tennis	7	1
Tennis	31	N/A
Tenpin Bowling	6	N/A
Volleyball	2	0

Source: Speech Day Booklet and *Quest* of respective years.

Omega Rosebowl/Bauhinia Bowl/Rising Star Awards

The Hong Kong Schools Sports Association Omega Awards were first introduced in September 1965 to bolster interschool competition. The awards were divided into two sections—the Omega Challenge Rose Bowl, awarded to schools achieving the best all-round performance in all sporting events, and the Sports Boy/Girl of the Year, awarded to an individual for outstanding abilities and contribution to sports. In 2003, the HKSSF announced that the Omega Rose Bowl Awards would be replaced by the Bank of China Bauhinia Awards and expanded to include the most outstanding sports boy and girl in each of the fifteen interschool sports categories, in addition to the overall all-round award.[38] As of 2019, the number of competing schools stands at 175, an increase from 85 in 1965. To date, DGS has won the overall award sixteen times, and since 1985 has been runner-up for thirty-four consecutive years. Notably, a DGS girl has been selected as Sportsgirl of the Year a total of thirty-three out of the fifty-two years since this category has been available. The inaugural Omega Sportsgirl of the Year was won by Pamela Baker, multiple track and field record holder for Hong Kong and the school's first Asian Games representative. DGS also boasts Hong Kong's only multi-generational, mother–daughter Omega Sportsgirl Award recipients, with Kim Fenton winning in 1969, followed by Robyn Lamsam in 1994 and 1995. From 2005 to 2008, Rainbow Woo won the Bank of China Hong Kong (BOCHK) Bauhinia Bowl Sportsgirl of the Year a record four times for her exceptional all-round performances in volleyball, life-saving, badminton, basketball, and athletics. Her forte was in track and field in which she broke the Hong Kong Javelin Record an impressive six times.[39]

The HKSSF also established the BOCHK Rising Star Awards to encourage school participation in development sports, and is given to the school achieving the best all-round performances in archery, beach volleyball, indoor rowing, rugby sevens, and tenpin bowling. Since the launch of this award in 2010, DGS has been the Overall Girls School Champion every year for the past ten consecutive years.[40] Furthermore, DGS has had a

Figure 13.9: Four-time BOCHK Bauhinia Bowl Sports Girl winner, Rainbow Wing Tung Woo (2007) receiving the award in 2008.
Source: Rainbow Wing Tung Woo.

---

38. "Rose Award Turns over New Leaf", *South China Morning Post*, 9 September 2002, accessed 11 November 2020, https://www.scmp.com/article/390739/rose-award-turns-over-new-leaf.
39. Personal communication with Rainbow Woo, 12 December 2020.
40. BOCHK Rising Star Award, accessed 28 November 2020, http://www.hkssf-hk.org.hk/hk/sec/general-rules/rising-star%20rules.pdf.

Figure 13.10: First Dragon Boat Overall Championship, 2015. Source: School Archives.

winning representative every year in the BOCHK Rising Star Athlete Award, created in 2014 to recognise athletes from S1–3 who have achieved outstanding performances in events held by the HKSSF, Jing Ying Tournaments, and Interport, Asian, and International Schools competitions.[41]

University Scholarship Athletes and Old Girls Who Remain Active in the Hong Kong Sports Scene

Given the internationally recognised calibre of DGS athletes, it is not surprising that a few of them have been awarded scholarships to attend some of the world's best colleges and universities. Three-time Olympian Sherry Tsai led the way in 2004 when she was granted a scholarship to the University of California, Berkeley, one of the United States' top college swimming programmes. Sherry is now a professional swim coach in Hong Kong, and was presented with the Hong Kong Swimming Coaches Association Harry Wright Coaching Award in 2019.[42] In 2011, Claudia Lau was the first Hong Kong swimmer to receive a scholarship into the celebrated University of Michigan swimming programme where she trained alongside multiple Olympic champions and world record holders.[43] Claudia was also the

---

41. BOCHK Rising Star Athlete Award, accessed 28 November 2020, http://www.hkssf-hk.org.hk/hk/sec/general-rules/rising-star%20athletes.pdf.
42. Personal communication with Sherry Tsai, 11 January 2021.
43. Personal communication with Claudia Lau, 25 January 2021.

first DGS swimmer to attain an Olympic "A" Qualifying Time which she achieved in the 200-metre backstroke ahead of the 2016 Rio Olympic Games.[44] DGS golfers to receive college scholarships include Kitty Tam to San Diego State University and Tiffany Chan, who was the first Hong Kong player to qualify for the Ladies Professional Golf Association Tour. Tiffany received a scholarship to attend the University of Southern California, which at the time was the number one ranked US college for golf, and highly regarded for its long history of having one of the world's best women's golfing programmes.[45]

A number of old girls remain active in Hong Kong's sporting scene, led by Mrs Stella Lau who is the Chairlady of the Board of the HKSSF, Vice Chairperson of the Secondary School Sports Council, and member of the Multi-Purpose Sports Complex Task Force of the Sports Commission, which is overseeing the immense Kai Tak Sports Park Project.[46] Professor Anna Wai-Kwan Wong (DGS graduate, 1976) of HKU is a Director on the Board of the Hong Kong Sports Institute, a government-mandated academy for elite athletes, and a member of the Home Affairs Bureau Sports Commission's Major Sports Events Committee; and Robyn Lamsam is serving her third term as a member of the Elite Sports Committee, which provides policy direction to the Hong Kong Sports Institute and advises the government on matters pertaining to high performance sport and athletes.[47]

Modern Approach to PE

Modern school life at DGS remains extraordinarily vibrant, guided by the underlying principle that a good education encompasses many aspects, including opportunities for students to improve their physical health and self-discipline through sports.[48] In 1991, PE was formalised as a subject in the Hong Kong Certificate of Education Examination, which transitioned to the Hong Kong Diploma of Secondary Education in 2011. Candidates are expected to exhibit a high level of personal fitness as well as demonstrate communication and collaborative skills and a clear understanding of the theoretical concepts of PE.[49] Accordingly, PE lessons at DGS have expanded to include a broader and more balanced school curriculum. Fundamental sporting skills are introduced in S1 to S3 in areas such as

---

44. "Claudia Lau Makes the Olympics in the Nick of Time", *South China Morning Post*, 2 July 2016, accessed 23 January 2021, https://www.scmp.com/sport/hong-kong/article/1984538/claudia-lau-makes-olympics-nick-time.

45. Personal correspondence with Tiffany Chan, 30 January 2021.

46. Personal communication with Mrs Stella Lau, 2 February 2021.

47. "Elite Sports Committee", Home Affairs Bureau, accessed 8 January 2021, https://www.hab.gov.hk/en/policy_responsibilities/arts_culture_recreation_and_sport/sport3.htm.

48. Personal communication with Mrs Stella Lau, 12 December 2020.

49. Hong Kong Examination and Assessment Authority, HKDSE Elective Subjects: Physical Education, Assessment Framework & Curriculum, accessed 11 November 2020, https://www.hkeaa.edu.hk/en/hkdse/hkdse_subj.html?A2&2&19.

athletics, ball games, gymnastics, aquatics, dance, and indoor rowing. In the senior forms, girls have the option of further developing those skills, or exploring alternatives such as squash, tenpin bowling, and rock climbing. In addition to hiring professional coaches and trainers, the school has also integrated modern technology into its PE and sports programmes. In 2004, the Fitness Award Scheme was introduced to improve students' fitness index, with activities tailor-made to suit the levels and needs of DGS students.[50] In 2013, the school set up an E-Classroom for students to record personal information and fitness data to keep track of the development of their physical stamina.[51] Two years later, the school incorporated applications using Swift programmes to video and evaluate students' fitness data to improve both teaching and learning outcomes. And in 2019, Polar heart rate monitors were also introduced to analyse and monitor fitness and health data during PE lessons, training sessions, and fitness assessments.[52] Upon completion of the school's immensely ambitious redevelopment project in 2011, new state-of-the-art sporting facilities for the next generation of DGS girls included a top-of-the-line equipped fitness centre; an indoor, six-lane, 25-metre swimming pool equipped with FINA-standard competition diving platforms; two indoor games halls for basketball, volleyball, dodgeball, fencing, table tennis, and handball; two outdoor courts for archery, netball, and tennis; and a 2,700-square-metre artificial turf sports field equipped for a wide variety of sports, including a three-lane track and three-bay, golf-driving range.[53]

DGS sport has blossomed from only twelve teams in the 1980s to twenty-three sports teams with nearly 500 participants. To broaden students' horizons, the school has organised seminars and workshops with ex-DGS athletes and internationally renowned athletes and coaches. In addition to sharing sessions from ex-DGS athletes about the challenges of balancing school life, academic achievement, and a high-level sporting career, students have also had the opportunity to meet Olympic Gold Medallists: Ian Thorpe, Leisel Jones, DeeDee Trotter, NBA All-Star CJ McCollum, and Valentina Vezzali, the first fencer in Olympic history to win three individual gold medals at three consecutive Olympic Games. Since the 1990s, the school has also arranged a number of sports camps, with the inaugural DGS Sports Camp at the HKSI in 1993, a large-scale sports camp at Tsinghua Experimental School in 2007, and the 2008 Beijing Olympic Tour sponsored by Mr Charles Wong and Mr Yu Kam Kee, which afforded 124 students a unique opportunity to watch world-class competitions and experience the Olympic spirit first hand.[54] DGS has also organised two Walkathons to enable all girls, regardless of sporting abilities, to enjoy a healthy activity

---

50. "PE Report", Speech Day Booklet, 2004, 48.
51. Speech Day Booklet, 2013, 102.
52. Information provided by Mrs Rosa Santos, January 2021.
53. "Physical Education", Speech Day Booklet, 2013, 102.
54. Speech Day Booklet, 2009, 55.

Sports 333

Figure 13.11: Group photo taken in the Centenary Hall prior to Beijing Olympic Tour, 2008. Source: School Archives.

together and to promote the spirit of cooperation among students, staff, and old girls.[55] The first Walkathon took place in 1993 as part of the school's Building Extension Appeal, and the second Walkathon Family Day was organised in May 2008 as a final opportunity for students, parents, and friends of the school to explore the old campus along special designated paths prior to the commencement of the school's extensive redevelopment project.[56]

Parent Teacher Association and DOGA Support

DGS Sports is also very fortunate to have a strong internal support network, including the Diocesan Girls' School Parent Teacher Association (PTA) and the DOGA. The PTA was established in June 1951[57] as a partnership between parents and the school, with the inten-

---

55. Speech Day Booklet, 1992, 10.
56. *Quest* (2007–2008): 67.
57. PTA Minutes, 15 June and 10 July 1951.

tion of enhancing student learning and enriching the lives of students.[58] PTA support for the school's sports programmes began in the 1970s with the tradition of supplying trophies and flowers for the school's Sports Day and Swimming Gala.[59] Since then, PTA assistance has expanded further to include sponsorship of sports training and coaching fees, as well as contributions to improve the school's sporting facilities and equipment. The Swimming Subcommittee of the PTA also provides support for all pool-related matters such as daily operational expenses, maintenance, and running of swimming courses arranged by the school's Aquatics Club.[60] Similarly, the DOGA has also shown staunch support for the school's athletes. In addition to sponsoring interschool celebratory dinners for the Swimming and Athletics Teams, DOGA also hosts the annual interhouse alumni netball tournament, and organised Netball Club training for both the Senior and Junior schools from 2001 to 2016.[61]

DGS has long been a pioneer in providing its students with the all-rounded education and balanced foundation necessary for them to become productive and high-achieving members of society. In 2019, the International Olympic Committee awarded DGS the Achievement Diploma in recognition of the school's outstanding contribution to promoting the development of women and girls in sport. This great honour from the world's highest sporting body was an affirmation of the school's legacy, and an inspiration to ensure that sport at DGS remains synonymous with excellence in the years to come.

---

58. Personal communication with Sheilah Chatjaval, Chairperson of Parent Teacher Association, 2000–2009, 28 January 2021.

59. "Gifts to the School", Speech Day Booklet, 1975, 11.

60. Personal communication with Christine Nip, Chairperson of Parent Teacher Association, 2019, 27 January 2021.

61. Personal communication with Anna Wong, 9 December 2020.

Chapter 14

School Life

Amy Ng (1991)

From its chequered beginnings as the Diocesan Native Female Training School, through its evolution into an orphanage, then the school of choice for Eurasian families, to its current status as one of the leading girls' schools in Hong Kong, school life in DGS has always been shaped by the wider social and political forces in Hong Kong, especially in terms of gender, race, social expectations, and religious affiliation.

Gender

The school—originally established to educate Chinese girls—was quietly radical in its very concept. In 1860, most Chinese families did not send their daughters to school. In richer families, they were tutored at home and prepared to be housewives. This social conservatism doomed the earliest incarnation of DGS, which had to be shut down. Later, although girls from upper- and middle-class families joined the school, "most girls left school to work as unqualified teachers, nurses, or eventually as typists and secretaries".[1] Alternatively, they got married. In stark contrast to DBS, which in the interwar years aimed to be the most illustrious school in the Far East in the British public school tradition, and from where many old boys went on to the University of Hong Kong, or even Oxford and Cambridge, few girls aspired to university. When Miss Elizabeth Mary Gibbins was appointed DGS Headmistress in January 1939, she found DGS a "lame school" and resolved to raise its academic standards. Realising that the school "had the makings of a girls' public school", she introduced botany, biology, full mathematics, and a more professional approach to

---

1. C. J. Symons, *Looking at the Stars: Memoirs by Catherine Joyce Symons* (Hong Kong: Pegasus Books, 1996), 87.

the study of English Literature, history, and geography, "and in two short years the school changed direction".[2]

In the 1950s, as American and Canadian universities opened their doors to Hong Kong students, more girls considered tertiary education. In 1951, there were sixty-seven DGS alumnae at Hong Kong University (sixty girls and seven boys—DGS took in some boys before DBS reopened after the war). Of the sixty female graduates, thirty-six (60 per cent) were in the arts, fifteen (25 per cent) in medicine, five (8.3 per cent) in architecture, and four (6.6 per cent) in science.

However, university was still the exception rather than the rule for girls. In post-war Hong Kong, where the majority of families were too poor to send their daughters to school (though they would scrimp and save to pay for their sons' education), many DGS girls were expected to earn money as teachers, stenographers, and secretaries upon graduation to finance their brothers through university. In 1951, Miss Hurrell responded to this societal need by introducing the "modern" syllabus heavily focused on domestic science, typing, and shorthand skills, justifying the move by arguing that most DGS girls were not destined for higher education, since they "are not really interested in their work as it becomes more abstract and more difficult. They are not normally interested in Physics and Chemistry as such (whereas a boy is), and they just cannot cope with the higher branches of Mathematics."[3] The modern syllabus was deemed a success at the time. Most graduates of the programme were snatched up by big corporations as secretaries because of the school's reputation for excellent English language skills. Some did so well that they eventually became important members of the staff of major business corporations.

Not surprisingly, given the push and pull of different forces and attitudes, articles about the abilities and the proper role of women populated the pages of the school magazine in the 1950s—"Can Women Study Medicine?", "How to Raise the Status of Women?", and "The Advantages of Being a Woman", for example.[4]

The tide turned in the 1960s. DGS girls graduated from Hong Kong University "and from famous universities abroad with excellent degrees in almost every subject, including Medicine and Engineering", with many sixth formers winning prestigious scholarships to American universities.[5] Mrs Symons' avowed goal now was to "prepare girls for life as educated young women, able to contribute to the professional and business life of Hong

---

2. Symons, *Looking at the Stars*, 87.

3. *The Quest* (1949): 17.

4. *The Quest* (1951): 25–26; *The Quest* (Chinese) (1948): 5; *The Quest* (1954): 48.

5. Symons, *Looking at the Stars*, 58.

School Life   337

Kong",[6] albeit with "attributes of womanly patience, poise and gentleness".[7] Henceforth, almost all DGS graduates went on to higher education.

Race

In the matter of race, DGS was also unintentionally radical. Although the Diocesan Native Female Training School was set up exclusively for Chinese girls, its successor organisations were racially mixed. The Diocesan Girls' School and Orphanage founded in 1899 was for European and Eurasian girls. It was only in 1921, when Miss Ferguson became the Headmistress, that the school started admitting Chinese girls. There are few statistics about the precise racial mix in DGS in the 1920s and 1930s, and first-hand accounts differ. According to Mrs Symons, in 1926 the school had "about 150 students, with just a few Chinese amongst a crowd of Eurasians, Portuguese, Indians and expatriates".[8] Jean Gittins (née Ho Tung), who was at DGS between 1917 and 1923, concurs with Symons' memories of the school as predominantly for "European and Eurasian girls". However, Jean's older sister Irene Cheng (née Ho Tung), who entered the school in 1914, claimed that the DGS community included many Chinese girls, though both girls remembered the mixed community of the school with warmth.[9] Given heightened racial tensions in Hong Kong in the 1920s, especially towards Eurasians who were caught between and never fully accepted by either the Chinese or European communities,[10] DGS was seen as a haven from racial strife, which is probably why the Eurasian Ho Tung family elected to send their daughters there, although the daily commute consisted of a donkey ride to the tram station, the Peak tram down the mountain, followed by a sedan ride to the Star Ferry terminal, the ferry across the harbour, and finally a rickshaw ride to school. The Ho Tungs were willing to put up with this long and onerous commute because the Peak School, which was only a 15-minute walk away from their home, did not admit Chinese children, and the nearby St Stephen Girls' College, recognised as "the school for daughters of Chinese gentlemen", was deemed to have a lower standard of English instruction than DGS.[11]

The very existence of a mixed-race school was remarkable given the historical context—there was strong societal disapproval of racial mixing in schools and in society. Separate

---

6. Symons, *Looking at the Stars*, 54.

7. Symons, *Looking at the Stars*, 56.

8. Symons, *Looking at the Stars*, 9.

9. Vicky Lee, *Being Eurasian: Memories across Racial Divides* (Hong Kong: Hong Kong University Press, 2004), 202–203.

10. See Anthony Sweeting, "Hong Kong Eurasians", *Journal of the Royal Asiatic Society Hong Kong Branch* 55 (2015): 83–113, for a discussion of the increase of discrimination against Eurasians by both Chinese and European residents in the early decades of the twentieth century.

11. Jean Gittins, *Eastern Windows, Western Skies* (Hong Kong: *South China Morning Post*, 1969), 26.

schools had been set up for the Chinese, such as St Stephen's College in 1903, and for the Europeans, such as the Kowloon British School in 1902. The Peak District Reservation Ordinance was passed in 1904, reserving the Peak district for non-Chinese residents only. That a mixed-race school should have come into being under the aegis of the Anglican Church was a minor miracle. Notwithstanding, the Anglican Church was slower to integrate girls from different racial and social backgrounds than the Catholic schools in Hong Kong, probably as it closely identified with the colonial establishment.

Nevertheless, racial mixing was worn as a badge of honour by DGS:

> [W]hatever changes take place, the basic characteristic of this school is being and will always be maintained. It is that of harmony between girls of many different races. A glance at the class-registers is enough to show the international composition of the school . . . This fostering of real friendship between girls of Chinese, Indian and European parentage is undoubtedly the special contribution to the welfare of the community which the DGS has to offer.[12]

Indeed, DGS girls could even be seen as a secret weapon in the struggle for world peace:

> [A]s every month goes by, the need for racial harmony becomes more acute, so that the very future of the human race depends upon the determination of people everywhere to devote their whole strength towards preventing another and even more terrible fratricidal world war. The newspapers in many countries already vie with one another in deliberately encouraging the most virulent forms of thinly disguised racial hatred as a means towards the furtherance of their political ends . . . against such a background, the spirit of racial harmony at the DGS is like a tiny pin-point of flame in the dark.[13]

The racial demographics of the school changed after the Second World War. Eurasian students increasingly went to expatriate schools in Hong Kong or boarding schools abroad. The flood of refugees from China also reached the school, and soon Shanghainese became the second most common native dialect spoken in DGS after Cantonese. From 1956, the government picked one-third of the incoming Form 1 students, who were all from local Chinese primary schools, which further accelerated the trend towards racial homogenisation, though the boarding school remained a multiracial holdout of Eurasians and overseas students until its closure in 1973.[14] Currently, the overwhelming majority of students are Chinese.

---

12. *The Quest* (1949): 1.

13. *The Quest* (1950): 1.

14. Email from Dorothy Kent, a boarder at DGS from 1948 to 1957, 20 May 2020.

School Life   339

The Boarding School

The Diocesan Girls' School and Orphanage started as a boarding school. At the beginning, the majority of students were boarders. The percentage of students boarding at the school steadily declined, with a sharp drop in numbers after the Second World War, until the boarding school was shut down, given that there were only 19 boarders left out of a total student population of 1290 in 1971.

The boarding school originated in the school's mission as an orphanage, although it also took in students whose families were not in Hong Kong, those who simply lived too far away from the school. Discipline at the boarding school was strict, and there were complaints about bad plumbing. Florence Yeo (née Ho Tung), sent to boarding school at the age of four in 1919, recalls waking up screaming and crying every morning, and "of being given a bath in a cold concrete bathtub without any privacy". Coolies carried big wooden tubs of hot water up the back stairs to the bathroom as there was no running hot water. There were four concrete tubs in a row, and the children were "scrubbed down". She also vividly remembers always being hungry, with the last meal consisting of a teatime of bread and margarine or bread and jam.[15] However, other students (and staff) had fond memories of the close friendships formed and the kindness of teachers who took them out on hiking trips and expeditions in their own time during the weekends.[16]

In 2015, the school decided to reopen its boarding school to recruit girls from the larger region beyond Hong Kong, although the reopening plan has been put on hold until after 2019.[17]

Language

Founded by Anglican missionaries, from the start DGS modelled itself upon British schools. The teaching of Chinese was long regarded as secondary.

Prior to 1938, no Chinese was taught in the school, for it was essentially an English school with a minority of Chinese girls enrolled. As year by year the number of Chinese girls steadily grew, and as Chinese was a language required of Chinese pupils in the School Leaving and Matriculation Exams, its teaching was found to be indispensable, and hence a Chinese Department was created. At first, Chinese lessons were taught mostly in the afternoons, and pupils were allocated to different groups according to their Chinese standard.[18]

---

15. Florence Yeo, *My Memories* (Pittsburgh, PA: Dorrance Publishing Co., 1994), 17–18.
16. *The Quest* (1952): 21–22; email from Dorothy Kent, 20 May 2020.
17. Headmistress's Report, Speech Day Booklet, 2015, 11.
18. *The Quest* (1947): 18.

As the student body at DGS became predominantly Chinese, first Miss Hurrell and then Mrs Symons promoted the study of Chinese, including Chinese as a subject in the entrance examination that girls had to pass to be admitted. In 1952, Mr Y. C. Chan was hired away from Pui Ching Secondary School to teach Chinese and Chinese history, and during his twenty-six-year tenure laboured mightily to raise the standard of Chinese at DGS.[19]

However, Mrs Symons also determined that DGS should remain a school run along British lines. Right through the 1950s, students were punished for speaking Chinese on school grounds. Every subject apart from Chinese and Chinese history was taught in English, frequently by expatriate teachers. Successive incarnations of the school rules insisted that "English was to be spoken as much as possible", although the revised school rules in 2012/2013 updated the rule to "English and Putonghua are to be spoken as much as possible".[20] Despite the best efforts of the Chinese teachers, the level of Chinese in DGS lagged behind English, until the late 1970s when the percentages of pass and distinction for Chinese matched those of English. While English dramatic works were staged almost every year, Mr Chan only managed to stage four Chinese plays in his twenty-seven years at the school, despite his great love of drama.[21] In a bittersweet jest, he mandated that any student caught speaking English during his rehearsals would be punished.

Even after the 1997 handover, the standard of Chinese is still an issue for some of the girls with English-speaking backgrounds. In 2015/2016, the school started to offer an alternative curriculum for girls to sit for the GCE Advanced Levels in chemistry, biology, mathematics, geography, economics, history, and psychology. In 2017, both Chinese and English were added to the GCE A-Level curriculum. This proved to be particularly helpful for the small number of girls who did very well in other subjects but found it difficult to gain the HKDSE Level 3 proficiency in Chinese Language.[22] Other schools have also introduced this alternative curriculum.

As a Eurasian, Mrs Symons' choices reflected an identification with her British heritage more than her Chinese one. In her first year as Headmistress, she celebrated Coronation Day with enthusiasm, not only because she was an "unashamed royalist", but also because "many girls had been refugees from Communist China and I felt they should begin to absorb the underlying tenets of British administration in this their new home".[23] However, by the time of the school's centenary, she had already formed a set of new objectives, with

---

19. *Quest* (Chinese) (1977–1978): 6.

20. School Notices, 2012–2013.

21. *Quest* (Chinese) (1977–1978): 6; *Quest* (Chinese) (1979–1980): 13.

22. Headmistress's Report, Speech Day Booklet, 2017, 12.

23. Symons, *Looking at the Stars*, 49.

an intent "to send out into the world, girls who were conscious of their wonderful heritage of Christian thought, Western democratic ideals, and classical culture of China".[24]

Dr Symons, however, was antagonistic towards the emphasis on examinations and rote learning that prevailed in local schools, and was especially suspicious of the Education Department and their periodic attempts to "ram [their ideas] down our throats".[25] Academically, she expected sixth form girls to be "fellow-researchers of educational material with their teachers, and not mere sponges absorbing data without thought",[26] and pushed through plans to extend the general education of the sixth formers with seminars and conferences, debates and open sessions—even though the idea was not popular among the staff.[27] Not surprisingly, school trips have featured prominently in school life, although the geographical reach and duration has expanded dramatically in recent years. While expeditions in the 1950s took in Ma Wan Island and its fishing port, the manufacture of ceramics at Castle Peak, the cottage industry of making joss sticks using waterwheel power along the Tsuen Wan River Valley, and the Garden Bakery,[28] nowadays school trips have gone global, encompassing history trips to Germany, geography field trips to South Korea, and trips to Singapore, India, the USA, New Zealand, and Australia. The school has also partnered with different schools in China.[29]

For Mrs Symons, what happened outside the classroom was arguably as important as formal education in shaping the characters of her students. She insisted on the "intrinsic value of non-academic subjects like art, music, domestic science and physical education. These subjects were all taught by expatriate teachers, since no training facilities were available in Hong Kong at the time."[30] She built upon features imported from Britain, such as the prefect system, and a heavy emphasis on extracurricular activities, to foster leadership qualities, sportsmanship, and an all-round education.

Prefects

The prefect system goes all the way back to the fourteenth century in Britain.[31] It reached its heyday in the nineteenth century in British independent schools and was exported throughout the British empire. Traditionally, prefects were appointed from the sixth form

---

24. Symons, *Looking at the Stars*, 56.

25. Symons, *Looking at the Stars*, 57.

26. Symons, *Looking at the Stars*, 54.

27. Symons, *Looking at the Stars*, 58.

28. *The Quest (1950)*: 20; Symons, *Looking at the Stars*, 24.

29. Headmistress's Report, Speech Day Booklet, 2014, 14–15.

30. Symons, *Looking at the Stars*, 56.

31. Accessed 31 December 2020, https://www.britannica.com/topic/prefect-education.

based on their intellectual prowess and good character, and were given enormous powers to enforce discipline and the school rules, including the power of inflicting corporal punishment on the younger students.[32] Prefects in DGS were never given such extensive powers, and their duties mostly consisted of reporting on the infringement of school rules to the teachers and in helping to lead school assemblies. Historically, DGS school prefects were appointed from students in the sixth form but are currently appointed from S5 students so as to allow S6 students more time to focus on their upcoming examinations.

As the student body has grown, the number of prefects has also increased drastically and the system has become more hierarchical. When Joyce Anderson (Mrs Symons) was head girl in 1934/1935, she oversaw six other prefects. Currently there are thirty-five prefects, including two Head Girls, four Deputy Head Girls, eight Assistant Deputy Head Girls/ Assistant Head Girls, two Music Prefects, one Library Prefect, and two Sports Prefects.

Prefects have been variously appointed by the Headmistress alone (in Miss Sawyer's time, 1925–1939),[33] by the Headmistress and the bishop in Miss Gibbin's time (1939–1941, 1945),[34] and now by a combination of staff and current prefects. The school has also experimented with student democracy: in 1966, 1975, and 1977, students in the upper forms could vote for eight girls from a list of nominees shortlisted by the staff and school prefects.[35] Since 2016, all S5 and S6 students and teachers can vote for the prefect board before the next academic year commences.[36]

Extracurricular Activities

The importance accorded extracurricular activities means that student life is extraordinarily busy, with students frequently skipping lunch and staying on long after the end of the school day and at weekends for sports training, rehearsals, and club meetings. During the time leading up to the Speech or Music Festivals, classrooms empty out as students are taken out of regular lessons for extra rehearsals. Over the years, the number and variety of extracurricular activities have increased, resulting inevitably in greater specialisation and competitiveness. Through music and sports scholarships, the school has nurtured students with different talents, with the result that DGS dominates interschool competitions in most fields. The current nurturing of specialisation has helped some of the students to shine but has not lessened the emphasis on the general all-rounder. DGS has even won international competitions—for example, the DGS choir has won awards not only at the Hong Kong

---

32. Paul Nash, "Training an Elite", *History of Education Quarterly 1 (March 1961): 12–21.*

33. *Quest (1992–1994): 176.*

34. *Quest (1992–1994): 178.*

35. School Notices from 1966, 1975, 1977.

36. Headmistress's Report, Speech Day Booklet, 2016, 23.

School Life   343

Music Festival, but also at international competitions such as the World Choir Games held in Cincinnati, USA, in July 2012.[37]

Although the number of girls participating in extracurricular activities and the activities on offer have increased throughout the years, the school day has remained more or less constant and hence subject to ever increasing time pressure. To alleviate this pressure, in 2017 it was established that Other Learning Experiences (OLEs) should take place on designated Fridays throughout the year. On OLE Fridays, the fifth lesson is omitted and the afternoon is devoted to OLEs or extracurricular activities.[38]

Political Context

Despite the efforts to achieve true bilingualism, in the eyes of the broader public, DGS remained a British school. Indeed, Mr Y. C. Chan recalled that his colleagues at Pui Ching Secondary School urged him not to make the move, because Chinese could never be taught properly in a school such as DGS.[39] This perception became a liability during the 1967 riots in Hong Kong. The anti-colonialist riots in the vicinity of the school caused Mrs Symons to fear for the safety of DGS and the students. Although the school came through the crisis physically intact, the riots sparked a veritable exodus of students to boarding schools abroad, as anxious parents sought safe havens in the West. Somewhat defiantly, Mrs Symons proclaimed that the school would never transform into one that only prepared students for life abroad. Rather, she reaffirmed her commitment to providing leaders for Hong Kong:

> The day will come when the top posts in every aspect of the city's life may be taken by Chinese and local graduates . . . For this wonderful day the preparation . . . must begin now, in our secondary schools . . . [O]ur educational pattern must provide a sense of involvement; and part of that can be successfully met when our young men and women will serve their fellow Chinese with traditional charm and politeness, and a well-balanced mind that is international, not parochial, in its outlook.[40]

In the face of successive waves of emigration, both Mrs Elim Lau and Mrs Stella Lau have followed Mrs Symons' lead in educating students who can thrive both abroad and in Hong Kong.

Although Mrs Symons encouraged the study of politics in DGS, she did not believe that "the young should be too actively involved in matters that are not their business. I

---

37. Headmistress's Report, Speech Day Booklet, 2012, 15.
38. Headmistress's Report, Speech Day Booklet, 2019, 19; School Notices, 2017–2018.
39. Quest (Chinese) (1977–1978). 5.
40. Headmistress's Speech Day Address, Speech Day, 11 December 1967.

cannot accept the belief that student protests alone show genuine concern for others. If we adults have made serious mistakes it is by careful study of these mistakes that the young can prepare themselves for the reins of authority."[41]

As a member of both the Legislative and Executive Councils in Hong Kong, Mrs Symons herself was part of the political establishment. After the signing of the Sino-British Joint Declaration in 1984, she realised that the switch in political masters from Britain to China would necessitate changes in the school, and welcomed the appointment of Mrs Elim Lau, the first Chinese Headmistress of DGS, as her successor.

In her more optimistic moments, Mrs Symons believed that the school could play a beneficial role in the transition:

> I am certain that Hong Kong's hour has come: Hong Kong's new role will be the springboard of friendship between East and West. The educated Hong Kong person is a very important agent in this understanding—with his exposure to two very different cultures, he is able par excellence, to work for international understanding based not on narrow bigotry but a healthy and innate broad-mindedness. I rejoice that in this school we have always tried to produce this kind of person, and I trust this intrinsic aspect of genuine education will survive in the turbulent seas of adjustment in the future.[42]
>
> Is it too much a flight of fancy to suggest that if we get our educational policies right that China and the world will ultimately benefit? Can we not nurture this mustard seed?[43]

Mrs Symons' successors have also hewed to the principle of turning out informed citizens but discouraging participation in political protests.

Class

From the very beginning, when the dream of educating upper-class Chinese girls failed and successor institutions took in orphans and Eurasians from poor families, there has been tension around socio-economic class, much of it played out in the area of admissions. For most of its post-war history, the school's reputation has been so high it could easily have admitted only the daughters of the wealthiest and most powerful families in Hong Kong. However, Mrs Symons was determined that admissions would be meritocratic. She resisted pressure from the Anglican clerical establishment, old girls, and VIPs from all walks of life to favour "their" candidates and instead looked for "alert candidates, fluent in English and Chinese, preferably girls from the middle or lower middle-classes".[44] Despite her own deep

---

41. Headmistress's Speech Day Address, Speech Day, 10 December 1971.
42. Headmistress's Speech Day Address, 21 November 1984, Speech Day.
43. Headmistress's Speech Day Address, 6 November 1981, Speech Day.
44. Symons, *Looking at the Stars*, 55.

religiosity, Mrs Symons refused to limit admissions to members of the Anglican Church, fearing that this would result in a wave of inauthentic conversions. She looked upon the government scheme to select a third and later half of the Form 1 students with great suspicion, afraid that the government wanted to "destroy" or "water down prestigious schools", many of them old grant schools,[45] although she eventually acknowledged that the government scheme was undoubtedly "more democratic and Christian" by increasing class diversity in the school.

When the XYZ classes were first introduced in 1959 to replace ABC classes, they were filled alphabetically, which meant that X classes had many Chans, Y classes Lees, and Z classes Wongs. Soon, however, it became clear that the pupils from the Chinese primary schools lagged far behind girls from the Junior School in English. Hence, they were taught English separately, and the X class was reserved for the best students from the Junior School, with the rest of the Junior School intake going into the Y class, and the Chinese primary school students ending up in the Z class. In 1976, a "U" class was added to the mix when a fourth class of Form 1 was created. In 1979, to ease the teaching of English, X and U were reserved for girls who had come up through the Junior School, with Y and Z accommodating the new students. As the Junior School became a private school in 1959, school fees meant that with many Junior School alumni came more established families, whereas some students in Y and Z classes tended to come from more varied social and financial backgrounds. The differences in background and friendships already established over six years in the Junior School meant that it was not easy to assimilate the X/U and Y/Z classes in Forms 1, 2, and 3 together. However, this improved further up the school after the classes were mixed around from Form 4 onwards, by which time "the brightest from Chinese schools had matched our own best".[46]

The situation further improved with the help of Mrs Elim Lau as a teacher and later as head, who encouraged cross-curricular activities so that girls with similar interests from different classes and sets would have the opportunity to learn together and form a common identity. She also worked to change the mindsets of girls, teachers, and parents "so that the X class/Science classes were not the only best classes and the Z class/lower sets were not for the nobodies" as "everyone who enters DGS deserves to be given the opportunity and help to excel, each in her own way".[47]

However, autonomy and admissions remained a live issue. In September 2005, in order to deliver the "through-train" concept, DGS joined the government's Direct Subsidy Scheme (DSS) "so that the senior school would have more discretion to accept DGJS [Junior

---

45. Symons, *Looking at the Stars, 89*.
46. Symons, *Looking at the Stars, 89*.
47. Mrs Elim Lau, email communication, 7 January 2021.

School] girls into the school than under the current arrangement".[48] Since the switch to DSS status, the school has sought to mitigate the perception that it is an elite school only for those who can afford it, by providing bursaries for good students whose families could benefit from the extra resources.

Religion

The many ways in which religion permeated school life is covered more fully in Chapter 10. Assemblies featured daily Bible reading and hymn singing, clergy from St Andrew's came every week, and the Chapel was used for Holy Communion every Wednesday. The school's motto—"Daily Giving Service"—was rooted in the religious understanding of loving your neighbour as you love yourself. Mrs Symons felt strongly that since Hong Kong people equated academic prowess with success, and success with wealth, "it was therefore up to us in the School to present a counterbalance, by creating a respect for spiritual values such as love, honesty and concern for others".[49] Practically, this resulted in a tradition of community service: from the girls' club and Sunday schools for poor children in the 1950s, to the donation of two cottages for refugees in the 1960s, to the current array of community service projects ranging from teaching Cantonese to children of ethnic minorities in Hong Kong, volunteering in impoverished rural areas of China, and giving musical concerts in hospitals.

A school is a work in progress, always growing, never static. DGS has weathered many a crisis in its long history: war, political turbulence, societal upheavals, epidemics, and pandemics, but it has always adapted and thrived. However, in all the vicissitudes of history, DGS has never abandoned the school motto of "Daily Giving Service", and the Christian ethos behind that motto. As always, the school will be mindful of what kind of service is needed, to whom it is rendered and how it is delivered, especially in complex times.

---

48. Headmistress's Report, Speech Day Booklet, 2004,15.
49. Symons, *Looking at the Stars,* 67.

Chapter 15

Teaching and Non-teaching Staff

Andrea Lai (1990) and Moira M. W. Chan-Yeung (1955)

The first part of this chapter, by Moira M. W. Chan-Yeung, describes the composition of the teaching staff during various periods of the development of the school. The second part, by Andrea Lai, consists of students' reminiscences about their teachers and the non-teaching staff.

Part 1: Composition of Teaching Staff

All school records before the Second World War were destroyed during the Japanese Occupation when the school was turned into the headquarters of the Japanese Gendarmerie. In addition, during the redevelopment of the school in 2009–2011, all the buildings, except the newly built SIP (School Improvement Plan) building, were demolished. During the process of decanting to the hotel school, many documents from Mrs Symons's era were lost and presumably destroyed. As a result, most of the data before 1985 were incomplete.

The school enrolment and the number of teachers of the whole school from 1860 to the present are shown in Figure 15.1. Readers who are interested in the teaching staff of the Diocesan Home and Orphanage period should consult the school history of DBS, *To Serve and to Lead*.[1]

When the Diocesan Girls' School and Orphanage was founded in 1899, it only had two teachers, Miss Elizabeth Skipton and Miss Maud Hawker, for twenty-four boarders and

---

1. Yee Wang Fung and Moira Chan-Yeung, *To Serve and to Lead: A History of the Diocesan Boys' School* (Hong Kong: Hong Kong University Press, 2009).

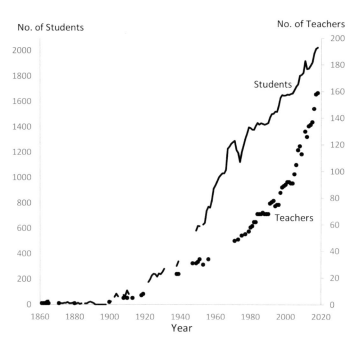

Figure 15.1: Number of students and number of teachers at DGS, 1860 to the present. Source: Compiled from the Female Education Society minutes of meetings and annual reports, *SCMP* historical newspapers 1903 to 1945, minutes of School Council meetings, *Quest*, and Speech Day Booklets. Note: Continuous line represents no. of students; dotted line represents no. of teachers.

two or three day students. It was only in 1900 when the school became a grant-in-aid school with financial support from the government that the school was able to expand and recruit more teachers. The Skipton period ended with about 180 students and six more teachers. Since the school only taught in English, all the teachers were from England.

Miss Catherine Ferguson, who became the next Headmistress in 1921, began to admit Chinese students. As a result, during her tenure and that of Miss Dorothy Sawyer, school enrolment had increased to 340 when Miss Sawyer retired in 1938. No record was found regarding the number of teaching staff. However, a photograph of the teaching staff taken in 1939/1940 (Figure 4.2 in Chapter 4) showed a total of twenty-three teachers, including Miss Elizabeth Gibbins, the next Headmistress, giving a student–teacher ratio of 14.7:1.

After the war, the rapid rise in student enrolment from the population explosion increased the student–teacher ratio, and when the school was separated into the Senior and Junior schools in 1947/1948, the student–teacher ratio in the Senior School was, as expected, lower than that in the Junior School. The ratios further increased reaching the highest level in 1971/1972 (Table 15.1).

The birth rate in Hong Kong gradually declined from the 1960s onwards. At the turn of the twenty-first century (2000/2001), the number of students in each class was reduced and the student–teacher ratios for both the Senior School and Junior School lowered. Further improvement in the ratio in the Senior School occurred after the school changed to the Direct Subsidy Scheme (DSS), dropping to 11:1 in 2018/2019. The ratio in the Junior School also decreased to 15.4:1. (Table 15.1) As a result, the students received a great deal more individual attention from the teachers, and streaming of the class for subjects other than English was possible.

Table 15.1: Student–teacher ratios in DGS and in other schools in brackets by year

Year	Senior School	Junior School	Whole School
1939/1940	–	–	14.7:1
1947/1948	17.1:1	23.8:1	18:1
1971/1972	23.1:1 (25.8:1)*	33.8:1 (35.8:1)*	26.8:1
1993/1994	18.7:1 (21.6:1)	23.5:1 (25.7:1)	19.3:1
2000/2001	17.4:1 (18.6:1)	19.9:1 (22.0:1)	18.3:1
2018/2019	11.1:1 (11.3:1)	15.4:1 (13.7:1)	12.7:1

Source: Hong Kong Education Bureau and Hong Kong Annual Digest of Statistics 1978, 2019 edition.
Note: ( ) Student–teacher ratios for schools in Hong Kong excluding ESL (English Language School) schools and international private schools; * for aided schools only.

During the days of Miss Skipton and Miss Ferguson, members of the teaching staff were all female. In the 1930s, Miss Sawyer appointed a Chinese male teacher, Dr Baldwin Lee, who had a US doctorate degree, to teach English. In 1939, there were seven Chinese teachers, three males and four females. Other than Dr Lee, the other two male Chinese teachers were appointed to teach Chinese, which was introduced by Miss Gibbins to the school curriculum for the first time. Two of the four female Chinese teachers, Miss Lee and Miss Wong, were physical education teachers; the third, was Miss Chiu who taught botany. There is no information on the fourth. We do not know the qualifications of the female teachers, but in the 1930s, there were a number of women who graduated from teachers' training colleges and universities in China.

In the Junior School, all the teachers were female—a practice of the school until only very recently when the Junior School had one to three male teachers for a couple of years. Until 2004, the qualification required for teaching in the Junior School had been training at one of the teachers' training colleges. After that, the Education Department required that all teachers be degree holders. By then, almost all of the teachers in the Junior School who were not degree holders had already upgraded their qualification and obtained a degree from one of the local universities.

In the Senior School, the proportion of male teachers was 36 per cent in 1949, but this dropped to about 5 per cent or even lower in the 1970s, when the school concentrated on liberal arts subjects and most female students were taking liberal arts subjects at university. Since the 1970s, with curriculum reform, science subjects have been made much more interesting and comprehensible. Moreover, increasing job opportunities in science and technology have resulted in more girls taking science subjects, and more male teachers were recruited to teach these subjects (Figure 15.2).

It was the policy of DGS and other Anglo-Chinese schools to appoint expatriate teachers from English-speaking countries to teach English subjects. The proportion of non-Chinese teachers, though forming about 50 per cent of the teaching staff in the 1950s and 1960s, gradually decreased as more young Chinese women graduated from one of the local teachers' training colleges or HKU and entered the teaching profession. Among them were several old girls who returned to the school to teach. The proportion of native English-speaking teachers progressively decreased from the 1980s, when there was a restriction on engaging expatriates to teach English in government and aided schools, reaching its lowest point in the early 2000s. The establishment of language laboratories had been helpful and compensated for the lack of native-speaking teachers to a certain degree. When DGS became

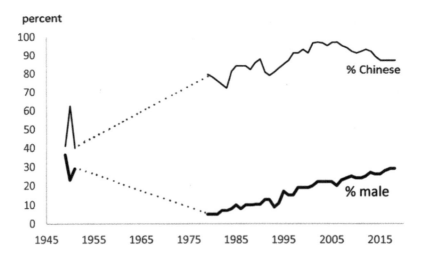

Figure 15.2: Gender and ethnicity of Senior School teachers, 1945 to 2018. Source: Compiled from minutes of School Council meetings, *Quest*, and Speech Day Booklets. Note: Dotted lines connect years without data; thin line represents percentage of Chinese teachers; thick line represents percentage of male teachers. For this graph, we classified an individual as Chinese based on her/his name and facial appearance, thus giving only a rough estimate of percentage of Chinese in the staff.

Teaching and Non-teaching Staff

a Direct Subsidy Scheme school in 2005, the number of native-speaking English teachers increased and reached 13 per cent in 2019.

In the Senior School, while only about 50 per cent of the teaching staff were degree holders after the war, the proportion increased to 100 per cent in the 2000s (Figure 15.3). In 2019, about 60 per cent of the teaching staff held a master's degree and a few a doctorate. After the school joined the DSS in 2005, both the quantity and quality of the teaching staff improved considerably.

As knowledge advances rapidly, teachers could no longer teach all the subjects on the curriculum. Specialisation in teaching occurred after the Second World War. At present, most teachers are expected to teach in their own area. The school has been divided into departments since the 1970s: in the beginning, there were only four. The number of departments increased over time as more resources became available and new subjects were introduced. At present, almost every subject has its own department and its own department head who is responsible for all matters related to teaching and learning of the subject, and for the teachers in the department as well as for communication with other departments. The departments and department heads over the years are shown in Table 15.2.

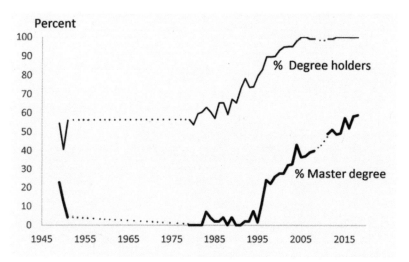

Figure 15.3: Qualification of Senior School teachers, 1946–2018. Source: Compiled from minutes of School Council meetings, *Quest*, and Speech Day Booklets. Note: Dotted lines connect years without data; thin line represents percentage of degree holders; thick line represents percentage of master's degree holders.

Table 15.2: Heads of subject groups/departments, 1980 to 2019

Heads of Groups/Depts	1980	1990	2000	2010	2019
English, French	Mrs P. C. Collier				
English		Miss R. Keung	Mrs A. Lee	Mr J. Oddie	Ms S. Yap
Chinese	Mrs H. S. Tang	Mrs H. S. Tang	Mrs H. S. Tang	Mrs K. Y. Lam	Mrs K. Y. Lam
Mathematics	Mrs M. Chan	Mrs M. Chan	Mr N. B. Wong	Mrs P. S. Tong	Mrs P. S. Tong
Biology, General Science	Mrs P. Kan	Mrs P. Kan			
Biology			Mr T. Man	Dr T. Man	Mrs J. Tang
Integrated Science			Mrs J. Chiu		
Junior Science				Mrs C. C. Wong	Miss P. M. L. Cheung
Chemistry, Physics	Mrs Y. L. Lam	Mrs Y. L. Lam			
Chemistry			Mr S. Chu	Mr S. Chu	Mr S. Chu
Physics			Mr S. K. Lam	Mr S. K. Lam	Mr B. Doherty
Geography, E.P.A., Social Studies	Mrs J. Yeung*				
Geography		Mrs J. Yeung	Mrs K. L. Shing	Mrs K. L. Shing	Mrs K. L. Shing
History		Mrs I. So	Mrs K. L. Shing	Mrs A. Lee	Mr A. Ebrahim
E.P.A., Economics, Principles of Accounts, Sociology, Psychology		Mr M. H. Au			
Economics, P.A., Psychology			Mr M. H. Au		
Social Sciences (Economics, Business, Accounting & Finance Studies, Psychology, Economics & Commerce)				Mr M. H. Au	
Economics					Mr M. H. Au
Business & International Studies					Mr A. Ebrahim
Music, Art, P.E.	Mrs P. Crosby				
Music		Mrs J. Oxley	Miss S. Ko	Mrs A. Lee	Miss G. Chiang

Heads of Groups/Depts	1980	1990	2000	2010	2019
Art		Miss P. Wong	Mrs P. Kam	Mrs P. Kam	Mrs P. Kam
Physical Education		Miss J. Clark	Mr K. L. Tang	Mr K. L. Tang	Mrs R. Santos
Home Economics		Mrs V. Chan	Mrs P. Hui		
Technology & Living				Mrs P. Hui	Ms P. Ho
Religious Knowledge		Mrs A. Hurst	Mrs A. Cheng		
Religious Education				Mrs A. Cheng	Mrs M. Fong
Liberal Studies			Mrs A. Cheng	Mrs A. Cheng	Miss N. Kitchell
Computer Studies			Mrs C. P. Ho		
Computer				Mrs C. P. Ho	Mrs C. P. Ho
Psychology					Mrs K. Tsang

Source: Prepared by Dr Alice Cheung based on school records; *Mrs I. So advised on History.

Part 2: Students' Memories of Teachers and Non-teaching Staff

Teachers

The diversity of teachers who passed through DGS over the decades reflected the educational philosophies of DGS and the evolving government policy guidelines set for grant-in-aid schools. The teachers, in turn, left a legacy of colourful memories to the students whose lives were often moulded by the examples they set.

Despite the disruptions and despair of the late 1930s and early 1940s, students had fond memories of their teachers. Students returning after the Second World War recalled that going to school was an intimate experience, owing to the small class size of around twenty, which included a few boys from DBS. The students enjoyed a special sense of camaraderie from their shared experience of the war, and were happy to survive and resume school again. The Headmistress, the staff, and students had a close relationship and everyone knew one another by name.

The classes remained small in the 1950s and there were not many teachers, so the connection between teachers and students was more personal. The teachers were instrumental in shaping the girls' characters and brought about lifelong impact on the rest of the students' lives. Stemming from the familiarity of the close-knit group, and as an act of affection for each other, outward appearance and idiosyncrasies were often the most prominent features that students took note of and became the rallying point for concocting nicknames. This was especially common among boarders, who wanted to have some youthful fun in their daily lives while living and studying together in close proximity to their teachers.

In the 1960s and 1970s, DGS girls were taught by an international coterie of teachers from England, New Zealand, Denmark, Scotland, USA, Ireland, and India who bred in the girls a global mindset of embracing both the East and the West. As a result, students from that era benefited from a cosmopolitan intellectual outlook, along with the capacity to enjoy the best of Western literature, art, and music. The teachers instilled a belief in the students that everyone had the potential to achieve if they wanted to, even if they did not attain top scores. Students were encouraged to be bold in their exploration of knowledge, to develop their own interests, and to have independent opinions.

In addition to academic achievements, many girls in the 1980s and 1990s aspired to excel in sports, music, and arts and eventually became all-rounders who were well prepared for university education both in Hong Kong and abroad. The dedicated and talented faculty at DGS, consisting mostly of local teachers plus several native English-speaking teachers, were not only demanding but also taught students to become resilient achievers equipped with a strong school spirit. This contributed to numerous successes in interschool competitions in subsequent years. Many girls also developed close relationships and special bonds with their teachers, which lasted even after their departure from DGS. Their interactions extended well beyond the classroom, with girls attending teachers' weddings, visiting their newborn babies, and even an entire class visiting a teacher's home during a weekend.

Stepping into the twenty-first century, education at DGS incorporated both traditional and innovative elements, and teaching became integrated with modern media, the Internet, and technology. Students were encouraged to dive into the virtual ocean of knowledge, to conduct self-learning under the one-student-one-iPad programme, and to increase their knowledge of science, technology, engineering, and mathematics (the STEM subjects). Yet the fundamentals of the school's mission never changed—to nurture girls to become women of excellence via an all-round education supported by the five pillars of DGS education: academics, art appreciation, sports, service, and spiritual learning.

Below is a collective memory of teachers and non-teaching staff from different decades, gleaned from selected anecdotes and quotes given by alumnae from across the class years. Although the memories from students go well beyond the names included, limitations on space meant that not all could be used, and quotes have been edited for clarity.

Mrs Daphne Quay Ying Blomfield (1978–1989)

Mrs Blomfield (Figure 15.4.1) taught English in the Junior School and became its Headmistress from 1978 to 1989. She was fondly remembered by one of her students:

> Mrs Blomfield was both my Headmistress and Primary 3 English teacher. She was the kind of headmistress who could call out your name in a crowded assembly hall and use the lunch hour to talk to students when she walked around the school. I loved her Grammar lessons with her magician puppet! I received my Hong Kong Speech Festival first prize because she trained me well and allowed me to add my own interpretations of the poem (which I still remember after almost 40 years)! —*Class of 1990*

Mr Lawrence S. L. Chan (1945–1964)

Mr L. Chan (Figure 15.4.20, front row L5), nicknamed *"Dai Chan"* (Big Chan), was a maths and translation teacher. He left a deep impression on students, as there were few male teachers at DGS in the 1950s and 1960s:

> I was in Form 3, Beginners' class in Translation. Mr Chan came into the classroom and gave us a translation assignment from Chinese to English: Yue Fei's *'ci' "Mang Jiang Hong"*. Amid the moans and groans, Mr Chan grinned and said, "Have a go at it. If you don't like it, do another exercise." I had a go at it. It was the most challenging assignment I have had. I had a tough time trying to save my hero from being translated into a blood-drinking cannibal! In the process, I was liberated into the world of translation! "Have a go at it!" is a wonderful attitude. I cannot thank Mr Chan enough!
>
> "Have a go at it!". I heard this nudge many times in DGS to take up something new, and it quite effortlessly opened doors to learning, doing new things and taking up what is often quite fearfully presented elsewhere as "challenges". I am indebted to our teachers, and to Mrs Symons, for the confidence they had in us that if we made the effort or took the trouble we could achieve something, or at least learn something. That is a mindset which helps one through life. —*Class of 1956*

Mr Chan Yik Cham (1952–1979)

Mr Y. C. Chan (Figure 15.4.23, middle row L5), nicknamed *"Sai Chan"* (Little Chan), taught Chinese history and Chinese literature. He inspired his students to love these two subjects, as he made history come alive through his colourful recounting of historical tales. He was also a terrific director of plays:

> It was a major event when the school, under Mrs Symons, integrated Chinese subjects into the curriculum and counted the grades in the total assessment of student performance. Another was the recruitment of Mr Y. C. Chan from Pui Ching Middle School to teach at DGS. Mr Chan's Herculean effort to raise the standard of Chinese in the

school was amazing. I noticed his zeal in getting us interested in Chinese writing and through drama, to treat Chinese as a living language in our everyday life although we were not to use Chinese in school except during Chinese lessons. He worked on this goal by turning himself into a one-man stage production team for performance of Chinese plays. I was in the audience for one, on stage for two, and returned to join a fund-raising production, a third, after graduation from school. He worked even harder at our study efforts. He was visibly shaken when students did not take their work seriously and let him down, but he kept up his spirits until they improved. The first batch of Form 1 intake that came under his wing was the 1952 cohort. If my memory serves, that batch graduated with the first distinction in A-Level Chinese that DGS ever had.

He had a sharp eye on each individual student as well. When I graduated and asked him to write in my autograph book, he made the most astute and cogent comments and offered advice which has helped me in later years. —*Class of 1956*

Mr Chan produced and directed "Flowers of Martyrdom". For reasons known only to himself, he chose me to play the villain—a puny guy with a paint-on moustache. He showed me how to walk on stage and produce a long, low, continuous throaty laugh of a cunning and evil man. He even passed me a tape-recorder on which he recorded this unusual laugh and told me to practise it. I just couldn't imitate him! What came out of my throat was a strangulated growl! When I told him about my inability to imitate him, he just replied nonchalantly, "It'll come." I wished I had his confidence.

I was in real despair when the opening day of the play arrived. As the gangsters strode out onto the stage, I somehow managed this flow of continuous, raucous, evil laugh coming out of my throat! Every time I came onto the stage, the audience laughed! When I bumped into Mr Chan during a break outside, he laughed out loud as he saw me, so I guess that darn laugh was OK. —*Class of 1960*

Mrs Beatrice Cheung (1956–1961)

Mrs Cheung, a maths teacher at DGS, had a tough way of dealing with students who did not remember well what she taught:

Her most famous quote in algebra class was "Letters are used to represent numbers only." At the end of our very first lesson in Form 1, she asked girls to repeat this quote. Those who could not repeat it had to remain standing. As nobody was able to repeat this line, the entire class ended up standing! —*Class of 1964*

Mrs Clare Cheung (1975–2011)

Mrs Cheung (Figure 15.4.2) had a long tenure of thirty-six years teaching maths and English at the Junior School. She was also a Brownie Pack guider for a long time. An old girl reminisced:

Teaching and Non-teaching Staff

I remember on my first day of Primary 1, I had no idea how to buy lunch. I went to Mrs Cheung, my class teacher, and she bought me a chicken leg for lunch. I also appreciate how she would hug every one of us when we had to get our injections at school. It was very reassuring to have this motherly figure at school. Of course, I will never forget her signature Scholl sandals! —*Class of 1997*

Miss Peggy Man Lai Cheung (2006–Present)

As a biology teacher, Miss P. M. L. Cheung (Figure 15.4.3) would explain the structure of the cell by demonstrating the cell wall's collapse with dramatic body language. Her welcoming and calming presence, meticulous attention to detail, and keen eye for precision put her students at ease in the face of the seemingly indecipherable marking rubrics for Diploma of Secondary Education Biology. During numerous fire drills, her distinctive and serene voice was sufficient to quell impatient students waiting for dismissal. As an advisor to leading service programmes, her continuous devotion was a good illustration of the school motto "Daily Giving Service". One of her students wrote:

Although Miss Cheung's assessments were extremely challenging and her standards unflinching, she taught us what it meant to persevere towards excellence in academics, to altruistically contribute to society, to observe punctuality, and to respond promptly to fire hazards.—*Class of 2020*

Mrs Christina Chiang (1972–1982, 1993–2017)

In the roles of full-time music teacher at the Junior School, Music Director of the Senior and Junior schools (2010–2013), and part-time music teacher at the Junior School (2014–2017), Mrs Chiang (Figure 15.4.4), an alumna herself, spent more than thirty years teaching music at her alma mater. She enjoyed bringing out the best in students who were not necessarily possessed of talent by nurturing their love of music through singing. She instilled in her students to be lady-like on stage, and to "Chin up & smile". A student recalled:

To us she was Miss Chan, but she came back one day and declared she would now be called Mrs Chiang. She wrote "Chiang" on the board and said, "Don't call me Mrs *Jeung*. I am NOT Mrs *Jeung*, I am Mrs Chi-Ang, CHI-ANG!!"—*Class of 1986*

Mrs Poppy Crosby (1968–1981)

Mrs Crosby (Figure 15.4.5) taught music at DGS for thirteen years. Alumnae remembered her blonde hair in a "bird's nest" hairdo, her elegant spectacles, and her thick pile of notes on each classical music piece. They also appreciated her enthusiasm in exposing them to classical music:

> She would tape her notes on the blackboard and make us copy them while she played the music from a vinyl record on the turntable. She would narrate what was happening when a certain instrumental sound was played. If the sound didn't come out right, she would lick her finger and touch the turntable pin to fix the record! —*Class of 1981*

Mrs Emily Tin Mei Dai (1998–2016)

Mrs Dai (Figure 15.4.6) joined the Junior School as Deputy Headmistress/Headmistress Designate in 1998, became Headmistress in 1999, and retired in December 2016. She had a long association with DGS, having completed kindergarten to Upper Sixth in the school:

> It was our very last day at the old 1 Jordan Road campus. Though I was only in Primary 3, I vividly remember Mrs Dai walking into our classroom with the smile she always wore on her lips. She gave us colour pens to draw our dreams on the white classroom walls before the school building was demolished the next day. This was a very special moment for me, and her reminder to "dream big with faith" stays with me up till this day. —*Class of 2018*

Miss Norah Edwards (1950–1962)

Miss Edwards (Figure 15.4.20, front row R1), from New Zealand, taught music and was also the conductor of the school choir. She led the choir to many championships, and DGS won more competitions than the next two best schools combined. To celebrate DGS's centennial year in 1960, the girls were to stage an opera, *Dido and Aeneas* by Henry Purcell. The diminutive Miss Edwards took on the formidable task of producing and directing the opera to thunderous applause by the audience. Her nickname, "*Gai Zai*" (Little Chicken), was probably derived from her habit of using her index finger in a pecking motion as she conducted:

> One year, I was given the important role of Sound Effect Controller for the stage performance of a play based on *Vanity Fair*. The task was to be responsible for hitting, with a gramophone needle, a tiny unmarked spot on a micro-groove in a sound-effect black vinyl record, on an electrically operated gramophone, just once, when I heard my cue, "I think I heard a cannon shot! Listen!"
>
> After days of anticipation, and hours of practice at rehearsal, came the performance. I made dozens of run throughs and checked everything and went out for a sip of water. I came back backstage and waited. An hour passed. My cue came. I put the needle where it should go. Nothing moved. "Listen!" Nothing. "That was definitely a cannon shot! Let us leave now!" Quick thinking, girl. I had failed. I checked everything and found

Teaching and Non-teaching Staff

that the electricity was cut off; the gramophone plug was kicked out of its socket. I held my rage until the curtain came down.

"Who the hell did this?" I exploded, shaking the plug on the wire, like a severed head.

"If you are so angry, you make it impossible for people to apologise," said tiny Miss Edwards softly.

Miss Edwards did not teach me to sing. She taught me a life lesson that I never forgot. —*Class of 1956*

Miss Edwards shared with us wisdom from her life. She told us to try not to have any regrets in our lives. Precious advice. —*Class of 1960*

Mrs Kirkby (1923–1927, 1935–1938)

Mrs Kirkby was a Scotswoman who taught scripture at DGS during the 1930s. Her students came to realise her teachings became their salvation in later lives:

My most memorable teacher was Mrs Kirkby, form mistress of Class 5. She required us to learn the Psalms by heart. Even now, I remember them. My husband and I moved to China sometime after I left DGS. Life was hard and during times of strife, I usually recite "though I walk through the Valley of Death I shall fear no evil, for thou art with me". This helped me to solve my problems. —*Class of 1940*

Mrs Inger Kvan (1950–1980)

Mrs Kvan (Figure 15.4.7) taught history at DGS. The story was that she and her husband arrived in Hong Kong in the 1950s, all the way from Denmark, to be Christian missionaries in China. Given that China had just declared itself a People's Republic and restricted most foreigners from entry, Mrs Kvan came to DGS instead to become a history teacher, while her husband lectured in psychology at HKU. Mrs Kvan had high expectations of her students, but this was later appreciated by many of them:

Mrs Kvan was gentle, soft-spoken, and urbane. Her classes on Tudor England were wonderful. Somehow she made that period of history come to life. I used to hate history that was filled with dates and records of events that took place with no analysis of the causes or the effect. But not when Mrs Kvan taught Tudor England. Her classes were like university lectures softly delivered . . . sometimes not quite audibly. So we hung onto her every word. In order not to miss anything, some of us adopted an old mode of coping: employ dictation mode.

I remember an old legend passed down by my seniors about Mrs Kvan. It was a true event, but the details are blurred by the passing of over 60 years. I can only crave licence in reconstructing the details of the story.

One day, in the second term, Mrs Kvan walked into the classroom, sat down, and started giving a lecture on a battle in England in Tudor times.

"The army was ready and marched . . ." Scribble, scribble, scribble . . . "army . . . marched . . ."

"The general led the soldiers . . ." Scribble, scribble . . . scribble . . . "led . . . the soldiers . . ."

"The ships . . ." Scribble . . . scribble . . . "the . . . ships . . ."

"The supply line was supported by trains . . ." Scribble, scribble . . . "supported by . . . trains . . ."

"Meanwhile the planes joined in reconnaissance . . ." Scribble, scribble . . . "the planes . . . recon . . . nai . . . sance . . ."

Planes . . . planes? . . . planes in Tudor times? In the sixteenth century? And trains? Trains . . .

Puzzled faces looked up to see the glint of a mischievous smile on Mrs Kvan's face.

"April Fool's Day," she said. It was 1 April. —*Class of 1956*

Mrs Kvan emanated a silence, a serenity, and self-possession which was unique to her. She never inspired fear, but we were in awe of her, which oddly developed into admiration and affection. Mrs Kvan's lessons were university grade and she expected lengthy essays, based on reading and research of at least three books. All her students matriculated into university. She famously said that in high school if students fail it's the teachers' fault, but at university if the students fail, it's their own fault. She taught us how to read, but also to love reading for entertainment and for education. I believe she created a group of lifelong learners in us. —*Class of 1960*

Mrs Kim Fenton Lamsam (1984–1994)

Mrs Lamsam (Figure 15.4.8), a DGS old girl, taught English, English literature, history, and liberal studies at DGS for ten years. She never ceased to be a fun-loving teacher who would play a trick on her students on April Fool's Day:

The shock in no way diminished 30 years on, recalling that big fat zero for my first-ever dictation at DGS! My heart would have sunk to the ocean depths had I not noticed that smiley face squiggle at the corner of the page, with scribbles: "Great pronunciation, girl!" Incredible. That great teacher back then saw not just the nought, but the girl behind it trying her best who went onto Oxbridge and a high-pressure career. —*Class of 1994*

Mrs Veronica Lee (2007–Present)

Mrs V. Lee (Figure 15.4.9) has been teaching English and General Studies at the Junior School for more than fourteen years. She has touched the hearts of many students:

I was notorious for chatting with my neighbour and singing during lessons. I clearly remember the day when Mrs Lee announced that I was the class monitress. Everyone thought Mrs Lee made a mistake! Little did we know that it was her intention to instil discipline through assigning responsibility. As class monitress, I witnessed the difficulty of keeping a class of 40 young girls in control. Consequently, I became more cooperative and attentive in class. I am grateful for Mrs Lee's trust in me, which brought about the change in my learning attitude. —*Class of 2018*

Miss Marjorie S. Maneely (1963–1967)

Miss Maneely (Figure 15.4.10) was a music teacher who left a lasting impact on many of her students even after they left DGS. Her signature quotations were "To teach is to touch a life forever" and "Teachers shape the future", and she surely walked the talk:

> I will always remember
> ... your snowy white curls,
> ... your raised arms "blessing" the choirs,
> ... your warm smile, your gentle yet strict discipline.
> I decided to become a teacher because of the significant impact you made on my life. If I could affect just one life, as you did mine, then it would be worth it all. By virtue of your influence, more than 3,000 young lives were moulded and blessed over the course of my teaching career. Thank you, Miss Marjorie S. Maneely. —*Class of 1965*

Miss Margaret Mansfield (1947–1950, 1956–1973)

Miss Mansfield (Figure 15.4.11) was from England and taught biology at DGS. She also engaged her students by teaching them how to play bridge. She was well liked among her students because she was renowned for a genuine interest in them and there was never a dull moment in her classes.

> She was a superb teacher. I remember one of her favourite quips was, "The fatter the lens, the better it bends". —*Class of 1960*

Mrs Nancy O'Connell (1953–1974)

Mrs O'Connell (Figure 15.4.12) was well remembered by old girls for being very strict and demanding when it came to pronunciation. For twenty-one years at DGS, she taught oral English and trained the girls for the Speech Festival. Students deeply appreciated Mrs O'Connell for teaching them how to pronounce and project their voices to the end of the hall well enough to win public speaking contest awards:

When Mrs O'Connell joined the school, she was an active member of the Hong Kong Stage Club and, I think, of the Garrison Players—both were drama societies formed by expatriate members of the civil service, the militaries, and teachers. They were very active in performing plays, especially exciting new plays in those eras. Apart from trying her best to help us with our oral English, she tried to give us exposure to English as it was used in dialogue. She used to take those of us who were interested to these performances. We were in the upper forms, but frankly could not follow everything, or understand very much of plays like Ionesco's *The Bald Prima Donna*, Jean Anouilh's *Antigone*, or John Osborne's *Look Back in Anger*. But the exposure was exciting. We started from what we could understand and from that began to explore. I remember Anouilh's definition of Tragedy, thought about it and read about it, and found it exhilarating to think that one could redefine words and concepts that already had a dictionary meaning. Going to those plays also stimulated my interest in verbal music and the dramatic arts. —*Class of 1956*

Mrs O'Connell was my oral teacher. I remember her dramatic teaching of prose, her yelling when the result was not up to her standard, and the big smiles when she saw the trophies that we won in the Speech and Music Festival. —*Class of 1976*

Dr Or Man Wai (2000–Present)

Dr M. W. Or (Figure 15.4.13) is a chemistry teacher who joined the DGS staff team more than twenty years ago. His students enjoy his lessons tremendously:

He always tried to bring joy to his classes even when we were busy preparing for the HKCEE/HKALE exams. He used humour in his teaching and showed us examples of how chemistry was applied in real life. It was great to be a student of Dr Or. —*Class of 2005*

Mr Daniel Pang (2013–2019)

Mr D. Pang (Figure 15.4.14) taught history for six years and was highly praised for his teaching style:

Many conceive history as a dry subject, yet Mr Pang's history lessons were a source of infinite amusement to us. When discussing the Cold War, he transformed before our eyes from a drably dressed civilian to a flashy and mysterious espionage agent. When teaching the Hong Kong module, we gained insight on cultural interaction through viewing English-language Cantonese Opera—a surprisingly amusing art form. When he sadly had to bid farewell to our class, he, referring to the bear metaphor for Russia, warmly referred to us as "bear cubs". Mr Pang himself has made history in DGS. —*Class of 2020*

Miss Helen Macgregor Paterson (1959–1971, 1972)

Miss Paterson (Figure 15.4.21, back row L3) taught physical education (PE) and was nick-named "Helen of Troy" because she was considered very beautiful by her students. She used to lament that the girls were like elephants as she tried to teach them to dance waltzes. She also had a very pleasant personality—cheerful, lively, warm, and kind:

> As you know, Miss Paterson is big. But you'd be amazed how with her size, she could run with unbelievable grace! In her long black skirt and long-sleeved knit top for the fall, she would run across the hockey field so fast, smoothly, and gracefully! It's as though underneath her skirt she was wearing some kind of skates and not sneakers! She hit the ball with such force too that it went from one side of the field to the other!
>
> What I remember most was the number of suitors she had! As a boarder, I saw the stream of young men who came for a date with Miss Paterson right after our breakfast on Saturdays!! Miss Paterson would talk to them at the window of the dining room. You can imagine how early they had to wake up and drive across town to call on her at DGS! —*Class of 1960*

Miss Elizabeth Stewart (1957–1966)

Miss Stewart (Figure 15.4.22, front row R4), from Scotland, taught English and was an excellent teacher of Shakespeare. Students remembered her Scottish flair and style in both the way she dressed and the way she spoke. Her lessons were regarded as university level, and she expected the same high standard from her students:

> She always swept into the classroom in her well-tailored and well-designed "frock". She titivated herself with make-up and splashed on an abundance of perfume, which had fragrance that always prompted us of her arrival to the classroom.
>
> We "did" *Macbeth* under her. The words of that play full of blood and gore still ring in my ear. Her methodical teaching has enabled us to pursue, appreciate, and imbibe more Shakespeare besides *Macbeth*. We speckled quotable quotes into our conversations quite like Cambridge or Oxford dons: Nothing is good or bad except thinking makes it so; What wound heals but by degree; To be, or not to be: that is the question . . . and so on and so on. —*Class of 1960*

Mrs Karen Tsang (2006–Present)

Mrs Tsang (Figure 15.4.15) is a psychology teacher who constantly provides moral support and cares for the well-being of her students:

> As the first group of students to sit for the A-Level exam, my classmates and I lacked confidence in ourselves and often worried about our future. During our struggles, Mrs

Tsang always encouraged us with her warm smile and said, "I believe in you girls, don't give up!" Under her guidance, for which we are forever grateful, we were able to grow and enjoy our final DGS years under the new curriculum. —*Class of 2018*

Mrs Lydia Moo Wong (1941, 1945–1971)

Mrs Moo Wong (Figure 15.4.22, front row L4), known to the students as Mrs Wang, was an English teacher in DGS:

> I rushed back to the classroom after PE lesson on a particularly hot afternoon for the next lesson. I was perspiring like mad. My face flushed, beads of sweat rolling down my cheeks. My hair dishevelled. My school uniform damp and askew. I must have been a sight.
>
> Mrs Wong appeared at the door, eyed me for a second and came in. Keeping her eyes on me, she slowly walked towards me. I tensed up, ready for a lecture on . . . oh so many things!
>
> She walked towards me, slowly, stood in the aisle a step away, turned round to face me, smiled and said, "Would you like to borrow my comb?"
>
> That was when I started to learn the art of conversation. —*Class of 1956*

Mrs Renee Leung Wong (2006–Present)

Mrs R. L. Wong (Figure 15.4.16) is an economics teacher who makes her lessons fun:

> Mrs R. L. Wong is memorable for her energetic teaching methods and hysterical jokes. She found an opportunity for humour in all aspects of economics—referring to taxes as "bombs", using vivid analogies to describe price elasticity of demand, and comparing GDP to our report cards. She made every lesson fun, enjoyable, and full of laughter. Her patience and passion in teaching imbued us with a love for economics, and instilled in us an eagerness to learn and improve. —*Class of 2020*

Mrs Rebecca Luen Yuen Yip (1958–1969, 1979–1982, 1985–1999)

Mrs Yip (Figure 15.4.17) was much loved and respected as an old girl, a Junior School teacher for seventeen years, and Headmistress for ten years:

> I had a particularly meaningful experience with Mrs Yip. While she was the Headmistress, she also trained me for the interschool Bible reading competition. Given my initial concept of a headmistress to be a distant authority, I was hesitant to visit her office, but the true Mrs Yip's respectful yet firm style quickly calmed my fears. I recall specific instructions—say "there, not dare". She was patient, effective, and precise in improving my performance. —*Class of 2000*

Non-teaching Staff

Our DGS memories would not be complete without commending the dedicated non-teaching staff at the school. A smile on their faces, a simple "Good morning", or their willingness to help behind the scenes all contribute to making our DGS experiences special and memorable.

瓊姐 (1950s–1970s)

瓊姐 (King Tse) was responsible for ringing the bell for the change of lessons. She was always hard-working without any complaints and was always seen wearing a smile on her face. An alumna from the Class of 1955 shared a wonderful and inspirational story about 瓊姐: she got married in China, but not long after the wedding, her husband went to the US to study and to make his fortune. When the Second World War broke out, she became separated from the rest of the family. 瓊姐 and her little daughter made their way to Hong Kong, and she was hired as the school's seamstress for the boarders. She was later redeployed to work in the office and to ring the bell. She continued to work as the "office girl" for many years. 瓊姐 became a devout Christian who prayed to the Lord every day in hope of finding her husband. With the help of a long lost relative, she finally found the US address of her husband. 瓊姐's daughter wrote to her father, and before long, her father, who had never remarried, replied and made arrangements for a reunion. He finally took 瓊姐 to live with him in the US. Another alumna recalled:

> I can see her in front of me even today, in her Chinese jacket and pants [衫褲] very skinny but seemingly ageless, protecting one ear with her hand while ringing the bell in the courtyard with the other. —*Class of 1960*

根叔 (1980s–1990s)

根叔 (Gun Suk) (Figure 15.4.24, front row R5), lifeguard at the school, was fondly remembered for his tanned skin and white vest, holding a long net to clear the leaves in the swimming pool. Students were grateful that he taught them how to dive and that he worked through many summer holidays when they returned to school for swimming practice. An old girl from the Class of 1986 called him "the best lifeguard and teacher".

Ms Mok Yin Fong, 芳姐 (1997–2016)

芳姐 (Fong Tse) (Figure 15.4.18) was best remembered as a great assistant head chef:

She would help us patiently with our cooking so that at least we could make something edible, as sometimes we just lacked the ability to comprehend what Mrs P. Hui or Mrs A. Wong demonstrated. 芳姐 always cleaned up our big mess after cookery classes. We appreciated her help greatly. —*Class of 2005*

Mr Billy Chi Wah Woo, 細華叔 (2007– 2016, 2017– Present)

In the mornings, Junior School janitor 細華叔 (Sai Wah Suk) (Figure 15.4.19) would sit in the lift and say "早晨" (good morning) to each girl who walked into the elevator. This simple gesture lifted the spirits of many and gave the girls a cheerful start to the long day ahead:

After the last lesson every day, 細華叔 would come by the classrooms to "shoo us away". A school day is never complete without 細華叔 saying "快 D 啦!" (hurry up!) through the door before coming in to have a quick, friendly chat, handing us a few candies, and leading us to the stairs. —*Class of 2024 (left in 2017 after P5)*

Figure 15.4.1: Mrs Daphne Quay Ying Blomfield

Figure 15.4.2: Mrs Clare Cheung

Figure 15.4.3: Miss Peggy Man Lai Cheung

Figure 15.4.4: Mrs Christina Chiang

Figure 15.4.5: Mrs Poppy Crosby

Figure 15.4.6: Mrs Emily Tin Mei Dai

Figure 15.4.7: Mrs Inger Kvan and her daughter Elizabeth Kvan

Figure 15.4.8: Mrs Kim Fenton Lamsam

Figure 15.4.9: Mrs Veronica Lee

Figure 15.4.10: Miss Marjorie S. Maneely

Figure 15.4.11: Miss Margaret Mansfield

Figure 15.4.12: Mrs Nancy O'Connell

Figure 15.4.13: Dr Or Man Wai

Figure 15.4.14: Mr Daniel Pang

Figure 15.4.15: Mrs Karen Tsang

Figure 15.4.16: Mrs Renee Leung Wong

Figure 15.4.17: Mrs Rebecca Luen Yuen Yip

Figure 15.4.18: Ms Mok Yin Fong, 芳姐

Figure 15.4.19: Mr Billy Chi Wah Woo, 細華叔

Figure 15.4.20: DGS Staff 1956. Back row: Mrs Lydia Moo Wong (R4), Mrs Nancy O'Connell (R3); Middle row: Mr Chan Yik Cham (L1); Front row: Mr Lawrence S. L. Chan (L5), Miss Margaret Mansfield (R2), Miss Norah Edwards (R1).

Figure 15.4.21: Miss Helen Macgregor Paterson (back row L3) with the rounders team, 1960.

Figure 15.4.22: English (Arts) Class Lower Six, 1961. Front row: Mrs Lydia Moo Wong (L4), Miss Elizabeth Stewart (R4).

Figure 15.4.23: DGS Staff in 1971–1972. Middle row: Mr Chan Yik Cham (L5), Mrs Inger Kvan (R1); Front row: Mrs Nancy O'Connell (L1), Miss Margaret Mansfield (L2).

Figure 15.4.24: DGS Non-teaching Staff, 1985–1986; 根叔 (front row R5).
Source: From DOGA Archives, *Quest* of respective years and individual teachers.

Chapter 16

Diocesan Old Girls' Association

Yvonne Chan (1980) and Andrea Lai (1990)

The Founding Years

The Diocesan Old Girls' Association (DOGA) was founded in 1926 by an enthusiastic group of old girls, who were dedicated to building an alumnae body under the guidance of Miss H. D. Sawyer.[1] While no official records for the first year of DOGA are available, nine letters replying to a tea invitation on 12 July 1926 formed the first informal records of the association's activities. They revealed that Miss Irene Ho Tung (Class of 1917),[2] in the true spirit of DGS fellowship, had undertaken the recruitment of DOGA members over a tea gathering in Shanghai. The letters also disclosed the existence of an inaugural booklet that Miss Maria Kacker (Class of 1920) had circulated to old girls.[3]

Correspondence from 1927 onwards indicated that Miss E. D. Skipton assumed the role of DOGA president from April 1927 to 1929 after her retirement to London.[4] Although the identities of the other officers of its General Committee (GC) could not be confirmed, archives of meeting minutes from May 1929 showed that DOGA was well served by an elected GC of ten. This included a president, a DGS Headmistress as the first vice-president, a second vice-president, a secretary, a treasurer, and an associate member, who was a member of the DGS staff responsible for arranging DOGA activities at school. Convenors

---

1. "The Diocesan Old Girls' Association Section", *The Quest* (1941): 21.
2. 鄭宏泰、黃紹倫，《三代婦女傳奇：何家女子》（香港：三聯書店，2010），180.
3. "Old Girls' Section", *Quest* (1964): 92.
4. Letter to Miss E. D. Skipton from the DOGA Hon Secretary, 30 April 1927, DOGA Archives; Memorandum from Mrs A. E. Matthews to Miss M. Kacker, 9 May 1928, DOGA Archives.

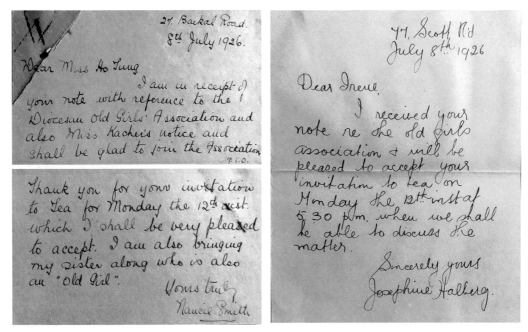

Figure 16.1: Letters from alumnae in Shanghai to Miss Irene Ho Tung, 1926. Source: DOGA Archives.

for sports, entertainment, and catering were also appointed from members to assist in the organisation of events.

The association's inception years were preoccupied with increasing alumnae membership through the organisation of activities. With fifty-eight members on board by its second year, DOGA's GC sought support for its first social function in 1927—a dance held at DGS on 27 May, with mah-jong and bridge available beforehand. Sporting activities, being at the heart of DGS culture, became the focus of the committee's efforts. Tailored blue sports blazers, badges, and brooches were made for sale, and a full range of sports activities were offered. These included tennis on DGS courts on Saturdays, hockey on Fridays and Saturdays, bathing launches (boating trips) leaving once a week on Thursdays from Queen's Pier at 5:20 pm, and physical culture (physical fitness) classes with instructors on request. An ambitious project was explored by the committee in August 1927—to build a members' clubhouse, modelled on the same lines as the Kowloon Football Club, which had a wooden structure with a veranda around it.[5] The pavilion was to be located on the new school playground, with permission from DGS. However, government grants in 1928 partially funded a new sports pavilion for the school on the same playground. This might have caused DOGA to eventually abandon its clubhouse project in April 1928.

---

5. Letter to Miss Grose from the DOGA Honorary Secretary, 16 August 1927, DOGA Archives.

Giving back was a priority of the association, and the annual school bazaar was an opportunity for old girls to raise funds through serving tea and selling handicrafts at the DOGA stall. However, astute investment of the association's reserves was seen as the best way of ensuring long-term support for the school. Under the stewardship of Miss W. Robinson, the president of DOGA, the association's reserves grew sufficiently in 1931 to allow a $2,000 investment in 6 per cent yielding Hong Kong Government Bonds. This funded the establishment of a DOGA scholarship in 1932, which enabled an award of $60 each year to a Class IV (equivalent to Form 3 from 1951 onwards) student of merit, as well as further donations towards sports shields and school activities.

To forge a closer bond with existing students, DOGA welcomed graduating classes as guests to annual dinners, and invited Classes I to IV (equivalent to Lower 6 to Form 3) to participate in "At Home" (events held at DGS) socials and sports matches. To further prepare them for life beyond graduation, DOGA offered extracurricular classes to students in cookery, hygiene, physical culture, science, and the arts. Moreover, alumnae members answered to appeals from the Headmistress, Miss H. D. Sawyer, for help towards DGS orphans and to train as Guide officers. Support was also pledged to the new kindergarten in Kowloon Tong, which would be opened to reduce the large class sizes on the Jordan Road campus.[6] As a testament to the service of the association, Bishop R. O. Hall remarked at a School Council meeting that the school was at a loss without a representative from DOGA on its committee. This led to the president of DOGA being invited to become a permanent member of the School Council from 1938 onwards.[7]

The Post-war Years

The Diocesan Schools were badly damaged during the Second World War and had to appeal for funds in the newspapers. Although DGS was able to restart classes quickly, funding was needed for a new concrete roof and the upkeep of thirty-one orphans.[8] In order to help the school get back on its feet again, Miss A. W. Hurrell, the DGS Headmistress, expressed a strong wish for DOGA to be restarted as soon as possible. Aside from re-equipping classrooms, her requests included support towards reviving the school magazine and sponsorship for school orphans. A special appeal was made to DOGA to seek replacement photographs of Bishop J. C. Hoare (Bishop of Victoria and South China 1898–1906), who revived the Diocesan Female School as the Diocesan Girls' School and Orphanage in 1899, the Rev. N. C. Pope and the Rev. G. R. Lindsay; three former headmistresses, Mses

---

6. Minutes of the Annual General Meeting of DOGA, 27 April 1933.

7. Letter to Mrs A. E. Matthews from Miss H. D. Sawyer, 21 June 1938, DOGA Archives; Miss A. E. Matthews's acceptance letter, 22 June 1938, DOGA Archives.

8. Minutes of a General Committee Meeting of DOGA, 8 January 1947.

Diocesan Old Girls' Association

E. D. Skipton, C. A. Ferguson and H. D. Sawyer; and benefactors such as Miss Margaret Johnstone, Miss Fletcher, Miss A. J. Dulmage, Miss N. Bascombe, and Miss M. Hawker.[9] Location of their photographs would allow their portraits to be restored to the DGS Main Hall.

Having lost all records of members' subscriptions, and retaining only two Government Bonds and $440 interest due from them, the association immediately called an Extraordinary General Meeting in October 1946, within two weeks of Miss A. W. Hurrell's requests. Mrs Winifred Penny was elected as DOGA president, and an appeal was made for voluntary donations and subscriptions to "resuscitate" the association.[10] In the same meeting, Mrs Maria Fincher (née Kacker) and Miss Irene Ho Tung undertook the redrafting of the DOGA constitution with the support of a special subcommittee. The essence of this document is still embodied in the constitution today, with a fourfold mission stated in its initial objects:

(i)   To foster and maintain contact between old girls of Diocesan Girls' School.
(ii) To promote and encourage social intercourse between them.
(iii) To further the interests and welfare of past and present members of Diocesan Girls' School and to create a bond of fellowship between them.
(iv) To establish, maintain and conduct a social club for the accommodation of members of the association.

To assist the school in its restoration, an Old Girls' Appeal was set up to solicit funds for school furniture and equipment from alumnae and parents, as well as donations of gifts in kind, such as school library books, which had all but disappeared. Conscious of a general sense of despondency after the war, Mrs Winifred Penny rallied the members in an impassioned plea to support the school at DOGA's annual general meeting (AGM) in April 1947. In her opinion, the challenges that they faced were:

> Something to live for . . . If we believed in something sincerely and thoughtfully, then let us do something about it. If we think the school is a good thing, then let us do something about it . . . The task was a stupendous one if we attempted to do it alone but as one of the greatest missionaries once said, I can do all things through Christ who strengthens me.[11]

On what was described by Miss A. W. Hurrell as the greatest day of the school year—Founders' Day on 18 Sept 1947—DOGA's donation of portraits of the founder, former headmistresses, and benefactors of DGS were fittingly unveiled. Fixtures such as benches

---

9. Minutes of an Extraordinary General Meeting of DOGA, 30 October 1946, and Minutes of a General Committee Meeting of DOGA, 8 January 1947.
10. Minutes, 30 October 1946.
11. Minutes of the Annual General Meeting of DOGA, 25 April 1947.

and candlesticks from the association and alumnae were also gifted in time for the hallowing of the new chapel.[12] By the next AGM in 1948, DOGA had raised $1,835 from members' voluntary subscriptions and donations, and $2,108 from the Old Girls' Appeal fund, of which $1,000 was used to furnish a boarders' sitting room. The incoming DOGA president, Mrs C. J. Symons, subsequently suggested the establishment of a Headmistress Discretionary Fund to either support disadvantaged girls through university, or to clothe the many orphans who were dependent on the school. After she became DGS Headmistress in 1953, Mrs Symons continued to work closely with DOGA to give guidance on the needs of the school, which resulted in DOGA's increased participation in the funding of school projects.

Membership

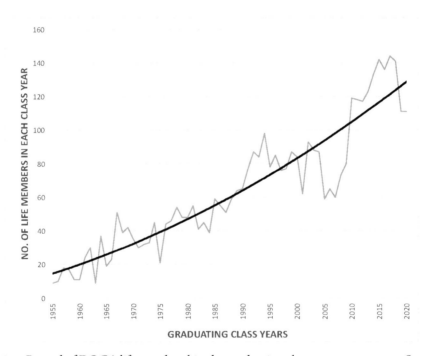

Figure 16.2: Record of DOGA life memberships by graduating class year, 1955 to 2019. Source: DOGA Archives.

The DOGA 1948 constitution, *Rules of the Diocesan Old Girls' Association, Hong Kong*, defined membership under four categories: Ordinary (annual), Life, Associate, and

---

12. Minutes of a General Committee Meeting of DOGA, 10 September 1947; *The Quest* (1947): 7.

Honorary Members. Any old girl of DGS who had completed at least one academic year at the school was eligible to become a member. To attract and retain members, annual subscriptions of $3 for Ordinary and Associate members and $50 for Life members were set in the post-war period. In spite of this, total membership only averaged around 250 per year by the mid-1950s, with three-quarters being Ordinary subscribers. To avoid an overdependence on annual renewals, Ordinary subscriptions were abolished in the 1960s and the association saw a steady migration to Life memberships. Subsequent membership drives and the establishment of class representatives have ensured the continuous growth of new members. With the advent of more activities catered for young alumnae, the proportion of students registering for membership in each graduating class since 2010 has increased to more than 70 per cent. Today, DOGA has over 4,000 members, including 122 junior members (under eighteen years old), who were welcomed to the association from 2014 onwards (Figure 16.2).

The Roles of DOGA

The primary goals of DOGA today remain largely similar to those under its 1948 constitution with extended objectives to encompass wider causes, such as aid to the disadvantaged and suffering to exemplify the ethos of the school motto, "Daily Giving Service". The association also commits to provide assistance to Junior and Senior School activities and projects, reflecting the role that DOGA has played in the history of the school—not only as a custodian of its past, but as a champion of its present and future.

Honouring the Past

In honour of the pivotal role played by former headmistresses, DOGA has acted as a facilitator for the reunion of retired headmistresses and the DGS community on many special occasions.

To commemorate the school's Centenary in 1960, DOGA answered to a call by Mrs C. J. Symons to bring back three former DGS headmistresses from the United Kingdom to celebrate with the school.[13] Together with old girls, DOGA sponsored the passages of Miss H. D. Sawyer, Miss E. M. Gibbins, and Miss A. W. Hurrell to Hong Kong for three weeks. In the first ever fashion show co-presented by DGS Parent Teacher Association (PTA) and DOGA in the DGS Centenary Hall and themed as "The Hong Kong Debutante", the association was able to raise funds for the headmistresses' passages by staging an event described by all as beautiful and innovative.

---

13. C. J. Symons, *Looking at the Stars: Memoirs by Catherine Joyce Symons* (Hong Kong: Pegasus Books, 1996), 57.

Figure 16.3: (Upper) Left to right: Mrs C. J. Symons, Miss A. W. Hurrell, Miss E. M. Gibbins, and Miss H. D. Sawyer (seated), attending DGS Centenary celebration; (Lower) DOGA's successful fundraising event "The Hong Kong Debutante" which supported the ex-headmistresses' passages to Hong Kong. Source: *DOGA Homecoming Carnival, 2000*, 10; *China Mail* and *Quest* 1960, 34.

In celebration of Dr C. J. Symons's thirty years as a DGS Headmistress, DOGA held a dinner in her honour in 1983, and on her retirement in 1985, organised a dinner of even grander proportions at the Regent Hotel in Hong Kong. This was attended by old girls from all over the world, including those from London, Vancouver, Toronto, San Francisco, Los Angeles, Sydney, and Melbourne—all bearing testimony to a Headmistress whom they loved and honoured. It was such a moving occasion for Dr C. J. Symons that she later wrote in her memoirs: "My heart nearly broke".[14] To commemorate her retirement, DOGA established the Dr C. J. Symons Overseas Scholarship (renamed the Dr C. J. Symons Scholarship in 1990), to be presented annually to a graduate who best exemplified the qualities of a DGS girl, as envisioned by Dr Symons in her memoir *Looking at the Stars*.[15]

After her retirement to the United Kingdom, DOGA sponsored Dr Symons's return to Hong Kong on many occasions, such as the school's one-hundred-and-thirtieth and one-hundred-and-fortieth Anniversary celebrations in 1990 and 2000. Unfortunately, ill health prevented Miss E. M. Gibbins from accepting DOGA's invitation to Hong Kong in 1990, so the association gifted her the equivalent cost of her passage and hotel accommodation instead. Mrs Rebecca Yip, a former Headmistress of the Junior School, was also sponsored by DOGA to return to Hong Kong to officiate at the one-hundred-and-fortieth Anniversary events in 2000. Upon Dr Symons's passing on 11 June 2004, DOGA created a guest book on its website in her memory, and lent assistance to the school at her memorial service at St John's Cathedral on 13 July 2004. In lieu of flowers, donations were requested to be made towards the Dr C. J. Symons Scholarship Fund.

Evolving in the New Millennium

The activities of DOGA today continue to flourish under the tireless efforts of its twelve subcommittees—Art, Careers and Scholarship, Choir, Community Services, Editorial, Finance, Information Technology, Legal, Membership, Secretarial, Social, and Sports. With the formation of the Choir, Sports, Community Services, and Art subcommittees after 2000, DOGA's role as a social club for alumnae expanded rapidly. Together with Social and Membership subcommittees, fellowship among old girls is now promoted through regular events such as Art Club workshops, annual dinners, music concerts, netball tournaments, and New Year visits to nursing homes.

The launch of DOGA's website (www.doga.org.hk) in 1998 marked the beginning of virtual updates of DOGA activities and alumnae news. This has been further supplemented by regular DOGA e-newsletters and features within *Kaleidoscope*, the school newsletter. To ensure that the DOGA community can stay connected by more than one means, DOGA later achieved another milestone by introducing online activities from its Art, Community Services, Social, Choir, and Membership subcommittees.

To advance the welfare of young graduates, the Membership subcommittee has provided study and career support to young members in recent years. A successful mentoring programme was initiated in 2006, which has nurtured close to 400 young alumnae over

---

14. Symons, *Looking at the Stars*, 90.
15. Symons, *Looking at the Stars*, 56.

Figure 16.4: DOGA subcommittee activities clockwise from top left: Social Subcommittee workshop, Diocesan Graduate Singers Concert, DGS Careers Fair, Art Club workshop, Flag Day for community services, DOGA annual dinner, Membership Mentoring Programme, Netball competition. Source: DOGA Archives.

fourteen years. University Groups and Professional Interest Groups have subsequently been formed, where young members can benefit from study and career guidance generously offered by their older "sisters" within the same university or field. The Careers and Scholarship subcommittee also supports current students by inviting alumnae to engage in informal career and college counselling at DGS career and university fairs. In addition, the subcommittee selects a student from the graduating class each year for the Dr C. J. Symons Scholarship, and awards the recipient $160,000 in support of her tertiary studies.

To cater for the broadening complexities of the twenty-first century, the association was incorporated in August 2001 as Diocesan Old Girls' Association Limited, a company limited by guarantee. DOGA's charitable activities, educational projects, and scholarship sponsorships were placed under Diocesan Old Girls' Association Foundation Limited, a wholly owned tax-exempt charity, to facilitate fundraising and to conserve the association's assets. To meet the obligations of corporatisation and to serve its growing membership, the operation of DOGA has become an increasingly complex affair that requires the combined efforts of the Finance, Information Technology, Legal, and Secretarial subcommittees to provide essential administrative support and guidance in compliance with relevant ordinances.

Table 16.1: New school buildings and major improvements of school facilities supported by DOGA from 1956 to the present*

Year	Projects
1956–1959	Centenary Building Development i) Assisted in the DGS Scheme B campaign and raised funds from old girls. ii) Donated a classroom named after DOGA.
1992–1993	DGS Building Extension (Phase 1) i) Co-organised the Walkathon at Shatin to fundraise for Phase 1, with DOGA coordinating logistics and event programmes. ii) Donated a Lecture Room named after DOGA HK.
1995–1996 1996	DGS Building Extension (Phase II) i) Co-sponsored the school fundraising musical The King and I.
1998–2006 1998 2000 2000 2001 2005 2006	DGS Upgrade of Teaching Facilities i) Donated a second computer room (Computer Room B) and hardware to the Senior School. ii) Raised funds from a Homecoming Carnival, for the upgrade of the Computer Room B to enable a second AS-level Computer Applications class. iii) Co-sponsored the school fundraising musical Wizard of Oz, with performance participation from old girls. iv) Donated DOGA Place, an extra venue for club meetings and relaxation at DGS. v) Co-sponsored the original school musical The DGS Girl at the Shatin Town Hall, with DOGA in the role of ticketing. vi) Donated funds to upgrade school computers with the latest software.
2007–2011 2007–09 2008 2010	DGS Quest: Building on Excellence Campaign i) Donated a Lecture Room for the new Senior School. ii) Co-sponsored the Walkathon Family Fun Day. Organised "Walk the Path", "Search the School" activities, and souvenir sales. iii) Co-sponsored the 150th Anniversary Fundraising Dinner, and entrusted with many roles, from legal counsel to the production of a symbolic "150" centrepiece cake.
2011–2013	DOGA Alumnae Wall Campaign i) Established the Alumnae Wall around the new DOGA Place on the redeveloped campus with funds raised from alumnae and students. ii) Donated a DOGA Bench in front of the Alumnae Wall.

Source: DOGA Archives and School Council Reports.

*Due to the loss of records between 1960 to 1990, some contributions from DOGA to the school may be omitted.

Figure 16.5: Unveiling ceremony of Alumnae Wall, 2013. Source: DOGA Archives.

Giving Back

With every school facility upgrade comes an opportunity for DOGA and its members to give back to their alma mater, through the association's own fundraising campaigns, as well as school musicals, walkathons, and dinners that DOGA co-sponsors with the DGS PTA and the School Council (see Table 16.1).

The unveiling of the Alumnae Wall, a beautiful curved wall around the new DOGA Place Garden on 17 January 2013, marked the completion of the largest fundraising campaign that DOGA had launched. This was in support of the 2007 DGS Quest: Building on Excellence Campaign for the redevelopment of the school campus. To raise awareness of the project, DOGA hosted a series of memorable homecoming events before the redevelopment, including an annual dinner for over 1,000 old girls, a Homecoming Lunch, and a DOGA Art Day. Through the collective efforts of old girls, $10 million was raised from the Alumnae Wall Campaign. A combination of 451 large and small dedication tiles were subscribed by current students, individual alumnae, and class groups spanning over nine decades, with the names of family and group inscriptions arranged in their own clusters on the Wall.

Growing from Strength to Strength

> Much has been achieved since we started but there is no reason we should rest on our oars . . . the boat DOGA is launched but it has to be manned as well as officed . . . If members will practise more of Tolstoy's idea of morality, by giving more than they get, the future of the association will be assured. —*Miss W. Robinson, DOGA president, 1934*[16]

Without doubt, the success of DOGA has greatly rested on the dedication of its officers and support from its members. A few exemplary officers devoted a large part of their lifetimes to serving the General Committee and have assured the continuity of the association. The late Mrs Maria Fincher served on the board from its founding (1926–1948, 1955–1961), and Mrs Grace Lam (née Lee) has served DOGA for more than five decades from the 1970s to the present. Dr. Vivian Wong (née Taam) was the longest serving DOGA president at thirteen years. Many ex-presidents continued their long service with the school through the DGS School Council (as shown in Table 16.2).

Over the early years of the association, the success of DOGA would not have been possible without the school's support, with DGS playing host to most of the association's activities on campus. In return, DOGA has not hesitated to step up to assist the school in times of need, in the pre-war period, and in its rehabilitation after the war. This reciprocal

---

16. Minutes of the Annual General Meeting of DOGA, 25 April 1934.

relationship continues to stand strong today. Since 2012, the school has provided DOGA with a dedicated room at the new campus, and many DOGA activities, including netball matches, choir rehearsals, concerts, and AGMs continue to be held at school. DOGA, on the other hand, is always a ready partner at school's events and fundraising exercises. From its modest origins as a social club for members, DOGA has evolved into an avid supporter for students and young graduates through the organisation of in-school career support, university groups for matriculated students, and mentoring programmes with alumnae. These efforts, together with donations of scholarships, underpin DOGA's aim to support our alumnae on a path to success beyond the school. In this way, the school and DOGA have been, and will continue to be, truly complementary partners in each other's success.

Table 16.2: Past and present presidents of DOGA

Year	Name
1927–1929	Miss Skipton Elizabeth D
1929–1930	Mrs Lo Man Kam (Ho Tung Victoria)
1930–1935	Miss Robinson Winifred
1938–1940	Mrs Matthews A M Ethne
1940–1941, 1946	Mrs D'Almada e Castro Leo*
1947–1948	Mrs Penny Winifred*
1948–1951	Mrs Symons Catherine Joyce
1951–1953	Mrs Yeo Florence (née Ho Tung)
1953–1955	Mrs Mackie Molly J B
1955–1961	Mrs Fincher Maria*
1961–1963	Mrs Leonard Eva
1963–1964	Ms Wong Betty
1964–1965	Ms Chan M
1965–1966	Mrs Lo M
1966–1969	Mrs Lo Hester*
1969–1974	Mrs Mok Gladys*
1974–1982	Mrs Fok Katherine*
1982–1991	Mrs Ho Doris*
1991–1993	Mrs Chang Josephine*
1993–2006	Dr Wong Vivian
2006–2010	Ms Pang Loretta
2010–2014	Ms Ng Jane
2014–present	Ms Chan Yvonne

Source: DOGA Archives.

Note: Due to incomplete records, we cannot confirm the identities of DOGA Presidents in 1926, 1936, 1937.

*These presidents continued to serve the school through the DGS School Council after retiring from their positions at DOGA.

Chapter 17

Diocesan Girls' School Parent Teacher Association

Sheilah Chatjaval (1978)

Beginnings

DGS has probably the oldest Parent Teacher Association (PTA) in Hong Kong. It was one of the first schools to recognise the importance of building a strong working relationship with parents, and the value of having parents from diverse backgrounds and different perspectives coming together to work with the school and its teachers for the benefit of the school and its students. DGS's PTA was formed in 1951, and at the school's one-hundred-and-sixtieth anniversary it will have entered its seventieth year of existence. It remains active and busy, and plays a vital role in many aspects of student life.

In a circular letter addressed to all parents of DGS in June 1951, Miss A. W. Hurrell, then Headmistress of the school, proposed starting a PTA. It was felt that closer cooperation and more frequent contacts between teachers and parents would be most desirable. The suggestion was to hold meetings during which a short talk on some aspect of school life, on careers, on problems connected with the children would be given, followed by informal discussion. It would thus afford an opportunity to ask questions on matters of common interest to teachers and parents.[1]

On 15 June 1951, the first gathering of teachers and parents was held in the School hall at 8:00 pm with about one hundred present. A motion in favour of organising the PTA was carried unanimously. An Executive Committee of eleven, including eight representatives

---

1. DGS PTA Booklet, 1955–1956.

Diocesan Girls' School Parent Teacher Association
385

of parents, was elected.[2] On 20 June 1952, at an Ordinary General Meeting of the PTA, the first Rules governing it were passed.[3]

Membership of the PTA quickly grew. By the third year of its inception, the PTA had a membership of well over 200. Among its activities, besides the social evenings and discussion meetings, the PTA published a parents' directory, offered help with the school's Annual Bazaar, and offered a number of scholarships to students of merit.[4] The PTA also started to hold meetings at which parents and teachers could meet and discuss students' progress in a more intimate setting and for a closer interchange of views.[5] A letter dated 19 June 1953 from Mrs Symons, then Headmistress of DGS, to the PTA extended an invitation for the Chair of the PTA to serve on the School Council, thus beginning a tradition by which the Chair of the PTA serves in an ex officio capacity as a Council member.[6]

By 1 June 1956, the PTA had officially been registered under the Societies Ordinance. On 11 April 1957, an Extraordinary General Meeting was held at which the Rules of the PTA were revised and amplified. Among the changes was an amendment to Rule 3 of the PTA's Rules, making all parents automatically members of the PTA without the need for an application and a change to Rule 7 eliminating the need for any membership fee.[7] The intention behind the changes was to increase the number of parents involved in the PTA.

In the initial years after the formation of the PTA, in addition to increasing parental membership and participation in the PTA, another concern was the raising of funds for the PTA scholarships and other expenses. In addition to membership subscription prior to their abolition in 1957, other methods of raising funds included collecting gate receipts at the annual school bazaars, manning a stall at the bazaar,[8] a tradition that started in 1954, soliciting parents' donations, as well as investing the PTA scholarship funds to achieve capital growth. It is interesting to note that a summary of the PTA accounts for the year ending 30 June 1957 revealed that almost 10 per cent of the revenues from the PTA Scholarship Fund came from dividends from the PTA's investment in 134 shares of China Light & Power.[9] In the following fiscal year, the PTA purchased an additional 26 shares of China Light & Power.[10] It was clearly a very enterprising PTA from the start!

---

2. Minutes of a Meeting of DGS Parents and Staff, 15 June 1951.

3. Minutes of an Ordinary General Meeting of the PTA, 20 June 1952.

4. Minutes of a Meeting of the Executive Committee of the PTA, 25 January 1952.

5. PTA Annual Report, 1955–1956.

6. Minutes of a Meeting of the Executive Committee of the PTA, 19 June 1953.

7. Minutes of an Extraordinary General Meeting of the PTA, 11 April 1957.

8. Minutes of a Meeting of the Executive Committee of the PTA, 25 June 1954.

9. Receipts and Payments Account of the PTA from 1 July 1956 to 30 June 1957.

10. Receipts and Payments Account of the PTA from 1 October 1957 to 30 September 1958.

PTA Fundraising Efforts

The PTA, along with the Diocesan Old Girls' Association (DOGA), was instrumental in helping the school with important fundraising projects. The first of such projects was the raising of funds for school expansion to mark the centenary celebration of the school in 1956, for which the PTA agreed to subscribe to the Centenary Building Fund Scheme B, calling for voluntary contributions by each parent of HK$200 or any sum payable two years from 1 April 1956.[11] This Centenary Drive by the school with the PTA's endorsement came into operation on 15 June 1956. By August 1956, $35,000 had been paid up for Scheme B with about $50,000 in additional pledges.[12]

The 1964/1965 school year saw the completion of the largest PTA project up to that date—the construction and completion of the school's swimming pool at the corner of the school grounds. The 25-metre swimming pool was made possible by a donation appeal to parents organised by the PTA, and it officially opened on 9 July 1965.[13]

In 1992, the PTA also assisted in the school's fundraising drive for a new building extension that would house the Junior School library, a computer room, an arts room, a medical room, and two classrooms. It organised a Walkathon with the objective of giving every student the sense of pride that they had personally contributed in a meaningful way to

Figure 17.1: *Quest* 1964 swimming pool cartoon. Source: *Quest* 1964, 7.

---

11. Minutes of a Meeting of the Executive Committee of the PTA, 24 February 1956.
12. Minutes of a Meeting of the Executive Committee of the PTA, 10 August 1956.
13. Speech Day Booklet, 11 January 1966.

help build the school extension. The Walkathon was held on 18 October 1992, and this successful event raised $2.2 million for the school. Together with $8.1 million from the parent appeal letters, a total of $10.3 million was raised for the building extension.[14]

In the summer of 1995, the PTA undertook a major project to renovate three Junior School toilets with seven cubicles each. These toilets were in their original state, dating from 1975. The PTA carried out the tendering process and financed the project with parent donations, while the design of the toilets was made possible by a parent architect who donated his services.[15]

The PTA again played an important role in the fundraising efforts of the school for the new building extension phase II in 1995/1996 to house a new Junior School Hall, extra classrooms for additional classes, and special rooms to replace the former special rooms; these were to be used as a staffroom, two audiovisual rooms, and new science laboratories for the Senior School. This fundraising drive culminated in the musical *The King and I*, and volunteer parents played a key supporting role in the production's success.[16]

In July 2000, the school celebrated its one-hundred-and-fortieth anniversary and presented a fundraising musical, *The Wizard of Oz*. Over 280 volunteer parents helped in the production, and the performances raised over $7 million over three days for the school's redevelopment fund.

Again in September 2005, in celebration of the school's one-hundred-and-forty-fifth anniversary and as a fundraising drive for the establishment of the DGS Foundation, the PTA co-organised and co-sponsored the original musical production of *The DGS Girl* in partnership with the DOGA. It was a massive undertaking with hundreds of volunteer parents helping in all aspects including costumes, make-up, catering arrangements, ticketing, and advertising. It was a resounding success.

In 2007, the school launched a major fundraising campaign entitled the DGS Quest: Building On Excellence Campaign, with a target to raise $250 million over the following few years for the school's redevelopment programme. The main focus of this programme was the redevelopment and modernisation of the entire school campus, upgrading resources and equipment, and adding to the school's scholarship fund, financial aid, and staff development fund. The PTA undertook a leadership role in certain projects under this campaign, including organising an annual summer Read-A-Thon for students of both the Senior and Junior schools. The objectives of this were not only to help the school reach its fundraising target but also to promote a love of independent reading in each student. All participants in Read-A-Thon were required to read a minimum of five books, and the PTA

---

14. Minutes of the Annual General Meeting of the PTA, 28 October 1992.
15. Minutes of the Annual General Meeting of the PTA, 18 October 1995.
16. Minutes of the Annual General Meeting of the PTA, 23 October 1996.

Figure 17.2: Read-A-Thon sticker (designed by Vanessa Leung). Source: PTA.

provided suggested reading lists that were age appropriate. The grand prize for the class in each school (Senior and Junior) that raised the most money was a pizza party for the entire class, and there were also individual book voucher prizes for the top five student fundraisers in each school. However, the best prizes were the ones the students could not see—all of the great stories they would read, the better reading skills they would gain, and the satisfaction of knowing that they had played a part in contributing to the school's redevelopment programme. In the first year alone, over 870 students participated in the Read-A-Thon and over $1.4 million was raised.

Another project undertaken by the PTA in the DGS Quest: Building On Excellence Campaign was a Walkathon held on 10 May 2008. The Walkathon took place on the school campus and was a good opportunity for students, old girls, and parents to walk around the school one last time before it was demolished. There were over 1,300 registrants and it was a fun day for all.[17] The PTA also ran a special raffle ticket draw for the campaign, which raised $781,000 for the school.[18] Through its various fundraising activities and direct donations, the PTA contributed significantly to this campaign.

---

17. Minutes of a Meeting of the Executive Committee of the PTA, 6 May 2008.
18. Minutes of a Meeting of the Executive Committee of the PTA, 18 March 2010.

Governance and Activities

From its inception in 1951, the PTA was governed by an eleven-member Executive Committee comprising the Headmistress, the Mistress-in-Charge of the Junior School, and the Senior Chinese Master, all as ex-officio members, along with eight parent representatives.[19] Over the years, as the activities and responsibilities of the PTA expanded and the school management evolved, the composition and size of the Executive Committee also changed accordingly. The number of parent representatives on the PTA was increased from eight to twelve, as passed at an extraordinary general meeting of the PTA in October 1956.[20] The number of parent representatives continued to increase as the PTA took up more responsibilities and, at present, the Executive Committee consists of the Supervisor, the Headmistress of the Senior School, the Headmistress of the Junior School, two teachers, one from the Senior School and one from the Junior School as nominated by the school, and up to twenty parent representatives elected at each annual general meeting of the PTA.[21]

Since the beginning, the PTA has become a vital and integral part of DGS life, overseeing and managing many aspects of student life. Its Executive Committee in recent years has overseen many subcommittees and activities, including but not limited to the following:

Library Subcommittee and Chinese and English Book Clubs

The Library Subcommittee is responsible for running the Junior School library, with volunteer parents taking turns to man the library during lunchtime every day and conducting storytelling sessions. The library volunteers also ensure that library books are maintained in good condition and are properly catalogued and shelved. The parents belonging to the Chinese and English Book Clubs are responsible for screening and making book recommendations to the Junior School students for summer reading and organising authors' talks and book signing events.

Uniform Subcommittee

This subcommittee is responsible for working closely with school uniform suppliers to keep a watchful eye on the pricing and quality of school uniforms and sportswear and for running a uniform recycling programme. Although the styling of the basic DGS school winter and summer uniforms has not changed much since the 1940s, there have been

---

19. Minutes of a Meeting of DGS Parents and Staff, 15 June 1951.
20. Minutes of an Extraordinary General Meeting of the PTA, 5 October 1956.
21. Rules of the PTA, as Adopted at the PTA's Annual General Meeting, 30 September 2020.

some changes to the fabric and some additional optional items added, particularly sports uniforms. The Uniform Subcommittee of the PTA oversees these changes and the design of the new uniform items, and monitors their costs and quality. For instance, the winter uniform was modified in 2000 to make use of a new fabric for the winter tunics, skirts, and school blazers that is of a softer and lighter quality, and the style was improved for a better fit. In January 2001, the PTA introduced new grey DGS logo-embroidered cardigans and sleeveless pullovers as part of the school's winter uniform. In the 2012/2013 school year, an optional winter trench coat was also introduced.[22]

For the purposes of conservation and education for the students, the PTA Uniform Subcommittee also undertook a pilot project of winter uniform recycling in the last week of October 2002. Girls and parents of the Junior School were encouraged to bring back used uniforms for exchange and recycling. Encouraged by the favourable response, the subcommittee then carried out a second uniform recycling programme at the end of March 2003 for summer uniforms, and the Senior School was included. This uniform recycling project serves a useful function and is now carried out by the PTA on a regular basis.

Transportation Subcommittee

Arrangements for school bus routes and supervision of the school bus service provider including safety issues fall within the purview of the School Bus Subcommittee, which acts as a liaison between the school and the school bus service provider. The subcommittee deals with parent complaints and problems, oversees the opening of new bus routes, and helps to monitor school bus charges. The subcommittee also arranges transportation for school outings.

Lunchbox Subcommittee

Similarly, the Lunchbox Subcommittee is responsible for coordinating with lunch caterers and monitoring the quality of the lunchboxes. This subcommittee shortlists and reviews lunch caterers, arranges for visits to the food production facilities, and conducts tasting sessions to ensure that students have access to healthy, nutritious school meals at a reasonable price. It also organises a healthy cooking club for Junior School students.[23]

---

22. Minutes of the Annual General Meeting of the PTA, 27 September 2013.
23. Minutes of the Annual General Meeting of the PTA, 15 October 2015.

Seminar Subcommittee

This subcommittee is in charge of organising seminars and workshops for parents every year. In the early years of the PTA, a social evening was held at the school three times a year for parents and teachers to meet and get to know each other.[24] Over the years, the social evenings evolved into parent seminar evenings. The earliest such parent seminar took place in March 1955 when Miss Clements, a lecturer from Hong Kong University (HKU), was invited to give a talk on child psychology.[25] In November 1956, Miss Beryl Wright, another HKU lecturer, was invited to give a talk on patterns of child rearing.[26]

Topics covered by parent seminars in recent years include communication with children and understanding their world through literature, emotional intelligence in our children, building resilience in our new generation, how to identify and handle crisis in teenagers, how to deal with children's emotions effectively, how to enhance our children's Chinese learning skills, how to raise gender-confident children, instilling healthy positive culture in the family, parents' role in nurturing and managing guidelines for cyber citizenship, and win-win communication in the family.

Brownies Subcommittee

Parents from the PTA Brownies Subcommittee are trained as Brownie guiders. They collaborate with teachers to run Brownie packs for the Junior School.

Figure 17.3: Brownies packs, c. 2000. Source: Sheilah Chatjaval.

---

24. Minutes of a Meeting of the Executive Committee of the PTA, 28 September 1953.
25. Minutes of a Meeting of the Executive Committee of the PTA, 28 February 1955.
26. Minutes of a Meeting of the Executive Committee of the PTA, 2 November 1956.

Computers Subcommittee

This subcommittee works closely with the school to advise and support the school's expanding information technology programme. It also oversees the donation of computer equipment to the school.

Newsletter Subcommittee

Formed in 2001, this subcommittee serves to publish and distribute a PTA newsletter free of charge to all parents twice a year to keep them apprised of school and PTA activities. The inaugural issue was published in February 2002. In 2007, the school decided on the publication of a newsletter, the *DGS Kaleidoscope*, twice a year to keep all school stakeholders informed of the latest news and activities of the school, the PTA, the DOGA, and the school's Redevelopment Project Office. Not only did PTA members collect information and write articles for the PTA section of the newsletter, but the printing design and costs were also borne by parents, so that the newsletter could be distributed free of charge. The inaugural issue of the *DGS Kaleidoscope* was published in January 2008.[27]

Outings Subcommittee

The Outings Subcommittee, formed in the 1995/1996 academic year, is in charge of organising special outings and educational visits for Junior School students throughout the year, particularly after examination time, to give teachers time to work on their post-examination duties. In recent years, visits have been arranged to the Science Museum; the Lee Kum Kee factory; the Museum of History; the Garden Farm in Sai Kung; the Green Produce Farm in Fanling; the Holiday Farm; Ocean Park for guided tours on butterflies, birds, and fishes; the Nestlé Dairy Farm; Police Museum; School for the Deaf; and a tour of the Legislative Council building. These visits are an enormous undertaking and involve the help of many volunteer parents.

Swimming Subcommittee

This subcommittee was formed to work with representatives of the school's Aquatics Club to deal with pool-related matters, such as daily operations, maintenance of the pool, and running of swimming courses. The Aquatics Club was formed in November 2012 by the school to provide opportunities for students, old girls, and parents to enjoy the indoor

---

27. Minutes of a Meeting of the Executive Committee of the PTA, 3 March 2008.

Figure 17.4: PTA outing to the Holiday Farm, c. 2003. Source: Sheilah Chatjaval.

heated 25-metre swimming pool during non-school hours. The Swimming Subcommittee also assists, along with the Legal Subcommittee, in the tender process for the service provider for pool maintenance and swimming/training courses.

Legal Subcommittee

This committee was formed in September 2011 to advise the PTA and the school on matters relating to legal activities such as tendering and contracting, copyright issues relating to the school's website, and personal data requirements concerning parental consent forms.

PTA Scholarships

In January 1952, the PTA Executive Committee resolved to start a scholarship fund to assist students whose parents could not afford to pay the full school fees and books. This scholarship was to be awarded annually, and the selection of the deserving students was left to the school. In July 1952, the PTA decided that a total of nine scholarships each for $100 would be granted each year, in the ratio of six for the Senior School and three for the Junior

School.[28] In September 1952, the PTA also resolved to award a PTA prize to the best scholastic student in the Junior School and a prize to the student who renders the best social service in the Senior School.

The number of scholarships and amount awarded have continued to evolve and increase over the years. In 1957, when for the first time 50 per cent of the intake of students into Form I was from "outside" schools based on the Secondary School Entrance Examination, three girls whose financial circumstances seemed most to warrant it received a grant of $200.[29] The selection criteria of the PTA scholarships also evolved over the years, and they are now awarded to students who show "good conduct and dedication to service". In the 2019/2020 academic year, a total of thirty PTA scholarships each worth $1,000 were given to a Senior School student in each class, and forty-eight PTA scholarships each worth $500 were given to two students in each class in the Junior School.

In 1998, the PTA donated the Mrs Rebecca Yip Shield to be awarded annually to a Primary 6 girl with outstanding performance in scripture, conduct, and service. Upon Mrs Elim Lau's retirement, the PTA established the Elim Lau Cup, which is awarded annually to a Senior School student for excellence not only academically but also in music, services, and sports.[30] Similarly, on Mrs Emily Dai's retirement in 2017, the PTA created the Mrs Emily Dai Award—a scholarship given annually to a Primary 5 student who shows continuous improvement in conduct, learning attitude, application, and effort, as well as in maturity and academic progress.

Summer Camps, After-School Classes, and Other Ad Hoc Programmes

In recent years, the PTA has helped to organise summer camps for students conducted on school campus, ranging from science adventure camps introducing science concepts through interactive experiments, fun activities, and take-home science projects, to workshops on the playing of African drum music and Western percussion workshops. Other summer camps included IT courses such as web media design and coding and programming courses, conducted on the campus of the Hong Kong Polytechnic University. For the Senior School, the PTA organises after-school classes, primarily in Putonghua and foreign languages.

From time to time, the PTA also suggests and sponsors special programmes. For instance, in June 2002, the PTA sponsored a three-day student learning enhancement programme for Primary 6 students at the Hong Kong University of Science and Technology

---

28. Minutes of a Meeting of the Executive Committee of the PTA, 8 July 1952.
29. Minutes of a Meeting of the Executive Committee of the PTA, 2 November 1956.
30. Minutes of the Annual General Meeting of the PTA, 28 October 1999.

Figure 17.5: Fiftieth Anniversary celebration of PTA with current and past chairpersons of the PTA at the Annual General Meeting. Source: Sheilah Chatjaval.

(HKUST) entitled "Creative Thinking and Expression Day Camps". This unique programme was designed by the Centre for Enhanced Learning and Teaching at HKUST to help Junior School Primary 6 girls to develop their creative thinking and expression skills in the context of environmental issues. The programme consisted of a series of workshops conducted on campus at HKUST, with instructors from the university teaching the community using a mix of presentation, activities, and hands-on practice.

In addition to the activities described here, the PTA purchases teachers' retirement gifts, sponsors extracurricular activities such as coaching fees for sports, donates equipment, and improves facilities at the school. Each year, the PTA also donates trophies for athletics and swimming competitions, a tradition that started in 1954.[31]

Without a doubt, the PTA's strongest asset is its cadre of parent volunteers who help in so many ways with their time, donation, and sponsorship. With its active and multi-faceted contributions, the PTA plays a vital role within the school, supporting the school in many aspects, enhancing the communication between parents and teachers, and enriching the lives of the students. The PTA is a much-loved feature of the school and a significant factor contributing to the success of DGS.

---

31. Minutes of a Meeting of the Executive Committee of the PTA, 21 January 1954.

Table 17.1: Past and present PTA chairpersons

Year	Name
1951–1954	Mr Barma H T
1954–1955	Mr Cunningham E S
1955–1957	Dr Pan Francis K
1957–1958	Mr Cunningham E S
1958–1960	Mrs Wong Nancy Y H
1960–1961	Mr Lee E A
1961–1963	Mr Rainbow F E
1963–1964	Mr Pang K C
1964–1967	Mr Taylor D
1967–1970	Mr Bokhary S D S
1970–1971	Mrs Wilking J
1971–1975	Mr Lee Hon Wing
1975–1976	Mr Kwong William
1976–1979	Mr Sun Jeffrey
1979–1982	Mrs Lo Elizabeth
1982–1984	Mrs Lai Cordelia
1984–1987	Mr Billingham Nick I
1987–1989	Ms Cheung Stephanie
1989–1991	Mrs Chang Josephine
1991–1997	Mrs Ng Saw Kheng
1997–1999	Mrs Yeh Yolanda
1999–2000	Mrs Tang Lisa
2000–2009	Mrs Chatjaval Sheilah
2009–2013	Mrs Ho Yvette
2013–2015	Mrs Tcheng Fu Deirdre
2015–2019	Mrs Wong Chan Sherlynn
2019–present	Mrs Nip Christine

Source: PTA Archives.

Appendixes

Appendix 1

Chronicle of Major Events

Year	External	DGS
1842	Ceding of Hong Kong Island to the British	
1843	Ying Wa College moved to Hong Kong	
1858		Founding of **Day Girls' School (DGS)** by Mrs Lydia Smith in Albany Terrace
1860	Convention of Peking; cession of Kowloon	**Diocesan Native Female Training School (DNFTS)** founded by Mrs Lydia Smith with Ms Wilson as superintendent
1862	Central School founded	
1863		Miss M. A. W. Eaton took over as superintendent of DNFTS; DNFTS moved to new premises on IL831, corner of Bonham Road and Eastern Street
1864		Miss Eaton attacked
1865		Miss Eaton resigned
1866		Miss M. J. Oxlad became the superintendent; name of school changed to **Diocesan Female School (DFS)**
1869		DFS closed due to funding problem
1870		**Diocesan Home and Orphanage (DHO)**, coeducational, established in January 1870 in the same premises with Mr W. M. B. Arthur as headmaster
1873	Grant-in-aid Code introduced	

Year	External	DGS
1878		Mr Arthur left; crisis in DHO; attempts to reorganise as the DFS under the Female Education Society failed; the business community faction of DHO School Committee gradually changed DHO to a boys' school; DHO joined grant-in-aid scheme
1879		Mr G. H. Piercy became headmaster. Only day girls in DHO
1886	Cambridge Local Examinations introduced in Hong Kong	
1889	Oxford Local Examinations replaced Cambridge Local Examinations	
1892		All day girls transferred to Fairlea School; DHO renamed **Diocesan School and Orphanage** (**DSO**) and subsequently became Diocesan Boys' School
1894	Bubonic plague hit Hong Kong; First Sino-Japanese War	
1898	New Territories leased to the British for 99 years	
1899		**Diocesan Girls' School and Orphanage** founded at Rose Villa West; Miss E. Skipton as headmistress
1900		Diocesan Girls' School and Orphanage renamed **Diocesan Girls' School** (**DGS**); DGS became a grant-in-aid school
1901	Education Committee appointed to review education	
1903	1903 Grant Code introduced	School expanded to include Rose Villa East
1911	HKU established	
1912	Republic of China founded	
1913	First Education Ordinance passed; all schools with 10 or more pupils had to be registered; Subsidy System introduced for vernacular schools	DGS moved to new campus at 1, Jordan Road, Kowloon
1914	First World War began	
1918	First World War ended	New extension completed
1921		Miss Skipton retired, succeeded by Miss C. A. Ferguson; two DGS girls entered HKU for academic year 1921/1922
1922–1924		School motto "Daily Giving Service" and extracurricular activities introduced
1924	School Health Programme: medical examination of students and inspection of premises	Miss Ferguson left for England due to illness; Miss H. D. Sawyer as acting headmistress

Appendix 1   401

Year	External	DGS
1925	Strike-boycott began and ended the following year	Miss Ferguson died, and Miss Sawyer succeeded as headmistress
1926		Diocesan Old Girls' Association formed; the land west of the school was granted to the school as playground
1928		A pavilion (covered playground) for PE built
1931	Japanese aggression in Manchuria	
1932		Bishop Ronald O. Hall, Chairman of School Council, arrived in Hong Kong
1933		Off-site DGS kindergarten founded in Kowloon Tong
1937	China declared war with Japan; School Certificate Examinations at the end of Class 2 and Matriculation Examinations end of Class 1	Business course introduced for those who passed the School Certificate Examination and did not wish to enter university
1938	Fall of Guangzhou to Japan	Miss Sawyer retired at the end of 1938
1939		Miss E. M. Gibbins succeeded as headmistress
1940		1940 Wing built; Chinese introduced to the curriculum
1941	1941 Grant Code enacted; Second World War broke out; fall of Hong Kong on Christmas Day; Japanese occupation began	First volume *The Quest Magazine of the Diocesan Girls' School* (*The Quest*) published; Miss Gibbins interned in Stanley Camp; the school taken over as headquarters of Japanese Gendarmerie
1945	Liberation of Hong Kong	Miss Gibbins repossessed the school and left for England; school reopened on 1 October 1945 by Miss C. J. Anderson, acting headmistress until December; Mr J. L. Young Saye acting headmaster until March 1946
1946	1941 Grant Code amended	Miss A. W. Hurrell arrived in March to be headmistress; house system started; covered playground converted to a dormitory
1947	Amended 1941 Grant Code implemented and further amended	DGS separated into Senior School and Junior School
1948		Semi-permanent Junior School built
1949	PRC founded; Hong Kong Schools Music Festival began; Joint Primary 6 examination implemented; expansion of primary education began	No more small boys admitted to DGS
1950	Korean War began, UN embargo on China	Modern stream introduced; 1950 Wing built; school divided into an academic stream and a modern stream

Year	External	DGS
1951	Fisher's Report published on government expenditure on education; Anglo-Chinese primary schools changed to 6 years instead of 4	Junior School reorganised to 6 years; Parent Teacher Association formed; Miss Hurrell retired; Miss M. Fisher as acting headmistress
1953	Upper 6 form added to secondary schools	Mrs C. J. Symons became headmistress
1954		New kindergarten in the Green hut
1956	All grant schools to have 30%–35% of Form 1 places for "outside" students who passed the Joint Primary 6 Examination	Senior School increased from 2 to 3 classes per form; old 1913 building to be replaced
1959		Centenary Building, Assembly Hall, and Gymnasium completed; Junior School became a private school from September 1959
1960		Centenary celebration
1962	Joint Primary 6 examination renamed Secondary School Entrance Examination (SSEE)	
1964		The kindergarten was abolished
1965	White Paper on Education Policy in Hong Kong published	Swimming Pool built
1966	Bishop Hall retired, succeeded by Bishop Gilbert Baker; Star Ferry Riots; Cultural Revolution in China began	
1967	1967 riots in Hong Kong	Sex education introduced; expansion of the Junior School to 2 classes per level for all levels
1968	Compulsory SSEE for all primary 6 students	Junior School students started taking SSEE
1969		The Council of the Diocesan Girls' School Incorporation Ordinance (Chapter 1124) enacted; lectures on civic responsibilities and political theories introduced
1971	Compulsory free primary education	
1972	President Nixon's visit to China; Sir Murray MacLehose announced 10-year housing programme	Sixth Form Centre opened
1973	Unified Code of Aid	Closure of boarding school
1974	White Paper on Secondary Education in Hong Kong over the Next Decade; expansion of secondary education; ICAC established	
1975		New Junior School built. Mrs R. Benton became Junior School headmistress (half-time); Junior School officially known as DGJS

Appendix 1

Year	External	DGS
1976		Senior School increased from 3 to 4 classes per form, admitting "outside girls" to 50% of Form 1 places, in anticipation of the introduction of Secondary School Places Allocation (SSPA)
1978	SSEE replaced by Academic Aptitude Test and students allocated secondary places by SSPA System. In grant schools 50% of Form 1 places allocated to "outside" students by 1982; compulsory free nine years education; White paper on Senior Secondary and Tertiary Education	Mrs Benton retired; succeeded by Mrs D. Blomfield (full-time)
1981	Junior Secondary Education Assessment (JSEA) examination for Form 3 students for places in senior secondary schools	Form 3 students began to participate in JSEA
1982	Llewellyn Report of a review of education in Hong Kong	Edmund Cheung hut and China Light and Power hut added
1983		School celebrated Dr Symons 30th anniversary as headmistress
1984	Sino-British Declaration signed; Education Commission formed; seven Education Commission reports (ECR1-7) published between 1984 and 1997	
1985		Dr Symons retired; succeeded by Mrs Elim Lau as Senior School headmistress; Mrs Doris Ho appointed supervisor of both Senior and Junior Schools
1989	Tiananmen Square Incident	Mrs Blomfield retired; Mrs Rebecca Yip succeeded as Junior School headmistress
1990		DGS 130th anniversary celebration
1993		Extension Phase I completed; *VA magazine* published for the first time
1994		Science class per form increased from 1 to 2 from Form 4 upwards; computer literacy programme and development of information technology (IT) began
1996		Extension Phase II completed; Junior School increased from 2 to 3 classes per level
1997	Hong Kong returned to China; Avian influenza; Asian financial crisis	
1999		Mrs Elim Lau and Mrs Rebecca Yip retired. Mrs Stella Lau and Mrs Emily Dai took over as headmistress of Senior and Junior Schools respectively

Year	External	DGS
2000		140th anniversary celebration
2001		DOGA Place built
2003	Severe Acute Respiratory Syndrome (SARS) pandemic	School closed for a period between March and May because of SARS epidemic.
2005		SIP Building completed; Senior School changed to Direct Subsidy Scheme; Junior and Senior schools in "through train" mode; Senior School increased from 4 to 5 classes per level
2006		DGS became an "Affiliated Member" of the Anglican (Hong Kong) Secondary Schools Council Limited (Anglican Council)
2008	Global financial crisis	DGS *Kaleidoscope* first published
2009/ 2010	Hong Kong education system to become 6-3-3-4 by 2011/2012; introduction of New Senior Secondary (NSS) curriculum	School Redevelopment Project began; both Senior and Junior schools moved to "hotel schools"; NSS curriculum began
2010		150th anniversary; DGS's first comprehensive review by Education Bureau
2011/ 2012	Hong Kong Diploma of Secondary Education Examination replaced Hong Kong Certificate of Education Examination and Hong Kong Advanced Level Examination	Moved back to redeveloped campus at 1, Jordan Road in July 2011; Junior School increased enrolment from 3 to 4 classes per level, starting from Primary 1
2014	Occupy Central or Umbrella Movement	
2016		Mrs Emily Dai retired in December 2016
2017		Mrs Annie Lee succeeded as headmistress of the Junior School in January 2017

Appendix 2

Members of the School Council
from 1860 to the Present

The Diocesan Native Female Training School (DNFTS) was governed by a Lady's Committee and there was no documentation of its composition. When the DNFTS was replaced by the Diocesan Home and Orphanage (DHO), there was a School Committee and the membership of the Committee can be found in the history of Diocesan Boys' School, *To Serve and To Lead*, published by Hong Kong University Press in 2009, p. 13.

The composition of the School Committee (School Council) of the Diocesan Girls' School and Orphanage in 1899 can be found in Chapter 2. It changed in 1969 when the school was incorporated (Chapter 6) and a new constitution was given and again in 2005 when the school was changed to a DSS school (Chapter 8). The following list laid out in two columns gives the names and years of service of those who served on the School Council. The years given are the first and the last years in which individual members served the School Council. Over the years, some members have changed their titles; their last titles before resignation are used in the table. The abbreviations used are as follows: C—chairman, VC—vice-chairman, HS—honorary secretary, HT—honorary treasurer, HM—headmistress, AC—acting chairman, AHM—acting headmistress, HMJ—headmistress of Junior School, and SS—school supervisor. For example, Bishop Alford was Chairman from 1867 to 1869; Mr Hatam T. Barma was Honorary Treasurer from 1959 to 1979; and the Reverend R. K. Hyatt served as a member from 1969 to 1973, and 1974 to 1978 as Vice-Chairman of the School Council.

Name	Year
Revd Aldis J	1988–1999 (VC)
Mrs Alexander	1860–1861
Mrs Alford	1868–1869
Bishop Alford Charles R	1867–1869 (AC)
Ms Avasia J	1950
Bishop Baker Gilbert J H	1966–1980 (C)
Mr Barma H T	1953–1959, 1959–1979 (HT)
Ms Baxter	1863–1865
Revd Beach W	1868–1869 (HS,C)
Mr Benson D	1952–1967 (VC)
Mrs Bernard	1863–1864
Mr Billingham Nick I	1984–1987
Mr Bokhary S D S	1967–1971, 1972–2011 (HT)
Mrs Bremridge J H	1975–1980
Bishop Burdon, John Shaw	1894–1897 (C)
Mrs Campbell I J	1959–1967
Archbishop Chan Andrew	2012–present (C)
Ms Chan Barbara	2011–2015
Ms Chan M	1964–1965
Ms Chan Yvonne	2014–present
Mrs Chang Josephine	1989–2011, 2011–present (HT)
Mrs Chatjaval Sheilah	2000–present
Prof Chen Nelson	2011–2017
Mr Cheng Ronnie	2012–2020
Ms Cheung Stephanie	1987–present
Ms Chiu Bak To	1950–1963
Mr Chu Man Wai	1972–1999
Major Churn Samuel Macomber	1945–1947, 1956–1959
Dr Clasper P	1979–1980
Revd Coleman K	1979–1984 (VC)
Mr Cunningham E S	1954–1955, 1957–1958

Name	Year
Mrs D'Almada e Castro Leo	1940–1941, 1946–1968
Mrs Dai Emily	2005–2016 (HMJ)
Mr Davies	1866–1869
Mrs Davies	1866–1869
Revd Eva O V	1957–1961
Mrs Faid J	1947–1950
Ms Ferguson	1921–1924 (HM)
Mrs Fincher Maria	1955–1992
Ms Firth	1864–1869
Ms Fisher Molly	1951–1953 (AHM)
Mrs Fok Katherine	1974–2012
Ms Fu Tcheng Deirdre	2013–2015
Lady Fung Ping Fan	1950–1967, 1971–1973
Ms Gibbins Elizabeth M	1939–1941, 1972–1973 (AHM)
Mr Glennie E L H	1947–1949 (HT)
Mrs Goodban Mary G	1947–1955
Mrs Gowler	1867
Mrs Grey	1865 (HT)
Mr Grose J F	1946–1960
Mrs Hacola	1864
Revd Hague Eric	1953–1957
Bishop Hall Ronald O	1932–1966 (C)
Bishop Halward Nelson V	1946–1947 (C)
Revd Hanson Dale R	2015–2016 (VC)
Mrs Hawke	1864
Mrs Herklots	1947–1948
Mrs Heywood G A C	1946–1955
Bishop Joseph Charles Hoare	1899–1906 (C)
Mrs Ho Doris	1982–1985, 1985–2021 (SS)
Mrs Ho Yvette	2009–2013, 2015–present
Ms Howell B	1950
Mrs Hunter	1860–1861

Appendix 2

Name	Year
Ms Hurrell Alice Winifred	1946–1951 (HM)
Revd Hyatt R K	1969–1973, 1974–1978 (VC)
Mrs Ingram A W	1946–1951
Mrs Irwin	1860–1863
Revd Irwin J J	1865 (AC)
Mr Jardine R	1946–1947 (HT)
Dr Kane	1865–1867
Revd Kenchington Paul	2000–2005 (VC)
Mrs Ko Elizabeth	1968–1979
Ms Kotewall Patsy	1950
Archbishop Kwong Peter K K	1980–1999 (C)
Mr Kwong William	1975–1976
Mrs Lai Cordelia	1982–1984
Mrs Lau Elim	1985–1999 (HM)
Mrs Lau Stella	1999–present (HM)
Mrs Lee Annie	2017–present (HMJ)
Mr Lee Hon Wing	1971–1975
Mr Lee Richard Charles	1950–1955
Mrs Leonard Eva	1961–1963
Prof Li Arthur	2011–present
Mr Li Fook Tai	1968
Mrs Lo Hester	1966–1987
Mrs Lo Elizabeth	1979–2011
Mrs Lo M	1965–1966
Mr Lok Hardy	2017–present
Mr Long H K	1959–1965
Colonel Lovell	1865–1866
Mr Mackenzie J J	1863 (HT), 1863–1864
Mrs Mackenzie J J	1860–1861
Mrs Mackie Molly J B	1953–1955
Mrs Maclean	1860–1861, 1864 (HT)
Mrs MacMurdo	1863–1864
Ms Mansfield Margaret B	1957 (AHM)

Name	Year
Mrs Masson	1865 (HT), 1865–1867
Mrs Matthews A M Ethne	1938–1940, 1945–1950
Revd McCoy Alex	2016–present (VC)
Mr Mellish	1866–1868 (HS, AC)
Revd Menear John L	1985–1989 (VC), 2006–2015 (VC)
Mrs Mercer	1864 (HS), 1863–1864
Revd Michell J R S	1961–1968 (VC)
Mrs Mok Gladys	1969–2007
Mrs Murray	1863
Ms Ng Jane	2010–2014
Mrs Ng Saw Kheng	1991–2021
Mrs Nip Christine	2019–present
Ms Oei A	1950 (HS)
Revd Ogilvie J H	1946–1955
Dr Pan Francis K	1955–1996
Mr Pang Kwok-chan	1963–1964, 1968–1975
Ms Pang Loretta	2006–2010
Mr Penn Y W	1958–1959 (HT), 1960–1967
Mrs Penny Winifred	1946–1959
Mrs Perceval	1860–1861
Mrs Perry V	1940–1950
Ms Peters E	1950
Mrs Phillips	1867
Revd Pope Norman C	1952–1953 (HT)
Mrs Prew A G F	1940 (HT)
Mr Rainbow F E	1961–1963
Mr Randall B C	1949–1958 (HT)
Lady Robinson	1860–1861 (Patron), 1864
Ms Sawyer H Dorothy	1925–1938 (HM)
Mrs Sharp	1866–1869
Revd She George	1945–1954
Prof Shen Helen	2011–2016

Name	Year
Mrs Simpson	1864 (HS), 1863–1867
Ms Skipton Elizabeth	1899–1921 (HM)
Mr Slade C D	1950–1956
Mrs Smith Lydia	1863 (HS), 1863–1864
Bishop Soo Thomas	1996–1999 (VC), 1999–2011 (C)
Mr Stewart A	1945
Mrs Stringer	1864
Mr Sun Jeffrey	1976–2011
Dr Symons Catherine Joyce	1945, 1948 (AHM), 1949–1952, 1953–1974 (HM), 1975–1985 (HM/SS)
Mrs Tang Lisa	1999–2000
Mr Taylor D	1964–1967
Mrs Tcheng A	1950
Mrs Tien Frances	1979–1989
Mrs Townsend	1863–1864
Mr Tsang K C	1969–1970
Mrs Vaucher	1860–1861
Mrs Walkinshaw	1860–1861
Mrs Warren	1865 (HS), 1865–1869
Revd Warren C F	1865–1867 (AC)
Ms Wentworth Norah M	1940 (AM)
Mrs Wilking J	1970–1971
Revd Wilson J	1865–1866 (AC)
Ms Wong Betty	1963–1964
Mrs Wong Chan Sherlynn	2015–2019
Mrs Wong Nancy Yat Hung	1958–1959
Mrs Wong Susanna	2011–present
Dr Wong Taam Vivian	1993–2006
Ms Woo Nellie	1950 (HT)
Mr Wood	1865–1866
Mr Wu Marco	2011–present

Name	Year
Mrs Yeh Yolanda	1997–1999
Mrs Yeo Florence	1951–1953
Dr Yeo Kok Cheang	1945–1957
Mrs Yew H P	1959–1990
Mr Young Saye J L	1945–1946 (AHM)
Ms Yu Benita	2011–present
Madam Justice Yuen Maria	2011–present

Appendix 3

The Teaching Staff, from 1860/1861 to the Present

In preparing the tables for the teaching staff of DGS, we followed certain rules: (1) All part-time staff and those who served for less than one year are not included because of the large numbers in these two categories. Those who had served for one year or more are included in the table. (2) The staff of the Senior School and the Junior School are presented separately. The staff, who had worked in both the Senior School and the Junior School, are indicated by an asterisk in both columns (Column 1—name of staff; Column 2—year starting to work and year ending). When there is only an asterisk in Column 1, it is because there is no record as to when the staff member switched over from the Junior School to the Senior School or vice versa. The asterisk in Column 2 indicates the initial years of teaching in the Senior/Junior School. (3) Male staff are denoted by Mr before their names; single female staff by Ms, and married female staff by Mrs. All married female staff are presented as Mrs followed by their married name and their maiden in brackets when available. Staff with a doctorate degree are denoted by Dr after their names. For example, Mrs Symons is presented as Mrs Symons (Anderson) Catherine Joyce (Dr). (4) The year starting and the year ending denotes the academic year. For example, 1978–1997 means that the teacher started working at the school during the academic year 1978/1979 and ended during the academic year 1996/1997. Because we decided to pause our record of the school history at the end of the academic year 2018/2019, the word "present" means that the staff were still teaching in the new academic year 2019/2020. (5) For teachers who left the school but returned later, the years for both periods are presented. There are some teachers, particularly those before the war, whose records are incomplete; their year of ending at the school might not be recorded, but they taught in the school for over one year as shown in the school magazines Quest or speech day booklets; only the years of starting are presented. There are also some teachers in the early years for whom we have only their surname on record.

Senior School

Name	Year
Ms Abbey Sarah Louise	1998–2001
Ms Abdullah Sarah	1945–1968
Ms Abesser B	1978–1979
Mrs Adams Sharon	1991–1997
Mrs Adamson (Mitchell) Francessca	2015–2019
Ms Ahuja Radhika	2013–present
Ms Allen Ethel*	1915–1955
Mrs Amiss G	1973–1975
Ms Armstrong	1934–1936
Ms Aspinall*	1921–1925
Mrs Au (Hung) Wai Yi Helen 區洪慧儀	1992–2007
Mr Au Ka Lok Paul 歐家樂	2006–2012
Mr Au Man Hin 區文顯	1990–present
Ms Au Nui Oi Camilla 區女愛	2012–present
Ms Axbey Susan	1965–1966
Mr Baldwin Rupert	1926–1937
Mrs Barber (Bedford) Molly	1924–1941, 1947–1948
Mr Barry Jarrod Alexander	2015–2018
Mrs Bartles Kate	1982–1985
Ms Barty Jennifer	1963–1965
Ms Bascombe Nora	1915–1919
Ms Baxter Jean	1968–1972
Mrs Beckett C	1969–1971
Mrs Bird C M	1941, 1947–1948
Mrs Birdsall S	1971–1972
Mrs Birley (Bird) Jennifer M	1954–1974
Mrs Bland V*	1954–1955
Mr Blofeld John 蒲樂道	1948–1951
Mrs Blunt E M	1953
Mrs Booker	1940–1941
Mrs Bowes O	1948–1949
Mrs Bradley G K	1970–1973
Ms Braga Caroline	1947–1948
Mrs Bramwell J G	1956–1957

Name	Year
Mrs Brazendale G	1964–1965
Mrs Briscoe H M	1968–1969
Mrs Brooker B	1967–1968
Ms Brown C	1955–1957
Mr Bugaj Tomasz Andrzej	2017–present
Ms Burbidge Brenda	1955–1956
Mrs Carter Samantha Lee	2006–2008
Mrs Cartildge (Day)	1915–1918
Ms Carvalho C	1947–1956
Ms Chan Alice	1984–1994
Mrs Chan (Au) Chi Kwan Alice 陳區芷君	1996–2010
Mrs Chan (Au) Yvonne Chi Ying 陳歐芷盈	2008–present
Mr Chan Billy	1994–1996
Mrs Chan (Cheung) Mei Ling Mary 陳張美梨	1970–1998
Ms Chan Fung Ming 陳鳳鳴	1998–2000
Mr Chan Hin Chun 陳顯俊	2007–present
Ms Chan Ka Ki 陳嘉琪	2014–2015
Mrs Chan (Ko) Synthia 陳高德儀	1997–2006
Mrs Chan (Lau) Siu Yee Connie 陳劉小儀	1995–present
Mr Chan Lawrence S L 陳世諒	1945–1964
Mrs Chan (Lee) Hoi Yan Laura 陳李凱茵	2002–present
Ms Chan Man Ling Maggie 陳漫玲	2006–2007
Ms Chan Oi Nei 陳愛妮	2018–present
Ms Chan Po Yee 陳寶儀	2013–2018
Ms Chan Sau Chi Debbie 陳秀姿	2011–2012
Mr Chan Tak Ching Eric 陳德正	2017–present
Mrs Chan (Tsang) Wai Fan Jennifer 陳曾惠芬	1995–2012
Mrs Chan Valerie	1987–1995
Ms Chan Wai Ting Viyon 陳慧婷	2012–present
Ms Chan Wing Hei Grace 陳穎希	2016–present
Mrs Chan Winnie	1995–1996

Name	Year
Mrs Chan (Wu) Diana	1973–1979, 1983–1994
Ms Chan Yee Durn Selina	1967–1970
Mr Chan Yeuk 陳約	1940–1950
Ms Chan Yi Man 陳伊玟	2017–2018
Mr Chan Yik Cham 陳翊湛	1952–1979
Ms Chan Yuk Ting	1992–1993
Ms Chang Chi Lok Charlotte 張芷諾	2012–2014
Ms Chang Mary Ann	1965–1969
Mrs Chau (Au) Wai Chun 周歐惠珍	1993–2001
Ms Chen	1940–1941
Ms Chen J J	1973–1974
Ms Chen Pierra	1990–1991
Mrs Chen S	1958–1964
Ms Chen Wei Beth 陳薇	2015–present
Mrs Cheng (Cheung) Shuk Yee Alice 鄭張淑儀 (Dr)	1994–2011, 2018–present
Ms Cheng Elenor	1983–1984
Ms Cheng J	1971–1973
Mrs Cheng (Kiang) I	1967–1968
Mrs Cheng (Kiang) Oi King Molly 鄭姜愛琼	2011–present
Mr Cheng Kwok Hung 鄭國雄	2011–2016
Mr Cheng Lok Yee Louis 鄭樂怡	2016–present
Mr Cheng Mang Kit Tom 鄭孟傑	2013–2015
Ms Cheng Wing Chi Winnie 鄭穎芝	2015–present
Ms Cheung Ah Yuk Iris 張阿旭	2014–2016
Mrs Cheung Beatrice	1956–1961
Mrs Cheung C	1977–1981
Ms Cheung Chi Kwan Angela 張志軍	1996–1998
Ms Cheung Chi Li Alice 張至勵	2006–2009
Mr Cheung Ching Po 張正甫	1992–2000
Ms Cheung Ivy	2001–2002
Mrs Cheung (Lo) Wan Ching Jane 張盧允晴	2010–2018

Name	Year
Mrs Cheung M L	1970–1972
Mrs Cheung (Ma) Pui Haan	1956–1961
Ms Cheung Man Lai Peggy 張敏麗	2006–present
Ms Cheung Phebe 張明華	2006–present
Mr Cheung Tom	2005–2006
Ms Chiang Grace 蔣頌恩	2011–present
Mr Chiang Lo Fung Tommy 蔣路楓	2006–2007
Ms Chien Amelia	1964–1966
Ms Chin M	1951–1953
Ms Ching H	1969–1970
Ms Ching M W	1951–1953
Mrs Chitson (Ng) Chun Yuk Janet 吳珍玉	1989–1990, 1992–1998
Ms Chiu Bak To	1946–1948
Mr Chiu Chi Yeung Ken 趙之揚	2013–2014
Mrs Chiu (Lee) Shiu May	1958–1966
Mrs Chiu (Mok) Siu May Juliet 趙莫少湄	1967–2004
Mrs Chiu (Sitt) Wing Yee Winnie 趙薛穎儀	1990–2006
Mrs Chiu (Tang) Wing Sze Cecilia 趙鄧詠詩	1992–2007
Ms Cho Janny	2007–2008
Ms Cho Yee Tak Joan 曹懿德	2013–2017
Ms Choa Lip Chee	1915–1917
Ms Chow S	1973–1974
Mr Chow Sau-on	1976–1977
Mrs Chow Tang (Leung) Hoi Ling Helen 梁愷玲	1976–1998
Mrs Choy (Poon) Siu Lan Daisy 蔡潘笑蘭	1966–2001
Ms Choy Suen Kee	1969–1970
Ms Choy Y W*	1972–1974
Mrs Christiansen I*	1946–1950
Ms Chu	1940–1941
Mr Chu Chun Pong Steve 朱振邦	1995–present
Mr Chu Hiu Fung Anson 朱曉峯	2018–present

Name	Year
Mrs Chu (Lo) Sau King	1959–1963
Ms Chu Teresa	1989–1995
Mr Chu Wing Chiu Vincent 朱永超	2007–2009
Ms Chua	1940
Mrs Chui (Chiu) Mo Wan 趙慕蘊*	1958–1987
Ms Chung Chi	1958–1968
Mrs Chung (Ho) Shiu Van Alice 鍾何秀雯	2012–present
Ms Chung Pak Ling 鍾百靈	2008–2009
Mr Chung Wah Yiu Francis 鍾華耀	1947–1948
Mr Chung Wing-on 鍾榮安 (Dr)	1991–1992
Ms Clark Jill*	1976–1995
Mrs Clynes (Paterson) Helen Macgregor	1959–1971, 1972
Mrs Cochrane R	1979–1980
Mrs Collier (Moore) P	1971–1982
Ms Cook Louise	1988–1989
Ms Corbett Jane N	1982–1984
Mr Cortes Pedro Henrique	2016–present
Ms Coulter Maureen Elizabeth (Dr)	2014–2015
Mrs Cowie T	1955–1956
Ms Cox	1933–1935
Ms Crawshaw	1940
Mrs Crosby Poppy	1968–1981
Ms Crossly	1915
Ms Cunningham	1939–1946
Ms Curreem H C	1946–1947
Ms Dalziel	1936
Mr Danenberg Emilio FX (Prof)	1917–1920
Mrs De Biere	1933
Mrs Deacon Lynne	1978–1987, 1995–1997
Ms Deva P L	1970–1975
Mr Dibbs Geoffrey	1946–1947
Ms Dick Jean	1977–1979

Name	Year
Ms Doble A S	1910–1915
Mr Doherty Brendan Patrick	2011–present
Mrs Donnan Beryl	1984–1990
Ms Dowbiggin	1934
Mrs Drust	1964–1966
Ms Dulmage Agnes Jean	1925–1926
Mrs Easterbrook Joyce	1949–1952, 1963–1964
Ms Eaton Mary Anne Winifred 伊頓	1863–1865
Mr Ebrahim Azeem	2009–present
Ms Eddis S J	1989–1990
Ms Edwards H A	1972–1974
Ms Edwards Norah Mary 聞慧中	1950–1962
Mrs Edwin	1952–1954
Mrs Eggleton M	1948
Mrs Engel Joyce	1963–1964
Mrs Evans Irene	1969–1970
Ms Ferguson Catherine A	1915–1924
Mrs Fernandez	1933
Ms Fernie Janet	1908
Ms Fisher Molly*	1947–1953
Mrs Fletcher G I	1956–1957
Ms Foley M	1966–1967
Mrs Fong (Wong) Suk Wai Martha 方黃淑慧	1992–2006, 2011–present
Ms Fong Yvone	1971–1972
Mrs Freedlander Erne	1940–1946
Mrs French	1946–1947
Ms Fung	1969
Mr Fung Chi Tim 馮自添	1998–present
Mrs Fung (Fong) Tsz Mann Joannie 馮方祉文*	2017–present 2016–2017*
Ms Fung Tak Ki	1992–1993
Ms Fung Ying Irene	1996–1997
Mrs Galin (Cheung) Suet Mui Mary 張雪梅	2014–present
Mrs Gardener A C	1977–1984
Mrs Gavriloff V	1945–1948

Appendix 3

Name	Year
Ms Gibbins Elizabeth Mary	1936–1945
Mrs Gillham (Lee) Wai Han Betty 李慧嫻	1994–1997
Mrs Goodfellow W	1946–1947
Ms Gourdin K	1915
Mrs Gourdin R	1948
Mrs Grady-Hammond Karyn Lee	2000–2004
Ms Gray K S	1983–1984
Mrs Greenburgh S	1962–1963
Mrs Grieve M	1964–1965
Ms Griffiths Rhian	1986–1988
Mrs Griffiths Sheila Margaret	1995–1999
Ms Grindley I S	1953–1954
Ms Grose	1925–1931
Ms Hall Catherine Anne	1989–1993
Mrs Harris Hilda*	1958–1961, 1952–1954*
Mrs Harvey	1959–1962
Mrs Hau (Wong) Kwok Yan Jessie 侯王幗欣	2006–present
Ms Hawker Maude Isabel	1899–1910
Ms Haynes	1940–1941
Mrs Haynes Barbara	1969–1971
Ms Hazeland	1917
Mr Hemery S Gordon	1949–1950
Ms Henderson E F	1947–1951
Mr Heung Chun Yu 香震宇	2016–present
Ms Hewer S	1968–1972
Mrs Hindes P J	1983–1984
Ms Ho A	1973–1974
Mrs Ho (Chan) Wai Ha*	1947–1967
Ms Ho Chi Man Claudia 何智雯	1991–present
Ms Ho Ching Ni Jenny 何靜妮	2011–2013
Mr Ho Dit Sang	1969–1970
Ms Ho Hiu Yen Olivia 何曉欣	2010–2012, 2015–present
Ms Ho J	1970–1972
Ms Ho Man Chee Charlotte 何敏知	2008–2009

Name	Year
Mrs Ho May	1964–1967
Mrs Ho (Poon) Kar Ling Carmen 何潘嘉凌	1994–present
Mr Ho Shiu Cheung Eric 何紹璋	2009–present
Ms Ho Suet Ying Peony 何雪瑩	2017–present
Ms Ho Sylvia 何粹華	1996–1997
Ms Ho Wing Yee 何詠儀	2011–2012
Mr Hoh Kaak Yan	1947
Mrs Holland	1940–1941
Mrs Holmes	1959–1960
Ms Hong Kwai Chun 康貴珍	1991–1992
Mrs Hooper	1923–1926
Ms Hopkins P	1947
Mrs Houston Ruth	1988–1989
Mrs Hoy	1925
Mrs Hu Viveca	1958–1967
Mrs Hughes J	1980–1983
Ms Hui A	1970–1974
Ms Hui Flora	1956–1959
Ms Hui Ka Lok Dorothy 許加樂	2012–present
Mrs Hui (Lun) Yin Kan Paulina 許倫燕勤	1978–present
Mrs Hui P	1983–1985
Mrs Hui (So) Sylvia	1986–1992
Ms Humphreys Robyn Jean	2017–2019
Mrs Hung Gloria	1969–1975
Mrs Hung (Quah) Cecilia	1971–1989
Ms Hunt	1916
Ms Hurrell Alice Winifred	1946–1951
Mrs Hurst Aileen	1980–1994
Mr Hyam Daniel Ross	2008–present
Ms Ip Margaret	1966–1967
Ms Janne P	1958–1963
Mrs Jeffries	1924
Mrs Jenkins J	1951–1952
Mrs Jenkinson	1918–1923
Ms Johnson Cynthia	1972–1973
Mrs Jones (Nisbet-Jones) Sheila	1962–1964

Name	Year
Ms Joyce	1948–1954
Mr Kam Ming Yuen Edmund 甘鳴遠	2007–2013
Mrs Kam (Wong) Pui Wa Pearl 甘黃佩華	1989–present
Mrs Kan (Ho) Pauline	1973–1993
Ms Kan Lai Bing	1960–1962
Mrs Kehl D	1968–1969
Ms Kelly S	1970–1972
Mrs Kemp	1952–1954
Mrs Kennedy	1925
Mr Kennedy-Skipton	1959–1961
Mrs Kent G	1963–1965
Ms Keung Ronnie	1980–1993
Ms Killin Janice	1979–1980
Mrs Kilshaw	1964–1968
Mrs Kirby	1965–1967
Mrs Kirkby	1923–1927, 1935–1938
Ms Kishinchand Sundri	1965–1968
Ms Kitchell Norrie Pegeen 柯穎賢	2005–present
Ms Ko Denise 高志恆	2005–2006
Ms Ko P	1967
Mr Ko P M	1959–1964
Mr Ko Wing Hang Derek George 高穎恒	2008–2010
Ms Ko Yeung Katherine 高洋	2010–2011
Mrs Kong N L	1955–1965
Mr Kong Paul (Dr)	2005–2006
Ms Kong Wing 江穎	2018–present
Ms Kong Yin King Oriana 江燕婷	2015–2017
Ms Kotwall Hazel 葛美慈	1958–1959
Mrs Kun (Lin) Wai Ying Suzanna 靳連慧影*	2011–2018, 1989–1993*
Mrs Kung (Ng) Y M	1977–1982
Revd Kvan E	1949–1954
Mrs Kvan (Busted) Inger Kristine	1950–1980
Ms Kwan Kitty	1991–1993

Name	Year
Mrs Kwan (Ng) Shiu Yan Michelle 關吳小茵	1997–2010
Ms Kwan Sin Yee Cindy 關善怡	2002–2007
Ms Kwan Yan Oi	1960–1961
Ms Kwok Hiu Lam Helen 郭曉琳	2013–2017
Ms Kwok Julian	1967–1970
Mrs Lai (Cheng) Melissa 黎鄭兆清 (Dr)	2007–2008
Mrs Lai Diana	1984–1990
Ms Lai Hiu Wai Johanna	2005–2006
Ms Lai Mo Yu Alice 黎務愉	2017–present
Ms Laidlaw E	1978–1980
Ms Lam Amelia	1959–1961
Ms Lam Chak Yan Jessie Teresa 林澤欣	2004–2008
Mrs Lam Greta	1965–1970, 1981–1987
Mrs Lam (Ho) Kit Yee 林何潔儀	1996–present
Ms Lam Ka Yee Patricia 林家怡	2007–2008
Mr Lam Kwok Wai Tony 林國瑋	2012–2013
Mrs Lam (Lee) Yee Ling	1960–1992
Mrs Lam (Ma) Sze Wan Daphne 林馬思蘊	2006–2019
Mrs Lam Margaret	1964–1970
Mrs Lam (Ng) Mei Po Mabel 林吳美寶	2010–present
Ms Lam S Y	1984–1987
Ms Lam Sau Shun 林守純	1989–1992
Mr Lam Siu Keung 林紹強	1989–2019
Mrs Lam Wai Huen	1962–1976
Ms Lamb Kirsten Emma Wai-Ling	2007–2010
Mrs Lamb Winifred	1985–1986
Mrs Lambert C I	1964–1968
Mrs Lamsam (Fenton) Kim	1984–1994
Mrs Lane F	1964–1965
Ms Lang Phyllis	1946–1947
Mrs Langworthy J L	1956–1957
Ms Last Irma	1939–1941
Mrs Latham (Burke) Siobhan	1993–1995

Appendix 3

Name	Year
Mr Lau Fei 劉飛	2015–present
Ms Lau Ga Yee 劉嘉宜	2014–2017
Ms Lau J	1968–1972
Mrs Lau J	1972–1973
Ms Lau Ka Yue Jenny 劉嘉渝	2014–present
Ms Lau Kam Fung Annie	2007–2008
Mrs Lau (Kun) Lai Kuen Stella 劉靳麗娟	1990–present
Ms Lau Lai-fong Maria	1976–1983
Ms Lau Lai-yee Liza	1976–1995
Mrs Lau (Pong) Elim 劉龐以琳	1964–1966, 1985–1999
Mr Lau Wai Keung Raymond	1984–1993
Mr Lau K S Thomas	1992–1993
Mr Lau Wai Keung Dennis	1986–1993
Mrs Lau Y W	1971–1973, 1977–1995
Mrs Lau (Yao) Shui Chun Tiffany	1976–1983
Ms Lau Yuen Cheuk	1946–1953
Ms Law B	1986-1987
Ms Law Kin Chong Zoe 羅健莊	2016–present
Mrs Law Lisa	1984–1986
Mrs Law May	1998–2007
Ms Law Mei Fong	1986–1987
Mrs Lawrence	1959–1960
Mrs Lee A	1978–1989
Mrs Lee A A	1965–1966
Mr Lee Baldwin (Dr)	1932–1948
Ms Lee Bong Sil 李奉實	2006–2007
Ms Lee Bonnie	1987–1992
Ms Lee Bui Ki Becky 李貝琪	1999–present
Mrs Lee (Cheung) Wing Yi Winnie 李張詠怡	2006–2014
Mrs Lee E B	1971–1974
Ms Lee Eleanor	1964–1966
Ms Lee F J	1930
Ms Lee Fook Wah Margaret	1963–1965
Mrs Lee (Fu) Eva 李傅翠華	1957–1966, 1970–1989

Name	Year
Mr Lee Ka Ming 李嘉銘	2017–present
Ms Lee Marjorie 李節芬	1964–1970
Mrs Lee M	1967–1968
Mr Lee Pak-shing Matthew 李伯成	1993–1994
Ms Lee May	1979–1990
Mrs Lee Monique	1965–1968
Mrs Lee (Poon) Kit Ming 李潘潔明	1990–2009
Ms Lee Pui Shan Joyce 李佩珊	2010–2011
Mrs Lee R	1987–1988
Mrs Lee (Shea) Violet	1940–1941
Mrs Lee Sheila	1958–1961
Ms Lee Shuk Wah 李淑華	2011–2012
Mrs Lee W K	1959–1976
Ms Lee Wai Huen 李為絢	1959–1960
Ms Lee Wing Yin Juanita 李詠賢	2012–present
Mrs Lee (Yau) Kwai Ching Prisca 李丘桂貞	1996–2007
Mr Lee Yuen Kang 李元鏡	2008–2009
Mrs Leitch*	1961–1964
Ms Leung	1939–1941
Ms Leung Wai-see Ally	1993–1995
Ms Leung Pui Yee Angela 梁沛儀	1999–2005
Ms Leung B	1970–1975
Mr Leung Gilbert	1976–1977
Mr Leung Ho Yin	1987–1989
Ms Leung Hoi Kei Karen 梁凱祈	2001–2004
Ms Leung I	1963–1965
Ms Leung Jacqueline 梁維芝	2008–2009
Mrs Leung Jane	1961–1964
Ms Leung Kam Har Yvonne 梁錦霞	2001–present
Mr Leung King Man 梁景文	2017–2018
Mrs Leung (Kwok) Suk Yin Angela 梁郭淑賢	1997–2007
Mrs Leung (Lee) Hsin Yin Sharon Anne 梁李善殷	2010–2014, 2017–present

Name	Year
Mrs Leung (Li) Pak Ling Heidi 梁李柏齡	2018–present
Mrs Leung M	1970
Ms Leung Man Na Helena 梁敏娜	2015–2016
Mr Leung Martin	2006–2007
Ms Leung Mei Po Mable	1990–1992
Ms Leung P C	1967–1974
Ms Leung Pui Chun	1980–1981
Ms Leung Shin Nga Shina 梁善雅	2013–2019
Mr Leung Tat Wing 梁達榮 (Dr)	2001–2012
Mrs Li A	1963–1964
Ms Li Ching Man Sarah 李靜文	2010–present
Mr Li Hong Yi 李康怡	2014–present
Mr Li Ngai Dennis 李巍	1999–2000
Mrs Liang Wang Djeng	1950–1956
Mrs Liao (Yuen) Christine 廖袁經綿	1963–1964
Ms Lim Elvera	1956–1959
Mrs Lim M R	1957–1981
Mr Lin C Y	1939–1941
Ms Lin Sui Ching 連彗晶	2008–2009
Ms Liu Wai-yee Alice 廖慧兒	1993–1994
Ms Liu Ka Lei 廖嘉莉	2011–2013
Mrs Liu (Tin) Nim Yu 廖田念如	2007–2013
Ms Liu Yung Hwei Clara 劉詠暉	2011–2013
Ms Lo Amy	1962–1963
Ms Lo Eileen	1980–1993
Mrs Lo (Ho Tung) Grace 盧何堯姿	1945–1948
Mr Lo Kwun Chung 盧冠忠	2015–present
Mrs Lo (Wong) Siu Ling 盧黃小玲	1998–2002
Mrs Loasby (Pang) Yee Lam Elaine 彭綺琳	2009–2014
Mrs Lodge (Rowley) Jean Margaret	1952–1954
Mrs Loh Fi-ngo	1962–1963
Ms Lok Kwan Wai Emily 陸筠慧	2015–2018
Mrs Long C	1957–1958

Name	Year
Ms Lovegrove Nelly	1910
Mr Lowcock S J	1963–1965
Ms Lui Jacqueline Ashley 呂凱盈	2007–2012
Mr Lui W K	1979–1980
Mrs Lung (Wong) Esther	1967–1988
Mrs Lyal	1933–1934
Mrs Ma (Au) Ho Vanessa 馬區皓	2006–present
Mrs Ma (Chow) Tuen Yi Alice 馬周端兒	1980–1992
Ms Ma Grace	1965–1970
Mrs Ma (Lau) Man Choi 馬劉文采	1984–1996
Ms Ma Nancy	1967–1968
Mr Ma S W	1983–1986
Ms Ma-Cunanan Theresa	1991–2001
Mrs MacArthur Mary F	1972–1973
Mrs Mack Ruth M	1951–1955
Ms Maclean P	1976–1979
Ms Mak Hang Wun Stella 麥幸媛	2008–present
Ms Mak Man Yee 麥敏儀	2014–2017
Mr Man Wai Hin Thomas 文惠顯 (Dr)	1993–2011
Ms Maneely Majorie S	1963–1967
Ms Mansfield Margaret Brunt	1947–1973
Mrs Mar (Chu) Christine	1970–1971, 1968–1970*
Ms Mark Priscilla 麥婉怡	1961–1962
Mrs Marquand J	1960–1962
Mrs Marr	1966–1968
Mrs Mason C M Katherine	1969–1977
Mr Mason Frederick	1926
Ms Matheson	1933
Ms Mathieson Margaret Mckie Wilson	2008–2009
Mrs Matthews (Dunbar) E	1908
Mr Matthews Philip A	2000–2001
Ms McGarvey L	1966–1967
Ms McGill	1923–1932
Ms McHardy R	1976–1978

Appendix 3

Name	Year
Ms McLachlan D	1961–1970
Ms McMullin D	1968–1969
Ms McQueen A	1961–1962
Mrs McTavish	1961
Mrs Meffan I	1959–1967
Ms Melbye F	1963–1965
Mrs Merry M	1972–1973
Mrs Millar	1924, 1934
Mrs Milnes Sally	1993–1995
Ms Moir Elizabeth	1964–1967
Mr Mok Chiu Yu Augustus 莫昭如	1974–1979, 1980–1990
Ms Mok E	1946–1947
Ms Mok Ida	1983–1990
Mr Mok Kai Yuen Simon 莫繼元	2001–2014
Mrs Monks	1940
Ms Moodalie-Huennemeyer Nhyacinth Thul	1992–1995
Ms Moore J	1973
Mrs Morris B	1970–1971
Mrs Morris G	1967
Ms Moy Kit Yu Catherine 梅潔榆	2013–present
Ms Nee Dok Sing Mary 倪鐸星	1985–1992, 1995–2000
Ms Ng Angel 吳安琪	1990–1994
Mrs Ng D	1958–1960
Ms Ng Wai Ling Kathleen 吳慧玲	2002–2012
Mrs Ng (Lau) Ching 吳劉静	2017–present
Mrs Ng (Leung) Wai Yung Joanne 吳梁慧容	1999–2013
Mr Ng Philip	1985–1986
Ms Ng Sau Way Cynthia 吳秀衛	1999–2003
Mr Ng Siu Wah Jack 吳少華	1998–present
Mr Nip Chun Kit Michael 聶俊傑	2013–present
Ms Nolasco Guida	1966–1967
Mrs Norris	1957–1958
Mrs O'Connell Madeline Nancy*	1953–1974
Mr Oddie Joseph Salawood	1995–present
Ms Odell Ada Lillian	1927–1929

Name	Year
Mrs Old A	1962–1965
Mrs Olsen	1933–1941
Mr Or Man Wai 柯文偉 (Dr)	2000–present
Ms Oxlad M J 岳士列	1866–1869
Mrs Oxley Jean Valerie	1981–1997
Mrs Paces (Higgs) Sybil Eugenia	1948–1952
Mrs Pakenham-Walsh	1952–1954
Ms Pang Chi Kwan 彭芷君	2011–2013
Mr Pang Yen Kiu Daniel 彭恩橋	2013–present
Ms Pang Hiu Wai 彭曉慧	2015–2018
Mrs Pang (Wong) Sau King 彭黃秀瓊	2005–2016
Ms Patel Nargis Badruddin	1988–1990, 1994–1998
Ms Paterson	1922–1928
Ms Paterson H M	1963–1965
Mr Pau Kwok Wan 鮑覺幻	1947–1951
Ms Paul P A V	1973–1977
Mrs Pearce	1929–1930
Mrs Pearson	1937–1938
Mrs Pegg J	1970–1971, 1987–1988
Mrs Pei (Chu) Regina	1973–1989
Ms Perkins Mary Elizabeth	1999–2000
Ms Pite E S R	1961–1967
Mrs Poole E	1952–1957
Ms Poon Why May	1915–1920
Ms Pope	1952–1954
Mrs Pope	1919
Ms Portman Christine	1997–1999, 2008–2012
Mr Powell James Kent	1991–1992
Ms Pragnell May	1952–1954
Ms Quon Maple	1948–1949
Mrs Rathmall (Mason)	1924–1940
Mrs Rebuck	1965–1967
Mrs Reeve Monica	1964–1966
Mrs Reid J	1963–1965
Ms Reilly N P	1965–1966

Name	Year
Mrs Renard B	1967–1968
Ms Rendle 蘭德爾	1867–1868
Mrs Ritchie	1935
Ms Roberts	1918–1921
Mrs Robertson M	1963–1966
Ms Roden M	1948–1953
Ms Rogers-Tillstone Belina K	1955–1957
Ms Rose Patricia M	1974–1976
Mrs Rowlands C	1958–1964
Ms Rowley K	1961–1962
Ms Royle Pamela J	1982–1983
Mrs Sadler Pamela	1954–1955
Mrs Santos (Yip) Yuen Shan Rosa 山度士葉婉珊	1989–present
Ms Sawyer H Dorothy	1922–1938
Ms Schaller K B	1963–1967
Mrs Seyer	1946–1948
Mrs Shaddock E H	1955–1958
Mrs Shann Dewing	1927
Ms Sharma Seetal	2004–2005
Ms Sharp Eleanor	1953
Mrs Shea (Batalha) E I	1929–1940
Mrs Sheeham	1959–1960
Ms Shem	1937–1941
Ms Shen Margaret 沈燕民	1993–1996
Mrs Shen (Yuen) Jane 沈袁經楣*	1967–1968 1956–1967*
Ms Shih Joan	1956–1957
Mrs Shing (Chow) Kit Ling Lena 成周潔玲	1993–present
Ms Shiu K M	1957
Ms Shu Amy	1981–1982
Mr Shu H T (Dr)	1950–1953
Ms Sia Yen Ping Mandy	2011–2012
Mrs Sinn C	1970–1975
Ms Sinn Phyllis	1940–1958
Ms Sinton V	1968–1971
Ms Siu S	1969–1970
Ms Skipton Elizabeth	1899–1921

Name	Year
Mrs Smart	1961–1962
Mrs Smith J	1970–1971
Ms Smith Joan	1935–1937
Ms Smith Marie	1936–1941
Mrs Smith Mary	1966–1972
Ms Smith Middleton	1917
Mrs So (Fan) Irene	1962–1993
Mrs So Grace*	1946–1968
Ms Soo Betty 蘇曼瑩	1958–1959
Ms Sowerbutts S	1968–1972
Mrs Stanley H F	1964–1966
Ms Steel	1936–1938
Mrs Stephens (Ngan) Chi Kwan Vivian 顏芷筠	2015–2018
Mrs Steven Joan*	1946–1959
Mrs Stevens	1925
Mrs Stevenson J	1960–1961
Ms Stewart Elizabeth H	1957–1966
Ms Stone D	1923–1939
Mrs Stout	1925–1927
Ms Striker Diane A	1983–1986
Mrs Sum (Tse) Shuk Ping 沈謝淑平	1993–2006
Ms Sun Lok Hei Pearl 孫樂熹	2014–present
Mr Sung I	1957
Ms Suthiphongchai Kacinee	2000–present
Ms Swan Dorothy	1961–1962
Ms Swanston Mona	1967
Ms Swinton	1912
Ms Sy Man Nor Amber 施敏娜	2010–present
Mrs Symons (Anderson) Catherine Joyce (Dr)	1939–1985
Mrs Takasugi (Liu) Yung Ye Beatrice 劉詠怡	2008–2010
Mr Tam Ho Lun Jacky 譚浩麟	2017–present
Ms Tam Shuk Shan 譚淑姍	2017–present
Ms Tam Siu Fung	1975–1976
Mr Tang C K	1974–1975
Mr Tang Chun Wai 鄧振威	2011–2013

Appendix 3

Name	Year
Mr Tang Kun Loi 鄧根來	1986–1989, 1992–1993, 1994–2018
Mr Tang Kwai Nang	1967–1968
Mrs Tang (Li) Wai Ting Joanne 鄧李慧婷	2004–present
Mrs Tang Louisa	2000–2002
Mrs Tang (Ng) Hung Sang 鄧吳洪生	1965–2001
Ms Tang Vivian 鄧麗韞	2012–2014
Madame Tavastjerna	1940–1941
Ms Taylor D H	1983–1984
Mr Taylor David Richard	1964–1966
Mrs Taylor Margaret R	1957–1963
Mrs Taylor P	1978–1979
Mr Taylor Richard David	2015–2017
Ms Teague Rebecca Justine	1995–1997
Ms Tengvall Kaisa Tania	2014–present
Mrs Thomas (Madge) Clarke	1927–1939
Mrs To (Fang) Siu Yu 杜方小茹	2001–present
Mrs To (Kam) Yee Tuen 杜金義端	1994–2006
Mr Tobin David	2015–2016
Ms Tong	1948
Mrs Tong (Ho) Pui Shan Gloria 湯何佩珊	1992–1995, 1997–present
Ms Tong Kwai Fan Eva 湯桂芬	2007–2008
Ms Townend M K*	1954–1957
Mrs Triggs T M*	1953–1963
Mrs Tristram Joyce	1969–1970
Ms Tsang Alice	1970–1971
Mrs Tsang (Chong) Ka Yan Karen 曾莊嘉恩	2006–present
Mrs Tsang (Chung) Wai Yee	1963
Ms Tsang H	1972
Mr Tsang Hing Kee	1946–1948
Mrs Tsang J	1960–1980
Mr Tsang Kwai-ming	1939–1941
Ms Tsang Rose	1986–1987

Name	Year
Mrs Tsang T	1973–1974
Ms Tsang Wai Yee Phoebe 曾慧宜	2008–2010
Mrs Tse (Chow) Sin Ling Nancy	1998–1999
Mr Tse Wai Lok Timmy 謝煒樂	2013–2015
Ms Tsui Hiu Yan 徐曉欣	2008–2010
Mr Tsui Kam Tong Anthony 徐錦堂	2014–present
Ms Tsui Kit Ming 徐潔明	1993–2015, 2018–present
Mr Tsui Kwok Hing	1948
Mrs Tsui (Yeung) Mei Wai May 徐楊美慧	1975–1997
Ms Tuck Amanda	1981–1982
Ms Turbett	1934–1937
Mr Turner-Robson Jason Mark	2018–present
Ms Upsdell	1916
Ms Vaughan	1933–1934
Mrs Vere Man Yin Christine 蕭文燕	2013–2014
Mr Visick T H	1952–1953
Ms Wade J	1967–1968
Mrs Wai (Li) Kit Wa Jenny 韋李潔華	2006–2011
Mrs Wallace-Jones J	1962–1965
Mrs Walls Margaret Anne	1989–1995
Mrs Walsh P	1952–1954
Mr Walsh Robert James	2007–2008
Ms Walters E K*	1920–1933, 1947–1949
Ms Wan	1917
Ms Ward Phyllis J	1948–1950
Ms Watt Joyce E	1949–1962
Ms Wei Phoebe	1954
Mrs Welsh C*	1971–1972
Mrs Weng Carolyn	1988–1999
Ms Wentworth Norah	1920–1946
Ms Whattam L	1967–1971
Ms White	1934
Mrs Whitton	1964–1965

Name	Year
Mrs Wickens Helen	1981–1996
Mrs Wiggham M	1962–1963
Ms Williams Molly*	1965–1976
Mrs Williamson	1970–1971
Ms Willis	1925
Mrs Wilson	1927
Ms Wilson A	1965–1968
Ms Wilson Barbara A V	1966–1968
Ms Wilson Nancy	1951–1957
Mrs Wilson S	1959–1964
Ms Wilson 韋以信	1860–1862
Mrs Winfield	1962–1971
Mrs Winfield R E	1911–1915
Ms Wong A	1988–1989
Ms Wong Betsy 黃冰斯	1958–1959
Ms Wong Bik Yuk Daisy 黃碧玉	1989–2012
Ms Wong Carmen	2007–2008
Mrs Wong (Chan) Lai Wan Lily 王陳儷尹	1997–2018
Ms Wong Hau Yiu Charlotte 王巧瑤	2009–2010
Mrs Wong (Cheung) Ka Lee Carrie 黃張嘉莉	2007–2017
Mrs Wong (Cheung) Wai Shan Ida 黃張惠珊	2010–2014
Mr Wong Chi Yung Michael	2010–2011
Ms Wong Ching Yee Jenny 王菁儀	2009–2011
Mrs Wong (Chiu) Wai Yee Rosalind 王趙慧儀	1977–1990, 2001–2008
Ms Wong Jessie	1940–1941
Mr Wong Ka Ho 王家豪	2018–present
Mr Wong Ka Lok 黃家樂	1998–1999
Ms Wong Ka Yi Anissa 黃嘉怡	2005–2006
Mr Wong Kam Yiu Jimmy 黃金耀 (Dr)	2002–2006
Mrs Wong (Kan) Shuk Ching Theresa	1959–1995, 2007–2009, 2011–2012
Ms Wong Karen	1987–1988

Name	Year
Mrs Wong Lyndia	1946–1971
Mrs Wong (Leung) Renee 黃梁穎妍	2006–present
Mrs Wong (Leung) Suk Ying Anisa 黃梁淑英	1997–2014
Mrs Wong (Ling) Betty	1979–1986
Mrs Wong M	1964–1966
Ms Wong Ming Ming Elsie	1955–1956
Mrs Wong Moo Lydia*	1941, 1945–1971
Mr Wong Nam Bo 黃南波	1989–1992, 1995–2017
Ms Wong Pui Sze Catherine 黃珮詩	1995–present
Ms Wong See Pui Lilian 黃詩蓓	2018–present
Mrs Wong (Tam) Wing Cheung Bonnie 黃譚詠璋	2006–2013
Mr Wong Wah Alvin	2007–2008
Mr Wong Wai San 王偉新	2011–present
Mrs Wong (Wu) Elin 胡綺蓮	2000–2001
Mr Woo Chi Shan 胡之薪	1948–1955
Ms Woo Jannie	1959–1960
Ms Wood Constance	1931–1932
Mrs Woodhouse	1969
Mrs Wright M*	1949–1963
Ms Wun Tsz Sum 溫梓琛	2015–present
Ms Yam Sau Yin Candy 任秀然	2017–present
Mrs Yang S H	1946–1947, 1949–1953
Mrs Yao	1957
Ms Yap Set Lee Shirley 葉雪莉	2018–present
Mrs Yau Anita	1951–1987
Ms Yau S W	1995–1996
Ms Yeung Florence	1955–1956
Ms Yeung In Leng Elaine 楊燕玲	2018–present
Mrs Yeung Julia	1967–1973, 1974–1994
Ms Yeung Lily	1971–1973
Ms Yeung Patcy 楊佩詩	1993–1996
Ms Yeung Po Ki Dora 楊寶琪	2006–present

Name	Year
Mr Yeung Tsz Chun Raymond 楊子俊	2016–present
Ms Yim Tsz Yan Michelle 嚴子昕	2017–2019
Mrs Yip Anthony	1969–1975
Mrs Yip (Cheng) Tung Ying Ada 葉鄭東熒	2010–2011
Ms Yip Chui Man 葉翠雯	2015–present
Mr Yip Chun Yu Frank 葉震宇 (Dr)	2012–2014
Ms Yip Pui Ling 葉佩玲	2015–present
Mrs Yip (Tong) Wai Yun Leslie 葉唐慧茵	1998–2010
Ms Yiu E	1970–1975
Mrs Young Lydia	1960–1962
Mr Young Saye J L 楊俊成	1945–1946
Ms Yu I	1947
Ms Yu Ming Ka Gladys 余明珈	2011–present
Ms Yu Rosanna	1970–1972
Mrs Yu (Woo) Nellie*	1946–1947, 1949–1963, 1965–1967
Ms Yuen Becky	1989–1991
Mr Yuen Chu-hei	1967–1970
Ms Yuen Jean 元碧利	1964–1968
Mr Yuen Roy	1979–1986
Mr Yung Chi Ko 容志高	2012–2017
Ms Zheng Min Michelle-Priscilla 鄭敏	2006–2008

Junior School

Name	Year
Ms Ahwee Isolde	1952–1953
Mrs Au (Chan) Hoi Ki Karina 區陳凱琪	2012–present
Mrs Au (Tam) Oi Ling Ellen 歐譚藹靈	2009–present
Ms Auyeung Shirley	1971–1976

Name	Year
Mrs Baker M	1959–1963
Mrs Barnes J L	1947–1948, 1951
Mrs Benton Rachel	1970–1978
Mrs Bland	1953–1955
Mrs Blomfield Daphne Quay-ying	1978–1989
Mrs Calton S M	1987–1988
Mrs Chan (Barrett) Lisa Katherine	1996–1999
Mrs Chan (Cheung) Man Yan 陳張文欣	2007–present
Mrs Chan (Cheung) Wing 陳張穎	2001–2007
Mrs Chan (Chin) Mo Chun Yvonne 陳陳慕珍	1981–2000
Ms Chan Diana	1962–1963
Ms Chan Julia	1986–1987
Mrs Chan (Lo) Lai Kuen 陳盧麗娟	1999–present
Mrs Chan (Lui) Oi Man Enrica 陳雷藹雯	2005–2009
Mrs Chan (Luk) Chueck Wah Stella 陳陸卓華	2002–2005
Mrs Chan M	1974
Ms Chan Wing Yun Winnie 陳詠欣	2004–2009
Ms Chan Yuen Chi	1996–1999
Ms Charter	1976
Ms Chau Wai Yee 周慧儀	2013–present
Mrs Cheng Grace	1976–1980
Ms Cheng Chui Lin Lyn 鄭翠蓮	1994–present
Mrs Cheng M L	1973
Ms Cheng Nancy 鄭朗思	1984–1986, 1988–1993
Mrs Cheng Paulina	1961–1972
Ms Cheng Yuen Yu	1955–1958
Mrs Cheung (Chan) Yuk Ching Clare 張陳玉貞	1975–2011
Mrs Cheung (Cheung) Ella Christine 張張鎧靈	2017–present

Name	Year
Ms Cheung Kim Man Agnes	2001–2002
Ms Cheung Tsz Ting 張芷婷	2016–present
Mrs Chiang (Chan) Hung Mui Christina 蔣陳紅梅	1972–1982, 1993–2018
Mrs Chiang (Leung) Sui-ping Lourdes 蔣梁瑞萍	2002–2004
Ms Ching H	1969–1970
Mrs Chiu (Lau) Wai Ka 趙劉媁嘉	2011–present
Ms Choi Irene	1982–1985
Ms Choi Yat Wah	1973–1980
Ms Chong P	1971–1973
Ms Chow Kam Fun	1963–1964
Ms Chu Kit Yee Rosanna 朱潔儀	2005–2015
Mrs Chua (Lo) Fung Wa 蔡盧鳳華	2008–2011
Mrs Chui (Chiu) Mo-wan	1957–1967, 1977–1988, 1991–1992
Mrs Chui (Lam) Hiu Ying 崔林曉瑩	2013–present
Ms Chung	1917
Ms Chung Emily	1981–1983
Ms Chung Man Ping 鍾文萍	2014–present
Ms Chung Pik Yan Peggy 鍾壁茵	2009–2011
Mrs Chung (Wong) Chan Kim 鍾黃燦劍	1996–2017
Mrs Dai (Ho) Tin Mei Emily 戴何天美	1998–2016
Ms Der Irene	1953
Ms Dick	1977
Mrs Digby Susan	1982–1985
Mrs Dinsley	1953
Mrs Fan (Lam) Pui Yan Connie 樊林佩恩	1991–present
Ms Fok Hiu Tung Dorothy 霍曉彤	2011–2012
Mrs Fong (Lau) Oi Ling Henrietta	1994–1995
Mrs Fong Nina	1975–1989
Mrs Fraser H C	1947–1948

Name	Year
Mrs Fuhn J	1949
Mrs Fung (Hui) Yu Ning Elaine 馮許宇寧	2018–present
Mrs Fung (Li) Suk Han Liliane 馮李淑嫻	1978–2016
Mrs Fung (Soo) Kam Yee Winnie 馮蘇錦兒	2012–2018
Mrs Fung (Yam) Kim Man Teresa 馮任劍曼	2001–present
Mrs Gonzalez (Yu) Tinya 余淳茵	2007–2009, 2011–2015
Ms Goodair Doreen	1957–1961
Mrs Goodman K M	1954
Ms Hadfield Bethany Jan	2017–2018
Mrs Hai (Tsui) Oi Man Karen 奚徐凱文	2004–present
Ms Ho M	1972
Mrs Ho (Ng) An Yue	1972–1977
Ms Ho Wing Nga 何咏雅	2017–present
Mrs Hodgson Jane	1993–1994
Ms Hoffman Jeannette	1968–1981
Mrs Holdefer (Lee) Joan 李苑芳	1992–2004, 2010–2015
Ms Hui Flora	1956–1959
Ms Hui Mimi	1982–1985
Ms Hydes Sarah	1992–1993
Ms Imamura Yuri 今村有里	2017–present
Ms Ip Pui Ky Peggy 葉珮琪	2017–present
Ms Johnston Kelly Eric	1998–1999
Mrs Kan (Lui) Mei Ling Millie 簡呂美玲	2007–present
Mrs Kang (Cheung) Lai Yu 耿張麗瑜	2011–present
Mrs Kent (Taylor) Dorothy	1959–1985
Ms Koo Wai Yee Amy 顧慧怡	1998–2009
Ms Ku H Y	1948–1954
Ms Kung E	1967–1972
Ms Kwai Joan	1967

Appendix 3

Name	Year
Ms Kwok	1917
Mrs Kwok (Chan) Yin Ling Vivian 郭陳彥伶	2018–present
Ms Kwok Kit Yee	1993–1994
Ms Lai C	1972–1974
Ms Lam Ada 林欣欣	2012–2017
Mrs Lam (Chan) Shuk Fong Brenda 林陳淑芳	2002–present
Mrs Lam (Leung) Wei Yan Crystal 林梁為恩	2009–present
Ms Lam Sin Ying May 林善嬴	1996–2010
Ms Lam Yi 林懿	2018–present
Mrs Langley	1932–1941
Mrs Langworthy J	1956–1957
Ms Lau Kam Fung Annie 劉金鳳	2007–present
Mr Lau Ho Hin Kelvin 劉灝顯	2017–present
Ms Lau Kar Lok 劉嘉諾	1992–1993
Mrs Lau (Kong) Tik Sze Daisy 劉江廸詩	2008–present
Mrs Lau (Pang) Hoi Li 劉彭凱莉	2010–present
Ms Lau Sau Kwan	1964–1965
Ms Lau Wing Yiu Winnie 劉穎瑤	2011–present
Ms Lau Yuen Cheuk	1946–1953
Mr Lee Born Ting Otto 李邦珽	2000–2002
Mrs Lee (Chang) Lai Yee Polly 李鄭麗儀	2000–2011
Mrs Lee E B	1971–1974
Ms Lee Elizabeth	1983
Mrs Lee Esther	1977–1979
Ms Lee Hung-kun 李洪瑾	1993–2002
Ms Lee Ka Ki 李家琪	2010–2014
Mrs Lee (Lee) On Lai Annie 李李安麗*	2017–present, 1997–2016*
Ms Lee Woon-yee Peggy 李媛怡	2002–2003
Ms Lee Sun Min 李宣旼	2018–present
Mrs Lee (Tang) Ying Chi Veronica 李鄧瀅芝	2007–present
Mrs Lee Violet	1954–1968

Name	Year
Mrs Leung (Chou) Kam-ngan 梁曹錦顏	1994–present
Ms Leung H	1968
Mrs Leung (Lai) Ka Po Amanda 梁黎嘉寶	1992–1993
Mrs Leung (Li) Man Ki Mandy 梁李文璣	1972–2012
Ms Leung Rosanna	1969
Ms Leung Vivian	1985–1989
Ms Leung Wai Ming	1980–1982
Ms Leung Yuen Ying Lily 梁婉瑩	1993–2007
Ms Li Ka Yee 李嘉瑜	2011–present
Ms Li Man Yi Kitty 李敏儀	1995–2010
Ms Liang A	1951–1956
Ms Lim Elvera	1956–1959
Mrs Lim R	1957–1981
Mrs Liu (Au) Suk Han 廖歐淑嫻	2012–2017
Ms Lo Hau-yee	1987–1988
Ms Lo R	1967–1968
Ms Loh T	1967–1968
Ms Luk Hoi Yin Harmonie 陸凱妍	2015–present
Ms Ma Oi-lin 馬靄蓮	1967–2018
Ms Ma Sze Cheung Sabrina 馬仕章	2001–2002
Mrs Mak (Li) Wai Kwan Joyce 麥李慧君	2011–present
Mrs Marcham	1949
Ms Mcgrandle Kimberley Ruth	1997–2001
Ms Moore D	1967–1968
Ms Moore J	1973
Mrs Nam (Liu) Hoi Ying April 南廖海英	2002–2016
Ms Ng Alice	1993–1994
Ms Ng Mien Yin Christine 黃敏音	2015–2018
Ms Ng Iris	1989–1993
Mrs Ng (Liang) Wing Yun Vera 吳梁永恩	1996–2002

Name	Year
Ms Ng Sin Tung 伍倩彤	2012–2018
Mr Ng Tsing Wah 吳清華	2018–present
Mrs Phillips L	1947
Ms Poole Doreen	1991–1992
Ms Poon Clara	1986–1987
Ms Poon Ka Hing Erika 潘嘉馨	1996–present
Ms Seen M L	1953
Ms Shee	1917
Ms Shih Joan	1956–1957
Ms Shing Ka Ling 成嘉玲	1996–2010
Mrs Shum (Wong) Shuk Hung Alice 岑王淑紅	1995–present
Mrs Sin (Yeung) Christine	1970–1972, 1975–1980
Mr Sit Hoi Fai 薛海暉	2013–2015
Ms Siu King Yue Carina 蕭敬瑜	2005–2008
Mrs Smyly Diana	1962–1968
Mrs Snoswell	1940
Ms Spurrier A L	1982–1983
Mrs Stanis Nicola	2007–2009
Ms Stephens Lyla Dawn Lynnette	1999–2001
Ms Suen Yin Shin 孫嬿善	2018–present
Ms Sze Yu Mui 施玉妹	2011–2014, 2016–present
Mrs Tam (Wan) Yuet Kwan	1988–1994
Ms Tam Yee Man Joanne 譚綺旻	2002–2004
Mrs Tang (Tsui) Wai Yee Agatha 鄧崔慧儀	1983–1991, 1992–1993
Ms Tang Tsz-wan 鄧芷雲	1994–2008
Ms Tay M	1961–1962
Mrs Taylor Jill	1999–2012
Mrs Telfer K	1947
Ms To Angela	1991–1992
Mr Tong Yik Him Jacky 唐亦謙	2012–2018
Ms Trainor V O	1963–1964
Ms Tsang H	1972
Ms Tsang Mo Ching	1965

Name	Year
Ms Tsang Wai Mui	1980–1983
Ms Tsao Kwai-king	1989–1991
Mrs Tse Elizabeth	1983–1991
Mrs Tse (Lee) Chi Yan 謝李芷茵	2015–present
Ms Tsui K	1968–1971
Mrs Tyrrell V	1973–1974
Ms Tyson Cheri Lee	1960–1961
Mrs Watt (Yam) Ka Ling Katherine 屈任珈齡	1967–2005
Ms Watts Lesley	1957–1960
Ms Weilerscheid T	1995
Ms Winyard Barbara	1968
Mrs Wong Becky	1970–1990
Mrs Wong (Chan) Ying Tung Jasmine 王陳映彤	2014–present
Ms Wong Chi Kwan Denise 黃芷筠	1996–2001
Ms Wong Dorothy	1972–1977
Ms Wong Esther	1953–1955
Ms Wong Fung Yee Alice	1990–1991
Mrs Wong G	1967–1972
Ms Wong Heau In Esther 黃曉恩	2017–present
Ms Wong Ming Ming Elsie	1955–1956
Ms Wong Ming Yan 黃明茵	2001–present
Ms Wong Pui Sze 黃沛施	2017–present
Mrs Wong (Shen) Wing Yee Jane 黃冼泳儀	2009–present
Mrs Wong (Tam) Wing Yee Winnie 黃譚詠儀	2011–present
Mrs Wong Wendy	1985–1995
Mrs Wong (Wong) Kuen Kuen Ruby 黃王娟娟	2015–present
Mrs Wong (Yeung) Florance	1956
Mrs Wong Yip Wing 黃葉穎	2005–2011
Ms Woo Karen	1983–1986
Mrs Yau (Chu) Lai Ching Nina 邱朱麗清	1989–present
Ms Yau Oh Ee Hua	1963–1964

Appendix 3

Name	Year
Ms Yeung C	1967
Mrs Yeung (Tse) Kun Yee Cynthia 楊謝芹兒	1970–2012
Mrs Yih O	1962
Ms Yim R	1967–1971
Mrs Yip (Lit) Rebecca 葉列鸞琬	1957–1969, 1979–1982, 1985–1999
Mrs Yip (Wu) Yuewen 葉吳月文	2017–present
Mrs Yu	1949
Mrs Yu (Chan) Wing Shan Ella 庾陳泳珊	2004–present

Name	Year
Ms Yu Ellen	1993–1994
Mrs Yu (Ng) Wing Man 茹吳詠雯	2010–present
Ms Yu Sau Ying	1946–1949
Mrs Yu (Wong) Erh Tsung Rachel 余王爾聰*	2015–present, 2009–2015*
Mrs Yue Lydia	1971–1972
Ms Yuen Ka Sin 袁嘉善	2014–present
Ms Zhang Qiyun 張綺芸	2014–present

Appendix 4

Head Girls, 1922 to 2019

Year	Name
1922	Wong Pansy
1923	Fincher Maria
1925	Anderson Phyllis
1935	Anderson Catherine Joyce
1941	Kotewall Patsy
1947	Chan William, Oei Alice
1948	Howell Bertha
1949	Oei Yvonne
1950	Pillai Mina
1951	Ashby Clara
1952	Drew Lilian
1953	Ramsay Mary
1954	Shing Laura
1955	Yang Mirion
1956	Tsien Elaine
1957	Taylor Dorothy
1958	Lai Jane
1959	Ma Dorothy
1960	Yuk May
1961	Chang Mary Ann
1962	Ip Shirley

Year	Name
1963	Liu Stella
1964	Lee Evelyn
1965	Leung Violet
1966	Yue Agnes
1967	Wilking Sandra
1968	Cheung Stephanie
1969	Wilking Virginia
1970	Wilking Sylvia
1971	Duh Eileen
1972	Lam Adrienne
1973	Chen Mary, Chang Iris, Ngai Jessie
1974	Chan Wendy, Wu Elizabeth
1975	Hui Carol, Wong Jean
1976	Cho Amy, Lee Alice
1977	Cheung Antonia, Lo Cynthia
1978	Li Susanna, Wong Priscilla
1979	Cheng Eva
1980	Chen Annie
1981	Chan Mabel, Lee Joanna
1982	Yu Benita
1983	Chiu Wendy

Year	Name
1984	Morris Fiona
1985	Ng Jane
1986	Ann Karin, Chan Mary
1987	Po Winky
1988	Tsoi Selene
1989	Tsang Jennifer
1990	Lam Judy, Chan Anne Gigi
1991	Dasani Seema, Chan Evelyn
1992	Tsang Janice
1993	Chan Susanna
1994	Tsang Diana
1995	Lau Hynn Ming
1996	Woo Denise, Lau Vivien
1997	Lau Mandy
1998	Fung Wan Yi Winnie
1999	Chan Eleanor 陳雅詠
2000	Lau Hiu Yan Stephanie 劉曉欣
2001	Ho Wing Yan Janet 何詠欣
2002	Liu Yung Ye Beatrice 劉詠怡
2003	Nip Lok Tin Winnie 聶樂天
2004	Chow Theresa Lena 周廷勵
2005	Chan Man Hei Michele 陳敏熹
2006	Cham Wing Chi Lillian 覃穎芝 Kuok Yen Kwong 郭燕光
2007	Chan Mary Jean 陳瓊瑪 Chan Wing Tung Jasmine 陳泳彤
2008	Ko Yan Long Phoebe 高昕朗 Lam Chaminade 林澄
2009	Luk Jody Ching Sze 陸正思 Chan Wing Yan Joyce 陳詠欣
2010	L6 2010–2011: So Yik Ka 蘇奕嘉 Leung Wing Sum 梁詠心 S5 2010–2011: Hwang Chin Amanda 黃晴 Chen Pui Yin Yolanda 陳沛諺

Year	Name
2011	So Tsz Ching Natalie 蘇子晴 Yip Hoi Ching Cherie 葉愷晴
2012	Ng Lam Wai Zoe 伍琳煒 Yiu On Ying Angela 姚安盈
2013	Liu Hui Kay Nicole 廖煦琪 Yung Wai Man Regina 容慧雯
2014	Ma Yuen Kwan Vanessa 馬沅鈞 Qiu Jennifer Zijun 丘紫君
2015	Chan Lok San Kate 陳樂山 Chow Yik Yee Eunice 周易兒
2016	Yep Cheuk Hei Charlie 葉綽希 Fung Ying Ka Odessa 馮螢珈
2017	Wong Janus 王婕 Yeung Man Kei, Helen 楊文琦
2018	Fong Sin Hang Jada 方善珩 Fung Wai Yee Queenie 馮湋栭
2019	Liu Tin Nam Katrina 廖天藍 Yu Chin Hang Carina 余芊衡

Bibliography

Primary Source

Archives

Bishop's House Archives: DGS Minutes of School Council meetings files and general files from 1945 to 1998. The general files include correspondence of DGS with other institutions such as the Education Department, the Anglican Church, as well as parents and potential teachers from the UK.

Church Missionary Society (CMS) Archives
> Section I, East Asia Missions: Annual Letters 1917–1959
> Section II, East Asia Missions, 1859–1917: Minutes of Society for Promoting Female Education for Girls in the Far East (FES) and Annual Reports of FES
> Section III, Part 1: CMS/C/CH/O90/36. Annotated Reports and Letters of Missionaries

Diocesan Girls' School Archives: Minutes of School Council meetings 1999 to present, Headmistress's Reports, Speech Day Booklets, and old and recent photographs of the school and activities of students 1945 to present

Diocesan Old Girls' Association Archives

Colonial Office Records

Series CO129/242, CO 129/255, CO 129/388 and CO1030/571 and CO1030/1094, from Special Collections of HKU Libraries

Government Reports

Hong Kong Administration Report—Online

Hong Kong Annual Reports

Hong Kong Blue Book—Online

Hong Kong Sessional Papers—Online

Hong Kong Old Newspapers, Hong Kong Public Library, Multimedia Information System

China Mail

Hong Kong Daily Press
Kung Sheng Daily
Telegraph
Wah Kiu Yat Po
Proquest Historical Newspaper: *South China Morning Post* 1903 to 1946, from Hong Kong University Libraries

Hong Kong Public Records Office

HKRS94-1-06, HKRS58-60, HKRS156-1-280

Historical Laws of Hong Kong online

Special Government Reports

Kowloon Disturbances 1966, Report of Commission of Enquiry, Hong Kong Government, J. R. Lee Acting Government Printers, 1967.

Hong Kong Legislative Council Debates Official Report, in the Session of the Legislative Council of Hong Kong which opened on 17 October 1973. https://www.legco.gov.hk/yr73-74/h731017.pdf.

Annual Report by the Commissioner of the Independent Commission Against Corruption, 1974. Prepared by J. Cater, CBE, JP, Commissioner of the ICAC, for submission to His Excellency Governor Murray MacLehose in accordance with Section 17 of the ICAC Ordinance, 1974.

White Paper, Secondary Education in Hong Kong over the Next Decade, Tabled in the Legislative Council, 16 October 1975, https://www.eduhk.hk/cird/publications/edpolicy/02.pdf.

"The Development of Senior Secondary and Tertiary Education in Hong Kong," October 1978, Hong Kong Government, https://www.eduhk.hk/cird/publications/edpolicy/04.pdf.

K. W. J. Topley, Secretary for Education, "The Hong Kong Education System," June 1981, Government Secretariat, Hong Kong Government.

Education Commission Report No 2, Education Bureau, HKSAR, https://www.e-c.edu.hk/doc/en/publications_and_related_documents/education_reports/ecr2_e.pdf.

Education Commission Report No 3, Education Bureau, HKSAR, Education Commission Report no. 3, Education Bureau, HKSAR, https://www.e-c.edu.hk/doc/en/publications_and_related_documents/education_reports/ecr3_e.pdf.

Education Commission Report No 4, Education Bureau, HKSAR, https://www.edb.gov.hk/attachment/en/curriculum-development/major-level-of-edu/gifted/guidelines-on-school-based-gifted-development-programmes/ecr4_e.pdf.

Education Commission Report No 5, Education Bureau, HKSAR, https://www.e-c.edu.hk/doc/en/publications_and_related_documents/education_reports/ecr5_e.pdf.

Education Commission Report No 6, Education Bureau, HKSAR, https://www.e-c.edu.hk/doc/en/publications_and_related_documents/education_reports/ecr6_e.pdf.

"Information Paper—Curriculum Development Institute," Panel on Education, Paper 17 October 1997, Legislative Council, HKSAR, https://www.legco.gov.hk/yr97-98/english/panels/ed/papers/ed1710-6.htm.

Secondary Source

Books

馮以浤。〈學運的歷史意義及評價〉。載香港專上學生聯會編，《香港學生運動回顧》。香港：廣角鏡出版社，1983。Fung, Yee Wang, "Student Activism—A Force Not to Be Ignored." In *Hong Kong Student Activism in Retrospect*, edited by Hong Kong Federation of Students. Hong Kong: Wide Angle, 1983.

馮以浤。〈麥理浩年代的社經政策與課外活動的發展〉。載曾永康、黃毅英編，《香港學校課外活動發展史》。香港：香港城市大學出版社，2021。Fung, Yee Wang, "The Socio-economic Policy and Development of Extracurricular Activities in MacLehose's Era". In *The History of Extracurricular Activities in Hong Kong Schools*, edited by Tsang Wing Hong and Wong Ngai Ying. Hong Kong: City University of Hong Kong Press, 2021.

鄭宏泰、黃紹倫。《三代婦女傳奇：何家女子》。香港：三聯書店，2010。

梁雄姬。《中西融和：羅何錦姿》。香港：三聯書店（香港）有限公司，2013。Leung Hung Kei, Lady Victoria Jubilee Lo. Hong Kong: Joint Publishing Hong Kong Co Ltd, 2013.

Boyd, Robin. *The Witness of the Student Christian Movement*. London: Society of Promoting Christian Knowledge, 2007.

Castells, M. *The Shek Kip Mei Syndrome: Economic Development and Public Housing in Hong Kong*. London: Pions Ltd, 1990.

Chan Lau Kit-ching, and Peter Cunich. *The Impossible Dream: Hong Kong University from Foundation to Re-establishment 1910 to 1950*. Hong Kong: Oxford University Press, 2002.

Chan-Yeung, Moira. *A Medical History of Hong Kong 1942–2015*. Hong Kong: Chinese University of Hong Kong Press, 2019.

Chan-Yeung, Moira. *The Practical Prophet: Bishop Ronald O. Hall and His Legacies*. Hong Kong: Hong Kong University Press, 2015.

Chau, L. C. "Economic Growth and Income Distribution in Hong Kong." In *25 Years of Social and Economic Development in Hong Kong*, edited by Benjamin K. P. Leung and T. Wong, 494–503. Hong Kong: Centre of Asian Studies, the University of Hong Kong, 1994.

Chen, Ping, and Nanette Gottlieb. *Language Planning and Language Policy: East Asian Perspective*. Cornwall: Curzon Press, 2001.

Cheng, Irene. *Intercultural Reminiscences*. Hong Kong: Hong Kong Baptist University, 1996.

Cheng, Joseph. *Hong Kong in Transition*. Hong Kong: Oxford University Press, 1986.

Chiu, Patricia P. K. "Female Education and the Early Development of St. Stephen's Church, Hong Kong [1865–1900s]." In *Christian Encounter with Chinese Culture: Essays on Anglican and Episcopal History in China*, edited by Philip Wickeri, 47–64. Hong Kong: Hong Kong University Press, 2015.

Chiu, Patricia P. K. *A History of the Grant Schools Council*. Hong Kong: Grant Schools Council, 2013.

Chiu, Patricia P. K. *Promoting All-Round Education for Girls: A History of Heep Yunn School*. Hong Kong: Hong Kong University Press, 2020.

Choi, Susanne Y. P. Choi, and Fanny M. Cheung. *Women and Girls in Hong Kong: Current Situation and Future Challenges*. Hong Kong: Hong Kong Institute of Asia-Pacific Studies, the Chinese University of Hong Kong, 2012.

Emerson, Geoffrey Charles. *Hong Kong Internment, 1942 to 1945: Life in the Japanese Civilian Camp at Stanley*. Hong Kong: Hong Kong University Press, 2008.

English, Jean. *A Vanished World: My Memories*. Private circulation, n.d.

Bibliography

Featherstone, W. T. *The Diocesan Boys' School and Orphanage: The History and Records, 1869 to 1929*.

Fung, Yee Wang. "Education." In *Hong Kong in Transition*, edited by Joseph Cheng, 300–330. Hong Kong: Oxford University Press, 1986.

Fung, Yee Wang, and Moira Chan-Yeung. *To Serve and To Lead: A History of the Diocesan Boys' School*. Hong Kong: Hong Kong University Press, 2009.

Gittins, Jean. *Eastern Windows, Western Skies*. Hong Kong: South China Morning Post, 1969.

Gittins, Jean. *Stanley: Behind Barbed Wire*. Hong Kong: Hong Kong University Press, 1983.

Goodstadt, Leo. *Poverty in the Midst of Affluence: How Hong Kong Mismanaged Its Prosperity*. Hong Kong: Hong Kong University Press, 2013.

Hoe, Susanna. *The Private Life of Old Hong Kong: Western Women in the British Colony, 1841–1941*. Hong Kong: Oxford University Press, 1991.

King, Gordon. "An Episode in the History of the University." In *Dispersal and Renewal: Hong Kong University during the War Years*, edited by Clifford Matthews and Oswald Cheung, 85–103. Hong Kong: Hong Kong University Press, 1998.

Lee, Vicky. *Being Eurasian: Memories Across Racial Divides*. Hong Kong: Hong Kong University Press, 2004.

Luk, Hung-kay. *A History of Education in Hong Kong*. Hong Kong: Hong Kong Lord Wilson Heritage Trust, 2000.

Ng-Lun, A. N. H. *Quest for Excellence: A History of the Chinese University of Hong Kong*. Hong Kong: Chinese University Press of Hong Kong, 1994.

Scott, I. *Political Change and the Crisis of Legitimacy*. Hong Kong: Oxford University Press, 1989.

Sinn, Elizabeth, and Christopher Munn. *Meeting Place: Encounters across Culture in Hong Kong 1841–1984*. Hong Kong: Hong Kong University Press, 2017.

Smith, Carl. *Chinese Christians: Elites, Middlemen, and the Church in Hong Kong*. Hong Kong: Hong Kong University Press, 2005.

Sweeting, Anthony. *Education in Hong Kong, 1941–2001: Visions and Revisions*. Hong Kong: Hong Kong University Press, 2004.

Symons, C. J. *Looking at the Stars: Memoirs by Catherine Joyce Symon*. Hong Kong: Pegasus Books, 1996.

Tsang, Steve. *A Modern History of Hong Kong*. Hong Kong: Hong Kong University Press, 2006.

Wang, Ping. *Aching for Beauty: Foot-Binding in China*. Minneapolis: University of Minnesota Press, 2000.

Wong, Frances. *China Bound and Unbound: History in the Making—An Early Returnee's Account*. Hong Kong: Hong Kong University Press, 2009.

Yeo, Florence. *My Memories*. Pittsburgh: Dorrance Publishing, 1994.

Periodicals

The China Medical Journal, Vol. XXX, 1916.

China Review or *Notes and Queries on the Far East*, Volume XIX, 1892.

Education International, 23 January 2006, accessed 28 June 2020, https://www.ei-ie.org/en/detail/54/hong-kong-teachers-protest-following-stress-related-suicides.

The Female Missionary Intelligence, 1859 to 1864.

History of Education, 17, 2008.

International Journal of Educational Management, 23(1), 2009.

An Irish Quarterly Review, 2, 1913.

Journal of the Royal Asiatic Society Hong Kong Branch, 57, 2017.

Journal of Social Issues, 59, 2003.

The Outpost, 1922 to 1975.

The Quest Magazine of the Diocesan Girls' School 1941, 1947–1959. Because of space limitation, the name has been shortened to *The Quest* in this school history. In 1960, the school magazine was renamed *Quest*. In 1972, the Chinese section of Quest was given the name 研幾.

Thesis

Morris, Erin. "Participation in Extracurricular Activities and Academic Performance: A Comprehensive Review". master's degree dissertation, Western Kentucky University, 2019.

Interviews

From the DOGA website, information was obtained for the following old girls based on interviews by members of the DOGA over the years: Cecily Kotewall, Patsy Kotewall, Frances Wong, Sarah Liao, Karen Lam, Stella Lau, Eva Cheng, Solina Chau, Vivian Yam, Helen Meng, and Karen Morris. http://www.doga.org.hk/index.php/doga-news/conversations/old-girls-profiles/112-interviews/.

Twenty-one individuals were interviewed by Moira M. W. Chan-Yeung by email or telephone:

Mrs Ho (Ko) Suet Yiu Doris 何高雪瑤	Ms Wong Bik Yuk Daisy 黃碧玉
Mrs Lau (Kun) Lai Kuen Stella 劉靳麗娟	Mr Chu Chun Pong Steve 朱振邦
Mrs Lau (Pong) Elim 劉龐以琳	Dr Or Man Wai 柯文偉
Mrs Yip (Lit) Rebecca 葉列鷺琬	Mrs Chan (Lau) Siu Yee Connie 陳劉小儀
Mrs Dai (Ho) Tin Mei Emily 戴何天美	Mrs Chan (Cheung) Mei Ling Mary 陳張美梨
Mrs Lee (Lee) On Lai Annie 李李安麗	Mrs Santos (Yip) Yuen Shan Rosa 山度士葉婉珊
Mrs Hui (Lun) Yin Kan Paulina 許倫燕勤	Mrs Kam (Wong) Pui Wa Pearl 甘黃佩華
Prof Lai Chui Chun Jane 黎翠珍	Mrs Shing (Chow) Kit Ling Lena 成周潔玲
Dr Man Wai Hin Thomas 文惠顯	Mr Lam Siu Keung 林紹強
Mr Tang Kun Loi 鄧根來	Mr Mok Chiu Yu Augustus 莫昭如
Mr Wong Nam Bo 黃南波	

It is not possible to give all the details on the timing of the "interviews" because, with some individuals, the email communications and telephone calls were carried out on many occasions and over a period of time.

Index

Note: Page numbers in italics refer to figures or tables.

130th Anniversary, 180–181, *181–183, 403*

140th Anniversary, 191, 387, *404*

1940 Wing / Science Wing or Block / Gibbins Wing, 47, *76,* 131–132, 137, 166, 180, 205, 257, *401*

1950 Wing / Domestic Science or Chapel Wing or Block / Hurrell Wing or Block, 103, *103,* 108, 131–132, 137, 166, *173,* 205, 258–259, *258,* 284, *401*

Academic Aptitude Test (AAT), 130, 199, 222, *403*

Albany Terrace, xvii, 7, 9, 11, *399*

Alford, Richard Charles, 15, 18, 20–24, 29, *405, 406*

all-round education, 118, 234, 236, 288, 321, 341, 354

Allen, Ethel A., 47, *75,* 82, 94, 120, *410*

alternative curriculum, 294, 340

Alumnae Wall, *379, 380,* 381

Anderson, Phyllis, 69, 71, 82

Arthur, William M. B., 22, *22–*25, 237, 281, *399–400*

AS Computer Applications Course, 177

Asian Games, 185, *185,* 225–226, 317, 323, 325–326, *326,* 329

Avian Influenza (H5N1), 192, *403*

Baker, John Gilbert Hyndley, 109, 138, 156, *402, 406*

Baker, Pamela, 151, *152,* 319, *320,* 325, *325,* 329

Bascombe, Nora, 37, 45, 47, 373, *410*

Basic Law, 193

Baxter Mission, 26, 35

Baxter, Robert, 8, 17

Baxter, Susan Harriet, 8–11, 13, 15–17, 23, *406*

bazaar, 18, 58, 70, 105, *106,* 137, 372, 385

Beijing Olympics, 226, 332

Belilios Public School, 70, 85

Benton, R., 128, *128,* 235, *402–403, 421*

Bishop's Diocesan Girls' School, xviii, 8, 8n5, 30

"Blest are the Pure in Heart," 64–65, 182, 298

Blomfield, Quay Ying, Daphne, 127–128, 161–162, *162, 183,* 235, 355, *367, 403, 421*

Board of Education, 8n5, 19, 63, 74, 156

boarding school, xviii, 7–9, 13, 25–26, 29, 49, 51, 61, 88, 92, 96–97, 109, 119, 131–132, 135–136, 166, 269–270, 338, *339,* 343, *402*

BOCHK Bauhinia Bowl, 328–329, *329. See also* Omega Rose Bowl

BOCHK Rising Star Awards, 329

Bokhary, S. D. S., *168, 183,* 235, *396, 406*

Boxer Rebellion, 32

Boys' and Girls' Club, 52, 107, 160, 234

Boys' Club, 70, 150

Brownies, 108, *150,* 153, 160, 188, 231, 391, *391*

Burdon, John Shaw, 24–25, 29, *406*

Cambridge Local Examinations, 48, *400*

Cantonese, 10, 219, 221, 248, 338, 346, 362

Career Committee, *150*

Centenary Block / Symons Block, 166, 171, *173,* 205, 209, 285

Centenary Celebration, xix, 88, 108–109, 134, *136,* 376, 386, *402*

Central School / Queen's College, 19, 23–24, 34, 85, 303n31, *399*

Chan, Amy, 292, *293*

Chan, Andrew, 213, 276, *406*

Chan, Ho Wai Rebecca (née Chung, 陳可慰), 82, 246

Chan, Lawrence S. L. (陳世諒), 104, 120, 355, *368, 410*

Chan, Mary Jean (陳瓊瑪), 245, *427*

Chan, Mo Wah Moira (陳慕華), xiii, 246, 347

Chan, Tiffany, 331

Chan, Yik Cham (陳翊湛), 120, 146, 178, 355, 368–369, *411*

Chan, Yvonne, xvi, xviii, xx, 213, 383, *406*

"Change and Challenge," 288

Chapel of the Holy Spirit, 136–137, 259, 268

Chatjaval, Sheilah, xvi, 213, 396, *406*

Chau, Hoi-shuen Solina (周凱旋), 249

Cheng, Eva (鄭汝樺), 246, *426*

Cheng, Irene (née Ho Tung, 鄭何奇姿), xvii, 37, 44, 46–47, 49–50, 50n57, 64, 237, 240, 283, 337, 370, *371*, 373

Cheng, John, 305

Cheng, Nancy (鄭朗思), *301–302*, 307, *310*, *421*

Cheng, Ronnie, *28*, 213, 226, 312, *314*, *406*

Cheung, Beatrice (née Ma), 356, *411*

Cheung, Clare (née Chan, 張陳玉貞), 356–357, 367, *421*

Cheung, Man Lai Peggy (張敏麗), 357, 367, *411*

Chiang, Grace (蔣頌恩), xvi, xx, *301*, *314*, *411*

Chiang, Hung Mui Christina (née Chan, 蔣陳紅梅), *301–302*, 305, 311, *315*, 357, 367, *422*

Chien, Chi-lien Elizabeth (錢其濂), 245

China Light and Power hut, 137, 166, *260*, *260*, *403*

China Mail, xvi, 10

Chinese Department, 78, 103–104, 147, 178, 284, 339

Ching, Man Fai Lucy (程文輝), 248

Ching, Sansan, 114

Chiu, Kai Keung, 312

Chiu, Yee Ha (趙綺霞), 243, 305n49, 316

Choy, Suk-fan, 312

Christ Church, 60, 148, 269

Church Missionary Society (CMS), 17, 19, 36, 45

Churn, S. M. Major, 87, 99, 131, 133–134, 143, *406*

Citizens' Club, *150*, 153, 186, 278

Clark, Jill, *164*, 185, 321, 323, 353, *412*

Cobbold, R. F., 35–36

Code of Aid, 115, *402*

Community Youth Club (CYC) Outstanding Member Award, 189

Council of the Diocesan Girls' School Incorporation Ordinance 1969, 122, *402*

Counselling and Guidance Team, 188, 273

Crosby, Poppy, *154*, *301*, 305, 352, 357–358, 367, *412*

Crozier, Douglas James Smyth, *133*, 135

Curriculum Development Institute, 176, 197

Dai, Tin Mei Emily (née Ho, 戴何天美), xviii, xxi, 189, 195, *195*, 215, 225, 230, 235, 243, 358, 367, 394, *403–404*, *406*, 422

"Daily Giving Service," xiv, xix, 4, 52–53, 80, 109, 135, 155, 157, 232, 236, 250, 252, 277–278, 300, 346, 357, *375*, *400*

Daily Press, 16

DGS Plaza, 209, *210*

DGS Quest: Building on Excellence, 379, 381, 387–388

Dido and Aeneas, 304, 358

Diocesan Boys' School and Orphanage, 30, 31, 41

Diocesan Boys' School, *28*, 30, 31, 41, 74, *400*, 405

Diocesan Girls' Junior School (DGJS), 128, 161, 195, *231*, *301*, 307n64, 345, *402*

Diocesan Girls' School (DGS), xiii, xv, xvi, 4, 8, 26, 29–30, 31, 36, 52, 233, 282, 373, *400*

Diocesan Girls' School and Orphanage, 29–30, 31–32, 36, 41, 53, 101, 282, 337, 339, 347, 372, *400*, 405

Diocesan Girls' School Management Committee Limited (DGSMC), 211, 213–214

Diocesan Home and Orphanage (DHO), xvi, 19, 21–24, 26, 28–30, 35, 237, 267, 280–282, 298, 347, *399–400*, 405

Diocesan Native Female Training School (DNFTS), xvi–xviii, xx, 8n5, 8–11, *12*, 13–16, *17*, 22, 25–26, 28, 29–30, 31, 34, 40, 237, 280–282, 296, 335, 337, 399, 405

Diocesan Old Girls' Association (DOGA), xviii, 70, 105, 123, 167, 206, 235, 319, 321, Chapter 16, 386–387, 392, *401*, *404*

Diocesan School and Orphanage (DSO), 28–30, 31, 39–40, 97, 122, *400*

Diocesan School and Orphanage Incorporation Ordinance 1892, 29, 97

Diocesan Schools' Choral Society, 106, 303, *304*, 308, *308*

Direct Subsidy Scheme (DSS), 161, 174–175, 196, 199–201, *202*, 203, 213–214, 216–217, 232, 234, 251, 294, 312, 345–346, 349, 351, *404*, 405

DOGA Place, 209, 261, *261*, 379, 381, *404*

"Double Cohort," 218
Dr C. J. Symons Scholarship, 377–378
Dunbar, E. (Matthews), 45, 99, *416*
Duppuy, Charles Ridley, 52, 58

Eastern Street, 11, *399*
Eaton, M. A. W. (伊頓), 10–11, *12*, 13–16, 23, 281, *399*, *412*
eClass, 215, 224
Edmund Cheung hut, 166, 260, *260*, *403*
Education (Amendment) Ordinance 2004, 211
Education Action Group, 114
Education and Manpower Bureau (EMB), 200–201, 205–206, 217, 222
Education Bureau (EDB), 206–207, 213–214, 217, 220, 225, 274, 292, 313, *404*
Education Commission Report (ECR), 160, 163, 171, *403*
  ECR1, 171, 174
  ECR2, 174
  ECR3, 174
  ECR4, 175
  ECR5, 175
  ECR6, 176
  ECR7, 171, 191, 193
Education Commission, 115, 160, 171, *403*
Education Conference 1878, 20, 281
Education Department (ED), 33, 91–92, 97, 99, 102, 104, 112, 117, 120, 124–127, 129, 132, 138, 141, 145–146, 152, 156, 160–161, 163, 167, 174–177, 182, 184, 188, 190, 193, 199–200, 203, 216–217, 219, 222, 233, 285–286, 288, 303n31, 307n61, 305, 341, 349
Education Ordinance 1913, 32, *400*
Edwards, Norah (聞慧中), *301*, 303–305, 358–359, *368*, *412*
Eitel, Ernest John, xviii, 8, 8n5, 16, 20, 30, 34, 298n2
English, Jean, 64
Eva, Owen V., 132, 135, *406*
Extension Phase I, 166–167, *168*, 169, 177, 203, 261, *261*, *403*
Extension Phase II, 169, 171, *172–173*, 261, *261*, 387, *403*
Extension Phase III / School Improvement Plan (SIP), 196, 203, *204*, 205, 262, *262*, 263, 347, *404*

extracurricular activities (ECA), 50–53, 67–70, 79, 104–108, 116–118, 149–155, *150*, 160–161, 167, 181, 184–189, *187*, 191, 198, 207, 214, 225–232, 342–343, *400*
Extradition Bill, 193

Fairlea House, 26
Fairlea School, 26, 28–29, 35, 39, 41, *400*
Featherstone W. T., xvi, 62, 298
Female Diocesan School, xvii, 21
Female Missionary Intelligencer, 13, 237
Fenton, Patricia (née Kotewall), 56, 64, 75, 319
Ferguson, Catherine, 37, 45, 48, 51–53, 55, 234, 282, 318, 337, 348–349, 373, *400–401*, *406*, *412*
Fincher, Maria (née Kacker), 37, 41, 140, *183*, 370, 373, 381, *383*, *406*, *426*
Fisher, Molly, 93, *94*, 108, 118, *402*, *406*
Founders' Day, 46, 98–100, 373
Fung, Wan Yi Winnie (馮韻兒), 250, 279, *427*

General Certificate Examination, Advanced Level (GCE-A), 217–219, *241*, 286, 294, 340
General Certificate Examination, Ordinary Level (GCE-O), 143, 219, 286
General Certificate of Secondary Education (GCSE), 219
Gibbins, Elizabeth M., 71, 73–74, *75*, 76–79, 83–85, 87–88, 98, 118, 134–135, *136*, *144*, 234, 239, 251, 282–283, 335, 348–349, 375, *376*, 377, *401*, *406*, *413*
Gillard, G., 188
Girl Guides, 52, 58, 69–70, 81, 107–108, *150*, 160, 181, 229
Girls' Club, 107, *150*, 277
Girls' Day School, 7–9, 8n5, 30
Gittins, Jean (née Ho Tung), xvii, 38, 44–45, 83, 337
Goodban, Gerald Archer, xxi, 80, 87, 92, 95, 125, 300
Gospel Week, 275
Grant Code, 33, 41, 74, 90–91, 93, 115, 125, *400–401*
Grant School Council (GSC), 74, 85, 91–92, 125
Grant-in-Aid 1873, 8n5, 20–21, 23, 32–33, 39–40, 48, 57, 61, 63, 73, 84, 282, 348, *399–400*
Grantham, Alexander, 108
Grantham, Lady, 107, *129*, 287
Green hut, 123, *124*, 258, *258*, *402*

"Greek Temple" / "Greek Parthenon," *59*, 96, *97*, 169, 256, 258

Hall, Ronald Owen, 72, 76, 86–88, 91–93, 95–96, 98–100, 107, 109, 118–119, 135, *136*, 137–138, 140, 149, 156, 234, 259, 268–269, 372, *401–402*, *406*

Hawker, Maud I., 36–38, 347, 373, *413*

Hazeland, Doris, 237, *413*

Heep Yunn School, 28, 41, 92, 132, 162–163

Hemery, Gordon, 106, *301*, 303, *413*

Ho Tung, Eva, 44, 49, 50, 50n57, 64, 82, 237, 283

Ho Tung, Lady, 37, 44, 46, 48, 78

Ho Tung, Robert, 35, 37, 44, 46, 52

Ho, Helen, 75, 82

Ho, Suet Yiu Doris (née Ko 何高雪瑤), 161, 167, *168*, 180, 195, 213, 235, 243, *383*, *403*, *406*

Hoare, Joseph Charles, 29, 31, 35–36, 46, 100, 372, *406*

Hoare, Mrs, 35–36

Hong Kong Academy for Performing Arts, 160, 245, 313

Hong Kong Advanced Level (HKAL) Examination, *148*, 174, 179, 194, 218, 220, 238, 240, *241*, 292, 362, 307, *404*

Hong Kong Arts Festival, 304

Hong Kong Certificate of Education Examination (HKCEE), 147, *148*, 174, 178–179, 179n54, 194, 218, 220, 237, 238, 240, 250, 273, 288, 291–292, 293, 307, 331, 362, *404*

Hong Kong Diploma of Secondary Education Examination (HKDSE), 194, 218–220, 223, 240, *241*, 273, 294, 311, 340, *404*

Hong Kong Junior Local Examination, 49, 63, 283

Hong Kong Outstanding Young Student Award, 292

Hong Kong School Sports Association (HKSSA), 327–328

Hong Kong Schools Music Festival, 152, *154*, *155*, 160, 179, 185–186, 188, 226, 243, 303, 303n31, *401*

Hong Kong Schools Sports Council (HKSSC), 327

Hong Kong Schools Sports Federation (HKSSF), 232, 319, 322, 327–331

Hong Kong Schools' Musical Association (HKSMA), 300, 302, 303n41

Hong Kong Senior Local Examination, 47, 283

Hong Kong Sheng Kung Hui (HKSKH, Anglican Church of Hong Kong), 156n137, 156, 191n80, 202, 203, 211, 312

Hong Kong Sports Institute (HKSI), 327, 331–332

Hong Kong University of Science and Technology (HKUST), 220–221, 296, 394–395

Hong Kong's National Sports Associations (NSAs), 327

"Hotel School" / "Hotel Schools," 206–207, *208*, 271, 347, *404*

Hui, Yin Kan Paulina (née Lun, 許倫燕勤), xviii, xx, 185, 322, 324, *413*

Humbug, 167, 311

Hurrell, Winifred Alice, 87–88, 89, 92–93, *93*–94, 96, 98–103, 105, 108–109, 118, 134–135, *136*, 140, 146, 149, 234, 239, 268, 284–285, 288, 336, 340, 372–373, *375*, *376*, 384, *401–402*, 407, *413*

Hurst, Aileen, 164, 273, 291

information and communication technology (ICT), 218, 221

Institute of Education, 175, 194, 216

International English Language Testing System (IELTS), 219–220

Irving, Edward Alexander, 50

Irving, Rachel, Miss 50

IT Department, xvii, 214–215, 224

Johnstone, Margaret, 26, 35–36, 373

Joint Primary 6 Examination, 113, 124–126, 130, *401–402*

Kaleidoscope, 228, 377, 392, *404*

Keswick, William, 25

kindergarten, 45, 51, 60–61, 69, 71, 81, 99, 100, 104, 119, 123–124, 161, 258–259, 269, 285, 298–299, *302*, 358, 372, *401–402*

Kirkby, Mrs, 359, *414*

Ko, Faith (高文蘊), 243

Ko, Synthia (高德儀), 227, *301*, 312, *314*, *410*

Kotewall, Mrs, 49

Kotewall, Robert, 49

Kvan, Inger, 120, 359–360, *367*, 369, *414*

Index 437

Kwong, Kong-kit Peter, 156–157, 156n137, 180, 182, *183*, 190, 202, *407*

Kwong, Paul, 211, *212*, 268

Ladies Committee, 8–11, 13–16

Lai, Andrea, xvi, xx, 347

Lai, Chui Chun Jane (黎翠珍), xvi, xviii, xxi, 243, *426*

Lam, Grace (née Lee), 381

Lam, Siu Ling Karen (林小玲), 247

Lam, Yee Ling (née Lee), 120, *414*

Lamsam, Kim (née Fenton), 164, 360, *367*, *414*

Lamsam, Robyn, xvi, 184, *185*, 225, 323, *324*, 329, 331

Lander, Gerald Heath, 42–43

Lander, Mrs, 43

Lau, Claudia, 330

Lau, Elim (née Pong, 劉龐以琳), xviii, xxi, 157, 158, 161, *162*, 163, 165, *168*, 180, 189–191, 234, 243, 277, 291–292, 308, 343–345, 394, *403*, *407*, *415*

Lau, Lai Kuen Stella (née Kun, 劉靳麗娟), xvi, xviii, xx–xxi, 190–191, 195, *195*, 205, 213, 225, 232, 234, 243, 292, 331, 343, *403*, *407*, *415*

Lee, Baldwin, 60

Lee, Elton, 312

Lee, Ho Ching, 326, *326*

Lee, Joanna C. (李正欣), 316

Lee, Kit Ming (née Poon, 李潘潔明), 178, 227, *415*

Lee, Man Yee Virginia (李文渝), 247

Lee, On Lai Annie (née Lee, 李李安麗), xviii, xxi, 195, *195*, 213, 225, 230, 232, 235, *404*, *407*, *423*

Lee, Quo-wei, 167, *168*

Lee, Ying Chi Veronica (née Tang, 李鄧瀅芝), 360, *367*, *423*

Legge, James, 6, 8n5, 19

Leung, Kin Fung, 311, *313*

Leung, Lydia (one of the two graduates before 1900), 11, *12*, 13, 237

Leung, Vanessa, xvi

Li, Chi Ho, 137

Li, Wai Yee (李惠儀), 244

Li, Yuen Mei Emmy, 250

Li, Yuet Ting, xviii, xxi, 180

Liao, Sau-tung Sarah Mary (廖秀冬), 246

liberal studies, 194, 217–219, 294, *353*, 360

Liu, Yan Wai, 326

Lo, Man Kam Mrs, 49, 71, 100, *383*

Lo, Shiu-ching Katherine (羅兆貞), 245

Lo, Victoria Jubilee (née Ho Tung), 44

London Missionary Society (LMS), 5–6, 19, 268

Looking at the Stars, xvii, 157, 377

Lowcock, Jimmy, 151, 325

Lugard, Flora Lady, 40, 298

Lugard, Frederick, 40

Lynn, Margaret (林敏柔), 305, 316

MacLehose, Murray, 111–112, 116, 155, 288, *402*

Man, Si Wai (文思慧), 248–249

Man, Wai Hin Thomas (文惠顯), 214, *416*

Maneely, Marjorie, 120, *301*, 305, *306*, 361, *367*, *416*

Mansfield, Margaret, *94*, 120, *121*, 361, *367*–369, *407*, *416*

Mason, Katherine M., 120

Menear, John, 188, *407*

Meng, Mei Ling Helen (蒙美玲), 248

Mercer, W. T., 11

mini-bazaar, 105, 207, 228

Ministering Children's League (MCL), 70, 300

modern stream, 101–102, 142, 284, 288, *401*

Mok, Chiu Yu Augustus, 146, *164*

Mok, Man Wai Karen (aka Karen Morris, 莫文蔚), 167, 249

Mok, Yin Fong (芳姐), 365–366, *367*

Money, Margaret, 305

Morrison Education Society, 5

Multimedia Learning Centre (MMLC), 177

New Senior Secondary (NSS) Curriculum, 194, 217–219, 274, 292, *404*

New Territories Schools Sports Association (NTSSA), 327

Ng, Saw Kheng (née Yeoh), 167, 213, *396*, *407*

Ng, Tsui Yan Amy, xvi

Nissen huts, 99–100, 123, *124*, 132, 258, *258*, 302

O'Connell, Nancy, 120, *121*, 304–305, 361–362, *367*–369, *417*

Ogilvie, J. H., 269, *407*

Olympic Games, 323, *324*, 331–332

Omega Rose Bowl Sportsperson-of-the-Year, 189

Omega Rose Bowl, 151, *152*, 155, 328. *See also* BOCHK Bauhinia Bowl

Opium War, 4, 14, 19, 33

Or, Man Wai (柯文偉), 362, 367, *417*

Organisation for Economic Cooperation and Development (OECD), 115, 160, 171

Ost, J. B., 26

Other Learning Experience (OLE), 194–195, 218–219, 225, 343

other learning programs (OLP), 220

"Our Father by Whose Servants," 79, 298

Outpost, xvii, 38, 51, 64, 64n29

Oxford Local Examinations, 47, 49, 283, *400*

Oxlad, M. J., 16–19, *17*, 23–24, 281, 399, *417*

Oxley, Jean, *164*, 167, 180, *301*, 307–308, 352, *417*

Pan, Francis K., 137, *396*, *407*

Pang, K. C., 137, *396*, *407*

Pang, Samuel, 312

Pang, Yen Kiu Daniel (彭恩橋), 362, 367, *417*

Papageno, 304

Parent Teacher Association (PTA), xvii, 108–109, 123, 137, 142, 145, 166–167, 200, 206, 221, 228, 235, 259, 276, 285, 333–334, 375, 381, Chapter 17, *402*

Paterson, Macgregor Helen, 151, 363, *368*, *412*, *417*

pavilion, 58, 371, *401*

Pedagogy for Scientific Investigations, 294

pedagogy, 140, 146, 217, 219–221, 280, 282, 294

Penny, Winifred, 373, *383*, *407*

People's Republic of China (PRC), xi, 89, 95, 109n62, 112, 115, 136, 156n137, 158, 191n80, 226, 234, 245, *401*

Piercy, George, 26, *27*, *400*

Piercy, Mrs, 27

Pong, Shi, 9

prefect system, 105, 341

private school, 5, 32, 84, 87, 90, 124–127, 132, 162, 164, 174, 196, 200, 202, 251, 345, *402*

Public Works Department, 100

Pui Ching Middle School, 85, 160, 340, 343, 355

Putonghua (PTH), 129, *150*, 193, 197, 219, 221–222, 340, 394

Quality of Education, 193, 216–217

Quest / the Quest, xvii, 51, 81, 105, 150–151, 228, 237, 297n1, *386*, *401*, 409

Read-A-Thon, 387, *388*

Redevelopment Project, 196, 203, 205, 272, 332–333, *404*

"Remove" Class, 51, 61

Rendle, Miss (蘭德爾), 18, *418*

riots (1966 or 1967), 111, 114, 116, 145, 343, *402*

Robinson, Hercules, 19

Robinson, W., 71, 372, 381, 383

Rosary Hill, 83, 96, 96n14

Rose Villa East, 38, *400*

Rose Villa West, 29, 36, *400*

Rose Villas, 39, 42, 44

Rowell, Thomas Richmond, 90–91, 100, 102

Royal Reader, 282

Santos Yuen, Shan Rosa (née Yip, 山度士葉婉珊), *198*, 322, 353, *418*

Sawyer, Dorothy H., xvii, 51, 53, 55–58, *56*, 60–66, 71–72, 91, 102, 134–135, *136*, 234, 271, 282–283, 299, 348–349, 370, 372–373, 375, *376*, *400*–*401*, *407*, *418*

School Certificate Examination, 63, 90, 102, 142–144, 147, 174, 179n54, 283, *401*

School Council, xvi–xviii, xx, 36, 40–41, 45, 71, 76, 87, 95, 99–100, 118–120, 122–123, 125–127, 131, 135–137, 140, 153, 156–157, 161, 166, *168*, 169, 175, 190–191, 201–202, 205, 211, 213–214, 232, 235, 261, 268–269, 276, 372, 381, 385, *401*, *405*

school house system, 105

school hygiene programme, 62

School Management Initiative (SMI), 175

school uniform, 38, *56*, 59, 67, *68*, 180, 364, 389–390

Science Committee, 219, 294

Science Enhancement Programmes, 176

science, technology, engineering, and mathematics (STEM), 194, 216, 220, 230, 234, 294, 354

Secondary School Entrance Examination (SSEE), 126, 130, 140–141, 286, 394, *402*–*403*

Secondary School Placement Allocation System (SSPA), 130, 141–142, *403*

Severe Acute Respiratory Syndrome (SARS), 192, 224, *404*

sex education, 145, 157, 286, *402*

She, George, 86, *407*

Shen, Jane (née Yuen, 沈袁經楣), *301–302, 305, 418*

Shuen, Felix, 312, *314*

Sinn, Yuk Yee Elizabeth (冼玉儀), xviii, xxi, 244

Sino-British Agreement / Sino-British Joint Declaration, 112, 158, 193, 344, *403*

Sishū (四書), 104n37

Sisters of St. Paul de Chartres, 6

Sixth Form Centre, 136, 143, *144*, 286, *402*

SKH Kei Fook Primary School, 207

Skipton, Elizabeth D., xvii, 36–38, 45–46, 48, 51–53, 55, 64, 71, 234, 282–283, 347, 349, 370, 373, *383, 400, 408, 418*

Smith, George, 7, 11, 18–19, 29

Smith, Lydia, xvii–xviii, 7–11, 8n5, 13, 24–25, 29–30, 31, 34–35, 233, 249, 399, *408*

So, Fong Suk Jenny (蘇芳淑), 244

Society of Promoting Female Education for Girls in the East (FES), xvi, 7–8, 10–11, 13, 16, 18, 23–26, 36, 249

Songs of Praise, 298

Soo, Thomas, *172*, 191, 191n80, 206, *408*

South China Morning Post's Student-of-the-Year awards, 189

Southorn, Mrs, 58

Southorn, Wilfred Thomas, 58

St. Andrew's Church, 45, 81, 98–99, 100, 123, 132, 148, 188, 202, 222, 236, 269, 271, 273, 274, 276–278, 299–300, *301*

St. Christopher's Home, 273

St. John's Cathedral, 10, 13, 18, 23, 35, 80, 98, 135, 181, *183*, 269, 281, 299–300, *301*, 303n31, 307n64, 377

St. Paul's Coeducational College, 70, 200

St. Paul's College, xviii, 6, 8, 13, 18, 20, 35, 46, 200, 280–281, 327

St. Paul's Convent School, 6

St. Peter's Church, 45, 60

St. Stephen Girls' College, 337

Stanton, Vincent, 6

Stewart, Elizabeth, 363, *368, 418*

Stewart, Frederick, 19–20, 23

streaming, 141, 286, 349

Student Christian Association, 148, *150*, 270, 278

student-teacher ratio, 74, 120, 163, 169, 196, 216, 348–349, *349*

Subsidy Code, 90, 115

swimming pool, 108, 123, 137, 205, 209, 259, *259*, 322, 332, 365, 386, *386*, 393, *402*

swine flu (H1N1), 192

Symons, Catherine Joyce (née Anderson), xvi–xvii, xix, 61, 65–67, 74, 78, 87–88, 93, 96, 108, 110, 117–121, *119, 121*, 125–132, 134–135, *136*, 141, 145–149, 152, *152*, 155–157, 161–163, 161n9, 180–182, *182–183*, 231, 234, 237, 239, 243, 268, 273, 284–286, 288, 291, 309, 336–337, 340–347, 355, 374–378, *376, 383, 385, 402–403, 408, 409, 418*

Sze, Hang Yu Rosanna, 225, 323

Tam, Kitty, 331

Tang, Hung Sang (née Ng, 鄧吳洪生), 147, *164*, 178, *352, 419*

Tang, Kun Loi (鄧根來), 151, *164*, 185, *198*, 322, 353, *419*

Tang, Wai Yee Agatha (née Tsui, 鄧崔慧儀), *301–302, 307, 424*

Tao Fung Shan, 149, 188, 273

Target Oriented Curriculum (TOC) Programme, 175

Target-Related Assessment (TRA) Programme, 175

"Te Deum," 180, 206

Territory-Wide System Assessment (TSA), 222

The Anglican (Hong Kong) Secondary Schools Council Limited (or the Anglican Council), 202–203, *404*

The Chairman of the Committee of the Diocesan School and Orphanage, 29, 40, 122

The Chinese University of Hong Kong (CUHK), 116–117, 123, 159, 174, 176–177, 190, 239, 244, 248–250

The Council of the Diocesan Girls' School, 41, 76, 122, *405*

The DGS Girl, 226–227, 312, 379, 387

The Duke of Edinburgh's Award Scheme / Hong Kong Awards for Young People, 151

"The Hong Kong Debutante," 375, *376*

The Hong Kong Polytechnic University, 394

The House of Wonders, 227, 312

The Invisible Duke, 106

The King and I, 186, 227, 309n68, 311, 379, 387

The Last Rose of Summer (曲終人杳), 146

The Pirates of Penzance, 106, 226–227, 304

The University of Hong Kong (HKU), xvi–xviii, xxi, 5, 40–41, 44, 47–51, 50n57, 53, 63–64, 72, 74, 77–78, 82, 84, 87, 115–116, 118, 123, 142–143, 156, 159, 161, 163, 189, 237, 239–240, 243–248, 283, 285, 331, 335–336, 350, 359, 391, *400*

The Wizard of Oz, 227, 312, 379, 387

Theseus and the Minotaur, 311

"through-train" mode, 200–201, 345

Tiananmen Square Incident, 158, *403*

Tom Sawyer, 180, 311

tong fai, 91, 120–121, 164

Training College (of Education)

    Grantham, 113

    Northcote, 90, 303n31

    Sir Robert Black, 113

Trench, David, 116

Trinity College of Music local examinations, 69, 299

Tsai, Sherry, 225, 323, *324*, 330

Tsang, Ka Yan Karen (née Chong, 曾莊嘉恩), 353, 363–364, 367, *419*

Tsang, Kwai-ming, 78, *419*

Tsang, Wing Hang Janice (曾詠恆), xvi, 250, *427*

VA Magazine, 228, *403*

virtual classroom, 215, 224

walkathon, 167, 333, 379, 386–388

Warren, the Reverend, 17, *408*

Weng, Carolyn, *164*, 228, *419*

White Cap System, 323

White Paper on Secondary Education Over the Next Decade, 1974, 114, 130, *402*

White Paper on the Development of Senior Secondary and Tertiary Education, 1978, 115, 142, *403*

Williams, Molly, *152*, 321, 323, *420*

Wilson, Miss, 9–11, *399*, *420*

Wilson, Wilberforce, 25–26, 29

Winyard, Barbara, 151, 318, *320*, *424*

Wong, Chi-woon Vivian (née Taam, 黃譚智媛), 247, 381, *383*, *408*

Wong, Hoi-yan Joyce (黃凱欣), 249–250, 279

Wong, Jenny (王菁儀), *301*, 314, 316, *420*

Wong, Lydia (née Moo), 85, 94, 364, *368*, *420*

Wong, Renee L. (née Leung, 黃梁穎妍), 364, 367, *420*

Wong, Sing Frances (黃星), xvii, 66–67, 70, 245, 250

Wong, Wai Kwan Anna, 331

Wong, Winnie, 326, *326*

Woo, Chi Wah Billy (細華叔), 366, 367

Woo, Wing Tung Rainbow, 329, *329*

World Championships, 317, 323, 326

World Choir Games, 226, 312, *314–315*, 343

Wun, Tsz Sum, xvi, *420*

xiucai (秀才), 44

Yam, Wing Wah Vivian (任詠華), 248

Yang, Margaret (楊惠), 316

Yau Tsim Mong District School Principals Committee, 191

Yeo, Florence (née Ho Tung), xvii, 45, 339, *383*, *408*

Yeo, Kok Cheang (K. C.), 87, 108, *408*

Yeung, Kai-yin, 180

Ying Wah College, 6, 74

Yip, Luen Yuen Rebecca (née Lit, 葉列鸞琬), xviii, xxi, 162, *162*, 165, 169, 172, 175, 180, 183, 188–189, 191, 235, 243, 364, 367, 377, *394*, *425*

Young Saye, James Lawrence (楊俊成), 87, *401*, *408*, 421

Young Women's Christian Association (YWCA), 55, 70, 81

Youth Fellowship, *150*, 188, 229, 270, 274–275, *276*, 278

Yu, Chiu For, 309

Yuen, Ching-wan Gina (袁青雲), 250, 279

Zimmern, Cecily (née Kotewall), 64, 69

瓊姐 (King Tse), 365

根叔 (Gun Suk), 365, 369